THE
FEMALE
ORGASM

THE FEMALE ORGASM

PSYCHOLOGY
PHYSIOLOGY
FANTASY

SEYMOUR FISHER

BASIC BOOKS, INC., PUBLISHERS

NEW YORK

© 1973 by Basic Books, Inc.
Library of Congress Catalog Card Number: 72-89173
SBN 465-02373-8
Manufactured in the United States of America
DESIGNED BY VINCENT TORRE

72 73 74 75   10 9 8 7 6 5 4 3 2 1

ACKNOWLEDGMENTS

This book was constructed on the trust and verve of women who were willing to participate in a scientific study of sexual behavior. They were willing to "take a chance" on a potentially threatening experience and displayed remarkable patience in putting up with gross intrusions into their psychological and physical privacy. With few exceptions, they not only accepted the sometimes stressful and also occasionally boring demands that the experiments made upon them but extended themselves in a gracious fashion to be cooperative and informative. They were admirable in their commitments to describe their sexual behavior and feelings openly and frankly. Considerable credit for the trust that was inspired in these women must go to the laboratory personnel who worked with them. The men and women who collected the psychological and physiological data were typified by their ability to deal with others in a dignified fashion. They were warm and receptive but not intrusive. Robert Curtiss, who supervised important aspects of the data collection, must be particularly singled out for the example he set in this respect. In addition, his technical and electronic skills were invaluable in almost every experiment that was undertaken.

I would like to thank Dr. Howard Osofsky for first making me aware of the need for research in the area of sexual behavior and actually getting me involved in a study that eventually led to the series of investigations that comprise the core of this book.

My wife has played an important role in the evolution of this work. She has given me all the sympathy and support that wives are known to give when husbands are engaged in long and arduous enterprises. But as a psychologist and clinician in her own right, she has also offered ideas, made literally hundreds of helpful suggestions, and actively participated in the collection of data. She conducted intensive interviews with a considerable number of the women who were involved in the studies, and her reflections on this material were invaluable to me as I tried to understand what it all meant.

Special acknowledgments are due to Dr. Harvey Taub, who read and criticized a large part of an early version of the manuscript. He uncovered a variety of inconsistencies, particularly of a statistical and logical nature, and I am indebted to him for his thorough analysis. If there are any defects of this nature remaining, they are my own fault.

Others have read large portions of the manuscript and offered suggestions that were sufficiently persuasive to lead to revisions. In this respect, I would like to express my thanks to Drs. Marc Hollender, Sidney Cleveland, George Fabish, Roger Greenberg, and Jay Land.

I wish to recognize the invaluable assistance of the Computer Center of the Upstate Medical Center as well as the financial aid provided by the National Institute of Mental Health.

My secretary, Mary McCargar, who had seen me through a previous book, managed the typing and retyping of a procession of pages with her usual calm efficiency.

Finally, let me express my pleasure about the helpful and cordial attention I have received from Erwin Glikes of Basic Books.

CONTENTS

LIST OF TABLES

THE
FEMALE
ORGASM

A GENERAL VIEW OF

THE BOOK

This book seeks to understand the psychological aspects of the various kinds of sexual behavior studied by Kinsey, et al. (1953) and Masters and Johnson (1966). It is concerned with how a woman's personality influences her sexual responsiveness as well as her experiences with body functions such as menstruation and pregnancy. Speculations concerned with these matters are abundantly touted in the literature, but it is fair to say that our real fund of knowledge concerning them is fragmentary. One should add that learning more about the psychology of sexual responsiveness in women is important not only in its own right but also because it offers us an opportunity to find out more about how a basic drive or appetite becomes integrated into an individual's life style.

A good deal of material is presented in this book. The material is complex and covers a broad range of topics. As the reader burrows into it, the details begin to fill his vision and obscure his broader comprehension. It is easy to lose the overall analytical view needed to keep the details in proper perspective. The purpose of this introductory section is to provide enough of a preliminary look at the major components of the book so that the reader will have a frame of reference for assimilating its diverse inputs.

One of the principal tasks the writer set for himself in preparing this book was to review and make sense out of all of the available scientific literature concerning the nature of femininity and sexual responsiveness in women. As far as can be ascertained, this has not been previously done in a comprehensive fashion. It was hoped that in the process of putting together all of the accumulated information some new and dependable conclusions about the nature of female sexuality would emerge. There were a number of major issues that were examined. Some of the questions that were evaluated within the context of the pool of information available in the literature were as follows:

Does a woman's ability to be sexually responsive have anything to do with how psychologically disturbed or maladjusted she is?

Do women who differ in their ability to attain orgasm also differ in personality?

Is it true, as psychoanalytic theory proposes, that women perceive their own
bodies as inferior to those of men?

Can a woman's orgasm potential be predicted from such factors as education,
religiosity, and social class?

What is the impact of early traumatic sexual experiences upon a woman's ability to be orgasmic?

To what extent do the traits and qualities of a woman's sex partner influence
her ability to be sexually responsive?

Do sexual practice and experience improve a woman's ability to attain orgasm?

Does a woman's mother or her father have the most influential role in the development of her femininity and her orgasmic potential?

Is there any relationship between how sexually responsive a woman is and the
manner in which she copes with menstruation and pregnancy?

Do women who prefer clitoral stimulation differ in personality from women
who prefer vaginal stimulation?

The analysis of previous studies produced a sheaf of interesting and
often surprising findings. It became evident that there are many widely accepted ideas about the nature of feminine sexuality that are erroneous.
These erroneous ideas exist not only in the popular mind but also in the
theories and procedures of professional disciplines. Whereas it is beyond
the scope of this introductory summary to describe in detail the conclusions that were extracted from the literature, it will be helpful to the
reader to have an overview of several conclusions that have major implications.

A particularly striking discovery that was made was that a woman's
ability to be sexually responsive is not related to how psychologically
"healthy" or "unhealthy" she is. No evidence could be found that women
with neurotic or even schizophrenic symptomatology are any less orgasmic
than normal women. Contrary to psychoanalytic theory, it cannot be said
that a woman's sexual responsiveness is an index of her emotional maturity or stability. This finding plus others to be presented later indicated that
a woman's ability to be sexually responsive is only one aspect of her life
and should not be used to classify her in any general sense as a psychologically adequate or inadequate person.

It was difficult to find any qualities or traits that will predict a woman's
orgasmic potential. Age, religious membership, characteristics of the
husband, religiosity, ordinal position in the family, and other variables all
proved to be largely nonpredictive. Surprisingly, two of the best predictors
were education and social class; orgasm potential is positively correlated
with both. The more years of education a woman has had or the higher
her social class the more orgasmic she is. The finding with regard to education is especially interesting because it contradicts current stereotypes
about education having a masculinizing or desexualizing effect on women.

Another major finding that emerged from the study of the literature was
that practice, as such, has *relatively* little effect on a woman's ability to be
orgasmic. Although Kinsey, et al. (1953) reported some increases in

orgasm consistency during marriage, they are quite small and occur only after years of marital sexual practice. It is doubtful that a woman's ability to be sexually responsive can be looked upon as a simple motor or "athletic" skill. The evidence argues, on the contrary, that sexual responsiveness is linked to feelings and attitudes about people.

It is also interesting that no support was discerned for the idea that a woman's ability to be orgasmic is impaired by traumatic sexual experiences. Empirical studies have consistently obtained negative results in this area. One such study that might be mentioned by way of example is the Gebhard, et al. (1958) report that unmarried women who have an abortion to rid themselves of an unwanted pregnancy do not subsequently, in their first year of marital intercourse, display unusual difficulty in attaining orgasm. The trauma of the abortion experience apparently did not produce any long-term effects capable of inhibiting orgasm.

One other conclusion derived from the literature that should be mentioned is that, as yet, no one has been able to demonstrate that a woman's sexual responsiveness is related to the attributes and traits of her husband. There have been several studies of this matter; all have largely failed to find significant relationships. Terman (1938, 1951) studied the husbands of a large number of women in exquisite detail. Measures were obtained with regard to each husband's personality, interest patterns, and early background; all turned out to have basically chance correlations with measures of his wife's sexual responsiveness. As suggested at a later point in this book, it is possible that studies that focused not on the traits of the individual husband but rather upon his style of interaction with his wife might prove to be more meaningfully related to her sexual behavior. However, at this point, those who would assert that the sexual responsiveness of the average woman is significantly dependent upon the characteristics of her sex partner will have to come up with some new convincing facts.

In scanning the literature dealing with the development of feminine identity, it was possible to isolate some of the parental attitudes and strategies that play an important part in shaping a girl's view of herself as a feminine object. Contrary to common-sense assumptions, it was found that the father may play a relatively more important role than the mother in the female sex-typing process. Several studies have reported closer corelations between father attitudes and daughter femininity than between mother attitudes and daughter femininity. As will be seen, the writer's studies have also uncovered data that show that a woman's attitudes toward her father are more related to her sexual responsiveness than are her attitudes toward her mother.

Samples of noteworthy findings sifted out of the scientific literature dealing with feminine sexuality have been cited not only for their intrinsic content but also because they suggest that a good many widely held assumptions about female sexual behavior are incongruent with the available facts. There seems to be good reason for questioning practically every accepted idea about femininity and placing a serious burden of proof upon anyone who declares that a woman's sexual behavior is determined by one variable rather than another. As will be seen by the reader after digesting the details of the literature analysis presented in the chapters that follow, there is an urgent need for fact rather than unsupported opinion in this area.

A part of this book deals with the writer's own research that appraised the sexual behavior of multiple samples of women. Each woman participating as a subject in the research was intensively studied both with respect to her sexual behavior and psychological characteristics. Some women were also studied from a physiological point of view. In most of the samples, elaborate attempts were made to win the confidence of the women so that they would truthfully and accurately describe intimate aspects of their own sexual behavior. They were asked to provide information about such matters as intercourse frequency, orgasm consistency, amount of subjective satisfaction from sexual arousal, preference for clitoral versus vaginal stimulation, masturbation frequency, and so forth. Both questionnaires and interviews were used to compile such information. It can be said with confidence that the women who were studied were extremely open and frank about themselves. A large array of psychological tests, inventories, and laboratory procedures was used to investigate their personality attributes. They were asked to respond to questionnaires that tapped traits and values, to produce fantasies about inkblots and other more structured pictures, to give spontaneous word associations, and to interpret stimuli presented at high speed (tachistoscopically). At the level of actual sensory experience, they were studied with reference to sensitivity to light touch and response to tickle in sexual (for example, breast, thigh) and nonsexual body regions. Physiological measures, such as heart rate, vaginal and rectal temperature, and skin resistance of the breast, were obtained in response to erotic and nonerotic stimuli. Most of the measures were taken in a variety of contexts. These measures were obtained during and after pregnancy, and also before, during, and after menstruation. The range of women studied permitted comparisons of younger and older women; those with and without children; and those employing different contraceptive techniques.

Many positive and negative results as well crystallized out of the findings compiled from the procedures just outlined. One of the primary facts that became clear is that a woman's sexual behavior is exceedingly complex. Any one aspect of it is not easily predictable from other aspects. To know that a woman has a high intercourse rate does not predict whether her ability to attain orgasm is high. To know that a woman easily achieves orgasm does not predict whether she feels happy or unhappy during or after the orgasm. To know that a woman enjoys masturbation does not predict her feelings and attitudes during intercourse with her husband. To know that a woman uses a large repertory of intercourse positions does not predict her orgasm potential. As discussed in detail later, there are many aspects of a woman's sexual behavior that do not seem to be related. They have in common only the fact that they are labeled as "sexual."

One of the most significant pieces of information that came out of the writer's studies had to do with the psychological correlates of orgasm consistency. It was observed that the greater a woman's difficulty in reaching orgasm the more likely she is to be concerned about the lack of dependability of love objects. She is concerned about how transitory relationships are and how easily loved ones can be lost. This concern was particularly revealed in the fantasies she produced when responding to inkblot and pictorial stimuli. On the basis of such information and other material presented at a later point a model was constructed conceptualizing the impact of psychological factors on the orgasm process. The essence of the model is that sexual excitement, by diminishing a woman's sensory awareness of the outer world (see Kinsey, et al., 1953), creates in her a feeling that objects "out there" are "fading" and less real; this, in turn, elicits exaggerated concern about object loss in those who already feel that objects are undependable. The perceptual fading process set off by sexual excitement presumably alarms the woman who is doubtful about object stability, and this reaction in turn prevents sexual arousal from continuing to build up to orgasmic levels. Various kinds of direct and indirect evidence seem to support the validity of this model.

Another phase of the writer's studies relates to whether women prefer clitoral or vaginal stimulation in the process of reaching orgasm. It was discovered that the majority of women regard clitoral stimulation as contributing more than vaginal stimulation to their sexual arousal. Furthermore, no support could be found for the psychoanalytic theory that clitorally oriented women are more immature or psychologically disturbed than vaginally oriented women. In fact there was evidence that the former were *less* anxious than the latter. The vaginally oriented woman was also found to experience her body as being more alienated and depersonalized than the clitorally oriented woman. The overall results pertaining to the clitoral-vaginal distinction were in agreement with psychoanalytic theory insofar as they revealed a psychological differentiation between the two stimulation preference modes, but they contradicted the theory with reference to its more specific statements. The findings also contradicted the Kinsey, et al. (1953) and Masters and Johnson (1966) viewpoints that all orgasms in women are directly or indirectly based on clitoral stimulation. The women who were studied could distinguish differences between the experiential quality of orgasms based upon direct clitoral manipulation versus those primarily induced by direct penile intromission. There are probably kinesthetic sensations and feelings of body fusion produced by penile penetration that may constitute a major component of the so-called vaginal orgasm and impart to it a fairly unique quality. Similarly, there are certain unique qualities associated with the orgasm produced by direct manual manipulation of the clitoris. For example, women described the "clitoral" orgasm as producing a greater "ecstatic" feeling than the vaginal type. This was, of course, quite an unexpected finding because it is widely believed (despite the Masters and Johnson [1966] statement to the contrary) that the "vaginal" orgasm is the most exciting of all. In any case, there seems to be reason to say that the so-called clitoral and vaginal orgasms, at least in their extreme forms, do differ experientially. Also, they seem to differ in terms of their psychological correlates, but it should be cautioned that orgasm for many women is probably an indistinguishable blend of vaginal and clitoral elements.

In the previously mentioned review of the literature dealing with female sexuality, one intriguing finding was that women who have an unusual amount of menstrual discomfort are *not* particularly disturbed psychologically. This finding clashes with assumptions that are rampant in clinical papers that menstrual distress is often a sign of underlying poor "mental health." Incidentally, an interesting sidelight is that schizophrenic women were found to have, if anything, fewer symptoms of menstrual distress than the nonschizophrenic. When the writer obtained psychological measures from women during menstruation in the various samples he studied, no consistencies could be demonstrated. There was no indication that women were unusually anxious or in an especially poor state of psychological equilibrium or preoccupied with specific conflicts during menstruation. It is pertinent to add that the writer similarly failed to detect any special degree of psychological disturbance in a sample of pregnant women who were studied; if one analyzes the previous literature concerned with the psychological aspects of pregnancy, one finds that it has come up with similar results. In short, one can discern no real reason for assuming that the average woman experiences reproductive related functions such as pregnancy and menstruation as being psychologically traumatic. It is a popular stereotype that such functions have an alien, unacceptable quality and are a continuing source of crises for women. Although there are certainly extreme cases where this would be true, it is doubtful that it applies to the average woman.

Many other aspects of female sexuality were studied by the writer. Their scope and diversity can best be conveyed by citing the following illustrations:

Personality correlates of masturbation frequency.
Factors involved in feeling satisfied after orgasm.
Differences in physiological arousal of the genital area in women varying in their ability to attain orgasm.
Correlates of intercourse frequency.
Relationship of sexual responsiveness to individual differences in sensitivity to tickle.
Voice quality of high versus low orgasmic women.
Differences in clothing preferences among women displaying various patterns of sexual behavior.
Relationship of sexual behavior to other appetites, such as eating, drinking alcohol, and smoking.
Degree of femininity and sexual responsiveness.
Conservatism-liberalism and sexual behavior.
Sexual responsiveness and contraceptive practices.

Effects of erotic stimuli on patterns of physiological arousal.
Body image and orgasmic potential.

The writer would like to think of his work and findings as ultimately having significance for the psychology of women in general. But it must be emphasized that the studies that are described actually involved selected samples. The information gathered was derived from a relatively limited number of women living largely under the canopy of a university world (Syracuse University) in Syracuse, New York. The selective nature of the samples is indicated by the fact that they consisted of women who had at least a high school education, were married to well educated men, had volunteered to serve as experimental subjects, and were willing to undergo such discomforts as having physiological measuring devices attached to, and even inserted inside their bodies. Because of the special character of the populations appraised, which will become even clearer as the details of the studies unfold, no claims will be made concerning the generalizability of the findings to other women. It is true that the writer privately believes that his studies will prove to be validly applicable to middle-class women in the United States, but it remains for future work to ascertain whether this is so.

The basic research strategy used by the writer was to obtain measures from repeated samples of women and to report as valid only those findings that were reaffirmed with at least a moderate degree of consistency. However, the reader will undoubtedly detect instances in which the writer has allowed his enthusiasms and prejudices to carry him away and in which he has generalized beyond the facts. It is urged that this entire research enterprise concerned with the psychological aspects of female sexuality be regarded as exploratory and that the results be viewed as tentative. One of the lessons the writer has learned from his analysis of the previous literature is that generalizations about the nature of sexual responsiveness in women are risky.

PART
I

What Is Known about
Sexual Behavior
and Sex Role
in Women?

INTRODUCTION

This book limits itself to the matter of sexual responsiveness and sex role definition in women. Its prime aim is to clarify the factors that modify a woman's ability to enjoy sexual stimulation and to ascertain how she integrates sexual experiences into her style of life. Basically, it represents an attempt to understand the manner in which a major appetitional system influences and also reflects an individual's personality. What are the ways in which an important appetite is given human meaning?

The review of the pertinent literature, which begins in Chapter 1, conscientiously attempts to examine the full extent of the known data. Although there may have been accidental oversights, it is believed that all published sources of consequence have been given serious attention. Theories, speculations, anecdotal observations, and careful empirical studies have been appraised and, hopefully, sorted into some sensible order. The most fanciful of psychoanalytic speculations, at one extreme, and the tightest, simplistic learning theory declarations, at the opposite pole, have been spanned.

The literature review ranges over a series of topics. It, for example, inquires about our existing stock of facts concerning the process of establishing feminine identity, the body experiences that characterize womanhood, the various forms of adaptation to menstruation and pregnancy, and the nature of the fantasies linked with sexual arousal.

1

SEXUAL RESPONSIVENESS

AND DETERMINANTS OF

ORGASM CAPACITY

The first major topic surveyed concerns the matter of individual differences among women in their ability to respond to sexual stimulation. It is, of course, a well documented fact that some women are little aroused by sexual stimulation and incapable of achieving orgasm. Others respond intensely and report multiple orgasms. To what degree are such differences a function of psychological attitudes, traits, values, and conflicts?

Rather grim statistics are often presented concerning the numbers of women who apparently cannot experience satisfying sexual arousal. Illustratively, many citations (Terman, 1951; Kinsey, et al., 1953; Terman, 1938; Slater and Woodside, 1951) indicate that in samples of married women about 30 percent either never achieve orgasm or do so only occasionally. One can also find more extreme reports (for example, Stone and Stone, 1937; Yarros, 1933) suggesting that as many as 50 percent of married women do not achieve orgasm more than occasionally. Such data strongly suggest that large numbers of women are not capable of intense arousal when sexually stimulated. It should be cautioned at this point that one cannot make simple deductions from the absence of orgastic response about whether a significant degree of satisfaction is obtained from sexual stimulation. There are findings that indicate (for example, Kinsey, et al., 1953; Chesser, et al., 1957) that, although many women do not attain orgasm, they do obtain enjoyment and satisfaction from intercourse and other forms of sexual stimulation. As discussed in some detail later, the nature of the correlation between experiencing orgasm and enjoying sexual interaction is a complicated one that is not as high as one might expect.

Incidentally, with reference to the "grim" statistics of sexual dissatisfaction, it might be useful to ask what rate of dissatisfaction one would find in a survey of almost any category of body functioning. For example, would not a fairly high percentage of persons indicate that eating was often much less satisfying than had been expected and perhaps even unpleasant? Or what percentage would describe the degree of rest and relaxation derived from sleep to be frequently unsatisfying?

Effect of Psychological Maladjustment on Sexual Responsiveness

One of the most common speculations about limited sexual responsiveness is that it represents a form of psychological maladjustment. Freud (1959) and other psychoanalytic theorists (for example, Fenichel, 1945) have been leaders in equating psychological maturity with the ability to become sexually aroused—and even more specifically to achieve orgasm.[1] Presumably a woman cannot obtain orgasm unless she has successfully mastered the major conflicts associated with each of the psychosexual phases that preceded the genital stage. A mastery of Oedipal problems is often particularly emphasized as a prerequisite for adequate sexual arousal. It would be fair to note, however, that a movement away from this position has begun in some analytic circles. For example, Barker (1968) in reporting on a recent psychoanalytic symposium, indicated that several participants explicitly recognized that high orgasm capacity can be found in some schizophrenic women and low orgasm capacity can be found in other women who seem by most criteria to be mature and stable.

If the level of sexual responsiveness were indeed linked with general psychological adjustment, one would expect women who have neurotic or schizophrenic symptoms to show low responsiveness. For example, they might be able to attain orgasm less often.

What does the existing literature tell us about this matter?

One of the most pertinent studies, completed by Winokur, Guze, and Pfeiffer (1959), involved interviewing 50 neurotic, 50 psychotic, and 100 normal women (nonpsychiatric medical patients) concerning various aspects of their sexual behavior. The findings indicated that the three groups did not differ significantly in the frequency at which they experienced orgasm when engaging in intercourse. Reported frequencies of intercourse were largely similar in the three groups, although there was a significant trend for the psychotics to report the most extreme low frequencies.[2] No differences appeared among the groups in reply to an inquiry whether they enjoyed coitus as much as their partners. However, in reply to the question whether they considered their sex life to be "satisfactory," the normals were found to be significantly more satisfied than the neurotics and the psychotics. Winokur, et al. were skeptical about this last finding because they felt that many of those interviewed interpreted the question to refer not only to the literal matter of sexual experience, but also to whether their marriage itself was a satisfactory one. Overall, they concluded that there were no convincing differences in the sexual responsiveness of the psychiatric patients and the normals. One might question this conclusion in view of the fact that a few statistical differences between the three groups did emerge. But it is quite impressive that orgasm rate, which has often been regarded as one of the most basic indices of sexual responsiveness in women, does not differentiate psychotic and neurotic persons from those without gross psychiatric symptomatology.

Another noteworthy set of observations was made by McCulloch and Stewart (1960), who compared several aspects of the sexual histories of 100 female psychiatric outpatients (for example, neurotics and schizophrenics) with those of the normal subjects in the Kinsey, et al. (1953) samples. This information was secured by means of a questionnaire. (Male psychiatric patients were also studied.) One of the most pertinent questions asked was, "Have you generally found sexual intercourse satisfying?" [3] When the responses of the female psychiatric patients to this question were compared with responses to a similar question obtained by Landis, Landis, and Bolles (1940) from normal women, no difference could be shown. Apparently, too, no differences could be demonstrated in "satisfaction" between the neurotic patients and the more seriously disturbed schizophrenics. Interestingly, among those women in the sample without a college education, the psychiatric patients began premarital coital activity at a significantly earlier age than reported for comparable normals by Kinsey, et al. (1953). The authors concluded from their results that (p. 73) "females who subsequently become psychiatric patients and who do not go to college, arrive at sexual maturity with less inhibiting attitudes to coitus than their nonpsychiatric counterparts."

One of the most comprehensive perusals of the problem under consideration was initiated by Landis, et al. (1940), who used interview and questionnaire techniques to compare the sexual adjustment of 142 hospitalized women who were psychiatric patients and 153 normal volunteers. The psychiatric sample contained 41 diagnosed as schizophrenic, 41 manic-depressive, 50 psychoneurotic, and 10 psychopathic personalities. Analysis of the interview data did not reveal any consistent differences in the "psychosexual development" of the psychiatric and normal subjects. Landis, et al. stated (p. 144), "The psychotic, that is, dementia praecox or manic-depressive patient, gives little or no evidence of a consistent type of deviation from the normal course of psychosexual development." However, some differences were noted with respect to adult sexual responsiveness. It was observed that a significantly larger percentage of the married psychiatric patients had "never" experienced orgasm than the married normals. Furthermore, a significantly larger percentage of the married normals experienced orgasm "most of the time" than did the married psychiatric patients. There were no differences between the married groups for the middle categories of sexual responsiveness, nor were there differences between these groups with respect to their ratings of how much guilt is aroused by heterosexual contact; verbal statements about how generally attractive sex is considered to be; the age at which first date occurred; amount of sexual instruction received; affective response to first menstruation; amount of masturbation; and amount of heterosexual experience prior to marriage. However, with respect to the issue involving premarital experiences, the patients recalled such experiences as having been less pleasant and more emotionally traumatic than did the normals. One point emphasized by Landis, et al. was the fact that many of the women in their psychiatric sample had been able to attain what appeared to be normal levels of sexual responsiveness despite the presence of severe schizophrenic symptomatology. They also noted the complicating fact that in certain instances what appears to be inadequate sexual responsiveness in a psychiatric patient is simply a manifestation of the *general* disablement produced by her anxiety and disturbance.

Winokur (1963b) reported, without providing any detail, that a systematic inquiry had revealed no greater incidence of disturbed sexual functioning in 18 women with a diagnosis of anxiety neurosis than is typically found in normal populations.

To the contrary, Purtell, Robins, and Cohen (1951) reported (on the basis of a standardized interview) that 86 percent of conversion hysteric patients, as compared to 29 percent of a control group, were sexually unresponsive. Marked revulsion to sexual interaction seemed to characterize the hysterics.[4] Winokur (1963a,b), after reviewing the general pertinent literature, considers that this is the only psychiatric category for which "sexual pathology" has been specifically demonstrated.[5]

A trend for sexual inhibition to be associated with psychopathology has been described by Coppen (1965), who compared reported orgasm consistency in a variety of English female psychiatric patients (neurotics, schizophrenics, and affective disorders) with that in a normal group. One problem in interpreting these findings is the fact, pointed out by Coppen, that the normal subjects were not matched in age with the psychiatric patients and, in addition, different methods were used to obtain sexual information from the two groups. But within the limits imposed by such methodological problems, it was noted that the normals reported attaining orgasm significantly more consistently than any of the categories of psychiatric patients. However, the largest difference found was between the normals and the neurotics rather than between the normals and psychotics. In fact, there was a clear trend for the neurotics to show *lower* orgasm consistency than the schizophrenic and affective disorder patients. That is, there was apparently more difficulty in attaining orgasm among women with relatively mild (neurotic) than those with extremely severe (for example, schizophrenic) psychiatric symptomatology. One is left in a quandary about how to interpret the overall findings of this study. Because of sample and methodological discrepancies, the normals and psychiatric patients were not really comparable; one wonders whether it would not be best to regard the observed orgasm consistency differences between them with a skeptical eye. On the other hand, the neurotics and psychotics were quite comparable, and so the orgasm differences between them, which are the reverse of that which would be expected if psychopathology produced sexual disturbance, appear to be fairly reliable.

Sexual behavior was appraised by Burton and Kaplan (1968) in the case of 16 couples who had applied for marital counseling. In each instance the husband had a severe alcoholism problem. Sixteen couples without gross psychiatric difficulty served as controls. Both husbands and wives responded to questions concerning their frequency of intercourse, orgasm frequency, and ability to communicate about sex. No differences in sexual responsiveness for either the women or men were found between the pairs comprised of the alcoholic husband and his spouse and the control pairs. Thus, the maladjustment that one would associate with alcoholism and the disturbance one would presume to exist in a husband-wife pair that included an alcoholic did not seem to be linked with disturbance in sexual responsiveness.

Somewhat analogously, Slater and Woodside (1951) could detect no differences in orgasm frequency between the wives of hospitalized neurotics and the wives of soldiers hospitalized for nonpsychiatric reasons. These findings take on greater force when one considers that the wives of the neurotics were actually found to be more "neurotic" than the other wives, as defined by frequency of "nervous" symptoms (Woodside, 1948). Despite their greater "neuroticism," they were apparently no less able to attain orgasm.

Further, James and Pike (1967) concluded from questionnaire responses secured from 50 couples, who had sought long-term marriage counseling for their difficulties, that these individuals evidenced no greater disturbance in sexual responsiveness than typifies normal samples.

Finally, in the same vein, Winokur and Gaston (1961) remarked that in two studies (Dickinson and Beam, 1931; Terman, 1938) it was reported that unhappy couples, even though on the point of divorce, have intercourse just about as frequently as happy couples. But this must be tempered with Gebhard's (1966) analysis that indicated that in marriages that ended in separation or divorce, wives' orgasm rates were lower than those of wives in intact marriages.

Shope and Broderick (1967) described a study involving female college students: 80 virginal, 40 nonvirginal but nonorgastic, and 40 nonvirginal but orgastic. A number of personality variables (for example, sociability, impulsiveness, stability) were measured in these groups by means of the Adams Marital Happiness Prediction Inventory (1951). Actually, an index of predicted marriage happiness is one of the prime derivatives from this inventory. Few significant differences emerged between the various scores of the orgastic and the nonorgastic. One of these differences was in the direction of the orgastic showing *less* personal stability than the nonorgastic as defined by a Stability subscale.[6] In an earlier analysis of this finding, Shope (1966) had conjectured that it might indicate (p. 87) "that a tendency toward neuroticism is positively related to female orgasm among subjects in this study." This comment, if anything, does not support the notion that the inability to experience orgasm is linked with maladjustment.

Winokur and Gaston (1961) interviewed the wives and husbands of 20 marriages and ascertained the presence or absence of 20 different symptoms of anxiety. These individuals were without gross psychiatric symptomatology. Their average frequency of intercourse was determined; no relationship could be established between amount of anxiety and intercourse frequency.

Raboch and Bartak (1968a,b) appraised personal and background factors in the lives of 279 married women with little or no orgastic capacity, and 316 married women with good orgastic capacity. These women were Czech and were obtained from a group of medical patients. They were each interviewed for an hour and asked a standard series of 170 questions. Special inquiry was made concerning the presence of neurotic symptoms (for example, depression, feelings of inferiority, and anxiety). No differences could be established between the two groups with regard to the occurrence of neurotic symptoms.

Cooper (1969) administered one questionnaire measuring neuroticism and another that tapped attitudes about expressing hostility to 41 women who had serious difficulties in attaining orgasm. These women had no apparent anatomical or "organic" defects that would explain their lack of response. They were seen in a hospital setting, but it is not clear how they were recruited. Their neuroticism scores were not found to differ significantly from what is considered to be "normal." Also, those women with the most severe orgasmic difficulties did not differ in neuroticism from those with less severe difficulties. Psychiatric interviews failed to elicit the presence of serious personality pathology in most of the sample. There was a significant trend for the nonorgasmic to be characterized by significantly elevated anxiety and "intropunitive" hostility scores; Cooper had difficulty in integrating these findings with the more negative ones relating to neuroticism. However, one of his conclusions was that (p. 154) "the present results may suggest that frigidity is not generally a neurotic response. . . ."

Another perspective on the issue is provided by Pomeroy's (1965) investigation of sexual responsiveness in prostitutes. Many have theorized (for example, Fenichel, 1945) that a woman who would "choose" to become a prostitute is basically an immature, disturbed person, and that she must lack the ability to respond with a normal degree of sexual excitement. Clinical reports about prostitutes have underscored their depreciated self-concepts, their vague identity, and masochism. In fact, it is widely speculated that a majority of prostitutes are frigid. Pomeroy systematically interviewed 175 prostitutes and found that they experienced orgasm and multiple orgasm more frequently in their personal "noncommercial" intercourse than did normal women (as defined by the Kinsey, et al. norms). Over 20 percent of the prostitutes even reported frequently experiencing orgasms while having intercourse with customers. If the data presented by

Pomeroy are dependable, one is confronted by the fact that a group of women who occupy an extremely depreciated role in the culture and who are considered to have made an obviously maladaptive adjustment to life are even more sexually responsive than normal women, who are generally considered to occupy a better adjusted life role.

More in line with psychoanalytic expectation are the findings of Graham (1960), who compared the reported frequency of intercourse and the satisfaction derived from it in 65 married women and men who were about to begin psychoanalytic therapy with the same parameters in 142 married women and men who had been in psychoanalytic therapy from several weeks to 49 months. Those in therapy were found to engage in intercourse more frequently and to enjoy it more than those about to begin therapy. Graham concluded (p. 95), "The results of this study seem to bear out with certain reservations the assumption that psychoanalytically oriented psychotherapy does free the individual for more frequent and more satisfactory coital experience."

In a particularly intensive study carried out by Schaefer (1964) with a group of psychologically maladjusted (but not psychotic) women ($N = 30$) who had sought psychotherapeutic help, Schaefer, a woman, interviewed (and tape-recorded) each subject for approximately eight hours and systematically obtained information about a wide range of sexual behavior. Schaefer chose women who had had the experience of being in psychotherapy because she felt they would have learned to talk freely about sexual matters. After analyzing her data impressionistically, she concluded that there was no relationship between "mental health" and sexual responsiveness. One of her surprising findings was that all of the women in her sample had experienced some kind of orgasm. This contrasts with earlier cited findings in which sizable percentages of women in various samples have reported never having had an orgasm. Schaefer speculates that this discrepancy may be caused by the fact that most studies have been conducted by men in settings where only a superficial relationship was established, thus preventing the kind of communication needed to collect valid information.

Overview

It would be an overstatement to say that the existing empirical literature indicates no relationship at all between degree of maladjustment and sexual responsiveness. There have clearly been instances in which some links have been observed. Thus, Landis, et al. (1940) did find married psychiatric patients represented more often than normal married controls at the extreme of "never" experiencing orgasm. Winokur, et al. (1959) did report that neurotics and psychotics were overrepresented at the extremes of low intercourse frequency, and that they verbalized less general satisfaction with their "sex life" than normals. Purtell, et al. (1951) did find an extremely high frequency of inadequate sexual responsiveness in women with conversion hysterical symptomatology, and Coppen (1965) did observe a trend for normal women to report more orgasm consistency than psychiatric patients, although there are methodological issues that make this observation questionable. Finally, Graham (1960) did report that persons with psychiatric symptoms who were in psychotherapy enjoyed intercourse more than persons with such symptoms who had not yet begun therapy.

But, on the other hand, consider the following: Winokur, et al. (1959) could discern no difference between psychiatric patients and normals in orgasm frequency or ratings of their degree of enjoyment of intercourse as compared to their partners. McCulloch and Stewart (1960) reported that psychiatric patients did not differ from normals in the amount of satisfaction they derived from sexual intercourse. Winokur (1963b) indicated that anxiety neurotics showed no greater incidence of disturbed sexual functioning than normals. Coppen (1965) discovered less orgasm consistency in neurotics than in psychotic patients. Three studies (Burton and Kaplan, 1968; Slater and Woodside, 1951; James and Pike, 1967) did not observe significantly impaired sexual functioning in husbands and wives who constituted families in which one or the other had manifested serious maladjustment. Shope and Broderick (1967) detected a slight trend for unmarried orgastic girls to appear *less* personally stable (as defined by a questionnaire) than unmarried nonorgastic girls. Winokur and Gaston (1961) failed to show a relationship between level of anxiety in husbands and wives and their intercourse frequency. Raboch and Bartak (1968a,b) discerned no difference in the frequency of neurotic symptoms between normal women with low orgastic capacity and normal women with high orgastic capacity. Cooper (1969) did not detect significant elevations in the neuroticism scores of women with orgasmic difficulties. Pomeroy (1965) could not affirm the expectation that prostitutes, because they occupy such a depreciated role that apparently implies serious maladjustment, would be less sexually responsive than normal women. Schaefer (1964) found no evidence that "mental health" and orgastic ability were linked in her study of maladjusted women who had sought psychotherapy.

The weight of the empirical evidence favors the view that one can be seriously maladjusted [7] and even schizophrenic and still enjoy a normal amount of sexual responsivity.[8] The existing data are not persuasive that general psychological maladjustment, as such, plays a major role in sexual responsiveness.[9] It may prove to be true that certain types of maladjustment linked with specific symptom syndromes, such as conversion hysteria, do result in disturbed sexual responsiveness; but this remains to be seen.

Basic Factors Defining
Sexual Responsiveness

The next logical step in probing the determinants of sexual responsiveness in women is to look at some of the more obvious possibilities by reviewing what is known about the contributions of a series of simple defining factors. How is sexual responsiveness modified by variables such as education, social class, religion, and age? Can one, for example, show that the shaping process that goes along with attaining a certain level of education or the training that is traditional in particular religious systems affects sexual responsiveness in women?

Each of several factors is reviewed in light of what the existing literature has to say about them.

Education

Do women who differ in level of education also differ in sexual responsiveness? Four studies (Landis, et al., 1940; Terman, 1938; Terman, 1951; Thomason, 1951) have given negative answers to this question. Thus, in none of these instances was orgasm capacity correlated with formal educational attainment. However, Kinsey, et al. (1953), who conducted the most extensive investigation of the educational variable, did find a significant trend for orgasm capacity to be higher at the upper as compared to lower levels of education in married women. Kinsey, et al. state (p. 378), "In every period of marriage, from the first until at least the fifteenth year, a larger number of the females in the sample who had more limited educational backgrounds had completely failed to respond to orgasm in their marital coitus, and a smaller number of the better educated females had so completely failed." It should be added, though, that there were no consistent differences between educational levels with reference to intercourse frequency. One must give greater weight to the Kinsey data pertaining to the orgasm differences between educational levels than to the negative studies cited previously. This is so not only because the size of the Kinsey sample far exceeds that of all the other samples combined but also because the Kinsey sample contains a much wider range of educational levels than all of the other studies. The other studies included a very narrow range of educational differences. One should add that the care taken by Kinsey, et al. in collecting their sexual responsiveness information easily matches that exercised in the other studies.

Actually, the Kinsey, et al. study is not the only one that has shown a positive relation between education and sexual responsiveness. Ranker (1967), in studying a group of sexually adjusted ($N = 49$) and a group of sexually unadjusted ($N = 48$) married women, reported a borderline trend for the adjusted to have the higher educational levels. Also, Raboch and Bartak (1968a,b) found in a Czech sample that the educational level of a group of highly orgastic married women was significantly higher than that of a group of married women of low orgastic capacity.

The association of orgasm capacity with educational level is a puzzling and intriguing one.[10] There is no existing theory about the nature of sexual responsiveness in women that would explain it. Indeed, many stereotypes about the masculinizing effects of education upon women might have led one to expect a quite opposite sort of relationship.

Social Class

Does a woman's sexual responsiveness vary as a function of her social class? Kinsey, et al. (1953), who completed one of the most comprehensive surveys of this question, found a definite trend for married women from lower-class homes to attain orgasm less consistently than women from white-collar or professional homes. This trend held persistently for the first through the fifteenth years of marriage.

Relatedly, Chesser, et al. (1956) studied, by means of questionnaires, the sexual attitudes and behavior of 6,034 English women. The questionnaires were distributed through physicians in the National Health Service plan who volunteered to ask patients to fill them out. Chesser, et al. noted a trend for married women whose husbands were of higher occupational status (for example, managerial, professional) to have orgasm more consistently than married women whose husbands were of lower occupational status. The same kinds of results were obtained when wife's orgasm consistency was related to husband's income; the higher the husband's income the more likely was the wife to experience orgasm.[11]

However, one must note that Terman (1938, 1951) could not, in two different studies, detect a relationship between the wife's orgasm consistency and the husband's occupation or income. It should be added that the populations evaluated ($N=556$, $N=792$) were considerably smaller than either the Chesser, et al. (1957) or Kinsey, et al. (1953) samples. Also, one of the Terman (1938) samples was particularly restricted and unrepresentative in that it consisted of married pairs in which either the husband or wife had been designated as "gifted" by virtue of having unusually high intelligence.

Actually, one of the most thorough and theory-based analyses of the relationship between orgasm capacity in women and their social class status was completed by Rainwater (1965). It involved 409 subjects (including 207 women) who were intensively interviewed concerning their sexual standards and behavior, among other things. White and black representatives of three different social classes participated. It was found that whereas 50 percent of the middle-class married women had a "very positive" attitude toward sex relations, only 20 percent of the "lower-lower" subjects felt such a strongly positive attitude.[12] Conversely, whereas 20 percent of the "lower-lower" "rejected" sex, only 3 percent of the "middle-class" women did so. Rainwater interpreted these differences as reflecting the contrasting nature of the wife-husband relationship in the lower and middle classes. He pointed out that spouse roles in the lower classes were highly differentiated, with a minimum of mutuality and motivation for intimate interchange. The division of labor within the family unit was carefully defined. In the middle classes, husband-wife roles appeared to be less segregated and differentiated, and there was emphasis upon close communication between spouses. It was the factor of greater intimacy and closeness that Rainwater considered to account for the fact of relatively greater favorableness toward sex among middle-class women. He says of nonsegregated middle-class conjugal relationships (p. 77):

> The emphasis on sharing in such relationships extends to sex so that it becomes important that the wife also find enjoyment in sexuality, and that the husband not be "selfish" by taking pleasure only for himself. The husband must help his wife to achieve gratification, and the wife must achieve it to prove to herself that she is really participating as she should and to provide her husband with the fuller gratification that is believed to come when the wife achieves orgasm also.

Congruent with his formulations are other studies of lower-class Puerto Rican (Stycos, 1955), Mexican (Lewis, 1951), and English (Spinley, 1953) groups that have indicated that wives in such samples are not expected to experience much sex gratification and, in fact, do not generally enjoy sexual intercourse. Rainwater (1964) raises the interesting question whether a high degree of sexual responsiveness on the part of wives in the lower-class, role segregated family unit would not require a degree of intimacy between husband and wife that would be antagonistic to the system in which it is embedded insofar as it would interfere with other solidarities and values important to the system. The apparent influence of social class upon a woman's sexual responsiveness reminds one of Mead's (1949) statement that (p. 219): "the human female's capacity for orgasm is to be viewed much more as a potentiality that may or may not be developed by a given culture. . . ." [13] But what is especially striking about the Rainwater social-class findings involving samples of persons from the United States is that they indicate that even the magnitude of differences in conditions that exists between subcultures within the same basic culture is sufficient to produce differences in the sexual responsiveness of women living in these subcultures.

Religion

In view of the emphasis that has been placed by some theorists (for example, Fenichel, 1945; Freud, 1959) upon the influence of moralistic and religiously derived beliefs in inhibiting sexual behavior, one might expect sexual responsiveness in women to be linked with their degree of religiosity or their religious affiliation. But as one examines the array of pertinent studies, this expectation is not generally fulfilled. Kinsey, et al. (1953) could discern no differences in orgasm consistency or intercourse frequency between married Protestant, Catholic, and Jewish women, or between the religiously devout and nondevout within each religious sect. The relative lack of a *general* relationship between religious variables and the sexual responsiveness of married women has been borne out too in observations made by Landis, et al. (1940), Terman (1938), Terman (1951), Thomason (1951), and Rainwater (1965) in a diversity of populations and subcultures. Chesser, et al. (1957) even found a slight trend, opposite to what one might expect, for English women who attended church with some frequency to show more orgasm consistency than women who never attended church. Shope (1966, 1967) could find no correlation in a group of unmarried college girls between orgastic consistency and religiosity.

It is true that Kinsey, et al. (1953) observed a trend during the first year of marriage for Catholics of very *high* devoutness to attain a lesser level of orgasm consistency than "inactive" Catholics and Protestants and Jews in general.[14] But the highly devout Catholics were *not* less orgasmic than Catholics of moderate devoutness. Hamblin and Blood (1957) reported that devout Catholics were less orgasmic than "inactive" Catholics. However, the difference between devout and "inactive" Protestants was not statistically significant. Also, Goshen-Gottstein (1966) reported that in an ultraorthodox Jewish group living in Israel the women seemed rarely or never to attain orgasm. Perhaps unusual *extremes* of religiosity are associated with reduced orgasmic response, but one must remain skeptical in view of the Kinsey, et al. observation that Catholics of moderate and high devoutness do not differ in orgasm consistency.

In summarizing, one may say that among married women who, in contrast to the unmarried, have an equal opportunity for legally and morally approved sexual intercourse, religion does not generally affect orgasm consistency.[15] There are suggestions that women who are at the far extreme of religiosity may display reduced orgasmic response.[16] Perhaps at the extreme of religious indoctrination, as typified by the very devout Catholic or Jew, religiosity does exert an inhibitory effect upon a woman's sexual responsiveness, but this is still a matter of considerable uncertainty.

Age

To what extent does a woman's sexual responsiveness depend upon her age? Within a wide age span, Kinsey, et al. (1953) concluded that there was little relationship between age and sexual responsiveness as defined by orgasm consistency. If anything, a trend was found for married women in the 16–20 age range to have lower orgasm consistency than married women in older age groups (even those in the age category of 51–55 years). Of course, one of the complications in analyzing such data is the fact that older women are likely to have been married longer, so that the variables of age and length of marriage are confounded. Kinsey, et al. felt impressionistically that women who, in their younger years, had found intercourse stimulating and who had the opportunity for regular stimulation, were able to maintain high levels of responsiveness, even into their sixties and occasionally into the seventies. Masters and Johnson (1966) arrived at a similar conclusion on the basis of their study of the sexual responses of older women in a laboratory situation, although they detected some changes in the character of the physiological response to sexual stimulation in women of advanced age.

It is of further interest that Landis, et al. (1940) and Terman (1938, 1951) reported no apparent relationship between age and orgasm consistency within a relatively wide age range (that did not include women in their sixties or seventies).

There is no real indication, within a large range, that women lose their ability to be sexually responsive as they grow older. Kinsey, et al. (1953) state (p. 353), "There is little evidence of any aging in the sexual capacities of the female until late in her life." They suggest that some of the decline in intercourse frequency and responsiveness that has been attributed to aging married women may be caused by the more obvious physiological decline of their husbands.

Pfeiffer, et al. (1968) found on the basis of a longitudinal study of aged married couples in their sixties and seventies that some women actually show an increase in sexual interest and activity during their period of advanced aging. However, it should be added that Chesser, et al. (1957) noted in a sample of English women, who were contacted via a questionnaire distributed by physicians to their patients, that orgasm consistency and enjoyment of intercourse declined consistently over the age range from 21 through 51.

Indirectly pertinent to the matter of age is the fact that Kinsey, et al. found that married women born after 1900 displayed greater orgasm consistency than women born before 1900. Also, married women in each of the three decades following 1900 showed a marked trend to attain greater orgasm consistency than in each of the preceding decades.[17] The increase in orgasm consistency over the sequence of decades probably represents another example of how cultural conditions may affect sexual responsiveness in women. That is, one may presume that the increase reflects the effects of changing social conditions during this time period.

Family Constellation

Considering the importance that an individual's ordinal position in the family has turned out to have in predicting various aspects of his behavior (Schachter, 1959), one must ask whether it predicts sexual responsiveness in women. Does such responsiveness vary in terms of whether a woman is the youngest, the oldest, an only child, and so forth? Attempts to answer this query have been made by Terman (1938, 1951), who in two studies consistently observed a significant trend for the orgastic to be "only" children (14.4 percent versus 9.4 percent; 18.8 percent versus 11.8 percent) more often than the nonorgastic.[18] None of the other usual indices of ordinal position differentiated the two categories of women.[19] However, these findings are contradicted by those of Thomason (1951) who presented findings that indicate that a group of sexually "well adjusted" married women did not exceed a "poorly adjusted" group in the frequency with which they were "only" children. Because the Thomason study involved a large sample and seems to have been carefully done, one does not find it easy to resolve the contradiction between its findings and those of the Terman studies.

Practice Effects

Is a woman's sexual responsiveness affected by the amount of sexual experience that she has had? To what extent is a woman's sexual responsiveness merely a function of practice? [20]

There are two findings that might initially suggest that sexual practice plays a role. Schofield (1965) reported that 28 percent of a sample ($N = 102$) of teen-age girls indicated that they experienced orgasm at the time of their first intercourse. This figure contrasts with the considerably higher proportion (namely, 49 percent—Kinsey, et al., 1953) that apparently attains orgasm even after only one month of marriage. One might interpret this as a practice effect, although other explanations (for example, increased physiological maturity and decreased tension associated with the legalization of intercourse for the married) could be offered. Secondly, there is the Kinsey, et al. (1953) observation that 75 percent of married women attained at least occasional orgasm during the first year of marriage, 83 percent by the fifth year, and 89 percent by the twentieth year. Even more pertinently, they discovered that whereas only 49 percent of women had attained orgasm in the first month of marriage, 55 percent had in the second month, and 59 percent by the third month. In a three-month span there was a 10 percent increase. Relatedly, 39 percent of females were reaching orgasm in all or nearly all of their coitus during the first year of marriage, and by the end of the twentieth year of marriage, this percent had increased to 47 percent. Thomason (1955) reported comparable results for 641 married women. Such increasing proportions of successful orgasm sound like they could be based on practice effects. The term "practice" would be used in a broad sense to include repetition, learning new techniques, and obtaining reinforcement for successful performance.

But once again, contrary to the Kinsey, et al. and Thomason data, Chesser, et al. (1957) found that in a sample of English women orgasm consistency and satisfaction from intercourse declined gradually in marriages as they increased in duration from one to over 20 years. Chesser did not know whether to attribute this decline to some aspect of the duration of a marriage or to the increasing age of the wife, which was accompanied by a biological loss in her ability to be responsive. Also, contrary to the Kinsey, et al. and Thomason (1955) results, Terman (1938, 1951) reported in two studies that orgasm consistency in women was not related to how long they had been married.

Another line of argument that has been offered for the practice effect is the fact that the Kinsey, et al. results indicated that the frequency of orgasm in premarital intercourse predicts frequency of orgasm during marital intercourse. Similarly, premarital petting to orgasm and premarital mastur-bation to orgasm also successfully predicted marital orgasm frequency. Thus, one could say in terms of the Kinsey, et al. observations that the at-tainment of orgasm premaritally by almost any means served as a method of practice that facilitated orgasm attainment after marriage. Burgess and Wallin (1953) collected material on 616 women and showed that orgasm capacity during marriage was higher in those who had had premarital in-tercourse with their husbands or with other men. Also, Landis, et al. (1940) stated that orgasm capacity in married women was positively corre-lated with whether they had engaged in premarital intercourse.[21] Of course, a flaw in attempting to explain such findings in terms of practice effects is the possibility that women who are most responsive to sexual stim-ulation are those who premaritally are most likely to seek out contacts and experiences that will produce orgasm, and also those who after mar-riage are most likely, because of their responsiveness, to attain orgasm. In fact, Hamblin and Blood (1957) after a detailed analysis of the Kinsey, et al. data bearing on the correlation between premarital and marital orgasm rates concluded that nothing could be reliably said about causal effects. These data could not be used to argue for the facilitating effects of prac-tice or for alternative explanations (for example, that early orgasm experi-ence prevents the formation of lasting inhibitions about sex).

There is a fair probability that practice effects facilitate sexual respon-siveness to some degree. But the effects seem to be variable and in some populations have not been detectable. Even in the Kinsey, et al. data where these effects have been most clearly evident, they have been really impressive only with respect to the category of "no orgasm." From the first to the fifth year of marriage there was a reported 8 percent decrease in women who could not attain orgasm at all. There was a 3 percent decrease from the fifth to the tenth year of marriage, a 2 percent decrease from the tenth to fifteenth year, and a 1 percent decrease from the fifteenth to the twentieth year. Over the entire span (from first to twentieth year of mar-riage) there was a 14 percent decrease in women who could not attain or-gasm at all. The average difference between marriages of one year and 20 years' duration with respect to the number who achieved orgasm in "nearly all" of their coitus was merely 8 percent. Only a small percentage had been able to increase their ability to attain orgasm with a high consis-tency.[22]

Traumatic Episodes

It is widely conjectured and believed that a woman's sexual responsive-ness may be permanently adversely affected by individual episodes in which sexual trauma was experienced. For example, it is thought that an encounter with a sexually aggressive man during adolescence or an inept husband during the honeymoon may grossly inhibit a woman's sexual re-sponsiveness. But the existing literature makes one skeptical about such suppositions. Many of the studies that have investigated sexual responsiveness in women and inquired about previous traumatic sexual experiences have all largely failed to detect a convincing link between orgasm consistency (or any other indices of sexual responsiveness) and reports of previous sexual experiences that were disturbing—either because they were frightening or inept in character. In one study conducted by Hamilton (as described by Ferguson, 1938a), it was found that married orgastically adequate women had had fewer "sex aggressions" committed against them premaritally than had the orgastically inadequate. However, quite contrastingly, in two studies Terman (1938, 1951) could not find a significant difference between the orgastic adequates and inadequates in the frequency with which they had had shocking premarital sexual encounters. Landis, et al. (1940) obtained similar negative results. Actually, contrary to what one might expect, Shope (1966) discovered that unmarried orgastic girls in his sample had had significantly *more* shocking sexual encounters before the age of 16 than had the unmarried nonorgastic girls. Kanin and Howard (1958), who studied early marriage and honeymoon behavior, could find few instances in which long-term marital sex adjustment was disturbed by the negative or disappointing quality of initial sexual interactions. Finally, and importantly, Gebhard, Pomeroy, Martin, and Christenson (1958) observed in a large sample of women that those who had an abortion performed upon them prior to marriage were not less capable of orgasm during their first year of marriage than were those who had not had an abortion. This was true despite the fact that the abortion experience was probably, in most instances, a disturbing and traumatic one—with obvious implications about the difficulties that may ensue from intercourse.

Motherhood and Responsivity

Does the experience of becoming pregnant, producing a child, and functioning as a mother affect a woman's sexual responsiveness? Certainly there are popular stereotypes that might lead one to expect an affirmative answer. There are also theoretical formulations that might lead to a similar expectation. However, all investigators of this problem have unanimously concluded that a woman's sexual responsiveness has only a chance relationship with the number of children she has borne. Kinsey, et al. (1953), Terman (1938), Terman (1951), Chesser, et al. (1957), Landis, et al. (1940), and Thomason (1951) have all been in agreement on this matter.[23]

Physical Attributes and Responsivity

Is sexual responsiveness in women correlated with individual differences in physique, physiology, hormonal levels, and developmental history? That is, can it be related to definable variations in body structure or function? Definitive answers to the various aspects of this question are largely not yet available. In some instances, there have not been sufficient reliable data assembled and in others contradictory findings have already come into view. Much has been written in this area, but an attempt will be made to cut through the complexity of the details and to state in a few words the essence of what has and has not been established with regard to the matter.

As to the relation between responsivity and developmental history, no consistencies have been observed. For example, neither Kinsey, et al. (1953), nor Landis, et al. (1940), nor Terman (1938), nor Hamilton (see Ferguson, 1938a,b) have found a significant association between sexual responsiveness in married women and their age of onset of menstruation. This was also true in Shope's (1966, 1967) study of sexual responsiveness in *unmarried* girls. Further, Fisher and Osofsky (1967) failed to detect a link between sexual responsiveness and indices such as age of breast development, age when pubic hair first appeared, and age of onset of menstruation. Generally, one cannot see a connection between sexual responsiveness and how early or late pubertal changes began.

Simple measures and ratings of body configuration do not correlate with sexual responsiveness.[24] One should mention, parenthetically, there are some older findings by Landis, et al. (1940) involving physique parameters that may deserve further evaluation. First, they reported that significantly more women with "gynecoid pelves" than "anthropoid pelves" had made a "satisfactory sexual adjustment" in marriage. The terms "anthropoid" and "gynecoid" refer to the configuration of the pelvis (viewed through X-ray). The "gynecoid" is the pelvis that conforms best to the accepted female configuration and "anthropoid" is the narrowed pelvis resembling that seen in anthropoid apes. Secondly, Landis, et al. reported that sexual adjustment was negatively correlated with the distance from the urinary meatus to the clitoris. This finding was actually a cross-validation of a previous report by Narjani (cited by Landis, et al., 1940) and one wonders why it has not been given more serious attention by other investigators. These are the only significant findings of this nature of which the writer is aware, and so one is hardly encouraged at the moment by what seems to be known concerning the role of body physique and structure in a woman's response to sexual stimulation.

The question whether estrogen, androgen, and other hormonal levels of women are, within the normal range, predictive of sexual responsiveness remains open, but the existing evidence is not promising.[25] Although Benedek and Rubenstein (1942) first presented data in which estrogen levels derived from vaginal smears seemed to predict sex drive and sexual imagery in women who were in psychoanalytic therapy, a later study by Waxenberg, et al. (1959) failed to support these findings. Masters and Johnson (1966) have also pointed out that postpartum women whose estrogen levels are extremely low may show high levels of sexual responsiveness. Analogously, menopausal women who are characterized by gross decreases in estrogen levels do not show a comparable decrease in sexual responsiveness. There are actually examples cited in the literature of women who have, as the result of trauma or surgery, suffered major losses of estrogen (and other hormones), but who have continued to function sexually in the same fashion as they had prior to the loss. Analogously, it is fairly well established that some castrated men continue to display orgasm adequacy in their coitus. One may add that Kinsey, et al. (1953), after reviewing the available evidence, concluded that there was no correlation between patterns of increase in estrogen levels in females as they matured and their ability to be aroused by sexual stimulation. Money (1961b, p. 296) stated, "The direction or content of erotic inclination in the human species is not controlled by the sex hormones."

In general, it is fair to say that few or none of the obvious and gross indices of body size and structure, rapidity of maturation, and hormonal levels (for example, estrogen, androgen) seem able to predict a woman's sexual responsiveness.[26] To have arrived at this conclusion is in no way intended to attack the possibility that physiological measures may prove in the future to have considerable predictive value.[27]

Influence of Sex Partner on Sexual Responsiveness

In pondering the ingredients that contribute to a woman's sexual reactivity, the question inevitably arises as to the importance of her sex partner's attributes. Is a woman's responsiveness largely an individual matter or is it typically dependent upon the behavior of her partner? There are anecdotal reports about women who have not been able to attain orgasm for years with a particular spouse, but who, upon shifting to a new partner, become orgasic. Examples of this sort are cited by Kinsey, et al. (1953). However, they may possibly represent extreme instances and may not have real pertinence for what is generally true.[28]

It bears upon the question under consideration that Kinsey, et al. (1953) concluded from an analysis of some of their data that techniques of sexual stimulation, as such, did not have much influence on a woman's orgasm capacity. They stated (p. 364): "We are not convinced . . . that any limitations or extensions of pre-coital petting are of primary importance in establishing the effectiveness or satisfactoriness of coitus." [29] This implies that variations in the sexual partner's mechanics of stimulation are not important in determining the woman's level of responsiveness.[30] Some support for this view has come, first of all, from the Terman (1951) findings that the amount of time spent by the husband stimulating his wife does not correlate with her orgasm frequency. Support has also come from the fact that Terman could find no relationship between how much sexual experience the husbands had had premaritally and the subsequent orgasm consistency of their wives. Burgess and Wallin (1953) similarly could not discern a link between a wife's orgasm consistency and how extensive her husband's sexual experience had been premaritally. Relatedly, reporting on a Czech sample, Raboch and Bartak (1968a,b) indicated that interview data revealed no differences in the potency of husbands of women differing in orgastic capacity.

Another point to consider with regard to the importance of a woman's sexual partner is the repeated finding (for example, Terman, 1938; Terman, 1951; Kinsey, et al., 1953; Chesser, et al., 1957) that marital happiness and orgasm capacity are positively correlated.[31] Generally, the happier a woman's marriage, and therefore presumably the better her relationship with her husband, the higher is her orgasm consistency. This could mean that the fact of relating to a man who has qualities that are attractive and productive of friendly interaction plays a role in a woman's ability to respond sexually. The ability of her spouse to relate to her harmoniously would, from this perspective, influence how she responded to being sexually stimulated by him. However, a difficulty with this perspective, well recognized by those who have published results showing a significant positive correlation between orgasm capacity and marital happiness, is that one cannot specify which is cause and which is effect. That is, whereas one can assert that a happy relationship with one's spouse increases a woman's ability to achieve orgasm, it can just as logically be suggested that the more a woman is capable of responding orgastically to her spouse, the more they will be satisfied and therefore the happier their marriage will be. The mutual satisfaction derived from the wife's responsiveness might even be basic to marriage compatibility. One complication with this view, insofar as it presumes that positive feelings evoked from the husband in a happy marriage play a role in the wife's responsiveness, is that the Terman data (1938, 1951) have not indicated a significant relation between wife's orgasm adequacy and the *husband's* marital happiness. This brings to mind, too, the earlier mentioned observation (Burton and Kaplan, 1968) that women with troubled and disturbed husbands (for example, alcoholics), who would probably be difficult to relate to, do not display limited orgasm adequacy. In any case, researchers such as Terman (1951), who have given much thought to the matter whether the wife's marital happiness is basic to her orgasm adequacy or whether the obverse is true, have not felt comfortable about definitely favoring one alternative explanation over the other.

There are several studies in the literature that have specifically examined the relationships between a woman's orgasm capacity and a variety of attributes of her spouse. Numerous aspects of the husband's behavior and background have been scanned with respect to this matter. By way of illustration, one may mention the following:

His degree of childhood happiness.
His religious training.
His current interest in religion.
His early sex instruction.
His childhood discipline experiences.
His age.
The number of his sibs.
His parents' attitude toward sex.
The amount of sexual experience he had in high school.
How shy he was with the opposite sex in high school.
His premarital sexual behavior.
His favorite parent.
Various formal measures of his personality.

Generally, these variables have proven to be unrelated to the wife's orgasm capacity.

The most careful appraisals of the husband's role in wife responsivity have been carried out by Terman (1938, 1951), who studied one population of married couples ($N = 792$) and then another ($N = 541$ couples) in an attempt to cross-validate those significant results that did emerge. Information concerning the consistency of attainment of orgasm was obtained from the wives in both samples. In addition, wide ranging data were secured about each husband's childhood, religious training, degree of marital happiness, and vocational and financial achievement. The husbands also responded to the Bernreuter Personality Inventory (1931), items from the Strong Vocational Interest Blank (1966), and scales requiring self-ratings of various aspects of oneself. Of several hundred statistical tests of differences between husbands of wives with high orgasm consistency and wives with low consistency, only a relatively few were supported across both the original and the cross-validating studies.

One negative finding that ought to be immediately highlighted is the fact that the wife's orgasm consistency had only a chance correlation with how happy or satisfied the husband reported *he* was with the marriage. This implies that (within the affect limits encountered in marriages that persist for a number of years) the husband's general feeling tone about his wife and their marriage does not appreciably affect her ability to attain orgasm. If this were to be definitely confirmed, it would do much to establish that a woman's orgasm adequacy is a relatively self-contained and independent capacity.

Of 32 items pertaining to the husband's childhood and family background, only one differentiated those married to orgastic versus nonorgastic wives. This one difference was for husbands of the nonorgastic to report having experienced "exceedingly strict" discipline more frequently than the husbands of the orgastic wives.[32] There was also a borderline trend for the husbands of the nonorgastic wives to have had more strict religious training. This trend may be given some weight by virtue of the fact that in the earlier Terman (1938) study the same relationship appeared at a statistically significant level.

Thirty-five items pertaining to the background of the marriage (for example, number of the opposite sex with whom he kept company before marriage, how long he knew his wife before marriage, his health since marriage) to which the husbands responded did not distinguish those with orgastic as compared to nonorgastic wives.

Of the numerous Bernreuter personality items, only three distinguished the husbands of the nonorgastic wives from the husbands of the orgastic: the former indicated that they more often seek advice, are more often made discontented by discipline, and are more inclined to rebel at orders. Of 34 Strong Vocational Interest Blank items, only a few distinguished the two classes of husbands and even these were not in the same direction as the Strong results obtained in the earlier Terman study.

Ratings of husbands by their wives with respect to 14 personality traits revealed several differences. Orgastic wives more often rated their husbands as sociable, "better natured," less moody, more definite of purpose, and less subject to inferiority feelings. (These ratings had not been obtained in the first Terman study.) Of course, the usual question could be raised whether the more unfavorable husband ratings by the nonorgastic wives simply reflected their chronic frustration and anger about not achieving orgasm. Overall, Terman felt that his results demonstrated that the wife's orgastic consistency was linked only to a minor degree with her husband's attributes.

Despite the negative data cited to this point, one has to give serious thought to the previously described Rainwater (1965) report that enjoyment of sex in women is less common in lower-class than middle-class samples because of the greater differentiation of roles and lesser communication and intimacy characterizing the lower-class family culture. That is, Rainwater regarded the limited enjoyment of sex among lower-class women as a reflection of their poor relationships with their spouses. This represents an explicit statement that the nature of a woman's relationship with her husband plays an important role in her sexual responsiveness. Rainwater's original observations were derived from interview materials that were somewhat impressionistically interpreted; but, as earlier mentioned, other observers (for example, Stycos, 1955; Spinley, 1953) have also been impressed with the low sexual responsiveness in lower-class women in different cultures. However, even if it were eventually well established that lower-class women are limited in their responsiveness, there would still be a question about whether Rainwater's explanation, which focuses on the idea of an impaired relationship between wife and husband, is a valid one.

Scattered findings from a few other studies (Landis, et al., 1940; Chesser, et al., 1957) concern differences between husbands of orgastic versus nonorgastic wives. For example, Chesser, et al. reported a trend for the husbands of the nonorgastic more often to take full responsibility for contraception. But such findings have typically constituted a few positive ones among a much larger number tested and could be regarded as probably caused by chance.

Overall, the empirical findings do not give much weight to the assertion that the attributes of a woman's sex partner play a major role in determining whether she will experience orgasm consistently.[33] The Terman studies, described previously, were carefully done and involved fairly sizable samples yet they produced few significant results. At the moment, the burden of proof rests upon those who would assign appreciable importance to the husband's attitudes and personality in limiting or enhancing his wife's orgasm adequacy.

Overview

It is remarkable how few of the obvious factors that one might think of as likely to influence a woman's sexual responsiveness have actually been shown to do so. Such factors as age, religion, degree of religiosity, number of pregnancies, source of sex education—and even a variety of maturational and hormonal indices and perhaps even more surprisingly the attributes of one's sex partner—have not, except in a few special extreme categories, been predictive of orgasm consistency. The only significant correlates of responsiveness that have been demonstrated involve education, social class, practice effects, and perhaps being an only child.

Apparently, the practice effects of regular intercourse, as it occurs in marriage, do provide a facilitating effect upon a woman's ability to attain orgasm (particularly to shift from a state of "no orgasm" to "occasional orgasm"). The relative insignificance of the effect suggests that each woman has, by the time she becomes involved in regular intercourse, already acquired certain attitudes and other attributes that set broad limits to her sexual responsiveness. The fact that her responsiveness parallels, to some degree, her educational level and her social class implies that the broad limits are particularly a function of social learning. That is, one would presume, in terms of the voluminous literature in this area, that education and social class are likely to define the learning of certain values, standards, and modes of interpreting the world. One would presume, in addition, that at some level they are represented by interiorized systems roughly corresponding to "personality traits," cognitive styles, and life-orienting attitudes. Basically, what the education and social class data suggest is that women experiencing different kinds of socialization backgrounds develop different potentialities for attaining orgasm. A detailed evaluation of this proposition is presented in terms of an analysis of the existing empirical literature concerned with the personality and value correlates of orgasm adequacy.

NOTES

1. Actually, the analytic position has been to insist that in women even orgasm is not a sign of maturity, unless it is achieved by so-called vaginal rather than clitoral stimulation.

2. In one of the most thorough studies of sexual behavior in male schizophrenics, Lukianowicz (1963) did not find that intercourse frequency in this group was lower, either before or after the onset of acute symptomatology, than in a normal male control group.

3. There are complications about interpreting such self-ratings by psychiatric patients when one considers the Shatin and Southworth (1961) report that the judgments

of male patients as to the adequacy of their sexual adjustment and the same judgments by their psychotherapists were *negatively* and significantly related!

4. O'Neill and Kempler (1969) have presented experimental evidence that conversion hysterics are particularly disturbed by words with sexual connotations that are presented to them under "sexually seductive" conditions. They concluded that conversion hysterics show special "conflict involving sexual motives and sexual behavior."

5. It should be parenthetically added that Winokur, Guze, and Pfeiffer (1959) have also found an as yet unexplained tendency for neurotic and psychotic women to experience nocturnal orgasm to a significantly greater degree than normal women.

6. It is apropos to note that Swenson (1962) found that college girls who had sought psychotherapy engaged in more sexual intercourse than college girls who had not found it necessary to seek treatment. However, the groups did not differ in orgasm frequency or consistency. One should add, though, that Freedman (1965) detected no relationship between Minnesota Multiphasic Personality Inventory (MMPI) indices and amount of overt sexual behavior (for example, intercourse) in a sample of college girls. Even further, Miller and Wilson (1968) observed no relationship in a sample of college girls between a MMPI measure of maladjustment and reported amount of sexual behavior.

7. Gelfman (1969) suggests (p. 656): ". . . if the otherwise maladaptive behavior patterns of the patient do not prevent the establishment of some form of friendship, no matter what level the interpersonal relationship may be, mature or immature, and if the person's neurosis is in a great measure indulged, adequate sexual functioning may indeed be very possible. In other words, if in a sexual setting, a neurotic person is accepted on his terms, adequate functioning may well be within the realm of possibility."

8. The complexities involved in relating sexual adequacy to adjustment adequacy are pointed up by the Heyder and Wambach (1964) finding that men who were rated as having most effectively dealt with the rigors of a difficult and stressful "frogman" training course were apparently most fearful of women and doubtful of their own sexual adequacy.

9. It is of tangential pertinence to this point that Fink (1970) has recommended the revival of Freud's old idea that an inability to attain sexual relief may produce psychological disturbance. In support of his view he cites not only examples from his clinical practice but also the findings of Masters and Johnson (1966), which he interprets as indicating that women who do not achieve orgasm in the sexual act develop pelvic vasocongestion that can produce somatic and psychological distress.

10. Wallin (1960) indicates that highly educated women are less likely than those with limited education to report "complete relief of sexual desire" from intercourse if they fail to attain orgasm. This suggests, of course, that education may play a role in how important it is to a woman to attain orgasm.

11. Blood and Wolfe (1960) showed, on the basis of interview data, that wives of high social class or high education or with husbands in the high income categories were more satisfied with the amount of love they were obtaining from their husbands than were wives in the corresponding low social class or low education or low income categories.

12. "Lower-lower" blacks were more favorable toward sex than "lower-lower" whites.

13. It is apropos of this remark to cite Klausner's (1964) findings that Jewish women who migrate from Iraq to Israel shift their intercourse frequency and responsiveness in the direction of the higher norms in Israel.

14. Kinsey, et al. (1953) found that among *unmarried* samples the religiously devout had lower intercourse frequencies and less orgasm consistency than the nondevout.

15. Of course, it is well established that the amount of premarital intercourse and degree of liberality toward premarital intercourse are negatively correlated with

religiosity (for example, Kinsey, et al., 1953; Chesser, et al., 1957; and Reiss, 1964a).

16. Masters and Johnson (1970) assert on the basis of their impressionistic clinical experience that religiosity that assigns negative value to sexuality is a significant factor in limiting sexual responsiveness in women they have interviewed and treated for sexual problems.

17. This increase in orgasm consistency took place at the same time that there was a trend for actual frequency of intercourse to decline over the sequence of decades. Kinsey, et al. attribute this decrease to the fact that males have gradually taken a less exploitative attitude toward their wives and do not insist on such high coitus frequencies.

18. Kilpatrick and Cauthen (1969) ascertained that female firstborns had less liberal attitudes about sex than lastborns. However, onlyborns and middleborns were very similar in their sexual attitudes, and they were about midway between the other two birth order groups.

19. It is of interest that Gundlach and Riess (1967) found an unusually high percentage of homosexual women to be firstborns. But at the same time, Raboch and Bartak (1968a,b) reported that in a group of married Czech women of high orgastic capacity there was a significantly greater number of firstborns than in a married group of women of low orgastic capacity.

20. It is pertinent to the matter of practice and learning effects to note that the manner in which girls first learned the facts of reproduction and coitus seems not to be predictive of their later sexual responsiveness. Whereas individual studies (for example, Chesser, et al., 1957; Terman, 1951; Shope, 1966, 1967) have found significant correlations between source of sexual information (for example, peers, books, and parents) and sexual responsiveness, the overall results from all studies must be interpreted as being either negative or inconclusive.

21. On the negative side, one must indicate that Terman (1938, 1951) in two studies did not find a relationship between amount of premarital "petting" and orgasm capacity in married women. Also, Shope (1966, 1967) did not find a significant correlation between orgasm consistency in unmarried college girls and the total amount of dating or sexual experiences they had had. Finally, Ranker (1967) reported a trend for sexually well adjusted married women to have been less overtly erotic and liberal in their sexual behavior premaritally than were matched poorly sexually adjusted married women. In view of these studies, one must maintain some skepticism about whether, in fact, the sexually adequate married woman was typified by either more sexual experience or more successful sexual experience premaritally than the sexually inadequate married woman.

22. The difficulties involved in attaining adequate sexual response are pointed up by the fact that Landis (1946) found that after couples married they required longer to adjust satisfactorily to the sexual demands of their relationship than to any of its other aspects (for example, sharing family income and social activities).

23. These results are not supportive of Sherfey's (1966) speculation that the permanently increased pelvic vascularity produced by pregnancy enhances orgasmic response.

24. Landis, et al. (1940) could find no relation between how masculine the body configuration appeared to be and orgasm adequacy. Shope (1966) did not find significant correlations between height and weight and orgasm adequacy.

25. Waxenberg, et al. (1959) and Schon and Sutherland (1960) have shown that adrenalectomized women are characterized by a loss in sexual responsivity because of a deficit in androgens.

26. Severe body disablement or crippling of women that originated in childhood has been described by Landis and Bolles (1942) as resulting in "hyposexuality" and gross lack of interest in sexual stimulation. Terman (1951) also noted a trend for more orgastically adequate than inadequate wives to report "perfect" health since their marriage.

27. Of course, many important relationships between hormonal levels and sexual behavior in animals have been demonstrated (see, for example, Beach, 1965).

28. It is interesting, though, that Hamilton (1929) stated on the basis of his observations that women with serious difficulty in attaining orgasm rarely improve after a change in sex partners.

29. But this finding may require some modification in terms of a later publication by Gebhard (in Shiloh, 1970) who reanalyzed some of the original Kinsey, et al. findings and detected a significant trend for unusually lengthy foreplay (for example, 21 minutes) and unusually lengthy intromission (for example, 16 minutes) to be accompanied by high orgasm rates. Gebhard felt that only extremely brief intromission (less than one minute) and extremely lengthy intromission might significantly influence the wife's orgasm consistency.

30. It is of related interest that Terman (1938) failed to find a significant correlation between husband's preferred frequency of intercourse and wife's orgasm consistency.

31. One should add the caution that a few observers (for example, Landis, et al., 1940) have not been able to support the existence of such a correlation.

32. This reminds one of the Goodrich, Ryder, and Raush (1968) study that found that there was less interest in sexual interaction among those newly married couples in which the husband continued to maintain close contact with his mother and father.

33. This view does not agree with the recently stated Masters and Johnson (1970) position that the difficulty one spouse has in responding sexually is usually a function of the relationship between the two of them. Operating within this perspective, they state that they have significantly helped about 80 percent of women with sexual responsiveness problems who have come to them for treatment.

2

PERSONALITY AND

SEXUAL RESPONSIVENESS

The next step is to review the empirical work that has dealt with differences in personality and value orientation among women who are at various points on the orgasm adequacy continuum. Have consistent personality differences been convincingly shown? Do particular patterns of personality seem to facilitate or inhibit sexual responsiveness? Many speculative and theoretical statements may be encountered in the general literature that are pertinent to this question. However, only that information will be considered that seems to have been devised with at least a modicum of empirical or scientific rigor. Attention will be directed to sources that have appraised the differences between orgasm "adequate" and orgasm "inadequate" women with reference to such variables as family background, socialization experiences, attitudes toward parents, and personality structure.

The two most ambitious studies in this area were carried out by Terman (1938, 1951). The first involved a large sample of married women (and their husbands) and was highly saturated with members of the middle and upper-middle classes of urban and semiurban California. The second also involved a California sample, composed of wives who were either married to men with unusually high intelligence quotients or who were themselves of superior intelligence. It was intended that this study would provide an opportunity to cross-validate any findings that emerged from the first. An elaborate array of information was obtained, largely via questionnaires, from all subjects. They were asked to provide details about their sexual attitudes, sexual behavior, degree of sexual satisfaction, attitudes toward their parents, and the nature of multiple aspects of their childhood experiences. In addition, they responded to the Bernreuter (1931) Personality Inventory, which presumably taps dimensions pertinent to personality traits and emotional stability, and the Strong Vocational Interest Blank (1966), which defines the individual's preferences for various occupations and activities. Even further, in the second study each of the wives rated herself and was rated by her husband with reference to a series of trait attributes.

The results from these elaborate inquiries were rather disappointing. Although some meaningful consistencies were demonstrated, the large majority of the findings did not successfully differentiate women with relatively high versus relatively low orgastic adequacy.

In the first of the studies orgastic consistency was *not* significantly correlated with reported happiness of parents, attachment to father or mother, conflict with father or mother, happiness of childhood, discipline during childhood, and parental attitudes toward sex. On the more positive side, and largely derived from the Bernreuter and Strong criteria, it was found that the orgastic adequates exceeded the inadequates in being:

Less conforming and more individualistic.
Less willing to drive themselves steadily in their work and to plan their work in detail.
More disapproving of methodical work or methodical people.
More motivated to fill "player roles" than "audience roles."
Less often "grouchy."
Less often "lonely."
Less often "miserable."
More favorable toward practical things and occupations such as arithmetic, geometry, physiology, dentistry, and policeman than toward those with "aesthetic" or "sentimental" connotations such as YWCA worker, poet, magazine writer, and music teacher.

Incidentally, a trend was also observed for the adequates, less often than the inadequates, to use response alternatives in the questionnaires that indicated either "indifference" to, or indecisiveness about, the issue in question. Terman concluded from the data of the first study that the adequates differed from the inadequates in being less "neurasthenic," more "responsive," more "vigorous," more "zestful," and more "colorful" in personality.

To digress momentarily, one should indicate that an interesting auxiliary analysis of the data was carried out that involved a comparison of so-called passionate and nonpassionate wives. The passionates ($N = 65$) were those who reported a preference for 12 or more copulations per month and the nonpassionates ($N = 81$) were those indicating a preference for only 0, 1, or 2 copulations. They were contrasted on 50 variables relating to background, values, personality traits, and sexual attitudes. Orgasm consistency was significantly higher in the passionate than nonpassionate groups. The former also exceeded the latter in having had premarital intercourse with their spouses, in their amount of adolescent petting, in describing themselves as not being puritanical about sex, and in attaining orgasm at time of first intercourse.

Furthermore, the passionates (at or close to a significant level) were found more often than the nonpassionates:

To be strongly attached to father and to rate him as above average in attractiveness.
To report their childhood discipline as mild or irregular.
To describe their childhood happiness as above average.
To marry husbands not physically the "opposite" of their fathers.

Terman, after appraising the various differences between the groups, indicated that (p. 412): "the passionate wives have the more desirable personality traits: their feelings are less easily hurt by criticism, and they are less touchy, less often feel miserable, have more self confidence, are less critical of others, and lose their tempers less easily."

In the second of the Terman studies referred to previously (Terman, 1951) background factors pertinent to early socialization and family background once more proved to be almost entirely nondiscriminating between those orgastically "adequate" and "inadequate." In this second study only the husbands of the women were asked to rate their wives for a number of traits. (The women also rated themselves.) Significant trends were found for the husbands of the adequates to rate their wives as happier and more self-confident, and less possessed of feelings of inferiority than did the husbands of the inadequates. No differences occurred in the ratings for persistence, definiteness of purpose, sensitiveness, and egotism.

A number of differences between the adequates and inadequates emerged, too, in terms of responses to the Bernreuter items. The adequates exceeded the inadequates in asserting they were:

Not much affected by the praise or blame of many people.
Not frequently burdened by a sense of remorse.
Not often "just miserable."
Not frequently "grouchy."
Not often "lonely."
Not likely to worry "too long over humiliating experiences."
Not lacking in self-confidence.
Not usually likely to drive themselves steadily in their work.
Not avoidant of asking others for advice.
Often sought out by others asking for advice.
Inclined to be made discontented by discipline.
Likely to rebel inwardly at orders issued to them when working for someone.
Likely to feel they were well dressed and making a good appearance.
Careful to avoid saying things that would hurt the feelings of others.
Not inclined to find it hard to be optimistic where others are greatly depressed.
Not likely to make excuses more often than the average person.

Actually, a final tabulation indicated that only five Bernreuter items consistently differentiated the adequates from the inadequates across both studies.[1] Of the hundreds of items studied, only these few survived. The five surviving differences indicated that the adequates exceeded the inadequates in asserting:

They do not often feel "miserable."
They do not often experience "periods of loneliness."
They do not frequently feel "grouchy."
They can be optimistic when others around them are "greatly depressed."
They do not usually drive themselves "steadily" in their work.

None of the Strong items consistently distinguished the two groups across both studies.

Terman (1951), after sifting his relatively few significant findings, decided that women of low-orgasm consistency are characterized by being dependent on others, having a negativistic orientation, and being generally apprehensive.

Note his summarizing comments (p. 153):

Despite large overlap of the two wife groups the inadequate wife tends to be less happy, less self confident, less secure, less persistent, and less well-integrated, more sensitive, more moody, more exclusive in her friendships, and more apt to conform to authority and conventions.

Some indirect support for the Bernreuter derived findings of the Terman studies could possibly be seen in the work of Thomason (1951). This investigator compared 150 wives characterized by a good sexual adjustment (and high orgasm capacity) with 150 wives typified by a poor sexual adjustment (and limited orgasm capacity). Multiple variables were analyzed, for example, education, religion, perception of spouse, and complaints about spouse, but only a few were specifically pertinent to personality or characterological attributes. A number of the findings pertinent to the nonpersonality variables have already been described in earlier sections of this chapter. Among the personality-oriented measures was a cluster of questions, similar to several in the Bernreuter, concerned with feelings of personal isolation and unhappiness. Thomason was able to show that the sexually well-adjusted women significantly *less often* than the poorly sexually adjusted indicated they were lonely when with other people, felt "miserable," often had bothersome "useless thoughts" run through their minds, and felt a lack of self-confidence. The findings pertaining to feeling "lonely" and "miserable" and not self-confident seem to be in the same direction as several differences between "adequates" and "inadequates" that Terman had been able to show. However, it must be kept in mind that Thomason's definition of good and poor sexual adjustment included not only criteria involving orgasm capacity but also others involving degree of conflict with husband. Therefore, it is doubtful that Terman's and Thomason's findings are really directly comparable. None of the other findings of the Thomason study was directly pertinent to the question of personality differences between high and low orgastic women.

A number of other studies, none of the magnitude of the Terman efforts, have assayed possible correlates of orgasm adequacy. One of the earliest was carried out by Hamilton (1929), who evaluated 200 married persons (110 of whom were husbands and wives) by means of intensive interviews, and considered that he had been able to isolate a variety of background and attitudinal differences for the women that were linked with variations in orgasm capacity. Ferguson (1938a,b) later evaluated Hamilton's report and pointed out that he had not statistically tested the significance of the apparent findings. When such tests were performed, only 12 of the 53 originally described findings were found to be actually significant. These 12 significant findings were diverse and do not lend themselves to meaningful generalizations. The following are examples of their diversity (p. 301):

A higher percent of the adequate group than of the inadequate group have fathers who are physically unlike their husbands.

A higher percent of the adequate group than of the inadequate group never had sex day dreams.

A higher percent of the adequate than of the inadequate group have a lapse of sex curiosity, or a latency period before puberty. . . .

One can discern little in the Hamilton data that helps clarify possible psychological differences between high and low orgastic women.[2]

Landis, et al. (1940) conducted a study of the correlates of sexual responsiveness in normal women ($N=153$; 44 married) and women with psychiatric symptomatology ($N=142$; 41 married). Intensive interviews and questionnaires were used to obtain information about numerous aspects of sexual behavior as well as background and personality parameters. Within the normal sample only a few of the multitudinous measures that were derived significantly differentiated those women who were orgastically adequate from those who were orgastically inadequate. None of the differentiating measures pertained to the individual's background, socialization experiences, attitudes toward parents, or trait characteristics (for example, narcissism, maturity, aggressiveness), but were actually indicators directly relating to sexual behavior (for example, number of positions used in sexual intercourse) and therefore not truly independent of the orgasm index itself.

In an English sample of married women ($N=3,705$) Chesser, et al. (1957) explored, among many other things, the background correlates of orgasm adequacy. All information was obtained by questionnaires distributed by physicians in the National Health Service system in England. Only a tiny fraction of the background variables seemed to distinguish those with adequate versus inadequate orgasm capacity. The inadequates more often than the adequates reported that they were early made to feel that sex was unpleasant, that their parents had an unfavorable view of sex, that their parents did not enjoy the "physical side" of marriage, and that their parents' marriage had been an unhappy one. One could interpret such results as indicating that low orgasm adequacy was related to a childhood background in which sexual and marital transactions had been negatively depicted and experienced.

Shope (1966) undertook a study that is unique insofar as it dealt with *unmarried* (rather than married) women in the following categories: sexually active and orgastic ($N=40$), sexually active and nonorgastic ($N=40$), virgins ($N=80$). The sexually active groups were college students who were attending the Marriage Clinic at Pennsylvania State College for counseling on various problems and who volunteered to participate in the study. The virgins were also college student volunteers (from a marriage course). All subjects were matched for age, social background, religious affiliation, and grade-point average and intensive interviews were utilized to obtain information about sexual behavior and attitudes. In addition, the Adams' Marital Happiness Prediction Inventory was administered to measure various personality parameters, and the Adams' Sexual Attitudes and Responsiveness Inventory was given to secure detailed information about sexual response patterns. The personality dimensions presumably tapped by the first of these inventories variously included: Sociability, Dominance, Sensitivity, Realism, Impulsiveness, Flexibility, Prejudice, Normalcy of Thought Processes, and Stability.

None of these dimensions, except Stability, successfully distinguished between the sexually active orgastic and nonorgastic. In commenting upon this one successful finding, Shope states that the Stability score refers primarily to evenness of temperament and adds that (p. 71): "the orgastic girls . . . may have also been more neurotically inclined than the non-orgastic girls since the stability score . . . is made up of many items usually found in neuroticism scales." He suggested that the orgastic might be less "even" in temperament and more interested in change and innovation.[3] It should be indicated, too, that the virgins showed greater Stability than either of the two sexually active samples.

Two other findings by Shope with tangential personality implications involved attitudes about coitus and one's sex partner. First, orgastic girls most often said that they first engaged in coitus either out of "curiosity" or "just for fun," whereas the nonorgastic ascribed their motivation to "love or intention to marry" or "to hold date." Shope phrased this difference by noting (p. 81), "Girls who engage in coitus more for an interest in the activity itself than as a method of promoting interpersonal relations were most likely to be orgastic." Secondly, the nonorgastic significantly more often than the orgastic felt that when they agreed to engage in intercourse they were "giving in" or "submitting" to the male's demands. They seemed to perceive coitus as a means of exchange on their part to secure affection or friendship or status as a "girlfriend." Both of these findings suggest that the nonorgastic women are particularly oriented to use coitus and sex as a means of securing affection or "holding on" to someone.

What most typified the Shope results was their negative quality, which indicated the existence of only a few links between orgastic capacity and personality attributes, as they had been measured in that context.

One of the pioneers in empirically analyzing the personality correlates of sexual responsiveness was Maslow (1942), whose research leaned particularly on an inventory that he developed for measuring dominance-submission. In a number of different samples of women Maslow found that the higher their dominance scores the more "free" and uninhibited they were in their sexual behavior and sexual attitudes. For example, he found that high-dominance women were more likely than low-dominance women to experiment with a variety of intercourse positions, to enjoy nudity, to be gratified by masturbation, and to participate in oral-genital contacts. De-Martino (1963) was able to cross-validate successfully the general tenor of these observations. However, in none of the studies was a significant correlation demonstrated between dominance and orgasm adequacy or any other index of sex drive. Shope (1966), Terman (1938, 1951), and Fisher and Osofsky (1967) have likewise not found correlations between various measures of dominance and orgasm capacity. Apparently, one cannot anticipate whether a woman will be orgastically high or low merely from a knowledge of how dominant she is.

Overview

What reasonable conclusions can one synthesize from these studies? The two large-scale Terman (1938, 1951) enterprises tenuously pointed up a difference between the orgastic and nonorgastic in the degree to which they admit to negative affects such as feeling "miserable," "lonely," "grouchy," and "depressed." That is, the nonorgastic more often testified (via the Bernreuter inventory) that they are subject to unpleasant, unhappy psychological states. The Terman data also showed, across both studies, that the orgastic are less likely than the nonorgastic to state that they feel a need to "drive" themselves steadily in their work. Additionally, the orgastic appeared (as defined by husband's ratings) to be more happy and self-confident and less possessed of feelings of inferiority than the nonorgastic. Piecing these findings and a number of borderline trends together, Terman felt justified in describing the orgastic as being more happy, more self-confident, more secure, more well-integrated, and less likely to conform to authority and conventions than the nonorgastic. It will be recalled that the Thomason (1951) study might be viewed as indirectly supporting the Terman findings with respect to high orgastic women being less lonely and unhappy and more self-confident than the low orgastic women—but it is actually doubtful that the two studies are comparable.

Do any of the other studies concerned with the correlates of orgasm consistency provide support for any of the Terman observations? The answer must be in the negative. Other studies have either not dealt with variables pertinent to Terman's observations, or when they have done so (as in the instance of Shope, 1966, 1967) came up with nonsignificant findings. The few positive results from these other studies have a patchwork quality that cannot be symmetrically knitted together.

What can one say about the results from the Terman (1938, 1951) study that indicate that feelings of loneliness, depression, and lowered self-confidence characterize low-orgastic women? If one were to accept these results as reliable, they suggest at first glance that the low orgastic are more disturbed and maladjusted. If so, this would paradoxically contradict the results of most of the previously cited studies that have not been able to isolate sexual responsiveness differences between psychiatric patients and normal controls. But one must caution that the subjects in the Terman study were normally functioning women who had not developed gross psychiatric symptomatology. The statements about being "lonely" and "miserable" emanating from the low-orgastic women were not paralleled by serious clinical symptoms. In addition, since low-orgastic women were found by Terman in both of his studies to experience their marriages as unhappy (contrasting with the happy marriages of the high orgastic), it is possible to regard their "lonely" and "miserable" affects as direct reactions to their unhappy marital state. That is, one could view the low-orgastic women not as basically "maladjusted" but rather as experiencing negative feelings arising out of chronically poor relationships with their husbands. Of course, there is also the additional logical possibility that their unhappy affects and moods reflect their frustrations about being chronically unable to obtain orgastic satisfaction from their sexual relationships.

If one looks beyond the differences between the high- and low-orgastic women that concern matters of happiness and maladjustment, one may possibly discern a few characterological consistencies. The Terman data imply that the high orgastic may be more self-confident, less conforming, more individualistic, less preoccupied with work obligations, and perhaps, by implication, more zestfully interested in the "nonwork" side of life than are the low orgastic. But it must be kept in mind that these conclusions are precariously based on a relatively few positive questionnaire findings, which were part of a much larger pool of chance findings. It must also be emphasized at this point that the writer could not, in later studies of his own that are described, find support for Terman's conclusion.

Theories and Speculations
about Female Sexual Responsiveness

A distillation of the empirical findings in the literature bearing upon sexual responsiveness in women has been presented. Reasonable evidence emerged that a woman's orgasm capacity is linked with several general factors (namely, educational level, social class, and sexual practice effects). Much more tenuously, there have been suggestions that it may be linked with a few specific affect and characterological variables (namely, depression, irritability, self-confidence, individualism versus passive conformity, and compulsive preoccupation with work-type activities). Also, a fair amount of negative evidence accumulated that indicated that a woman's orgasm capacity is *not* related to quite a range of variables (for example, religion, number of pregnancies, spouse attributes, manner in which sex education was obtained, and psychological maladjustment as defined by clinical symptomatology). One cannot be too impressed with what has emerged up to this point. The findings have either been too tenuous or too general to lend themselves to explanatory models. What can one, for example, conclude from the fact that women of high orgastic capacity tend to be of higher educational and social class? The categories involved are too crude to offer much clarification. One could variously and with equal justification speculate that women of high educational and social class levels exhibit high orgastic capacity because they possess a superior and therefore more secure self-concept; because their status has given them unusually good lifelong opportunities to be consistently gratified and therefore to have acquired positive attitudes and expectations about being gratified; because their status has protected them from serious life traumas; because their relative superiority permits them to feel equal to men and therefore less potentially threatened by them as social and sexual objects; and so forth.

Theoretical Models

Although the present empirical findings about female sexual responsiveness are limited and offer little opportunity for theory construction, there is a large clinical and theoretical literature that has proposed explanatory models of great complexity. This literature, which has been mainly unconcerned with scientific verification of its statements, has often been preoccupied with prolix trains of deductions. It offers multilevel, intriguing, and fanciful ideas about how particular modes of socialization and patterns of personality may facilitate or inhibit a woman's reaction to sexual stimulation. Because of the richness of these ideas and their potential value in providing a framework for interpreting future research findings concerning sexual responsiveness, it was considered important to undertake an analysis of them. The task was set of reviewing the theoretical literature in order to classify and evaluate the multiple views proposed.

This section involves such a review. Diverse viewpoints are classified and attempts are made to trace what is common and different among them.

Most of the theories that have evolved concerning the causes of limited sexual responsiveness (frigidity) in women have been directly or indirectly based on psychoanalytic concepts. It is logical, then, to begin an exposition of these theories by summarizing Freud's formulations concerning female sexual inhibitions. Subsequent to this summary, other theories are classified and appraised in terms of a number of major categories.

Freud's Formulations

Freud (1959) thought that frigidity in women reflected their inability to cope with forces in their personalities preventing acceptance of a conventional feminine role. As is well known, Freud theorized that the development of the little girl into a woman with capacity for satisfying heterosexual love was an arduous process bristling with complications. A brief review of this developmental schema is in order to facilitate discussion.

Freud pictured the little girl as initially attached to her mother, who was her prime love object. He regarded this attachment as analogous to that of the little boy to his mother. Indeed, at this point he could see no apparent differences in the psychosexual developments of the two sexes, but he went on to say that the little girl typically proceeds to discover (for example, by observing her brother or father) that she lacks a penis and reacts with sharp feelings of inferiority and resentment. Presumably, she then fantasies that she once possessed a penis and lost it through castration, with the consequence that she feels degraded and thereafter is chronically susceptible to feelings of body inferiority. Invariably, states Freud, this deep disappointment is blamed on the mother, who is depicted as providing an irresistible target for blame because as "mother" she can be held directly responsible for the missing penis (that is, she produced her daughter with female rather than male attributes). A long list of grievances also exists about the mother not having provided sufficient supplies ("did not suckle her long enough"—as Freud puts it, [in Ruitenbeek, 1966, p. 96]) or having favored other sibs. Moreover, the mother is usually the one who first arouses sexual feelings in the child by her manipulation of her body (for example, when touching and cleaning it) but then (says Freud) inhibits the feeling aroused by forbidding masturbation and other sexual activities. For all these reasons and others the little girl turns away from the mother as a love object and replaces her in this respect with her father. Further, she begins to identify with the mother's role and to regard her as a competitor for the father. The Oedipal confrontation is thereby initiated. The little girl is in love with her father and her mother confronts her as a rival. Also, the child begins to fantasy producing a baby by her father. At one level, this fantasied baby takes on a reparative meaning and somehow becomes a substitute or compensation for the lost penis. Normally, in the long run, says Freud, a woman is able to assuage her disappointment about her penis lack by finding a man who will impregnate her and permit her to produce the substitute child. The shift from mother to father as a love object also involves giving up the clitoris as a prime erogenous zone and attaching greater importance to receptive rather than phallic erogenous body areas. This prepares for what Freud considers a fundamental step in the development of femininity, namely, minimizing the clitoris as a sexual response mode and learning to respond vaginally. In any case, the Oedipal relationship itself is described as arousing great anxiety and guilt in the little girl. She develops intense fear that her mother will retaliate against her for being her rival in relation to her father. Over a period of time her Oedipal aims are repressed and given up because of such fears (which emphasize the consequences of losing mother's love) and also guilt about the badness of her aims. A "latency period" (beginning at age six or seven) is then said to follow, during which the child's sexual wishes are held in abeyance. Finally, there is a revival of sexual interest at puberty; and if all goes normally, a sexually gratifying relationship with a man will be eventually established. As mentioned earlier, it is considered that a prerequisite for such a gratifying heterosexual interaction is to renounce the clitoris as a focal sexual arousal area and to learn to experience excitement from vaginal stimulation. Freud also specified that the manner in which a girl deals with the conflicts and tensions of the original Oedipal confrontation shapes the style of her interaction with her adult male sexual partner.

As evident from this summary, Freud regarded the route to heterosexual femininity as circuitous. It involves shifting from the mother love object to the father; being able to absorb the disappointment of lacking an important body organ (penis); shifting from one prime erogenous zone (clitoris) to another (vagina); and coping adequately with the complications, ambivalences, and guilt of the Oedipal confrontation. These are just some of the major adaptation tasks along the way to feminine sexual maturity that have been cited. Freud actually pointed up many other potentially complicating variables, such as how intense and ambivalent was the original (pre-Oedipal) relationship with mother and even possible constitutional differences in degree of masculinity-femininity. Freud did not really spell out, in a specific sense, how difficulties in getting through the feminine sex role sequence eventuated in an inhibition of sexual responsiveness. He only suggested that such difficulties produce disturbing fantasies, anxiety, and fear of being hurt—which then block and overwhelm the sensations aroused by sexual stimulation in general or those arising in localized body areas (for example, the vagina). However, he and some of his associates (Jones, 1927; Lample-De Groot, 1928) did focus on certain kinds of disturbances in the sex-role identification sequence as most likely to eventuate in symptoms of frigidity. These are reviewed briefly.

1. When, in the developmental sequence, the little girl presumably turns away from her mother as a love object and substitutes the father, she is simultaneously called upon to give up her active-phallic-clitoral sexual orientation in favor of one that is more passive and a precursor to the vagina becoming the prime erogenous zone. Freud noted that in the course of this renunciation of what had been the little girl's dominant style of sexual expression, there was the danger of a more general renunciation of all sexuality, which could lead to frigidity. He says at one point (in Ruitenbeek, 1966, p. 101): "Frequently, with the turning away from the mother there is a cessation of clitoral masturbation, and very often when the little girl represses her previous masculinity, a considerable part of her general sex life is permanently injured." That is, the shock and disappointment of discovering that one form of sexuality is inappropriate may generalize to an expectation that all sexual experience will be disappointing and ultimately frustrating.

2. Another major source of difficulty may derive from the little girl's refusal to give up her mother as a love object or from her retreat back to the mother as an object if she finds her passive (feminine) mode of relating with father too frustrating or disturbing. Such an adaptation may result in homosexual problems and a rejection of heterosexual stimulation. Lample-De Groot (1966, p. 43) notes at one point: ". . . a woman may form relationships with a man, and yet remain nevertheless inwardly attached to the first object of her love, her mother. She is obliged to be frigid in coitus

because she does not really desire the father or his substitute, but the mother."

The persistence of mother as an object may also signal the persistence of a phallic-orientation that is a defense against the passive "castrated" role implicit in taking father as a love object. It is theorized that resentments and anxiety about lacking a penis may result in compensatory illusory fantasies on the girl's part that she does possess one. There may also be an accompanying acting out of attitudes that are concerned with depreciating men and denying their phallic superiority. This may express itself, at one level, in a "refusal" to be sexually aroused by a man. In this way men can be made to feel frustrated and disappointed.

3. The complications and potential negative effects upon sexual responsiveness of the Oedipal interaction are often underscored. The little girl is confronted by her wishes to relate sexually to the father and to eliminate the mother as a rival. Her fantasies about her father make her feel guilty, fearful, and expectant of punishing retaliation. Indeed, if she cannot give up her father as a love object and accept some other nonfather male image as a substitute, her ability to respond sexually will be curtailed. This is so because her sexual interactions will be experienced as if they were with the father and thus be contaminated by all the tension and guilt such an idea evokes. Apropos of this point, Jones (1966, p. 28) states: "The girl must choose, broadly speaking, between sacrificing her erotic attachment to her father and sacrificing her femininity. . . . Either the father or the vagina . . . must be renounced."

4. The bisexuality of the female is said by Freud to add unique burdens to her problem of responding adequately to sexual stimulation. Note the following excerpts from one of his papers (in Ruitenbeek, 1966, p. 91): ". . . there can be no doubt that the bisexual disposition which we maintain to be characteristic of human beings manifests itself much more plainly in the female than in the male. The latter has only one principal sexual zone—only one sex organ—whereas the former has two: the vagina, the true female organ, and the clitoris which is analogous to the male organ." As indicated in this quotation, Freud was strongly impressed with the fact that the male has only one major genital arousal area and the female has two, and that therefore the female finds herself with a strong and often threatening bisexual potential. The female has to learn to integrate two polar forms of arousal, and in order to attain normal femininity must ultimately "transfer" from experiencing the clitoris as a prime center of sexual satisfaction to the vagina as the major center. Erotization of the clitoris must be substantially decreased and that of the vagina greatly increased. This transfer process has emerged in the psychoanalytic literature as one of the most difficult steps for most women to take. Inability to achieve orgasm via vaginal stimulation is cited as a major manifestation of female frigidity. Indeed, as defined by some (Hitschmann and Bergler, 1936), the only proper definition of frigidity is whether vaginal orgasm can or cannot be attained.

There is obviously quite an array of elements that Freud, both explicitly and implicitly, regarded as influential in modifying a woman's sexual responsiveness. Let us quickly scan the diversity included in this array:

Ability to give up mother as a love object.
Suitability of father as a love object.
Possessing sufficient strength not to be overwhelmed by the discovery that one is castrated (that is, lacking a penis).
Ability to "renounce" the satisfaction of clitoral stimulation without renouncing all sexuality.
Tolerance for the passivity associated with the feminine role.
Avoiding the temptation of acting as if one did possess a penis.
Being sufficiently flexible and adaptive to resolve the temptations, guilt, and contradictions of the Oedipal confrontation.
Coping with the confusion of the bisexuality represented by possessing two prime genital arousal areas (namely, clitoris and vagina).
Learning to minimize clitoral and maximize vaginal erotogenicity.

Freud's formulations about female sexuality, which appeared in scattered publications over a period of 15 years, stirred many others to try to understand the origins of female frigidity. They were almost all disciples of Freud, and their publications, which consisted largely of clinical observations of patients in analysis, seemed to support what Freud had had to say. But, as has been well described elsewhere (Sherfey, 1966), a number of female analysts (Thompson, Horney, Deutsch, Benedek) did register disagreement with Freud's conception of the female as someone mainly preoccupied with her lack of a penis and having no real pride in her own unique feminine attributes (for example, her ability to produce a child, and her nurturant and child-rearing talents). Increasingly, other analysts (Marmor, Keiser, Greenacre, Rado) have joined in criticizing what they regard as Freud's simplistic views about the determinants of a woman's sexual responsiveness. The publications of Kinsey, et al. (1953) and Masters and Johnson (1966) added impetus to this criticism because they offered empirical evidence that challenged one of the mainstays of Freud's theories about feminine sexuality—namely, that the ability to achieve vaginal orgasm is an indicator of sexual maturity. They cited anatomical and physiological data that they interpreted as indicating that a vaginal orgasm, as such, is a myth and that orgasm almost necessarily has to be mediated by clitoral stimulation.

These criticisms are only mentioned in passing, since there is no intent at this point to critique Freud's formulations systematically. But having summarized Freud's views, which provided the springboard for much of the subsequent speculation about female sexual responsiveness, we can now proceed to a survey of the major lines of thought involved in such speculation. This is done in terms of the following major categories: Body-Experience Distortions, Loss of Control, Phallic Defenses and Aspirations, Oral Attitudes, Guilt and Badness, and Miscellaneous.

Body-Experience Distortions

One cannot but be impressed with the frequency with which the literature suggests that disturbances in a woman's sexual responsiveness are traceable to distortions in the way she experiences her body. In numerous contexts, it is theorized that the changes in body experience produced by sexual arousal may be threatening and therefore inhibitory of satisfactory responsivity. The threat is often said to be a derivative of preexisting defects in the body image (concept of one's own body), particularly with reference to the genital sectors. Many women are portrayed as having poorly integrated concepts of their bodies that render them vulnerable to alarm and even disorganization when they are confronted by the gross shifts in body perception initiated by sexual excitement. Psychoanalytic writers often underscore the importance of such body image distortions, which is not surprising in view of the fact that Freud's formulations about the difficulties in attaining normal femininity heavily implicated distorted attitudes about one's body. Thus, Freud spoke of "castration anxiety" (fear about damage to the genital area), phallic fantasies (images of possessing an illusory penis), and anxiety about vaginal penetration (involving unrealistic images about the nature of the vagina) as affecting a girl's ability to make her way successfully through her psychosexual development.

To provide background for the presentation of body-image theories that follows, a word is in order at this point about the concept of "body image" and the part that body attitudes play in behavior. Freud (1959) and other psychoanalysts (for example, Fenichel, 1945) stated that an individual's identity and ego structure are importantly founded upon body experiences. They suggested that the first and primary core of self is the matrix of sensations linked with "my body." The awareness of one's own body as a separate object could be regarded as the foundation of the self. Further, the process of psychosexual development was outlined as involving a series of stages during which energy is successively invested in different sectors of the body (oral, anal, genital) that correspondingly vary in their importance in the body scheme and their influence in coloring interpretations of the world. For example, when, during the oral stage, the mouth and associated oral regions are psychologically accentuated they also become perceptually prominent in the individual's image of his body; and, as such, lead him to respond selectively to "oral" elements in his environs. One of the pioneers in really elaborating a formal superstructure of theory about body image was Paul Schilder (1935), who proposed that each person has to learn to integrate his multifarious body experiences, and each person evolves a fairly unique way of doing so. He conceived of the organized body image as having a significant impact in shaping conduct and providing a persistent frame of reference into which other experiences are assimilated and accordingly modified. He noted that the individual's existence is represented by his body which he carries with him into all situations. It is a constant source of sensations and experiences that help to guide his judgments. Over the years, a sizable scientific literature has accumulated (Fisher and Cleveland, 1968; Fisher, 1970; Shontz, 1969) that demonstrates that body attitudes do, in actuality, affect behavior. Body-image parameters have been variously shown to predict aspects of social interaction, response to stress, adaptation to threatening body incapacitation, patterns of physiological reactivity, and so forth. Clear evidence has accumulated that persons vary in the ways in which they integrate and interpret their body experiences and that, in turn, these adaptations affect their personality style.

One of the best descriptions of the body-experience alterations associated with sexual arousal has been provided by Fried (1960, pp. 3–4):

> Sexual arousal does not affect merely the sexual zones. The whole body is involved. . . . breathing, perspiration, vocalization and equilibrium sensations are all affected. . . . the ability to accept physiological changes is one of the important prerequisites of sexual enjoyment. Fear of such change is one of the greatest impediments to sexual functioning.
> A *sexually aroused person feels different all over. Expansions or distentions occur in various* body zones, not only in the genital area. . . . The experience of *equilibrium* undergoes a marked change. The customary, relatively automatic feel of body weight gives way to *floating and flying sensations.*

One may add, as detailed by Masters and Johnson (1966), that there are also changes in sensory acuity, throbbing of body parts, a temperature (heat) increase that suffuses over the body, muscle tension alterations, itching, sustained skin contact with another individual, and intense excitation emanating from mucous membranes.

Observers have pointed out that such changes present a sexually excited woman with a perception of her body that is radically different from the way in which she typically perceives it. Her excited body is, in the literal sense, hardly recognizable as the same body she knows most of the time from day to day. If she is a person who feels insecure about her body and has not organized a stable body concept, the gross "distortions" induced by sexual arousal may be frightening and therefore ultimately inhibitory of the attainment of orgasm.[4] On the other hand, these distortions may, as proposed by Fried (1960), appeal to another woman as being novel and enjoyably "different," thereby facilitating orgasm.

Multiple theories have been advanced concerning the forms of disturbance in body image that are likely to render a woman vulnerable to being traumatized by the sensations of sexual arousal.[5] A number of writers converge in emphasizing that fear of intrusive body penetration and of losing body boundaries is a prime cause of disturbed response to sexual stimulation. They suggest, each with his own phraseology, that a woman's conviction that her body is too "open," insufficiently protected, and incapable of resisting invasion can make her interpret sexual sensory experiences, with their accompanying expectation of being entered by the penis, as destructive. Directly or indirectly, they stress that each individual needs to experience her body as possessing a boundary because it not only delineates self-identity but also serves as a protective shield against outer dangers. Without an adequate boundary there is faulty differentiation between self and nonself. It is the threat to the fundamental boundary that is confronted in sexual interaction that is said to be so disturbing to many women.

Some have argued that the very nature and location of the female genital cause the girl, from the beginning, to have the feeling that a part of her body is hazy, incomplete, and essentially a "rent" through which outside forces can uncontrollably gain entry to her interior. Barnett (1966), Keiser (1956), Moore (1964), and others have expressed this view. It is said that because the girl, until the onset of menstruation, has little evidence of the existence of her vagina, which unlike the penis cannot be readily inspected visually, she attains only a hazy, tenuous concept of its form. For the little girl it is a mysterious "hole" in her body that has no apparent function.[6] Thus, she cannot easily perceive herself as possessing a complete, enclosing boundary, and an important region of her body is experienced as poorly defined and therefore insubstantial.[7] Incidentally, even the onset of menstruation, which is said to help define the existence and locale of the vagina, because of the associated flow of blood may be viewed as increasing fears about the vulnerability of the vagina and the dangers of penetration (Horney, 1967). Rheingold (1964) comments, apropos of this matter (p. 296): "In the anxieties provoked by the sight of blood . . . the idea of being torn and dismembered internally plays an extremely important part." But one should add that some writers (Kestenberg, 1956) state that the repeated practice effect of dealing with menstrual bleeding may have a reorganizing and stabilizing effect on a woman's body concept.

Barnett (1966) has pointed out that the vagina is one of the few body openings that has no sphincter and no protective "closing off" mechanism. She notes with respect to both the oral and anal orifices that (p. 131): "the child has initially, or develops within a very short time, some voluntary effective muscular means of preventing penetration. . . . *There is no such similar apparatus for control of the vaginal orifice,* so that penetration via this organ remains a constant threat over which the little girl can have no active control." She elaborates (p. 140) that the following conditions make it difficult for the girl to incorporate the vagina into her body image: "(a) There is no voluntary control of the orifice; (b) There is nothing contained in the cavity, the nature and activity of which would help the girl learn about this organ; (c) There are no contents which can be viewed by the girl as an actual part of herself."

These special attributes of the vagina, as outlined by Barnett, presumably maximize body anxiety. The girl is made to feel that the very existence of her vagina is a "threat to body integrity." [8,9]

It should be cautioned that despite the forceful way in which psychoanalytic theorists have called attention to the woman's potential difficulties in integrating the vagina into her body image, and also underscored her susceptibility to anxiety about being penetrated and losing her boundaries because of the nature of the feminine sex role, there is little scientific support for this perspective. Indeed, the empirical studies that have concerned themselves with comparing boundary definiteness and stability in males and females (for example, Fisher and Cleveland, 1968; Fisher, 1970) have consistently found the latter superior to the former. Using a well-validated index (Barrier score) that measures how clearly and definitely an individual experiences his body boundaries, Fisher (1970) concluded that both in children and adults the female feels more secure about her boundaries than does the male. In fact, other empirical findings (Fisher, 1970) indicate that the woman may generally feel more secure about her body and see it as more directly linked with her identity than does the man. These findings stand in direct opposition to the view long held by psychoanalytic circles (but also now increasingly doubted by many analysts) that a woman typically considers her own body to be a castrated (inferior) version of the male's, and is therefore chronically beset with doubts and fears about it.

Another primary body image difficulty ascribed by psychoanalytic theorists to women relates to a sense of being dirty and defiled. Freud (1949a,b), Horney (1967), Bonaparte (1953), and others were impressed with the spatial proximity and analogous forms of the vagina and rectum.[10] They believed that the separation of the anal and genital zones was less clearly defined in females than in males. Indeed, it was considered that sensations from the rectum were, throughout childhood, dominant over vaginal sensations, and that modes of adaptation to these sensations often provided a prototype for adaptation to vaginal sensations when they became more prominent at the time of menarche. Analysts have reported that in the fantasies of female patients in psychotherapeutic treatment, one finds a confusion between vagina and anus, with the result that "dirty" attributes associated with anality become linked with the vagina. Presumably as a consequence of this sense of body dirtiness, women may react with disgust to certain of the body changes, such as vaginal secretions and associated odors, produced by sexual arousal. They may perceive their body changes as dirty and having anal rather than sexual meaning. One of the most thorough discussions of this matter may be found in a paper by Needles (1961), who, in describing one of his patients who had unusually vivid feelings of genital dirtiness, notes (p. 706), ". . . she regarded the sexual act as one of defilement and soiling, with herself as the victim. . . . The vagina was regarded by her as filthy."

The girl's perception of her genitals as dirty apparently receives strong reinforcement at the time she begins to menstruate. Deutsch (1946) asserted that girls often interpret menstruation as an eliminative (anal type) function. Thompson (in Ruitenbeek, p. 59) states: ". . . I have frequent evidence that the inability to control not only menstruation but all secretions of the female genitals has contributed to a feeling of unacceptability and dirtiness. . . ." She adds that the general tendency to treat women as inferiors intensifies their sense of being unworthy and therefore dirty. Silbermann (1950), Rheingold (1964), Lederer (1968), and others indicate that the concept of the menstruating female as dirty has wide currency, not only in the Western world but in almost every culture ever studied. It is the basic shame about her body being dirty, especially in the genital region, that presumably causes a woman to react with disgust and inhibition when she perceives sexual stimulation releasing excretions and odors from her.

Many other exotic kinds of body image effects and distortions related to sexual arousal have been described. To exhaustively catalogue them would be an extended task, but their range can be illustrated as follows.

Agoston (1946) notes that following orgasm some women develop a feeling of bodily "emptiness" (lack of sensation) and seem to feel an internal "void" subsequent to orgastic release that is so unpleasant and threatening that it introduces anxiety into all of their sexual encounters.

Fried (1960) speaks of the perspiration and other liquid secretions at the time of sexual arousal as setting off concern about sphincter control. For example, fantasies about losing bladder control may parallel the sudden appearance ("gushing out") of so much liquid on one's body.

Some writers (Fried, 1960) report instances in which sexual arousal is so traumatic to a woman that she responds with defensive depersonalization of her body. That is, she begins to experience her body as "not mine," like a foreign and alienated object. It seems to belong to someone else and to be incapable of feeling anything.

One writer (Eisenstein, 1949) indicates that (p. 165) intercourse "brings about tremendous shifts in libidinal cathexes that bear directly on the nature of subsequent dream formation." The shifts in body excitation patterns produced by intercourse are described as vectors that are so powerful that they circumvent the dream defenses and find unusually direct representation in the manifest content of postcoital dreams.

Keiser (1947) refers to psychiatric patients who perceive sexual arousal as if it had filled their bodies with "electricity." He remarks that some react to such sensations with a "fear of bursting." Keiser describes still other women who react to their sexually excited bodies as though a force had "taken control" over them and that their bodies had been overpowered.

One can see from the material presented in this section that luxuriant consideration has been devoted to how a woman's attitudes toward her body may affect her reactions to sexual stimulation. Amidst the welter of material is an emphasis on anxiety about being penetrated and losing one's boundaries as one of the prime body image factors in sexual inhibition. It is impressive how frequently this factor is mentioned in the literature. Many observers claim to have demonstrated its importance in terms of the fantasies, dreams, and even conscious fears verbalized by women with problems in attaining sexual arousal. Whether these affirmations represent diverse valid observations or, on the contrary, simply reflect the fact that there is widespread adherence to psychoanalytical theories about the importance of "penetration" fears remains to be seen. Fisher's (1970) empirical finding that women's boundaries, rather than being less definite than men's, are actually relatively more clearly delineated does not seem to be congruent with the view taken in the speculative literature that the nature of a woman's psychosexual development and the structure of her genitals maximize feelings of penetrability and vulnerability. Clarification of this issue should be one of the high priority goals of future research concerned with feminine sexuality.

This discussion of body attitudes would not be complete without considering one other related topic. In various publications it has been proposed that a woman may find herself inhibited sexually because of her fears of the reproductive consequences of intercourse.[11] That is, intercourse signals the possibility of impregnation, which in turn means nine months of pregnancy and ultimately the delivery of a child. This process may be seen as being fraught with danger. Pregnancy may be perceived as something that can weaken and harm one's body, and the act of delivery as one that can tear the body and even eventuate in death. Obviously, anxiety that pregnancy may inflict damage or death on one's body is a species of body image disturbance.

Deutsch (1945) and Benedek (1968) have been particularly prominent in calling attention to the intimate link between sexual and reproductive fantasies in women. They suggest that a woman's concept of intercourse is quite different from the man's in the extent to which the woman experiences it as just one phase of the total reproductive sequence. Presumably, a man is focused, during intercourse, on the immediate sexual gratification aspects of the experience, whereas a woman is more likely to react to it as one phase of the larger reproductive process. In so doing, she links sexual arousal with pregnancy and is faced with all of the biological consequences of her sexuality. If these consequences have dangerous implications to her, they may "turn her off" sexually.

Apropos of this matter Heinman (1963, pp. 373–374) remarks: "Some psychoanalysts have postulated the unconscious analogy between coitus and birth. This unconscious analogy is present in the woman regardless of the degree to which she consciously wishes to separate sexual pleasure from reproductive function." Moore (1961, p. 572) adds: ". . . the vagina is the bearer of the deeper anxiety—of death—which is mobilized in pregnancy and accompanies all biological acts of motherhood.[12] Although there are individual factors which provoke the anxiety, the biological destiny is to a high degree responsible for preventing sexual responses in the vagina."

It is of related significance that several writers (Deutsch, 1945; Benedek, 1968) have conceptualized the learning of the feminine role as necessarily involving the acceptance of a masochistic definition of self, a feeling that a woman is destined to suffer and be damaged. Presumably, she expects that being a woman and a sex object means she cannot escape the ultimate pain and body damage that go along with menstruation, "defloration," and the sometimes unpleasant vicissitudes of pregnancy (abortion, death). In fact, the very definition of the feminine sex role is often said to contain the assumption that sexual intercourse requires a submission to the stronger male who will master, and even hurt, one's body.[13]

It is pertinent to add that some indirect support for the importance of masochistic attitudes in a woman's orientation has come from the work of Douvan and Adelson (1966), which was based on interview data obtained from samples of adolescent girls. They concluded (p. 239): "Our evidence supports the psychoanalytic notion that feminine women tend to accept and tolerate, even take pleasure in, a measure of pain. We find that feminine girls are more intrapunitive, more self blaming, than nonfeminine girls."

Loss of Control

The excitement that builds up during sexual arousal may, according to some writers, result in a woman's feeling that she is losing control of herself. She is depicted as finding herself in a psychological state that is so intense and "gripping" that it appears to have the potentiality of overwhelming her usual rational controls. She may feel that the reasoning part of herself will be swept away and that as a result she will "go out of the world," do something "crazy," or behave like an animal. This concern about losing control may be reinforced by the fact that sexual arousal tends to decrease consciousness and diminish articulated awareness of external objects, aside from one's sex partner. Indeed, Keiser (1956) believes that orgasm is often accompanied by a momentary loss of consciousness (although Kinsey, et al. [1953] did not find many women who reported this to be true). Fried (1960) in discussing the fear of loss of self-control arising out of sexual arousal states (p. 17): "The intensity of sexual passion is determined partly, though not altogether, by the individual's capacity for enduring and enjoying regressive processes. Nearly all acquisitions the ego has made are temporarily and partially given up. . . . Certain ego defenses which have been built up and used since childhood are shed and so the organism is in a rather vulnerable position." She adds (p. 21): "If the regressive processes are experienced as too pronounced, the temporarily dissolved ego functions, defenses, and boundaries are resurrected.[14] . . . The individual man and woman, sensing that the ego, which is usually in the driver's seat, is about to dissolve, even though only partially, anticipates a permanent loss of ego, or, to put it differently, insanity."

Actually, what Fried is suggesting is that when the fear of ego dissolution becomes too great, anxiety is aroused that "shuts down" and blocks further sexual arousal.

Many other psychoanalytic observers have reported that they find in the fantasies of their patients that fear of loss of control and madness are linked with orgastic arousal. Here are two examples. Keiser (1947) describes the fear (p. 382), ". . . that sexual tension will lead to 'insanity' (loss of all inhibition with the release of the id). . . ." Benedek (1968) notes with exceptional clarity (pp. 445–466): "Transient ego regression is a constituent of the orgasm capacity in both sexes. . . . Unconscious fear of ego regression may impede the orgasmic capacity of men as well; this, however, happens more frequently in women. Since her sexual experience is diffuse, this regression often feels to her as a loss of herself. Many women experience this regression in the ego state—a psychological precursor to orgasm—as an intolerable threat."

Although the foreboding implications of "losing control" have been pointed to by some, others (for example, Fried, 1960) consider that the sensation of potential loss of control is for many women a piquant enrichment of the sexual arousal experience. It is the opening of self to a sense of undisciplined excitement that presumably makes sexual interaction especially enjoyable. Paradoxically, some (Feldman, 1951) even suggest that *fear* which is set off by sexual arousal may itself further energize, rather than inhibit, the arousal process. A variety of examples are cited by Feldman of instances in which orgasm seemed to be produced by fear and anticipation of danger. It is explicitly assumed that fear can be "sexually exciting." [15] Freud himself proposed that sexual impulses could be turned into fear, and Ferenczi thought the process was reversible (see Feldman, 1951).

Fried (1960) and others suggest that it is the rigid woman, who has lived narrowly and avoided change, who is most upset by the loss of control implications of intense sexual arousal. [16] Although there is no direct evidence for this view, it is pertinent to note that studies have shown that personal rigidity does inhibit involvement in novel perceptual experiences. [17] For example, Snyder (in Ittelson and Kutash, 1961) reported that the greater an individual's personality rigidity the less capable he was of detecting the unusual visual changes produced in his surroundings when he looked through distorting (aniseikonic) lenses. Rigidity has also proven to be predictive of a reluctance to becoming involved with novel and adventurous activities. As will be described in a subsequent section, the present writer has undertaken empirical studies of the correlation between sexual responsiveness in women and their preferences for novel experiences.

If anxiety about loss of control can be stirred by the fact of attaining a high degree of excitement, is this phenomenon specific to sexual excitement? Or is the response to sexual excitement merely a special case that applies to all forms of extremely high arousal? Would there be a correlation between the amount of anxiety about loss of control elicited by sexual arousal and the amount provoked by other forms of arousal (for example, drug induced; intense hostility)? A number of writers (Fried, 1960) would probably anticipate the correlation to be fairly substantial.

Phallic Defenses and Aspirations

As outlined earlier, Freud assumed that a crucial component of a woman's psychosexual development is learning to shift from a phallic (clitorally oriented) mode of sexuality, in which the mother is the prime object, to a more passive (vaginal) mode involving identification with the mother, and taking the father (and eventually another man) as a prime object. Presumably, this shift involves the following steps: the girl discovers that she lacks a penis; therefore she feels hurt and disappointed; she blames her mother for her deficiency because her mother produced her and also because of accumulated grievances against her; she identifies with her mother and takes her father as a love object; and simultaneously turns away from the clitoris and gives intensified importance and prominence to the passive-receptive vagina. This is regarded as the normal sequence of adaptation. However, women are said to have real difficulty in "giving up" their phallic orientation and accepting vaginal passivity. The sense of being castrated consequent upon such acceptance is apparently too painful to some, and they continue to strive for phallic modes of expression.[18] Freud (Ruitenbeek, pp. 95–96) said apropos of this point: "When a little girl . . . discovers her own deficiency, she does not accept the unwelcome knowledge without hesitation and reluctance . . . she clings obstinately to the expectation of acquiring a similar organ sometime, and the desire for it survives long after the hope is extinguished." The fact that a woman clings to phallic hopes has been cited frequently in the literature as a cause for frigidity. It is theorized that phallic attitudes may be inimical to the sort of passivity presumed to be necessary for real femininity and, more specifically, for the development of sensitivity of the vagina to penile stimulation. Further, a woman's phallic attitude is said to express itself often in an aggressive, avenging attitude toward men designed to demonstrate that they are not superior because thay possess a penis. This avenging attitude may utilize frigid unresponsiveness as a way of disappointing men. It is even suggested that symptoms such as vaginismus (spasms of vaginal musculature) may be unconsciously directed toward frustrating the male by making intercourse painful for him (Moore, 1964).

The factors considered to influence a woman to adopt a phallic orientation have been conceptualized in multiple ways in psychoanalytic publications. It would not be pertinent to the present discussion to consider them in detail, but the following brief listing illustrates the range of views that may be found.

Unusually strong attachment to the mother is regarded by Jones (1966) as preventing a woman from shifting so that she can see her mother not as a love object but as someone with whom she can identify—and thus be enabled at the same time (in a nonphallic way) to take her father as a love object.

Fenichel (1945) indicates that a mother who is unusually aggressive and phallic may provide her daughter with a phallic feminine model that she then emulates.

Horney (1967) suggests that phallic fantasies may paradoxically be a way of denying heterosexual (Oedipal) fantasies involving father. She states (p. 67): "The fiction of maleness enabled the girl to escape from the female role . . . (which is) burdened with guilt and anxiety."

Horney (1967) also suggests that phallic fantasies may not literally represent wishes to possess a penis, but rather express symbolically the desire to possess the superior privileges and status of the male.

The reparative functions of phallic fantasies have been stressed by both Ovesey (1956) and Keiser (1947). Ovesey indicates (p. 342): "The castration-anxiety may give rise to magical reparative fantasies through which a new penis is acquired." Keiser (1947) speculates that an illusory penis may be unconsciously sought by a woman in order to repair the rent in the body boundary apparently represented by the female genital.

Ovesey (1956) proposes that any crisis that a woman encounters (for example, pregnancy, loss of an object) that disappoints her with regard to her femininity may revive phallic attitudes.

Greenson (1955) refers to women assuming phallic attitudes (p. 250) "in order to avoid anxiety or disappointment in their own sexual role."

As these illustrations indicate, the psychoanalytic framework has offered a number of different levels of explanation for phallic attitudes in women. Possibly without exception, the theorists maintain that such phallic attitudes interfere with a woman's heterosexual responsiveness. This would, of course, be expected in view of the fact that the psychoanalytic developmental scheme considers the phallic phase to precede real femininity and to represent a relatively early state of immaturity. The possibility of challenging this view has presented itself since the publication of the Kinsey, et al. (1953) and Masters and Johnson (1966) work indicating that the clitoris continues to play an important role in the sexual responsiveness of normal women. That is, since the clitoris is equated in psychoanalytic theory with a phallic mode of responsiveness and since it does play a significant part in the sexual arousal of the normal woman, one must begin to consider the possibility that adequate feminine sexuality is a fusion of both the phallic and nonphallic. Some data pertinent to this issue are considered at a later point when the writer's studies of feminine sexuality are presented.

Oral Attitudes

Whereas the original psychoanalytic formulations did not coherently say much about the part played by oral experiences and attitudes in a woman's sexual responsiveness, this has become an increasingly popular topic in the analytic literature. There has been a growing trend to assume that the little girl's earliest experiences with eating, and the whole province of oral appetite, may influence how she later adapts to the demands of her sexual appetite. Early oral experiences are considered significant not only at the literal level of satisfaction of appetite but also in terms of what is learned about "feeding" figures, as exemplified in mother's behavior while she provides oral satisfactions. It is generally assumed that if a woman's experiences with eating and incorporation have been too frustrating or disappointing, she will respond defensively (and with inhibition) to sexual stimulation. The rationale for this view is reviewed in a subsequent section.

The establishment of an early relationship between orality and sexuality has been depicted by some as occurring as the result of an association between the baby girl's sucking experiences (while eating) and sensations supposedly aroused in her vagina simultaneously by the sucking. Brierley (1932) conjectures, on the basis of clinical observations, that vaginal contractions and sensations are induced in the infant while it is sucking in nourishment. Brierley even proposes that only those babies whose vaginas receive the stimulation arising out of happy sucking will eventually achieve satisfying femininity. Actually, a number of psychoanalysts have reported that female psychiatric patients frequently equate mouth and vagina in their fantasies (Lorand, 1939; Langer, 1951; Jones, 1966). Lorand (1939) has been particularly explicit in attributing female frigidity to an equation of vagina and mouth and an acting out of oral deprivation feelings via vaginal experience. Thus, he states, with reference to sexually unresponsive women he had studied (p. 433): "The inability to cope with the reality of sexual functioning had its roots in the earliest mother fixation. The constant hunger for affection, guidance, and dependence, the need to be 'filled up,' characteristic of all these patients, was mainly responsible for the failure to attain sexual gratification. In all, the equation of 'Vagina = Mouth' was dominant."

Kestenberg (1956) provides an interesting model for the manner in which mouth and vagina might become equated (pp. 458–459): [19]

> The ability to open or close the mouth at volition establishes permanent boundaries between oneself and the outside. Such oral experiences are used by analogy in the body-image formation of other openings. . . . The mouth . . . as the model opening becomes the symbol for all "holes" of the body. Thus, the vaginal opening becomes endowed with oral representations stemming from a direct equation with the mouth as well as from an indirect one, which emerges from oral admixtures incorporated in the image of other openings with which the introitus is successively equated.

This formulation proposes that the vagina is endowed with mouth attributes because the two areas are analogous in being openings into the body. Freud explicitly recognized the possibility of this sort of equation.

Clinical accounts abound that describe women who are said to experience intercourse in a context of oral fantasies (Lorand, 1939). These reports assert that it is not uncommon to find women who unconsciously perceive the vagina as sucking in or incorporating the penis during intercourse. Presumably such perceptions can interfere with sexual intimacy, especially if they are destructive in character and therefore arouse inhibiting guilt (Moore, 1961). It is pertinent to mention also that Hamburger (1959) reports that food and eating are frequently symbolically substituted for sexual aims in dreams.[20,21]

Some (Lichtenstein, 1961) trace the interplay between orality and sexuality back to the original intimacy between the child and the nurturing mother. They suggest that no other relationship, except that between mother and child, approaches the closeness of sexual interaction. It is conjectured that in the original intimacy of being fed and cared for by mother, attitudes are shaped that are ultimately basic to sexual intimacy. Hitschmann (1952, p. 426) comments that Freud assumed that "the sucking of the child at the breast of the mother is the model of every love relationship. . . ." Congruent with this view, the assumption is made that if the original transactions between mother and child were faulty, there will be a resultant lack of trust about closeness that will interfere with future sexual enjoyment that requires a related species of closeness.[22]

It should be reiterated that the import of oral factors in female sexuality has come under wide consideration in the psychoanalytic literature. There is serious belief that the original interaction with mother may be a prototype for future sexual intimacy. Also, there is serious belief in the possibility of unconsciously equating vagina and mouth.[23]

Guilt and Badness

One finds the concept of guilt appealed to strongly as an explanation for inhibited sexual responsiveness in women. This was earlier touched upon in the section dealing with body image distortions and frigidity. It will be recalled that feelings of body dirtiness, which would appear to involve guilt, were discussed in terms of their presumed negative impact upon responsivity. The psychoanalytic literature usually portrays the guilt of women as growing out of difficulties in coping with the Oedipal confrontation. Presumably, when the little girl takes her father as a love object (simultaneously giving up her mother), she also sees her mother as a rival and jealously fantasies getting rid of her. It is the rivalry with the mother and the fantasies about destroying her that are said to create great guilt in the little girl. If the girl does not relinquish the father as a love object, it is assumed that her later relationships with men will be heavily suffused with Oedipal significance—with the consequence that sexual interaction will activate the guilt tied to the original Oedipal rivalry with the mother.

Moore (1964, p. 345) has succinctly summarized this view:

Normal identification with mother is accompanied by the desire to be loved by father and, like mother, to have a child by him. This wish can be fulfilled provided the girl exchanges her infantile object, the father, for another man. Otherwise, instead of successful identification, she develops spiteful rivalry with mother accompanied by a grave sense of guilt which requires renunciation of the maternal role.[24]

Rado (1955), a psychoanalyst, proposes that sexual guilt may, even more directly, be traced to the way in which the culture imparts knowledge to the child about sexuality. He notes that not only does it try to keep children "ignorant of sexual matters" and "to deter them from sexual activity and interests," but it presents sex as a "sin or something that a nice child should not even think of doing." He conjectures that the sexual fears so engendered are converted into "guilty sexual fears" because the underlying repressive orientation of the culture arouses rage that cannot be expressed and is turned back reproachfully upon the self.[25]

Deutsch (1945) feels that a woman's sexual guilt is likely to be mobilized in situations that accentuate her femininity or reproductive functions. She speaks of pregnancy as having such an impact. Apropos of this view, it is interesting that Horney (1967, p. 67) believes that some women take refuge from their sexual guilt by denying their femininity and identifying with masculinity. ("The fiction of maleness enables the girl to escape from the female role . . . burdened with guilt and anxiety.")

Hollender (1963) describes instances in which women protect themselves against sexual guilt by focusing their attention upon certain defensive fantasies during intercourse. For example, he cites a woman who, in order to obtain sexual pleasure, found it necessary to picture herself as being raped by a Negro. He interprets this (p. 105) as a maneuver to "replace her husband with someone completely remote from the father in order to overcome the incestuous taboo (and resulting guilt) that sexual relationship with her husband brought forth." [26]

Greenson (1955) enumerates ways in which sexual foreplay rituals may be developed that are designed to neutralize sexual guilt. The basic principle involved seems to be to get the sexual partner to do things (for example, kissing of genitals) that demonstrate that he does not regard one's body as dirty or bad or unworthy.

Another defense against sexual guilt is mentioned by Kestenberg (1956), who conjectures that when the little girl turns to the father as a love object she gets rid of her guilt by ejecting it on him. The girl supposedly assigns to him all kinds of seductive and sexually bad intentions and is then left free of blame or evil sexual intent.

The impact of guilt on sexual behavior has actually been demonstrated empirically by Mosher and Cross (1971), who were able to show in terms of a measure of sex guilt derived from responses to a questionnaire that the greater a woman's guilt the less sexually active she was premaritally.

Miscellaneous

Traversing the literature, one can find many other theories that seek to explain the nature of a woman's sexual reactivity. There are explanations that give weight to constitutional factors, and others (Comfort, 1963) that blame sexual inhibition upon the generally high level of tension and the depersonalized atmosphere said to typify Western culture. Still other explanations are offered that assortedly blame poor sex education, "honeymoon trauma," fear of becoming addicted to orgasm (Keiser, 1947), and so forth.

This perusal of the theories about feminine sexual responsiveness has turned up quite a melange. With minor exceptions, these theories have been of psychoanalytic origin and have called upon the full repertory of psychoanalytic concepts—from orthodox Oedipal factors, to the intricacies of clitoral-vaginal shifts, and again to speculations about orality and mouth-vagina equations. One is presented with a matrix of theories in which ideas crowd each other. There is no immediate way to decide which are the most reasonable or even the most logical. Some may very well turn out to be verifiable when pertinent empirical findings accumulate. At this point, without further information one can only admire their ingenuity and complex concatenations.

N O T E S

1. As described in more detail later, the present writer found in the course of checking Terman's findings further that a score based on these items was not significantly correlated with a woman's ability to attain orgasm.

2. Other early pioneering studies by Dickinson and Beam (1932) and Davis (1929) likewise contain little empirical data that help to clarify possible psychological distinctions among women with varying orgastic capacities.

3. Reevy (1954) has similarly reported that in a group of unmarried college girls, orgastic capacity seemed paradoxically to be linked with test responses indicating low potential for stability in future marital relationships.

4. Benedek (1968, p. 446) says apropos of this matter: "To endure passion the individual must be able to submit to increasing sexual tension without anxiety; she must be able to accept changes in her behavior and in her body without shame."

5. It is pertinent to mention that Landis and Bolles (1942) found that women who had had serious body defects from early childhood did not seem to be motivated to seek out sexual stimulation or interaction.

6. Kestenberg (1956) conjectures that the little girl projects her poorly understood and mysterious vaginal sensations upon her doll and seeks to gain mastery over them in the course of her doll play.

7. Glenn and Kaplan (1968) speculate that the perceived site of greatest sexual arousal and even orgasm may be influenced by fear of being penetrated. They offer the clinical example of a woman who apparently "restricted" her orgastic sensations to "external" body sites because to experience them internally was too threatening insofar as it implied that something had gained access to the interior of her body.

8. It would be superfluous to enumerate in detail the multiple other statements in the literature concerning the role of anxiety about boundary loss and body penetration in diminishing a woman's sexual responsiveness. Numerous other writers could be cited. Illustratively, Bonaparte (1953) felt that women have a dread of being sexually penetrated that is as biologically based as the resistance of a cell wall to being penetrated. Fliess (1956) and Ferenczi (1938) speculated that during intercourse there is an experience of "fusion" between the male and female genitals— which can be reacted to as though it meant a dangerous loss of individuation. Friedman (1962) reported that fear of the destructive effects of penile penetration played an important role in cases where women had refused for years to consummate their marriages. In addition, disturbance linked with sexual penetration in women has been discussed by Benedek (1968), Deutsch (1945), Keiser (1947), Kestenberg (1956), Weissman (1964), and others.

9. But as might be expected, Kaplan (1970) has found in his review of a number of clinical cases involving congenital absence of the vagina that this condition produced great distress and conflict about sexual identity and about being "different."

10. Note Jones' (1938) opinion on this matter. "The anus is evidently identified

with the vagina to begin with, and the differentiation of the two is an extremely obscure process, more so perhaps than any other in female development."

11. Whereas this is an interesting and apparently logical speculation, it should be pointed out that Rodgers and Ziegler (1968) did not find an increase in sexual responsiveness in women who shifted from relatively nondependable to dependable forms of contraception. They state (p. 503), "Our data thus do not support the generalization that change to effective, noncoital contraceptive procedures markedly alters such sexual problems as frigidity. . . ."

12. Keiser (1947, 1952) has pointed out that the momentary loss of consciousness associated in some instances with orgasm may be equated with death.

13. Freud (in Ruitenbeek, 1966) and other analysts refer to the passive masochistic fate of the female. They see it as partially a mode of countering previous active, phallic (even sadistic) wishes that would interfere with being sufficiently passive to attain normal femininity. Rado (1933) even suggests that the "hurt" experienced by the little girl when she discovers she lacks a penis may become a substitute source of gratification. She somehow paradoxically derives gratification from the fact that she has been and will be hurt.

Deutsch (1944) has nicely summarized one aspect of the psychoanalytic view concerning the role of masochism in feminine psychosexual development (p. 251): ". . . the girl gives up her aggressions partly as a result of her own weakness, partly because of the taboos of the environment, and chiefly because of the love prize given her as compensation . . . activity becomes passivity, and aggression is renounced for the sake of being loved. In this renunciation the aggressive forces that are not actively spent must find an outlet, and they do this by endowing the passive state of being loved with a masochistic character. . . . The absence of an active organ brought the turn toward passivity and masochism in its train."

14. There are obvious parallels between a reference such as "dissolved ego functions" and the concept of "disturbed body boundaries," which was the topic of the previous section.

15. The energizing effects of anxiety upon learning and other functions have been well documented in the psychological literature (Hilgard, 1948).

16. Even more striking is her statement that some psychotic persons are able to appreciate orgasm to an unusual degree because they have learned to accept states of extreme regression and disorganization without becoming alarmed. She says (p. 23): "Familiarity with ego regression is one of the reasons for the sexual advantages which such severely damaged individuals as the borderline patient or psychotic may have over the neurotic. . . . Those we look upon as most disturbed are accustomed to transitions from ego control to regression and frequently tolerate ego recession in the sexual act better than do neurotics." Obviously, this observation is also relevant to the discussion, earlier in this chapter, concerning the relationship of sexual responsiveness to psychopathology.

17. If living within a rigid, closely defined set of values does increase the likelihood of disturbance about the loss of control implications of sexual arousal, one might have expected that religiosity would have an inhibiting effect on orgasm capacity in women. But, in fact, neither Kinsey, et al. (1953) nor others have been able to find consistent general support for such an expectation.

18. Levin (1966) was able to show in an empirical study that made use of Rorschach Inkblot measures that unmarried women with masculine social roles have more "castration anxiety" than married women not filling such roles.

19. Kestenberg (1956) suggests that Freud, in his contention that the child's earliest concept of intercourse is that of fellatio, recognized the oral involvement in discharge of sexual tensions.

20. Weakland (1956) indicates that the Chinese strongly associate sexuality and orality. The vagina is seen as capable of exhausting a man and also of providing strengthening supplies.

21. MacLean (1962) has called attention to the close anatomical contiguity of oral and sexual response areas in the limbic cortex.

22. It has even been imaginatively speculated that women may unconsciously perceive the penis as a (motherly) breast and therefore intercourse as a "nursing" experience (Moore, 1961, 1968).

23. Rosenblatt (1967), making use of cross-cultural data, was able to show that the greater the early oral frustration in a culture the more importance was assigned to romantic love as a basis for marriage. It was considered that early oral frustration resulted in a compensatory need for later heterosexual relationships to supply closeness and affection. One can view such findings as providing some support for the idea that oral attitudes and sexual behavior are somehow linked. It is pertinent to the same issue that Harlow (1958) found that infant monkeys who were not receiving grooming attention and contact from the mother were unmotivated to engage in sexual activity as adults.

24. Van Ophuijsen (1966) adds that the little girl may experience guilt because she interprets her lack of a penis as a "result of wrongdoing," "punishment for a sexual lapse."

25. Ellis (1958) has likewise focused upon the general message given by the culture about how bad and shameful sex is.

26. Words in parentheses introduced for purposes of clarification by the present writer.

3

BEING A WOMAN

There is still another place to look in trying to build up notions about what shapes a woman's ability to be sexually responsive. One can take the view that if the ability to respond adequately sexually is a normal phenomenon, it should be associated with normal femininity. This view has been put forth by Brown (1958) who suggests that without a normal sex identification process in childhood there cannot be normal sexuality in adulthood. Obviously, a similar perspective characterizes psychoanalytic theory. If this basic assumption is correct, it should be informative to examine the process of attaining modal (normal?) femininity in our culture. Possibly in tracing this process one can find clues about what facilitates or hinders a woman's reaction to sexual stimulation. Information pertinent to feminine responsiveness might emerge if the findings available concerning the nature of femininity, the "feel" of what it is like to be feminine, were reviewed and appraised. The objective of this section is to range through the available empirical data on feminine personality structure and the course of feminine socialization, hopefully to help at eventually arriving at some clarification of the responsivity issue.

One should add that, in more general terms, it seemed important to review what is soundly known about how femininity evolves in order to provide a context for interpreting research findings to be presented at a later point.

What Is Modal Femininity?

Are there attitudes, feelings, and traits that are uniquely feminine in Western societies? In agreement with what would be the common-sense answer to this question, one can find a fair number of studies that have isolated attitudinal and personality dimensions that do, indeed, typify femininity.

Body Concept

It would be well to begin with the most obvious, and perhaps most fundamental statements that seem to derive from the anatomical differences between the sexes. A woman experiences her body differently than does a man. Her body image or concept of her body has unique feminine connotations. Freud and other psychoanalysts suggested this in a negative way when they theorized that the female forever feels that her body is inferior because it lacks a penis. More recent empirical studies have shown that the female experiences her body as nonphallic, in contrast to the male whose body feelings are saturated with phallic qualities. The terms "phallic" and "nonphallic," as they are used here, do not simply refer to the feeling that one literally does or does not have a penis. They pertain to a more generalized sense of one's body possessing phallic or nonphallic qualities. The phallic-nonphallic dimension, in this generalized sense, includes sensations of phallic shape, strength, large size, toughness, and so forth.

Erikson (1951), in an early often-cited investigation, provides a good introduction to the question of the body concept dimension. Erikson requested adolescent boys and girls in the 11–13 age range to construct "imaginary" scenes with an array of standard play materials that were available to them. The play scenes so produced were photographed and later analyzed by means of objective scoring categories. It was found that there were marked differences between the sexes with reference to what they had fashioned. The boys more often depicted scenes involving moving vehicles, elevated structures, and settings of linear motion. The girls typically represented interior settings (for example, of homes), open structures, and static situations. Erikson regarded these differences as analogous to the sex differentiation in the structure of the genitalia.[1] That is, the boy was presumably expressing his phallic perception of his body in his upright and moving play representations, whereas the girl was expressing her vaginal (and perhaps uterine) concept in her portrayal of areas that were open and accessible. Erikson, in another publication (1964), summarized the contrast as follows (p. 10): ". . . sex differences in the organization of a play space seem to parallel the morphology of genital differentiation itself: in the male, an *external* organ, *erectible* and *intrusive* in character, serving the channelization of mobile sperm cells: *internal* organs in the female, with vestibular *access,* leading to *statically expectant* ova."

Honzik (1951), in a further analysis of play constructions of boys and girls, reaffirmed the nature of the sex differences reported by Erikson.

Even in dreams obtained from males and females there are differences in content that resemble some of the Erikson and also Honzik findings. Brenneis (1967) studied the manifest content of dreams of male and female college students and found (among other things) that those of the females more often occurred in an inner space (for example, home) and those of the males more often involved themes of "extended forward motion." Brenneis himself commented upon the similarities between his results and those of Erikson. Ward, Beck, and Rascoe (1961), in discussing sex differences in dream content, stated that themes of flying were significantly more often mentioned by males than by females. Colby (1963) reported that in a collection of dreams from 75 tribal societies those of men more often involved themes of "intensified penetration of space" than did those of women.

Other investigators have continued to report male-female differences that seem to be congruent with the idea that the sexes experience themselves differently with respect to the phallic-vaginal paradigm. Franck and Rosen (1949) have shown that males and females, when asked to complete a series of standard drawings, differ significantly in their styles of completion. The males compose phalliclike, angular, closed completions whereas the females tend to elaborate the drawings internally and to leave them open. Such differences have been substantiated by a number of investigators and have been observed across several cultures (Kohlberg, 1966). Franck and Rosen and others have interpreted these contrasts between the sexes as analogous to the difference between male and female genitalia. There have been cross-cultural studies (McClelland, 1964) that indicate that males tend to prefer designs with "simple," "direct" qualities, and females to prefer designs with "open" attributes.[2] Relatedly, Kagan, et al. (1961) and also Osgood (1960) have found in several cultures that angularity is attributed to males and roundness to females. Finally, McClelland and Watt (1968) demonstrated that men prefer "upright" rather than slanted figures to a greater degree than do women.

The idea of forward motion is often associated with a phallic attitude. The phallic approach implies free, unrestrained movement in space. Erikson (1951), as earlier indicated, found more themes of vehicle movement in the play constructions of boys than in those of girls. Honzik (1951) affirmed these results when she analyzed the play constructions of boys and girls. In addition, as mentioned, Brenneis (1967) showed that there were significantly more themes of "extended forward motion" in the manifest dream content of boys than of girls.[3,4] DeMartino (1953) reported that female college students, in replying to questionnaires concerning the character of their dreams, indicated more often than males that they dreamed of situations in which they were unable to move.

Thus, results from diverse sources converge in suggesting that there is a greater sense of free motility in males than in females.[5] It should be underscored that this evidence was derived entirely from fantasy material (namely, play constructions and dreams). However, Wittreich and Grace (1955) and also Fisher (1964) performed studies involving an entirely different methodology, which is supportive of the findings derived from fantasy material. Wittreich and Grace had boys and girls of various age levels view themselves in a mirror while wearing aniseikonic lenses. These lenses bring images of different sizes to the two eyes and can produce a variety of unusual distortions in the appearance of perceptual objects. Interestingly, it has been shown that the greater the anxiety evoked by a perceptual target the less likely it is to be perceived as distorted when viewed through aniseikonic lenses. Somehow, the association of anxiety with an object motivates the individual to keep it perceptually stabilized and un-

changed. For example, when subjects were asked to look through aniseikonic lenses at a person dressed to look like an amputee (and therefore
presumably evocative of anxiety), he was less often seen as perceptually
distorted than a person without a gross body defect. In the Wittreich and
Grace study, when subjects viewed themselves through aniseikonic lenses,
it was observed that the girls perceived their legs and feet as less distorted
than did the boys. This could, within the context just mentioned, indicate
that the girls had more anxiety about their legs than did the boys. Fisher
(1964) later replicated this finding in two samples consisting of college
men and women. Fisher summarized the findings as follows (p. 5):

> It would appear that there is a basic difference between the male and female
> in our culture in their ability to experience perceptual change in the legs; and
> it extends into the early years. In terms of the available research regarding the
> factors underlying aniseikonic change this strongly suggests that the female
> finds her legs as perceptual targets to be a source of anxiety. She is not suffi-
> ciently secure about them to take a chance on their visual transformation—her
> anxiety stems from the fact that she has learned that mobility and movement in
> space, which are closely associated with the legs, are unsafe for a female—her
> anxiety would be a reflection of the limitations conventionally placed upon the
> female role.

The woman's anxiety about motility has also been indirectly detected in
terms of her fears about being separated from, or losing, love objects. Several studies have shown that women fear "loss of love" and "desertion"
more than men. Bradford (1968), in an analysis of the Thematic Apperception Test protocols of male and female college students in terms of a
"Loss of Love" scale that included such subscales as "Abandonment," "Isolation," "Separation," and "Loss of Dependent Support," found that females exceeded males in the number of such themes produced. Analogously,
Gleser, Gottschalk, and Springer (1961) analyzed the spontaneous verbalizations (during a five-minute span) of male and female psychiatric
patients, and discerned, on the basis of an objective scoring system, that
the females expressed more "separation anxiety" (that is, fear of being separated from their loved ones) than the males. In a normal group there
was a similar trend, but it was not statistically significant. If one conceptualizes "separation anxiety" and related terms such as "Abandonment"
and "Loss of Dependent Support" in spatial terms, they would seem to be
pertinent to the matter of female anxiety about motility. The categories
just enumerated can be thought of as portraying situations in which the
female is left by love objects who go off into another area of space where
she cannot venture. That is, they go off "there" and leave her "here." The
love object has motility and leaves; but she has to stay where she is and
therefore finds herself alone.

Messer and Lewis (1970) have even observed a male-female difference
in spatial motility as early as the first year of life. They appraised the behavior of 15 boy and 15 girl infants in the presence of their mothers in a
free-play situation. Girls remained closer to their mothers than did the

boys. They stated (p. 11), "The boys took longer before they returned to mother, returned fewer times, and spent less time in physical contact with her." Goldberg and Lewis (1969) similarly detected a tendency for mothers to maintain greater physical closeness to their 6-month-old girl infants than to boy infants. It would appear that the male-female difference in attitudes about "staying close" versus moving off "out there" may be fostered by parental attitudes very early, even before there is much individual ability to be mobile.

Another quality that is often linked with a phallic orientation is a wish to be large rather than small. To be of large stature rather than small is a typically masculine (phallic) attribute. It has, in fact, been demonstrated that men prefer to perceive themselves as large and women wish to experience themselves more diminutively. Several studies employing the Secord-Jourard (1953) technique, which asks subjects to rate their degree of satisfaction-dissatisfaction with various parts of their bodies, have discerned significant trends for men to hold before themselves the idea of being big and for women to prefer smallness (except with reference to their breasts).[6,7]

The most systematic theoretical exposition of the role of the body concept in defining one's sex role has been offered by Kohlberg (1966), who proposes that a fundamental step in evolving the sex role is the learning that one's body, as a physical object, is either of the class male or female. Taking a Piaget orientation, Kohlberg suggests (p. 83) that "children develop a conception of themselves as having an unchangeable sexual identity at the same age and through the same processes that they develop concepts of the invariable identity of physical objects." He refers to data he has collected that show a significant positive correlation (in children ages 4–6) between recognition constancy of nonself objects and recognition of the sex constancy of one's body. He theorizes that the process of acquiring sex identity begins with learning the terms "boy" or "girl" as being applicable to self and then recognizing various aspects of one's body as typically characterizing a given sex. The child discriminates his genitals as being either male or female and also makes analogous discriminations that involve body differences in such attributes as muscle strength and body size. Kohlberg feels that even the social-role differences between men and women that the child observes become translated into concrete body terms. Thus, the greater apparent social power of the male is rephrased in terms of the greater strength attributed to the male body. What is unique about Kohlberg's view is that he would regard, for example, the girl's identification of her body as female as the fundamental step in establishing her sex identity. Once the girl labels her body as having a specific sex (which is presumed to occur almost irrevocably by age three or four), she is depicted as henceforth reacting selectively to her mother, father, and other figures in terms that will reinforce her own body gender labeling. She is presumed to assimilate selectively from the environment that which will reinforce her gender identity. Hence, she will want to be like and to emulate her mother because her mother's body (and sex labeling) is most like her own. Or she will want to accept certain values rather others because they make her feel "good" or "better" about the fact that she has a female body. Kohlberg's summary of his position is as follows (p. 164):

> Gender identity . . . as boy or girl is the basic organizer of sex-role attitudes. This gender identity results from a basic physical reality judgment made relatively early in the child's development. . . . Basic self categorizations determine basic valuings. Masculine-feminine values develop out of the need to value things that are consistent with or like the self. . . . Sex-role stereotypes develop early. . . . These stereotypes arise from the child's conceptions of body differences. . . . These basic sex-role stereotypes, then, lead to the development of masculine-feminine values in children.

Kohlberg and others who stress that body feelings contribute to sexual identity would, of course, expect that an important component of the sense of being female or male derives from the differential structure of the female and male genitalia. Presumably, for example, one of the important contributors to a girl's feeling that she is a girl is the fact that she possesses a vagina rather than a penis.[8] It is therefore surprising to learn from the few empirical studies that have been done that many children still do not have an understanding of the difference between female and male genitalia even by age 7 or 8. But with few exceptions, children do know their general sex classification at a much earlier age (about 3 or 4). Apparently, their acquisition of a clear image of the difference between their genitals and those of the opposite sex proceeds at a slower pace than their learning of the fact of a *general* difference between the sexes. Conn (1940a,b) and Conn and Kanner (1947) evaluated children's knowledge of genital sex differences in a doll-play interview. They found in the 4–6 age range that only 50 percent of the children evidenced an accurate concept of such differences. The corresponding percent in the 7–8 age range was 72 percent; and in the 11–12 range 86 percent. Butler (1952) found that only 30 percent of a sample of children aged 4–5 displayed convincing knowledge of genital distinctions. One of the most ingenious studies with reference to this matter was carried out by Katcher (1955), whose subjects consisted of 149 boys and 117 girls in the 6–9 age range. In order to determine their knowledge of genital differences the children were asked to identify pictures of portions of male and female figures. For example, they would be shown a male head and a female head and asked which was the man. Similar judgments were requested for nude representations of male and female genital areas. A series of such judgments was obtained. By means of this procedure it was possible to sample knowledge of genital differences in a directly verifiable form without requiring much verbalization from the child. Incidentally, Katcher reported that only a few of the children seemed to be embarrassed or disturbed by their confrontation with pictures of the genitals. A large proportion of those in the 3–4 age group made significant errors in identifying genital regions. By age 5, only 50 percent made no errors in genital judgments. However, by age 6 about 70 percent were without error. Kohlberg (1966) points out that the awareness of genital differences may, at various stages of development, contribute to different degrees to the sense of sex identity. This awareness may be of special import when it first becomes sharply clear at the age of 6 or 7; it may acquire new significance when a knowledge of sexual intercourse and its role in sex functioning is later learned; and its contribution to self-definition may, at adolescence, be even further magnified when sexual drives and sexual experiences become physical realities paralleling new body maturation.

One striking finding of the Katcher (1955) study was that in the young age groups the girls were significantly more accurate than the boys in identifying girl's genitals and boy's genitals. Katcher speculated that young girls had superior knowledge of genital differences because of their special intimate relationship with their mothers.[9] He stated (p. 141):

> Girls erred less than boys because mothers are the principal adult models during early childhood and they usually see their mothers dress, bathe, and toilet; they thus receive considerable experience with female characteristics. Boys neither have this opportunity nor experience comparable relationships with their fathers. They are therefore more confused about sex differences. After all, children only need to know one of the sexes in order to differentiate accurately on the basis of experience.

The relative superiority of the girls in their knowledge of genital distinctions anticipates a paradoxical matter that is discussed shortly. Namely, the fact that whereas much has been written about the inferiority of the female's body concept, there are many empirical findings that point to a contrary position.

As mentioned earlier, it has been popular to assume that the average woman feels that her body is somehow inferior to that of the man. It has even been suggested that a sense of body inferiority is an integral element of feeling like a woman. Freud fostered this idea when he theorized that the little girl is deeply disappointed upon discovering that she lacks a penis and therefore is left with a chronic feeling that her body is devalued and depreciated. Some impetus to this position was indirectly provided by the work of Witkin and his associates (Witkin, et al., 1954). As is well known, they found that if persons are asked to adjust a luminous rod to the correct position of vertical in a darkened room, while experiencing conflicting cues (for example, a tilted luminous frame around the rod) that interfere with the perception of verticality, men consistently show greater skill at this task than do women. Witkin, et al. theorized that men do better than women in this test because they are better able in an unstructured spatial context to use kinesthetic cues from their bodies to define the spatial coordinates. This, in turn, was interpreted as evidence that men have a "better" or more efficiently functional body concept than do women. Indeed, Witkin, et al., in one of their publications (Witkin, et al., 1954), speculated that Freud's theory about the female's chronic sense of body inferiority might help to explain why the female's spatial judgments were less accurate than the male's. This perspective regarding the "inferiority" of the woman's body experiences has grossly pervaded thinking in the behavioral sciences.

It would seem to be important to the present task of analyzing what it "feels" like to be feminine to ascertain whether the feminine body concept is really inferior. Do women perceive their bodies as inferior to those of men? Do women feel like castrated men? Do women feel more insecure about their bodies than men? Are women less capable than men of integrating body experiences and using them sensibly to guide their behavior?

There are several different levels at which these questions can be approached. Let us begin with a review of what is known about sex differences in body anxiety. Are women more concerned than men with the possibility of their bodies being hurt? The available evidence suggests a negative answer. In fact, the accumulating data indicate that males have more anxiety about body damage than do females. Consider the following. Pitcher and Prelinger (1963) found that when young children were asked to make up spontaneous stories, the boys introduced significantly more themes than the females pertaining to getting physically injured. Gottschalk and Gleser (1969) reported that when males and females were asked to speak spontaneously for a brief period of time and their verbalizations were objectively analyzed, the males produced significantly more themes pertaining to "mutilation" and "death." Blum (1949) observed a sex difference in castration anxiety when he applied the Blacky Test to college students. This test requires subjects to describe and make judgments about a series of pictures portraying a dog in typical crisis situations as they are spelled out by psychoanalytic theory. For example, there is a castration picture in which a dog is threatened with the loss of his tail. In his analysis of responses to the pictures, Blum discovered that the males displayed more "castration anxiety" than the females. Friedman (1952) had children complete a story that concerned a monkey involved in adventures in which he might or might not lose his tail. Scoring the stories for castration anxiety, he found that at ages 5–7 the boys seemed to be more disturbed by the potential body loss than the girls. However, he also noted that at ages 11–12 the trend was significantly reversed, whereas at ages 8–9 the two sexes did not differ. Friedman suggested that the difference in results for the 5–6 versus the 11–12 age periods reflected the fact that at the earlier age girls had already resolved their Oedipal conflicts and boys were still struggling with them, therefore experiencing more castration anxiety; but at the later age girls were entering adolescence, with its attendant anxieties about body changes, earlier than the boys who had not yet developed as far. Hall and Van de Castle (1965) observed that a greater percentage of women than men evidenced no castration anxiety in the manifest content of their dreams. Schwartz (1955) devised a measure of castration anxiety that could be derived from Thematic Apperception stories. In a college population, males turned out to have higher castration scores than did females. It should be added, though, that Bradford (1968) could not distinguish between the sexes in terms of a Thematic Apperception Test castration index. Lane (1966) objectively evaluated the dreams of patients before and after surgery in an unusually intensive fashion, and discovered that those of men contained much more castration material than those of women. Relatedly, Schneider (1960) who used the Thematic Apperception Test, Figure Drawings, and Story Completions to study children awaiting surgery, found that boys are more concerned with castration themes than are girls.

Still another finding mentioned earlier, which reinforces the idea that the female feels more secure about her body than the male, is Fisher's (1970) observation that women experience their body boundaries as more definite and secure than do men. They experience their bodies as more clearly differentiated and better protected. The male perceives his body as relatively more open to intrusion. The index employed by Fisher to measure body boundary definiteness was the Barrier score, which has shown itself to be predictive of an ability to cope adequately with body threat and gross body disablement.[10] Somewhat analogously, Fisher and Fast (1971) demonstrated that when male and female subjects were injected with adrenalin, which often produces disturbing body sensations, the body boundaries of the men were more disrupted by the impact of this experience than were those of the women.

These overall findings, whereas far from conclusive, may be sensibly interpreted as indicating that females are probably characterized by less anxiety [11] about, and preoccupation with, body damage than are males.[12]

Do females have more difficulty than males in organizing or dealing with body experiences? Once again the answer is in the negative; indeed, the obverse is true.

Several investigators have shown, first of all, that women are more aware of their bodies than are men. They exceed men in the relative perceptual vividness of their bodies. Van Lennep (1957) reported that females refer more than men do to body themes in stories they create. Even further, women show an increasing amount of body interest as they mature beyond adolescence, whereas the trend for men is toward decreasing interest. Secord (1953) found women to be more bodily aware than men when he compared the number of "body" words given by the two sexes in their associations to homonyms that have both body and nonbody meaning. Korchin and Heath (1961) indicated that women report more sensations of body arousal than do men in various situations.

In a series of studies, Fisher (1970) compared body awareness of men and women by means of a Body Prominence score, a well-validated index based on a count of the number of body references elicited from an individual when he is asked to list "twenty things you are aware of right now." He found that females obtained higher Body Prominence scores than males, which adds to the unanimity of the various results pertaining

to this issue that have been mentioned. But what is of even more importance is the differential he demonstrated in the significance of body awareness to women and men. In women, significant positive correlations were
observed between degree of body awareness and the definiteness or sub-
stantiality of body boundaries. The measure of boundary definiteness utilized (Barrier score) has been shown to be positively linked with a clear
sense of identity, ability to tolerate stress, and facility in maintaining an
individualistic and self-determining style of behavior. In the case of
women one can say that those who are most body aware are probably high
on the attributes just enumerated.[13] Fisher detected a quite different pattern for men, whose degree of body awareness had only a chance relationship with boundary definiteness and, in fact, was positively correlated with
a number of indices indicative of concern and perhaps conflict about oral
issues. The man with a high awareness of his body was not, as is true of
women, characterized by attributes of a positive and adaptive type; instead
he seemed to be concerned about matters relating to orality and incorporation. This contrast between women and men with respect to the significance of body awareness is suggested too by data collected by others. For
example, Korchin and Heath (1961) reported that women who have high
awareness of autonomic arousal in their bodies are active and aggressive,
whereas men with such awareness are passive-dependent and ineffectual.
Relatedly, Mordkoff (1966) demonstrated that men with high awareness of
their body sensations were maladjusted, but such was not true for women.

The underlying theme of these studies is that women exceed men in
body awareness and that the significance of such awareness differs in the
two sexes. In women, the act of being aware of one's body has positive implications, whereas in men it seems to have negative connotations. One
might say that body awareness is more congruent with the feminine than
the masculine; it is the woman with clearly demarcated boundaries and a
well-articulated sense of identity who is most aware of her body. Why
should women be more positively oriented toward awareness of their bodies than men? The present writer has suggested elsewhere (Fisher, 1970)
that this is probably caused by the rather obvious differences in the way
the two sexes are socialized with reference to their bodies. From an early
age the girl is encouraged to decorate herself, to experiment with different
kinds of clothing, and to be aware of the impression her body is making
upon others. Also, she is continuously challenged to learn to adapt to the
cyclic changes in her body produced by menstruation. But, even further, as
she matures she receives the implicit or explicit message that her principal
life role will revolve about having a body sufficiently attractive to interest
a man in marrying her and ultimately to fulfill a child-bearing role with
her body.[14] Fairly early in her development a female can see an obvious
link between her body and her principal life roles. She can draw parallels
and assign significance to her body in terms of future goals. This is much
less true for the male. It is considered unusual for the little boy to experiment much with his body appearance or his clothing. Likewise, the adult

man has much less freedom than the woman to direct attention to his body and to practice changing and decorating it. The man who shows more than moderate interest in his own body courts the suspicion that he is feminine or strange. But even more important is the fact that the average man cannot see a real relationship between his body and his most important life roles. A man is evaluated largely in terms of his achievement and forms of work success, which (except in the case of the athlete) have little to do with the state of his body.[15] He cannot easily trace a connection between his body and the roles that become the badge of his identity. Therefore, he experiences his body as alienated from his life transactions. He is uncomfortable about his body.

A study by Fisher should be mentioned at this point because it illustrates the difference between the sexes in their ability to cope with unusual body experiences. This was an experiment in which normal subjects were made to perceive their appearance when it had been altered in a novel fashion and their reactions to the alternation could be evaluated. As will be seen, women proved to be more skillful than men in their adaptation. Fisher (1964) asked each subject (college students) to stand in front of a mirror and to describe his appearance, as a series of masks were placed on his face. This was done in a darkened room, and when each new mask was placed on his face, the subject was only allowed to see his or her mirror image for a brief interval (one second). Eight rubber masks were used; four depicted male faces and four depicted female faces. It was found that if one takes as a criterion of disturbance the number of errors made in identifying the correct sex of the masks, males were more negatively affected by their changed appearance than were females. This same finding emerged in two separate samples that were studied. To be confronted by the changed image of his face, which suddenly had female rather than male qualities, was sufficiently disquieting to the male so that his ability to make an accurate perceptual identification of the sex of the mask he was wearing was impaired. The female seemed to be relatively unruffled by the radical and potentially threatening alteration in her appearance.[16]

By way of generalization, what can be said about how the feminine body concept is distinguished from the masculine? One immediately has to recognize that only modest conclusions can be drawn, simply because empirical investigation of this area is such a new enterprise. Relatively little is solidly known. But, in any case, one may begin by saying that the obvious phallic versus vaginal (nonphallic) differentiation between the sexes does find representation in contrasting modes of body experience. A number of studies have been enumerated that suggest that the female experiences her body as rounded, nondefensively "open" (but not in the sense of being fragile), smallish, and "designed" to be relatively stationary rather than in forward or upward movement. This contrasts with the apparent phallic feelings of the male, who perceives his body as angular, large, protrusive, guarded, and possessed of special potential forward and upward motion. A second conclusion that may be derived is that the female seems to experience her body as less vulnerable and less subject to attack than the male does. She is less anxious about getting hurt and more confident that she possesses boundaries that will differentiate her and protect her from nonself objects. Thirdly, she is relatively more aware of her body, as against the other objects in her perceptual field, than is the male. She is probably also more comfortable than the male about receiving and interpreting body experiences. One might say that she is relatively more "at ease" with her body. As earlier remarked, her harmonious relationship with her body may reflect the fact that a woman can, more easily than a man, see a direct connection between her body and her important life goals. A man's body tends to be alienated from his prime social roles that typically embrace his achievement and success.

Obviously, our understanding of sex differences in body experience is only beginning to crystallize. There are probably unique body feelings and fantasies that the average woman entertains with regard to her potential for producing a child, menstrual periodicity, wanting certain modes of sexual stimulation from a man, possessing breasts, and so forth that remain to be spelled out and studied.

Personal Traits and Attitudes

Having explored the findings with regard to differences between the sexes in body perception, the next step will be to consider what is known about personality and temperament differences. An informative and useful literature has become available about this matter. Sensible studies have been completed in diverse cultures around the world, and we have some reasonable leads about the principal ways in which females and males differ in their personality styles. At first sight the maze of findings is bewildering. Studies have isolated sex differences relating to aggression, dependence, passivity, suggestibility, tendermindedness, sociability, and so forth. In fact, almost all psychological studies of personality variables turn up with significant sex differences, if the trouble is taken to look for them. A number of very good attempts have been made to summarize the essence of the pertinent findings. Let us look at the cogent and direct summary offered by Kagan (1964, p. 143):

> In sum, females are supposed to inhibit aggression and open display of sexual urges, to be passive with men, to be nurturant to others, to cultivate attractiveness, and to maintain an effective, socially poised, and friendly posture with others. Males are urged to be aggressive in face of attack, independent in problem situations, sexually aggressive, in control of regressive urges, and suppressive of strong emotion, especially anxiety.

Kagan cites numerous studies that particularly highlight the female's tendency to be less aggressive than the male and to take a softer, more nurturant, more helpful attitude toward others. The female is less aggressive than the male no matter whether one considers the matter from the perspective of overt behavior or measures derived from fantasy productions. Such aggression differences emerge very early and persist throughout adulthood. Even in the doll play of children as young as age three and four, boys introduce more aggressive action than the girls. To be female is equated with being relatively low in aggression; and parents expect girls to carefully screen their output of hostility (Kagan, 1964).[17] An important aspect of sex differences in aggression relates to achievement. Girls and women have been found to be less motivated than their male counterparts to gain recognition by personal achievement, and it is more difficult to arouse achievement imagery in them.

Parents also expect girls to be kind, gentle, friendly, soft, and empathic. The girl is supposed to be nurturant according to the model of the good mother figure. In fact, she has much greater freedom to act in gentle nurturant ways than the boy. A boy who is too kindly or motherly is regarded as a sissy and treated like a nonboy. The girl's nurturant orientation has been documented in social interactions, in questionnaire measures, in doll play, in projective fantasies, in sensitivity to tachistoscopically presented nurturant pictures, and so forth. The evidence concerning her special orientation in this respect is beyond dispute. Investigators have varied in their evaluative labeling of the girl's nurturant attitudes. Some (McClelland, 1964) have underscored their positive, "motherly," helpful aspects. Others have referred to them negatively by focusing on the fact that the female is more "suggestible," "passive," and "yielding" than the male. Obviously, how positively or negatively one casts the difference is merely a value judgment.

An especially interesting study bearing on the differences just described was carried out by Barry, Bacon, and Child (1957), who compared the sex differences in socialization practices of 110 cultures. Detailed information about these cultures had been collected by anthropologists and judges were asked to make ratings concerning various aspects of the ways the two sexes were treated in each. In a majority of these cultures girls were taught to be more nurturant,[18] more obedient, and more responsible (dutiful) than boys; and, contrastingly, a majority of the boys were expected to be more achievement oriented and self-reliant than the girls. Despite the extremely disparate character of the many cultures represented in the samples studied, they showed great consistency with regard to what was differentially expected of females and males. The basic contrast between the nurturant orientation of the female and the more active achievement-directed stance of the male was almost everywhere apparent.

Barry, et al., in discussing the observed differences, were inclined to attribute them to economic factors and to some degree to biological elements. Note their comment (p. 328):

The observed differences in the socialization of boys and girls are consistent with certain universal tendencies in the differentiation of adult sex role. . . . men are more frequently allotted tasks that involve leaving home and engaging in activities where a high level of skill yields important results; hunting is a prime example. Emphasis on training in self-reliance and achievement for boys would function as preparation for such an economic role. Women, . . . are more frequently allotted tasks at or near home that minister most immediately to the needs of others (such as cooking and water carrying). These activities have a nurturant character. . . .

Ranging over the many distinct personality attributes of the female that have been isolated, one looks for a generalization that will unite them. Can one cut through the detail with an integrating concept? McClelland (1964) has made an impressive effort to do so in terms of "interdependence" by suggesting that the outstanding characteristic of the woman is that she is "interdependent." He points out that she is interested in people and social interaction, and continuously sensitive to the nature of her relationships. She is presumably continuously ready to adjust in order to balance the changes in others. McClelland would classify many disparate feminine attributes as falling within this conceptual scheme. For example, the special skill shown by women in fine motor adjustments, such as finger dexterity, is seen by him as part of an ability to be "more finely tuned to make adjustments to stimulus changes." Relatedly, what appears to others as the woman's dependence is interpreted by McClelland as an expression of her degree of involvement in relationships. McClelland further illustrates his view as follows (p. 176):

. . . Women disclose more of their secrets to others, feel less dislike for all sorts of odd people . . . and are most attached to fiction and movies that deal with interpersonal relationships. . . . Many tests like the Allport-Vernon-Lindzey Study of Values show women as more concerned with the welfare of others and as more moralistic. . . . In both instances they are simply expressing their social concern which covers all sorts of interrelationships of people from child care to proper social behavior. . . .

McClelland succinctly adds at another point (p. 177):

. . . Women are quicker to recognize their own interdependence; they are more interested in situations where interdependence is important; they enter jobs where this characteristic is salient. . . .

As part of this concept, he emphasizes that women are more interested in people whereas men invest more energy in things. He documents his viewpoint with published empirical findings.

One can easily find data in the literature that corroborate McClelland's formulation about the woman's "interdependent" orientation. Many studies have reported that women are relatively highly interested in people. Witryol and Kaess (1957) report that they have better memory for human faces than do men and are more easily influenced by other people (Walker and Heyns, 1962). It is relevant, too, that women are to a greater extent than men interested in, and sensitive to, the context or setting of any stimulus they encounter. They seem less motivated (or capable) of isolating a stimulus in an abstract way that does not consider its relationship with its setting.

One may pertinently mention that Johnson and Knapp (1963) concluded after a study of sex differences in aesthetic preferences that "in terms of content women tend to prefer the personal rather than the impersonal, the intimate rather than the grand, the sensuous rather than the abstract." Relatedly, Berger (1968) empirically concluded that females are more dependent than men on social feedback in arriving at self-evaluations. Their degree of self-esteem is apparently more influenced by how they feel others regard them. Men seem to be less "interdependent" on others in arriving at an evaluation of self. In a study of children, Yi Guang-Lin (1961) was able to conclude similarly (p. 163): "The early and late adolescent girl seems to fuse her self esteem more on personal traits such as popularity and warmth, while the male bases his more on individual achievement and status." One could at random cite many other pertinent findings, such as Baker's (1968) demonstration that girls are more "tenderminded" and "sensitive" to others than boys; Goodenough's (1957) observation that even at nursery-school age girls are more "person oriented" than boys; Stein's (1969) report that the learning of *social* skills is perceived by adolescents as more a feminine than a masculine activity; and Becker's (1968) conclusion that women are more interested than men in obtaining "social approval" (with men more concerned about "self-approval"). It is striking that even with regard to the likelihood of engaging in immoral acts (for example, cheating), the female is more affected than the male by the social context (Ganley, 1968).

A large-scale study by Douvan and Adelson (1966) adds some new highlights to these perspectives. They used interview and questionnaire techniques to evaluate a national sample ($N = 3,000$) of adolescents (age range 14–16). Emerging with sharp clarity from their findings was the fact that girls are more concerned than boys with the nature of their relationships with others. They state (p. 48):

> The desire for popularity . . . tends to turn the girl's attention to the external world . . . and toward the reactions of other people to her. This tendency toward "other-direction" is a consistent distinguishing characteristic of interviews with girls. . . . Girls . . . are more sensitized to interpersonal relationships, to the opinions of others, to meeting the demands and judgments of important people in their surroundings. These concerns are functional to the adult feminine role—they are adaptive for wife and mother. . . .

They found that girls are keenly sensitive to how others perceive them and even "put off" completing the contours of their personality in a definitive way, lest this prove to be a handicap in their future adjustment to an as yet unknown husband with unknown personality traits. They reported that girls form more intimate relationships during adolescence than do boys ("The individual friendship transcends the group," p. 344). They unfold an intriguing account of how the very concept of being feminine revolves about aspirations to develop complex interpersonal skills that contrast with the mastery and autonomy aims of the male. The girl's goals, fantasies, and vocational choices were found to be dominated by the intent to forge close relationships with others, but the boy's goals focus on detachment and independence. Apropos of this, Douvan and Adelson noted that 76 percent of the girls in their sample admired personal qualities such as kindness, generosity, thoughtfulness, and understanding, whereas only 34 percent of the boys were positive to such qualities. They add that as part of the girl's investment in the interpersonal she develops her intraceptive and introspective skills. She needs to be able to look at herself, to understand her motivations, to be aware of her feelings—in order to relate sensitively to others. Within their sample of girls, Douvan and Adelson discovered that those whose interests were the most feminine were also those who had the best cultivated interpersonal skills. The feminine girl apparently exceeded the nonfeminine girl in placing high value on personal relationships and in being "more sophisticated and subtle" in handling interpersonal conflicts. The feminine girl was actually found to participate more in social organizations and to display more poise and self-confidence while she was being interviewed.

A carefully designed study by Gottschalk and Gleser (1969) may be appropriately mentioned at this point. They tape-recorded spontaneous five-minute samples of speech from male ($N = 75$) and female ($N = 54$) college students and analyzed the content of these samples by means of an objective and reliable scoring system they developed. One of the scoring categories they were particularly interested in was labeled "Human Relations," which was designed to evaluate motivation for constructive, mutually satisfying human relationships. They discovered that the average Human Relations score for the females was very significantly higher than that for the males.

The personalized and "interdependent" mode of adaptation of the woman has been looked at from another perspective by Gutmann (1965) and Brenneis (1967), who conceptualize the woman's mode as one that involves a personalized extension of self into all that is encountered. Guttman's view is that women see the world as flavored and permeated with self qualities and therefore populated by familiar and largely friendly people. Presumably, men see the world as alien, difficult to predict, and fluctuating in dangerous ways and therefore requiring that they impose their mastery over it. Women, by contrast, experience it as self-related and familiar and assume the possibility of a comfortable interdependence. Brenneis (1967) examined this proposed distinction by evaluating the manifest content of dreams collected from female and male college students. His empirical analysis of the dream content revealed significant differences between the females and males that were congruent with that distinction. Brenneis found that the dreams of the females more often than those of the males portrayed friendliness, being with familiar people, and getting personally involved with others. Whereas the people in the men's dreams are often unfamiliar and strange, those in the women's dreams were typically depicted as comfortable to be with and close. In generalizing about the data pertaining to the females, Brenneis stated (p. 92):

. . . We find that female ego modalities cluster about the issue of intimacy or domesticity. Sensitivity, physical closeness, and familiar company all set in a stable enclosure (like a house) are important facets of this intimacy. . . . The women of our sample also create in their dreams an atmosphere of personal closeness full of people one knows and can refer to by name.

The special nature of the female orientation is more dramatically conveyed if one views it against the contrasting backdrop of what Brenneis concluded about the dream content of his male subjects (p. 90):

There are simply not as many people in the dreams of these men as there are in the dreams of our female subjects. When people appear in their dreams they are unfamiliar, unknown, or nameless figures. . . . The male . . . finds himself alone in an alien world.

Carlson (in press) undertook several studies of a number of aspects of Guttman's formulations concerning the importance of interpersonal involvement in defining the feminine orientation. In one sample of college students (39 female, 37 male) he tested the formal hypothesis that women represent self in terms of "interpersonal relatedness," whereas men do so "in individualistic terms." He did so by asking each subject to choose ten adjectives (from a larger list) that were best descriptive of self. Analysis of the adjective selections indicated that the women significantly exceeded the men in choosing those adjectives in which self-definition required an implicit social object. The women more often chose terms such as "friendly" and "persuasive," whereas men chose terms such as "ambitious" and "idealistic."

A second form of evaluation of the hypothesis was undertaken in a sample of 20 male and 21 female college students. The subjects were asked to indicate their degree of similarity to a variety of other figures (for example, mother, like-sexed friend, admired person), and it was shown that the females judged themselves to be more like others ("to experience themselves as intrinsically related to others") than the males. This was considered to reaffirm the special interpersonal (other-related) orientation of the females.

At still another level, the hypothesis was tested by asking college students (18 males, 23 females) to describe a series of life incidents in which they had experienced specific emotions (for example, shame, fear, or joy). These descriptions were then scored to determine the degree to which the theme of independence (being separate or individual) versus social interdependence (being together or dependent) predominated. As anticipated, the interdependence theme was significantly more often found in females than in males.[19]

An excellent case can be made for representing the essence of the feminine personality style in terms such as "interdependence," "mutuality," "intimacy," and "agreeable closeness." Evidence from a myriad of sources highlights the woman's investment in creating a world for herself in which she is personally in contact with others and particularly able to express herself by the skill with which she can respond to, and nurture, them.[20] She might be said to weave her identity in the richness of her mutuality and in the understanding contained in her communications. This is obviously not passivity in its simplistic sense; it is an active and complicated form of striving.

If women are so invested in successful mutuality with others, it should come as no great surprise that their anxieties tend to concentrate around fears of being rejected and losing love.[21] Manosevitz and Lanyon (1965) reported that in their questionnaire study concerned with the fears of women and men, women obtained their highest scores in responding to questions about "Being rejected by others." Of twelve questions that evoked the greatest admission of fear from the women, seven pertained to interpersonal issues. Gleser, Gottschalk, and Springer (1961) analyzed five-minute samples of spontaneous speech of male and female psychiatric patients and demonstrated that concern with fears about being separated from others was significantly higher in the females than in the males. Bradford (1968) devised a reliable scoring system for evaluating anxiety about loss of love, as expressed in Thematic Apperception Test stories, and affirmed the hypothesis that women would manifest more such anxiety than men. In discussing the possible origin of "loss of love" anxiety in women, Bradford conjectures (p. 88): "It might be argued that from infancy on, females are encouraged to be people and home oriented; that parents tend to use withdrawal of love rather than physical punishment in disciplining girls and thus their extreme sensitivity to this threat. . . ."

Lewis (1969) exposed females and males to a film containing a loss of love theme and found that the former were made more anxious by it (as defined by their Thematic Apperception Test stories) than were the latter. Conversely, when exposed to a film dealing with a castration theme (subincision ceremony), the males evidenced more anxiety than the females.

Lowery (1965) has even found that the woman's concept of death conforms to her special investment in interpersonal contact and avoiding loss of love. He concluded on the basis of an empirical analysis of imaginative productions that (p. 183): ". . . females tend to see death as a force which threatens to rob them of love or . . . to put them out of communion with the objects of their love." By way of contrast, he noted that males tend to see death as a form of failure or mutilation ("castration").

This analysis of sex differences in personal orientation would not be complete without considering what is known about sex differences in response to stimuli with sexual significance. Masters and Johnson (1966) contradicted persistent assumptions about the female orgasm being less real or based on different physiological principles than the male's. In fact, they showed that women have (if anything) greater orgasm capacity than men. But a good deal of discussion is to be found in the literature concerning the female's presumed lesser response than the male's to the whole spectrum of visual sexual stimuli. Kinsey, et al. (1953) cited considerable evidence from their interview data supportive of such a contention. In the course of their interviews they found that males more often than females reported the following to be sexually stimulating: observing the opposite sex, looking at portrayals of nude figures or erotic art, observing genitalia of others, looking at own genitalia, watching sexual actions, and observing burlesque and floor shows.

They were led to the conclusion that men are generally more responsive to "psychosexual stimuli," particularly those that are visual in nature. But they did specify that there was no apparent sex difference in the ability to respond to tactile stimuli.

As one studies the original Kinsey, et al. data, a few puzzling facts come into view that lead one to raise questions about their conclusion regarding a *general* difference between the sexes in response to psychosexual stimuli. First, one finds that females reported romantic "commercial moving pictures" to be more erotically arousing than did males. Secondly, females found "literary materials" (poetry, novels) to be just as erotically stimulating as did the males. Thirdly, about 2 or 3 percent of the females (p. 688) "were psychologically stimulated by a greater variety of factors and more intensely stimulated than any of the men in the sample. Their responses had been more immediate. They had responded more frequently, and they had responded to the point of orgasm with frequencies that had far exceeded those known for any male. A few of the females were regularly being stimulated by psychologic factors to the point of orgasm, and this almost never happens among any of the males." Kinsey, et al. indicated puzzlement about these observations, but such data suggest that it is an oversimplification to state that women are basically less responsive to psychosexual stimuli than are men. Not only do the Kinsey, et al. data indicate that some specific stimuli ("commercial movies" with romance themes) are more erotically stimulating to women than men, but also that there are women who experience more erotic arousal to a variety of psychological stimuli than do any men.[22] The last finding implies that women do, under certain conditions, have the potential for responding with just as high intensity as men to a range of psychosexual stimuli.

The question of how women react to psychosexual stimuli has been explored by several investigators from different perspectives.

Loiselle and Mollenauer (1965) sought specifically to ascertain how women ($N=20$) would respond to clothed and nude pictures of males and females. The Galvanic Skin Reflex (GSR) was employed as a measure of responsiveness. It was found that the nude figures elicited considerably greater GSR response than did the clothed figures. The women were physiologically aroused by the nude stimuli. The Mf Scale of the Minnesota Multiphasic Personality Inventory had been administered to all subjects and so an index of masculinity-femininity was available. When the Mf scores were correlated with the GSR response scores, it was noted that the greater the subject's masculinity the larger was her GSR response to both the clothed and nude figures.

Levi (1969) compared women ($N=53$) and men ($N=50$) in their reactions to two films depicting sexual intercourse. There were also two control films concerned with bland natural scenery. Subjective reports and also chemical measures derived from urine samples were used to evaluate the film effects. Both sexes rated themselves as significantly sexually aroused by the intercourse movies, but the level of subjective arousal was significantly higher in the male than the female sample. However, it is also interesting that the males showed a significant increase in anxiety from a baseline period to the intercourse film period. The females did not show a significant increase, which Levi attributed to the fact that they were already high in anxiety during the control period. Both sexes showed a significant increase in adrenaline and noradrenaline excretion during the intercourse film, with that for adrenaline being significantly greater in the male than the female group. Levi regarded these findings as indicating that whereas both sexes were aroused by the sexual film, the men were more aroused than the women. However, it helps to keep one's perspective on these findings to quote one of Levi's observations (p. 263): "Our data indicate that *some individual females actually are more responsive to the stimuli used than any of the men* (italics by present writer) in the sample, both with respect to psychological and catecholamine reactions."

Mosher and Greenberg (1969) asked a group of women ($N=72$) to read an erotic literary passage. Previous to and following the reading of this passage they rated the women's moods and degrees of sexual arousal. The same ratings were made of a control group before and after reading a neutral literary passage. The results demonstrated a significant increase in sexual arousal following reading of the erotic passage but not after the neutral one. These results agree with the Kinsey, et al. (1953) data that indicated that women do respond with sexual arousal to written erotic material. An affirmation of the female's responsivity to written erotic material has come from Jordan and Butler (1967), who observed a significant change in skin resistance in a group of females ($N=32$) after reading a literary passage describing sexual seduction. Affirmation has also come from Jakobovits (1965), who found that females ($N=20$) were just as aroused (as defined by self-ratings) by erotic stories as were men ($N=20$).

It is appropriate at this point to mention the work of Beardslee and Fogelson (1958), which indicated that unmarried women are higher in symbolic sexual arousal to music than are unmarried men. Subjects were asked to listen to musical selections and to create stories suggested by the music. The stories were then scored for symbolic sexual imagery ("back and forth rhythm," peaks and declines in tension) by means of validated criteria. Significantly more sexual imagery was produced by females than males, and Beardslee and Fogelson speculated that music might be intrinsically more sexually stimulating to women than to men.

Wallach and Greenberg (1960), who later worked with the same music arousal technique, commented on the sex difference obtained by Beardslee and Fogelson as follows (p. 16): "The stricter societal prohibitions against girls for direct sexual expression should lead to a stronger need in the case of unmarried women than men for displacement arousal in response to music." One could say that women, because of their frustration with regard to overt sexual expression, actually react to sensory stimuli such as music with an exaggerated (but concealed) focus on their sexual implications. Parenthetically, one may mention that Wallach and Greenberg discovered in the data from their own experiments that the extent to which women utilized music as a means of indirectly expressing sexual motivation was a function of the degree to which they were uncomfortable about social interaction and lacked the means for dealing with their discomfort via introversive mechanisms.

The pupillary response of women and men to nude pictures has been appraised in two studies. Scott, Wells, Wood, and Morgan (1967) could not distinguish the responses of the two sexes in terms of pupillary measures. Similar results were found in a study by Lawless (1968).

Two particularly decisive studies concerned with female-male differences in response to stimuli with sexual significance will now be described. Sigusch, Schmidt, Reinfeld, and Wiedemann-Sutor (1970) exposed 50 female and 50 male German college students individually to slides depicting sexual themes (nudes, kissing, petting, coitus). The subjects rated how much sexual arousal each picture produced. The subjects also provided information about their body reactions while looking at the sexual pictures and filled out questionnaires in which they described their sexual behavior during the 24 hours previous to the experiment and the 24 hours subsequent to it. There was a significant trend for the men to report greater sexual arousal than the women. However, the mean difference was small and there was considerable overlap. For example, one-third of the women rated the petting and coitus pictures as more arousing than did the average man. The largest difference between the sexes was for pictures depicting nudes and the smallest for those with romantic content. It was found that when the reports of actual body arousal (particularly genital sensations) in response to the pictures were considered, the females indicated just as much arousal as the males. A considerable number of the subjects reported increased sexual activity in the 24 hours following the experiment (for example, petting, coitus, masturbation), but the increase was not significantly greater in the male than female group.

In another study involving the same researchers (Schmidt and Sigusch, 1970) which employed a similar design, almost identical results were obtained. Particular emphasis was placed on the fact that whereas the women tended to express less overt favorable responses to the sexual pictures, they evidenced as many or more signs of high emotional reaction to and involvement with them. It was the overall conclusion of this research group that the Kinsey, et al. original statements about women being less aroused than men by visual sexual stimuli were exaggerated. Indeed, they consider that true sex differences in this respect probably do not exist, and where they seem to occur are probably artifacts of the woman's tendency to conform to social stereotypes that pressure her to conceal her sexual feelings (especially publicly).

Barclay and Haber (1965) had a male experimenter frustrate and anger male ($N=36$) and female ($N=28$) subjects and then had them compose stories about Thematic Apperception Test pictures highlighting various dominance-submission relationships. Control subjects who had not been angered also composed stories about these pictures. The stories were scored for aggressive imagery, sexual imagery, and apparent degree of defensiveness aroused by each of these categories of imagery. It was discovered that the experimental anger situation aroused more sexual imagery than the control situation in both women and men. Also, significantly more sexual imagery was aroused in the men than in the women. Barclay and Haber underscored the fact that the arousal of anger elicited sexual fantasy in both sexes. But further, the data showed that the males were significantly *more defensive* about their increment in sexual imagery than were the females. Barclay and Haber remarked that (p. 472):

Women responded to aggressive arousal by a male with an increase in sexual imagery, not an inhibition of it. Further, there seemed to be little defensiveness attached to this arousal, at least as compared to men. It appears that women respond with sexual arousal to an angry man who in fantasy they see as making sexual rather than hostile advances. Thus, from the female's point of view, aggression is an important aspect of a male's sexual appeal.

In another study (Paris and Goodstein, 1966) samples of female and male subjects were asked to read literary passages that were either neutral, sexual, or concerned with death, and were then asked to rate their feelings and reactions while reading one of these types of material. The females rated themselves as more sexually aroused following the reading of the sexual material than following either the death or neutral material. This was also true for the males. The two sexes did not differ significantly in their relative degree of arousal by the erotic passage. However, it was found that the women rated themselves as significantly more sexually aroused by the death themes than did the men. Paris and Goodstein point out that McClelland (1963) similarly observed that women regarded the image of death as having more sexual connotations than did men.

The fact that death material was said by the women in this study to be sexually stimulating and the fact that in the Barclay and Haber (1965) study just cited hostility aroused sexual fantasies (with little accompanying defensiveness) in the female subjects indicates that a rather esoteric range of stimuli has psychosexual meaning to women. This does not match the Kinsey, et al. (1953) view that women respond to only a few kinds of psychosexual stimuli. Evidence has been cited here that such diverse stimuli as sexual literary passages, sexual movies, hostility, and death themes elicit in women either overt feelings of sexual arousal or more disguised fantasies with sexual implications. In addition, one must also keep in mind that in at least two studies an extreme group of women has been found to be more sexually aroused by "psychosexual" stimuli than any of the male subjects. It may be that women are less willing than men to talk about the feelings of arousal produced by psychosexual stimuli and therefore appear to be less arousable in this respect. Or it may be that women find it more appropriate and satisfying to experience psychosexual stimuli within a romantic or affectionate context and therefore do not seek them out in situations where they are displayed in a fashion that dramatizes sex as anonymous or not requiring real interpersonal warmth. Perhaps it is the lack of interpersonal warmth in such settings that is inhibiting to a woman rather than there being an absence of arousal value in the psychosexual stimuli themselves. There are certainly a number of studies (Ehrmann, 1959) that indicate the relatively greater importance to a woman than a man of romantic or friendly involvement as a basis for sexual interaction.

The presentation in this section represents a conscientious effort to convey the highlights of what is actually known about sex differences in personal orientation and personality.[23] Although much material has been condensed, this was done with the intent of clarifying what is otherwise a bewildering maze of research detail.

NOTES

1. In a later publication Erikson (1964) reinterpreted these differences as less literally representing male-female body distinctions, but he still emphasized the contributory role of unlike body experiences.

2. However, McElroy (1954) reported that in a Western sample males *prefer* symbols that are "rounded" and females prefer symbols that are "angular."

3. McClelland (1964) mentions that when the Thematic Apperception Test stories of males and females are analyzed, those of males more often than those of females contain themes in which a figure is on a "straight line *projecting upward* to a peak of glory until his assertiveness fails. . . ." (Italics added).

4. There is also good evidence that males and females differ in the degree to which they manifest a right versus left bias in their spatial perceptions. As Fisher (1962) has indicated, males show a directional bias to the right and females a bias to the left. The meaning of this difference remains obscure.

5. Weaver (1968) concluded that one of the major aspects of a father's long-term communication with his daughter relates to how permissive he is about her "expanding her psychological space" as she matures.

6. It is paradoxical that evidence has accumulated (Fisher, 1970; Bradford, 1968) that men experience more anxiety about potential damage to their bodies than do women. Such fear about body damage has been labeled by some as "castration anxiety." One recalls, in this respect, that Freud and other psychoanalysts have pointed out that men, because they actually possess a penis and have a phallic-body concept, are more likely to have castration anxiety (which literally refers to phallic damage) than women who lack phallic attributes.

7. It is an intriguing, but basically unexplained, phenomenon that females are more accurate than men in identifying abstract symbols with phallic attributes (in the Freudian sense) and males are more accurate than females in identifying symbols

with female characteristics (Richardson, 1967; Lessler, 1962). Lessler (1962) has offered two tentative explanations for this difference. He suggests that possibly the difference reflects satisfaction derived from heterosexual cues. He theorizes that perhaps
the adolescent males in his study obtained some heterosexual stimulation from attending particularly to the female symbols and the adolescent females some
stimulation from focusing upon the male symbols. Alternatively, he speculates that
adolescents who are "struggling with their sexual identity . . . found like-sexed symbols more threatening and anxiety-provoking than heterosexual symbols."

8. However, Stoller (1968a,b), who has studied girls congenitally lacking a vagina, finds that the presence of a vagina is not necessary to develop a firm sense of
feminine identity. He does admit that the absence of a vagina probably has some
negative effects. Note his comments (p. 61): "I am not alleging that the body ego of
this girl (without a vagina) is the same as that of an anatomically normal female, for
she has not had that vaginal awareness which is dimly present in anatomically normal little girls. I presume that with the latter there is a sense of space within . . .
produced especially by the vagina and even more vaguely by the uterus. . . ."

9. Katcher (1955) points out that Freud regarded the boy (at age four or five) as
likely (because of castration anxiety) to deny differences between male and female
genitals and the girl (because of penis envy) to be sensitive to genital differences.
Thus, the actual observed superiority of the girl in identifying genital differences is
"in the direction of expectation" as one would derive it from Freud's views.

10. As described earlier, the Barrier score is based on responses to inkblot stimuli. It represents the number of percepts produced in which the periphery is ascribed unusual protective, containing, or decorative properties.

11. D'Andrade (1966) asserts that if one surveys the projective and semiprojective
data gathered in various cultures, one finds (p. 199): "In general, females appear to
have a better psychological adjustment than males."

Spiegel, Brodkin, and Keith-Spiegel (1969) reported that males showed more signs
of disturbance about sexual themes in their projective responses (for example, Thematic Apperception Test) than did females. Barclay and Haber (1965) came to a
similar conclusion.

12. A noteworthy example of this phenomenon is Rainwater's (1960) observation
that men seem to be more threatened by the potential body damage that might be
produced by a "male pill" taken for contraceptive purposes than women are by the
idea of taking a "female pill."

13. Compton (1969) found that body awareness, as measured by the Fisher Body
Prominence score, was negatively correlated with anxiety in a female sample.

14. A large-scale study of adolescent girls by Douvan and Adelson (1967) documents their preoccupation with marriage as a life goal.

15. Douvan and Adelson (1967) report that adolescent boys are much more concerned than girls about successful achievement. Girls, on the other hand, express
more concern about being physically attractive. One could argue that the girl's concern about physical attractiveness reveals underlying anxiety about her body. But
one could also regard it as a realistic recognition that body attractiveness will be important to her in attaining her prime life goals.

16. The fact that the female is probably less likely than the male to be negatively
affected by body changes is also indirectly supported by the observation that the age
of onset of pubertal body alterations seems to be more important psychologically in
boys than girls. Several studies (Weatherley, 1964; Peskin, 1967; Jones and Bailey,
1950) have shown that boys who develop pubertal body changes early differ psychologically from boys who mature late. That is, the timing of the body changes seems
to have an impact psychologically. However, in girls (Weatherley, 1964; Faust, 1960)
consistent and significant psychological consequences of early versus late body maturing have not been demonstrated.

17. May (1966, 1969) asserts that denial of aggression and an underlying mas-

ochistic orientation are characteristic of women. He concluded that there is actually a pattern of feminine expectation about the world that starts with the assumption that there must first be suffering and failure and only then can there be joy and success. In two studies involving the use of the Thematic Apperception Test he has shown a significant trend for the action in women's stories to exhibit such a sequence.

18. Helson (1968) has even found evidence that creative women and creative men differ in their intellectual styles, with the women being more "open" and "nurturant" to new ideas.

19. This study actually grew out of Bakan's (1966) statement that the male is "Agentic" (emphasizing differentiation of self from the field) and the female is "Communal" (merging self with the field).

20. The flexibility of the female in setting up closeness and intimacy is ironically documented by studies showing that women have a tendency to be erotically aroused by the image of Death (McClelland, in S. White, 1963; Paris and Goodstein, 1966). Barclay and Haber (1965) have even shown erotic arousal in women in response to aggressive and hostile imagery.

21. Freud (1905, *Three Contributions to a Theory of Sexuality*) proposed that the female counterpart to "castration anxiety" in the male is "anxiety over loss of love." Indeed, he theorized that what he considered to be typical feminine traits, such as narcissism and need for social approval, stemmed most from a concern about loss of love.

22. Kinsey, et al. found that more women than men attained orgasm by merely fantasying about sexual themes.

23. Many other interesting sex differences could have been cited. One could mention differences in smiling and laughter behavior (Bugental, Love, and Gianetto, 1971; Leventhal, 1970); differences in humor preferences (Felker and Hunter, 1970); differences in response to "outsiders" (Feshbach, 1969); differences in expressive styles (Stein and Lenrow, 1970); and differences in patterns of psychopathology (Garai, 1970); and so forth.

4

HOW IS THE FEMININE ROLE

ACQUIRED?

Attention is now turned to research findings bearing on how a feminine identification is acquired. Do we know what conditions foster or inhibit the learning of a feminine role? Is femininity more or less difficult to learn than masculinity? What parental attitudes most influence the girl as she evolves her sex role? These are some of the prime questions that are explored.

Let it be said from the outset that there is still considerable controversy about how anyone acquires sex identity. Most theorists agree that sex identity arises in the course of a learning process and that one of its core components, namely, recognition that "I am a girl" or "I am a boy," crystallizes out by the age of 3 or 4.[1] It is also widely agreed that learning one's sex identity is part of a broader process of establishing one's overall identity. Sex identity is viewed as a component of general identity. Multiple models have been offered concerning the nature of the identification process. These have ranged from the extravagant complexity of the psychoanalytic account of how each child integrates the bristling difficulties of the Oedipal encounter to emerge with a sense of being like the same-sex parent—to the much simpler schema in which identification is a straightforward learning to imitate parent figures. One of the best summary accounts of the multiple views that have been proposed concerning how identification proceeds has been presented by Lynn (1969). He concluded that these views, which relate to the forces that result in the child adopting and integrating within himself the attributes of his parents, may be reduced to the following categories:

1. The child adopts attributes of the parent model because he fears that he will be punished if he does not do so.
2. The child is made to feel that he will lose parental love if he does not learn to be like them.
3. The child will emulate the parents because he is rewarded for doing so and punished for not doing so.
4. A child imitates his parents because he perceives that they receive rewards for their modes of behavior and he vicariously shares in their experience.

5. Relatedly, a child tries to be like his parents because he envies the rewards they receive from others.
6. A child fashions himself after his parents because they apparently have powers that he lacks.
7. Finally, a child may choose to take on various parental attributes because he is stimulated by his perception that he already shares certain basic similarities with them.

Actually, most of the formulations about the identification process may be loosely integrated into a simpler form. The major forces in stimulating identification may be represented as part of a continuum, one pole of which involves the child's positive feelings about the warmth and power of his parents and the other pole the child's anxiety about being punished or hurt if he does not behave like his parents. Some theories, for example, psychoanalytic, see both of these extremes as not only simultaneously involved in the child's learning his identification but also varying in their importance at different stages of the evolution of the child's identity.

A persistent problem to those interested in sex identification has concerned the actual elements or attributes of the child's parents that the child learns to make part of himself. Does the child learn fairly small units of behavior (a specific way of reacting to a specific object)? Does he learn broad attitudes and traitlike orientations? Or can he even learn a pervading life style that goes far beyond any one or more specific ways of reacting to things? Gewirtz (in Goslin, 1969) has argued for the view that largely discrete bits of behavior are learned, whereas the psychoanalytic position takes the opposite view.

When one begins to discuss specifically the question of how the child learns *sex identity,* some complicated issues present themselves with regard to how the child selects the proper proportion of attributes from two parents of opposite sex in order to arrive at a harmonious blend that is congruent with being a person with one prime sex role. That is, since the mother and father together represent both female and male elements, how does the child of one given sex learn to take over their traits and attitudes in a fashion that results either in an integrated male or female identity? How does the child dampen the identity impact of the opposite-sex parent and maximize the influence of the like-sex parent? Although at first sight one might expect that it would not be difficult to provide a simple, straightforward explanation for this phenomenon, it has in actual fact turned out not to be an easy task.[2] The very same complications, related to the fact that both male and female children have shifting patterns of relationships with mother and father at different life stages, that persuaded Freud to fashion his complex theory about the nature of sex identity have plagued other theorists. How does the boy who spends so much of his early life in intimate contact with his mother escape becoming feminine? How does the girl who has initially taken her mother as her most intimate object of relationship ever learn to shift so that her eventual major bestowal of affection is upon masculine figures?

Slote (1962) has succinctly highlighted the complications that confront anyone trying to think through the process of sex identification (p. 82):

The actual process by which a girl or boy learns sex-role identification is . . . only partially understood. . . . There are many questions that arise. Do girls have stronger identifications with their mothers than boys do with their fathers? . . . Do girls and boys perceive themselves as, or actually assume traits of, both the same-sex and opposite-sex parent in their sex-role development? Do children, in fact, incorporate the sex role of the parental figure(s) or do they, indeed, identify with a cultural stereotype of masculinity and femininity which they, in turn, superimpose on or offer as representative of their parents?

Let us consider what is known about the factors that contribute to the girl becoming psychologically feminized. To begin with, one should keep in mind Kohlberg's (1966) injunction that what is basic to sex-role differentiation is that boys and girls enter life with structurally different bodies and that these differences consistently evoke "girl" versus "boy" labels from others. The girl learns the "girl" label and her girl appearance evokes rather consistent "You are a girl" reactions from the important people in her world. The core of her feminine identity is the fact that her body is labeled as female. Apropos of this point, it is interesting that the hermaphroditic child who, in actuality, does not possess a body that is clearly male or female, will develop a clear sense of sexual identity if the people in his world consistently label the child as masculine or feminine during the first three years of the child's life (Stoller, 1968; Money, Hampson, and Hampson, 1957). That is, what seems to be crucial is the decision of the appropriate adults that the child's body will be called masculine or feminine. Once this decision is made and consistently enforced the child gets communications from others and also from himself that his behavior must conform to specific sex-role expectations.

Hartley (1964) presents a particularly clear exposition of the ways in which girls are psychologically feminized. She "informally" studied the "sex-typing" techniques used in 22 young families and made the following observations:

Mothers indicate that they "fuss with" the baby girl's hair, dress her in a feminine way, and tell her how pretty she is. This is a form of "handling" that may gradually "mold" parallel self-regarding attitudes. Relatedly, the girl's play and interests are "canalized" in a feminine direction by providing her with toys such as dolls and carriages. Hartley notes apropos of such toys (p. 4): "Opportunity to manipulate these with satisfaction, to incorporate them into early imitative sequences, provides the basis for both heightened awareness and anticipation of pleasure in relation to similar objects." She adds that likewise feminine colors, certain styles of body movement, and so forth are selectively brought to the girl's attention through objects and perceptual experiences frequently made available to her.

Importance is assigned by Hartley to such verbal designations as "That's a good girl," "Don't be a bad girl," "There, now, you really are a good girl." The repetition of such statements is said to serve as a sign to the child that she is of a specific sex identity and the term "girl" acquires experiential and feeling qualities associated with parental attitudes at the times the parents apply the "girl" labels. With time, the label "girl" also conveys to the girl that she belongs to a general category of "other girls" and she gains a sense of *general* "girl" identification.

Quite early, the girl is encouraged to emulate mother—to be "just like Mommy." She receives communications that when she grows up she will be like mother, that it is fun to dress up like mother, and that mother's activities are a worthy model. By doing things "like Mommy" she learns feminine ways. The imitation of mother extends to learning the appropriate body posture for urination. Hartley underscores the apparent import of this bit of learning by remarking (p. 6):

The observant little girl who wants to urinate from an erect position is told, "No, little girls don't do that. You must sit like mommy. Only daddies and boys stand." This may be the first direct negatively phrased sex-oriented limitation the young female has encountered. It not only emphasizes further her kinship with women, but calls attention insistently to her separation from men.

Analogously, the girl is told that she cannot shave the way her father does, but that she can apply cosmetics and perfumes the way her mother does. More practically, the girl is initiated into household chores and encouraged to invest herself in learning to use the tools basic to "female housekeeping." Hartley comments that if Piaget is correct about the importance of imitation, supplying the little girl with tools for carrying out traditional female activities may contribute much to sex typing. The tools may encourage long-term imitation and practice of behavior examples provided by the mother model. Sensory-motor experiences may be encouraged that convey the "feeling" of femininity even before there is real appreciation of the verbal labels that apply to the mother's behaviors. In general, the girl's continuous contact with the mother's feminine activities results in a preference for imitating such activities.

Komarovsky (1964) asked a group of college girls to reminisce about their childhoods and scanned their reports to ascertain what had been the primary feminizing influences in their lives. One of the earliest of these influences seemed to be the expectation that a little girl will select "girl's toys" to play with and that she will be more "quiet" and "restrained" in her play than boys. Presumably, girls who deviate too much from this expectation are made to feel they are "queer" and different. The pressure exerted on girls to be restrained in their activities is illustrated by the report of one girl who participated in the study (p. 217):

When I was 12, my mother was boasting one day to some friends about my swimming. . . . This friend remarked, "Don't let the child swim so much.

Large muscles are very unattractive in a girl." From then on the fear of becoming unfeminine cooled my interest in swimming.

The restraint imposed was said to extend to a feeling that it was wrong to do things independently. Many of the girls felt that they were "sheltered" and that any movement away from home was disapproved. Parallel with an emphasis upon staying close to home was the expectation that a girl has obligations to be close to, and do things for, her family and kin. The injunction not to move about "out there" fits well, of course, with Fisher's (1970) observation that women have more anxiety than men about movement in space.

Colley (1959) has, perhaps more than others, emphasized the idea that each parent facilitates sex-role learning in the child by "projecting" onto it certain modal sex-role concepts. Thus, presumably each parent "projects" femaleness into female children and maleness into male children. Colley illustrates this view by portraying the selective attitude of a mother from the first occasion that she sees her new child. She knows that her child is of a particular sex and her view will be conveyed in how she touches it, the tone of her voice, her manner of handling the genitalia, and the kinds of responses she tries to evoke. Empirical support for Colley's view has come from a study by Rothbart and Maccoby (1966), who had parents listen to a tape recording of a child's voice that was ambiguous as to sex. One group of parents were told they were listening to a boy and another that the voice was a girl's. The child's voice uttered a series of separate statements (for example, "Daddy, help me"; "Mommy, come look at my puzzle"). The parents were asked to imagine that they were at home with the child and to write the response they would make to each of the statements. It was found that both fathers and mothers reacted differently to the fictitious child if they thought it was a boy than if they thought it was a girl. For example, the fathers showed more permissiveness with regard to dependency and aggression when they thought the child was a girl rather than a boy. Mothers showed more permissiveness to the child when they presumed it was a boy rather than a girl. Parents obviously had certain sets or stereotypes about a female versus male child. When the experimental conditions were right, they elicited a projection of these stereotypes from the parents onto the neutral child's voice.[3]

Douvan and Adelson (1966) concluded, after a careful study of the attitudes and values of thousands of adolescent girls, that a core component of feminine identity is the goal of becoming a wife and mother. There are few aspects of a girl's development that do not somehow seem oriented toward this core image. The wife-mother concept serves the same sex-role integrating function for girls as occupational goals do for boys. Despite the widespread assumption that the female role is changing radically, the wife-mother ideal is still a paramount definition of femininity. Incidentally, Hartley (1959–1960) has similarly shown on the basis of studies of young children that their concepts of both the female and male roles do not really differ from older, long accepted stereotyped versions. It is of interest to examine what Douvan and Adelson found to be the basic components of the widely accepted mother-wife image. They state with regard to the young girl's concept of womanhood (p. 232): "She looks forward to being an attractive, active woman in the family setting. . . . She will be married to a man of her choosing with whom she shares a romantic and permanent love." Even the traditional feminine vocational goals, such as being a nurse or a stenographer, are visualized as temporary excursions in the process of waiting for the mother-wife fulfillment. It cannot be overemphasized how much importance Douvan and Adelson assign to the part played by the wife-mother feminine ideal in integrating a girl's sex-role development.

One of the puzzling questions about learning femininity relates to how much is taken from the mother and how much is taken from the father. Actually, as is discussed later, there is also a further question with regard to how much is taken from one's sibs and even one's peers. At first sight, there would not seem to be much of a problem in deciding about the relative importance of the mother and father in providing a model for the girl in structuring her sex identity. Presumably, a girl gets the core of her sexual identity by modeling herself after her mother. Most empirical studies (Beier and Ratzenburg, 1953) demonstrate that when girls are asked to rate themselves with reference to a variety of attributes and also analogously to rate their parents, they turn out to perceive themselves as more similar to their mothers than to their fathers. However, there are both theoretical and empirical reasons for doubting the assumption that acquiring femininity is simply a matter of the girl learning to be like her mother.

A number of theorists have proposed that the father is a crucial participant in the feminization of his daughter. As is well known, most psychoanalytic writers see the girl's early relationship with her father as an essential experience in learning to accept the passive aspects of the feminine role. That is, she presumably has the opportunity in her interactions with him to try out passive-feminine strategies and to obtain some reassurance (in terms of his responses) that will compensate her for giving up her earlier (more phallic or clitoral) sexual orientation.

Kohlberg (1966) suggests that whereas boys test out their masculinity in terms of their acceptance in male groups, girls do not primarily define their femininity in terms of acceptance by other females but rather with reference to being approved by males. From this perspective, learning to obtain the approval of the first significant male in her life, namely, her father, would be an important element in the girl's feeling about her sex role.

Johnson (1963) takes the rather extreme position that the father rather than the mother is the prime source of sex typing for girls (also for boys). She argues that there is an initial identification with the mother by girls (and boys), but that it is not sex typed because the mother does not vary her behavior toward her children in terms of their sex. Presumably, after the stage of infantile dependency upon the mother, the girl establishes a relationship with the father in which she learns how to relate to a man. The father is said to take the lead in interacting with her in such a fashion as to highlight her femininity. Johnson's explanation of the limited participation by mother in sex typing (p. 320) is as follows:

Although the mother does share common cultural values with the father about what is appropriate and masculine and feminine behavior . . . there is considerable evidence that she does not make a basic differentiation in her attitude toward male and female children. She neither plays wife to her son nor does she urge her daughter "to buck up and get in there and be a woman," rather she thinks of both sexes as "children". . . .

Johnson specifies that the father's contribution to his daughter's learning her sex role takes the form of rewarding her for being "attractive," in the entire sense that this term applies to being girlish and feminine. She cites a number of empirical studies to support her views about the father's large and the mother's small sex-typing contribution. For example, Johnson refers to the work of Brodbeck (1954), which demonstrated that mothers do not have differential effects on the moral standards of their child, whereas fathers do. Relatedly, she mentions that Goodenough (1957) concluded, after interviews with parents about their conceptions of masculinity and femininity, that fathers are much more concerned than mothers with the sex typing of their children. She refers further to the work of Bronfenbrenner (in L. Petrullo and B. M. Bass, 1961) who, after studying the relation of parental behavior to leadership and responsibility behavior in adolescents, concluded (p. 249): ". . . generally speaking, it is the father who is especially likely to treat children of the two sexes differently . . . girls receive more affection, attention and praise than boys—especially from their fathers. . . ."

If one scans the literature, one can also find other studies that reaffirm either that the mother contributes little to sex typing or that the father contributes relatively more than mother does. For example, Sears, Maccoby, and Levin (1957), after an intensive analysis of the child-rearing practices of mothers, expressed their surprise at how few differences they could detect in maternal modes of dealing with girls as compared to boys. Sopchak (1952) reported that "feminine girls" were more identified with their fathers than were "masculine girls." Osgood, Suci, and Tannenbaum (1957), in a series of studies making use of the semantic differential technique to explore identification phenomena, discovered that young women were as much identified with their fathers as their mothers. This contrasted with the findings for young men, who were more identified with their fathers than their mothers. Mussen and Rutherford (1963) discovered that measures of a girl's femininity were positively correlated with indices of her father's masculinity and his expectations of femininity in her.

A rather unique study by Grayson (1967) dealt with the effects upon a girl's psychosexual attitudes of losing (by death) a parent in early childhood. It evaluated the differential impact of mother versus father loss. High school and college-age girls whose parents had died responded to the Rorschach Inkblot, Thematic Apperception, Draw-A-Person, and Cole Animal Tests, and measures of psychosexual conflict were derived from these tests.[4] Analysis of the data indicated no consistent tendencies for either mother or father loss to have a greater negative effect than the other on the conflict indices. Actually, the one significant result obtained was in the direction of finding more sex-role conflict in the Thematic Apperception stories of girls who had lost a father rather than a mother.

A clearer indication of father's influence emerged when Fish (1969) found that the degree of femininity in a group of female college students was positively correlated with estimates of how much time the father spent at home and was actually available for a relationship. One could interpret this finding to mean that the girl who had the greatest opportunity to interact with her father was likely to become the most feminine.

Heilbrun (1965) too provided support for the proposition that the father can provide adequate cues for his daughter's sex typing. Thus, he found that girls closely identified with a masculine father were just as feminine as girls identified with a feminine mother.

Even more impressively, Sears (1970) reported that in a sample of 84 girls, degree of femininity was positively correlated with the father's (but not with the mother's) "warmth." The measure of warmth was derived from interview data (from the mother) collected seven years earlier.

Relatedly, Lawrence (1968), while comparing a group of college girls who were categorized as "father identifiers" (because they see themselves as more like their fathers than their mothers) and another categorized as "mother identifiers," discovered that the former were more home-oriented and less interested in a career than the latter. He was surprised by these results and speculated that the greater apparent femininity of the interest pattern of the "father identifier" might represent some kind of a defensive maneuver. This speculation was partially stimulated by the fact that "father identifiers" were also found to do relatively better than the "mother identifiers" on the Embedded Figures Test, a task in which males usually excel over females.

We lack sufficient reliable research findings to state definitively how influential the father is in his daughter's sex-role development.[5] But one can say that there is now good evidence that the father is probably much more influential in this respect than many theorists had thought.[6] In fact, he may have a unique responsibility in the family for enforcing sex-role differentiation. After a comprehensive review of the literature concerned with father-daughter relationships, Biller and Weiss (1970) concluded (p. 90): "The father's role in the family seems to be of great significance in the process of feminine identification and personality adjustment in the female."

A number of observers have found that a girl's ordinal position in the family and the number of female versus male sibs she has may affect her

sex-role definition. Kammeyer (1966) reported that firstborn girls (as compared with later-born girls) have a more traditional concept of the feminine role and are more likely to prefer marriage over graduation from college if a choice has to be made between the two. Sutton-Smith, Roberts,
and Rosenberg (1964) found that girls who had only a female rather than
a male sib were also relatively higher in their feminine interests (as measured by the Strong Vocational Interest Blank). Kammeyer (1967) noted
that girls with an older cross-sex sib are more likely than girls without
such a sib to have a concept of the female personality that minimizes its
difference from the male's. Koch (1956) and Rosenberg and Sutton-Smith
(1964a) have both shown that the presence of opposite sex siblings tends
to diminish identification with one's own sex and the presence of like-sex
sibs apparently augments identification with one's own sex.[7] Even further,
Fagot and Paterson (1969) present some interesting data about the impact
of extrafamily figures on sex role. They have demonstrated that the child's
peers and his teachers in the school setting have a significant effect in
shaping his sex-role behaviors.

What kinds of mother and father attributes are most likely to shape
femininity in the female child? Although only limited solid information
pertinent to this question is available, it is worth reviewing.

Probably one of the most thorough studies of the matter was carried out
by Sears, Rau, and Alpert (1965), who intensively observed, rated, and
tested children in a nursery school with a variety of procedures. Their parents were interviewed, and tapes of these interviews were rated by judges.
Measures of sex-role identification and traits related to sex role were obtained from the children. For example, standardized doll-play situations
were presented in which attitudes about sex-linked activities could be evaluated. Preferences for "boy" versus "girl" toys were measured, and the
so-called "It Test" (Brown, 1956) was administered that considers the
kinds of sex-role attributes the child projects onto a sexless stick-figure
drawing of a child. Nineteen girls and 21 boys (plus their parents) participated in the study.

Analysis of this data revealed that the degree of femininity of the girls
was not related to either how warm and nurturant their mothers were nor
to the degree of power the mothers appeared to have in the family. Girls
with "warm" mothers were no more feminine than girls with "cold" mothers. Girls whose mothers were relatively passive, as defined by submission
to the fathers' authority, were no more feminine than girls whose mothers
were dominant over their fathers.[8] In addition, the girl's degree of femininity was not related to how clearly her parents seemed to differentiate
between what kinds of activities are properly feminine and those that are
properly masculine. But there was a trend for girls in families believing
strongly that little girls should be different from little boys to be more
feminine than girls from families not adhering to such a belief. A girl's degree of femininity showed a consistent relationship to how permissive her
parents had been about sexual play. The more permissive mothers and

fathers had been about "sexual" matters (for example, letting the child go nude, providing sexual information) the *less* feminine were their daughters.[9] Incidentally, the correlation was no greater with respect to the influence of the mother than that of the father. Sears, et al. (1957) interpreted the findings in the context that masculinity is associated with an active orientation and therefore (p. 189) "any qualities of the child-rearing experiences that tend to provoke active sexual play would conduce to masculinity, whereas parental attitudes that tend to inhibit a child's exploration and seeking would conduce to femininity." In the same vein, Sears, et al. discovered that femininity was highest in those girls who came from families that discouraged aggression and required passive submission to rules and demands. Thus, the higher a girl's femininity the more her parents had punished her for aggression toward them, imposed strict toilet training on her, expected proper table manners from her, and so forth. Femininity seemed to be maximized by a parental orientation that was nonpermissive and punitive. Another way to look at this finding was that femininity was encouraged by parents who cultivated passivity and submissiveness in their daughters. Sears, et al. summarized their perspective as follows (p. 198):

> A closed, anxious, non-permissive attitude on the part of either or both parents was conducive to femininity in both sexes of children, as were the use of physical punishment and severe control of aggression. . . . permissiveness encourages the development of the active, adventurous, free-ranging quality of behavior that characterizes the male role, and . . . punitiveness creates pressure toward the more passive and conforming behavior that typifies the female role.

One other finding of this study should be described. Sears, et al. devised an index that defined how encouraging each parent was of dependent behavior in the child. It turned out that the more dependency was encouraged by the father the more masculine was his daughter. (Analogously, the more the mother encouraged dependency in her son the greater was his feminization.) However, paradoxically, the daughter's degree of femininity was *not* related to how much her mother encouraged her to be dependent. An adequate explanation for this pattern of results has not really been provided, but it is obviously pertinent to the earlier discussed issue of the part that the father plays in structuring the sex role for his daughter. Here one sees that the father may be able to inhibit his daughter's femininity by encouraging her to behave dependently toward him.

A longitudinal study of personality development reported by Kagan and Moss (1962) offers some material that bears on the Sears, et al. results. Kagan and Moss examined, among numerous other things, the relationship of maternal behavior in early life to the child's later sex role behavior—in adolescence and also early adulthood. Numerous kinds of naturalistic and controlled measures were obtained with regard to both mother and child over a period of years. It was found that the mother's behavior was minimally predictive of her daughter's later sex behavior or degree of femininity (as defined by interests and activities).[10] One significant trend that did emerge indicated that the more girls were "protected" by their mothers in early childhood the greater was the likelihood they would exhibit feminine interests during later childhood and adulthood as well. The "protective" behavior of the mothers referred to their encouraging dependence. It was also true that the more protective mother was during the time that her daughter was in the six–ten age range the higher was her daughter's anxiety about sex during adulthood. A final significant finding was that girls whose mothers were most hostile toward them (pushing them toward independence) during the first three years of life were those most likely to adopt masculine activities when they became adults. These findings are roughly congruent with the Sears, et al. results just cited. That is, in both instances it would appear that encouraging dependence increases femininity and applying pressure to be independent increases masculinity. However, these findings are contradictory insofar as the Sears, et al. data indicated that the mother's behavior with respect to dependence did not affect her daughter's degree of femininity, whereas the Kagan and Moss data did show the mother to be influential in this respect. Incidentally, the fact that encouraging dependence, in the Kagan and Moss sample, seemed to lead to increased anxiety about sex might appear to be contradictory to the finding that it also increased femininity. But there is no contradiction. As discussed later, some findings suggest that the stereotyped "feminine" role may encourage certain forms of fearfulness and anxiety.

Mussen and Rutherford (1963) determined the sex-role preferences of first-grade girls in terms of their choices of toys and activities, as projected onto a neuter stick-figure representation called It (Brown, 1956). They also studied the girls' feelings about their parents by evaluating doll play involving "mother" and "father" dolls. Further, the parents of the children were evaluated by means of questionnaires, and in the case of the mothers, interviews were obtained. Analysis of the material indicated that the greater a girl's femininity, as depicted by the It measure, the more likely she was to portray her mother (during doll play) as nurturant, warm, and affectionate. In addition, a girl's degree of femininity was positively correlated with the extent to which interviewers judged her mother to display "warmth" toward her child and how "self-accepting" her mother was, as measured by her responses to a questionnaire. Her femininity was not related to her mother's own femininity scores on a standard measure (Gough, 1957) of this dimension, nor was it related to ratings of how much her mother encouraged her to engage in feminine activities. Data concerning the fathers of the girls indicated that a girl's femininity was positively correlated with the amount of masculinity of the father (as measured by the Gough questionnaire) as well as the degree to which the father encouraged her to engage in feminine activities.

Lynn (1961) had earlier looked at the relationship of girls' (5–6-year-old range) sex-role preferences (defined by the It test) to attitudes toward their mothers and fathers, as revealed in doll-play observations. It was *not* possible to show a significant positive correlation between degree of femininity and the amount of nurturance or protectiveness ascribed to the mother, although the correlation was positive when the girl's femininity was compared to the combined degree of warmth of both her mother and father. Also, the apparent hostility ascribed to the mother and father in the doll-play situation had only chance correlations with sex-role preferences.

Slote (1962) studied adolescent girls who responded to a questionnaire measure of femininity as well as to a questionnaire involving the rating of mother, father, self, and other figures with regard to a variety of attributes. Borderline trends were discerned for a girl's level of femininity to be positively correlated with how much she perceived her mother to be "warm," "considerate," and "ready to forgive a wrong."

Preston (1965) measured femininity in adolescent girls by means of a standard questionnaire and the Franck-Rosen Drawing Completion Test. Presumably, the former measures "conscious" femininity and the latter (based on whether drawings are completed in a phallic versus nonphallic fashion) taps unconscious attitudes about femininity. A questionnaire also inquired concerning parental attributes, the relative dominance of mother and father, and the clarity with which the parents differentiate specific tasks as being masculine versus feminine. The findings of the study were as follows. The "unconscious" measure of femininity did not correlate with any of the girl's apparent feelings about her parents. The "conscious" measure of femininity was negatively correlated with the mother being described as being more punitive (punishing) than the father. That is, the more punishing the mother was said to be, as compared to father, the more her daughter depicted herself as having masculine attitudes. In addition, the girl's conscious femininity was positively correlated with how clearly her parents differentiated tasks as being typically feminine or masculine."[11] Integrating these findings, Preston concluded (p. 56): "The more traditional and differentiated parental roles with regard to degree and mode of punishment and to specific behaviors which our culture defines as masculine or feminine are shown to be associated with conscious femininity. . . ."

Looking back at the studies just reviewed, what stands out most clearly? A large majority of the studies have found that a girl's degree of femininity is positively related to the perception of her mother (or in one instance both her mother and father) as warm, nurturant, or protective.[12] Apparently a girl's femininity is fostered by the feeling that her mother wants to help or protect her. The one major contradiction to this finding is represented by the Sears, et al. (1965) data which found no correlation between femininity and maternal warmth. Indeed, the trend of their results suggested that femininity was greatest in those girls whose mothers (and fathers) were strict in their socialization demands—rather than lenient. Of course, it is possible that the "strictness" represented a form of protectiveness that had underlying nurturant intent. Another point to consider is that the children in the Sears, et al. study were among the youngest of those involved in the various samples. Femininity at age 4 or 5 may be differently related to the mother's behavior than is femininity in adolescent girls. Some support for this idea can be derived from the longitudinal Kagan and Moss (1962) study. Although they found no relationship between maternal protectiveness and femininity in the age range 4–6, which is equivalent to the Sears, et al. sample, they did find these variables to be positively correlated at later ages closer to adolescence. The role of the mother's nurturance or protectiveness stands out, at the present stage of empirical research, as one of the really important variables in shaping her daughter's femininity.

One may add that in two of the studies (Sears, et al., 1965; Preston, 1965) cited, in which attention was directed to whether the girl's femininity was linked with how clearly her parents differentiated things that are masculine and feminine, a positive relationship was observed. These results imply that parental standards and feelings about sex-role differentiation may also, upon further investigation, turn out to be significant variables in shaping femininity.

Is it more difficult or more complicated for the girl to construct her feminine identity than it is for the boy to build up his masculine identity? Are there special obstacles to a girl's learning the feminine role? Some differences of opinion exist about these questions.

Freud, who was one of the first to speculate systematically about the matter, was convinced that the girl's sex-identification task is more difficult than the boy's. He felt that this was true because he assumed that since boys and girls both start out with the mother as their first love object, the boy can continue, even as he matures, to hold to an opposite-sex love object; whereas the girl must, as she develops, shift from mother to a male object (father). Presumably, the need for the girl to shift from the mother to a male object introduces an extra step and an extra complication into the process of her learning her sex role. Others (especially Mowrer, 1953) proposed, in opposition to Freud's formulation, that the child's original relationship with the mother is more in the nature of identifying with her rather than taking her as a love object. From this view, it would be the boy who must shift when he turns to father and identifies with his masculinity. The girl, on the other hand, would continue, throughout her development, to adhere to the same feminine figure for her identification. The identification task would, therefore, be more difficult for the male than for the female.

Lynn (1969) has been particularly prominent among those who argue for the Mowrer perspective. Actually, he takes a rather complex position. Lynn proposes that girls have an easier time in arriving at a like-sex identification than boys do, but that with increasing age both sexes come to live in a world in which the male and his values are considered to be superior to that which is female—with the consequence that the female becomes less secure and the male more secure about sexual identity. He notes (p. 66), "When the girl leaves infancy she goes from a woman's world of mother care to a man's world. Being feminine, she thus moves from a same-sex to an opposite-sex-oriented world, whereas the boy moves from an opposite-sex to a same-sex-oriented world . . . the girl . . . is, in a sense, punished simply for being born female, whereas the boy is rewarded simply for being born male." In discussing the differential problems of the female and male in learning the sex role, Lynn suggests that their tasks are almost qualitatively different. He compares the identification task of the girl to that of following a map containing much detail, whereas the task for the boy is that of trying to grasp a map in which there are only sketchy outlines of main features. He points out that when the girl is acquiring sex-role information, it is continuously available to her in great detail because she is almost always with her mother whom she can observe and imitate. This he contrasts with the situation of the boy whose identification model, father, is away at work most of the day and who, even when he arrives home, is not as intimately and easily available for interaction as is mother. Little empirical support has been offered for this concept that the tasks of the girl and boy in learning sex role are radically different.[13] It is based largely upon the observation that the mother is more consistently and perhaps intimately available as an object of identification than is the father.

There are alternative pathways and criteria that can be considered in the course of judging comparability of sex-role identification problems for girls and boys. One may ask which of the two sexes more quickly arrives at a concept of its sex role. One may ask which experiences more difficulty and anxiety during the identification process. One may ask which is able to construct the most definite and consistent definition of its sex role. And there are still other alternative questions pertinent to this issue that could be raised. It is difficult to find research data that consistently answer such questions in a unidirectional way.

Let us explore the matter of which sex is the first to arrive at a definition of sex role. One approach to the issue has involved studying the relative frequencies with which girls and boys sketch a same-sex figure, rather than one of the opposite sex, when asked to draw a picture of a person. The assumption has been made (without solid empirical support) that an individual with minimal conflict about his sex role has a set or readiness to produce a like-sex figure when the instructions leave him a choice as to which of the two sexes to draw. Several investigators have actually examined the relative frequencies with which females and males depict their own sex first in their drawings. Bieliauskas (1960, 1965), Brown and Tolor (1957), and others have reviewed findings that indicate that at younger age levels (5–11) girls draw same-sex figures more often than boys. But, interestingly, this trend shifts with increasing age, and there are data indicating that college-age males draw same-sex figures more often than females. This pattern of results is, of course, nicely congruent with the theories of Lynn (1969) and others who theorize that girls have an easier task than boys in initially arriving at a sex-role definition because they can, from the very beginning, remain identified with their mothers whereas boys have to shift from mothers (their first models) to fathers in order to adopt male models. These investigators have proposed, congruently with the figure-drawing findings, that as individuals advance to adulthood they increasingly encounter a world in which masculinity has higher prestige than femininity; and so the male's sex identity is bolstered and the female's is attenuated (which is paralleled by the fact that in the figure-drawing data a shift occurs so that adult males draw same-sex figures more often than adult females, rather than less often).

Numerous studies have considered how early and how consistently girls and boys show preferences for female versus male toys and activities. As indicated by various papers (Slote, 1962; Hall and Keith, 1964; Rabban, 1950) there is fairly good consensus that boys adhere earlier and more definitely to same-sex preferences than do girls.[14] Girls typically indicate relatively more preferences for masculine activities than do boys for feminine activities. Some have interpreted this fact to signify that boys more quickly evolve a clear concept of their sex role. However, others (Brown, 1958; Minuchin, 1965) have argued that it indicates that girls have more freedom than boys in defining their sex roles. Brown refers (p. 235) to the *"greater latitude* of the girls compared to the boys in sex-role development. It appears somewhat paradoxical that, although restricted much more in practically all other respects, girls are allowed more freedom than boys in sex-role learning. . . . For a girl to be a tomboy does not involve the censure that results when a boy is a sissy. With little, if any, embarrassment or threat, girls may show strong preference for the masculine role; this is not true in the case of boys." Brown points out that behaviorally girls may without real criticism wear masculine articles of clothing, have masculine names, and play with masculine toys—but boys would receive severe disapproval for equivalent kinds of feminine behavior. The findings pertaining to feminine versus masculine preferences are obviously open to divergent interpretations. It is interesting, though, that there have been a few studies that, upon examining aspects of sex role in terms of actual performance measures (rather than mere preference), found girls to be more knowledgeable (or "expert") about sex differences than boys. Thus, Katcher and Levin (1955) reported that when young children were asked to make size judgments concerning miniature child and adult representations, the girls seemed to be more realistically aware of their femininity (as defined in size terms) than the boys were of their masculinity. Similarly, as noted, Katcher (1955) found that young girls could, more realistically than boys, identify the difference between female and male genitals.[15]

Kagan and Lemkin (1960) and others have been impressed with the potential conflict that confronts the girl as she attempts to identify with her mother who, in terms of cultural stereotypes, may be regarded as the less competent sex and also as less capable than her father. She is told by the culture to model herself after a woman called mother, but she is simultaneously informed, state Kagan and Lemkin, that being a woman implies inferiority. They add that this is reflected in the fact that surveys find more females who state they would prefer to be males than males who would prefer to be females. Although there is probably some validity in the point made by Kagan and Lemkin, the identification dilemma faced by the female child may not be as great as they visualize it to be. Hartley, Hardesty, and Gorfein (1962) studied attitudes about female and male children in a group of 132 children (ages 8–11). The subjects were asked to complete a story about a couple who wanted to adopt a child and had to choose between a girl and a boy. They were also asked direct questions about whether they would prefer to have female or male children when they grew up and got married. The findings indicated that they were most likely to assume that adults prefer to have children the same sex as themselves. Fathers were seen as wanting boys and mothers as wanting girls. A majority of the directly expressed preferences of the subjects followed an analogous pattern. Girls wanted to have female children and boys, male children. These results imply that although there is a broad cultural stereotype about female inferiority, girls somehow learn to regard their own sex as "preferred" by mothers and themselves.

Similarly, Kohlberg (1966) comments that despite the general assumption that females are less competent than males, the concept of "woman" still retains many other positive connotations that makes it attractive to a young girl.[16] For example, it is attractive as a model even on the basis of the simple fact that an adult woman is superior in power to a child of either sex. Adult femininity represents to the little girl a certain measure of power and competence. In addition, there are positive connotations linked with femininity that contrast with certain negative connotations of masculinity. Femininity is associated with being nurturant and "nice," which have positive significance; whereas the aggressiveness of masculinity has "bad" implications. Kohlberg also points out that women are often perceived as superior to men in terms of their attractiveness and physical beauty. Outside of the realm of power there are important qualities associated with femininity that could make a girl feel that identifying with mother is a positive and advantageous thing to do.

The work of Douvan and Adelson (1966), previously cited, is appropriate to introduce into the discussion at this point because it bears on the matter of how clearly girls structure their sex identity. They studied a large sample of female adolescents and found that it was common for such girls to postpone a crystallization of their values and attitudes in anticipation of the time when they will meet a future husband and better be able to judge what style of behavior on their own part would be most harmonious with his attributes. If their findings are valid, this would mean that the feminine sex role requires, as a normative process, the maintenance of a certain degree of ambiguity in self-definition. Paradoxically, then, any vagueness in the girl's sex-role definition might represent a standardized ambiguity with adaptive value in terms of the kinds of demands made upon women. Apropos of this point, Tryon (1939) reported that the values of girls change much more than boys between the ages of 12 through 15. She remarked (p. 79), "There is much greater demand upon these girls . . . as compared to the boys for flexibility, for capacity to readjust their ideals, for ability to reorient themselves to new goals."

In spite of the "ambiguity" that may be built into the feminine role, there is evidence that females are probably as consistent and integrated as men in their sex-role attributes. For example, Sears, Rau, and Alpert (1965) administered a battery of measures of gender role to male and female nursery school samples and found much more consistent intercorrelation among the girls' scores than the boys'. The median correlation for the girls was .36 and that for the boys .15. Sears, et al. were so impressed with this difference that they concluded that the girls at this age had a more stable gender role structure than the boys. One can also cite the work of Zuk (1958) who reviewed the stability of measures of "sex appropriate" behavior during adolescence in girls and boys who were studied longitudinally (in the California Adolescent Growth Study) for several years. He found that (p. 30), "Boys did not match girls in increase in sex-appropriateness of behavior during the period of adolescence studied; nor did they demonstrate in their behavior the year-to-year consistency or stability of girls." Another interesting pertinent study was carried out by DeLucia (1960), who evaluated the differential effects upon girls and boys (ages 5–6) of being praised or censured for their choices of pictures depicting either "masculine" or "feminine" toys. He demonstrated that the sex-appropriate choices of the boys were more unstable and more easily manipulated by the experimental procedure than were those of the girls. The results were seen as indicating that the girls had less difficulty than the boys in structuring a same-sex identification.

Kagan and Moss (1962) were able to look at the stability of sex-related behaviors in girls and boys who were followed in a longitudinal study from the beginning of childhood into adulthood. Elaborate observational and test data were available at many time points in the developmental sequence. It was found that in both girls and boys the amount of interest displayed during adolescence in activities that were not traditional for their own sex could be significantly predicted from the amount displayed very early in childhood. As Kagan and Moss state (p. 159), "The boys who preferred music and reading to team athletics and mechanical interests— the girls who preferred climbing trees to baking cookies—retained this orientation from school entrance to adolescence." One particularly interesting aspect of these findings was the fact that failure in boys to adopt masculine interests during ages 3–10 was predictive of high sex anxiety as an adult; but for girls the amount of interest invested in masculine (nonfeminine) activities did not predict adult level of sex anxiety. This was interpreted by Kagan and Moss to mean that girls have more freedom than boys to indulge in opposite-sex activities without violating their definitions of proper sex role. However, it should be added that they also found that whereas the amount of interest in opposite sex activities during childhood predicted the nature of such interests for males during adulthood, similar predictions could not be made for females; the female pattern was less consistent. One possible way of interpreting these findings is to assert that women are less stable than men in sex-role related interests.

If one reviews the information presented in this section concerning the differential problems and difficulties of females and males in structuring sex roles, it is apparent that our present stage of knowledge does not permit simple generalizations. It would be premature to say that one sex has more difficulty than the other in this structuring process. The emphasis that psychoanalytic theorists have put upon the idea that the girl's sex-role identification problem is more complex than that of the boy's has not been empirically corroborated. Indeed, one might be able to argue persuasively from the known facts for a view that would be the opposite of the analytic position.

There is one other aspect of sex-role identity in women that needs to be discussed. This pertains to some puzzling correlations that have been observed to exist between personal maladjustment and identification with conventional femininity. Although it has been reported in a number of studies (Lazowick, 1955; Cosentino and Heilbrun, 1964) that good personal adjustment in men is positively linked with close identification with a masculine model (father), it has not been possible to demonstrate an analogous pattern for women. There is no evidence that the best adjusted women are those who identify with feminine models. In fact, somewhat out of step with what one might expect, there have been reports that apparently indicate that the more conventionally feminine and more mother identified woman is likely to show signs of greatest maladjustment. Heilbrun has devoted considerable attention to this matter. In several publications (1968a,b) he has plotted the ways in which indices of maladjustment vary in women with respect to their measured femininity as well as their perceived similarity to each of their parents. He found in one study (Heilbrun and Fromme, 1965, p. 55) that "identification with a less feminine mother is associated with the best adjustment, whereas increasingly poorer adjustment is found with the use of more feminine maternal models by adolescent girls." In another study (1962) Heilbrun concluded (p. 854) that "higher identification with the mother is associated with poorer adjustment for college females." Webb (1963) discovered that high anxiety in adolescent girls was significantly linked with high-femininity scores (as measured by the Gough [1957] Femininity Scale). Gray (1957) found that anxiety in girls (grades 6–7) was positively correlated with their rated femininity. Milton (1957) was able to support the hypothesis that the ability of girls to solve a series of complex problems was negatively correlated with their degree of femininity (as defined by the Terman-Miles [1936] M-F Test). Other studies could also be cited that indicate similar kinds of results (Helper, 1955; Rosenberg, Sutton-Smith, and Morgan, 1961). These various findings could be interpreted to mean that the more feminine a girl is, the more anxious and maladjusted she is. Sears, Rau, and Alpert (1965) have, in this spirit, proposed that a core component of conventional femininity is "fearfulness" and "inhibition." Before acquiescing to this view let us consider the findings of Douvan and Adelson (1966), which apparently stand in opposition to it. They used interview and questionnaire techniques to evaluate various personality and attitudinal parameters in a large sample of adolescent girls. On the basis of responses to a questionnaire concerning interests and goals (for example, Do you want to get married some day?, What kind of work would you like to do as an adult?) high-feminine and low-feminine samples were determined and the characteristics of each sample were appraised. One conclusion arrived at was that high-feminine girls have more ego integration than low-feminine girls. It is important to note, however, that Douvan and Adelson use the term "ego integration" in a special way. They define it with reference to several variables: exhibiting high poise and confidence in an interview, having an extended time perspective (looking into the future), feeling a sense of self-importance, having a clear adult model in mind to be emulated, and being socially active. Interestingly, at the same time that they report high-feminine girls are high in ego integration, as just defined, they also state that such girls exceed low-feminine girls in being self "blaming," "worrying," experiencing discomfort during menstruation, being "narcissistic," and worrying about their physical appearance.[17] It is these last-named variables concerned with "worrying" and "discomfort" that come closest to the criteria of maladjustment used in other studies that have, in contrast to the Douvan and Adelson work, found femininity and maladjustment to be positively linked. In this sense, the Douvan and Adelson findings do not really contradict the other studies. They only indicate that the matter is more complex than previously visualized. That is, at the same time that a girl indicates that she frequently worries and experiences discomfort she may also display other behaviors and attitudes that indicate that she has achieved unusually good mastery in effectively being feminine and fulfilling a woman's role. It may even be that heightened awareness of internal discomfort is part of a general intraceptive attitude that facilitates feminine role mastery. Douvan and Adelson point out (pp. 240–241), "The girl who is consciously integrating feminine goals is also generally more intraceptive than other girls. . . . In response to interpersonal problems the feminine girls bear more conflict internally. . . . They tend to be more aware of internal stimuli and more tolerant of their own feelings, wishes, anxieties, and fantasies. . . . A distinguishing feature of feminine girls is their acceptance of internal conflict." [18] Douvan and Adelson actually propose that awareness of tension and conflict in self, insofar as it indicates a special sensitive, intraceptive orientation, is a positive component of the ability to solve the kinds of problems with which women deal.

Their observations help to clarify the puzzling results of the other studies mentioned that relate to this general issue. They point up that one needs to adopt an interpretative perspective of considerable sophistication. What is regarded as a sign of maladjustment in a man may not be indicative of the same in a woman. The accumulated data that reveal a positive link between femininity and anxiety (maladjustment) may be empirically sound, but the interpretations that have been offered concerning their real significance seem to be too narrow. Feminine women may readily admit to anxious and conflictual feelings, but this may tell us more about their orientation toward the world of feeling and emotion than about how maladjusted they are. In fact, strangely, it may turn out that the readiness to admit to inner turmoil may betoken a clear identification with the goals of femininity.

Overview

Pondering the diverse material that has been sifted bearing on the formation of normal feminine identity, one would be foolhardy to declare that the process is really understood. We know that it is quite complicated. Despite the fact that nurturant and warm attitudes on the part of the mother do help to facilitate the development of her daughter's femininity, one cannot adequately explain the origins of femininity in terms of a simple "being like mother" model. We know that learning to be a woman involves more than just observing and liking mother and trying to imitate her. Clearly, the father is also importantly influential. There is good evidence that the father probably has a central "sex-typing" role in the family and that he normally mirrors back to his daughter interpretations of her behavior that facilitate the shaping of her femininity.

To assert that the girl's acquisition of feminine identity is complex is not to acquiesce to the idea that it is more difficult or painful than the equivalent process is for the boy. If anything, the existing empirical findings suggest that it may be a bit less circuitous for the girl. Actually, she may have relatively less tension about the sex-identification process and feel under less obligation to learn her "part" in a rigid narrowly defined way. Girls seem to have more latitude than boys to experiment with interests and behaviors that are of the opposite-sex category. As mentioned, there are those (Lynn, 1969) who accept the idea that girls have no more and perhaps less difficulty than boys in structuring a sex role, but propose that the girl's maintenance of sex role becomes more difficult (and the boy's less so) as she grows older and moves into a world in which masculine superiority is emphasized in various ways. Others have pointed to this problem of "female inferiority" as having, from the very beginning, a negative effect on the girl's ability to identify with her "depreciated" mother model. There is little doubt that the idea of male superiority has wide currency in our culture, and this may very well painfully affect the girl who is trying to define herself. However, as Kohlberg (1966) and Hartley, Hardesty, and Gorfein (1962) have pointed out, the superiority of the male is largely represented in terms of his power and strength, and there

are numerous other ways in which femininity has sufficient positive prestige to make it an attractive model for a girl. The feminine model is superior insofar as it is visualized as a carrier of nurturance, attractiveness,
beauty, warmth, and so forth.

Perhaps there is one level at which the feminine sex role does call forth
a special degree of discomfort. Reference is made to the finding, earlier
cited, that femininity is positively correlated with conventional measures of
anxiety, and to the Douvan and Adelson (1966) observation indicating
that feminine girls have a heightened awareness of internal discomfort
(partially expressed as worry) that seems to be part of a general intraceptive orientation. These findings may signify that learning the feminine role
also involves learning certain kinds of sensitiveness to feelings and emotions that are not comfortable to hold in awareness. Possibly, the emotionally expressive role, which the woman is said by some (Parsons and Bales,
1955) to hold in the family group, requires that she cultivate introspective
skills that make shutting out of unpleasant affect difficult. A number of
studies were reviewed earlier that indicate that the female is, in general,
more invested than the male in establishing and maintaining good interpersonal relationships with others. To do so she may need to be able to monitor emotional nuances within herself with heightened clarity, and may consequently experience discomfort. If this were so, one would need to be
cautious in making predictions about how women varying in femininity
would behave with reference to a normality-abnormality continuum. For
example, one might be tempted to predict that the more feminine a woman
is the lower her anxiety will be in various situations that particularly involve womanly behavior (for example, during sexual interaction, caring for
her children). But in light of what has been said there might be justification for making quite the opposite prediction.

In various ways it has been suggested that the female's sex role is more
flexible than the male's.[19] This view was implicit in data showing that the
girl has more "latitude" and freedom than the boy to experiment with opposite sex behavior. It was also implicit in the Douvan and Adelson (1966)
observations indicating that girls seek to postpone crystallization of their
attitudes until they can form a stable relationship with a man and then determine how best to arrive at congruence with him. Since the culture
apparently supports such ambiguity ("freedom") in the girl's evolving sex-
role concept, she may not find it anxiety provoking. In fact, as already
stated, she may find satisfaction in her relative freedom, especially since
this is one of the few instances in which she has a greater range of choice
than the male. Another point to consider is that whereas there may be relative ambiguity about a girl's sex-role definition for certain periods of
childhood and adolescence, she is offered some rather distinctly patterned
images about womanhood. Being a wife and mother, which is paramount
in self-definition for most women, presents itself in a very articulated way,
and constitutes for the developing girl a clear, future goal that probably exceeds in specificity the vision that the boy has about his future role. These

are only speculative thoughts, but if true, they would portray learning the feminine sex role as a process that presents the female with tasks of both considerable ambiguity and concrete specificity.

From the work that has thus far been done, can we deduce anything about the kind of sex-role definition that is likely to facilitate or inhibit a woman's sexual responsiveness? It would be difficult to point to one or more specific research findings and declare that they are pertinent to this matter. But what if one were, in an entirely speculative fashion, to propose that sexual responsiveness is likely to be greatest in those women who approach the norm attributes of femininity. If this were true, what characteristics would one expect to typify the high-responsive woman? Looking back over the literature reviewed, one could list the following: [20]

1. A prime characteristic of femininity seems to be an investment in setting up warm, nurturant relationships with others. The feminine mode is to trust oneself to interpersonal intimacy and to expect reciprocal affection and love from such self-investment. To fear interpersonal involvement is the antithesis of femininity. Indeed, one might say that aggression has a similar antithetical significance. A trusting orientation might, then, be one of the major determinants of the ability to be aroused by a man.

2. A second quality, which is really related to the first, would be deduced from the Douvan and Adelson (1966) findings that girls suspend the crystallization of certain aspects of their personality with the idea of trying to balance, or to be congruent with, the attributes of a future spouse. The feminine woman seems to be motivated to *accommodate* to her important love objects, as part of her general motivation to have "good" involvements. Some such willingness to "accommodate" to a man might be an elementary prerequisite for the establishment of an adequate sexual relationship.

3. A third factor one could cite concerns the woman's original pattern of relating to her parents. Although femininity certainly evolves from contact with a warm, nurturant mother, it would also seem to be true that important aspects of sex typing are facilitated by a good relationship with father. One would, therefore, expect that the ability of a woman to respond sexually might be appreciably enhanced by having learned from her father how to behave in a feminine fashion vis-à-vis a man.

4. A fourth and probably fundamental variable that should be included in the list pertains to the body feelings (body image) typifying femininity. A number of studies were described earlier that indicated that women tend, modally, to experience their bodies as rounded, nonphallic, small, and better adapted to closed intimate settings than to the requirements of swift movement in space. In addition, the modal feminine body orientation seems to involve a relatively high degree of awareness of one's body, an investment in body attractiveness and importance. Douvan and Adelson (1966) did find that investment in body was particularly characteristic of the most feminine girls in their adolescent sample. Also, the typical wom-

an's attitude toward her body seems to be one of relative confidence in its security. She is not anxiously concerned about her body being attacked or invaded. This may be a very significant attitude in view of the literal penetration of the female body that occurs during intercourse, which could arouse fantasies about body encroachment. Overall, the ability to be sexually responsive might depend to some degree upon a woman's ability to experience her body with a certain degree of psychological intensity or investment, to perceive it as having nonphallic rather than phallic functions, and to be convinced that it is adequately protected against potential attack or invasion.

As seen in later chapters dealing with the author's empirical investigations of the personality correlates of sexual responsiveness in women, a few of these speculations did turn out to be on the right track.

NOTES

1. This is true despite the recognition that endocrine variables may also play a significant role.

2. A broad sociological view of the factors affecting ability to establish adequate sexual identity is provided by Cottrell (1942). Four of the primary variables he mentions are as follows: (1) How well and clearly does the society itself define the sex role? (2) How consistently do people communicate to the individual what is expected of him in the context of his sex role? (3) To what degree does the individual possess the skills required of him by his sex role? (4) How much chance is there for intimate contact with persons who function in such a sex role—which facilitates the opportunity for identification and rehearsal?

3. The probable impact of parents' sex-role expectations is revealed in the Fauls and Smith (1956) finding that 5-year-old children perceive their parents as having specific undifferentiated expectations about how girls and boys should behave. Vener and Snyder (1966) report similar perceptions by children as young as 2½ years old.

4. This test is based on responses to questions about which animals the subject would most and least like to be.

5. Leonard (1966) has summarized psychoanalytic views about the role of the father in the girl's development of sex identity.

6. The potential complexity of evaluating the relative influence of father is exemplified by the Doherty (1970) report that among girls who consciously feel that they are like their mothers there is a positive correlation between the degree to which they perceive their mothers as "controlling" and the degree to which their concept of what is feminine is similar to their fathers' concept of what is feminine! The complexity of the matter is further illustrated by Bennett's (1968) finding that white girls but not black girls are more feminine in mother-only families.

7. The sex composition of the family (that is, number of male and female children) may, in turn, also affect the masculinity-femininity attitudes of the parents (Lansky, 1964; Rosenberg and Sutton-Smith, 1968). For example, there are findings that indicate that in families with a high concentration of female children the father is "defensively" high in his degree of "masculinity."

8. Hetherington (1965) similarly found that the relative degree of dominance of mother versus father was unrelated to measures of girls' sex-role preferences.

9. In boys, parental sexual permissiveness likewise produced less femininity (that is, resulted in a more masculine gender orientation). Indeed, all parental attitudes that encouraged submissiveness in the boy had a feminizing influence upon him.

10. Surprisingly, in both the work of Leslie and Johnson (1963) and the cross-cultural studies by Whiting and Child (1953), it was reported that there was little relationship between how parents undertake sex-role training and how they manage other aspects of socialization (for example, toilet training). In view of the positive relationships between dependency training and sex-role measures that Sears, et al. (1965) and Kagan and Moss (1962) described, one might have expected that a parent's behavior with regard to his child's sex-role training would be linked with his behavior toward other aspects of the child's training (for example, dependency, hostility). It is, of course, possible that the behavior of the parent that is formally concerned with sexual matters is relatively unimportant in the sexual socialization process. Apropos of this point, it may be recalled that previous studies that have been cited indicated that important aspects of a girl's sexual behavior are unrelated to the manner in which her parents communicated the "facts of life" to her.

11. Apropos of the effect of mother-father role differentiation, Broverman, Broverman, Clarkson, Rosenkrantz, and Vogel (1970) found that college girls whose mothers had customarily worked outside the home (that is, had not adhered to the usual housewife pattern) perceived smaller differences to exist between the female and male roles than did girls whose mothers had not so worked.

12. Sears, Maccoby, and Levin (1957) report on the basis of intensive interview data that mothers may treat baby girls more "warmly" than baby boys.

13. Emmrich (1959a,b) proposes another scheme that differentiates the sex-role identification task of the two sexes. He sees the girl as identifying with those aspects of the mother that will help her to differentiate the role of female adult from that of female child. But the boy is depicted as having for his primary identification task the learning from the father the essentials of what it means to be masculine.

14. An interesting exception is the Vener and Snyder (1966) study that found that when children were asked to identify and state their preferences for a series of common articles with obvious sex linkage (for example, screwdriver, hosiery) girls made same-sex choices earlier and more consistently.

15. It is apropos to add that Guardo (1970) found on the basis of a semistructured interview with young children that (p. 7): "Girls more often than boys evidence a sense of personal identity by the age of nine."

16. Hartley (1969) has actually found on the basis of her survey of four cultures that five-year-olds and eight-year-olds tend to perceive the girl as more favored than the boy. She states (p. 387): "The composite picture is overwhelming. Not only is the girl prettier, less troublesome, someone 'Mum' enjoys looking after . . . and Dad likes to play with, but she is a useful creature in the house, as boys are not in a sex-separated society."

17. Douvan and Adelson indicated that one portion (5 percent) of their sample consisted of girls who took the extreme position that they would never want to get married. They labeled this group as "antifeminine." The antifeminine girl was found to be poorly adjusted, constricted, and of limited imagination. She was, with unusual frequency, the oldest child in a large family who had heavy responsibilities, and who depicted her parents as having been unusually restrictive, denying of autonomy, and concerned about exacting obedience.

18. Bradford (1968) speculates that the reason why girls generally have higher scores than boys on conventional questionnaire measures of anxiety is because they are less defensive about experiencing anxiety. They are also less defensive about admitting to anxiety. From this view, the greater admission of anxiety by feminine girls would parallel the greater admission of anxiety by girls as compared to boys.

19. Interestingly, this may even extend to patterns of relationship with one's parents. Ban and Lewis (1971) discovered that whereas boys tend to be either high or low in their degree of attachment to *both* parents, girls are inclined to favor either one parent or the other.

20. These conclusions are considered to apply only in Western cultures.

5

ADAPTATION TO FEMININE
BODY FUNCTIONS

A woman's reproductive system occupies a good amount of her body space. Also, it is extremely complex in its functioning, and becomes a source of sensations and experiences that are both gratifying and trying. Perhaps to a degree greater than any other body system, it normally initiates radical, often recurring physiological alterations that vividly affect the individual's perception of herself and require a good deal of adaptive energy. The gross transformations in body that accompany pregnancy or the cyclic changes linked with menstruation confront a woman with multifarious adjustments to phenomena such as weight change, pain, discomfort, blood loss, feeling the movements of a real internal object of remarkable size, and so forth. There are real physiological stresses involved in menstruation and pregnancy. Despite the attempts of some to argue that the pain and discomfort associated with reproductive processes are largely neurotic complaints of women who suffer from distortions produced by Western culture, there are reports (Freedman and Ferguson, 1950) that indicate that similar pain and discomfort may be observed among women of all cultures.

Sexuality in women would seem to be particularly strongly bound up with their reproductive capacity, and it would thus be an oversight not to consider the nature of the relationship. What do we know about the possible influence of reproductive attitudes upon sexual responsiveness? Does the manner in which such physiological events as menstruation are experienced affect sexual reactivity? Does the woman adopt sets or attitudes toward the reproductive functions of her body that reflect the overall manner in which she has learned to define femininity? Is her ability to define herself as feminine affected by the amount of pain and discomfort chronically or cyclically emanating from the reproductive areas of her body? There are many speculations in the literature about these questions. In the pages that follow, such speculations are reviewed, and, in addition, existing pertinent research findings are presented.

Menstruation

Menstruation and pregnancy are two unique badges of femininity. Particularly universal for all women is the experience with menstruation. The recurring cycle that prepares a woman's body for the possibility of pregnancy is a vivid accompaniment of a major portion of her adult existence. This cycle is produced by hormonal changes that alter a variety of physiological processes and give rise to intense body sensations and mood states. The literature abounds with speculations about the relative contributions of organic and psychological factors to menstrual phenomena. There is also much discussion concerning the role that menstruation, as a psychological experience, plays in feminine identity and more generally in personality functioning.

Some of the speculations about the psychological impact of menstruation are reviewed below, and followed by an analysis of what is known empirically in this area.

It is easy, after a quick scanning of the literature, to conclude that menstruation is largely a negative, unpleasant experience for most women. It is portrayed as imposing a chronic burden, which, because of the suffering it evokes, tests a woman's commitment to the role of being a female. With few exceptions, the emphasis is upon the universal taboo or disgust associated with the menstruating woman, her inclination to assign distorted significance to her body experiences, and her vulnerability to being upset. However, as will be shown, a more careful consideration of the facts reveals that menstruation also has important positive significance to women. The discomfort linked with menstrual and premenstrual sensations may not infrequently be integrated into a broader attitude that equates menstruation with being feminine and capable of reproducing.

Much that has been said about menstruation as a psychological phenomenon has been concerned with explaining why it so often seems to be a source of distress. Observers have argued that since the typical woman reacts psychologically in such a disproportionate manner to the physiological changes that constitute menstruation, one must assume that she assigns disturbing symbolic meaning to them. Let us consider the major views that have been expressed about the psychological meaning of menstruation.

The first and perhaps most obvious implication of menstruation relates to its association with the process of reproduction.[1] Deutsch (1944), Benedek (1952), and others have analyzed the implications of this fact. They point out that menstruation is tangible evidence of the possibility of becoming pregnant and being a mother.[2] Several possible reasons have been offered as to why this should be disturbing. One relates simply to the idea that a girl and even an adult woman may find it threatening to be faced with a clear statement, in body terms, that she is no longer a child and is biologically qualified to function as a mother. This implies giving up all sorts of dependent gratifications and assuming the role of the giving and nurturant one. Menstruation may repetitively highlight the imminence or reality of roles that are demanding and stressful.

In more psychoanalytic language, it has been said that the "proof" of feminine maturity conveyed by menstruation may activate a woman's Oedipal conflicts and competitive feelings toward her mother. Presumably, each menstrual period, whether it be the first or merely another in the repetitive cycle, may arouse old Oedipal fantasies (described earlier) about being capable of replacing mother and becoming a sex partner for father. Each menstruation is, from this view, a reaffirmation of her sexual potential and therefore a fantasied challenge to mother's old sexual role in the family. The early rivalry is considered to be revived in fantasy, and becomes a source of anxiety, turbulent irritability, and guilt. Each menstruation is, in this sense, a stimulus to a reliving of an earlier traumatic experience that Freud theorized is never really fully resolved.

The equation of menstruation with reproductive potential has been interpreted by some psychoanalytic observers (Deutsch, 1944) as threatening because the whole process of gestation and delivery implies possible body damage and death. It is well known that pregnancy involves hazards to the mother's health, dysplastic alterations in her appearance, much pain, and even death. Each menstruation may remind a woman that her reproductive capacity exposes her to serious future hazards. Deutsch states that each menstruation strengthens the associative bond between death and birth because it brings blood flow (linked with injury and death) into association with the process of conception.

The prominence of a bleeding discharge in the menstrual process may dramatize the danger of suffering body damage. As Deutsch and others point out, blood is associated with being hurt or wounded; when blood begins to issue from a body orifice, it arouses concern about body destruction. Some refer to such concern as being analogous to "castration anxiety" (fear of genital mutilation or loss). Abraham (1948) proposed that each menstruation stirs up old fears about having been castrated, which, it will be recalled, psychoanalysts assume to be typical of all women as part of their normal development. The mutilating connotations of vaginal bleeding have been noted in numerous cultures (Devereux, 1950). Abel and Joffe (1950) provide anecdotal accounts of how commonly different ethnic groups interpret menstruation as an illness and a time of special body fragility. The body threatening significance of menstruation, both as a symbol of future dangers linked with pregnancy and as an immediate process involving blood flow from a body orifice, has been one of the most widely commented upon as a cause for disturbance and anxiety in menstruating women. With few exceptions, observers have been impressed with how disconcerting it is to women that menstruation produces an uncontrollable flow from a body orifice that can produce soiling and odors analogous to those associated with loss of bowel control. Deutsch (1944) states that it is common for women to experience menstruation as something "filthy." She emphasizes how often the pubertal girl interprets her first menstruation as a "new eliminatory function" that is "dirty and distasteful." Apropos of this point, Rheingold (1964, p. 299) remarks: "The discharge of blood from a sphincterless organ with possibility of 'accident' reactivates the conflicts of early childhood over imperfectly controlled bladder and bowel function. . . ." Benedek and Rubenstein (1939) suggest that the menses are often equated with feces. It is, of course, a common phenomenon, across many cultures, for the menstruating woman to be labeled as "unclean" and therefore unqualified to participate in important procedures that she would presumably contaminate.

One could enumerate many other speculations in the literature concerning the reasons why menstruation is responded to with anxiety and exaggerated emotion. It has been diversely proposed that during menstruation women become intensely angry and resentful (of their inferior status), unusually ambivalent about men and sexual stimulation, guilty about their masturbation fantasies, overpowered by sensations of being controlled by an ever-repetitive force, and so forth. There are few conflicts or problems that have not at some time or another been said to be activated or aggravated by the menstrual experience.

Although a large proportion of the pertinent publications focuses on the negative impact of menstruation, comments about its more positive aspects may also be found. Deutsch (1944) makes such remarks as (p. 172), "Menstruation becomes a decisive experience in the process of feminization," and (p. 162), "The young girl's narcissistic ego may welcome menstruation as a satisfying step along the road to adulthood." Also, Langer (as cited by Rodrigue, 1955) states, "Each menstruation . . . symbolizes the youth and fecundity for the woman, her capacity for continuous regeneration, and a promise of future maternity." Presumably, a girl may see the onset of menstruation as a demonstration that she is well on her way to being a woman and achieving full femininity. The adult woman may analogously regard each menstruation as an affirmation of her femininity and her continued future potentiality for being fertile. Kestenberg (1961) theorized that the menarche acts as an "organizer" in the girl's feminine development and introduces a regularity into her life that has stabilizing and integrating effects.

Drellich and Bieber (1958) have presented some important interview data concerning the positive significance of menstruation. They studied 23 women who had undergone hysterectomies. Somewhat surprisingly, they found that one of the disturbing things to these women about the loss of the uterus was the fact that they would no longer be able to menstruate. When confronted with the loss of the ability to menstruate, they became aware of certain positive values thay had assigned to it. Evidence emerged that menstruation was seen as an important means for excreting "wastes" from the body, as an organizing event introducing a chance for regular renewal, and generally as a sign of being normally feminine.[3] Drellich and Bieber conclude (p. 324):

Menstruation is valued as a cleaning or excretory function, as a part of the "rhythm of life," as a source of reborn strength and vitality, and as a periodic occurrence deemed necessary for the maintenance of health and well-being. . . .

The loss of this regulating device is unconsciously viewed as threatening to disrupt other bodily functions which are dependent upon the menstrual cycle for regulation, as well as disrupting pre-existing patterns of adaptation, patterns of work, sexual and social activities which have been organized within the periodicity of the menstrual month.

Some experimental evidence for the "positive" effects of menstruation may be found in the work of Housman (1955).[4] He administered psychological measures to a sample of 39 hospitalized schizophrenic women during their second day of menstruation and again nine days later. The measures administered consisted of the Rorschach Inkblots and the Blacky Test (which involves interpreting pictures depicting a dog in various crucial situations with psychoanalytic significance). Housman found evidence from the Blacky Test results that during menstruation the subjects were *less* confused about their sexual identity. He suggested that this was caused by the fact that the menstruation presented to each individual an "undeniable sign of femininity." This finding is certainly congruent with the previously mentioned Drellich and Bieber (1958) report that women who have lost the ability to menstruate experience this as diminishing their femininity. Housman also reported that the Rorschach results indicated (p. 82) that during menstruation the "women . . . experience an intensification of passive, affectional needs, an increased sensitivity to approval and therefore to rejection." Furthermore, he found hints of increased anxiety during menstruation. Thus, although menstruation had a positive impact insofar as it reinforced the woman's sense of femininity, it apparently aroused some anxiety about other issues. It is apropos to add that Coppen (1965) discovered that many of the women in a psychiatric sample ($N = 151$) that he examined showed improvement in their symptoms during menstruation. This observation, when taken in conjunction with Housman's data indicating decreased confusion about feminine identity in schizophrenic women during their menses, raises the possibility that the menstrual experience is somehow specifically helpful to women with serious psychiatric symptomatology. Indeed, one is reminded of previous reports (Cowden and Brown, 1956) that intense body experiences (for example, physical illness) may lead to an improvement in psychiatric disturbance. It may be pertinent to this same issue that two investigators (Coppen, 1965; Silbermann, 1950) have found that schizophrenic women seem to have less pain and discomfort during their menses than neurotic or normal women.[5] Further, Gregory (1957a,b) noted that schizophrenic women have less menstrual discomfort than neurotic women. One could interpret this to mean that the schizophrenic woman finds relatively more positive than negative elements in her menstrual experience, especially as compared to nonschizophrenic women. Perhaps those who are psychologically most disorganized paradoxically find the sheer sensory impact and significance of menstruation to have an "anchoring" or self-defining function.

In samples of normal women a large percent report discomfort linked with the *onset* of menses. Most studies (Moos, 1968) indicate that the proportion of women experiencing such discomfort ranges from 40 to 90 percent. Some of the most frequent symptoms reported are edema, abdominal bloating and pain, backache, moodiness, irritability, depression, nervousness, and hyperactivity. Both Tiffany (1964) and Moos (1968b) have systematically factor-analyzed menstrual complaints and ordered them into dimensions. Moos, for example, classifies them in the following categories: pain (for example, backache), concentration (for example, forgetfulness), behavioral change (for example, avoid social activities), autonomic reactions (for example, faintness), water retention (for example, swelling), negative affect (for example, crying), arousal (for example, excitement), and control (for example, feeling of suffocation).

It has been customary to assume that the degree of menstrual discomfort experienced is positively correlated with neuroticism or maladjustment. But what do we actually know about the validity of this assumption? To begin with, and as already mentioned, one must consider the fact that menstrual discomfort (dysmenorrhea) is relatively low in schizophrenic women, which would not be expected if there were a simple positive correlation between amount of menstrual disturbance and personal maladjustment. At the very least, as indicated by studies by Landis, et al. (1940), Gregory (1957a,b), Coppen (1963), and Silbermann (1950) involving large numbers of schizophrenic patients, one can say that schizophrenic women do not have more menstrual discomfort than neurotic or normal women. Further, one can say rather specifically, in terms of data reported by Gregory (1957a,b), Coppen (1963), and also Silbermann (1950), that persons classified psychiatrically as neurotic have more discomfort than either schizophrenics (or normals).

If one reviews the actual results of studies concerned with the relationship between menstrual complaints and measures of maladjustment in normal populations, it becomes clear that its nature is a debatable one.

Let us first consider those studies in which a link between maladjustment and dysmenorrhea does seem to be suggested. Moos (1969b) found in a sample of 839 women that complaining about menstrual symptoms was positively and significantly correlated with complaining about symptoms occurring during nonmenstrual times. This could mean that menstrual symptoms stem from a preexisting low threshold for experiencing discomfort and this low threshold might be said to reflect "neuroticism." Moos, however, felt that other kinds of explanations (for example, involving pain thresholds) might be equally justified.

Shainess (1962) obtained questionnaire responses concerning menstrual complaints from 22 neurotic patients and 81 normal controls. She reported, without providing details or information about statistical tests, that the patients had more symptoms and tension related to menstruating than did the normals.

Levitt and Lubin (1967) administered psychological tests (for example, Edwards Personal Preference Schedule) and a menstrual questionnaire to 221 student nurses. They discovered a significant trend for the number of menstrual complaints to be positively correlated with degree of emotional instability, paranoid hypersensitivity, and a lack of ability to understand the motives of others.

Paulson (1961) studied 255 normal women to whom were administered menstrual questionnaires and others he had devised that sought to measure four personality variables (intrafamilial relationships, acceptance of the feminine psychosocial role, acceptance of the feminine psychosexual role, and self-concept) and two others specifically related to psychological attitudes toward menstruation. Answers to the questionnaires were found not to vary as a function of the stage of the menstrual cycle of the respondent. (Moos [1969b] similarly reported that responses to a menstrual complaint questionnaire did not differ in relation to the phase of menstrual cycle in which they were given.) In any case, Paulson was able to show that the greater the tension reported by women premenstrually the more they depicted themselves as psychosexually and psychosocially inadequate, involved in tension-producing family relationships, holding negative attitudes toward self, and, further, perceiving menstruation as a stressful, unhappy experience.

Wittkower and Wilson (1940) interviewed 55 women with painful menstruation and compared them with 30 women without appreciable menstrual pain. It was concluded that the dysmenorrhea group showed four times as much maladjustment as the control group.

Rose (1949) administered the Bell Adjustment Inventory to 266 college women and found a significant trend for amount of reported menstrual pain to be positively correlated with degree of maladjustment.

In contrast to these findings, note the character of the following studies.

Coppen, Carshalton, and Kessel (1963) administered the Maudsley Personality Inventory and menstrual complaint questionnaires to 465 normal women. They could not detect a significant relationship between an index of neuroticism derived from the Maudsley inventory and dysmenorrhea.

Rees (1953) used the interview as well as the Maudsley Medical Questionnaire and Word Connection Test to evaluate degree of neuroticism in a group of 61 normal women. It was shown that neuroticism was not significantly correlated with the amount of premenstrual tension. Rees was impressed with the fact that some women who seemed to be extremely neurotic experienced little or no menstrual distress, whereas others who appeared to be emotionally stable reported severe dysmenorrhea. It should be added that in another phase of this study he did find more dysmenorrhea in a psychiatric sample of neurotic patients than he did in the normal group.

Hirt, Kurtz, and Ross (1967) appraised 105 nursing students who responded to questionnaires concerning dysmenorrhea as well as the Cattell 16 PF Test. They found very low, but statistically significant, positive relationships between dysmenorrhea and measures of anxiety and neuroticism. Although the results were statistically significant, the authors chose to emphasize how low the obtained correlations were (.20 and .22). They considered them to be "relatively negligible."

It is particularly important to cite the already often referred to work of Douvan and Adelson (1966), who studied a very large sample of adolescent girls. On the basis of a number of indices they classified the girls into high and low femininity groups. When they related a girl's femininity to her menstrual symptomatology, they concluded that the greater her femininity the greater her discomfort during menstruation. Whereas femininity is obviously not a measure of emotional stability, it does designate an attribute that is usually considered to have positive connotations with reference to women. Here one is confronted with the paradoxical fact that menstrual discomfort is highest in those who conform best, rather than least, to the definition of desirable femininity.

A number of studies (Ferguson, 1938b; Shope, 1966; Landis, et al., 1940; Terman, 1951) have looked at the relationship between dysmenorrhea and sexual responsiveness. Contrary to widely accepted assumptions in the psychoanalytic and gynecological literature concerning this matter, it has not been possible to demonstrate that women with serious dysmenorrhea are characterized by unusual difficulties in sexual adjustment.[6]

If one examines the cited scattering of studies, it is clear that one cannot with confidence assert that dysmenorrhea is or is not caused by neuroticism or some species of personality maladjustment.[7]

By way of contrast to these findings about dysmenorrhea, a review of what is known about the role of psychological factors in the *delay* or *cessation* of menstruation (amenorrhea) in women who are within the age range when they would normally be capable of reproduction suggests that psychological variables are involved in this syndrome. It has been anecdotally widely observed that psychological stress or danger will produce amenorrhea. Exposure to air bombardment, imprisonment, separation from home, and similar conditions have variously been reported as capable of triggering amenorrhea (Osofsky and Fisher, 1967).

There is evidence, contrary to the case for dysmenorrhea, that psychiatric patients (both neurotic and schizophrenic) experience amenorrhea significantly more often than normal women (Landis, et al., 1940; Coppen, 1965; Ripley and Papanicolaou, 1942; Allen and Henry, 1933).

Interestingly, Housman (1950) in a previously mentioned and rather unique study, established that schizophrenics characterized by amenorrhea differed psychologically from schizophrenics with regular menses. He administered the Rorschach Inkblots and the Blacky Test to a schizophrenic sample ($N = 39$) on the second day of onset of menses and again nine days later. Daily observation of the patients for a period of four months permitted determination of those with regular ($N = 19$) and those with irregular ($N = 20$) menses. When the psychological data available for the patients were analyzed, it was found that the "regulars" differed from the "irregulars" primarily in terms of how they shifted in their response patterns when they experienced the actual onset of menstrual flow. The prime difference was that the flow elicited increased ego control and integration in the regulars and diminished control in the irregulars. This was particularly true for the expression of impulses relating to anality and dirt. Indeed, the regulars not only were more controlled about expressing anal-dirt fantasies but reported being more careful about keeping themselves "clean" during menstruation. In general, the irregulars seemed to be less concerned about conformity than the regulars. A trend was also observed for the irregulars to become more conflicted about masturbation fantasies and the regulars to become more conflicted about oral fantasies during menstruation. Finally, it was suggested (p. 105) that whereas the irregulars superficially professed to be less conflicted about their feminine role than the regulars, they actually gave "less evidence of a genuine identification with the feminine role than the regulars." It should be added that no differences between the regulars and irregulars were discerned with respect to subcategories of diagnosis. Of the various findings, Housman emphasized the fact that the regulars responded to menstruation with increased ego control, whereas the irregulars manifested decreased control, particularly with reference to fantasies relating to anality and dirt.

In other studies, Coppen and Kessel (1963) showed that normal women with amenorrhea obtained higher neuroticism scores on the Maudsley Psychological Inventory than women without amenorrhea. Engels, Pattel, and Wittkower (1964) reported on the basis of an impressionistic study employing interviews and projective tests that psychological conflict is basic to many cases of amenorrhea. However, they were not able to discover any particular "core" conflict that was most characteristic of the group. Kelley, Daniels, Poe, Easser, and Monroe (1954) interviewed a series of patients with amenorrhea and a control group without such symptoms and concluded that the amenorrhea group showed more signs of "psychosexual immaturity," "oral conflict," and "schizoid thinking." Hain, Linton, Eber, and Chapman (1970) administered the Minnesota Multiphasic Personality Inventory to a class of nursing students and found statistically significant trends indicating that those with menstrual irregularity were (p. 84) "more immature and impulsive with numerous neurotic symptoms including somatic ones, and . . . they tended to have more difficulties in interpersonal relationships." Loftus (1962) reported that when five women with persistent amenorrhea were treated with psychotherapy, four began to menstruate spontaneously. The response occurred within 3–6 months of therapy. It was presumed that working through of certain psychological conflicts (particularly related to lack of identification with a mother perceived as hostile) was responsible for the improvement.

Osofsky and Fisher (1967) conducted a study that attempted to predict the occurrence of amenorrhea in a group of freshmen student nurses ($N =$ 66). On the basis of observations by others it could be anticipated that a number of the girls in the group would develop amenorrhea under the stress of their new duties and responsibilities. Each subject was asked to maintain a menstrual diary for four months from which the presence of amenorrhea symptoms could be evaluated. Measures were administered to subjects (on the first day of arrival at the school) that were designed to evaluate certain body-image dimensions. One was concerned with the degree to which the individual perceives the boundary regions of her body as definite and clearly articulated. It is represented by the well-validated Barrier Index (Fisher and Cleveland, 1968; Fisher, 1970), which is based upon responses to inkblot stimuli. Considerable data indicate that the more definite an individual's body boundaries are, the greater is her ability to cope adequately with stress. A second measure (Body Prominence) tapped the degree to which the subject was aware of her body as compared to other objects in her environs. It is determined by asking the subject to list "twenty things you are aware of or conscious of right now" and then ascertaining the number of references made to one's own body. Fisher (1970) has shown that the greater a woman's awareness of her body the more articulated are her boundaries and presumably the better defined her sense of identity. The prediction was made that the more definite a woman's boundaries and the greater her awareness of her body the less likely she would be to develop symptoms of amenorrhea. Both of these predictions were significantly supported by the data. Amenorrhea was most likely to occur in those subjects who experienced their bodies as lacking adequate boundaries and having relatively low prominence or sensory vividness. Fisher and Osofsky emphasized that the results demonstrated a link between psychological parameters and vulnerability to amenorrhea. Incidentally, variables such as age of onset of menses, weight, height, breast size, and frequency of other medical complaints did not predict the occurrence of amenorrhea.[8]

Although conclusive data are not yet available, it does seem reasonable to say that the tenor of the results cited supports the proposition that psychological disturbance may be involved in the causation of amenorrhea. However, it should also be noted that earlier cited data suggest that psychological factors may not play an appreciable role in the causation of dysmenorrhea. That is, psychological factors seem to contribute to irregularity or cessation of menstruation; but perhaps they contribute much less to menstrual discomfort.[9] Little is known about the actual mechanisms whereby psychological disturbance might affect the menstrual cycle, but there is abundant evidence that psychological stimuli can, indeed, affect uterine response (Bardwick and Behrman, 1967; Kelly, 1962a,b) as well as endocrine processes basic to ovulation (Rothchild, 1967). That is, potential pathways for the action of psychological vectors upon menstrual functions are known.

Peskin (1968) suggested that the matter of occurrence versus nonoccurrence of menstruation may be linked in some ways to the duration of menses. He conjectures that psychological factors may be involved in both classes of phenomena. Considerable variability in the duration of menses has been found. Levy (1942) was the first to examine some of the psychological correlates of short versus long menstrual flow. He found in several samples a trend for those typified by long menstrual flow (6 or more days) to be more maternal in orientation than those characterized by short menstrual flow (4 or fewer days). Peskin had an opportunity to investigate this problem further in a sample of 55 women who had been studied from early childhood into adulthood. Not only was long-term menstrual information available about these women but also elaborate personality data (based on interviews and observational ratings) were obtained even before the onset of menses. The data antedating the onset of menstruation were uniquely valuable because they could be considered not to have been influenced by any differences produced by the differential length of menstrual flow itself. Peskin was able to discern clear personality distinctions between those women with long- and short-duration of flow. The short-flow women were found to exceed the long-flow women in being more active, vigorous, achievement oriented, reality testing and cognitively efficient.[10] The long-flow women were more domestic, artistic, conforming, and dependent in their orientation. The vigorous and achievement-oriented short-flow women were found to relate in a more maternal fashion to their children than the long-flow women. Peskin concluded that the long- versus short-menstrual flow durations reflected different styles of personality organization. He proposes that (p. 386) menstruation is "channeled into already established ego styles of tension discharge." Peskin goes on to hypothesize that the differences in personality observed between the long- and short-duration women may be conceptualized as a difference in tendency to discharge tension inwardly (into the body interior) as opposed to outwardly. The action and achievement oriented short-duration women would be regarded as "outward" energy dischargers, and the more passive long-duration flow women as "inward" energy dischargers. Peskin states (p. 388), "The longer menstrual period in adulthood could be traced to an earlier reliance on tension-discharge into the interior of the body . . . whereas the shorter period appeared connected to tension-discharge in the form of action." He literally proposes that duration of menstrual flow will somehow be influenced by a preexisting personality-based style of energy expression. This is an intriguing theory that deserves further attention and investigation. Incidentally, Peskin also raises the question whether amenorrhea and other forms of menstrual inhibitions may not actually be adaptive and constructive (rather than maladaptive) under certain circumstances.[11] If the external situation is unusually threatening, such as might occur during aerial bombardment or imprisonment, it may be more realistically adaptive for body functions that could produce pregnancy or blood loss to be inhibited or suspended.

It has been a long-debated issue whether the phases of the menstrual cycle are paralleled by periodicities in mood, psychological attitude, and sexual arousal. Benedek and Rubenstein (1939) were the first to assert, on the basis of systematic research, that such relationships exist. They described data derived from women in psychoanalytic therapy in which the occurrence of certain psychodynamic themes in the patient's therapy verbalizations seemed to be related to phases of the menstrual cycle as determined from vaginal smears. Essentially, they found that as estrogen production increased during the first part of the cycle there was an increase in verbalized material pertaining to active, heterosexual, object-seeking wishes and goals. Following ovulation (in the progesterone phase) the verbal material seemed to contain more themes of relaxation and passivity and fewer themes with sexual connotations. Finally, during the premenstrual phase themes of discomfort and tension appeared.

Since the appearance of this work, numerous other investigators have discerned consistent mood and attitudinal variations paralleling menstrual phases in individual women who were studied during repeated menstrual cycles. Gottschalk, Kaplan, Gleser, and Winget (1962) evaluated the variations in affect content of five-minute samples of spontaneous speech obtained from women during different phases of the menstrual cycle. Although they did not find group consistency, they did establish that individual women showed consistency in certain affects for given phases across several different cycles. There was even a general trend for anxiety and hostility directed toward self to decrease around the time of ovulation. This finding is analogous to the Ivey and Bardwick (1968) observation (based on the same five-minute samples of spontaneous speech) that general anxiety and concern about death are lower at ovulation than during the premenstrual phase. There was a significant trend for the material produced during ovulation to express self-satisfaction over success or capability for coping with problems. Using a similar approach, Paige (1969) obtained results roughly corroborative of those of Ivey and Bardwick. Moss, et al. (1969) discerned definite trends for self-rated aggression to be high during menstruation as well as the end of the cycle, but relatively low during the middle of the cycle.[12] Self-rated anxiety followed a similar pattern. When self-ratings of sexual arousal were analyzed, it was noted that such arousal was low during menstruation and then had a sharp rise until the middle of the cycle, after which it decreased somewhat and then leveled off. This last pattern may be compared with other reports in the literature concerning shifts in sexual interest during the mentrual cycle. For example, Wineman (1967) could find no phase differences for sexual receptivity. Hart (1960) discovered that a majority of the women in her sample experienced an increase in sexual desire at the time of menstruation.[13] Shader, DiMascio, and Harmatz (1968) found that large shifts in sexual interest occurred primarily in high-anxious women, and that these shifts were in the direction of greater sexual interest in the immediate premenstrual phase. Overall, it is apparent that there is no consistency in the reports cited concerning variations in sexual interest at different points in the menstrual cycle.

A few tentative attempts have been made to ascertain whether dreams occurring during menstruation differ from those of nonmenstrual phases.[14] Van de Castle (1967), who has been particularly enterprising in this respect, has, for example, shown that references to babies, children, and temporal events appear significantly more often in menstrual than nonmenstrual dreams. Speculating about these findings, he states (p. 6):

> Although I have not examined the context in which these baby references appear, it would be intriguing if an emphasis upon past events were also associated with these dreams. If this were the case, it would suggest that the infantocentric orientation of women at this time might be related to unconscious grief over the loss of the potential baby they harbored and whose demise was now confirmed by the menstrual flow.

One of Van de Castle's findings concerning menstrual versus nonmenstrual dreams stimulated the present author to some speculation about the integrative effects of the menstrual sensory experiences. Van de Castle demonstrated a significant trend for the figure of the dreamer to be more socially active and initiatory in menstrual than nonmenstrual dreams. This activity encompassed both aggressive and friendly behavior. One is reminded of a rather analogous finding by Castaldo and Holzman (1967), who studied the dreams of subjects who, while asleep, were exposed to recordings of their own voices as well as the voices of others. It was found that in the dreams occurring while the dreamer was listening to his own voice, the principal figure was unusually likely to be active, assertive, and independent. One of the explanations that Castaldo and Holzman offered for this effect was that it might be caused by the fact that one's own voice produces a special degree of physiological arousal (they had earlier actually demonstrated this to be true), which, because of the motor inhibition associated with sleep, is translated into the enhanced fantasy activity of the dream. Might the enhanced socially active role of the dreamer during menstruation be explained in analogous terms? Does menstruation similarly produce a series of specific, novel, and yet periodically familiar patterns of physiological arousal during sleep that cannot find expression and therefore increase fantasy activity? One is further reminded of Housman's (1950) data in which it was found that the menstrual experience had an ego integrating effect upon some schizophrenics. Could this integrating effect be at least partially caused by the same kind of influence that has been theorized to result in the menstruating dreamer (or the dreamer hearing his own voice) appearing in the dream in an unusually active social role? In these various instances, body arousal appears to function as a stimulus to vigor or to a socially active orientation (rather than the retreat characteristic of schizophrenia). Menstruation may, as suggested by some (Kestenberg, in Lorand and Schneer, 1961), serve as a periodic reinforcer of body awareness and body vividness that intensifies self-awareness and therefore encourages self-assertive and ego integrating attitudes.[15] This possibility gains support from Fisher's (1970) experiments that have shown that enhanced body awareness in women is accompanied by well-defined boundaries. Indeed, Compton (1969) has also shown that the greater a woman's body awareness the lower are her scores on measures of psychological maladjustment.

Many guesses and speculations have been made about the significance of the menstrual experience to women. Most of these speculations have been derived from clinical interviews with psychiatric patients or medical patients with menstrual pathology. In actuality, we know little about the fantasies and feelings that menstruation arouses in the average woman. We have yet to learn how this periodic gross alteration in body physiology and body experience is integrated into the normal woman's style of adaptation. To understand this phenomenon is important not only in its own right but also because it may help to clarify the more general case of how adaptation to radical changes in any body-experience pattern occurs.

Producing a Baby

There are few things that happen "normally" to the human body that compare in magnitude with the changes produced by pregnancy. This is particularly true if one considers the relatively brief time span within which pregnancy grossly alters the body configuration. A process such as aging also results in drastic body changes, but they are attenuated over time. As contrasted with pregnancy changes, they occur gradually and are not compressed into a matter of months. The transformations produced by pregnancy have numerous biological and psychological effects that are stressful. There is good agreement in the literature that most women are, to some degree, frightened by pregnancy and are called upon to muster adaptive defenses. Bibring and her associates (1961), who have intensively studied pregnancy, regard it as a time of psychological crisis for all females. Klein, Potter, and Dyk (1950) found in their interviews with pregnant women that (p. 32), "no patient irrespective of whether the baby was wanted or unwanted, was not without anxiety at some time during pregnancy." One should add that problems in adapting to pregnancy are not unique to our culture. Freedman and Ferguson (1950) documented the difficulties that women in cultures around the world experience during pregnancy. Incidentally, it has turned out to be a myth that women in so-called "primitive" cultures, in contrast to their Western counterparts, experience little pain during delivery. The amount of anxiety and pain occurring during delivery by the modal Western woman is probably about average for a wide range of cultures.

Although there is agreement that pregnancy is stressful, there is also considerable agreement that it has integrative and maturing functions in the life cycle of the woman. Deutsch (1945) and others propose that most women see their first pregnancy as a demonstration of their full womanhood. Deutsch remarks that (1945, p. 164), "A woman who has never been successfully pregnant is deprived of an important experience—the joy of anticipation, the pride of achievement, the anxious tension and its mastery. . . ." Deutsch suggests, too, that pregnancy offers an opportunity to the woman for fantasying and expecting fulfillment of many aspirations and wishes. That is, she can visualize in the child being formed a special and superior creation capable of attaining things she feels have escaped her.

Those who focus upon the stressful aspects of pregnancy have not been at a loss for theories to explain why this should be a disturbing time. Many of these theories are, directly or indirectly, of psychoanalytic origin, and often represent elaborations of either Freud's views about the nature of femininity or Helene Deutsch's (1945) finely etched theorizing concerning motherhood. A brief review of the range and character of these theories follows.

Competition with the Mother

In various guises, one frequently encounters the formulation that pregnancy is stressful because it revives old conflicts with the mother. It is stated that when a woman finds herself pregnant this may symbolically give reality to old repressed fantasies about taking over the mother's attributes and replacing her (for example, in her relationship with the father). That is, pregnancy may signal to a woman that she has finally been able to attain the mother's envied status and qualifications; presumably it may even unconsciously represent the long wished for impregnation by the father, which is conjectured in psychoanalytic theory to be one of the aims of the girl during her Oedipal struggles. She suddenly finds it possible to say, "I am the mother now, not you." If so, anxiety would be aroused because pregnancy then comes to represent what is forbidden and potentially provocative of serious retaliation. Several writers (Deutsch, 1945; Lomas, 1960a,b) have placed emphasis on the destructive significance of equating one's pregnancy with a hostile act toward the mother. They ascribe many instances of serious psychological disturbance during pregnancy to fantasies about the mother's jealousy and to feeling that one is alienated from the mother at a time when her approval and support seem particularly important. Alienation from the mother in this sense is assumed to be doubly threatening if there is a history of unusual dependence upon her.

Related to the matter of pregnancy reviving old conflicts with the mother is the more general view that pregnancy provides a context for animating and projecting dormant problems. The very complexity of the pregnancy changes and the fact that they betoken altering the character of important contemporary relationships create unstable conditions in which one may find reminders of past crises. These "reminders" may presumably reinstate and energize old conflicts. Deutsch (1945) has even noted how the multiplicity of the body changes accompanying pregnancy may provide reminders of, and initiate, analogues of previous psychosomatic or pain experiences.

Introversion and Enhancement of Narcissism

Another explanation offered for the stressful impact of pregnancy relates to its so-called introversive or narcissism-enhancing effects. It is conjectured that pregnancy causes a woman to decrease her investment in outside activities and objects and to reinvest more strongly in herself (Deutsch, 1945; Blitzer and Murray, 1964). The pregnant woman is described as becoming more preoccupied with herself, more concerned about her own experiences and feelings, and more convinced of her own importance. Deutsch (1945, p. 138) says:

> The fact that pregnancy is accompanied by intensified introversion can easily be demonstrated. Pregnant women themselves complain that their former lively and sincere interest in various outside events seems to wane. . . . They may continue their accustomed occupations automatically, but inner participation is lacking. The diversion of the psychic energies from the outer world means the first more or less decisive step in the process of turning inward, i.e., introversion.

Implicit in this orientation on the part of the pregnant woman is an increased expectation that others will want to give to, and devote themselves to, her.[16] The stress or potential disturbance associated with the increased investment in self is regarded by Deutsch (1945) and others as growing out of the fact that such investment represents "regression." That is, the intensified interest in self as compared to outside objects is viewed as a less mature mode of adaptation that leaves the individual in a weakened state.

Regression in the pregnant woman is said by some to be encouraged by the fact that she is chronically tempted to identify with the regressive and uncontrolled state of her baby that is psychologically so close to her. Presumably, she is drawn to identify with the passivity of the baby and may envy his "privileged" way of life. Deutsch remarks that in situations where the pregnant woman can mobilize others to satisfy her increased narcissistic demands she may fare well, but her frustration tolerance will be acutely tried if she cannot elicit the magnified contributions from others that she expects.

Body Attitudes and Fantasies

A number of theorists have underscored the threat that pregnancy poses for the integrity of a woman's body image. In several different ways the body changes initiated by pregnancy seem to raise significant adjustment problems.[17] There is, first of all, the slowly initiated but then sharply accelerated increase in body size and change in body shape that accompany the development of the fetus. This is climaxed by a precipitous reversal when the body shrinks in size at the time of delivery. Such changes may be experienced as disfiguring, or they may be seen as so distorting as to exceed recognizable limits of what can be identified as self and so give rise to feelings of depersonalization. Or they may, through the very fact of introducing radical shifts in perception in a region where shifts of such intensity are rare, create feelings of instability and inconstancy. Deutsch (1945) and Schilder (1945) have been among those who have referred to such phenomena.

Relatedly, it has been pointed out that pregnancy body changes are threatening because they signal a biological process that can, in reality, lead to serious illness and even death.[18] They may also, because of their reactivation of old childish fantasies about the nature of pregnancy, arouse fears that certain organs will be damaged. Thus, a child's concept of pregnancy might be based on the notion that it occurs in the stomach or that delivery of the fetus occurs anally. When pregnancy is actually initiated and unusual body sensations are aroused in specific body areas, they may reinforce the old childish ideas about the participation of such areas in pregnancy. Fantasies that the fetus is implanted in the stomach, when reinforced by strange new stomach sensations, may arouse anxiety about the ability of the stomach to accommodate to something as large as a baby without being injured. Apropos of this example, a number of clinical reports have purported to implicate distorted fantasies about the role of the stomach and other oral areas in pregnancy in the etiology of excessive pregnancy vomiting.

Deutsch (1945) was among the first to attempt to define explicitly the problems that arise as the pregnant woman is confronted with the task of integrating the internally contained fetus into her body concept and yet at the same time of maintaining realistic differentiation between it and her own body (identity). The fertilized egg, representing the future fetus, starts out really indistinguishable from the woman's own body. She probably perceives it as completely fused with herself. However, as the fetus develops, increases in size, and begins to move, it takes on an obvious identity of its own and the woman must learn to distinguish it as an object separate from her own body. If she does not learn to make the distinction with some clarity, says Deutsch, she is faced with a serious dilemma at the time of delivery because she may interpret the departure of the child from her body as a loss of part of herself. She may feel so fused with the child that delivery has the implication of an actual excision of one's own body substance, with resulting fear and also resentment.[19] But, on the other hand, some writers suggest that if a woman too sharply distinguishes the fetus from her own body she may experience it as too different from self and therefore as something alien and potentially dangerous. To have something inside of one's body that is perceived as alien might be expected to arouse defensive, expulsive reactions. Such formulations picture a woman as faced by a fairly complex task in properly balancing her perception of the fetus as part of her own body and yet as separate and distinguishable. One may pertinently add that there are some interesting speculations in the literature about conditions that might unconsciously motivate a woman to rotate roles between her body and that of the fetus; and in so doing to confuse self with fetus. She might, for example, recurrently equate the fetus with herself and regard her own body as a representation of her own mother— as part of a fantasy in which she is taken care of by mother rather than having the obligation of nurturing her own child.

Guilt

Diverse species of guilt are described as permeating and complicating pregnancy adaptation.[20] At one level, guilt is said to attach itself to pregnancy because of its obvious equation with sexual activity. To be pregnant is to show openly and visibly that sexual intercourse has occurred. If there has been guilt attached to sexuality in the course of a woman's socialization, it will presumably also adhere to her pregnancy. Deutsch (1945) suggests that a woman's guilt about masturbation is often similarly transferred to her pregnant appearance. In the same vein, one should refer back to the fact that guilt looms large, too, in the idea that pregnancy may be experienced as a way of competing with the mother and renewing old Oedipal rivalries with her. Such guilt would be related to sexual guilt because, as defined by Freudian theory, the core elements of Oedipal conflict with the mother involve wishes to replace her as the father's sexual partner. Guilt during pregnancy has also been prominently attributed to hostile fantasies about the fetus that are expressed in wishes to destroy or expel it. It is said that the fetus may, because it represents future hardship or interference with long-term goals or demands for nurturant attention, evoke intense anger in the pregnant woman; and this anger, by exceeding acceptable limits of negativity toward one's child, can evoke feelings of guilt and unworthiness.

Altered Relationships with Husband

One way to conceptualize a first pregnancy is that it introduces a third party into what was previously a largely two-person system (Lomas, 1959). This immediately shakes up old equilibria and calls for new forms of response from each of the marriage partners. The pregnant wife suddenly finds that she has a new object (barely distinguishable from self) in which to invest herself, and may in the process withdraw an equivalent amount of interest from her husband. However, even as she does so she may signal to him that she expects greater support from him because of the stress imposed upon her by her pregnant condition. The husband is simultaneously stressed by the new responsibilities the pregnancy bodes for him and would probably like some extra support from her. The old two-person system comes under great strain, with each partner expected to face greater responsibility and difficulty, but each being threatened by the possibility of being unable to get as much support from the other as normally available in times of noncrisis.

Lomas (1959) presents clinical illustrations of instances in which serious psychological disturbance in women linked with pregnancy seemed to be caused by the stress placed upon the husband-wife relationship by the pregnancy.

Flapan (1969), after intensively interviewing a series of women, noted with reference to pregnancy attitudes that might be linked to the husband-wife relationship (p. 413):

> A woman may be reluctant to bear a child by a husband whom she neither loves nor respects, or she may be concerned that a child might resemble her disliked husband. Her husband's lack of interest in having a child may undermine her childbearing motivations. . . . If she thinks her husband wouldn't be a good father, she may be concerned about the harmful effects he would have on her children. . . .
>
> A woman may be conflicted about childbearing because she anticipates that a child would intrude upon or disrupt the functioning relationship she has established with her husband.

Obviously, the disturbance thought to arise from husband-wife strain is not a unique category in itself and can be viewed as overlapping with other categories that have been enumerated. For example, husband-wife difficulties might be aggravated if the wife were made extremely introversive or narcissistic by her pregnancy and had an unusually low amount of energy to invest in her husband; and conversely an unusually adverse mode of relating to him might lead her to retreat defensively into an exaggerated introversive state.

These speculations concerning the psychological stresses associated with pregnancy do not exhaust the full array to be found in the literature. There are others that diversely speak of how pregnancy tempts a woman to play a "sick role" (Brown, 1964), of the possibility that it evokes regressive anal fantasies in which the fetus may be equated with feces (Fenichel, 1945), and of the manner in which it may evoke exhibitionistic wishes (Lomas, 1962).

Motivation for Pregnancy

As suggested in the previous section, complex attitudes and fantasies may be involved in a woman's reaction to becoming pregnant. Pohlman (1969), who surveyed the literature dealing with empirical studies of motives for parenthood, concluded that such motives were extremely variform. Note the range of those that he discussed (pp. 80–81):

> Desires to be a parent and to have a family of a particular size are heavily influenced by social pressures. Family size seems to have aspects of "fad" or fashion within a given culture.
>
> Motherhood provides a role for the woman; it may be the chief means of establishing her identity.

A person may wish to express happiness and love felt toward a partner by sharing in procreation.

People may seek to identify with their parents by producing the same general size of family as did their parents.

Parents sometimes report having additional children because of a belief that large families are somehow better for existing children.

Centers and Blumberg (1954) arranged for interviews with a cross-section sample ($N = 1,021$) of persons in Los Angeles, California, concerning their reasons for desiring children. The sample consisted of equal numbers of men and women. It was found that the desire for children was positively correlated with church membership, but not with education or race. Furthermore, this desire was linked to rated happiness of one's childhood; the more one's childhood was recalled as having been happy the greater was the expressed desire to have children. Pertinent to this last finding is a report by Rabin and Greene (1968) who developed a semiprojective questionnaire that measures motivation for parenthood in terms of four scoring categories: altruistic (unselfish), fatalistic (one is brought into the world to procreate), narcissistic (child will reflect glory on the parent), instrumental (child is a vehicle to some goal). They administered these questionnaires and others concerned with attitudes toward one's parents to a sample of 33 males and 33 females, and found that, especially among the females, those who perceive their parents as loving are more likely to have "altruistic" motives for parenthood. Those who recall their parents as rejecting or demanding give more "narcissistic" reasons for procreating. It is an interesting sidelight on this study that a sex difference occurred, such that females were more often characterized by the "fatalistic" motivation and the males by the "instrumental" one.

A novel approach to evaluating motives for pregnancy was undertaken by Flapan (1969) with a sample of 82 women. He asked each woman to perform a series of tasks, one of which involved recalling "all the thoughts and feelings" she had had about "having and not having children" at various points in her life. Another task involved her formulating (on a tape recorder) a series of questions to herself about her reasons for having children (for example, "Are you reluctant to have a child because—?") and then responding to these questions. An impressionistic analysis of the material obtained in this fashion resulted in the following motivations for pregnancy:

1. There are social expectations that a woman will bear a child. To be "normal" one must conform to such expectations.
2. A woman may seek pregnancy to emulate her peers who already have children.
3. Childbearing may represent a way of affirming one's feminine identity and of proving one's fertility.
4. A woman may anticipate and want a child because it will represent her and perpetuate her identity in the future. This future representation of self may be a way of compensating for present feelings of inadequacy.

There may be a hope of rearing a child who will be strong rather than weak in the areas of one's inadequacies.

5. To produce children may be a woman's way of emulating an admired mother. "She may look forward to experiencing the fulfillment that her own mother experienced through motherhood, and want to reproduce the relationship with her children that she had with her mother" (p. 410).

6. Childbearing may represent a chance to produce someone whom a woman can love, touch, fondle, and nurture.[21]

7. A woman may see having a child as a way of becoming more mature, interesting, and responsible.

8. Pregnancy may provide a woman with a means to produce a replica of her husband; to offer him a "gift" of something he desires; to cement their relationship.

9. Becoming pregnant may enable a woman to please her parents who want grandchildren.

10. Pregnancy may provide a means for satisfying a woman's curiosity about what the experience of pregnancy is like.

If one carefully examines this list one is less tempted to arrive at simple formulations concerning the nature of pregnancy motivation. Each individual might have a rather unique combination of these reasons for becoming pregnant.

Empirical Studies

Psychological States Characterizing Pregnancy

What solid facts are available concerning the psychological feelings and attitudes characteristic of pregnancy? Do we actually have empirical evidence that the average pregnant woman is unusually anxious or preoccupied with special sorts of conflicts, or that she is different from others in the way she experiences the world?

Let us inquire concerning the basic question whether pregnant women are unusually anxious or psychologically disturbed. There have been a number of interview and questionnaire studies (for example, Klein, Potter, and Dyk, 1950; Kartchner, 1950) that have systematically inquired concerning the degree to which pregnant women are worried about the pregnancy itself. With rare exceptions, such studies find that pregnant women are typically worried about matters such as whether they will suffer injury or death during delivery, whether their child will be born deformed, whether they will be capable of caring adequately for the new child, whether they will be able to tolerate the pain of delivery, and so forth. Although there is no question concerning the fact that pregnant women have such anxieties, what justification do we have for assuming that their overall levels of anxiety are greater than those found in nonpregnant women? Perhaps special worries about pregnancy simply replace others that fade into the background during the pregnancy period.

Various kinds of empirical information are available concerning the psychological "condition" of the pregnant woman. One can look at studies that compare pregnant women with nonpregnant controls. Comparisons are to be found of how pregnant women shift psychologically from the prepartum to the postpartum period. Finally, one can find systematic observations of the psychological changes occurring within the prepartum time period itself.

Contrary to what has been reported in clinical and anecdotal papers, it has not been possible to convincingly demonstrate empirically that pregnant women are different from nonpregnant controls with respect to anxiety level or an assortment of other psychological parameters. The results in the literature present quite a contradictory picture. Consider first those studies that depict the pregnant woman as more psychologically disturbed than the nonpregnant woman. Treadway, et al. (1969) reported concerning a sample of pregnant women ($N = 21$) to whom the Minnesota Multiphasic Personality Inventory (MMPI), the Cattell Neuroticism Scale Questionnaire, and a Mood Adjective Check List had been administered. They found that the pregnant women had significantly elevated Hypochondriasis and Social Introversion scores and lowered Femininity scores.

Riffaterre (1961) obtained responses to the MMPI and the Rorschach Inkblot Test from pregnant ($N = 48$) and nonpregnant ($N = 48$) subjects, and found that whereas the MMPI Depression scale did not distinguish them, a depression score derived from the Rorschach Test was significantly higher in the former than in the latter group.

Simon (1964) asked pregnant women ($N = 16$) and nonpregnant controls ($N = 8$) to give their associations to a series of neutral words as well as to a series referring to delivery and "taking care of a baby." Speed of associations was measured, as was the Galvanic Skin Reflex (GSR). Analysis of the GSR data indicated that the pregnant women were more "emotionally labile," as measured by GSR variability. This heightened variability (emotional instability?) applied to responses to both the neutral and the pregnancy relevant stimulus words.

Goodman (1967) compared 15 pregnant women and 30 women who were nonpregnant (but had one child) with respect to scores on the Edwards Preference Schedule and measures of attitudes toward self and one's body. The pregnant women were found to have a significantly more negative attitude toward self than did the nonpregnant women. However, this may have been a chance finding because it was the only significant one in a large series of comparisons.

Jarrahi-Zadeh, Kane, Van de Castle, Lachenbruch, and Ewing (1969) compared the MMPI and Cattell Neuroticism Scale Questionnaire scores of pregnant women ($N = 86$) seen in the last three months of pregnancy with nonpregnant controls ($N = 21$). They found that the pregnant women reported more depression and psychological disturbance than did the controls. They also administered measures of intellectual functioning to the two groups (for example, Porteus Mazes) and noted "slightly impaired cognitive functioning" in the pregnant sample.

Several studies, however, portray the pregnant and nonpregnant woman as not differing psychologically. Hooke and Marks (1962) found that MMPI scores from a group of pregnant women ($N = 24$) were not indicative of unusual disturbance. They state (p. 316), "The most striking find of these data is . . . the absence of (even) mild subjective discomfort (that is, anxiety and/or depression) as late in pregnancy as the eighth month. Also of interest is the low incidence of psychopathology *of any sort* at this time." McDonald and Parham (1964) likewise observed in a sample of pregnant women ($N = 160$) that their MMPI scores were not significantly elevated in the direction of disturbance or psychopathology.

Brodsky (1963) asked pregnant women ($N = 29$) and various nonpregnant controls ($N = 48$) to respond to the Jourard Self-Ideal Questionnaire that evaluates the individual's self-concept as well as her ideal self-concept. He could detect no differences in degree of self-acceptance between the groups. The pregnant women felt just as positively toward themselves as did the nonpregnant women. Relatedly, one finds that when Edwards (1969) measured anxiety by means of various techniques (for example, Speilberger State-Trait Anxiety Inventory) in pregnant women ($N = 53$) as well as a control group of nonpregnant student nurses, a difference between the two groups failed to appear. The pregnant women were not more anxious than the nonpregnant controls.

Obviously, it would be difficult on the basis of the studies just enumerated to conclude that pregnant women do or do not differ from nonpregnant women in their degree of anxiety or psychological disturbance. This is an instance in which the familiar sentiment that more research needs to be done applies with special aptness. Although clinical studies (for example, Bibring, 1959) have unhesitatingly labeled the pregnancy period as one of unusual disturbance, it is unfortunately true that they have rarely employed proper control groups. Perhaps one can observe considerable psychological disturbance in pregnant women, but it might be just as easy to observe such disturbance in nonpregnant women.

Another approach that has been taken to the issue under discussion involves tracing changes in anxiety during the course of the pregnancy and into the postdelivery period. This permits consideration of such questions as whether anxiety intensifies as pregnancy alterations become more pronounced and whether it diminishes significantly after the baby has been delivered.

A particularly careful study by Grimm (1961) may first be appropriately described. This investigator was interested in measuring anxiety at five points in the pregnancy sequence. She studied five groups, each consisting of 40 pregnant women and each evaluated at a different point over the three trimesters that constitute the pregnancy period (namely, last half of first trimester and first and second halves of the second and third trimesters). The Thematic Apperception Test and a modification of the House-Tree-Person Drawing Test were administered to all subjects. Scores indicative of tension and disturbance about pregnancy that were derived were found to be of similar magnitudes at most of the time points sampled, but they were observed to be significantly higher during the last three months and especially during the last eight weeks. Grimm concluded that the peak of anxiety occurs during the last three months of pregnancy. She did indicate, though, that there was considerable individual variation. She cites examples of women who, because they have had a previous miscarriage, feel unusually high anxiety at a time corresponding to that at which the miscarriage occurred rather than at the point characteristic of most women.

In a subsequent study Grimm, collaboratively with Venet (1966), administered Pregnancy Questionnaires to a sample of pregnant women ($N = 92$) first at a time before the sixteenth week and again during the thirty-sixth week of pregnancy. The questionnaires were considered to measure a number of dimensions, for example, neuroticism, worry about the baby, dependence, and feelings of being "sick." Surprisingly, a comparison of questionnaire scores for the early and late phases of pregnancy indicated no significant shifts. These pregnant women did not show the kind of increase in disturbance late in pregnancy that had manifested itself in the Grimm study just cited in which projective measures of anxiety and tension were employed.

A similar lack of consistency in tension patterns was found by Simon (1964), who asked pregnant women ($N = 16$) to give word associations to stimulus words with neutral as well as pregnancy implications at three time points of the pregnancy period (13 weeks, 18 weeks, and 6 weeks after delivery). Responses were measured both in terms of speed of reaction and physiological arousal (as defined by the GSR). No differences in apparent degree of tension or activation were found among the three time points sampled. The average pregnant subject did not respond differently at an early as compared to a late phase of pregnancy, and her responses prior to delivery were not distinguishable from those given postdelivery.

Zemlick and Watson (1953) obtained measures of anxiety, body symptoms, and attitudes toward pregnancy from pregnant women ($N = 15$) early in their pregnancy as well as six weeks prior to delivery. No significant shifts in the measures occurred during the pregnancy.

Poffenberger and Poffenberger (1952) asked 212 women to recall how anxious they had been during various stages of their pregnancies. Their responses indicated a significant trend for anxiety to be recalled as having been greatest during the early months of pregnancy. The elevated anxiety that Grimm reported to be associated with the last weeks of pregnancy was not apparent in the data.

Erickson (1967) perused in fine detail the complaints of women during their pregnancy. She asked these women ($N = 18$) to maintain a record of their complaints or symptoms (by checking a list with 31 complaints) each night during the entire course of the pregnancy. Her results made it evident that rating psychological variations during pregnancy is probably a more complex task than most researchers have realized. She found that some complaints (for example, backache and tension) do not vary in any consistent fashion during the nine months, but complaints such as vomiting, headache, and "euphoria" decreased after the fourth month; at the same time complaints such as fatigue, depression, irritability, and anxiety were high both during the first four or five months and during the last month of pregnancy. One sees here that some kinds of difficulties increase, others decrease, and still others vary quite erratically during the pregnancy sequence.

As indicated, it is premature to declare that the period of pregnancy is generally typified by up or down shifts in tension states.[22]

Surveying the pertinent literature, one finds that actually most of the work concerned with psychological change during pregnancy has focused on comparing predelivery and postdelivery feelings and attitudes. As will be seen, the results of this work suggest that most women become less anxious and perturbed after the delivery. Consider the following.

McDonald and Parham (1964) obtained MMPI records from pregnant women ($N = 160$) during the seventh month of pregnancy and again within one week to ten days following delivery. They reported that the predelivery scores were generally higher and therefore indicative of greater psychological disturbance.

Davids, DeVault, and Talmadge (1961a) administered the Taylor Manifest Anxiety Scale, the Thematic Apperception Test (TAT), a Sentence Completion Test, and other measures to pregnant subjects ($N = 48$) during the seventh month and about six weeks after delivery. Analysis of the data indicated a significant decrease in anxiety, as defined by the Taylor Anxiety Scale. In addition, there was a decrease in feelings of alienation presumably measured by TAT and Sentence Completion indices. An interesting sidelight was the fact that following delivery the subjects less often identified a specific female figure (whose possible pregnant condition is ambiguously depicted) in a TAT picture as looking pregnant. There was an alteration in the degree to which stimuli with pregnancy connotations were perceptually important.

McDonald and Gynther (1965) appraised changes from the seventh month of pregnancy to two weeks postpregnancy in 177 women. The primary psychological measure used was the Leary Interpersonal Check List, which involves ratings of self and parents by means of adjective choices. The only gross difference that was discerned between the predelivery and postdelivery scores was that the latter tended to define self as "stronger." This finding would seem to be congruent with the idea of diminished fearfulness following delivery. When the sample was split into those women who had "normal" deliveries and those who had experienced "abnormal" complications, it was discovered that the "abnormals" described their parents less favorably after delivery and the "normals" described them more favorably.

The finding by McDonald and Gynther concerning the sense of being "stronger" following delivery is congruent with results reported in two other studies by Kogan, Boe, and Valentine (1965) and Kogan, Boe, and Gocka (1968). Both of these studies used versions of the same Interpersonal Check List technique that McDonald and Gynther employed. In each instance the findings indicated that the women felt more positively toward themselves postdelivery than they had predelivery.

Jarrahi-Zadeh, Kane, Van de Castle, Lachenbruch, and Ewing (1969) analyzed shifts in a variety of test scores occurring in 86 women who were seen once during the last three months of their pregnancy and again three days after delivery. A number of personality (for example, MMPI) and intellectual tests (for example, Porteus Mazes) were administered on both occasions. Significant trends were observed for depression and general psychological disturbance to decrease from the time of pregnancy to the postpregnancy period. No differences in intellectual functioning could be detected.

Edwards (1969) examined the predelivery to postdelivery changes in a sample of 53 women. The following measures were obtained early in the pregnancy and within ten days after delivery: anxiety (based on questionnaire and inkblot responses, body-boundary attributes and hostility (derived from inkblot responses), repression-sensitization (questionnaire), and attitudes toward pregnancy (questionnaire). The results indicated significant shifts from predelivery to postdelivery in the direction of decreased anxiety, decreased hostility, increased favorableness toward pregnancy, and decreased sensitization toward threatening stimuli.[23] It was concluded that the shifts represented an overall increase in adequacy of adjustment. One of the rather unique aspects of this study was that it considered the shifts in two scores developed by Fisher and Cleveland (1968) for measuring how the individual perceives the boundaries of his body. As described earlier, Fisher and Cleveland suggested the persons differ in the degree to which they experience their body boundaries as clear and well-delineated versus vague and insubstantial. They validated two indices, Barrier and Penetration scores, which measure boundary attributes in terms of the properties ascribed to the boundary regions of percepts elicited by inkblot stimuli. The higher the Barrier score the more definite are the individual's boundaries, but the higher the Penetration score, which taps another aspect of the boundary, the greater is the sense of boundary vulnerability. Edwards found that both the Barrier and Penetration scores decreased significantly from prepregnancy to postpregnancy. The decrease in Penetration represented a cross-validation to a previous finding by McConnell and Daston (1961), who reported that in a sample of pregnant women ($N = 28$) Penetration decreased from the last weeks of pregnancy to the third day after delivery. They interpreted this shift to mean that the sense of boundary vulnerability diminishes following delivery. They suggested that prior to delivery (p. 453), "Fantasies of body boundary disruption may . . . arise as the mother anticipates the actual penetration of body boundaries during the birth experience." One difference between their original results and those of Edwards was that whereas they found no shift from predelivery to postdelivery in the Barrier score, they did observe a significant decrease in the Penetration score. Edwards interpreted the Barrier decrease to mean that after delivery a woman had less need to think of her body walls as having protective and containing properties than she did when the fetus was still within her. This may be so, but it remains puzzling that both the Barrier and Penetration scores, which presumably measure partially obverse aspects of boundary definiteness, should both decrease.

The studies outlined have all consistently represented women as better adjusted and feeling more secure after delivery than before.[24] However, findings by Yalom, Lunde, Moos, and Hamburg (1968) seem to be contradictory. They undertook to observe women for ten days following delivery and found an unusual amount of depressive affect present, and concluded that this period was actually a "time of great vulnerability" and even of "regression." They noted that women were three times as likely to cry during the immediate postdelivery period than either during the late phases of pregnancy or eight months after delivery. Self-ratings of depression indicated a similar pattern of heightened depression in the days immediately following delivery. Because of the detailed observations of *overt* behavior (for example, reports by nurses concerning frequency of patients' crying) that were employed in this study, one must give it special weight. But at the moment one cannot easily reconcile the findings of this study with those that have indicated a decrease in tension and disturbance after delivery.[25]

This is probably a logical place to introduce a discussion of the so-called postpartum psychosis. There are reports indicating that psychosis may occur with unusual frequency during the period just subsequent to delivery. Psychosis is more likely to occur just subsequent to delivery than during the period of gestation itself (Shainess, 1966; Ostwald and Regan, 1957).[26] Such observations are obviously congruent with the Yalom, et al. (1968) assertion that the postdelivery period is one of heightened vulnerability and disturbance. Considerable speculation may be found in the clinical literature concerning the type of woman who is most likely to become seriously disturbed just subsequent to delivery. One of the most widely known theories concerning this matter was formulated by Zilboorg (1928a,b), who proposed that the woman most vulnerable to postdelivery breakdown is one who has incompletely resolved her Oedipal conflicts and been unconsciously preoccupied with wishes to possess a penis ("penis envy")—identifying more with masculine than feminine goals. As Zilboorg sees it, pregnancy provides such an individual with a substitute penis in the form of the fetus contained within her body, which by so doing, fulfills for her a long unsatisfied wish and provides an object (the fetus), which takes on extreme value as something that must be retained as part of her body. Presumably, the delivery of the child (penis equivalent) in such an individual is extremely disorganizing because it unconsciously means the loss of the long-sought-after penis.

Ginsparg (1956) seems to be the only investigator who has attempted to test Zilboorg's theory empirically. She studied women who became psychotic postdelivery ($N = 15$), women who had become psychotic at a time other than in association with pregnancy ($N = 15$), and normal women who had just delivered ($N = 15$). The Thematic Apperception Test, the Blacky Pictures Test (which involves interpreting pictures about a dog involved in situations with psychoanalytic pertinence), the MMPI, and the Franck Drawing Test, which evaluates masculinity-femininity, were administered to all subjects. Measures were derived that tested hypotheses concerning the special likelihood of finding Oedipal conflict, penis envy, psychosexual immaturity, and "female masochism" in those women with postdelivery psychosis.[27] The results indicated that the postdelivery psychotic women differed from normal postdelivery women in many of the ways that had been predicted, but they did *not* consistently differ from women who had become psychotic outside of the pregnancy context. It should be especially indicated that none of the groups differed significantly with respect to degree of penis envy, which is one of the prime concepts in Zilboorg's theory about vulnerability to postdelivery breakdown. Thus, the overall findings did not support the idea that the postdelivery psychotic is characterized by a unique etiology or set of personal attributes different from that found in other psychotics. The data were not really supportive of Zilboorg's formulation, although one should note that Ginsparg considered some of the trends in the data to fit his views.

The available empirical information simply does not justify glib generalizations concerning the nature of the average woman's psychological state during pregnancy, immediately following delivery, or during specific phases of pregnancy. True, a fair amount of evidence exists that tension declines from the predelivery to the postdelivery phase; but why do depression and psychotic breakdown appear with increased frequency after delivery? This represents a contradiction that requires investigation. Is it possible that most women do, indeed, experience less anxiety and tension postdelivery, but that there is a special subgroup which for some reason reacts to delivery as unusually traumatic? [28] Another possibility worth considering derives from the fact that all of the studies showing a decline in tension from predelivery to postdelivery utilized questionnaires and psychological tests that are concerned with subjective feelings and fantasies, whereas the studies that emphasize the presence of disturbance postdelivery are largely based on overt behavior (for example, crying, psychotic symptomatology). Perhaps there is a marked decrease in the subjective tension level of most women postdelivery, but it may be the sudden nature of this shift that leads to the overtly observed disequilibrium.[29] The sudden gross shift in the subjective economy, independent of whether the direction of shift is a positive one, may require the establishment of a new equilibrium that is paradoxically stressful.

Psychological Attitudes and Reproduction

A good deal of research effort has gone into ascertaining whether psychological attitudes and conflicts play a role in phenomena such as pregnancy, delivery, infertility, spontaneous abortion, and so forth. In essence, the question has been asked whether psychological variables are capable of influencing the physiology of the reproductive system. Can psychological attitudes influence the likelihood of becoming pregnant? Can they affect the length or difficulty of delivery? Can they instigate spontaneous abortion? Numerous attempts have been made to find correlations between psychological parameters and reproductive functions. More will be said about these studies later, but it may be noted in advance that, although a variety of significant correlations have been demonstrated, they have been difficult to interpret in terms of cause and effect.

One of the most direct ways to consider cause and effect possibilities is to examine instances in which investigators have tried to alter reproductive physiology by changing psychological attitudes. Several investigators have looked at the effects of giving psychotherapeutic treatment to pregnant women. Essentially, their objective has been to determine whether decreasing psychological disturbance during pregnancy will decrease the occurrence of physical complications often associated with this period (for example, nausea, prolonged labor, kidney disease). For example, Carpenter, Aldrich, and Boverman (1968) arranged for medical students to interview pregnant women ($N = 52$) several times during the course of their pregnancy in order to provide "emotional support." The behavior and symptoms of this sample were compared with those of a control group of pregnant women ($N = 50$) who did not receive "support." The findings revealed that the experimental subjects differed significantly from the controls insofar as they were less "nervous" during pregnancy and delivery, and they less often required tranquilizing or narcotic medication prior to delivery. However, the two groups did not differ in duration of labor, frequency of postpartum complications, or frequency with which postpartum sedative medication was given. Destounis (1962) considered the effects of psychotherapy on pregnancy complications in ten women and compared the results with those found for 52 pregnant women who received only the regular care of a physician. The women receiving psychotherapy were seen once a week from the second or third month through the completion of pregnancy. During therapy support was given, emotional problems were clarified, and reassurance was provided concerning the essentially "safe" nature of the pregnancy and delivery process. Only two (20 percent) of the women in the experimental sample developed pregnancy complications, whereas 43 (82 percent) of the controls manifested such complications. However, despite this dramatic difference, the results turned out to be ambiguous because the controls were found to be significantly less educated and to be of "lower" social class than the experimental subjects. One cannot, in this instance, know whether to attribute the difference in pregnancy complications between the groups to their differential treatment or to their differential social status.

Knobel (1967), in a short report, indicated that he arranged for a sample of pregnant women to receive brief psychotherapy and found that they had fewer pregnancy complications than a control group of pregnant women who did not receive psychotherapy.

Tupper and Weil (1962) interested themselves in the question whether psychotherapy could influence susceptibility to spontaneous abortion. They worked with an experimental group of 19 pregnant women who were habitual spontaneous aborters (three previous abortions), who were given supportive psychotherapy interviews throughout their pregnancy, and a control group of 19 pregnant women (also habitual aborters), who did not receive psychotherapy. In the experimental group, 84 percent of the pregnancies were successfully completed, but in the control group only 26 percent were successful. This difference is statistically significant.

A study by Mann (1957) is pertinent to this same matter. He provided brief, supportive psychotherapy to a sample of 39 pregnant women who were habitual aborters. Although 93 percent of their previous pregnancies had ended in abortion, only 20 percent ended in this fashion during the psychotherapy regimen. The treatment did appear to influence the likelihood of aborting.

Psychotherapy has also been used as a possible means of influencing infertility. Scattered papers may be found in the literature describing single cases in which psychotherapy seemed to permit women who were long infertile to become pregnant. Rothman, Kaplan, and Nettles (1962), who attempted a more formal study of this phenomenon, describe six women who had been infertile for relatively long periods and who showed no signs of organic pathology that would account for the infertility. A supportive type of psychotherapy was provided to each subject on a weekly basis. All of the patients successfully conceived within a year of the beginning of therapy and within at least a two-month period after therapy was stopped. Although a control group was not employed, the findings certainly suggest that psychotherapy facilitated conception in these women. Rubenstein (1953) provided individual psychotherapy to five infertile women and reported that four of them were thereby enabled to overcome their infertility.

Tangential to the work just cited, but also involving direct intervention from a psychological perspective in the reproductive process, is a study by Bergh, Taylor, and Drose (1966), who hypothesized that if a woman is a habitual spontaneous aborter because of emotional conflicts (for example, unwillingness to accept motherhood), there should be negative psychological repercussions if structural changes were made in the reproductive system that would prevent spontaneous abortion. They studied nine pregnant women who were habitual aborters, who had had sutures placed around the cervix at the level of internal os in order to prevent premature expulsion of the fetus, and who successfully delivered. Five of these women developed a postpartum psychosis. Of the four who did not develop psychosis, three had obtained psychotherapy. In a control group of pregnant women who successfully delivered after having the same surgical procedure, but who were not habitual aborters, only one patient manifested severe postpartum psychiatric symptomatology. The difference in disturbance between the experimental and control groups was significant. The authors concluded that the results supported their hypothesis that psychological attitudes may interfere with the pregnancy process as part of a strategy for defending self against threatening psychological consequences.

Most of these studies were exploratory and lack methodological sophistication. Yet, one cannot but be impressed with the consistency with which psychotherapy seemed to have an impact on some aspect of pregnancy or reproductive physiology.[30] A preliminary verdict would be justified that psychological attitudes can play a directive role in reproductive functions.

What Psychological Variables Are Correlated with Reproductive Phenomena?

Extensive literature reviews (McDonald, 1965a,b,c; Grimm, 1967) have concluded that there is good evidence of correlations between a woman's psychological state during pregnancy and her likelihood of developing various kinds of physical symptomatology. Phenomena such as prolonged labor, preeclampsia, and premature rupture of the membranes have been found to be significantly linked with psychological measures. Although many of the individual studies involved may be criticized for methodological shortcomings, the aggregate findings are rather convincing. One of the key psychological variables in such studies has been level of anxiety or degree of psychological disturbance. Those women who are most anxious and disturbed are most likely to end up with pregnancy difficulties. Anxiety and maladjustment have been diversely measured by means of interview, questionnaire, projective test, and epinephrine level. It has been found that the woman with greater anxiety tends to have prolonged labor (McDonald, 1965a; Kapp, Hornstein, and Graham, 1963); to manifest a high number of somatic complaints (Brown, 1964); to have an increased probability of bearing a child with an abnormality (Davids, DeVault, and Talmadge, 1961b); to be typified by a delivery that is particularly difficult or complicated (McDonald, 1965); and to have a child who weighs less than the average (McDonald and Parham, 1964).[31] In other words, anxiety has been linked with almost every kind of pathology that can occur as part of pregnancy and delivery. It is not a simple matter to interpret the meaning of such findings. One possible viewpoint is that psychological anxiety acts, through its somatic equivalent, to produce disturbance in physiological systems (for example, endocrine) that control the pregnancy process. Another perspective that has been proposed (Grimm, 1967) is that high anxiety in a pregnant woman is not the cause of her somatic difficulties, but rather a reflection of her perception that such difficulties exist. That is, a pregnant woman might receive barely liminal cues (pain, pelvic discomfort) that pathology was developing long before it became clinically manifest; and so a correlation between a measure of anxiety at a given point in her pregnancy and the later onset of a clinical symptom would have no real causal implication. It is apropos of this point to indicate that Fisher (1970) has shown that persons are good observers of their own bodies. They can render judgments about them that are congruent with formal physiological measures that have been secured from them and therefore may have the ability to detect very early pathological changes in their body functioning. Still another possibility to consider is that certain classes of anxious women might not cooperate well with prenatal instructions from their physicians and therefore have an increased possibility of complications. From this viewpoint, a correlation between anxiety and pathology would not be caused by the etiological role of anxiety, but rather the indirect effects of not accepting medical advice sensibly. It is likely that future research will demonstrate that all of the factors enumerated may contribute to the empirical correlations between anxiety and pregnancy pathology.

It is important to add, as noted by Grimm (1967), that although measures of anxiety and maladjustment are correlated with pregnancy pathology within normal samples of women, there is no evidence that women with severe psychiatric symptomatology (schizophrenics) are characterized by more pregnancy difficulties than are normal women. This is difficult to understand because one might logically expect, in terms of much of the data cited, that those who represent an extreme of psychological disturbance would be similarly extreme with reference to pregnancy disturbance.

In addition to anxiety and emotional instability, other parameters are mentioned in the empirical literature as being correlated with reproductive phenomena. Several studies refer to women with pregnancy complications as being unusually "immature" and "dependent" (Grimm and Venet, 1966). A number of investigators present data indicating that hostile tension and repressed anger typify women with certain kinds of pregnancy difficulties (McDonald and Christakos, 1963). Scattered studies have also associated pregnancy pathology with other variables such as "rejection of the feminine role," "Oedipal conflicts," "yeasaying," "hostility toward mother," "social introversion," and perceiving the role of the pregnant woman as a "sick" one. Contrary to widely held clinical assumptions, no consistent evidence has been obtained that pregnancy difficulties are linked with negative attitudes toward pregnancy or motherhood.[32]

It should be noted that although it has been possible to show that psychological parameters and pregnancy pathology are correlated, there has been little success in demonstrating specificity of relationship. Specific psychological measures are not consistently related to specific forms of pathology. We cannot say that premature rupture of the membranes is linked with a different psychological attitude than is prolonged labor. We only know grossly that certain psychological parameters (for example, high anxiety) are accompanied by an increased probability of pregnancy complications of some sort, but not of a particular class of complications.

It is surprising how little solid evidence has emerged that pregnancy pathology is correlated with sexual attitudes or sexual behavior. Many studies have evaluated the relative sexual responsiveness of women who do and do not manifest pregnancy difficulties and have been unable to discover differences between them. Grimm (1967) could not, in her review of the pertinent literature, discover any consistent deficiency in the sexual responsiveness of women with such difficulties as infertility, prolonged labor, habitual abortion, and toxemia. She did discern a trend for frigidity to characterize women with "pernicious vomiting" during pregnancy. It should, in fairness, be added that some studies have reported positive correlations between pregnancy pathology and sexual difficulties (for example, Brown, 1962; Newton, 1955; Heinstein, 1967; Coppen, 1958), but these are in a minority. Indeed, there is even one study (Hetzel, Bruer, and Poidevin, 1961) that found an unusually high degree of "sexual satisfaction" in pregnant women with "prolonged vomiting" or "toxemia." The authors speculated that this unexpected result was caused by greater "covering up of basic dissatisfaction about their sex life" in such women. If emotional factors do play a part in pregnancy difficulties, one might have expected an important contributing factor to have been a negative orientation toward sex as well as pregnancy, which is one of its derivative resultants. The fact that the available empirical findings do not support such a view suggests that the factors that control sexual responsiveness may be quite different from those that determine how a woman copes with pregnancy. Of course, one could argue that the failure of most studies to link sexual and pregnancy variables simply reflects their inadequate methodology. This may be so; and admittedly the state of the art in this area of investigation is limited. But as things stand, the burden of proof is upon those who have theorized that sexual attitudes significantly influence pregnancy phenomena.

Breast-feeding

Does the woman who chooses to breast-feed her baby differ from the woman who selects bottle-feeding? There are popular stereotypes that would label the former as more feminine and maternal than the latter. What does the empirical literature have to say about this matter? Before considering pertinent studies, it should be noted that broad cultural conditions have, year by year, decreased the prevalence of breast-feeding. Breast-feeding is less common in urban than in rural areas, more common in certain regions of the United States than others, and complexly related to education and social class (Newton and Newton, 1967). Heinstein (1965) was so impressed with such cultural and geographic variations that he stated (p. 22):

The presence in this study and others of geographic and socioeconomic differences in the incidence and duration of breast-feeding emphasizes not only the complex nature of the cultural factors associated with the decision and undertaking of breast-feeding, but also raises grave suspicions about any categorical statements of the relationship of breast-feeding to the mother's personality or her love of the child.

Despite Heinstein's warning, one can discern some meaningful trends in the studies that have examined the relationships between psychological parameters and breast-feeding behavior.

A number of studies assert that those women who breast-feed are relatively more maternal in their orientation than those who bottle-feed. Levy and Hess (1952) interviewed 19 mothers shortly after delivery and evaluated how maternal their attitudes were in terms of such criteria as how much they had enjoyed playing with dolls, caring for children, and indulging in fantasies about becoming a mother. It was found that those judged to be most maternal were most likely to breast-feed and to display effective and considerate behavior when actually nursing their babies (as defined by observers present during nursing). Potter and Klein (1957) appraised 25 women with the same techniques used by Levy and Hess and came to similar conclusions. They likewise observed that those with high maternal scores, as determined from interviews, were particularly likely to breast-feed and to show effective motherly behavior while nursing the baby. Brown, Lieberman, Winston, and Pleshette (1960) ascertained from 110 women, late in their pregnancies, whether they were going to breast-feed or bottle-feed their babies. In addition, questionnaire information was obtained from these women concerning their attitudes toward the two forms of feeding. It was concluded that the woman who prefers breast-feeding tends to be "nurturant" and especially interested in doing what will make the baby happy. Those preferring bottle-feeding were depicted as more "narcissistic" and interested in maintaining freedom for themselves from the "taxing demands" of breast-feeding.

Niles and Niles (1962) observed the first reactions of mothers to their new babies and classified such mothers into those who were "pleased" ($N = 157$) and those who were "indifferent" or "disgusted" ($N = 72$). It was then determined that a significantly larger number of the "pleased" group were "eager to breast-feed their babies" than was true of the rejecting group. Here one sees a positive correlation between a behavioral index of positive response to the child and intent to breast-feed it.

Newton (1955) interviewed a large sample ($N = 123$) of mothers of newborn babies and obtained information about their attitudes toward many aspects of feminine functioning (menstruation, pregnancy, the role of the woman). It was found that (p. 103), "Women who do not wholeheartedly desire to breast-feed are less likely to be motherly individuals . . . they are apt to feel that childbirth is hard . . . more apt to feel men have a more satisfying time in life, and are more likely to reject children."

One may also incidentally mention a study by Call (1959), who impressionistically evaluated 104 new mothers and concluded that those choosing to breast-feed were "slightly more anxious" than those choosing to bottle-feed. However, he also concluded that those who were successful at breast-feeding were "more calm" and "motherly" than those who were unsuccessful.

One study that contradicts those just described was carried out by Sears, Maccoby, and Levin (1957), who interviewed a sample of women with regard to their child-rearing practices and could discern no support for the view that women who bottle-fed their children were any more rejecting of, or cold toward, them than were women who breast-fed. Because this study was done with unusual care and with generally better controls than those employed in the other studies just described, one must take its negative results seriously. However, one still cannot dismiss the fact that several studies did independently attribute greater nurturant and maternal attitudes to the woman who breast-feeds. This perspective should logically hold the edge until further data accumulate.

There are scattered studies that have compared women who do and do not breast-feed in terms of their responses to formal psychological tests.

Brown, Chase, and Winson (1961) administered Rorschach inkblots to 110 women late in their pregnancies and evaluated the differences in responses between those choosing and those not choosing to breast-feed. Although the results were largely of a chance order, two significant differences did emerge. First, it was found that the group choosing to breast-feed made greater use of shading as a texture quality than did the group not making this choice. The difference was interpreted to mean that those favoring breast-feeding have greater needs for affection; and this, in turn, led to the speculative formulation that they unconsciously identify with the baby who is fed and who is the recipient of a special brand of maternal affection. Presumably, they indirectly gain gratification for themselves by identifying with the baby who will be given the breast. A second difference that was found indicated that the breast-fed group was less likely than the other group to respond to the blots in a global fashion. This was interpreted to mean that they had less "oral-incorporative ambitiousness and/or masculine strivings."

Adams (1959) obtained responses to the Blacky Test from 58 women (in the last phases of their pregnancy), each of whom had indicated whether she intended to breast-feed her child. Analysis of the data indicated that (p. 146), "The bottle choice group was significantly more disturbed on orality, anal expulsiveness, positive identification, sibling rivalry, guilt feelings, positive ego ideal, and narcissism. . . . The breast choice group was significantly more disturbed on the penis envy dimension." These findings were interpreted to mean, among other things, that the bottle-choice women were more dependent, more rejecting of the child, and more jealously competitive. It was also conjectured that the higher "penis envy" score of the breast-choice group indicates that they displace their desire for a penis onto a desire for a child (as proposed by orthodox psychoanalytic theory) and therefore seek "satisfaction in the child itself." Apropos of this same matter, it was speculated that breast feeding may permit the "passive nonfunctional breasts" to become "active and functional"—that is, to acquire phallic significance that would serve to express "penis envy" wishes. Call (1959) analogously conjectured that the breasts might have the "same psychological value in the female as is attributable to the penis in the male."

Converging observations imply that sexual factors may play a role in the decision whether to breast-feed. Newson and Newson (1962) found after interviewing 700 English mothers that many avoided breast-feeding because it involved exposure of the body that violated their mores regarding sex and modesty. Salber, Stitt, and Babbott (1959) found the same to be true in a sample of American mothers. Relatedly, Sears, Maccoby, and Levin (1957) reported that mothers who breast-fed were more tolerant of sexual play and masturbation in their children. The sexual implications of nursing were described by Masters and Johnson (1966), who indicated that postpartum women who nursed seemed to have a higher level of sexual interest than those not nursing. The nursing women were more interested in resuming regular intercourse with their husbands and described the nursing experience itself as being sexually stimulating.

Probably one of the most important and informative studies of breast-feeding was designed by Winter (1969), who asked women ($N=29$) to relate Thematic Apperception (TAT) stories (into a tape recorder) while nursing their babies. She similarly asked a control group of women ($N=30$), who had completed their period of breast-feeding, to relate TAT stories while their babies were awake and nearby. Analysis of the protocols and subsequent interviews with each woman revealed differences between the nursing and nonnursing conditions. During the nursing condition there were significantly more themes pertaining to orality (for example, food), feminine masochism (pleasure themes followed or associated with deprivation or pain), and positive feeling. Also, this condition was characterized by a description of time as being out of chronological order; by fewer references to instrumental activity (that is, undertaken to achieve specific goals); and fewer references to cognitive activities ("thinking," "considering," "studying"). No differences were found between the groups in number of sexual or narcissistic themes. The absence of difference for sex themes is a bit surprising in view of the earlier mentioned observations (Masters and Johnson, 1966) that breast-feeding may be sexually arousing to women. Winter interpreted the pattern of significant differences to mean that during nursing the mother feels unusually close to, or "fused" with, the infant, filled with pleasurable feelings, and functioning at a level that minimizes formal logical thinking (secondary process). She suggests that the diffuse pleasure characterizing the nursing mother is caused by a "weakening of the sense of separateness between mother and infant." Apropos of this suggestion, one recalls that Brown, Chase, and Winson (1961) speculated on the basis of Rorschach findings that the woman who chooses breast-feeding unconsciously gets her gratification out of identifying with the nursing child.

When the women who were no longer nursing were separated by Winter into those whose TAT's conformed to the pattern typical of the actual nursing state and those whose TAT's did not so conform, it was discovered that the former reported more success in their earlier breast-feeding experience as well as a more empathic relationship with their babies. This last finding lends some support to the idea that successful breast-feeding is facilitated to some degree by warm, maternal attitudes.[33]

A provocative question raised by Winter is whether the feelings typifying the mother who is nursing may not be present in people in any situation in which they are involved in close, interpersonal situations. The nursing relationship would become, from this perspective, only a special case of intimate personal interaction in general. If so, one could perhaps most economically think of the woman who is motivated to breast-feed her baby as one who is attracted to a certain kind of intimacy and closeness that can be defined within the context "I am a good mother who is willing to give of herself."

Contraception

Contraception takes on considerable importance in a woman's life as soon as she begins to have regular sexual intercourse. Improper use of contraception may obviously have serious repercussions for her.[34] There is evidence of considerable irrationality in the way women (and men) choose and utilize contraceptives (Pohlman, 1969). Unsafe contraceptive methods are frequently chosen or there may be a neglect to employ contraception at all, despite overtly not wanting to become pregnant. Some of this irrationality stems from religious indoctrination (for example, Catholic opposition to formal contraception), some derives from being poorly educated and lacking access to proper information, and some probably represents passive, "taking a chance" behavior.[35] Rainwater (1965) has shown that contraception is least effectively practiced in those lower class families in which the husband and wife have poor communication and are characterized by a "segregated" relationship in which they "go their separate ways." Scattered and inconclusive attempts have been made to relate contraceptive behavior to other variables such as relative dominance of husband and wife (Pohlman, 1969), neuroticism (Lehfeldt and Guze, 1966), degree of personality similarity between husband and wife (Bakker and Dightman, 1964), and personality of the wife (Rodgers and Ziegler, 1968).

It is particularly pertinent to one of the prime objectives of this book to ask whether contraception plays a role in a woman's sexual responsiveness. There are frequent assertions in the literature that fear of pregnancy inhibits women and prevents them from experiencing sexual stimulation positively. Landis, Poffenberger, and Poffenberger (1950) found that women who had one child and who feared becoming pregnant again suffered sexual inhibition as a result of this anxiety. Terman (1938) reported a similar finding, as did Rainwater (1965). Ferber, Tretze, and Lewit (1966) reported an improvement in sexual responsiveness in a sample in which the fear of pregnancy was banished because the husband had had a vasectomy. These studies seem to be unanimous in their implication that inadequate contraception may arouse anxieties that will interfere with a woman's sexual responsiveness.

However, it must also be reported that an unusually well-designed study by Rodgers and Ziegler (1968), which evaluated changes in sexual behavior of one sample of couples ($N = 36$) after the husband had received a vasectomy and in another sample ($N = 22$) after the wife began using ovulation-suppressing medication for contraceptive purposes, detected no changes in sexual responsiveness as a result of the greater safety from pregnancy that had been thus provided. In both samples interview and questionnaire data were obtained just before the new contraceptive procedures were instituted and follow-up data were then secured for four years. There were no indications that the women in the two samples showed a significant increase in sexual responsiveness or frequency of intercourse as a consequence of their increased immunity from unwanted pregnancy.

One source of irrationality in contraceptive behavior derives from the fact that some contraceptives require a woman to touch and manipulate her own body, which may in turn arouse anxiety and disturbance. Metzner and Golden (1967) discovered this fact in a study involving 100 women who were systematically interviewed concerning their contraceptive practices, sexual attitudes, and so forth. The interview also probed specifically concerning the woman's attitude toward the use of intrauterine devices (IUD). It should be added that a sentence completion test (containing incomplete sentences such as, "Birth control is probably ———") was administered to each subject. The analysis of the findings pertaining to which women did and which did not favor the use of IUD's revealed a general difference between them in terms of reluctance to use any contraceptive device requiring vaginal manipulation. To a significant degree, the pro-IUD group exceeded the anti-IUD group in their past use of such vaginal techniques as diaphragm, foam, and suppository. The former group also expressed significantly more positive attitudes than the latter with regard to insertion of other objects (for example, tampons) into the vagina. They were more favorable, too, toward masturbation and sexual intercourse. One may presume, from such findings, that some women either avoid using certain contraceptives or do so in an anxious (inefficient?) manner because they require touching the vaginal area. Apropos of this point, Ellis (1959) describes a patient who owned a diaphragm that she rarely used because it required touching her genitals that were repulsive to her. Relatedly, Rainwater (1960) noted in his interviews with working-class people that they had rather distorted concepts about the consequences of using an intravaginal device such as a diaphragm. For example, they feared that it might get "lost" within the woman's body or that it might produce internal injury.[36]

Rodgers, Ziegler, Prentiss, and Martin (1965) had 50 married couples rate various contraceptive dimensions (for example, masculine versus feminine, embarrassing versus unembarrassing) and discerned, among other things, that some were perceived as masculine and others as feminine. Thus, the condom is seen as masculine and the diaphragm as feminine. One of the chief determinants of whether a device is classified as masculine or feminine is whether the man or woman has control of, and responsibility for, it. Both Rainwater (1965) and Pohlman (1969) point out the irrationality in contraceptive behavior that may arise as the result of the obligations and demands made upon either a wife or husband as a function of the "masculine" or "feminine" quality of the contraceptive they employ. A wife who uses the diaphragm may resent the burden of deciding whether to insert the diaphragm each night because it implies a decision as to whether intercourse will take place. If she delays inserting the diaphragm until its need is apparent, her husband may become angry at the delay and inconvenience occasioned by the interruption. Clearly, there is the potential for considerable misunderstanding and role conflict. If a "masculine" form of contraception is used (condom), a woman may feel particularly insecure (and therefore unresponsive) because she has no direct control over what is done and has to trust that her partner is adequately protecting her. Her partner may sense her distrust and this may in turn influence the efficiency with which he applies the contraceptive device.

Some of the factors that might possibly determine whether a contraceptive will be acceptable to a particular husband-wife pair is illustrated by the observations of Rodgers and Ziegler (1968). They studied 39 couples (by means of interview and psychological tests) prior to their use of an oral contraceptive; and subsequently followed up their behavior for four years after contraceptive use had begun. Fifteen of the couples continued to use the oral contraceptive during the four-year period; but nine discontinued without any obvious logical rationale for doing so. Rodgers and Ziegler were interested in possible differences between such "continuous" and "discontinuous" couples. They found, particularly on the basis of psychological tests (p. 588) that the "continuous women are generally more socially competent, self satisfied, and independent than are the discontinuous women"; and they obtained lower femininity scores than the discontinuous. Further, the same tests indicated (p. 589) that the husbands of the continuous women were less "concerned about avoiding criticism than are their continuous counterparts"; and also less "conscientious about fulfilling their own social role obligations." When the attributes of husband and wife were compared, it was found that the use of the oral contraceptive was most likely to be continued in a marriage in which the wife had relatively more ascendant traits. One could interpret such a finding in the context of the fact that the oral contraceptive requires the woman to take prime responsibility. She must monitor herself and make sure that she takes the pill at specific points in time. Perhaps a woman who is low in ascendancy and who avoids assuming obligations becomes uncomfortable with the burdens placed upon her by the responsible role linked with the use of an oral contraceptive.

During their study, Rodgers and Ziegler became impressed with the complex interplay of motives between a husband and wife as they seek out a form of contraception that will be acceptable to both. Although they remarked that it is usually the one who is most "conscientious" and who tends to assume "ambiguous role responsibilities" who is also most likely to take the responsibility for contraception, they pointed out other potential complications that may develop. For example, a wife may reject the use of the oral contraceptive, not because she is a person who usually tries to evade responsibility, but rather because it results in more frequent sexual relations than she prefers. She may want a form of contraception that will make her less continuously sexually available or make it possible for her to use the excuse of fear of pregnancy as a reason for limiting intercourse frequency. This motive may cause her to exaggerate the side effects of an oral contraceptive and to declare them intolerable. It should be added, by way of a note of caution, that although there were individual cases in which degree of interest in sexuality seemed to play such a part in contraceptive behavior, it was *not* possible to demonstrate in the sample studied an overall significant relationship between continuing the use of the pill and intensity of sexual interest.

Concluding Comments

A labyrinth of studies concerned with feminine behavior has been explored in the course of this literature review. Attention has been directed to what is known about the personal correlates of sexual responsiveness in women, the nature of femininity and the manner in which it becomes part of the self structure during socialization, and the role of psychological attitudes in reproductive processes. Detailed analyses of the findings pertinent to these topics have already been presented. But a few further comments of a general nature will be offered.

As one becomes acquainted with the pertinent literature bearing on femininity, it becomes difficult to accede to easy generalizations about how women adapt to the feminine role. Sweeping theories that try to explain many different aspects of feminine behavior in terms of a few major variables or vectors become suspect for their oversimplification. Theories that tie the numerous phenomena of femininity to a few concepts (for example, "penis envy" and "Oedipal conflict") cannot embrace the known data. One prime fact that has emerged from the literature analysis is that the various classes of behavior roughly grouped under the rubric of "being a woman" do not easily lend themselves to portrayal as a unified general system. That is, it seems difficult to predict from one aspect of a woman's functioning to other aspects. To know that a woman has a good "feminine identification" does not seem to tell us whether she has much or little pain during menstruation. Similarly, the way in which she experiences menstruation does not apparently predict the way in which she will experience pregnancy. Her degree of sexual responsiveness seems to tell little, if anything, about her adaptation in most other sectors of femininity. It should be added that no evidence has emerged that there exists a generalized adequacy or inadequacy of feminine adaptation. This means that adequacy of various aspects of feminine function cannot currently be spanned within concepts such as "ego strength," "maladjustment," and "neurosis." The failure to find empirical evidence of a generalized relationship between maladjustment and such variables as sexual responsiveness and menstrual discomfort stands in opposition to a massive clinical literature that declares the obverse to be true. One finds especially that psychoanalytically-oriented observers have expressed conviction in their writings that lack of sexual responsiveness is caused by some deficit in ego strength. At the moment, it is fair to say that their view is supported only by case illustrations and faith in Freudian theory. Whereas it is true that really decisive empirical studies of the issues involved have not yet been carried out, there are clearly sufficient negative findings to offer a serious challenge to long accepted assumptions. However, there are some sectors of feminine functioning in which personal disturbance does seem to be significantly involved. For example, maladjustment seems to be greater in women with symptoms of amenorrhea (cessation of menses) than in those without such symptoms. Also, anxiety has been shown to be greater in women who develop pregnancy complications than those who do not. It is pertinent too that a number of studies have been cited that suggest that if disturbing tensions and conflicts can be decreased in women, they are less likely to manifest pathology in their reproductive functions. Psychotherapy has been shown to have potential for decreasing habitual spontaneous abortion, infertility, and delivery complications. Psychological tensions and conflicts do, from this perspective, seem to participate in certain forms of disturbance in the reproductive system. Actually, the initial evidence is sufficiently good that one wonders why psychotherapeutic methods have not been more widely used to assist women with specific types of reproductive difficulties (particularly infertility and habitual spontaneous abortion).

A succession of popularly accepted beliefs about the nature of a woman's sexual responsiveness and her feminine functioning have been challenged by the information tracked down in this literature review. Consider some of the doubts and new perspectives that have presented themselves.

As already indicated, significant doubt has been cast on the idea that a woman's ability to respond to sexual stimulation is related to her "mental health" or psychological maturity. Her responsiveness does not seem to be an index of her stability or degree of neuroticism. But at the other extreme, it does not seem to be highly related to the sheer amount of practice she has had in sexual intercourse. It is true that such practice may, over a period of years, decrease considerably the likelihood that a woman will not be able to experience an orgasm at least occasionally, but it does not appear to have more than a small effect beyond this threshold level. For example, years of practice only produce a small increment in those who experience orgasm "almost always." The limited effect of sexual experience itself is matched by the finding that previous exposure to sexual trauma (sexual aggression, submission to an abortion) does not seem to influence orgasm capability. Relatedly, the experience of carrying through a pregnancy and having a child does not, either via its physiological or psychological impact, facilitate sexual responsiveness.[37] What is striking about the findings just enumerated is that a woman's sexual responsiveness seems to be influenced only to a limited extent by the amount and character of her sexual experiences or the experiences she has had with her reproductive system. Apropos of this last point, the amount of pain or discomfort a woman typically has during her menstrual period does not seem to influence her sexual responsiveness. Orgasm capacity and indices of menstrual discomfort have not been found to be consistently correlated. Thus, although a woman may associate her vagina with recurrent painful sensations, this does not seem to affect her orgasm ability.

Still another pertinent fact to consider is that few, if any, studies have been able to link a woman's sexual responsiveness with the traits or attributes of her husband. The work of Rainwater (1965), which showed that lower-class women have diminished sexual responsiveness and which attributed this deficit to their poor communication with their husbands, stands as a notable exception. Another is the Masters and Johnson (1970) clinical report that asserts, although somewhat anecdotally, that sexual responsiveness problems in a woman can only be adequately treated within the context of her relationships with her husband. One may add that banishing the partner's attributes as an influential factor in a woman's responsiveness goes against many clinical as well as common-sense observations. But if one is to honor the bulk of the existing pertinent empirical data, one has to tentatively conclude that a woman's sexual responsiveness does not seem to be primarily a function of the kind of man who is stimulating her. Whereas there is a need for much further study of this whole issue, one cannot dismiss some of the careful work that has been done (for example, by Terman, 1938, 1951) which came up with negative results.

Actually, the two most positive leads that have been uncovered concerning correlates of orgasm capacity involve social class and education. Kinsey, et al. (1953) demonstrated that orgasm capacity is positively correlated with education and social class. As suggested earlier, there are a number of different ways that one can interpret such findings. Illustratively, one might propose that the life situation of the lower-class, less-educated woman is realistically such that she has to put up with an unusual amount of chronic frustration or fatigue or disappointment or pessimism, and that this interferes with her responding adequately to sexual stimulation. Apropos of the mention of pessimism, one is reminded that in the Terman (1938, 1951) studies of orgasm correlates, it was tentatively found (in middle-class samples) that women with the least orgastic capacity were those who were most inclined to lack optimism and to have low self-confidence. Another possibility to consider is that the orgasm difference related to education level and social class membership has to do with more general training or socialization factors. That is, women who are unable to obtain higher education or who come from a lower class may have learned to perceive the world differently from those at the other extremes of these two dimensions. They may have been given quite different ideas about the meaning of sexual intercourse, for example, whether it is potentially dangerous, whether it is a proper way to enjoy the world, or whether it enhances or depreciates a woman's status in the eyes of a man. They may have learned to adopt different attitudes toward self that encompass a woman's right to be gratified, to experience her body as a source of pleasure, and to perceive an intimate relationship as one in which there is mutual satisfying exchange.

Questions have been raised by this literature review concerning conventional interpretations of how such physiological processes as menstruation and pregnancy are experienced. Although there is little doubt that most women are exposed to uncomfortable sensations during menstruation, it is also true that they come to view it as a badge of femininity which, in that sense, has positive significance. Several studies have been reviewed that indicate that women value menstruation and may derive identity security from its symbolic meaning and its regular recurrence. Empirical observation has also cast doubt on the idea that pregnancy is typically a time of great psychological crisis. Although pregnant women worry about their health, the condition of the fetus, and so forth, it is not at all clear that they are overall more psychologically upset during pregnancy than during other phases of their lives. There is, however, some indication that the immediate postdelivery period may be a time of unusual psychological vulnerability, as indicated, for example, by an increased psychosis rate. It has been proposed that the uniquely sudden radical changes (for example, decrease in body size, no longer containing a fetus within self) that accompany delivery impose intense strains on a woman's adaptive abilities. Whether a woman likes or dislikes the changes that occur, they presumably tax her because they are so much swifter than changes of such magnitude usually are. This is, of course, a speculation.

Whereas a good deal of negative evidence has been presented with regard to the role of psychological forces in shaping sexual and reproductive processes, one should keep in mind that a considerable amount of positive evidence has also been offered. Anxiety does seem to predict the likelihood of pregnancy complications. Amenorrhea is positively correlated with indicators of personal maladjustment. Motivation for, and adequacy of, breast feeding seem to be linked with certain attitudes about personal intimacy. Psychotherapy does apparently diminish habitual aborting and helps women with infertility problems. The formation of feminine identity requires certain patterns of relationship with the mother and father. There can be no doubt of the importance of psychological factors in modulating feminine adaptation. The task is to ascertain which are the most prominent in specific areas of feminine functioning.

In closing this critique, one could pontificate about the deficiencies in past studies of femininity as one can in almost any area of behavioral research that one chooses to review. However, it must be recalled that investigators in this area have labored not only under the usual technical difficulties of finding proper measures and controls but also those arising from the basically negative attitude of the culture toward studying human sexual phenomena. The obstacles to effective investigation are considerable, as one can affirm by conversations with those who have tried to study sexual functions in humans and as the present author has learned in the course of his own work concerned with sexual behavior over the last several years.

N O T E S

1. Of course, it also signals that there has been a failure to reproduce in the immediate past. Rheingold (1964) suggests that disappointment and depression may stem from this fact.

2. Deutsch (1944) speculates that the body sensations associated with menstruation may in some instances activate "birth fantasies" and be experienced unconsciously as having birth analogies.

3. Deutsch (1944) also refers to the enjoyable regressive aspects of menstruation (p. 160): "There are women who admit that the days of their menses are the most peaceful and happiest for them. They achieve complete serenity and relaxation, allow themselves to be lovingly cared for, and free themselves from their usual obligations, including those toward their own children; often in the subdued light of her warm room this mature woman feels like a baby in its mother's lap or in the cradle."

4. The positive significance attached to the act of menstruating is indirectly highlighted by the well-documented negative reactions (Rheingold, 1964; Neugarten and Kraines, 1965) that occur, when at the time of menopause, menstruation ceases. Although the disturbance aroused by menopause is complexly determined (by anxiety about aging, loss of fertility, concern about loss of body beauty), it is at least partially a direct response to the cessation of menstruation, as such.

5. Silbermann would attribute the low degree of menstrual discomfort reported by schizophrenics simply to their impaired ability to introspect and communicate. But this seems unlikely in view of so many other instances in which complaints by schizophrenics about other symptoms exceed those of neurotics and normals.

6. An interesting sidelight to this matter is the fact that Greenblatt (1940) found a particularly low incidence of dysmenorrhea among prostitutes.

7. It should be added that there are a few scattered reports that behavior therapy (Mullen, 1968) can alleviate amenorrhea. Such reports are, however, tentative and involve a small number of cases.

8. A somewhat puzzling finding by Piotrowski (1962) should be mentioned. He compared psychological attributes of women whose amenorrhea was caused by demonstrable anatomical lesions with those of women whose amenorrhea could not be

traced to such lesions. The Rorschach Inkblot test, the Thematic Apperception Test, and the Kerman Cypress Knee test were employed as psychological measures. The findings indicated that the group with "organic" amenorrhea was more anxious and dependent and less productive than the group with "psychogenic" amenorrhea. Piotrowski did not have an explanation for the direction of the results.

9. Some studies report a link between age of onset of menstruation and psychological parameters. Thus, Shipman (1964) found that those with early onset of menses were as adults conservative, uncritical in their thinking, lax, inexact, trusting of others, and group dependent; whereas he observed that those with late onset of menses were dominant, aggressive, critical in their thinking, and ready to experiment. Others have offered conflicting findings concerning the correlation between early versus late maturing and the adjustment adequacy of girls (Jones, 1949; Weatherley, 1964; Faust, 1960). The entire matter remains unsettled. It is of interest, too, that Van De Castle (1967) found that the dreams of girls with early menarche differed from those of girls with late menarche. For example, the former more often dreamed of parents, sex, and being victimized by aggression, whereas the latter more often dreamed of friendly interactions, food, and social initiative. In another paper, Van De Castle (1967) described a higher occurrence of animal dreams in late than in early menarche girls, and conjectured on the basis of other data he had collected that this difference might be caused by the greater immaturity of the late menarche girls.

10. Apropos of the more vigorous and active stance ascribed to the short flow women, it is interesting that Yalom, et al. (1968) found that long flow women exceeded short flow women in the likelihood of showing discouraged and depressive behavior in the postpartum phase.

11. His views in this respect were partially stimulated by the findings of Shanan, Brzezinski, Sulman, and Sharon (1965), who studied the menstrual behavior of a sample of girls who had recently arrived in Israel. It was found that those who were most "active" in their orientation and most determined to come directly to grips with their new environment were those most likely to develop transient amenorrhea. They also showed a trend toward more "latent anxiety."

12. Swanson and Foulkes (1968) demonstrated that the rated hostility of dream content was maximal during menstruation. This was also true of self-rated dream unpleasantness.

13. It is apropos to add that Swanson and Foulkes (1968) reported that the rated sexuality of manifest dreams is greater during menstruation than during other phases.

14. Hartmann (1966) discerned a trend for amount of dream time (as indicated by EEG and Rapid Eye Movement criteria) to be greatest during the premenstrual phase of the cycle. He speculated that this might in part be a manifestation of tensions "pressing for discharge."

15. Reynolds (1969) discovered that women inclined to experience menstrual difficulties recalled past events more favorably (in a more positive mood) during menstruation than during a nonmenstrual phase. She interpreted this finding in terms of an "adaptation level effect." It was her assumption that because the women felt so discomforted during menstruation that events that had occurred at other times seemed, *by contrast,* to have been "better" or more positive in character. However, is it possible that the more positive interpretation of past events during menstruation reflected a basically more integrated level of ego functioning?

16. Loesch and Greenberg (1962) observed with respect to a group of pregnant women who had been interviewed (p. 631): "They all noted a conscious increase in wanting to be cared for and in irritation toward the husband for not adequately fulfilling this need."

17. Lerner, Raskin, and Davis (1967) speculate interestingly concerning varied meanings that may be ascribed by the pregnant woman to her changing body (pp. 295–296): "The swelling of the abdomen may represent a new inner growth, a penis,

that makes a pregnant woman feel complete 'down below' and overcomes an existing sense of castration. She may get support and help from the idea that she has part of a man, of her husband, or father, inside her. The bodily changes occurring during pregnancy may alleviate a painful sense of emptiness, hollowness and numbness and serve as a defense against depersonalization. The swollen and full abdomen and the engorged breasts may decrease anxiety concerning bodily adequacy. . . ."

18. Klein, Potter, and Dyk (1950) found fear of death to be the most prominently mentioned of the anxieties verbalized by pregnant women while being interviewed.

19. Psychoanalytic writers stress that the fetus may, as defined by some of Freud's formulations, unconsciously represent a substitute for the loss of penis that every girl presumably fantasies during the Oedipal period. As such, its exit from the woman's body could be symbolically experienced as the loss of an important body organ.

Deutsch (1945) feels that lack of differentiation between mother and fetus plays a role in the fear of death found in pregnant women. She remarks (p. 160): "To make it the being that is outside her, the pregnant mother must deliver the child from the depths of herself, and thus she discharges herself not only of it, but with it, of herself. She loses not only it, but herself with it. This, I think, is at the bottom of that fear and foreboding of death that every pregnant woman has, and this turns the giving of life into the losing of life."

20. Interestingly, Deutsch (1945) observes that (p. 158) some neurotic women show improvement in their symptoms during pregnancy because "the anticipation of the painful and sometimes dangerous process of birth produces a discharge of guilt feelings that is favorable to their condition."

21. Greenberg, Loesch, and Lakin (1959) reported that pregnancy in unmarried women was often preceded by loss of an important object and a period of depression. They concluded (p. 308), "The pregnancies of the subjects appear to us to partially represent attempts at reinternalization of an equivalent to the object loss. . . ."

22. It is difficult to generalize too about how sexual interest and responsiveness vary during pregnancy. Masters and Johnson (1967) found that during the first three months of pregnancy there was a decline in "sexual tension" in women who had not previously had a child and no change in sexual tension in women who already had a child. During the second three months of pregnancy a large proportion of all the women showed an increased "sexual desire" and then a decrease during the last three months of pregnancy.

Kane, Lipton, and Ewing (1969), who interviewed women ($N=89$) during the last three months of pregnancy, found that a large majority reported a decline in sexual desire and orgasm capacity during the course of the pregnancy. There seemed to be no differences in the reports of those who had and had not experienced a previous pregnancy.

23. Zemlick and Watson (1953) also found that pregnant women ($N=15$) expressed more favorable attitudes postdelivery than during the pregnancy period itself.

24. It is of parenthetical interest that Epstein (1969) did not detect significant differences in the amount of unpleasant or threatening affect in the manifest content of dreams that were obtained from a sample of women during pregnancy and following delivery.

25. The potential complexity of the whole matter of pre- to postdelivery changes is pointed up by the Wohlford and Jones (1967) finding that whereas anxiety decreases in firstborns after delivery, it remains unchanged in laterborn women.

26. Nilsson and Almgren (1968) offer findings that suggest that the use of oral contraceptives during the postdelivery period may increase the likelihood of developing psychiatric disturbance during this period.

27. Klatskin and Eron (1970) did find that women who were judged to be poorly adjusted during the postpartum period gave evidence in their predelivery Rorschach

and Thematic Apperception Test protocols of being less accepting of the feminine and maternal roles than women who showed a good postpartum adjustment.

28. A potentially interesting lead concerning the factors contributing to disturbance during delivery has been provided by Levy (1969), who found such disturbance to be greatest in women who had either received no information from their mothers about childbearing or had received extremely positive or negative communications about it. The role of the mother in conveying expectations about childbearing (and the likelihood of becoming disturbed during the process) was emphasized by the findings of this study.

29. Relatedly, McDonald and Parham (1964) seem to propose that psychological difficulties linked with pregnancy derive not so much from absolute levels of given attitudes or traits as from the disequilibrium or lability produced by the changes inherent in the pregnancy process.

30. The impact of life experience upon the reproductive system has been approached in several instances through an analysis of the frequency of pregnancy in women who have been infertile but who decide to adopt a child. Speculations abound that the decision to adopt represents the resolution of a psychological conflict about motherhood that removes inhibitory forces that prevent pregnancy. Although individual dramatic instances in which this phenomenon seemed to be exemplified occur, the weight of the formal evidence is against this proposition. Systematic studies by several investigators (Weir and Weir, 1966; Aronson and Glienke, 1963; Banks, Rutherford, and Coburn, 1961; Tyler, Bonapart, and Grant, 1960) have found only a chance relationship between the decision to adopt and a change in the fertility of women. It should be added that there is one study (Sandler, 1965) that reported that the act of adopting a child facilitated conception in previously infertile women.

31. Ferreira (1965) surveyed the literature concerned with whether the mother's emotional state during pregnancy affects the state of her child. He concluded that there is solid empirical evidence that such effects occur. He states (p. 114): "Seemingly, the mother's negative attitude toward the pregnancy may be, by many different means, conveyed to the fetus and reflected in complications of the pregnancy or in the child's early deviant behavior."

32. One exception to this statement may be toxemia of pregnancy. Grimm (1967) suggests that the evidence from the empirical literature supports the idea that the woman who develops toxemia has much hostility toward her husband (and by implication the pregnancy resulting from their relationship).

33. It is a curious and perhaps related fact that two studies (Newton, 1955; Jackson, Witkin, and Auerbach, 1956) have discerned significant positive correlations between favorable attitudes toward breast-feeding in women and actual ease of delivery.

34. With the advent of oral contraceptives these repercussions may possibly involve both serious physiological and psychological symptomatology. Several investigators have now reported psychological side effects from oral contraceptives (Kane, Treadway, and Ewing, 1969; Grounds, Davies, and Mowbray, 1970; Herzberg and Coppen, 1970).

35. Pohlman (1969) states, however, that formal studies of the relationship between a woman's degree of impulsivity and her likelihood of having unwanted conceptions have shown it to be of a chance order.

36. Parenthetically, it is of interest that irrational "unconscious" motives may be important in a woman's willingness to accept, and her subsequent responses to, artificial insemination (Heiman and Kleegman, 1966). Rubin (1965) observed in a group of women who had had artificial insemination that there was anxiety about who the sperm donor was and this anxiety seemed to be tinged with a vague dread that incest barriers had been violated (that the sperm had come from a man who was too close in terms of incest taboos).

37. Sexual responsiveness is equated with orgasm capability not because the author does not realize that there are many other important experiential aspects of sexual response but rather because this is really the only variable dealt with in the existing literature.

PART II

Psychological Studies
of Sexual Behavior
and Attitudes
in Women

INTRODUCTION

The remainder of this book will offer an account of a sequence of studies undertaken by the present writer to gain further knowledge about how psychological factors influence a woman's sexual responsiveness and her adaptation to requirements of the feminine role. These studies began in a tentative, exploratory fashion and then moved on to test specific hypotheses. During their course they examined the correlations between indices of sexual responsiveness and many psychological and physiological measures. Seven major studies were completed. The fine details of the procedures and tests employed in the major studies are presented in the Appendices, where one may find outlined the specific nature of the tasks and tests employed and the order in which they were administered within individual studies.

After the major findings have been presented, they will be summarized and integrated with the material presented in Part I. In other words, they will be related to the existing literature dealing with female sexuality. An attempt will then be made to raise some fundamental questions about sexual responsiveness in women and to offer a number of new perspectives concerning this area of behavior.

It is hoped that the reader will take a cautious, questioning stance and be encouraged to ask those who would offer glib generalizations about the nature of human sexuality, "What is your evidence?" We are only beginning to explore a subject of great complexity.

6

PERSPECTIVES:

BACKGROUND IDEAS,

SAMPLES, AND MEASURING

SEXUAL RESPONSIVENESS

As indicated by the literature review in the previous section, there are actually few solid empirical findings concerning the role of psychological variables in a woman's sexual responsiveness. The sparse tentative leads that have emerged appear to be especially insubstantial when one sets out to do research in this sector. They are not only insubstantial but also disparate and not easily unified within a theoretical scheme that would be productive of hypotheses. This is certainly true of the Terman (1938, 1951) reports that were reviewed earlier. Of course, the great mass of previous findings have been negative and they are helpful to the planning of new work only insofar as they indicate areas that are unlikely to yield profit from further investigation. For example, previous published work would suggest a low probability of finding a woman's sexual responsiveness to be linked to her "mental health," her habitual level of anxiety, her physical developmental history, the attributes of her husband, the manner in which she acquired her early sexual information, and so forth. It must be confessed, though, that when the planning of studies got under way it was difficult not to include some variables (for example, physical developmental history) for consideration which, although they did not look promising in terms of earlier work, seemed sufficiently important to require additional perusal. Realistically, it may be said that the present studies did not derive in any obvious logical fashion from previous research, although attempts were made to test some of the original Terman (1938, 1951) observations. Thus, particular attention was given to checking the specific differences he discerned between the low and high orgastic on a questionnaire inventory (Bernreuter), which had been interpreted as indicating that the latter were more free, zestful, and interested in experiencing life. Previous clinical and theoretical speculations in the literature did have considerable influence on the variables finally singled out for special investigation. Many factors that are assigned importance in psychoanalytic theory as determinants of sexual responsiveness were intensively appraised. Multiple techniques were used to measure degree of anxiety and conflict about oral, anal, and genital themes that represent major stages in the Freudian developmental scheme. Attitudes and concerns that are significant in the psychoanalytic frame of reference ("Oedipal conflict," "castration anxiety") were evaluated. Relatedly, a variety of measures were used to determine basic attitudes toward the mother and father that would presumably be important within the context of Freudian theory which proposes a developmental model emphasizing the role of parent-child interaction in producing sexual inhibition. In addition, the writer attached special import to theoretical speculations in the literature (for example, Fried, 1960) highlighting the role of body attitudes in sexual behavior; and so a considerable battery of body image techniques was consistently applied throughout the sequence of studies. Another source of theoretical influence was the general proposition, current in the literature, that an adequate sense of femininity (possessing a nonconflicted sexual identity) is basic to feminine functioning; and this resulted in the inclusion of measures pertinent to feminine identity in the experimental plan. It should be added that many procedures were employed purely in an exploratory spirit, simply because they are well recognized, relatively well-validated measures of personality and value orientation, and it seemed like a good idea to ascertain how sexual responsiveness is related to them.

Measuring Sexual Responsiveness

One of the first major difficulties that arose in planning studies of sexual responsiveness was to decide how such responsiveness could best be evaluated. Had it been feasible, it would perhaps have been ideal to observe subjects in the kind of setting devised by Masters and Johnson (1966) where overt behavior during intercourse was recorded. However, this was not feasible. One can argue rather persuasively (as have a number of critics of the Masters and Johnson work) that sexual behavior and sexual attitudes are artificially distorted in a laboratory situation. For example, can a woman having intercourse on the "scientific stage" feel tenderness or other shades of emotion toward her partner that might very well be of importance in more private, naturalistic settings? Could one ask a woman having intercourse on the "scientific stage" about her experiences and be able to differentiate those caused by the strange bypassing of her privacy from those specific to sexual arousal? Of course, it would be foolish to assert that objective measures of individual variations in physiological response and other overt manifestations of emotion in a Masters and Johnson type setting would not provide useful information about the psychological aspects of sexual arousal. But in the author's view such information would be supplemental rather than primary. Another possible approach to evaluating sexual responsiveness in women is to rely chiefly on "quantity" measures such as orgasm capacity and intercourse frequency, as has been customary in most studies (Kinsey, et al., 1953; Terman, 1938, 1951). However, such quantity measures obviously tell only a part of a complex story. Just as the gourmet could never adequately convey the nature of his gustatory experiences by recounting the amount he had eaten, a woman cannot communicate how sexual stimulation affects her by reciting the frequency with which she has an orgasm. This is not to say that the occurrence of orgasm is an unimportant aspect of sexual arousal, but it is only one aspect among many. Chesser (1957) and others have reported that a sizable group of women who do not attain orgasm still derive pleasure from sexual stimulation. Sexual arousal consists, among other things, of extremely complex patterns of sensations (tickle, warmth, pressure, muscle tonus increase), and like all such sensations are capable of being described on a potentially infinite series of descriptive continua. The approach to evaluating sexual responsiveness that was taken by the writer involved securing information about both the quantitative and the qualitative aspects of naturalistic sexual experience from women in settings where they felt free to be truthful. Like all sensations, sexual arousal registers in a private experiential domain; and so information can be obtained about it only if the perceiver is willing to examine this domain and be willing to talk openly about her observations. During the course of the studies to be described, special care was taken to create conditions under which the participating women would be motivated to scan their past sexual experiences carefully and to feel sufficient trust in those dealing with them to report their perceptions with minimal censorship or distortion.

The Samples and Their Recruitment

It would be well at this point to provide a detailed description of how women were recruited to participate in the studies and what was done to win their confidence. The first step in recruitment was to place an advertisement in the Syracuse University student newspaper that offered $50 to married women (with at least a high school education) in the 21–45 age range to participate in an experiment concerned with "reproductive and menstrual functioning." [1] Participation was limited to married women in order to be certain that subjects would have had ample opportunity for sexual experience and were currently engaging in regular intercourse. The requirement of a high school education was introduced because many of the experimental procedures called for a fair degree of literacy and verbal fluency. An age restriction was imposed so as to control for possible physiological effects related to aging. It is important to note that the advertisement placed in the newspaper made no direct mention of the fact that the study was concerned with sexual behavior. Subjects were explicitly told about the fact that they would be asked about their sexual behavior only after they had telephoned for an appointment and actually come in for an appointment to discuss the study. They were given the opportunity at that point to withdraw. About 10 percent of those who responded did withdraw. This general recruiting strategy was adopted in order to minimize biasing the samples with women who might, for their own reasons, be attracted to participating in a "sex study." As seen in data to be presented at a later point, a wide range of personalities was, indeed, obtained. For what it is worth, one may mention that the staff members in the laboratory who worked with the subjects were impressed with their diversity. There were the tense, the relaxed, the loud, the quiet, the shy, the exhibitionistic, the dull, the creative, the warm, and the cold. A great many participated primarily for the rather substantial financial remuneration, some came for the adventure, some were secretly looking for help for family and sexual problems, some volunteered because a close friend who had decided to participate persuaded them to do so, and some were genuinely altruistic in their desire to help a scientific enterprise.[2] Speaking impressionistically, the writer would say that the two prime motivations were, first of all, financial and, secondly, the wish to do something novel and exciting. It must be emphasized that although efforts were made to eliminate certain kinds of biased selectivity in the recruitment of subjects, there was obviously no intent to obtain a sample that was representative of the average American woman. As described shortly, the women in the samples collected were more educated than average, their husbands were predominantly students (55–70 percent) and eventually would attain high social status; they included only one black, and were largely Protestant in religious affiliation.[3] It would, of course, have been ideal if truly representative samples could have been recruited, but to do so was beyond the resources of the laboratory in which the research was undertaken. The more modest goal was set at studying sexual responsiveness in women living in a small segment of the culture. No claims will be made concerning the generality of the findings that emerged from this segment. Future work will decide this question.

Details concerning the characteristics of the samples that participated in the studies are presented as follows:

Table 6–1 indicates that the women in the samples were largely in their early or middle twenties. One can see that they averaged about two to three years of college education. They had generally been married about two or three years, and were typified by having one child or less. About 35 to 45 percent of most samples were Protestant, about 20 to 30 percent were Catholic; and from 0 to 20 percent were Jewish. A sizable percent (14–30) in each sample declared that they had no religious affiliation. There were one black and no Orientals in the samples. Using the same scheme as that employed by Kinsey, et al. (1953) to classify the occupational class of the parental homes from which the

TABLE 6-1
Characteristics of the Samples

Samples	Age		Education		Years Married		No. Children	
	M	σ	M	σ	M	σ	M	σ
1 (N = 42)	25.9	4.6	14.0	1.8	5.9	3.8	1.9	1.4
2 (N = 41)	27.4	5.4	14.8	1.9	5.7	4.9	1.7	1.3
3 (N = 43)	24.5	3.3	15.4	1.5	3.4	3.2	1.0	1.3
4 (N = 40)	23.1	3.2	15.3	1.7	1.9	2.0	.4	.7
5 (N = 30)	22.8	3.0	14.6	1.8	2.7	2.6	.6	.8
6[a] (N = 49)	24.6	2.7	15.1	1.8	3.3	2.6	.4	.7
7 (N = 40)	23.7	2.8	15.8	1.8	1.7	2.0	.2	.6
Total Average	24.6	3.6	15.0	1.8	3.5	3.0	.9	1.0

Samples	Religious Affiliation				
	% Protestant	% Catholic	% Jewish	% Special[b]	% None[c]
1 (N = 42)	59.3	23.8	0	2.3	14.2
2 (N = 43)[d]	46.5	30.2	4.6	2.3	16.2
3 (N = 42)	40.4	23.8	14.2	2.3	19.0
4 (N = 39)	35.8	28.2	15.3	2.5	17.9
5 (N = 30)	33.3	30.0	6.6	3.3	26.6
6 (N = 49)	38.7	20.4	16.0	0	24.4
7 (N = 40)	30.0	17.5	20.0	2.5	30.0
Total Average	41.0	24.5	11.2	2.1	21.0

[a]This sample consisted of pregnant women who were seen once during the pregnancy and again a month postdelivery.
[b]This category includes special, rare sects (for example, Bahais).
[c]This category consists of all persons who indicated they had no religious affiliation.
[d]Changes in sample size are caused by the fact that subjects sometimes did not answer a specific question or gave ambiguous unscorable replies. Such variations in sample size are common as different questionnaires and test scores are considered. They will not be specifically noted unless they are extreme in character.

women in their samples came, it was found that the average level (about 5.6) in the present samples was roughly midway between what is called "the lower white-collar group" and the "upper white-collar group."[4] Variations in age and education were not great among the samples.[5] The largest differences occurred for number of years married and number of children. One notes a trend for variability to decrease from earlier to later samples with regard to several of the attributes (for example, age, number of children). This was caused by the fact that the age range was deliberately limited to a greater extent as the studies evolved.

About 50 to 67 percent of the women in each sample were using an oral contraceptive as their mode of contraception. This is mentioned to provide a context against which to interpret other information about reproductive and menstrual functions described in the next several chapters.

When a potential subject came to the laboratory to inquire in detail concerning what would be expected of her, a standard explanation was offered that particularly focused on the fact that questions would be asked concerning her sexual behavior and attitudes. It is estimated that of all subjects who reached the stage of making detailed inquiry about the project, about 90 percent decided to participate. The women were told explicitly at the time they first inquired concerning the study and at the time they first came to the laboratory that all information they would give would be treated with the highest confidentiality. Furthermore, except in a few of the later studies, no questions concerning sexual behavior were asked until the women had spent at least three hours in the laboratory and had a chance to develop a sense of security in the situation. The technicians who administered the various tasks and questionnaires to them were typically women (although a few men were also involved) in the 20–40 age range with several years of college. With rare exceptions, the technicians were able to establish excellent, friendly relationships. There is little question that good rapport was, on the average, established with the women. They showed up for appointments on time, were obviously serious and thoughtful in their answers to inquiries, and acted friendly and cooperative. The best demonstration of their cooperative attitude was supplied when, at times subsequent to the completion of two of the projects, it was decided to obtain further information from them. When they were called and asked to fill out new questionnaires or to come to the laboratory for additional interviews, 90 percent of those still residing in the area readily agreed to do so. One of the most significant demonstrations of the reliability of the information obtained from the women was the fact that when a sizable number were asked to return for a series of intensive depth interviews (often involving several sessions and about five to seven hours of time), the information that emerged was consistently congruent with what they had revealed in their answers to formal questionnaires in the laboratory situation.[6] Actually, it became apparent in the course of the first study undertaken that the women were ready and willing to reveal more information about their sexual behavior than the investigators had intended obtaining. The original inquiries directed to the women were a bit timid and there were topics (for example, masturbation, details of intercourse behavior) that were avoided because it was thought they might be too threatening. However, many of the women spontaneously offered information and elaborations to questions that indicated that they were not only not threatened by sexual topics but eager to present detailed information about their sexual feelings and responses. There were a number of instances in which women spontaneously related facts pertaining to premarital and extramarital intercourse that they indicated they had never revealed to their husbands. Such occurrences encouraged the writer in the studies that followed to expand the range of inquiry about sexual behavior.

Sexual Information Obtained

The questionnaires used to obtain information about sexual behavior are presented in Appendices J and K. The women were asked to provide information about the following general topics: intercourse frequency, orgasm capacity, preference for clitoral versus vaginal stimulation, preferences with regard to foreplay stimulation of various body areas (for example, breasts), quality of the experience during orgasm, quality of the subjective state subsequent to orgasm, masturbation, techniques of intercourse, early sexual experiences, attitudes about nudity, attitudes about sexual freedom, nature of physiological changes during sexual arousal (for example, amount of vaginal lubrication produced), and importance of sex as compared to other activities.

Many of the items dealing with sexual behavior were taken directly from questionnaires used by previous investigators and others were suggested by comments and observations in the literature.

Among the various questions concerned with sexual response, there were several that were considered to be of prime importance; they will be highlighted in the presentation of the results.

1. Since so much of the literature has focused on ability to attain orgasm, the woman's self-rating with respect to this variable was given primary attention. As indicated in Appendix J, the women were asked to respond to the following format:

> Circle the number that best completes the following statement as it applies to you:
> During intercourse I experience orgasm:
> Always   Nearly always   Frequently   Occasionally   Rarely   Never
> 1   2   3   4   5   6

2. Another primary variable was intercourse frequency. The women indicated their frequency in terms of the following format:

> What is your average frequency of intercourse per week?
> More 7   10   9   8   7   6   5   4   3   2   1   0

3. A third primary variable involved the degree to which the women depended upon "clitoral" as compared to "vaginal" stimulation to attain orgasm. They rated themselves with reference to the following format:

> This question concerns the relative importance of clitoral as compared to vaginal stimulation in your attaining orgasm. Put a circle around the appropriate letter.
> A. Clitoral stimulation contributes much more than vaginal stimulation.
> B. Clitoral stimulation contributes somewhat more than vaginal stimulation.
> C. Clitoral stimulation contributes a little more than vaginal stimulation.
> D. Vaginal stimulation and clitoral stimulation make an equal contribution.

E. Vaginal stimulation contributes a little more than clitoral stimulation.

F. Vaginal stimulation contributes somewhat more than clitoral stimulation.

G. Vaginal stimulation contributes much more than clitoral stimulation.

4. A fourth major measure was concerned with the *quality* of the individual's experience during and after orgasm. The women were asked to rank order the following ten terms with reference to the degree to which they were descriptive of their feelings during orgasm:

_____ Strange	_____ Ecstatic	_____ Slightly Embarrassed
_____ Happy	_____ Tense	_____ Weak	_____ Tired
_____ Unsatisfied	_____ As if I would burst	_____ Not like myself

They were also asked to rank order the following ten terms with reference to how applicable they were to their feelings five minutes *after* the attainment of orgasm.

_____ Not like myself	_____ Satisfied	_____ Happy
_____ Weak	_____ Tense	_____ Unsatisfied	_____ Tired
_____ Relaxed	_____ Slightly Embarrassed	_____ Slightly Guilty

[The terms "satisfied" and "unsatisfied" were both included as a check on the consistency of the individual's rankings.]

As part of an effort to ascertain how openly and honestly the women responded to the sexual and the other questionnaires that were administered to them, two indices from the Minnesota Multiphasic Personality Inventory (Dahlstrom and Welsh, 1960) were employed. The first was the K scale, which is designed to evaluate how intent the individual is in making a good impression and denying negative or socially undesirable aspects of self. A second was the L scale, which similarly evaluates the degree to which the individual is motivated to deny possessing negative qualities (for example, bad thoughts, lack of control).

Table 6–2 shows the correlations of each of these scores with four measures of sexual responsiveness that might be considered to be particularly vulnerable to the effects of biased or defensive attitudes. One can see that only two of the entire matrix of 48 correlations attain statistical significance. It may be added that K and L are similarly not consistently correlated with a wide variety of other indices based on the women's responses to questions about their sexual behavior. It can be said, then, that insofar as the K and L scales are valid measures of response defensiveness, there is no evidence that the women participating in the various studies were usually responding to the questionnaires in a deceptive or self-protective manner.

It provides some perspective on the nature of the sexual information obtained from the women in the various samples to compare these data with those reported in the large-scale Kinsey, et al. (1953) study. Table 6–3 indicates the estimated intercourse frequency per week in each of the seven samples. These means range from 2.8 to 4.8 and the median of the seven is 3.4. This value does not differ greatly from the mean of 3.0 per week found by Kinsey, et al. in a comparable age group. Data from the present

TABLE 6-2

Correlations of Measures of Response Defensiveness (K and L)
with Sexual Responsiveness Measures

Sample		Orgasm Consistency	Actual Intercourse Frequency	Preferred Intercourse Frequency	Clitoral vs. Vaginal Preference
1 (N = 35)[a]	K vs.	−.08	−.05	−.15	−.04
	L vs.	.00	−.02	.28	−.06
2 (N = 41)	K vs.	−.13	−.09	−.28	.04
	L vs.	.04	−.27	−.06	.00
3 (N = 39)	K vs.	−.15	−.02	.12	.04
	L vs.	−.46[b]	.11	.01	−.03
4 (N = 40)	K vs.	−.19	−.01	−.09	.10
	L vs.	−.27	.11	.02	−.26
5 (N = 30)	K vs.	−.12	.04	.07	−.15
	L vs.	−.13	.35[b]	.26	−.12
6 (N = 45)	K vs.	−.09	−.06	.06	.17
	L vs.	.00	−.02	−.12	.21
7 (N = 36)	K vs.	−.31	.09	−.03	−.26
	L vs.	.00	−.17	−.03	−.11

[a]It should be repeated again that variations in N for a given sample as different scores are considered are a function of the fact that subjects either did not answer certain questions or gave unscorable responses.
[b]Significant at .05 level or better.

study concerned with ability to attain orgasm may also be considered with reference to the Kinsey, et al. (1953) findings.

Table 6–4 indicates that among the seven samples there was a range from 31–50 percent of those indicating that they experience orgasm always or nearly always. The median of these means is 38 percent. In the Kinsey, et al. data the roughly comparable value was 42 percent. The analogous value in the large-scale Terman (1951) study of well-educated women was 44 percent. Further, Table 6–4 shows that the range over the seven samples of those reporting never experiencing orgasm was 0–14.

TABLE 6-3

Intercourse Frequency in the Various Samples

Sample	Intercourse Frequency per Week	
	M	σ
1 (N = 37)	2.8	1.8
2 (N = 41)	3.8	2.3
3 (N = 43)	3.3	1.6
4 (N = 40)	4.6	2.4
5 (N = 30)	3.8	2.2
6 (N = 47)	3.4	1.9
7 (N = 40)	4.8	1.8

TABLE 6-4

*Percentages of Women Attaining Orgasm
with High Consistency and Never*

Sample	Always or Nearly Always	Never
1 (N = 42)	50	14
2 (N = 46)	39	13
3 (N = 44)	41	5
4 (N = 40)	31	0
5 (N = 30)	37	0
6 (N = 48)	37	8
7 (N = 36)	38	0

The median of the means is 5 percent. The roughly comparable value in the Kinsey, et al. data was 15 percent. In the Terman (1951) study this "never" category encompassed 8 percent of the sample. Therefore, it seems fair to say that with respect to certain aspects of their sexual behavior, the present samples are not grossly different from those seen at equivalent age levels in much larger scale studies containing relatively more representative samples.

N O T E S

1. In later studies the age range was 18–30. Also, fees paid to subjects were somewhat reduced in subsequent samples.

2. The small number recruited in this fashion did, of course, know that the study was primarily concerned with sexual behavior. However, it is reassuring that Diamant (1970), Siegman (1956), and Martin and Marcuse (1958) have not found substantial personality differences between persons who volunteer for a "sex study" and those who do not.

3. It should be noted, though, that the samples are very similar in many ways to those employed in previous major studies concerned with sexual responsiveness in women (for example, Terman, 1938, 1951; Thomason, 1951; Reevy, 1954).

4. Kinsey, et al. include small businessmen and clerical workers in the lower white-collar group. In the upper white-collar group they include persons in "more responsible, administrative white collar positions."

5. An analysis of replies to a question concerning how the "facts of life" had been first learned indicated that the majority of the women had obtained their initial sex education from books, mother, and girlfriends. Surprisingly, books were mentioned more often than any other source.

6. If one accepts as a criterion of accuracy of sexual information obtained from subjects by interview or questionnaire the amount of agreement between husbands and wives, one may conclude from several previous studies (for example, Kinsey, et al., 1953) that accurate information can indeed be obtained. Whereas there are small systematic differences in husband and wife reports of such behaviors as intercourse frequency, one is more impressed with the amount of agreement.

7. A value greater than 10 was coded as 11. Values greater than 10 were extremely rare.

7

PSYCHOLOGICAL DIMENSIONS

OF SEXUAL RESPONSIVENESS

AND ORGASM

This chapter is devoted to two major objectives: to ascertain the nature of some of the sensory and psychological experiences that occur during sexual stimulation and orgasm; and to explore the manner in which different aspects of a woman's sexual responsiveness are related or organized with reference to each other. This means considering the question whether each individual shows generalized consistency in her ways of responding to sexual stimulation or whether different aspects of sexual responsiveness are relatively independent of each other.

A variety of inquiries were directed to the women participating in the study that were designed to find out how they experience sexual arousal and orgasm. Let us now appraise the norm patterns of sexual response which were found in the seven samples.

SENSORY AND ORGASTIC EXPERIENCES

Foreplay

The first phase of sexual arousal occurs prior to onset of intercourse. This is the so-called period of foreplay. Kinsey, et al. (1953) and others have described the repertory (for example, deep kissing) that the male uses during this period to excite a woman (and she to excite him). One of the requests made of the women in the several samples was to describe how aroused different areas of their bodies became during foreplay. They were asked to rank the following body areas in terms of their degree of response to foreplay stimulation: breasts, outside lips of vulva, inside lips of vulva, vagina near clitoris, clitoris, and inside vagina. Each of these terms was precisely defined so that the women would clearly understand its meaning.[1]

As shown in Table 7-1, foreplay was rated as producing greatest excitement directly in the clitoris and least excitement in the outside lips of the vulva. The remaining body areas were rated in the following sequence (proceeding from greater to lesser excitement): vagina near clitoris, inside lips of vulva, inside vagina, and breasts. It is striking how relatively constant the ratings were from sample to sample. In all samples the "clitoris"

TABLE 7-1

Relative Excitement Experienced in Various Body Areas during Lovemaking and before Beginning Intercourse (Rank 1 = greatest excitement)

	Sample 1		Sample 2 (N = 38)[b]		Sample 3 (N = 43)		Sample 4 (N = 40)		Sample 5 (N = 30)		Sample 6		Sample 7 (N = 40)	
	M	σ	M	σ	M	σ	M	σ	M	σ	M	σ	M	σ
Clitoris	—[a]	—	2.0	1.4	2.5	1.6	2.2	1.3	2.8	1.6	—[a]	—	1.8	1.2
Vagina near clitoris	—	—	2.8	1.3	2.7	1.1	2.7	1.4	2.7	1.3	—	—	2.6	1.1
Inside lips of vulva	—	—	3.8	1.3	3.5	1.5	3.4	1.5	3.7	1.3	—	—	3.6	1.1
Inside vagina	—	—	4.0	1.8	3.8	1.8	3.9	1.5	3.3	1.8	—	—	4.2	1.6
Breasts	—	—	3.8	1.6	3.9	1.7	4.2	1.8	4.0	1.9	—	—	4.2	1.9
Outside lips of vulva	—	—	4.6	1.5	4.6	1.4	4.6	1.4	4.6	1.4	—	—	4.5	1.2

[a]This question was not asked in Samples 1 and 6.
[b]The size of each specific sample will occasionally fluctuate in succeeding tables because there are instances in which subjects either did not answer a question or did so in such a fashion that it could not be scored.

and "vagina near clitoris" were designated as the most excited of all areas. Also, "outside lips of vulva" was usually designated as the least excited. One notes too how relatively low is the excitement attributed to the "inside of vagina" in all of the samples. The fact that high excitement is ascribed to the clitoris and low arousal to the vagina is nicely congruent with the observations of Kinsey, et al. (1953) and Masters and Johnson (1966) that the vagina is relatively low in its sensory arousability, with just the opposite holding true for the clitoris. Note too that the finding that more excitement is experienced in the inside than the outside lips of the vulva fits with the apparently greater emphasis placed by Masters and Johnson on the changes in the labia minora as compared to those in the labia majora during sexual stimulation.

Another aspect of foreplay that was appraised concerned the amount of time typically devoted to it.[2] One can see in Table 7–2 that the mean times in the various samples range from approximately 11 to 16 minutes, with 12.5 being the median of the six means. Again it is striking how relatively constant the values are across samples. In the subculture from which the samples were taken there seems to be a convergence of conditions and expectations that results in a fairly standardized definition of what is a proper time period for foreplay. It is interesting to compare the foreplay time values in the present samples with those cited by Kinsey, et al. (1953). In the Kinsey, et al. sample it was found that foreplay was of 0–3 minutes duration for 11 percent; 4–10 minutes for 36 percent; 11–20 minutes for 31 percent; and 21 minutes or more for 22 percent; whereas in the present samples, the approximate corresponding values were 4, 50, 37, and 8 percents. The most obvious difference between the two sets of values is the greater occurrence of very low (0–3 minutes) and very high

(21 minutes or more) foreplay durations in the Kinsey, et al. data. About half of the women in the present samples indicated that their foreplay involved from 4–10 minutes. It was similarly true that a sizable percent of the Kinsey, et al. sample fell into this category. As noted by Kinsey, et al., the effort devoted by married couples to foreplay is generally brief and perfunctory.[2] In addition, they could find no relationship between length of foreplay and probability of attaining orgasm in the female.[3] This observation, as shown in greater detail later, also applies to the results obtained by the present writer.

TABLE 7-2
Minutes of Foreplay before Beginning Intercourse

	Sample 1	Sample 2 (N = 40)	Sample 3 (N = 41)	Sample 4 (N = 40)	Sample 5 (N = 28)	Sample 6 (N = 39)	Sample 7 (N = 39)
M	—[a]	11.7	14.0	12.5	11.4	15.7	15.6
σ	—	9.8	8.2	7.0	6.3	6.6	9.4

[a]This question was not asked in Sample 1.

Preferred Intercourse Frequency

Information was also collected about how the women in the various samples felt about the frequency with which they engaged in intercourse.[4]

Table 7–3 indicates that the average preference was for three to four intercourse contacts per week. This level of preference is higher than that observed in previous studies (Terman, 1938). One can see in Tables 7–4 and 7–5 that typically the women felt that their actual amount of intercourse per week did not really differ from their preferred amount; but they did indicate that they perceived their husbands as preferring about one more intercourse contact per week than they preferred.[5] In general, the picture that emerges is one of relative satisfaction on the part of these women with the amount of intercourse they experience.[6]

TABLE 7-3
Wife's Preferred Frequency of Intercourse per Week

	Sample 1 (N = 42)	Sample 2 (N = 41)	Sample 3 (N = 43)	Sample 4 (N = 40)	Sample 5 (N = 30)	Sample 6 (N = 47)	Sample 7 (N = 40)
M	3.1	3.9	3.3	4.3	3.5	3.3	5.0
σ	1.7	1.7	1.5	1.7	1.5	1.6	1.7

TABLE 7-4

Wife's Preferred Frequency of Intercourse
(per Week) Minus Actual Frequency

	Sample 1 (N = 37)	Sample 2 (N = 41)	Sample 3 (N = 43)	Sample 4 (N = 40)	Sample 5 (N = 30)	Sample 6 (N = 47)	Sample 7 (N = 40)
M	.3	.1	0	−.3	−.3	−.1	.2

TABLE 7-5

Husband's Preferred Intercourse Frequency per Week (As
Perceived by Wife) Minus Wife's Preferred Frequency

	Sample 1 (N = 37)	Sample 2 (N = 41)	Sample 3 (N = 43)	Sample 4 (N = 40)	Sample 5 (N = 30)	Sample 6 (N = 46)	Sample 7 (N = 40)
M	.9[a]	1.1	.7	1.3	.7	1.4	.8
σ	2.1	2.4	1.5	1.5	1.3	1.7	2.0

[a]A positive value means that the wife perceives her husband as preferring more intercourse per week than she does.

Sexual Responsiveness

How do the women feel about their own responsiveness to sexual stimulation? Table 7–6 indicates that in all of the samples the trend was to feel that one was slightly above average in this respect. Further, as Tables 7–7 through 7–9 indicate, the average woman across samples indicated that she rarely experienced pain during intercourse, rarely feared injury from intercourse, and almost never worried about getting pregnant during intercourse. That is, there was a minimizing of any of the negative or potentially threatening aspects of intercourse that are often mentioned in the clinical literature. However, this is not to deny that there were extreme

TABLE 7-6

Self-Rating of Sexual Responsiveness

	Sample 1 (N = 42)	Sample 2 (N = 41)	Sample 3 (N = 43)	Sample 4 (N = 40)	Sample 5 (N = 30)	Sample 6 (N = 47)	Sample 7 (N = 40)
M	2.7	2.6	2.4	2.5	2.3	2.8	2.4
σ	1.2	1.3	.8	.9	.8	1.0	1.0

Scale: 1 = Much above average; 2 = Above average; 3 = Average; 4 = Slightly below average; 5 = Considerably below average.

TABLE 7-7

Frequency of Pain during Intercourse

	Sample 1	Sample 2 (N = 41)	Sample 3 (N = 43)	Sample 4 (N = 40)	Sample 5 (N = 30)	Sample 6 (N = 47)	Sample 7 (N = 40)
M	—[a]	1.6	1.6	1.9	1.5	1.7	1.7
σ	—	.7	.7	.7	.5	.6	.6

Scale: 1 = Never; 2 = Occasionally; 3 = Often; 4 = Always.
[a]This question was not asked in Sample 1.

TABLE 7-8

Fear of Injury during Intercourse

	Sample 1	Sample 2	Sample 3 (N = 43)	Sample 4 (N = 40)	Sample 5 (N = 30)	Sample 6 (N = 42)	Sample 7 (N = 40)
M	—[a]	—[a]	1.5	1.7	1.5	1.5	1.7
σ	—	—	.7	1.0	.7	.7	.9

Scale: 1 = Never; 2 = On rare occasions; 3 = Sometimes; 4 = Often; 5 = Usually.
[a]This question was not asked in Samples 1 and 2.

TABLE 7-9

Worry about Pregnancy during Intercourse

	Sample 1	Sample 2	Sample 3 (N = 43)	Sample 4 (N = 40)	Sample 5 (N = 30)	Sample 6 (N = 42)	Sample 7 (N = 40)
M	—[a]	—[a]	1.4	1.6	1.4	1.5	1.4
σ	—	—	.7	.8	.5	.7	.6

Scale: 1 = Never; 2 = Occasionally; 3 = Frequently; 4 = Almost always.
[a]This question was not asked in Samples 1 and 2.

cases in all samples that were characterized by complaints of high anxiety and chronic pain sensations during intercourse.

Orgasm

When the women were asked to report on the consistency with which they attained orgasm, it became evident that a fairly large segment were limited in this respect. As already described earlier, many other investigators (Kinsey, et al., 1953; Terman, 1938) have also observed difficulty in attaining orgasm to be very common in women. Table 7–10 shows that the average woman across the seven samples stated that she attains orgasm "Frequently." Only about 39 percent (as described in Table 6–4) of the

TABLE 7-10
Reported Consistency of Orgasm

	Sample 1 (N = 42)	Sample 2 (N = 41)	Sample 3 (N = 43)	Sample 4 (N = 40)	Sample 5 (N = 30)	Sample 6 (N = 48)	Sample 7 (N = 36) [b]
M	3.1	3.2	3.1	3.3	2.9	3.2	3.0
σ	1.6	1.6	1.3	1.1	1.0	1.3	1.1

Scale: 1 = Always; 2 = Nearly always; 3 = Frequently; 4 = Occasionally; 5 = Rarely; 6 = Never.[a]

[a]Note particularly that a high numerical rating indicates low-orgasmic consistency.
[b]Four women who misunderstood the instructions with regard to this question are not included.

women indicated that they achieve orgasm "Always" or "Nearly always." In other words, for as much as 60 percent of the women orgasm does not occur consistently. About 5 or 6 percent have never experienced orgasm at all. It is pertinent to note in Table 7–11 that the average woman in the

TABLE 7-11
Time Elapsed in Marriage before Attaining First Orgasm

	Sample 1	Sample 2 (N = 39)	Sample 3 (N = 41)	Sample 4 (N = 39)	Sample 5 (N = 30)	Sample 6	Sample 7 (N = 40)
M	—[a]	3.3	2.3	2.0	1.6	—[a]	2.9
σ	—	2.9	2.2	1.7	1.3	—	2.6

Scale: 1 = Within 1 month; 2 = 2 months; 3 = 3 months; 4 = 4 to 6 months; 5 = 7 to 11 months; 6 = One year; 7 = Later; 8 = Have never had one.
[a]This question was not asked in Samples 1 and 6.

present studies attained her first marital orgasm within slightly more than two months of marriage. This is roughly comparable to the Kinsey, et al. (1953) observation that 55 percent of their sample attained first marital orgasm by the end of the second month of marriage. Looking negatively at such findings, one could comment upon the apparent difficulties so many women experience in attaining orgasm. About half of the women studied did not achieve even one orgasm during their first two months of marriage despite the fact that intercourse rates are usually very high during this period. In the Kinsey, et al. data, even after three months of marital "practice" about 41 percent of married women had not yet attained their first orgasm. These data revealed too that after 11 months of practice only 20 percent more women (69 percent) had managed to attain their first orgasm than had during the first month (49 percent) of marriage.

It should be added at this point that although the average women in the various samples of the present study did not attain orgasm consistently, there was good evidence that they did enjoy sexual interaction. As shown in Table 7–12, when the women were asked how much gratification they obtain from sex, the average response fell close to the category "Highly

TABLE 7-12

Gratification Received from Sex

	Sample 1	Sample 2 (N = 41)	Sample 3 (N = 43)	Sample 4 (N = 40)	Sample 5 (N = 30)	Sample 6 (N = 42)	Sample 7 (N = 40)
M	—[a]	4.2	3.8	3.7	3.7	4.0	3.9
σ	—	1.2	.6	.6	.8	.6	.6

Scale: 1 = Least gratifying of life experiences; 2 = Slightly gratifying; 3 = Moderately gratifying; 4 = Highly gratifying; 5 = Most gratifying of life experiences.
[a]This question was not asked in Sample 1.

gratifying." Similarly, as shown in Table 7–13 when two samples of the women were asked to indicate how much they preferred a series of seven activities (for example, sexual intercourse, eating, talking to friends, watching television), they designated sexual intercourse as their first choice. However, one may add that the second choice, "talking to friends," was a close second (not statistically significantly different from the first choice in Sample 6 but significant in Sample 7). Additional information about the importance of sex to the women in the various samples was sup-

TABLE 7-13

Rank Order of Enjoyment of Various Life Activities

Life Activities	Sample 5 (N = 30)		Sample 7 (N = 37)	
	M	σ	M	σ
Sexual intercourse	2.1	1.2	1.8	1.1
Talking to friends	2.7	1.4	2.8	1.4
Eating	3.4	1.2	2.9	1.2
Sleeping	3.7	1.6	4.0	1.7
Sports	4.4	2.1	4.8	1.8
Watching television	5.4	1.5	5.5	.9
Drinking alcoholic beverages	6.2	1.1	6.0	1.2

plied (as shown in Table 7–14) when they were asked how frequently they think about sex. The average response was just short of the "Often" category. Apparently, sexual themes are not an inconsequential part of the stream of thought of these women.

A serious attempt was made to find out from the women more than is presently known about the character of the experiences linked with orgasm itself. A range of questions were asked to elicit some of the basic experiential elements of what occurs subjectively in relation to orgasm. Some anecdotal information about the subjective aspects of sexual response in women is to be found in the Kinsey, et al. (1953) and the Masters and

TABLE 7-14
Frequency Think about Sex

	Sample 1	Sample 2 (N = 41)	Sample 3 (N = 43)	Sample 4 (N = 40)	Sample 5 (N = 30)	Sample 6 (N = 42)	Sample 7 (N = 40)
M	—[a]	3.0	2.8	2.8	2.7	2.6	3.3
σ	—	1.1	.8	.7	.8	.7	.8

Scale: 1 = Almost never; 2 = Once in a while; 3 = Often; 4 = Very often; 5 = A large part of the time.
[a]This question was not asked in Sample 1.

Johnson (1966) volumes, but little is known in terms of systematically processed information.

One approach in the present study to analyzing the experiential aspect of orgasm was to ask for ratings of the manner in which sexual excitement builds up and dissipates (see Table 7–15). Each woman was asked to rate her orgasm experience on a five-point scale ranging from "The excitement rises and then dies gradually" to "Excitement reaches such a high level that release is accompanied by collapse (possibly a faint)." [7] The average

TABLE 7-15
Manner in Which Orgasm Experienced

	Sample 1	Sample 2 (N = 37)	Sample 3 (N = 41)	Sample 4 (N = 39)	Sample 5 (N = 30)	Sample 6	Sample 7 (N = 38)
M	—[a]	2.6	2.5	2.2	2.2	—[a]	1.9
σ	—	1.1	1.0	1.1	1.0	—	.8

Scale: 1 = Excitement rises and then dies gradually.
2 = Excitement mounts to a high tension followed by sudden release.
3 = Excitement rises steadily to a condition of rigidity, followed by a very strong or cataclysmic release.
4 = Excitement increases to a point where release is accompanied by spasms or convulsions.
5 = Excitement reaches such a high level that release is accompanied by collapse (possibly a faint).
[a]This question was not asked in Samples 1 and 6.

in five samples that completed this rating was closest to the second of the five categories (namely, "Excitement mounts to a high tension followed by sudden release"). Examination of the percents of women endorsing each of the five rating categories is informative. Only about 1 to 2 percent indicated that they experience orgasm with the extreme intensity of excitement defined by the fifth point on the rating scale; but about 5 percent did rather consistently endorse the fourth rating alternative ("Excitement increases to a point where release is accompanied by spasms or convulsions").

The women in five of the seven samples were, in addition, requested to rate directly the strength of their orgasm (see Table 7–16). The typical judgment was that it fell beyond the midpoint of the five-point scale (about halfway between "strong" and "quite strong").[8] Relative to the matter of the excitement generated by intercourse, the women were asked to indicate how controlled versus uncontrolled their thinking and muscular movements were near the end of intercourse.[9] One can see in Tables 7–17 and 7–18 that the average judgment was that both movements and thinking approached a point at which they were only under limited voluntary control.

To ascertain whether conscious ideation or fantasy is very prominent during orgasm, the women in six of the seven samples were asked to respond to a four-point scale ranging from "During orgasm my mind is a complete blank" to "During orgasm I almost always have images or pic-

TABLE 7-16

Strength of Orgasm

	Sample 1	Sample 2 (N = 38)	Sample 3 (N = 41)	Sample 4 (N = 40)	Sample 5 (N = 30)	Sample 6	Sample 7 (N = 39)
M	_a	3.4	3.7	3.1	3.5	_a	3.3
σ	—	1.1	1.0	.8	.7	—	.7

Scale: 1 = Weak; 2 = Fair; 3 = Strong; 4 = Quite strong; 5 = Violent.
aThis question was not asked in Samples 1 and 6.

TABLE 7-17

Ability to Control Movements Near End of Intercourse

	Sample 1	Sample 2 (N = 39)	Sample 3 (N = 43)	Sample 4 (N = 40)	Sample 5 (N = 30)	Sample 6	Sample 7 (N = 39)
M	_a	2.0	2.1	1.9	2.1	_a	1.9
σ	—	.6	.6	.7	.6	—	.6

Scale: 1 = Controlled; 2 = Slightly controlled; 3 = Beyond control.
aThis question was not asked in Samples 1 and 6.

TABLE 7-18

Ability to Control Thinking Near End of Intercourse

	Sample 1	Sample 2 (N = 39)	Sample 3 (N = 43)	Sample 4 (N = 39)	Sample 5 (N = 30)	Sample 6	Sample 7 (N = 40)
M	_a	1.9	2.2	1.9	2.0	_a	1.9
σ	—	.7	.6	.7	.6	—	.6

Scale: 1 = Controlled; 2 = Slightly controlled; 3 = Beyond control.
aThis question was not asked in Samples 1 and 6.

tures in my mind." As Table 7–19 shows, the average judgment was that "images and pictures" only occur "occasionally." They do *not* seem to be a *regular* accompaniment of the orgasm experience.

Masters and Johnson (1966) observed a good deal of variation in the duration of orgasm in the women they studied. The women in five of the seven samples participating in the present study were asked to estimate the

TABLE 7-19

Imagery during Orgasm

	Sample 1	Sample 2 (N = 38)	Sample 3 (N = 42)	Sample 4 (N = 40)	Sample 5 (N = 30)	Sample 6 (N = 38)	Sample 7 (N = 39)
M	—[a]	1.9	2.2	2.1	2.1	2.1	2.1
σ	—	1.1	1.1	1.0	1.1	1.1	1.2

Scale: 1 = During orgasm my mind is a complete blank.
2 = I occasionally have images or pictures in my mind.
3 = I often have images or pictures in my mind.
4 = During orgasm I almost always have images or pictures in my mind.
[a]This question was not asked in Sample 1.

length of their orgasm. One cannot but be impressed, as depicted in Table 7–20, with how relatively consistent the estimates were. They largely clustered within the range 6–10 seconds. Apparently, as a subjective phenomenon, the typical female orgasm lasts from 6–10 seconds. It is noteworthy, though, that there were a few extreme cases in the various samples in which it was reported that orgasm lasts "more than 20 seconds." [10]

One of the special attempts made in the present studies to probe the feelings characterizing orgasm as well as the immediate postorgasm period involved asking the women in all of the seven samples to evaluate the accuracy of ten terms (by putting them in rank order) with reference to how well they describe their feelings during orgasm, and the accuracy of another ten terms with reference to how well they depict their feelings five minutes after orgasm. These terms, listed in Appendix J, were selected impressionistically on the basis of descriptions of sexual response presented

TABLE 7-20

Length of Orgasm

	Sample 1	Sample 2 (N = 33)	Sample 3 (N = 39)	Sample 4 (N = 40)	Sample 5 (N = 28)	Sample 6	Sample 7 (N = 37)
M	—[a]	2.6	2.7	2.3	2.2	—[a]	2.2
σ	—	1.1	1.2	1.1	.8	—	1.0

Scale: 1 = 1-5 seconds; 2 = 6-10 seconds; 3 = 11-15 seconds; 4 = 16-20 seconds; 5 = More than 20 seconds.
[a]This question was not asked in Samples 1 and 6.

in sources such as Kinsey, et al. (1953) and Masters and Johnson (1966).

One can see in Table 7–21 that typically the women in all of the seven samples thought that terms such as "ecstatic," "happy," and "as if I would burst" were most descriptive of how they felt during orgasm, and terms such as "tense," "slightly embarrassed," and "unsatisfied" as least descrip-

TABLE 7-21

Mean Rankings and Standard Deviations of Terms Descriptive of Feelings during Orgasm

Terms	Sample 1 (N = 33)		Sample 2 (N = 39)		Sample 3 (N = 42)		Sample 4 (N = 40)		Sample 5 (N = 29)		Sample 6 (N = 41)		Sample 7 (N = 40)	
	M	σ	M	σ	M	σ	M	σ	M	σ	M	σ	M	σ
Ecstatic	2.1	1.7	2.6	2.2	2.0	1.6	3.2	2.8	1.9	1.4	2.0	1.5	2.6	2.2
Happy	2.7	1.3	2.7	1.6	2.5	.8	2.4	1.4	2.5	1.3	2.2	1.1	2.6	1.3
As if would burst	3.6	2.5	3.0	2.2	3.1	2.2	3.5	2.5	3.9	2.5	3.5	2.2	3.6	2.5
Strange	4.8	2.0	5.0	1.7	5.1	1.8	5.0	1.6	5.1	2.4	4.9	1.9	4.8	2.1
Weak	5.4	1.8	5.9	1.4	5.9	1.5	5.5	1.8	5.7	1.5	5.5	1.6	5.7	1.8
Not like myself	5.6	2.0	5.6	2.3	5.8	1.9	5.9	2.4	5.3	1.7	5.9	1.9	6.2	2.2
Tired	6.8	1.7	6.4	1.8	6.2	1.6	6.2	2.0	6.3	1.7	6.2	1.8	6.1	1.9
Tense	6.9	2.4	6.7	2.4	6.4	2.2	6.3	2.1	6.7	2.1	6.7	1.7	6.3	2.5
Slightly embarrassed	8.5	1.7	8.6	1.5	8.9	1.2	8.3	1.9	8.7	1.1	8.6	1.9	8.2	1.8
Unsatisfied	8.5	1.9	8.5	2.4	9.3	1.0	8.9	1.8	9.1	2.0	9.4	.7	8.9	1.5

tive. In Table 7–22 the terms "happy," "relaxed," and "satisfied" are, across all samples, most often designated as being typical of the women's feelings postorgasm, and the terms "slightly embarrassed," "unsatisfied," and "slightly guilty" as being least typical.

Obviously, the evaluations by the women of the two sets of terms do not really reveal much about the orgasmic experience. The positive terms were consistently favored and the negative ones were not favored. It is hardly surprising that the judgments typically portrayed the orgasm and postorgasm experience as having favorable rather than unfavorable connotations. However, as seen at a later point, there was considerable individual variation in each sample with respect to the ranks assigned to the descriptive terms. There were women who said that feelings of being unsatisfied and tense were most, and feelings of ecstasy least, characteristic of their orgasm experience; and similarly some women depicted happy and relaxed

TABLE 7-22

Mean Rankings and Standard Deviations of Terms Descriptive of Feelings Five Minutes after Orgasm

Terms	Sample 1 (N = 33)		Sample 2 (N = 40)		Sample 3 (N = 42)		Sample 4 (N = 40)		Sample 5 (N = 29)		Sample 6 (N = 42)		Sample 7 (N = 40)	
	M	σ	M	σ	M	σ	M	σ	M	σ	M	σ	M	σ
Happy	2.6	1.3	2.3	1.7	1.6	.8	1.8	1.6	2.4	1.0	1.9	1.4	2.1	1.3
Relaxed	2.1	1.1	2.8	1.4	2.7	1.1	2.8	1.5	2.4	1.4	2.8	1.4	2.6	1.0
Satisfied	3.1	2.0	3.0	2.3	2.1	1.0	2.8	1.9	2.7	1.4	2.5	1.7	2.0	1.1
Weak	4.3	1.4	4.0	1.3	4.3	.9	4.7	1.5	4.0	1.3	4.1	1.0	4.2	1.0
Tired	3.8	1.4	4.5	1.4	4.9	1.0	4.5	.9	4.3	1.6	4.6	1.3	4.2	.9
Not like myself	6.1	1.0	6.5	1.4	6.0	1.4	6.2	2.3	5.9	1.1	6.0	.9	6.8	1.3
Tense	7.8	1.2	7.5	1.4	7.4	1.1	7.5	1.3	7.5	1.4	7.3	1.4	7.8	1.3
Slightly embarrassed	8.2	1.8	7.9	1.3	8.1	1.3	7.9	1.5	8.0	1.0	8.2	1.1	8.0	1.2
Unsatisfied	8.2	1.9	8.1	2.4	8.4	1.2	8.0	2.1	8.6	1.1	8.4	1.8	8.1	1.3
Slightly guilty	8.8	1.6	8.6	1.5	9.5	.7	9.0	1.8	9.4	1.0	9.2	1.0	9.1	1.2

as least, and slightly guilty and unsatisfied as most, characteristic of their postorgasm feelings. Such individual variations did prove to be of importance when analyzed with reference to various personality and attitudinal measures.

An inquiry was made concerning how long the women required to attain orgasm from the point that intercourse began as well as how long they estimated their husbands usually required to do so. The average woman in the six of seven samples who was questioned seemed to require about eight minutes to achieve orgasm, but it should be emphasized that there was remarkable individual variation, with some women requiring as few as one minute and others requiring as much as 30 minutes to reach orgasm. If one compares Tables 7–23 and 7–24, it is apparent that in every sample

TABLE 7-23
Minutes to Attain Orgasm after Intercourse Begins

	Sample 1	Sample 2 (N = 31)	Sample 3 (N = 39)	Sample 4 (N = 39)	Sample 5 (N = 28)	Sample 6 (N = 34)	Sample 7 (N = 35)[b]
M	—[a]	6.3	7.7	8.8	9.4	8.8	8.2
σ	—	4.6	5.5	7.0	6.6	5.8	5.3

[a] This question was not asked in Sample 1.
[b] A number of women misunderstood this question.

TABLE 7-24
Minutes for Husband to Attain Orgasm (As Estimated by Wife)

	Sample 1	Sample 2 (N = 37)	Sample 3 (N = 41)	Sample 4 (N = 40)	Sample 5 (N = 28)	Sample 6 (N = 37)	Sample 7 (N = 39)
M	—[a]	3.8	5.1	4.9	8.9	6.0	7.0
σ	—	3.0	3.4	3.6	9.0	3.1	4.7

[a] This question was not asked in Sample 1.

the women estimate that it takes longer for them to attain orgasm than it does their husbands; typically, from 40 to 80 percent more time. Kinsey, et al. (1953), in commenting upon the relatively longer time taken by most women to attain orgasm, stated that it was not caused by a lesser excitability on their part, but rather the relative inefficiency with which stimulation was applied during intercourse. They pointed out, for example, that during masturbation the average woman who could attain orgasm did so in just under four minutes.

In two of the samples (Samples 6 and 7) the women were requested to specify the exact procedure used in attaining orgasm.[11] They were asked to indicate which of the following alternatives best applied to them:

1. My husband stimulates me clitorally. He then inserts his penis and attains orgasm; and finally I attain orgasm after he stimulates me further clitorally.
2. My husband stimulates me clitorally until I reach orgasm and then he inserts his penis and attains orgasm himself.
3. My husband inserts his penis and attains orgasm and then stimulates me clitorally until I attain orgasm.
4. My husband stimulates me clitorally, inserts his penis, and we attain orgasm at the same time.
5. If none of the above statements apply, please give a description of what is true for you.

In one sample (Sample 6) 70 percent of the women indicated that they achieved orgasm through the sequence of being manually stimulated clitorally and then having their husbands insert the penis to stimulate them further, with both partners then attaining orgasm at approximately the same time. Twenty percent reported that orgasm was attained by the sequence of first being manually stimulated clitorally, having the husband insert his penis and attain orgasm, and then receiving further manual clitoral stimulation that finally produced orgasm level arousal.

In another sample (Sample 7), 55 percent said they attained orgasm through the process of husband stimulating them clitorally and then inserting his penis and continuing intromission until orgasmic excitement was achieved in both. Forty-five percent indicated that they reached orgasm through either alternatives 1, 2, or 3 listed previously. All of these variants involve primarily direct clitoral stimulation to orgasm, with the husband achieving his own orgasm by intromission either before or after his wife's orgasm.

If one averages the two samples, it can be said that about 63 percent of women reach orgasm by the sequence of clitoral stimulation followed by penile intromission, and about 35 percent reach orgasm by clitoral stimulation either before or after the husband attains orgasm by intromission.

In order to get an even more precise picture of the manner in which orgasm is attained, the women in one sample (Sample 7) were asked to answer the following questions.

What percent of the time that you attain orgasm does it occur *at the same time* that your husband attains his orgasm?
What percent of the time does your orgasm occur *before* your husband's orgasm?
What percent of the time does your orgasm occur *after* your husband's orgasm?
What percent of the time that you reach orgasm is the final stage of excitement that actually pushes you to the point of orgasm produced by your husband stimulating your clitoral area with his hand?
What percent of the time is your husband's penis still inserted in your vagina at the moment that you actually have your orgasm?

About 35 percent of the women indicated that they attain orgasm simultaneously with their spouses, approximately 41 percent said they reach orgasm before, and 23 percent said that their orgasm occurred after their husbands'.[12] That is, 64 percent of the women reach orgasm at a time other than their husbands do.

It is interesting that, on the average, the women indicated that about 30 percent of the time they require direct manual stimulation to give them the final push necessary to reach orgasm. Thirty-five percent of the women said they require such final direct manual stimulation 50 or more percent of the time to attain orgasm. Only 20 percent of the women said they never require a final push from manual stimulation to reach orgasm.

Finally, it was said by the women that, on the average, the husband's penis is still inserted in the vagina 57 percent of the time that the wife's orgasm occurs, and 33 percent said that the husband's penis is still inserted only 50 percent of the time that orgasm occurs. Only 33 percent of the women said that the husband's penis is always still inserted at the time of their orgasm.

Clitoral versus Vaginal Response

As outlined earlier, one of the issues concerning sexual responsiveness in women that has been prominently debated concerns the relative degree to which their sexual arousal is achieved by clitoral as compared to vaginal stimulation. Kinsey, et al. (1953) and Masters and Johnson (1966) consider that their data demonstrate little responsiveness to stimulation of the vagina, as such; they attribute a large part of sexual arousal in the female to direct or indirect stimulation of the clitoris. They indicate that clitoral stimulation may occur as a result of direct manual manipulation by the male or indirectly as a function of the penis or the male symphysis pressing upon structures (for example, labia minora), which in turn mechanically affect the clitoris. Attempts were made in the present studies to find out more about the role of clitoral and vaginal stimulation. The women in all seven samples were asked to indicate their perception of how much clitoral as compared to vaginal stimulation contributes to their reaching orgasm. The choices of response offered them are listed in Table 7–25. Table 7–25 shows that the average response was choice 3 (Clitoral stimulation contributes a little more than vaginal stimulation). In Table 7–26 one finds a summary of judgments about the overall importance of clitoral stimulation in attaining orgasm. The average response was about 3.6, which falls halfway between the category "I prefer a moderate amount of clitoral stimulation" and the category "I prefer a considerable amount of clitoral stimulation." Both the results in Table 7–25 and Table 7–26 indicate that the average woman in the range of samples attaches more importance to clitoral than to vaginal stimulation.[13] The difference, although not apparently great, is consistent. Actually, analysis of the percents of women endorsing the various specific clitoral versus vaginal judgment categories suggests that the difference may be even greater than the gross comparison

TABLE 7-25

Relative Contribution of Clitoral versus Vaginal Stimulation to Attain Orgasm

	Sample 1 (N = 32)	Sample 2 (N = 41)	Sample 3 (N = 42)	Sample 4 (N = 40)	Sample 5 (N = 30)	Sample 6 (N = 45)	Sample 7 (N = 40)
M	3.5	2.6	3.0	2.8	3.0	3.1	2.5
σ	1.7	1.8	1.8	1.8	2.1	1.5	1.7

Scale: 1 = Clitoral stimulation contributes much more than vaginal stimulation.
2 = Clitoral stimulation contributes somewhat more than vaginal stimulation.
3 = Clitoral stimulation contributes a little more than vaginal stimulation.
4 = Vaginal stimulation and clitoral stimulation make an equal contribution.
5 = Vaginal stimulation contributes a little more than clitoral stimulation.
6 = Vaginal stimulation contributes somewhat more than clitoral stimulation.
7 = Vaginal stimulation contributes much more than clitoral stimulation.

TABLE 7-26

Relative Importance of Clitoral Stimulation in Attaining Orgasm

	Sample 1	Sample 2 (N = 40)	Sample 3 (N = 42)	Sample 4 (N = 40)	Sample 5 (N = 30)	Sample 6 (N = 39)	Sample 7 (N = 39)
M	—[a]	3.5	3.6	3.8	3.2	3.4	4.0
σ	—	1.1	1.0	.8	1.2	.8	1.0

Scale: 1 = Not prefer; 2 = Prefer a little; 3 = Prefer moderate amount; 4 = Prefer considerable amount; 5 = Cannot attain without.
[a]This question was not asked in Sample 1.

of mean values indicates. As Table 7–27 shows, about 29 percent of the women across the seven samples studied indicated that "Clitoral stimulation contributes much more than vaginal stimulation" to attaining orgasm. Another 20 percent endorsed the statement that "Clitoral stimulation contributes somewhat more than vaginal stimulation." Contrastingly, approximately 7 percent across samples endorsed the statement that "Vaginal stimulation contributes much more than clitoral stimulation"; and only another approximately 5 percent indicated that "Vaginal stimulation contributes somewhat more than clitoral stimulation." Overall, one can see that about 49 percent of the women assigned high importance to clitoral stimulation in achieving orgasm, whereas only about 12 percent attributed equally high importance to vaginal stimulation.

Detailed analysis of the replies to the question (see Table 7–26) concerning the relative importance of clitoral versus vaginal stimulation in attaining orgasm also highlighted the relatively greater arousal potency ascribed to clitoral stimulation. In the six of seven samples studied, roughly 19 percent of the women indicated "I cannot attain orgasm without clitoral stimulation." Another roughly 35 percent stated that they prefer a "considerable amount" of clitoral stimulation in the process of attaining

TABLE 7-27

Detailed Analysis of Percentages of Women Endorsing Various Statements about the Relative Importance of Clitoral and Vaginal Stimulation in Attaining Orgasm

	Sample 1	Sample 2	Sample 3	Sample 4	Sample 5	Sample 6	Sample 7	Total Average Percent
1[a] N =	5	16	10	12	10	7	17	
% =	16[b]	39	24	30	33	16	43	28.7
2 N =	4	7	10	9	7	10	7	
% =	13	17	24	23	23	22	18	20.0
3 N =	6	4	7	11	2	7	5	
% =	19	10	17	28	7	16	13	15.7
4 N =	11	10	7	2	4	16	5	
% =	34	24	17	5	13	36	13	20.3
5 N =	1	1	3	1	1	2	4	
% =	3	2	7	3	3	4	10	4.6
6 N =	3	0	3	1	2	2	1	
% =	9	0	7	3	7	4	3	4.7
7 N =	2	3	2	4	4	1	1	
% =	6	7	5	10	13	2	3	6.6
Total N =	32	41	42	40	30	45	40	

[a]1 = Clitoral stimulation contributes much more than vaginal stimulation.
2 = Clitoral stimulation contributes somewhat more than vaginal stimulation.
3 = Clitoral stimulation contributes a little more than vaginal stimulation.
4 = Vaginal stimulation and clitoral stimulation make an equal contribution.
5 = Vaginal stimulation contributes a little more than clitoral stimulation.
6 = Vaginal stimulation contributes somewhat more than clitoral stimulation.
7 = Vaginal stimulation contributes much more than clitoral stimulation.
[b]Rounded off to the nearest whole number.

orgasm. Only about 3 percent across the six samples said that they do "not prefer" any clitoral stimulation when trying to achieve orgasm.

With regard to this same issue, the women in one sample (Sample 7) were asked to respond to the following question: "If you had the choice of receiving only clitoral or only vaginal stimulation, which would you select?" Sixty-four percent stated they would choose clitoral stimulation, whereas 36 percent gave their vote to vaginal.

To further clarify how women feel about clitoral versus vaginal stimulation, two samples were asked to respond to the following instruction:

Describe as best you can the differences between vaginal and clitoral stimulation. Enumerate any differences in body sensation, intensity, mood, and so forth that you can recall.

Here are some representative excerpts from those who wrote descriptions that emphasized the special importance of clitoral stimulation in attaining orgasm.

With vaginal stimulation I have a rather cool sweat all over my body. It is a very long and lingering feeling. There is no great intensity, only consistency of the mood and feeling. It can even become a sleeping feeling with no desire to continue. Clitoral is much more dramatic and intense. It is a hot, sweating feeling all over. It is more demanding and brings forth much better results.

This has changed since having my baby. I enjoyed vaginal as well as clitoral stimulation before being pregnant; . . . and now enjoy clitoral stimulation exclusively and find vaginal stimulation very uncomfortable. Clitoral stimulation, on the other hand, makes me feel very warm all over, very relaxed and at the same time eager, and is a very intense sensation.

Clitoral stimulation is more exciting because it tingles and makes the whole vaginal area pulsate. My body feels warm all over and as it is continued the intensity grows. Vaginal stimulation feels good but it can't make me achieve orgasm.

Vaginal stimulation works slower for me than clitoral stimulation. Clitoral stimulation tends to build the excitement faster and the orgasm is more intense. I feel I can grip the penis better. Vaginal stimulation is slower, so this can also be enjoyable if the need is not intense.

Clitoral stimulation is much more stimulating. There is hardly any sensation with vaginal stimulation. The (clitoral) feeling is highly intense. Sometimes it feels *too* good. Vaginal stimulation is much more sobering. It feels good but not in the same kind of way.

Vaginal stimulation is not as intense as clitoral stimulation. It is slower and less exciting. It seems only to affect that one part of my body, while clitoral stimulation makes almost my whole body react and is much more exciting and quicker.

Note the following representative comments from women in the group who obviously preferred vaginal over clitoral stimulation.

Vaginal stimulation is a more intense feeling and throbbing and an orgasm is reached faster with this, whereas clitoral stimulation is usually done in the beginning and the sensations are not as intense.

Clitoral stimulation can be felt more sharply. It is a tickling, uncomfortable feeling. Vaginal stimulation is more pleasing, more comfortable, less intense.

Vaginal stimulation is more deep and satisfying. Clitoral stimulation takes much longer to reach an equal amount of excitement. Vaginal stimulation causes faster orgasm and is definitely much more intense.

Vaginal stimulation is much more stimulating to me. It makes me excited rapidly, makes me feel ecstatic, like I can't control myself. Clitoral stimulation makes me feel good but doesn't excite as fast or as intensely as vaginal stimulation.

Vaginal stimulation is more gratifying than clitoral stimulation because it gives me a more whole and complete feeling. It is a deeper feeling than clitoral stimulation and I respond better. Clitoral stimulation does tend to aggravate me after a while.

Note the comments of several women who feel that they obtain important gratification from both clitoral and vaginal stimulation.

Clitoral stimulation is a more acute sensation; vaginal is somehow broader and vaguer though it may be just as exciting if I am desirous and ready for it. Clitoral stimulation can excite me at a much earlier phase of love making than can vaginal. Clitoral stimulation can completely physically satisfy me, as it does when I masturbate, but emotionally the vaginal is often necessary since it (intercourse) makes me feel closer to my husband. Vaginal stimulation before intercourse does not usually excite me, although it has sometimes.

Clitoral stimulation has a high intensity—feelings concentrated in one spot. It's a lightness, a spark, almost ticklish sensation. I feel sort of an electricity. I feel the pleasure is all physical. In a vaginal stimulation the pleasure is mental or spiritual, a feeling of depth or meaning. A wider area of pleasurable sensation. It produces a longing or hunger. It is a comforting pleasure. Vaginal stimulation is like a warm bath of pleasure while clitoral is a spark of pleasure. My whole body responds to vaginal stimulation; and it moves and it feels. In clitoral stimulation my body is rigid with expectation of continuing pleasure. Vaginal stimulation is like a hum but clitoral is a high pitched note. From clitoral stimulation my body demands to be satisfied, from vaginal my body is content even if it's not.

Clitoral stimulation seems to set off a reaction of feeling that shoots straight up through my entire body through the core of me. Vaginal stimulation feels like I am being filled up—not so much an exciting feeling as clitoral stimulation. Clitoral stimulation sends chills up and down me whereas vaginal stimulation is more of an emotional feeling, rather than a physical one. Clitoral stimulation is a much more intense feeling; presents a feeling of urgency more than vaginal stimulation.

Before sexual intercourse I am stimulated greatly by foreplay involving the clitoris. And even during intercourse, especially right after entry, I am very stimulated by strokes closer to the clitoris and direct stimulation. Right before orgasm, however, I enjoy deeper penetration and more vaginal stimulation. Vaginal stimulation at the very beginning of intercourse is not as pleasurable to me as it is right before orgasm.

Vaginal—full, warm, deep feeling. Can be prolonged. Clitoral—sharp, intense, almost uncomfortably pleasurable. Not enhanced by prolonging (like tickling), but by repetition.

Clitoral stimulation is more intensive and produces a more violent reaction. . . . Vaginal stimulation is much more relaxing and much less intense. I *like* it. I *love* clitoral stimulation. . . . Vaginal stimulation is soothing and produces a rhythmical rocking and rotating of the pelvis. . . . It is never intense as clitoral stimulation, yet feels extremely good in its own way. The best analogy I can contrive is the difference between someone lightly and caressingly stroking your bare back or arm or face and being violently, exhaustingly tickled. The former resembles vaginal, the latter clitoral stimulation. Vaginal stimulation soothes me and produces an involuntary contented hum deep in my throat. The vaginal stimulation of intercourse produces a closeness, a coordination, a sense of *oneness* unmatched by any other sexual activity.

Impressionistically scanning the comments the women offered, one is struck by how often clitoral stimulation is described with words such as "warm," "ticklish," "electrical," and "sharp," whereas vaginal stimulation is more often referred to as "throbbing," "deep," "soothing," and "comfortable." It is difficult to encompass such differences with a simple generalization; and it would be premature to do so without further studies. Interestingly, there were no differences between the clitoral and vaginally oriented with respect to the degree to which their excitement was felt to involve local or restricted body areas versus the body as a whole. It is also noteworthy that those who are apparently either clitorally or vaginally oriented may find the nonpreferred form of stimulation to be actually painful or uncomfortable. There were several women who so described the effects of the nonpreferred stimulation.

In any case, the material just cited clearly indicates that women do differ considerably in their reactions to stimulation applied manually to the clitoris and that experienced when the penis is inserted into the vagina. There may be strong preferences for one or the other but the overall trend is for clitoral stimulation to be experienced as contributing more to orgasm achievement than does vaginal.

Since Kinsey, et al. (1953) and Masters and Johnson (1966) cite evidence that the vagina has few sensory receptors and that penile stimulation does, in fact, indirectly produce a good deal of clitoral arousal, one is left a bit puzzled about why there should be different feeling states associated with clitoral versus vaginal modes of stimulation. One can only speculate that each of the two forms of stimulation does, in terms of its specific approach, evoke arousal in a somewhat special way. The vaginal form of stimulation may arouse more intense kinesthetic sensations, may more obviously represent being penetrated and holding a friendly object within one's body, may conform more to the conventional image of "sexual union," and may have more "comforting" connotations. If it is true that so-called vaginal arousal is (from a physiological perspective) primarily a form of clitoral arousal, the fact remains that it represents an approach that has unique psychological connotations (perhaps because the culture has so long had notions about there being such a uniqueness). The written comments of many of the women concerning their experiences during vaginal intercourse leave little doubt that they perceive it and "feel" it as more than just a variant on clitoral arousal.

Masturbation

A word may be said about the role of masturbation as a sexual outlet for the women in the samples studied. As depicted in Tables 7–28 and 7–29, the women in six of the seven samples were asked to state how frequently they engaged in masturbation and the amount of satisfaction they derived from it. The average response was to say that masturbation was "rarely" attempted and that a relatively low degree of satisfaction was derived from it. Only one woman in all of the samples combined indicated

TABLE 7-28
Masturbation Frequency

	Sample 1	Sample 2 (N = 40)	Sample 3 (N = 43)	Sample 4 (N = 39)	Sample 5 (N = 30)	Sample 6 (N = 39)	Sample 7 (N = 39)
M	$-^a$	1.6	1.8	1.8	1.6	1.4	2.1
σ	—	.8	.8	.9	.7	.7	1.0

Scale: 1 = Never; 2 = Rarely; 3 = Once in a while; 4 = Quite often; 5 = With great frequency.
[a]This question was not asked in Sample 1.

TABLE 7-29
Satisfaction from Masturbation

	Sample 1	Sample 2 (N = 35)	Sample 3 (N = 42)	Sample 4 (N = 39)	Sample 5 (N = 29)	Sample 6 (N = 38)	Sample 7 (N = 36)
M	$-^a$	1.8	1.8	1.8	1.7	1.6	2.2
σ	—	.9	.9	1.0	.9	.8	1.1

Scale: 1 = No satisfaction; 2 = Some satisfaction; 3 = Fair amount of satisfaction; 4 = Lot of satisfaction; 5 = Intense satisfaction.
[a]This question was not asked in Sample 1.

"great frequency" in the use of masturbation. Kinsey, et al. (1953) likewise observed in their married female sample that masturbation was quite an infrequent occurrence.

Relationship of Sexual Responsiveness to
Phase of Menstrual Cycle

A persistent unanswered question in the literature concerns the role of the menstrual cycle in sexual responsiveness. Several investigators have reported that sexual responsiveness in women is greatest just before or after menstruation (Terman, 1938; Davis, 1929; Winokur, 1963). Some have concluded that there is no real periodicity in the sexual arousability of women (Wineman, 1967; Thomason, 1951). Still others (Udry and Morris, 1967) pinpoint the midpoint of the cycle as the time of greatest sexual responsiveness. An attempt was made to clarify this issue in the present study by asking the women to respond to the following inquiry:

Please circle the answer or answers which most nearly apply to you:
During the menstrual cycle I notice greatest sexual responsiveness at the following times:
1. During menstruation.
2. The week after menstruation ceases.

3. During the middle of the cycle.
4. The week before menstruation begins.
5. No differences noted during the menstrual cycle.

When the answers of the women in the various samples were analyzed, as shown in Table 7–30, it was found that there was a definite trend to designate the week after menstruation and the week before menstruation as the points of greatest sexual responsiveness. Twenty-six percent chose the week after menstruation and 25 percent the week before menstruation as their times of greatest responsiveness. Note particularly that in four of the six samples the percents choosing the week after menstruation as the time of greatest responsiveness were the highest (or tied with the highest) of those in each array. Both the "middle of the cycle" and "during menstruation" alternatives were, on the average, chosen by 19 percent of the combined samples as their times of greatest responsiveness. The percents indicating that the women noticed no differences in their sexual responsiveness during the course of the cycle were fairly consistently among the lowest in each array.

TABLE 7-30

Percentage Analysis of Judgments Concerning Time during Menstrual Cycle When Sexual Responsiveness Is Highest

Time of Highest Responsiveness:	Sample 1	Sample 2	Sample 3	Sample 4	Sample 5[a]	Sample 7	Average Percent
Week after menstruation	24.5[b]	27.7	37.5	18.1	22.8	23.2	26[c]
Week before menstruation	24.5	18.5	16.0	36.3	22.8	21.4	23
During middle of cycle	24.5	14.8	17.8	18.1	20.0	16.0	19
During menstruation	13.2	20.3	17.8	16.3	17.1	28.5	19
No difference	13.2	18.5	10.7	10.9	17.1	10.7	14

[a]Sample 6 is not included because it was composed of pregnant women who, in many instances, did not respond to this question.
[b]Since many of the women chose more than one alternative as the time of "greatest sexual responsiveness," the percents represent total choices for a given time divided by the total number of all choices made.
[c]Rounded off to the nearest whole number.

These findings indicate that women do, in general, observe that their sexual responsiveness varies during the menstrual cycle. They further demonstrate that women typically feel most responsive in the week following menstruation and, to a lesser extent, during the week preceding menstruation.[14] Beach and Ford (1951), who arrived at similar conclusions concerning the points of greatest responsiveness, could see no reasonable hormonal explanation for the pattern, and speculated that it was related to the sexual deprivation that characterizes most women during the actual menstrual flow.[15] That is, since the menstrual period is usually a time of relative sexual abstinence, women emerge from this phase in a state of sexual deprivation that heightens their sexual responsiveness. Relatedly, during the week preceding menstrual flow, their awareness that a time of sexual deprivation is approaching may act as an extra stimulant when they are involved in sexual intercourse.[16]

Since only a small proportion of the women in each sample felt that their responsiveness did not vary during the menstrual cycle, one must conclude that most women have learned that they do consistently respond more to sexual stimulation at certain times as compared to others. Each woman may have a fairly unique pattern of her own. Although a sizable group of women apparently have found that they are particularly responsive before or after menstruation, others may consistently be more responsive during the middle of the menstrual cycle or during the time of menstrual flow. Incidentally, it would be interesting to find out whether women who have ceased to menstruate (either for menopausal or other reasons) continue to perceive themselves as having some pattern of consistent periodicity in their sexual responsiveness.

Overview

Looking back over the material that has been presented with regard to the sexual behavior and attitudes of the samples studied, the following general conclusions seem justified.

The average woman in these samples is, as defined by norms from other studies, quite sexually active. She engages in intercourse about three or four times a week, and this seems to be congruent with her own preferences. She does simultaneously have an awareness that her husband might prefer more intercourse than actually occurs, but she does not perceive the disparity as a large one. Indeed, she sees herself as rarely not agreeing to his requests for intercourse. Typically, the foreplay that precedes intercourse between her husband and herself is rather limited in time (about 12 or 13 minutes) and results in a build-up of arousal which is experienced as focalized in the clitoral area and the labia minora. Among the "sexual" areas of the body the inside of the vagina and the breasts are experienced as least excited during this foreplay phase. When intercourse begins, the typical woman in the sample indicates that she rarely concerns herself about the possibility of becoming pregnant, rarely experiences pain, and rarely worries that penetration will injure her. Usually, intercourse is experienced as "highly gratifying" and as having become more gratifying in the later as compared to the earlier years of the marriage. Those who attain orgasm say that it usually requires about eight minutes of stimulation to do so. This is roughly 40 to 80 percent longer than they feel that their husbands require to achieve orgasm.

About 39 percent of the women attain orgasm with high consistency, whereas approximately 60 percent do so more irregularly or not at all. Approximately 5 percent have *never* had an orgasm. Those who do experience orgasm describe their orgasmic feelings with terms such as "ecstatic" and "as if I would burst," and depict the orgasm process as one in which "excitement mounts to a high tension followed by sudden release." Only a very small percent experience orgasm as being of "cataclysmic" intensity or producing loss of consciousness. The duration of orgasm is usually regarded as being about six to ten seconds. It was typically felt that near the end of intercourse there is some loss of voluntary muscular control as well as loss of control of thinking. Few women indicated regular awareness of fantasies ("images" or "pictures") during orgasm. Ideation and fantasy do not seem to play a large or consistent role during the peak arousal phase for most of the women studied.

The detailed process by which orgasm is reached has been studied, but still remains a bit obscure. One can say that about 63 percent of the women (in two combined samples) indicated that the usual arousal sequence is for the husband first to stimulate the clitoris manually, and then to insert his penis to produce further stimulation, which finally results in both achieving orgasm. About 34 percent said they attain orgasm either before or after their husbands and primarily through manual clitoral stimulation. When very specific questions were asked about the timing of wife and husband orgasm, it was found (in Sample 7) that 35 percent of the women reach orgasm at the same time as their spouses, with 41 percent attaining orgasm before, and 23 percent after, their husbands do.

The women in the various samples indicated that clitoral stimulation is highly important to them in reaching orgasm. Over 50 percent ascribed either great or indispensable value to clitoral arousal. Further, it is clear that clitoral and vaginal stimulation are perceived quite differently by most of the women, who typically regard one of the two as relatively more exciting; or they experience one rather than the other as possessing some special quality (tickle, warmth, "deep feeling," throbbing). Although it may be true (as described by Masters and Johnson, 1966) that vaginal stimulation achieves much of its effect by its indirect arousal of the clitoris, one can still say that the *experienced* quality of the vaginal and clitoral experiences differs. They do not *feel* alike. Whether this is caused by differences in the kinesthetic and positional elements involved or by differences arising out of the psychological implications of being penetrated or not being penetrated (or holding an organ of another person within oneself versus not doing so) remains to be seen.

ORGANIZATION OF SEXUAL EXPERIENCE

Detailed Descriptions of Intercourse and Sexual Arousal

When women are asked to communicate the nature of their experiences during sexual arousal by giving brief answers or making numerical judgments in response to questionnaires, a good deal is lost by virtue of the abstraction and condensation inevitably required by such a format. Brief "objectified" replies lack affect, and when they concern a complex experience they may leave out basic emotional components. If one examines the existing scientific literature, one finds that no systematic attempts have been made to document in its full qualitative complexity the nature of sexual arousal in women as it is directly perceived by them. Various writers of fiction have tried to convey a detailed and finely etched picture of sexual intercourse and arousal in terms of the behavior and thoughts of characters in their stories, but there has been no way of knowing how representative or realistic their versions are.

In order to make a start in the direction of collecting more reliable data in this area, the writer gave women in one sample ($N = 40$, Sample 7) the following instructions:

> Please give a detailed description of how you usually attain orgasm. Describe particularly the body sensations you experience, the thoughts that pass through your mind, your feelings, your attitudes, any difficulties you have, and so forth.
>
> Also describe in detail how you feel about five minutes *after* you attain orgasm.
>
> Please write on the attached blank sheets. Try to fill at least two pages.

Most of the women who participated in this study were able to give rather full and meaningful descriptions of the arousal process and to convey well the inner subjective states accompanying it. Their descriptions are approached at two levels. First, a series of representative excerpts are presented that convey the qualitative richness of the data. Secondly, a systematic analysis of some of the prominent themes (for example, most typical sensations, frequently occurring fantasies) in the descriptions are offered.

Representative Excerpts

The following excerpts have been chosen so as to constitute a representative cross-section of the descriptions that were collected. They have been edited so as to eliminate extraneous material and to guarantee the anonymity of those who wrote them.

Excerpt 1

To have the *most* enjoyable time in bed I prefer the setting to be romantic and pleasant. My husband is usually in an aggressive mood—which I prefer. I like to feel in a playful mood—and to talk and fool around for a while instead of getting right down to serious sex. I like a wide variety of foreplay including cunnilingus, fellatio, some anal stimulation occasionally. I like to feel as if my husband is paying strict attention to me and my pleasure—treating me in regal fashion. This is a selfish attitude—and, of course, I'm not treated like this *all* the time—but it is important to me to at least have this frame of mind. The physical actions can really fit the mental actions if you really believe this is the way things are. I like to feel relaxed and secure. I prefer to be held, petted, and in general treated gently. The orgasm itself builds from the foreplay. Often I have an orgasm during the foreplay—but prefer to have one during intercourse.

Often I have orgasms—sometimes of lesser intensity—during foreplay and then experience another during intercourse. The sensation of the orgasm is one of mounting tension and warmth followed by a desire for more (whatever is happening at the moment) until finally a release and satisfaction is attained. When in a face to face position I prefer my husband to look at me—and this I find heightens the orgasm. It doesn't bother me too much if I don't attain orgasm—which isn't very often—because the sex was pleasurable anyway and I enjoy seeing my husband have fun. I do feel a little disappointed—but figure the next time will be better.

After lovemaking—I usually fall asleep—mainly because I'm tired. But if we do stay awake for awhile the sensation is one of laziness, euphoria—sort of a floating, drifting, luxurious feeling. It is probably the happiest time of the day. I feel very secure, time seems suspended, and I feel as if I have no cares.

Excerpt 2

I almost always attain orgasm during intercourse—the majority of the time I have multiple orgasms. My husband and I change positions about three times on the average during intercourse (sometimes this doesn't mean a total change, just a shifting in one position, e.g., I may lift my legs and wrap them around his waist after having them straight down when he's on top). This change in position stimulates different areas of our sex organs—fortunately, it works out that we both like the same angles of insertion at the same time. What happens many times is that I'll reach orgasm in one position and then we'll shift and I'll reach it again, etc., until my husband reaches a climax which in turn makes me climax again. The only times I don't reach climaxes like this are when my mind is on other things besides sex—if, for example, dinner is on the stove or I have a lot of things to do.

Sometimes I'll have climaxed a few times and be so tired I don't feel like continuing, but I want my husband to climax and I'll force myself—then I'm usually happy about it and I reach orgasm again.

Orgasm for me usually involves getting more and more tense until there is a final release and then it drops down slowly. Actually I wish that release were more violent at times. Usually my orgasms are short periods—about 15 seconds (although they have seemed much longer sometimes) of an intense tingling—all over—feeling. Sometimes it would be nice if they were only about 5 seconds but more violent. Once this happened—when it was like a convulsive thing and I involuntarily and unconsciously screamed—and I really enjoyed it. . . .

One thing about my orgasms—I feel like biting or grabbing something really hard and my husband's back sometimes gets pretty scratched.

Usually after orgasm, I feel like I have to urinate and almost always do go to the bathroom then. By the time I get out my husband is half asleep and I soon fall asleep myself. If we ball during the day we usually fall asleep then too (we don't get as much sleep as we need), but often we get dressed and go out if it's the beginning of the day. At any rate, we both like to relax together for a little while afterwards.

Excerpt 3

My husband and I usually start out side by side. He does some foreplay around my face and breasts but usually moves on quickly to more intense stimulation. Often we are holding a conversation at this point at which I won't allow him to stimulate me in any part of the pelvic area since I'm not really concentrating on sex. The conversations tend to put me in a good mood, though, and when stopped leave me relaxed and more sensitive.

When my husband starts foreplay in the pelvic region I begin being more responsive. Before this time I'll play with his hair and stroke his body but until I am relaxed enough I don't like to touch his penis. The only words I can put or a reason is I have the feeling that it's "ishy." After I have started responding I no longer feel this way and enjoy stroking his penis.

Occasionally I feel if my husband would just move his hands slightly over, up or down, I would be stimulated better and quicker. Sometimes he does and I'm wrong, often I can't get him to the "right" spot. Since I don't verbalize well at this time—still feeling embarrassed I think—this (my not opening my mouth and his inability to guess what to do) angers me and I end up impatient for the end. Also I often take quite long to become stimulated. If I feel my husband is anxious, or think he is, or believe I am just taking too long, I also get angry at myself and impatient. Either way the result is of course to slow things down even more—once or twice to a standstill.

When my husband stimulates me in the clitoral region I usually get a tickling sensation. It is next to this area I want him to do most of his fingering. I usually find myself quite intently concentrating on what sensation I am feeling and how I would like him to move over his stimulation and where.

After the tickling sensation—as my husband stimulates me faster—I get a tingling in my legs which spreads up and kind of like hits my head. This is of course stronger at some times than at others—occasionally it is almost painful. Immediate after this happens the clitoral region is extremely sensitive and I don't want it touched.

It is only after I am through that I pull my husband over at which time we have intercourse. During this time I usually get great satisfaction from his enjoyment—since I've had mine. (I found if I waited for intercourse I did not reach orgasm which left me very tense and irritable.) Rarely, I mentally wish he'd hurry up.

When we are finished I lie in the crook of his arm. I am very relaxed and in a good mood, feel very loving—not just sexually—toward my husband. I usually fall asleep quite quickly though occasionally I get the giggles and feel playful—but tired. I find that the next day I am also more cheerful and relaxed and friendly in general. (On the other hand, if I have not attained orgasm I lie awake for quite awhile, irritated—physically and mentally—and awake the next morning still irritated—consequently I don't allow this to happen.)

Excerpt 4

We kiss deeply. I usually prefer undressing each other, but this depends on the circumstances. My husband fondles and kisses my breasts a great deal which I find quite exciting early in the experience (later, when I'm in a more excited state, my breasts do not add much). Sometimes, early in the experience, I must concentrate on what we are doing and consciously rid my mind of other thoughts in order to be really responsive. I am nearly always successful in doing this. I like to have my husband breathing into my ear as it helps me if I'm having trouble concentrating and it excites me simply physically and emotionally in that he is excited.

We spend most of the foreplay manipulating and/or kissing each other's sexual organs. This kissing is extremely exciting and I often reach orgasm once or twice at this time. The sensation is that of a rigid knot bursting and flowing suddenly; I feel very appreciative and in love. If this is the case, my husband will wait for my orgasm to subside and then reexcite me with his penis by rubbing the clitoris and shallow insertions. We then have intercourse during which I sometimes have what I suppose is a mild orgasm—and I become tense and excited again, tho' not to as great a degree as earlier and there is a fainter bursting release about the time of my husband's orgasm. If at this point, I do not experience another release, I nevertheless find it quite easy to relax after my husband's climax.

If I do not reach orgasm before intercourse, intercourse lasts longer with my husband withdrawing a number of times during it. This intensifies my excitement and prolongs my husband's and we generally reach a climax together. However, there have been times when one or the other of us has not reached orgasm this way (which practically never happens the other way).

This orgasm is deeper somehow. It takes a great deal more physical energy and is more emotionally satisfying in that I feel more at-oneness with my husband.

Five minutes after either of these types of orgasms, I feel very relaxed, at peace, cleansed. I feel very affectionate in a very deep and meaningful (as opposed to flirtatious) way. I nearly always fall asleep, if only for one-half hour. I very much dislike having to get out of bed immediately for any reason (my husband often gets up to turn off the light or whatever and gets back in bed peacefully—I find that very difficult to do—when I try I feel uncomfortable —with the blood rushing to my head or even a suddenly hitting headache and/or a slightly nauseous, weak feeling). When I awake (if it's not during the night), I feel very replenished in a relaxed sort of way.

Excerpt 5

Before intercourse, during foreplay, which varies from one time to another, I go through a mental relaxation. My thoughts are on my body, my movements, my skin and my husband's. I concentrate on different things, such as the way our skin feels against each other and I concentrate on this for different areas of our bodies. It's as if I make every nerve in my body come alive and think.

Sometimes talking acts as a stimulus: talking about each other's bodies or sex organs, describing a certain feeling or even bringing up previous sexually satisfying experience.

Usually we are both quite active, moving legs and arms over each other's bodies—even before any genital contact. When genital contact does happen—I am so "psyched" for it that it's followed by a sigh. Then my thoughts are completely centered on how good his penis feels against my clitoris.

The way we approach intercourse depends a lot on our moods—if we are very quiet—i.e., if my love isn't expressed verbally but felt very deeply then we usually have much manual manipulation of the genitals or oral stimulation. If we are talkative and laughing before intercourse—we usually approach it more actively—using our entire body and body movements. At the time of genital contact with clitoral stimulation I begin to think about attaining an orgasm. It's as if all my feelings were condensed into one point. Sometimes I picture a plane with two dots—one is my brain and one my clitoris and there is an electric connection between the two.

Many times I try to picture what we look like and by doing so experience an exciting sensation.

With continued clitoral stimulation (and I am not only aware of my clitoris but his penis—I can concentrate on feeling one or the other). I finally seem to lose myself—or sink until it is no longer only the clitoris that is excited but the entire area. Occasionally I picture in my mind what my genital area looks like. I finally have an ache deep in my vagina so profound that I have to have the penis inside. With its entrance—it's as if I had to hold my breath till it becomes completely inserted and then I relieve it with a very loud sigh or cry. It is at this point that my thoughts are of our union—no longer only of myself and my own feelings—I am very aware of my partner's feelings too. There is usually a brief period of just feeling the penis filling me—a lack of body movement. Soon our bodies move very deliberately and mechanically—it is then that my thoughts revert back to my own sensations—and I am working to increase the physical pleasure. My husband usually attains orgasm first which is followed by a pause, clutching each other, my need to hold him. However, the pause does not decrease my sensation—I have the mental satisfaction of knowing he is physically satisfied and I completely let go. It is rare that we attain orgasm at the same time, perhaps because I am too conscious of his nearness to it, I can't "let myself go" knowing he is so close. However, once he has reached it—in no time I can also. As I again and completely concentrated on the feelings in my entire genital area, I reach a certain point when I know orgasm is inevitable and then almost hold it back to draw it out and cause a longer orgasm. I have absolutely no conscious thought of body movements or even of orgasm—I am only engrossed in the pleasurable sensation. The only images I have ever experienced at this time and during orgasm is a fuzzy blackness with red or white muted bursts coming through it. Orgasm comes with a dizziness, a loss of self—almost as if I didn't exist as a body but I exist on as a sensation. After orgasm my body completely relaxes—goes limp for a few seconds until I am conscious of what has really happened and how much my partner means to me. After intercourse we both lie close to each other quietly touching—talking some. I feel completely satisfied—almost relieved (as if there was a chance I might not attain orgasm). I feel very happy and full, close to another human being—amazed at the fact that there is such a pleasurable experience.

Excerpt 6

Attaining orgasm usually takes from 5 to 15 minutes. I usually enjoy some love-making before intercourse actually starts. I enjoy breast stimulation, I find oral-genital relations extremely satisfying. If I am excited, I experience no pain during intercourse. Orgasm is attained only by clitoral stimulation.

I sometimes worry because it often takes me as much as 15 minutes of stimulation before I can orgasm. The more I worry about how long it's taking, the longer it usually takes. I feel bad because, while my husband and I both agree that for me to orgasm is as important as for him, I feel that it must be tedious for him, and I have a hard time completely relaxing because I feel I am being selfish.

During orgasm I have no conscious thoughts, just a very pleasurable feeling of release.

After orgasm I usually feel very satisfied, somewhat letdown, usually tired, but very comfortably tired. I usually like some love-making afterwards such as hugging, kissing, etc.

I often feel that during orgasm I have sort of left my husband for a few seconds and I like love-making after orgasm to reestablish the secure feeling of oneness.

Physical sensations after orgasm are heartbeat return to normal, breathing returns to normal. Vagina pulsates and throbs very strongly in a steady beat and then gradually stops. The general body feeling is a loss of energy and a general tiredness, but a feeling of satisfied tiredness.

Excerpt 7

Well, I like to play around a lot before I like being romantic and my husband doesn't. He gets too excited and impatient. If we do play around a lot, he usually can't control himself. So, in that respect, I feel unsatisfied. We don't kiss and things for more than 5 minutes before he enters me. Before he does I usually like to play some more—but he gets his way. But then as soon as he does enter, I immediately feel extremely excited and become very passionate. It usually takes me quite a while to orgasm, but my husband can almost always stay with it. I usually feel a gradual buildup, but it is a very intense feeling of sexual excitement. We usually roll, twist and turn and sometimes quickly get into a different position—usually without coming out. Then my husband can usually tell what's happening with me by the way I squeeze him or move. Or sometimes I even tell him. The thing that's usually on my mind is what I can do to make him feel better. When I do orgasm, it's always intense and nothing is running through my mind. Hardly ever don't my husband and I orgasm together. We squeeze tightly and finally relax. He stays in me for a few minutes and usually by this time I'm still not thinking—just feeling ecstatic. There are usually no difficulties.

Afterward we separate and I feel completely relaxed and satisfied, calm and very womanly. I am usually conscious of not getting the bed messy now and usually feel the urge to urinate.

Excerpt 8

In attaining orgasm, some amount of foreplay is involved. It usually begins with kissing each other on the mouth, accompanied by each other fondling one another. After about 10–15 minutes of foreplay, during which I have been clitorally stimulated and vaginally stimulated, my husband inserts his penis. My feelings up until this time have been a gradual mounting of tension (physical), my whole body tingles, and I am very highly excited. There is involved also breast stimulation. Generally, the body sensations while attaining orgasm are a tightening, physical tension, tingling.

The thoughts that pass through my mind are fleeting, mostly associated with my physical feeling.

There are some difficulties occasionally. Sometimes I'm worried that I won't have an orgasm or that my husband won't be satisfied. These feelings do not last long and seem to have no effect on attaining orgasm.

Five minutes after orgasm I am usually feeling good—satisfied, happy, and tired. There are times when I get depressed after orgasm—some kind of letdown. The depression doesn't last long.

Excerpt 9

We usually start out with long French kisses while hugging each other tightly so that our bodies are pressed against each other. This generates a feeling of warmth and security between us. Then we engage in broad body caressing, which is the starting point of the actual stimulation. My husband fondles my breasts, often sucking on them. This doesn't arouse me greatly but brings on a feeling of satisfaction, as that of a mother breast-feeding a child. The breasts like this attention, making them become larger with erect nipples. He then stimulates my clitoris with his hand, often purposely avoiding at first while just caressing the surrounding areas, so that I build up excitement in anticipation of the moment when he will actually touch the clitoris. When I feel nearly ready for orgasm, he inserts his penis in the vagina and begins intercourse. When he finally does insert his penis, it brings on a feeling of satisfaction that you're on the "home stretch," after experiencing the anxieties and waiting for the overall stimulation of your body, so that you can easily receive the penis into the vagina. However, once he has entered me and started intercourse, I enter into another stage of anxiety waiting for the actual orgasmic climax. I often see myself climbing a mountain and finding it extremely steep at the top so that reaching the peak is more difficult than the climb thus far. My husband "comes" shortly after entering my vagina, stops for a moment in his ecstasy, and then continues the humping movement until I reach orgasm. Just before this point I enter deep concentration on attaining my goal and at the exact moment that orgasm begins, I draw a complete blank of thoughts and just "wallow" in the physical pleasure it derives. I sometimes have difficulty in attaining orgasm if I don't concentrate hard enough and find that my thoughts wander.

About 5 minutes after orgasm, I feel very peaceful and satisfied. I like to hug my husband tightly and hold him still inside me, symbolic of the feelings I have for our oneness and unity, and just lay in each other's arms, eking out every ounce of satisfaction from the act. After all the waves of physical feeling and emotion have succumbed, I like to start over, omitting the foreplay and just repeating the actual motion of intercourse.

Excerpt 10

My vaginal secretions are only moderate; therefore quite a bit of stimulation is required to lubricate me enough for intercourse. My husband stimulates my clitoris and breasts until I attain orgasm—sometimes I masturbate while he stimulates my breast. I *always* have sexual fantasies while doing this—usually about how other men view me sexually. Afterwards we rest very briefly— during which time I'm very tired, and feel intense affection for my husband. He then inserts his penis—there is usually some tightness, since orgasm has just been reached, but there is plentiful lubrication. But the tightness is alleviated with the body movements. My excitement mounts as his does, but my mind is more controlled; it's more of an intellectual excitement. I rarely fantasize at this point. I'm more aware of what *we* are doing as a unit and the gratification I'm giving him. The physical excitement that I experience at this time depends a lot on *pressure*—I feel the pressure of the penis and the more pressure the better. It only faintly resembles the same sensations as clitoral stimulation. The walls of the vagina feel practically nothing, the entrance feels more, the clitoris itself feels only a little tugging, a pleasant sensation, but not enough to induce a real climax. The most emotional sexual experiences occur when my husband enters me from behind—I feel a kind of subjugation to him— helplessness—the pressure is much greater as he goes much deeper—many times I reach an emotional peak—I feel ready to burst—and I end up crying hysterically for several minutes and recover after intercourse. It's a very happy and cathartic experience. But it's nevertheless a distinctly different experience from the preentry clitoral-stimulated orgasm. Afterward, we're both very relaxed and fall asleep almost at once.

Analysis of Descriptions

General Trends

Each of the women's descriptions of how she achieves orgasm was analyzed in detail and an attempt was made to determine both the common and unique elements among them.

In general, one could discern the well-known sequence that proceeds from foreplay, through orgasm, to relaxation. First, there was foreplay, during which most of the women were touched and kissed on various body areas (for example, lips, breasts) and received manual and often oral stimulation of the clitoral region; next the women entered into active intercourse; and subsequently they reached orgasm either through the husband's penile intromission or his direct stimulation of some other body area (clitoris, breasts). Within this general pattern there were, of course, many variations and idiosyncrasies. One woman preferred not to begin the usual foreplay until her feet had been tickled for about ten minutes by her husband. Another enjoyed the sensation of air blown in her ear as part of the foreplay. Still another found that foreplay was greatly enhanced by having her husband blow air into her vagina. Some women attained orgasm one or more times during foreplay and others required an extended period to achieve even the minimal excitement needed to begin intercourse. During intercourse some used only one position and others changed positions several times before attaining orgasm. There were women who never reached orgasm but who said they found their general state of arousal satisfying. Interestingly, there were a few who never reached orgasm but who still responded to stimulation with great, almost overwhelming excitement. Some found that the experience of holding the penis in the vagina was necessary for orgasm, while others considered penile insertion as only detracting from their enjoyment. There were a few who considered it an important part of the arousal process to immerse themselves in elaborate make-believe sexual fantasies. Individual preferences for stimulation of a specific body part in attaining orgasm were often prominent. Illustratively, one woman found breast sucking by her husband to consistently produce orgasm. For another woman rectal stimulation played such a role.

Following orgasm the typical pattern was to feel satisfied and sleepy and to cuddle up to the husband. But there were also many variations. Some women cried for a while after orgasm, stating that they needed an emotional catharsis to match the physical release attained. Others remained unsatisfied and wanted more stimulation and another orgasm. Several reported a preoccupation with potential loss of bladder control and the need to "clean up." There were instances in which women experienced the post-orgasm period as a time to communicate with their husbands and to discuss important problems with them.

Certain kinds of sensations were predominantly mentioned in the accounts of how excitement builds up during stimulation. Temperature sensations were particularly prominent. The women often referred to an increasing feeling of warmth that was at first localized in the pelvic region and then spread to the abdomen and thighs. Similar prominence was given to sensations described as "tingle" and "tickle." In about a sixth of the descriptions of the arousal process there were references to extreme arousal assuming some of the qualities of pain, but pleasantly rather than unpleasantly so. Orgasm itself was frequently described with such terms as "bursting," "exploding," "flooding," "flowing," "release," "pulsate," "melting," "getting relief," "spasmodic contraction," "something breaks." The build-up of tension reaches such proportion in some of the women that they become concerned about losing control of self and need to "hang on" to something. Experiences related to balance and equilibrium were often mentioned as associated with sexual excitement. Women described themselves as "drunk," "dizzy," "floating," and "lightheaded."

A number of the women indicated that they struggle with unpleasant feelings and tensions during the arousal process. Some worry that they will not attain orgasm at all. Others are irritated because their husbands are not properly stimulating them. One woman felt that she did not respond fast enough to her husband's stimulation and was chronically alarmed that this would drive him to seek other sex partners. Another woman worried that she was too sexually responsive and perhaps made unreasonable sexual demands on her husband.

About a fifth of the women articulated explicitly that intercourse and orgasm result in a loss of self. They indicated that at the height of intercourse they had sensations of "merging" with the sex partners ("like our bodies are one"). Several said that they could literally not tell where their bodies ended and those of their partners began. Sometimes this sense of being merged included a feeling of being unbelievably alone, as if nothing existed outside of what was taking place in the immediate room. There is no question but that in the majority of the women, intense sexual arousal meant a drastic change in the way they usually experience their bodies and also their usual way of regarding self. There were sharp changes in the state of consciousness, radical shifts in the apparent solidity of the self boundaries, and alterations in the immediate sense of one's relationship to the world "out there."

About a fifth of the women directly or indirectly emphasized the importance of intense concentration on oneself as a prerequisite to attaining orgasm. They reported that orgasm could be reached only if all "outside" distractions were banished from awareness and there was a single-minded focus on body arousal as it built up and finally peaked. The apparent importance that many women ascribe to being able to attend almost exclusively to the sensations occurring in one's own body as a necessary condition for achieving orgasm is interesting. It implies that they best achieve orgasm when they can forget about other persons and give up for a while their usual concerns and interests involving the world "out there." One woman humorously highlighted this matter when she reported that she could not get very sexually aroused if she was preoccupied with thoughts about "cooking supper."

Preferred Intercourse Conditions

Particularly pertinent to the last point are the results that emerged when the women in this same sample (Sample 7) were asked to respond to the following instructions:

> List the conditions (or example, your feelings, the physical surroundings) that seem to be most important in determining how sexually responsive you will be at any particular time that you have intercourse. Try to list at least five.

The various conditions enumerated by the women that they felt hindered or facilitated their sexual responsiveness were classified. It can be seen in Table 7–31 that one of the categories most frequently mentioned is "Privacy and freedom from intrusion." Many of the women stressed that they could not consistently build up excitement if they were aware of persons in adjoining rooms, heard loud sounds or voices nearby, or somehow felt they were not guaranteed complete assurance against being observed by others.[17] As already mentioned, this finding was regarded as being of special pertinence to the fact that a number of women had, in their spontaneous descriptions of how they achieve orgasm, emphasized the importance of freedom from distraction and of being able to focus exclusively on their body sensations during sexual arousal. Together, these observations

TABLE 7-31

Percentage Frequencies with Which Various Conditions Are Mentioned by Women As Facilitating Their Sexual Responsiveness

	%
Privacy and freedom from intrusion	18[a,b]
Good relationship between self and husband	18
Something "good" or "successful" occurred that day	8
Not tense or depressed	8
Not tired	8
Modulation of light (semidarkness)	7
Not sick	6
Be clean or smell good	5
No time limit	4
Proper temperature in room	3
Occur at night	3
Previously read sexy book or seen sexy movie	3
Be somewhere unusual (motel, woods, shower)	3
Good meal previously	2
Soft music	2
Have a few drinks	2
Occur during the day	2

[a]Rounded to nearest whole number.
[b]Since all women mentioned multiple conditions, each percent is equal to the total in that category divided by the total in all categories.

imply that the attainment of orgasm in a woman involves a rather unique degree of concentration upon self and a simultaneous shutting out of the outer world. The build up to orgasmic excitement seems to require an "insulated," "detached from the world," self-absorbed state.[18] This idea is considered further at a later point when its implications are discussed relative to some of the findings bearing on the personality correlates of orgasm consistency.

When one examines Table 7–31, one finds that a number of the major conditions cited by women as helping them to be sexually responsive have to do with feeling friendly (particularly toward husband) and perceiving the world in positive rather than negative terms. Thus, 18 percent of the citations mention "Good relationships between husband and self" and 8 percent "Something 'good' or 'successful' occurring that day" as facilitating. With reference to the second of these categories, a number of women indicated that if they had achieved a valued goal or received recognition for successfully doing something in the period prior to engaging in intercourse they were particularly likely to be responsive. A good feeling about self and the world seems to be central to such facilitation. A similar sense of feeling "good" is implied by the category "Not tense or depressed," which represents 8 percent of the statements about conditions that enhance responsiveness. Many of the other statement categories in Table 7–31 have to do with body feelings. Women say their responsiveness is greatest when they are not tired, not sick and clean—and to a lesser extent when they are experiencing an optimum room temperature and had good food, and a "few drinks." Scattered references are also found to the value of modulating the environment with "soft music" and semidarkness. A fairly low number of statements were made that concerned the value of novelty in stimulating responsiveness. Thus, 3 percent of the statements referred to the value of being in a different setting such as a motel room or the woods; and 3 percent indicated that their responsiveness was magnified if there had been previous exposure to sexually provocative material in a book or film.

Fantasies during Intercourse

As part of the effort to obtain material concerning the nature of the intercourse experience from the women in Sample 7, they were requested as follows:

> Please give at least two examples of thoughts or images or fantasies you have had more than once while having intercourse or during orgasm.

More than 75 percent of the women indicated that they have had at least one fantasy or image that recurred occasionally (but not frequently) during intercourse. When these fantasies were roughly categorized, it was found that about 40 percent involved scenes in which the woman was having a sexual contact or interchange with someone other than her husband. Within this category, more than half of the instances revolved about themes in which the woman perceived herself as being raped, sexually humiliated, or somehow sexually wicked. There were fantasies of being helplessly tied and having to submit to brutal rape, of being a cheap whore humiliated by men, and of having to expose one's genitals publicly in an embarrassing way. A number of the women fantasized that they were actresses on a stage and were performing sexually for an audience. Masochistic and exhibitionistic elements were strongly prominent in the fantasies that were collected. Another interesting category (10 percent) of fantasy portrayed self as being a royal or superior figure (for example, goddess, princess) with special power or prestige. Illustratively, one woman said, "I see myself like a queen in a fairy tale."

About 30 percent of the images reported by the women dramatized simple sensory experiences. There were references to "red flashes," "colors," "water rushing," and "things floating." In these instances the woman would, as she engaged in intercourse, conjure up images of intense colors or swiftly flowing water or of objects and persons floating in the air. Such images seemed to be simple representations of the arousal and excitement produced by sexual stimulation.

Other less common fantasies that were mentioned may be cited to illustrate the range obtained: a man climbing a steep mountain, a picture of husband and self combined into one person, an unknown male face, a religious ceremony, scene from a sexy movie, someone trying to "castrate" me, the word "love" on a valentine.

One of the interesting aspects of the fantasy material collected is the frequency with which it concerned being with someone other than one's husband or in a different place than the immediate situation. It seemed to represent an attempt to depict self as being with a new sex partner or engaged in a novel form of sexual activity. One could think of it as a means for adding spice to an experience that has grown repetitious or stale. At another level, it might be viewed as an attempt to remove oneself from the immediate situation, a way of distancing self from what is actually occurring. It might be a way of escaping unpleasant aspects of the immediate sexual intimacy. One woman explicitly stated that while having intercourse with her husband she imagined that she was with other men because she felt so negatively toward him.

There is a noteworthy contrast between such fantasies of escape from the immediate setting and the earlier described concern that many of the women have about carefully insulating the intercourse situation against intrusion from "outside." In one case the woman's emphasis is upon getting out or away and in the other it is upon keeping away from what is "out there."

Individual Interpretations of the Intercourse Experience

As one reads the descriptions the women (Sample 7) give of their intercourse experiences, it becomes apparent that each tells a different story with its own special dramatic quality and significance. Each woman perceives the events of intercourse within the context of her own unique problems and expectations. Although no attempt is made to analyze quantitatively the nature of the "self-presentations" in the intercourse descriptions, an impressionistic summary is offered of what seem to be the most common themes.

1. Some women present intercourse primarily as a great adventure in which there are new experiences and sensations to be sampled. Emphasis is placed upon the range of positions used, the novelty of some of the sensations aroused, and the potential for unlimited exploration by each spouse of the other spouse's body.

2. Related to this first theme is the perception of intercourse as a means of attaining ecstasy or going on a "trip" in which there are strange sensations and loss of identity. Included in this category are those who wish to ascribe a religious or mystical quality to sexual arousal.

3. For some women intercourse is an opportunity to prove their superior prowess in an activity that is highly valued. They dwell on their responsiveness, their ability to attain multiple orgasms, and the fact that they exceed their husbands in sexual capacity.

4. Another theme found in the intercourse descriptions portrays intercourse primarily as an opportunity for intimacy and blending oneself with a sex partner. Much is said about closeness, skin contact, cuddling, and feeling unbelievably united to another human being. The process of joining with someone is depicted as comforting and anxiety allaying.

5. A troubled martyred stance appears in some. The women in this category see intercourse as either painful or unpleasant. They picture themselves as victims of an inability to respond adequately to sexual stimulation. They dwell on their irritability during intercourse and their anticipation of ultimate frustration.

6. One interesting group characterizes sexual excitement as almost too intense to tolerate. They refer to their state of sexual arousal as painfully intense and suggest that they can barely control the tension that builds up. Illustratively, one woman said that when she became highly aroused sexually she was "ready to climb the walls." Reference is also made to excited body areas feeling "sore" and oversensitive. Sexual excitement seems to be regarded as a force greater than self, which has potential overwhelming and disorganizing properties.

7. There are also those who adopt a no-nonsense "businesslike" attitude. They describe intercourse as a routine, well-practiced procedure that provides adequate gratification, but which is simply one of a number of other important life activities. Several of the women who conveyed this idea indicated that shortly after intercourse they often resume some household task or work that needs to be done.

8. Those who experience intercourse as a reaffirmation of feminine identity should also be mentioned. They speak of how "womanly" they feel during and after sexual arousal. They experience sexual arousal as a demonstration that a man has accepted them in the role of "real" woman.

This brief review of the patterns discerned in the intercourse descriptions is not in any sense offered as a definitive classification scheme. It merely reflects the writer's impressionistic summary of the relatively small number of protocols collected in Sample 7. It should be added that the categories outlined are obviously not mutually exclusive and more than one pattern could easily characterize any particular woman.

How Are Different Aspects of Sexual Response Related to Each Other?

How unified are the various dimensions or aspects of a woman's sexual behavior? If she consistently achieves orgasm, does this mean that she prefers a high intercourse rate? If she has intercourse frequently does she also get a high amount of satisfaction from it? Does the relative degree to which she prefers clitoral versus vaginal stimulation correlate with her ability to attain orgasm? Do a woman's feelings during orgasm predict how she will feel after orgasm has occurred? Is a woman's masturbatory behavior related to other aspects of her sexual behavior? It is possible, on the basis of the data collected in the present studies, to offer answers to such specific questions as well as the more general one of whether various aspects of a woman's sexual behavior can be consistently predicted from other aspects. This involves looking at the interrelationships of the primary measures of sexual behavior and response that were obtained.

Orgasm Consistency

What does one find when the correlations of orgasm response consistency with other sexual indices are examined? Does the consistency with which a woman experiences orgasm during intercourse correlate with other aspects of her sexual behavior? To answer this question the correlations of the orgasm consistency index with the range of other sexual indices were analyzed across seven different samples.[19] The arbitrary convention is adopted here and in other data analyses that follow in this chapter of considering that noteworthy correlations exist only when they are statistically significant (.05 level) or borderline so (namely, .10 level) in at least 50 percent of the samples studied. The positive findings pertaining to orgasm capacity may be summarized as follows.[20]

The greater a woman's orgasm consistency the more likely she is:

To rate herself as being high in sexual responsiveness (6 of 7).[21]
To indicate that she feels satisfied *after* orgasm (4 of 7).
To describe her orgasms as being of high strength (3 of 5).
To experience more than one orgasm in an hour period (3 of 6).

A borderline trend may also be cited for orgasm consistency to be positively correlated with degree of satisfaction *during* orgasm (3 of 7). That is, the more consistently a woman experiences orgasm the more likely she is to perceive her orgasms as "strong" and satisfying and to view herself as a sexually responsive person. Those who consistently attain orgasm do feel more satisfied with their orgastic experiences than those who attain orgasm inconsistently. The rather limited nature of the relationships of orgasm consistency with other indices of sexual response is also interesting. Note that it is *not* correlated with time to attain orgasm, amount of pain during intercourse, amount of vaginal pulsation, presence of imagery or fantasy during intercourse, the degree to which foreplay excitement focalizes in any of a series of specific body regions, and so forth.

Intercourse Frequency and Sexual Responsiveness

The fact that orgasm consistency did *not* correlate with certain measures is in several instances more intriguing than any of the significant correlations that were obtained. One is struck with the finding that orgasm consistency is not correlated with either intercourse rate or preferred intercourse rate.[22] This means that the ability to reach orgasm, as such, is probably not a prime determinant of how much a woman wants or engages in intercourse. There is no indication that the capacity to attain consistent orgasm provides an incentive for a woman to seek a high frequency of intercourse. Conversely, there is no indication that the woman who attains orgasm inconsistently compensatorily seeks more frequent intercourse. These are, indeed, surprising findings that the present writer would not have predicted. They imply quite directly that a woman's ability to obtain what is an important component of sexual satisfaction does not determine her interest, or willingness to participate, in intercourse. However, still another perspective on this issue opens up if one considers the correlations of actual and preferred intercourse frequencies with another of the sexual indices that is based on the woman's rating of her own sexual responsiveness.[23] This index proved to be positively correlated (5 of 7) with preferred intercourse frequency and also actual frequency (5 of 7). Why should it predict such frequencies better than orgasm consistency does? The first thought that comes to mind is that, although the two indices are positively correlated (6 of 7), the self-rating of sexual responsiveness involves a judgment about how one responds *overall* to sexual stimulation, whereas the orgasm consistency measure concerns only one specific form of response to such stimulation. It is the woman who feels that she is, *in general,* most responsive or aroused when sexually stimulated who seeks intercourse, rather than the woman with the greatest probability of attaining the peak kind of excitement we label as orgasm. This obviously suggests that there are various arousal experiences produced by sexual stimulation that have more power to motivate a woman to enter into intercourse than does orgasm itself. This is true despite the already mentioned fact that a woman's likelihood of feeling satisfied after orgasm is greater if she is one who attains orgasm consistently and also despite the finding that satisfaction after orgasm is not related to how generally sexually responsive a woman judges herself to be.

Qualitative Feelings during and after Orgasm

It is important to specify that the consistency with which women attain orgasm does not seem to be related to the qualitative terms they use in describing their typical orgasm experiences. As earlier described, the women in all samples were asked to rank-order ten terms (see Appendix J) with respect to how well they depict one's feelings during orgasm and to do the same for another set of ten terms with respect to one's feelings five minutes after orgasm. Except for the fact that those attaining consistent orgasm were particularly inclined to state that they felt satisfied during and after orgasm, no other terms were significantly related to orgasm consistency. Those consistently reaching orgasm did not feel that descriptive terms such as "ecstatic," "as if I would burst," or "happy" were more applicable in describing orgasm than did those who reach orgasm inconsistently. Similarly, there were no differences with respect to more negative terms such as "tired," "weak," "slightly embarrassed," and "slightly guilty."

Foreplay and Elaboration of Stimulation

There was no evidence that orgasm consistency is related to the average number of different positions used during intercourse, the amount of time spent in foreplay, or the average duration of intercourse. An obvious implication is that, in general, orgasm consistency in women is not proportional to the elaborateness or duration of the sexual stimulation they receive. This, as may be recalled, is similar to the conclusion reached by Kinsey, et al. (1953). It is difficult to accept such a conclusion from a common-sense viewpoint; it obviously does not support many sexual "manuals" that promise higher rates of orgasm to women if they are provided with elaborate and extended sexual stimulation.

Clitoral-Vaginal Stimulation

Another issue of interest is the lack of correlation between orgasm consistency and a measure of how much clitoral versus vaginal stimulation is preferred.[24] Whether a woman is vaginally or clitorally oriented in her preference for sexual stimulation is in no way predictive of whether she will be able to reach orgasm. There is no apparent superiority of either form of stimulation over the other in its orgasm arousal potential. This observation is not in any way contradictory of the Kinsey, et al. (1953) or Masters and Johnson (1966) view that the vagina itself has low sensory excitability. As they point out, penile stimulation delivered to the vagina may indirectly transmit stimulation to the clitoral area. However, one must add that they may have underestimated the amount of nonclitoral arousal produced by vaginal stimulation in its own right via its kinesthetic effects (for example, sense of vaginal and muscle stretching) and its psychological meaning (intimacy and fusion of body parts). This would be an appropriate point to present other findings pertaining to the issue of clitoral versus vaginal arousal. Looking at the data, one finds that a woman's preference for clitoral versus vaginal stimulation is not related to how frequently she engages in, or prefers to have, intercourse, or her own rating of her overall degree of sexual responsiveness, or how satisfied she feels during and after orgasm, or the strength and duration of her orgasm, or the amount of time required to attain orgasm, or the likelihood of having more than one orgasm in an hour period, or whether she feels pain during intercourse, or whether she is aware of images or fantasies in her mind during intercourse. Interestingly, too, the clitoral-vaginal index has no relation to the degree to which vaginal pulsation is experienced during orgasm. These negative findings just enumerated underscore how difficult it is to distinguish basic differences between the response patterns of those differing on the clitoral-vaginal continuum. There was, however, one distinction observed with respect to the quality of the orgasm experience. It was found (at a slightly better than borderline level) that the greater a woman's preference for vaginal stimulation the less likely she is to characterize (by means of ranks) her orgasm as having produced an "ecstatic" feeling (4 of 7).[25] That is, the ecstatic sensations seem to occur relatively more often in those who prefer clitoral stimulation. If further work continues to substantiate this finding, it would stand in direct opposition to those (psychoanalytic theorists) who assert that vaginal stimulation produces a richer, more intense experience than does clitoral arousal. Another point worth mentioning with regard to clitoral-vaginal arousal is that there is a consistent positive relationship (4 of 5) between the degree to which clitoral stimulation is preferred during intercourse and the degree to which the clitoral area (as compared to other genital areas) is judged to be most aroused during foreplay.

Finally, it should be indicated that there is no relationship between clitoral-vaginal preference and either the amount of masturbation engaged in or the degree of enjoyment derived from it. This is interesting in view of the fact that clitoral stimulation involves manual manipulation in many ways analogous to masturbation; one might thus have expected the clitorally oriented to be more positive than the vaginally oriented to masturbation. However, this is not so. Apparently, it is just as important to the woman who is clitorally oriented as it is to the one who is vaginally oriented that the stimulation she receives be applied by a man rather than by herself.

Interrelationships of Orgasm and Also Postorgasm Feeling States

The data were scanned to ascertain if the presence of certain feelings during and after orgasm are related to the presence or absence of other feelings.[26] For example, if a woman says that orgasm makes her feel "ecstatic" does it also make her feel "happy" and "satisfied" but not "tense" and "strange"? In actual fact, the only two consistent findings for the "ecstatic" feeling were that it is greatest in those women who rank themselves lowest with reference to being "tense" (4 of 6) and feeling "strange" (4 of 6) during orgasm. However, it should also be added that other aspects of the data indicate that the woman who is most likely to feel "ecstatic" during orgasm is also likely to have orgasms of high strength (3 of 5) and to perceive herself as requiring a relatively brief period of time to reach orgasm (3 of 5).

When one looks at the feeling state correlates of "unsatisfied" during orgasm, one finds no consistencies. The woman who feels most satisfied during orgasm is *not* the one who feels most "ecstatic" or the most "as if I will burst" or the least "tense." Incidentally, she is the one most likely to feel satisfied five minutes *after* orgasm (6 of 6), and it should be added that she also tends to have orgasms of high strength (3 of 5). That is, greater satisfaction does go along with a perception of the orgasm as being physiologically intense.

There were miscellaneous consistencies in relationships among the various other qualitative terms used to describe feeling states during and after orgasm, but they were scattered and not particularly meaningful. Therefore, space will not be taken to specify them.

Strength of Orgasm and "Multiple" Orgasms As Predictors

Two aspects of a woman's orgasm experience stand out as being especially predictive of other of its aspects. One is the degree of strength she ascribes to her average orgasm.[27] The greater her rating of its strength the more consistently she achieves orgasm (3 of 4), the more overall sexually responsive she considers herself to be (3 of 5), the more she experiences orgasm as "ecstatic" (3 of 5), the more satisfied she is during (3 of 5) orgasm, the more intense her vaginal pulsations during orgasm (4 of 5), and the longer the duration of orgasm (4 of 5). A second noteworthy predictive aspect is the frequency with which more than one orgasm has been typically experienced within a one-hour period.[28] The greater a woman's frequency in this respect the more sexually responsive she rates herself (4 of 6), the greater her enjoyment of masturbation (3 of 6), the greater the average strength of her orgasms (3 of 5), and the greater the average duration of her orgasms (3 of 5). It is interesting that this variable did *not* prove to be correlated with consistency of orgasm. But note that it was positively correlated with enjoyment of masturbation, and, in fact, is the only sexual variable which correlates with any aspect of masturbatory behavior.

It is apparent that knowledge of the average strength of a woman's orgasms and, to a lesser extent, of whether she achieves more than one orgasm in a relatively brief period with any frequency provides a good basis for predicting a number of other primary aspects of her orgasmic related behavior. With these two indices one can predict her orgasm consistency, her overall feeling about her sexual responsiveness, the likelihood that she will extract "ecstatic" enjoyment from orgasm and feel satisfied after its occurrence, the average duration of her orgasms, and the intensity of accompanying vaginal pulsations.

Intercourse Frequency Correlates

It should be more clearly spelled out how actual and preferred intercourse frequencies are related to the other sexual variables. One finds that sexual intercourse frequency is positively correlated with how sexually responsive a woman considers herself to be (5 of 7), positively correlated with her preferred intercourse frequency (7 of 7), and positively correlated with the average number of intercourse positions she and her husband use per month (4 of 6). Preferred intercourse frequency shows exactly the same correlational pattern. What is striking about these findings is how limited are the relationships of the two frequency measures to any of the other sexual variables. Only a woman's feelings about her overall degree of sexual responsiveness tell us whether she will participate in a low versus high amount of intercourse. None of a multitude of other variables seems to have predictive value in this respect. One cannot anticipate a woman's intercourse frequency in terms of whether she finds intercourse painful or satisfying or productive of ecstatic sensations or leading to strong orgasms. More is said at a later point concerning personal determinants of intercourse frequency.

Miscellaneous

It is noteworthy that some of the sexual measures seem to be related to none, or, at most, to a few of the other measures obtained. Amount of imagery during intercourse correlates with none of the other sexual measures. Amount of pain during intercourse correlates significantly with only one other measure (negatively with how sexually responsive a woman considers herself to be). The degree to which arousal during foreplay is focalized in one area versus another (for example, vagina versus clitoris) is unrelated to any of the other measures. Number of minutes to attain orgasm after intercourse begins is unrelated to all other variables except one (the longer the time the lower the probability of feeling ecstatic during orgasm).

Overview

Retracing these results, one is *not* left with the impression that there is a unitary, consistent quality about a woman's responses to sexual stimulation. It is, in most instances, difficult to predict from one aspect of her sexual response pattern to another aspect. Consider the findings that have accrued for several of the major sexual variables. First of all, the consistency with which a woman reaches orgasm does not reveal much about how frequently she engages in (and wants) intercourse or the quality of her feelings during and after orgasm or her preference for clitoral versus vaginal stimulation. It also does not reveal much about whether she experiences pain during intercourse or has a lot of fantasy while being aroused or experiments with a variety of intercourse positions or engages in extended foreplay or practices (and enjoys) masturbation. Primarily, what it does predict of real consequence is whether there is a sense of being "satisfied" during and after orgasm, whether the average orgasm is experienced as being of strong intensity, and whether there is a perception of self as being a sexually responsive person.

In a similar vein, from a review of how consistently two indices such as actual and preferred intercourse frequency are related to other aspects of sexual behavior, one is again impressed by the lack of connectedness. The only major variable that the two indices are correlated with is self-rating of sexual responsiveness. The greater the women's actual and preferred frequencies of intercourse the more likely they are to rate themselves as having high sexual responsiveness. One might also incidentally mention a consistent trend for the two frequency indices to be positively correlated with average number of positions used in intercourse per month. But on the other hand, the two frequency indices had only chance relationships with such variables as amount of satisfaction derived from orgasm, intensity of pain felt during intercourse, degree of happiness produced by intercourse, preference for clitoral versus vaginal stimulation, and length of orgasm.

Still another example of the lack of coherence in the interrelationships of the various sexual measures is provided by the women's judgments of their relative preference for clitoral as compared to vaginal stimulation. Despite the central importance assigned to this variable in psychoanalytic theory, one finds that (with a few minor exceptions) it is not significantly correlated with other aspects of sexual behavior. Whether a woman prefers clitoral or vaginal stimulation tells us nothing about her orgasm consistency, her overall sexual responsiveness, her intercourse frequency, or the quality (with one exception earlier cited) of the feelings and body sensations aroused in her during intercourse.

The prime impression that emerges is that large sectors of what we call sexual behavior are relatively independent of each other. Sexual behavior is apparently a mixture of diverse elements, not infrequently having in common only their shared semantic designation. At first glance this conclusion may appear to be unreasonable. From a commonsense view we are inclined to think of people as having a sexual style or a typical way of responding sexually across a variety of situations. However, such oversimplified stereotypes may exist only because there is so little public empirical information available about sexual behavior. Where there is lack of knowledge, it is all too easy to evolve simplistic notions. If one shifts for a moment and considers a more public and less taboo area of appetite satisfaction such as eating, it becomes easier to see that unitary style is not typical. That is, it would probably be difficult to find a unitary quality in the overall eating behavior of a typical person. Any particular aspect of eating behavior is probably not easily predictable from other aspects. An individual may enjoy eating certain foods and not others, or get intense satisfaction from one style of cooking and not another. Two individuals may both enjoy eating very much but one eats only twice a day and the other eats five times a day. One gourmet may eat quickly and another very slowly. In all likelihood if multiple measures of various aspects of eating behavior were obtained, they would not show much consistency in their interrelationships.

Having made the basic point that large segments of sexual behavior in women seem unrelated to each other, it would be appropriate to repeat again that there are a few sexual measures that are superior to most others in predicting a number of aspects of sexual response. The most impressive of these measures is a woman's evaluation of her own overall degree of sexual responsiveness. One finds (as earlier reported) that it is significantly and positively linked with her orgasm consistency, her actual and preferred intercourse frequencies, several of the measures of her feeling state during intercourse (for example, ecstasy, pain), her orgasm strength, the average number of intercourse positions she and her husband use, and so forth. To a lesser but still noteworthy extent, orgasm strength also shows power in predicting other aspects of sexual response. It will be recalled that it is positively correlated with such measures as orgasm consistency, self-rating of overall sexual responsiveness, amount of satisfaction felt during orgasm, and degree of ecstasy experienced during orgasm. The fact that a woman's rating of her overall sexual responsiveness and her estimate of the average strength of her orgasms should turn out to be the two measures most related to other sexual response indices is interesting and a bit surprising.

Although there is little that comes to mind that would clarify the relative effectiveness of the orgasm strength index, one might conjecture that the effectiveness of the self-rating of overall sexual responsiveness stems from the fact that it called upon the women to mobilize and average their accumulated knowledge of many different phases of their own sexual behavior. In so averaging their observations of diverse phases of their own sexual response patterns they arrived at a judgment that was likely to have some commonality with a number of the individual phases. Of course, such an interpretation implies that if sufficient information is available, a certain amount of meaningful continuity can be extracted from the diversity of a woman's sexual behavior, and that this continuity can be expressed in terms of a dimension of lesser versus greater responsiveness to sexual stimulation. But at the same time, it must be cautioned that whatever continuity or commonality does exist is quite limited, as indicated by the fact that the correlations between self-rating of overall sexual responsiveness and the various other sexual measures are generally low.[29]

NOTES

1. This rating task was taken from the work of Shope (1966).

2. Despite this fact, it was found among the women in five of the seven samples who were questioned about the amount of lubricating fluid stimulated in the vagina by foreplay that the average response was midway between "moderate" and "considerable." This would suggest that the average woman does become quite excited during the foreplay phase.

3. Gebhard (in Shiloh, 1970) has tentatively raised the question, on the basis of additional analyses of the original Kinsey, et al. data, whether extended foreplay may not aid some women to attain orgasm who otherwise might not be able to do so.

4. The test-retest reliability of the basic sexual behavior indices is discussed in a later chapter.

5. Even so, the average woman in six samples who was asked indicated that she agrees to her husband's requests for intercourse "almost always." Thomason (1951) also found high acquiescence to the husband's requests for intercourse in a sample of wives with a college background.

It should be added that whereas a number of previous studies have observed that the wife estimates her husband's preferred intercourse frequency to exceed her preferred frequency, the average difference found in the present studies tends to be smaller than usually reported.

6. Six of the seven samples were asked how frequently they engage in intercourse during their menstrual periods. The average response was to choose the middle judgment category ("Once in a while") on the five-point scale ranging from "Never" to "Almost always."

7. This rating scale was adapted from Shope (1966).

8. Six of the seven samples were asked to indicate on a five-point scale how frequently they have experienced orgasm more often than once during a one-hour time span. The average response was midway between the second category "On rare occasions" and the third category "On scattered occasions."

9. These rating scales were adapted from Shope (1966).

10. Masters and Johnson (1966) also report extreme cases in which the duration of orgasm is as great or even greater than 20 seconds.

11. It is indirectly pertinent to this point that the average number of intercourse positions used per month in six of the seven samples was approximately three.

12. Thomason (1951) found in a large sample of college women that 38 percent said they attain orgasm at the same time as their husbands.

13. The women in five of the seven samples were asked to rate on a five-point scale (1 = Not at all; 2 = Slightly; 3 = Some; 4 = Strongly; 5 = Violently) how much "vaginal pulsation" they feel during orgasm. The average answer was "Some," but about a fourth of each sample said that vaginal pulsation was "Strongly" or "Violently" experienced. It is of importance that no relationship was found between the degree of such "vaginal pulsation" and the degree to which orgasm is induced by vaginal versus clitoral stimulation.

14. These findings do not mean that intercourse rates are higher during the week following and the week preceding menstruation. Ford and Beach (1951) cite information suggesting that intercourse rates for most married couples are rather regular from week to week. They conjecture that this is so because of the influence of the male spouse whose responsiveness does not vary cyclically. They also note that whereas women may be particularly responsive at certain times this does not mean that they are grossly unresponsive at other times.

15. The sexual deprivation usually associated with the menstrual period reflects cultural inhibitions about engaging in intercourse during this time. Masters and Johnson (1966) found no evidence for a significant physiological decrement in response to sexual stimulation during menstruation. Apropos of this point, it is interesting that an average of 19 percent of the women in the present samples said that the time of actual menstrual flow was one of the phases of the cycle during which they were most sexually responsive. Furthermore, in one sample (7) the percent of women choosing "during menstruation" as their time of greatest responsiveness was greater than for any other alternative time; and in another sample (2) the percent so choosing was the second highest.

16. An opportunity was presented for testing this view by examining the relationships between self-reported frequency of intercourse during menstruation with judgments concerning when one is most sexually responsive during the menstrual cycle. It was found that only for the extreme categories of those who have no intercourse during menstruation versus those who have a large amount of such intercourse were there differences in reported responsiveness. The former group more often indicated (at a statistically significant level) that they felt unusually responsive during the week

following menstruation. This result was derived from combining the extreme category women in all samples (except the pregnancy sample). It is supportive of the Beach and Ford view because it indicates that those women who had the least opportunity for sexual gratification during menstruation were the ones who felt particularly responsive following menstruation.

However, no relationship of consequence was found between designating the week before the menstrual period as a time of special responsiveness and being in one versus the other of the extreme categories of frequency of intercourse during menstruation.

17. It is obvious that such concerns could indicate the presence of guilt about sexuality. They could signify a fear of being discovered or apprehended in the midst of an "illegal" activity.

18. Although some women describe orgasmic build-up as one in which the boundaries between the sex partner and self dissolve, which would, in a sense, represent the opposite of increase of self-awareness, one finds upon careful reading of such descriptions that the emphasis is placed upon an enhanced self that "takes in" or includes the sex partner.

19. Based on self-ratings on a seven-point scale, ranging from "Never" to "Always," as to how consistently orgasm is experienced.

20. All correlational analyses to be described are based on the Pearson product-moment coefficient of correlation.

21. This designation 6 of 7 means that in six of seven samples a statistically significant (.05 level) or borderline (.10 level) correlation was found. This shorthand way of citing results is continued throughout the remainder of the chapter.

22. Neither linear nor curvilinear relationships were found.

23. A five-point scale ranging from the extreme "I am very much more responsive than the average" to the other extreme "I am considerably below average."

24. A seven-point scale ranging from the extreme of "Clitoral stimulation contributes much more than vaginal stimulation" to the other extreme of "Vaginal stimulation contributes much more than clitoral stimulation."

25. However, clitoral-vaginal preference was not consistently correlated with rated strength of orgasm or amount of loss of control of thinking or body during orgasm.

26. This analysis involved, of course, the previously described procedure in which the women ranked ten terms with reference to how well they described their feelings during orgasm and another set of ten terms with reference to their feelings five minutes after orgasm.

27. Rated on a five-point scale varying at one extreme from "weak" to the other extreme of "violent."

28. In six samples the women rated themselves on a continuum that extended from 1 (I have never had more than one orgasm during a one-hour span) to 5 (I have very often had more than one orgasm during a one-hour span). The average rating across the six samples was rather consistently about 2.7.

29. Only a very small percentage of the correlations were in the .40's or higher.

8

ORGASM CONSISTENCY

AND CONFIDENCE IN THE

PERMANENCE OF LOVE OBJECTS

This chapter is the first of several concerned with the personality correlates of the major sexual response dimensions that were studied. It inquires whether women who differ in their ability to attain orgasm also differ in personality.[1] Does the woman who usually achieves orgasm manifest special traits and attitudes that are absent in the woman who usually fails to do so? One can find glib assumptions and stereotypes in both the popular and clinical literature about the kinds of women who are most consistently orgasmic; but without exception they lack empirical support. It is hoped that the present studies will help to bring some order to this area of knowledge. As will be seen, a considerable array of investigations was undertaken to probe the personality correlates of orgasmic consistency.[2] Many different personality parameters were perused to see if they had pertinence. Initially, the studies were not guided by clear-cut hypotheses. They were frankly exploratory; only as directionalities began to emerge in the findings was it possible to develop a theoretical model that permitted specific formulations. The results of the various studies are presented here in two phases. First, those studies that are positive and significant and seem to pattern themselves in a meaningful way are described. Then, attention is turned to the numerous personality measures that do not seem to be correlated with orgasm consistency. These negative findings are, in their own way, just as important to analyze and assimilate as the positive ones.[3]

ASPECTS OF BEHAVIOR
RELATED TO ORGASM CONSISTENCY

Perceived Dependability of Love Objects

If one consults Appendices A–G, a detailed outline is provided of the tests and psychological procedures that were employed over the course of the multiple samples to study not only orgasm consistency but the other major sexual variables as well. In the very first sample that was appraised, collaboratively with Osofsky (Fisher and Osofsky, 1967), a number of apparently promising leads emerged concerning the nature of the personality differences associated with variations in orgasmic consistency, but they largely failed to hold up to cross-validation. It was observed in this sample that the greater a woman's orgasmic consistency the more likely she was to enjoy eating, to like a wide range of foods, to be low in hostility and irritability, to enjoy activities involving vigorous muscular movement, and to produce relatively more reference to female than male figures when interpreting inkblot stimuli. One of the major deductions originally made from these findings was that orgasm consistency is greatest in those women who generally enjoy physical satisfaction (for example, eating, vigorous muscular activity). More generally and in the language of the original paper (Fisher and Osofsky, 1967) it was concluded (p. 225): "The ability to obtain sexual gratification is but a single aspect of a more manifold capacity to feel positively toward objects and persons and to secure body satisfaction from them." However, the next study that was undertaken (Sample 2) failed, except in a few borderline instances, to support any of the major findings or conclusions cited; what had appeared to be a promising approach to understanding orgasm consistency suddenly seemed much less so.

Death Imagery

Therefore, a reappraisal was undertaken of some of the materials collected in Sample 1 to see if a new perspective might be extracted that could then be evaluated in further studies. Attention was turned to an impressionistic reanalysis of the imaginative projective test productions of the women. Specifically, interpretations the women had offered of a series of inkblots (Holtzman, et al., 1961) as well as the stories they had created when interpreting six Thematic Apperception pictures were available.[4] Detailed descriptions of each of these techniques are available in Appendix A. In the course of examining the women's inkblot responses, it became apparent that there was a relationship between the degree to which the fantasies they produced showed a preoccupation with themes pertaining to death and their orgasmic consistency. Those with limited orgasm consistency appeared more likely to conjure up inkblot references of the following character: dead, carcass, hanged, mummy, tomb, sacrifice, corpse, buried, extinct, and end of the world. Encouraged by such impressionistic observations, a formal scoring system was developed to measure the amount of death content in each woman's inkblot response protocol. A response was considered to have death significance if it fulfills either of the following two criteria: (1) Directly mentions death or dying (for example, dead, hanged, massacred, killed); (2) Refers explicitly to activities, objects, or symbols associated with death (for example, cemetery, gravestone, skeleton, reincarnation, mummy, heaven, hell, devil, funeral).

It was found that two judges, who independently applied this scoring system to 30 sets of inkblot responses, attained 94 percent agreement. There is little difficulty in identifying responses with death implications.

When the Death [5] scores were blindly computed for the inkblot protocols of the women in Sample 1, they were found to be related at a borderline level of significance with the orgasm consistency scores ($x^2 = 3.5$, $df = 1$, $p < .10$).[6] The greater a woman's Death score the lower was her orgasm consistency.

In order to further evaluate this borderline finding, the inkblot protocols collected in three additional samples were blindly scored for Death imagery.[7] It was found in Sample 2 that the greater the Death score the lower was the orgasm capacity ($x^2 = 6.4$, $df = 1$, $p < .02$); this was similarly true in Sample 3 ($x^2 = 9.8$, $df = 1$, $p < .005$)[8]; and Sample 5 ($x^2 = 3.9$, $df = 1$, $p < .05$).

The consistency of these results was encouraging. One could say with confidence that the greater a woman's difficulty in consistently reaching orgasm the more she was preoccupied with themes of death in her inkblot fantasies. In speculating about the meaning of this observation, the obvious association between death and loss presents itself. That is, death is amorphously linked with ideas of loss of life, losing one's friends, and losing gratification. It also conveys the theme that life is transitory and must ultimately be interrupted. From this perspective, it was speculated that the preoccupation of the low-orgasm woman with death represents her concern that her relationships with others, her sources of gratification, and her possessions are all transitory—finally to be lost. Presumably she is skeptical that relationships are dependable or can last, and anticipates the loss of the things that are dear to her.

Separation Imagery

To explore the generality of the Death findings, a blind analysis was undertaken of the Thematic Apperception (TAT) stories collected in Sample 1. Since the literal mention of death occurs rarely in TAT stories, it was decided to consider not only references to death but also equivalent themes involving loss or separation from others. A Separation score was formulated that embraces the following themes: death (or being near death); departure of friends or loved ones; being rejected, attacked, or ignored by others; having to be separated from, or distant from, loved ones. In preliminary independent analyses of 20 TAT protocols, two judges attained 86 percent agreement in their Separation scoring.

The Separation scores for all of the TAT records in Sample 1 were found to be significantly related to orgasm consistency ($x^2 = 8.1$, $df = 1$, $p < .005$).[9] The greater the Separation score the less was the orgasm consistency. This finding is obviously congruent with those involving the relationship of the inkblot Death scores to orgasm consistency.

The Separation scoring system was also blindly applied to two sets of imaginative stories that had been collected from other samples. In Sample 2 the women were asked to compose and write ten spontaneous stories and in Sample 4 they were requested to write eight spontaneous stories.[10] When (in Sample 2) the high-orgasm consistency women ($N = 15$) (who said they experienced orgasm "always" and "nearly always"), were compared with the low-consistency women ($N = 13$), who said they experienced orgasm "occasionally," "rarely," or "never," the latter were found to have higher Separation scores,[11] but only marginally so ($x^2 = 2.8$, $df = 1$, p .10, with Yates' correction).[12] An equivalent analysis in Sample 4 indicated that the low-orgasmic women ($N = 15$) obtained significantly higher Separation scores than the high-orgasmic women ($N = 10$) ($x^2 = 10.9$, $df = 1$, $p < .001$, with Yates' correction).[13]

The nature or flavor of the difference between the high and low orgasm groups can be more vividly conveyed by comparing two stories, one created by a high-orgasmic woman and the other by a low-orgasmic woman. Both of these stories were given in response to the instruction to make up a story about "a girl and her mother." The high-orgasmic woman responded as follows:

A girl and her mother did lots of things together. They went shopping and took trips together. They shared funny stories and humor together. They were sensitive to each other and they looked like each other. Many people who didn't know the mother but knew the girl said to the mother, when they saw her, that they knew she was the girl's mother just by looking at her.

The low-orgasmic woman said:

The girl and her mother had grown very close over the years. There had been many rugged times when the mother had to work hard to keep her daughter, as she (the daughter) was asthmatic and constantly ill. The *father had left to seek greener and younger pastures* and so the mother had full responsibility for caring for the ill girl and supporting her. At one period the child was so sick she could do nothing but vomit for a period of 24 hours and the mother had to work all day and sit with her child all night. There were several days like this and the mother became weak with fatigue. *She had to send her child to a home* where they could care for her professionally so she could keep her job. The girl cried and was unhappy but still knew her mother loved her and understood.[14]

One can see in these examples that although the mother and daughter are said to have a close relationship in both instances, it eventually turns out in the story of the low-orgasmic woman that mother and daughter become separated because the mother "had to send her child to a home." That is, despite the mother's apparent loving attitude she has to turn her daughter over to others and they are no longer together. Incidentally, it is also interesting that in this same story there was another reference to separation (of the mother and father) in the statement that "The father had left to seek greener and younger pastures. . . ."

Parental Loss or Absence

The difference between the high- and low-orgasmic women in their preoccupation with themes of death and separation was pursued at another level in terms of reports obtained from the women concerning their childhood. In Sample 2 (as described in Appendix B) the women were asked to think back to their childhood and to write down ten of the earliest memories they could recall. These memories were then blindly evaluated to determine the presence of the themes of loss and separation. A count was made in each woman's protocol of the frequency with which parents or possible parent representations (for example, uncle, grandfather) were recalled as having died, become seriously ill, been close to death, or separated themselves from the family (for example, by divorce or an extended trip from home). Several examples of such themes follow:

I remember my grandmother died on my birthday.
I remember the day I shot my father in the head with a BB pistol. It only grazed his skull but I was awfully scared.
I remember wishing my mother and father lived together.

When the number of Separation themes produced by each woman was related to her orgasm consistency score, a significant relationship was found ($x^2 = 6.0$, $df = 1$, $p < .02$).[15] The greater a woman's orgasm consistency the less likely she was to recall events of loss and separation as having occurred in her early childhood. Of course, this finding corroborated the others that were presented in this section.

Another opportunity to explore the link between orgasm consistency and concern about loss and separation was provided by autobiographical material that was collected from 43 women in Sample 3. These women were asked (as detailed in Appendix C) to write a rather extensive autobiography in which they provided information about the major events and persons in their lives. Each autobiography was examined to ascertain the frequency with which loss or separation from the mother and father were described as having occurred during childhood. The criteria for scoring loss or separation were as follows.

Death of a parent.
Parent chronically ill and frequently in danger of dying.
Explicit statement that a parent was not living in the house because of divorce.
Explicit statement that a parent was frequently away from home because of
    work or travel or other reasons.

Blind tabulation of references to Separation from mother indicated that they were so infrequent that an analysis could not be meaningfully made as to how they were related to orgasm consistency. However, references to Separation from father were more numerous.[16] When these father Separation scores were related to orgasm consistency, they were found not to be significantly linked. But, when the father Separation scores were examined with reference to the extreme low-orgasm consistency ($N = 16$) women (never, rarely, occasionally) and those of the extreme high-orgasm consistency ($N = 15$) women (always, nearly always), a significant relationship was found ($x^2 = 4.4$, $df = 1$, $p < .05$, with Yates' correction). The low-orgasm consistency women exceeded those with high consistency in the frequency with which they described their fathers as having been dead, separated, or absent during their childhood.

Delivery Experience

One of the studies, involving Sample 6, included women who were seen twice, first when pregnant and then again one month following delivery. A comprehensive account of this study is presented in a later chapter. The women who were involved were asked to write, as soon as possible after their delivery, a detailed description of the entire birth process. They were to discuss the major events of the delivery, including their feelings, thoughts, and annoyances. Thirty-eight women produced such accounts.[17] Since the whole process of delivery represents an event of dramatic proportions that confronts a woman with the need to adapt as an individual to difficult stress, it would seem to be an unusually opportune naturalistic situation in which to evaluate her feelings about loss and separation. That is, typically the woman who is about to deliver is brought into an alien hospital environment, separated from her husband, and forced to adapt to painful and threatening events involving her body with only one familiar face (that of her obstetrician) in view (and even he is present for only a limited part of the total sequence of events). One might expect that the woman with low-orgasm consistency, who apparently fears separation from love objects, would be particularly threatened by being placed in such a context. With this perspective in mind, a blind analysis was made of the description offered by each woman of her delivery in order to tabulate all statements indicating concern about being alone or deserted or ignored. When this analysis was first undertaken, it became apparent that there was an inverse relation between the frequency with which a woman made statements emphasizing a sense of being deserted or ignored (for example, disappointed by the delay in her obstetrician arriving on the scene or angry because hospital personnel were not sufficiently attentive to her) and explicit references to the fact that she missed her husband during the delivery and wished that he could have been present. That is, there seemed to be a tendency for a woman either, on the one hand, to clearly acknowledge that her husband is an important person in her life and that she would have liked to have him at her side during the delivery, or, on the other hand, to make diverse references to the fact that she was alone, deserted, and mistreated during the delivery process. Because of this difference, a separate tabulation was made of each category of response.[18]

An initial analysis involving the *total* sample indicated no relationship between orgasm consistency and reactions to the delivery situation. However, when a further analysis was made of the relative frequency of each type of response in the high-orgasm ($N = 13$) consistency (always, nearly always) and low-orgasm ($N = 12$) consistency women (never, rarely, occasionally), it was found that the greater the orgasm consistency the fewer were the statements made about feeling deserted or neglected by hospital personnel ($x^2 = 9.2$, $df = 1$, $p < .005$), but the greater were the number of explicit statements about wanting one's husband to be present during the delivery [19] ($x^2 = 4.8$, $df = 1$, $p < .05$).[20] In other words, the high-orgasm woman expressed less concern about feeling alone and deserted in the hospital than did the low-orgasm woman, but the former more often expressed an explicit wish to have her husband present during the delivery than did the latter. The fact that the low-orgasm woman is particularly concerned with a sense of aloneness certainly fits well with all of the other information that has been presented indicating her preoccupation with separation and loss of objects. The unexpected finding that the high-orgasm woman is particularly likely to state that she wanted her husband present at the delivery can only be interpreted tentatively. One may speculate that she is more likely than the low-orgasm woman to perceive her husband (just as she does other love objects) as a dependable source of support, and, therefore, when her anxieties about facing the labor process in a strange (somewhat alien) setting are aroused she can more easily formulate the explicit conclusion that his presence would alleviate her problem. Perhaps the low-orgasm woman is too disturbed by the particular brand of anxiety aroused by the alien delivery environment and too unsure of her husband to feel, as well as state, that his presence would be comforting.

Overview of Themes of Death and Separation

By making use of fantasy material and self reports, it has been possible to demonstrate repeatedly that low- versus high-orgasm consistency women differ in their preoccupation with themes of death and loss and in the degree of concern about being alone and deserted. The low-orgasm woman exceeds the high-orgasm woman in projecting death themes into her ink-blot interpretations; depicting characters in her fictional stories as likely to become estranged or separated; perceiving the father as unavailable for a close relationship during the early years; recalling her childhood as a time of loss of significant figures; and feeling deserted and alone after entering the hospital to have her child delivered. One of the most obvious ways of interpreting these findings is in terms of the idea that the low-orgasm woman feels insecure about the dependability of relationships. She could be said to expect that those she loves will die or leave or become separated from her. It is as if she assumed that union with someone else could not be counted upon to persist, but rather to be ultimately terminated unexpectedly. In essence, then, she might be said to view herself as lacking *dependable* attachment to people who really count. Of course, the question immediately arises as to how an orientation of this sort might play a role in inhibiting orgasm. At the end of this chapter a possible model is proposed. However, several other aspects of the findings from the various studies need to be considered first.

Parental Attitudes

Directly pertinent to the matter under consideration are findings that emerged when the women were asked to respond to questionnaires that systematically evaluated their attitudes toward their parents. In Samples 2, 3, and 4 the Parent-Child Relations Questionnaire (Roe and Siegelman, 1963) was administered (see Appendix B). Each woman filled it out once to indicate her recall of how her father had dealt with her during childhood and then again in an analogous fashion with reference to her mother. This questionnaire was designed to measure a number of different dimensions of the behavior of the parent, as it was recalled. The major dimensions and brief definitions of each follow.

Protective: Giving the child's interests priority; being indulgent, affectionate, and protective in the face of potentially threatening situations; rewarding dependency.

Demanding: Setting high standards; imposing strict regulations; being punitive; demanding unquestioning obedience.

Rejecting: Rejecting the childishness of the child; being cold, hostile, and derogatory; leaving the child alone.

Neglecting: Paying little attention to the child; forgetting promises made to the child; adopting a cold attitude.

Casual: Being easygoing; enforcing few rules; rarely planning deliberately for the child.

Loving: Being warm and loving; devoting attention to the child; encouraging independence.

Symbolic-Love Reward: Praising for approved behavior, giving special and affectionate attention.

Direct-Object Reward: Giving tangible rewards (for example, gifts, toys) for approved behavior.

Symbolic-Love Punishment: Shaming the child; isolating him; withdrawing love from him.

Direct-Object Punishment: Using physical punishment; taking away playthings; reducing allowance.

When the results of the application of this questionnaire to three different samples were analyzed, only two of the dimensions differentiated with any consistency among the women varying in orgasm response. Before describing these findings, it should first be noted that none of the Parent-Child scores as they apply to the behavior of mother was able to distinguish orgasm consistency levels reliably. There was no apparent relationship between a woman's recall of how her mother had treated her and that woman's current ability to attain orgasm. But some interesting trends were observed with reference to the Parent-Child Relations scores based on recall of how father had behaved. In Sample 2 a significant correlation was first observed between orgasm consistency and the Casual score.[21] The greater a woman's orgasm consistency the *less* she recalled her father as having treated her casually ($r = -.46$, $p < .05$, $N = 22$).[22] To put it another way, orgasm consistency was lower in those who perceived the father as having conformed to the following paradigm that describes how Casual parents treat a child (Roe and Siegelman, 1963, p. 357):

They (high Casual parents) will be responsive to him (the child) if they are not busy about something else. They do not think about him or plan for him very much, but take him as part of the general situation. They don't worry much about him and make little definite effort to train him. They are easy going, have few rules, and do not make much effort to enforce those they have.

The low-orgasm consistency woman depicted her father, then, as treating her "casually," without elaborate attempts at control or enforcing his will, informally, and easygoing rather than expecting conformity to well-defined rules.

This finding was evaluated by determining in a second sample (Sample 3) whether orgasm consistency and the Casual score were significantly correlated. They were found not to be. However, in still another sample

(Sample 4) they were significantly correlated ($r = -.33$, $p < .05$).[23] In this instance, it was again found that the greater a woman's orgasm consistency the less she perceived her father as having treated her casually. Overall, this relationship was observed in two of the three samples in which the Parent-Child Relations Questionnaire was administered, and may therefore be regarded as worthy of serious consideration.[24]

It is of related interest that orgasm consistency also showed a trend to be related to the father Demanding score of the Parent-Child Relations Questionnaire. In Sample 2 it was found that the greater a woman's orgasm consistency the *more* she described her father as high on the Demanding dimension ($r = .53$, $p < .01$, $N = 22$). This relationship failed to be supported in Sample 3, but it was reaffirmed at a borderline level in Sample 4 ($r = .27$, $p < .10$). One may regard the findings from these three studies as being indicative of a suggestive trend, but obviously requiring further confirmation. One of the reasons for citing this borderline trend is that it complements the relationships involving the Casual score cited previously in an interesting fashion. The Demanding dimension refers to the father's imposing strict regulations, being restrictive, and demanding obedience. Contrastingly, the Casual dimension refers to the father's being easygoing and enforcing few rules. These two dimensions, which represent opposite extremes of a Casual-Demanding continuum, were also reversed in their relationship with orgasm consistency.[25] The woman who is high on orgasm consistency tends to depict her father as not Casual but Demanding, and the woman with low-orgasm consistency characterizes her father as Casual rather than Demanding. One may more succinctly define this pattern by saying that the greater a woman's orgasm consistency the less permissive and the more controlling she perceives her father to have been. When this finding first began to emerge, the present writer was surprised. There is little in the literature that would prepare one for the possibility that the strict, controlling father is more likely than the casual, permissive father to "produce" a daughter who easily attains orgasm.[26] Although a detailed interpretation of this finding is postponed until later in the chapter, one tentative thought is offered at this point because it provides some continuity between the present results and those concerning preoccupation with death and separation described earlier. What was noted earlier is that the low-orgasm consistency woman is concerned about the lack of permanence and unreliability of her relationships with love objects. Is it possible that the father of the low-orgasm daughter, by acting "casual" and "permissive" toward her and not expecting her to live up to a fairly well-defined and enforced code of rules, gives her a feeling that their relationship is tenuous? Is his casual attitude interpreted as a lack of basic commitment to and self-investment in the relationship? The temptation to answer this question affirmatively is increased if one looks closely at the kinds of Parent-Child Relations Questionnaire responses that indicate a perception of the father as "Casual." A woman who depicted her father as clearly "Casual" would need to agree fairly strongly that the following statements applied to his mode of dealing with her before she had attained the age of 12.

He let me spend my money any way I liked.
He let me stay up as late as I liked.
He let me do pretty much what I wanted to do.
He did not tell me what time to be home when I went out.
He did not bother much about making rules stick.

Some of these behaviors on a father's part could be viewed as being thinly separated from indifference and lack of genuine concern about his daughter's welfare.

Oral Fantasy and Behavior

The first study initiated by the writer in collaboration with Osofsky (Fisher and Osofsky, 1967) that dealt with the correlates of orgasm capacity strongly implicated orality. That is, there seemed to be evidence that the woman who most consistently reaches orgasm also enjoys eating a wide variety of foods and entertains a good deal of fantasy or imagery concerned with oral themes (eating, drinking, sucking). For this reason many of the subsequent studies devoted significant effort to measuring numerous aspects of eating and other oral behavior. These studies eventually gave uneven results and, as is seen, the link between orgasm consistency and oral attitudes proved to be more complex and tenuous than had been expected. The primary reason that the findings pertaining to orality are being taken up at this point is because they may have pertinence to the whole matter of being concerned about the nondependability of love objects. They may be pertinent in the sense that persons who are chronically insecure about the dependability of relationships are often assumed to be "oral dependent" or "oral fixated" character types. Within psychoanalytic theory the oral character is one who had early frustrating experiences that induced anxiety as to whether necessary sustenance could be counted on from primary love objects. Presumably, the oral character doubts that anyone can really be depended upon and is chronically preoccupied with concerns about finding enough "supplies" to incorporate or "take in." If one accepts this formulation (which is made attractive by empirical studies linking certain types of oral imagery and dependent behavior—for example, Levitt, Lubin, and Zuckerman, 1962), it would be logical to expect that women who differ in orgasm consistency, and, therefore, also in their confidence in love objects, would show parallel differences in their concern about oral matters.

As indicated in Appendices A–G, the techniques employed in the present studies to measure attitudes about incorporation (for example, eating) and other aspects of orality have been diverse. They may be roughly classified into the following categories:

Measures of how much eating is enjoyed and the range of food preferred, as measured by the Byrne Food Attitude Scale (Byrne, Golightly, and Capaldi, 1963).

Judgments of whether drinking is pleasurable.

Responses to words and pictures referring to oral themes presented at high speeds (by means of tachistoscope).

Questionnaires concerned with traits of oral dependency and oral aggression.

Measure of the inclination to create words with oral connotations.

Number of references to oral themes in inkblot responses.

Number of references to oral themes in free expressions given in response to the instruction to write down "20 things that you are aware of or conscious of right now."

Many of the results obtained in relating these oral measures to orgasm consistency were of a chance nature. The orgasm index did not reliably correlate with questionnaire measures of oral dependency or oral aggression (Murray-David Affect Questionnaire), and did not correlate with the number of references to oral themes (for example, "I am hungry") in self-reports about what was in each woman's immediate awareness, the number of different foods liked, the speed at which a picture with a nurturant theme (parental figure caring for a baby) could first be accurately identified when presented tachistoscopically, the number of words with oral connotations produced when asked to complete a series of incomplete words, and the number of images with oral significance elicited by inkblot stimuli. However, there were several borderline significant findings that are briefly described.

General attitudes about eating were measured in four of the samples studied by means of the Byrne Food Attitude Scale (Byrne, et al., 1963) and related to orgasm consistency. The Byrne Scale evaluates the amount of enjoyment and positive feeling associated with eating experiences. It was found that orgasm consistency was positively correlated with enjoyment of eating in Samples 1 ($r = .25$, $p < .10$) and 6 ($r = .44$, $p < .01$), but not in Samples 2 and 3. At best, this is a borderline trend.

In a related vein, orgasm consistency was studied in two samples with reference to the amount of interest in oral activities such as eating and drinking, as measured by means of the Average Week (Fisher, 1970) technique (described in Appendix B), which is based on how frequently the individual refers to oral activities (for example, eating, cooking) when asked to write a description of how she spends an average week. A significant positive relationship was found between orgasm consistency and amount of references to oral activities in Sample 2 ($x^2 = 5.0$, $df = 1$, p .02), but in Sample 3 the relationship was of chance magnitude.[27]

There were two instances in which orgasm consistency was related to selective response to oral themes presented at high speed through tachistoscope.[28] In Sample 2 it was found at a borderline level ($x^2 = 3.7$, $df = 1$, $p < .10$) that the greater a woman's orgasm consistency the more quickly she was able to identify words pertaining to orality (for example, food, candy, soup, chew) as compared to words pertaining to other themes such as hostility and narcissism.[27] In Sample 2 it was also found at a borderline level ($r = .26$, $p.10$) that the more consistently a woman attains orgasm the more consistently she can correctly identify a picture with an oral aggressive theme (dog biting) as compared to pictures with other themes (for example, anal, masturbatory).[29]

Obviously, the results pertaining to oral variables that have been reviewed do not add up to much. There is a hint that the woman with low-orgasm consistency may have relatively low enjoyment of oral intake as well as react in a "shutting out" or defensive fashion to stimuli with oral connotations. But one speaks here of borderline trends that really need much more investigation.

Self-Report Personality Traits

Both the Thurstone Temperament Scale (1953) and the Edwards Personal Preference Schedule (1959) were used in an exploratory fashion to ascertain whether orgasm consistency is correlated with broad personality traits. Both of these questionnaires evaluate the presence of specific traits in terms of an individual's responses to a detailed and systematic inquiry about how he usually feels and behaves.

The Thurstone Scale (see Appendix A) measures seven dimensions.[30] In three different samples (1, 2, 6) orgasm consistency was not reliably related to any of these dimensions.

The Edwards Personal Preference Schedule (see Appendix B) measures 15 different variables.[31] Only one of these variables was found to be related with any consistency to orgasm consistency. This was Endurance, which was positively correlated with orgasm consistency in Sample 3 (.32, $p < .05$) and Sample 4 (.41, $p < .01$). Only in Sample 2 was there a nonsignificant correlation.[32] The significant coefficients in two of three samples are certainly suggestive of a real relationship.[33] Apparently, the higher a woman's Endurance score the greater is her orgasm consistency.

Edwards (1959) defines the Endurance dimension in the following terms (p. 11):

> To keep at a job until it is finished, to complete any job undertaken, to work hard at a task, to keep at a puzzle or problem until it is solved, to work at a single job before taking on others, to stay up late working in order to get a job done, to put in long hours of work without distraction, to stick at a problem even though it may seem as if no progress is being made, to avoid being interrupted while at work.

This would mean, then, that the more a woman can stick to a task and persist in dealing with a problem, even in the face of complication or interruption, the greater is her orgasm consistency. Does this finding have any immediate obvious relevance to other observations that have been presented concerning the attributes associated with orgasm consistency? Perhaps it does bear tangentially on the rather consistent link that has been noted between a woman's orgasm consistency and her trust in the dependability of objects to which she relates. One could speculate that a woman who sticks to tasks, persisting even in the face of complication and interruption, has a basic trust that her efforts will, over the long run, be rewarded. Presumably, her persistence reflects confidence in the trustworthiness of the world and a feeling that it can be depended upon to give a return if effort is invested in it. One could say that the high-orgasm-consistency woman who believes in the reliability of objects and relationships expresses this orientation in her willingness to persist at tasks that she assumes will be ultimately rewarding.[34] But the low-orgasm woman who doubts the permanence of objects would have less reason to expect that persistent effort would have a real payoff. A second thought offered at this point concerning the Endurance finding goes back to material presented in the previous chapter that contains women's descriptions of the process involved in their attaining orgasm. It will be recalled that many of the women emphasized that in order to reach orgasm they had to exclude outside stimuli that might be distracting, and there had to be an intense unwavering concentration on one's own body and the sensations being produced by sexual stimulation. One interpretation of such material is that the attainment of orgasm requires, to some degree, the ability to persist or concentrate, even if distractions occur. One could say that reaching orgasm demands of a woman that she be able to persist in a buildup process (gradual accumulation of muscular tension) despite momentary disappointments, distractions, and downward shifts in arousal.

Skin Response

There is a long history of anecdotal musing about whether a woman's sexual responsiveness is reflected in how ticklish she is. For example, Dunbar (1954) offered the view that many girls who were extremely ticklish cease to be so when they begin to engage in regular sexual intercourse. Ellis (1921) too suggested that the sexually inexperienced girl is likely to be particularly sensitive to tickle. Kepecs and Robin (1956, 1955) actually studied the responses of various kinds of personalities to tickle and concluded that they differ in the ways they adapt to continuous light stroking of the skin. The normal pattern, as they defined it, was for the initial tickle or itch to change within a two-minute period to a sensation of touch. One of their broad conclusions (1956, p. 340) was that:

The touch system is related to and subserves ego functioning. Responses of normal adaptation (to skin stroking) appear to be related to optimum balance between erotic, instinctual life, and ego control, insofar as this can be reflected in the skin.[35] Reactions of no adaptation (all itch or tickle) indicate excessive emotionality and deficient control.

Actually, observations have accumulated that skin contact and skin experiences can play a significant part in the maturation of the developing organism and the way in which it deals with affection in later life. Nissen, Chow, and Semees (1951) and Harlow (1962) have shown that monkeys deprived of sufficient early skin stimulation develop serious maladaptive behavior. Harlow reported that such monkeys had gross difficulties in the area of heterosexual behavior. Spitz (1955) has reported the disturbing consequences of babies not receiving sufficient skin stimulation from those who care for them.

There seemed to be good reason for investigating whether sexual responsiveness was correlated with the response characteristics of the skin. Findings will now be presented which specifically concern the relationship of orgasm consistency to two measures of skin sensitivity. One of the two measures of skin sensitivity evaluated response to tickle. As described in detail in Appendix B, a technique was used for measuring tickle response that involves delivering standard strokes to the skin with a piece of cotton.[36] Each woman was asked to report as soon as the stroking produced a feeling of tickle. Furthermore, she was to indicate exactly when the feeling of tickle disappeared and was replaced by some other sensation. Stroking was stopped at the moment that a woman indicated that the tickle sensation had disappeared. However, if tickle persisted beyond one minute, stroking was terminated at that point. In most of the samples in which this technique was employed, tickle measures were taken at a number of different body sites as well as systematically on the right and left sides of the body. The person administering the procedure used a stopwatch to determine the time of the first appearance of tickle and the time of cessation. As shown in detail in Table 8–1, the tickle stimulus was applied to such sites as wrist, cheek, breast, and thigh. The number of such sites varied from sample to sample.

A second measure of skin sensitivity involved light touch (pressure). A graded series of nylon filaments were used to determine each woman's ability to detect light touch. The filaments were calibrated so that the force they exerted was known. Each woman was asked, with her eyes blindfolded, to indicate each time she felt touch on a given body site.[37] The touch stimuli were applied in an irregular time sequence so that the women could not accurately anticipate them. As depicted in Table 8–1, light-touch stimuli were applied to such diverse sites as wrist, breast, and thigh, with the number varying in different samples.[38]

When the results pertaining to both perception of tickle and light touch were analyzed, a few interesting trends emerged. As portrayed in Table 8–1, the time required to experience tickle *on the wrist* was positively and significantly related to orgasm consistency in two of the three instances (although one of the positive correlations only attained the .10 level of significance) in which data relating to wrist responses were available.[39] The greater a woman's orgasm consistency the longer it required for the stroking *on her wrist* to be experienced as tickle.[40] However, the results for

TABLE 8-1
Correlations of Orgasm Consistency[a] with Tickle and Also Sensitivity to Light Touch

Body Sites	Tickle Correlations		Body Sites	Light Touch Correlations
	Time to Begin Sample 2	Duration Sample 2		Sample 1
Cheeks[b]	−.32*** (N = 40)	−.45*** (N = 20)	Wrist	.16
Breasts	−.33*** (N = 41)	N.S.[c]	Thigh	N.S.
Thighs	−.32* (N = 28)	N.S.		Sample 2
			Wrist	.34*** (N = 38)
	Sample 3	Sample 3	Breast	.28* (N = 41)
Wrists	.29** (N = 44)	N.S.	Leg	N.S.
Cheeks	.29** (N = 44)	N.S.	Thigh	.30*** (N = 41)
Breasts	N.S.	N.S.		Sample 3
Thighs	N.S.	N.S.	Wrist	.34*** (N = 43)
	Sample 4	Sample 4	Breast	N.S.
Wrists	.17 (N = 40)	N.S.		Sample 4
Cheeks	N.S.	N.S.	Wrist	N.S.
	Sample 5	Sample 5		
Wrists	.31* (N = 30)	N.S.		
Cheeks	N.S.	−.48*** (N = 17)		

[a]The original orgasm consistency ratings have been transformed so that a high value means high-orgasm consistency.

[b]A wrist tickle threshold was not obtained in this sample.

[c]N.S. = Not significant and not even attaining .20 level of significance.

*p .10 level.

**p .05 level.

***p < .05 level.

tickle responses on the cheeks, breasts, and thighs were of a chance order. It is also noteworthy that in two of four instances in which the *duration* of tickle on the *cheek* was measured it proved to be negatively linked with orgasm consistency. That is, the greater a woman's orgasm consistency the less did continuous stroking of the cheek produce persisting tickle.[41]

Looking at the results in Table 8–1 concerned with sensitivity to light touch, one notes that in two of four samples orgasm consistency was positively and significantly correlated with touch threshold *on the wrist*.[42] In other words, the greater a woman's orgasm consistency the less sensitive was the skin *on her wrist* to the pressure stimuli. Sensitivity of skin on other body areas, such as breast and thigh, was not correlated with orgasm consistency.[43] Just as was true for the tickle data, only the sensitivity of the skin on the wrist was meaningfully related to the orgasm index.[44]

Although the results for the tickle and touch sensitivity measures are not impressive, they do show the existence of a trend that is sufficiently definite to merit consideration. It would appear that response to a stimulus applied to the skin of the wrist is least in those who are most consistently orgasmic. One of the first questions that arises in appraising such findings is why consistent results appear only for the wrist and not for other sites such as breast, thigh, and cheeks of the face. At the moment, the most reasonable explanation derives from the amount of intimacy or potentially embarrassing closeness that goes along with applying a stimulus to the wrist as compared to the other body sites. The wrist is a less intimate or personal body area than any of the others. Therefore, one could speculate that when a stimulus is applied to it there would be less embarrassment or disturbing affect aroused that might interfere with accurate perception of the stimulus itself. In reacting to tickle or touch applied to her thighs or breasts, a woman might become so distracted by her embarrassment that this would seriously interfere with her ability to observe her sensations with clarity. Presumably, such embarrassment would be less likely for a stimulus applied to the wrist. If so, one would be able to get a more accurate measure, less complicated by extraneous influences, from the wrist than the other body areas.[45] The moderate consistency observed between wrist sensitivity and orgasm consistency would derive, then, in part from the relatively greater validity of the wrist measure as a "pure" or more specific index of skin sensitivity, as such. If one accepts what has been said about the skin sensitivity findings to this point, it becomes legitimate to ponder why a woman's orgasm consistency and skin sensitivity should be inversely related. Little in the scientific literature clarifies this issue, and so one can only fall back on speculation. But it seems sensible to let such speculation be guided by the multiple observations already cited that indicate that concern about maintaining ties with love objects plays a role in the orgasm process. Is it possible that the woman who fears loss of love objects (and who, of course, is also the one who has difficulty in reaching orgasm) expresses this concern in a chronic wishful expectation of *making contact* with objects? Could the heightened sensitivity of her skin be a manifestation of her persistent preoccupation with wanting objects to be close (to be "touching") so that she can be reassured of their presence? It is not unreasonable to assume that someone who has an unusual amount of concern about a body region (the skin), which plays an important role in contacting objects, should be particularly sensitive to stimuli impinging upon it.

Right-Left Directionality

Another parameter that was studied with reference to orgasm consistency concerned the differentiation between right and left. As noted by several writers (Fenichel, 1954; Fisher, 1962, 1970), one typically finds, across a range of cultures, that the dimension of right versus left is semantically associated with masculinity-femininity. Right is often linked with the masculine and left with the feminine. Empirical evidence has gradually accumulated that supports such an equation. For example, Sandstrom (1954), Bennett (1956), and Trites (1969) found that in adjusting a luminous rod to a vertical position in the dark, adult women show a left, and adult men a right, bias in their judgments. Relatedly, Groberg, Dustman, and Beck (1969) observed that, when making judgments about the vertical position of a luminous rod, women were more influenced by the fact of its first being viewed in a left starting position, and men by first perceiving it in a right starting position. Wapner and Werner (1957) noted that in the age range 10–17, boys more often locate the vertical to the right, and girls to the left. Chateau (1959) detected a trend for boys to exceed girls in their preference for right turns in a maze. Even further, Fisher (1962) demonstrated that beginning at the age of 11, boys are more often right directional than girls in their perception of autokinetic movement.[46] It should be added, though, that Fisher (1970) has not observed a difference between the sexes in the degree to which they focus attention on the right versus the left sides of their bodies. Overall, there is fairly convincing evidence that a bias to the right in structuring space is characteristic of the male and a bias to the left typifies the female.

It was with this viewpoint that a task was introduced into the studies that would make it possible to relate sexual responsiveness to right versus left directionality in spatial perception. This task had to do with adjusting a luminous rod to the vertical in the dark. Each woman was brought into a completely darkened room. She was positioned 16 feet from an apparatus consisting of a luminous rod surrounded by a luminous frame.[47] The rod and the frame were set at various degrees from the true vertical, and the woman was to instruct the experimenter how to move the rod until it was perfectly vertical ("straight up and down"). To evaluate right versus left bias in judgment of the vertical, a score was computed equal to the number of errors made to the right, minus the number to the left, of vertical.

In terms of the findings that have been reviewed that associate right spatial bias with the masculine and left with the feminine, it was tentatively expected that the greater a woman's orgasm consistency the more likely she would be to show left rather than right directionality in her perceptions.[48] Of course, this expectation indirectly implies that a feminine orientation in a woman indicates a greater potentiality for sexual responsiveness on her part to stimulation by a man than does a masculine one.[49]

The rod and frame technique was administered in Samples 2 and 3. It was found that orgasm consistency was negatively correlated with right minus left errors in Sample 2 ($r = -.28$, $p < .10$) and also Sample 3 ($r = -.45$, $p < .01$).[50] That is, as predicted, the greater a woman's orgasm consistency the less likely she was to show right directionality.

These findings do suggest that when a woman shows in her perceptions a spatial directionality that typifies the female rather than the male, she is likely to be relatively high in orgasm consistency. One way of interpreting the findings is simply within the framework of what is "normal" for women. That is, since left directionality is presumably a normal response for women, it can be said that any woman who displays this response pattern is behaving like a normal woman and consequently is able to respond as a normal woman should to sexual stimulation. Another approach to interpreting the findings is in terms of what has been learned in the growing literature on right-left directionality. Direct interest in relating right-left response patterns to personality may be found in the work of Day (1964, 1967), Duke (1968), Bakan (1969), and Fisher (1961). Other studies have examined right-left directionality with reference to perception, learning, and cognition (White, 1969). There has been a trend to find left-directional responses associated with a "subjective," emotional, imaginative, "humanistic," nonaggressive orientation, and right-directional responses with a "hard," achieving, "quantitative," less emotional stance. Bakan (1969) has suggested the interesting hypothesis that the left-directional individual responds to a special degree via the right cerebral hemisphere, with the right-directional person favoring the left hemisphere. He further points out that the right hemisphere tends to be dominant for certain functions that can be characterized as (p. 930) "preverbal, prelogical, subjective, intuitive, global, synthetic, and diffuse" whereas the left hemisphere seems to be specialized for more verbal and formal skills. From this perspective, right versus left directionality is a manifestation of the degree of influence of the right and left cerebral hemisphere in any particular person. Presumably, too, it denotes an inclination toward an intuitive as compared to a formal style of responses that is considered to be linked with dominance of the one as compared to the other hemisphere. There is no easy way of bridging between such a formulation and that involving anxiety about loss of love objects that has been so prominently invoked to explain other findings relating to orgasm consistency. However, as one immerses oneself in the scattered findings pertaining to right-left directionality, one cannot help but be impressed with how frequently the two extremes are distinguished in terms of concepts such as soft versus hard, informal versus formal, nonachieving versus achieving, nonaggressive versus aggressive, and interested in people as compared to things. One can read into this a difference in ease or comfort in relating to other persons. This difference might be described as having to do with whether one needs to be defensive or guarded in interpersonal contacts. The terms used in the literature to distinguish those who are left versus right directional remind one also of the many distinctions between the feminine and masculine style that were reviewed in an earlier chapter. It will be recalled that women have been observed in numerous studies to be "softer" and less defensive than men in their mode of interacting with others. Possibly, then, the difference in left-right spatial directionality associated with high- versus low-orgasm consistency reflects a difference in the degree to which a woman has adopted that special aspect of the feminine role that involves behaving warmly and nondefensively toward others. Of course, an obvious analogy exists between the concept of being nondefensive toward others and the concept of trust in the dependability and permanence of one's relationships with others.

This is the proper place to discuss those findings that were obtained with regard to right-left differences in tickle threshold.[51] In three samples (3, 4, 5) evaluations were made of differences in response to the stroking of the right as compared to the left side of the body. In some of the studies described in which stroking was applied, it was systematically alternated at right and left sites (for example, right wrist and left wrist, right breast and left breast).[52] The relative susceptibility of the right and left sides of the body to tickle was ascertained by averaging for all right-side sites the amount of time required for the stroking to be experienced as tickle and subtracting from it the equivalent average for left-side sites.

It was found that orgasm consistency was negatively related to the right minus left tickle-threshold score in Sample 3 ($x^2 = 3.8$, $df = 1$, p .05) [53] and Sample 5 ($r = -.49$, $p < .01$), but had only a chance relationship with it in Sample 4.[54] In two of three instances, then, one can say that the greater a woman's orgasm consistency the less quickly she responded to tickle on the left than on the right side of her body.[55]

It is difficult, if not impossible, at this point to decide in any logical fashion how to translate right-left differences in tickle threshold into right-left directionality terms analogous to those conceptualized for the rod and frame task. Does relatively quicker response to tickle on one side than the other mean that there is a directional bias favoring that side? The only empirical information available would argue to the contrary. As already noted, there was a borderline *positive* correlation between directionality of rod and frame response and directionality of tickle threshold. This means, for example, that the greater the rod and frame right directionality the relatively *less* responsive was the right side of the body to stroking. Thus, what was considered to be the feminine direction of bias for the rod and frame task (that is, left directionality) would be represented in the tickle task by being *less* responsive to tickle on the left side of the body. It is interesting that orgasm consistency was, indeed, positively correlated with the tendency to be less responsive to tickle on the left than right body sides.

There are obviously intriguing potentialities in further exploring the relationship of orgasm capacity to various right-left directionality patterns.

ASPECTS OF BEHAVIOR
UNRELATED TO ORGASM CONSISTENCY

The circuitous route to finding out what attributes of a woman are related to her orgasm consistency is dotted with many negative findings. Numerous developmental, personality, and physiological variables were discovered to be uncorrelated with the orgasm index. It is just as important to review these findings as the more positive ones considered earlier in the chapter. There are assumptions and stereotypes in the literature concerning the factors contributing to sexual responsiveness in women that are directly challenged by the negative findings that are now presented.

Developmental and Physique Factors

Information was obtained from each woman concerning her developmental background and physique. She provided data concerning such variables as the following: age of menarche, age at which breast development began, age of onset of pubic and axillary hair growth, age when attained maximum height, early and more recent menstrual regularity, age married, number of sibs, weight (actually measured), height (actually measured), dress size, and brassiere size.

Each woman was also asked to rate her own degree of physical attractiveness. Further, one group of judges rated the attractiveness of a sample of women on the basis of having observed them for several hours. The attractiveness of another sample was rated by judges who were given front- and back-view pictures of each woman. None of the measures enumerated was significantly correlated with orgasm consistency. One cannot predict how orgasmic a woman will be from a knowledge of how early she developed secondary sex characteristics, the regularity of her menstrual cycle,[56] or the size attributes of her body.[57] This is similarly true with respect to the attractiveness of her physical appearance, the size of her breasts, or her weight.[58] It would appear that the gross aspects of physique and body appearance do not have much to do with orgasmic capacity. Other investigators such as Terman (1951) and Landis (1940) have, with minor exceptions, come to essentially similar conclusions.

Femininity

There are widely accepted popular assumptions about the role of "femininity" in orgasmic response. It is thought that the more "feminine" a woman is the greater will be her orgasmic capacity. At some level, this may be true, but there is no support for the idea when one approaches it in terms of formal measures of femininity. The Femininity scale of the California Psychological Inventory (Gough, 1957) and a similar measure derived from the Strong Vocational Interest Blank (1966) had only chance correlations with orgasm consistency.[59] An analysis was also undertaken of the relative frequency with which male and female human figures appeared in the inkblot responses of the women studied. Although in an initial study (Sample 1) there was a significant trend for the more orgasmic women to perceive more female than male figures in the blots, it was not supported in several subsequent samples.

Another aspect of "femininity" that was considered had to do with degree of interest in cosmetics, perfumes, new clothing fashions, and varied hair styles. The women were asked to supply detailed information about such matters by filling out questionnaires (Appendices B and K). No consistent correlations of significance could be shown between these variables and orgasm consistency. A woman's orgasm consistency cannot be predicted from the degree to which she lavishes "beautifying" attention upon her body, or makes use of perfume, or seeks novelty in her dress or hair styles. This, by the way, is congruent with the earlier mentioned finding that a woman's appearance does not give any substantial clues as to her orgasm capacity.

There may be meaningful relationships between orgasm consistency and some aspects of what is called femininity.[60] However, the present studies have failed to find consistent links when femininity is defined either in terms of a woman showing interest patterns similar to those of the average woman, or producing more references to female than male figures in imaginative productions, or manifesting high investment in conventional forms of feminine body adornment and decoration.

Early Dating Behavior

Is the girl who begins to date early or who dates with relatively high frequency likely to become the woman who is relatively high in orgasm consistency? Inquiry was made in a number of samples concerning dating behavior in high school and college (for example, frequency, "going steady," being engaged); none of the derived indices correlated with the orgasm index. One cannot predict orgasmic potential from the sheer quantity of dating or the frequency of intimate alliances designated by terms such as "going steady" and "engaged."

Religiosity

The women in several samples were asked to fill out questionnaires in which they rated their own degree of religiosity and indicated not only their own frequency of church attendance but also that of their parents. Furthermore, in a number of other samples measures were available of the degree to which there was endorsement of religious values (as defined by the Allport-Vernon-Lindzey Study of Values [1960] Religious score). There was no hint of a relationship between orgasm consistency and any of the religiosity measures.[61] One qualification of the findings, the fact that only a few of the women who participated in the studies were highly religious, needs to be made.[62] The great majority of the women were of low to moderate religiosity, so that the possibility remains that differences in orgasmic capacity might emerge if one compared women representing the real extremes of religiosity. In any case, it will be recalled that Kinsey, et al. (1953) also found few solid differences in the sexual responsiveness of women with different religious orientations.

Psychological Disturbance

As noted in the early chapters devoted to reviewing the literature dealing with sexual responsiveness, there has been a strong inclination to link orgasm capacity with "mental health." It has been a prevailing view that the woman who has difficulty in reaching orgasm is psychologically maladjusted. In the present studies the findings did indicate that orgasm difficulties are particularly likely to occur in women who feel that love objects are not trustworthy. At first sight, this might be interpreted as an affirmation of the "maladjustment" theory, but such an interpretation would go beyond the facts. To say that a woman is concerned about loss of love objects or to specify her preoccupation with any other given problem does not indicate how adequately she is able to cope with her difficulty. Presumably, all persons have conflicts and problems that may vary over a wide spectrum. Psychological disturbance does not, then, simply mean the existence of a problem, but rather the inability to cope with it adequately. In relation to the matter of maladjustment, the proper question is not whether orgasm consistency is linked with the existence of a problem or conflict, but rather whether it is correlated with behavior indicative of anxiety, disturbance, and inability to cope.

A number of measures were included in the various studies that were designed to evaluate each woman's anxiety level.

1. One of the measures was based on a rating of each woman's degree of anxiety as manifested in her behavior in the psychological laboratory. In

three of the seven samples multiple laboratory personnel who administered tests to each woman rated her degree of anxiety (on a five-point scale). Further, the physician who administered a gynecological examination to the women in Sample 1 rated their degree of anxiety during this procedure, and the women themselves rated their own levels of anxiety at this time. When the various anxiety ratings were correlated with orgasm consistency, it was found that the relationships were of a chance order in all of the samples.

2. The Murray-David Anxiety Scale was administered in two samples (4 and 5). This calls for expressing one's degree of agreement with such statements as the following:

There are times when one is almost paralyzed by fear, sudden and senseless.
There is plenty to worry about in this life.

Although orgasm consistency was negatively and significantly correlated with the Murray Anxiety score in Sample 5 ($r = -.39$, $N = 30$, $p < .05$), the two measures were unrelated in Sample 4. One must therefore conclude that a dependable correlation between orgasm consistency and anxiety level, defined by the Murray Scale, has not been demonstrated.

3. The Stability scale of the Thurstone (1953) Temperament Schedule, which is said to measure "emotional stability," was administered in Samples 1, 2, and 6. It proved in all instances to have chance correlations with orgasm consistency.

4. Another approach to measuring anxiety, which was attempted in Sample 5, was based on a technique that has been used in previous studies of stress and anxiety effects (Lazarus, 1966). This technique involves the subject performing a motor task (Digit-Symbol subtest of the Wechsler Adult Intelligence Scale) under relatively quiet baseline conditions, imposing a stress upon him, and then having him repeat the task to ascertain the degree to which the stress effects disrupt the second performance.[63] Thus, in Sample 5 the women worked for 90 seconds on the Digit-Symbol task. They were then exposed to a five-minute segment of a movie that portrays automobile accidents in graphic and gory detail, and immediately afterward repeated the Digit Symbol task, with the film and its sound track continuing.[64] Scores were computed that indicated the degree to which performance subsequent to the stress film deteriorated. These scores proved to be completely unrelated to orgasm consistency; once again a presumed index of anxiety was not correlated with the orgasmic index.[65]

5. Anxiety was also appraised in terms of response to a learning task.[66] In three samples (2, 3, 4) the women were asked to learn lists of words that typically contained material with emotional connotations and that were presented under probably stressful, "hurry up" conditions. It was presumed that the greater the stress the more interference there would be with the learning and recall process and the smaller the number of words the individual would be able to recall correctly. When the average number

of words recalled by the women in each of the three samples was correlated with their respective orgasm consistency ratings, all of the relationships proved to be insignificant.

6. Each woman in Sample 3 was asked to write an autobiography.
These autobiographies were blindly evaluated by judges for the presence of
references to past episodes of psychological disturbance (for example, "I
had terrible nightmares," "I was very lonely and depressed").[67] No relationship of consequence could be discerned between the amount of such
disturbance and orgasm consistency.

7. Each woman in Sample 3 was also asked to watch a film depicting a
direct view of a woman in the delivery position with her genitals exposed
—as the child was being born and the afterbirth was subsequently ejected.
She was asked to rate her reaction to the film and to write a description of
its impact upon her. Anxiety indices computed from the ratings and descriptions had only chance correlations with the women's orgasm consistency.[68]

8. Inkblot protocols obtained in Samples 1, 2, 3, and 5 were analyzed
for the presence of images reflecting discomfort or disturbance (for example, themes of sadness, hostility, pain). Indices of inkblot discomfort that
were derived showed no significant links with orgasm consistency.

Across the range of techniques employed, there seems to be little evidence that women who differ in orgasm consistency differ correspondingly
in their degree of anxiety. It should be added at this point that intensive
interviews (described later in this chapter) with women representing extremes of high- and low-orgasm consistency did not turn up any indications of gross differences between them in neurotic symptomatology or
other kinds of maladaptive behavior.

Hostility

Considerable information was gathered concerning both the overt and
covert hostility of the women. One of the reasons this was done was to define the possible role of hostility in orgasmic response. Are there any indications that the hostile woman is less orgasmic than the relatively nonhostile woman? As shown in Appendices A–G, measures concerned with
anger and aggression were applied in all of the studies, ranging from appraisals of how much hostility was displayed in actual interpersonal situations to that detected in fantasies given in response to inkblots. The measurement techniques employed were roughly as follows:

Ratings by laboratory personnel of amount of hostility openly displayed.
Questionnaires that inquire concerning one's typical ways of experiencing and
    expressing anger (namely, Buss-Durkee [1957] Hostility scale, Murray
    Oral Aggression scale).

Indirect projective or semiprojective methods which involve sampling the presence of hostile imagery and fantasy (Thematic Apperception Test, Holtzman Inkblots [Holtzman, et al., 1961], word associations, tachistoscopically exposed pictures with aggressive themes, word completions, cartoons, Bass [1956] Famous Sayings Hostility score).

Analysis of the measures obtained from these several approaches did not yield even one reliable finding. There does not seem to be any relationship between how consistently a woman reaches orgasm and the amount of anger that typifies her either overtly or in her fantasies.

It is of parallel pertinence that several measures concerned with dominance and superiority were administered to some of the samples. It was considered important to include such measures because (as described in an earlier chapter) several previous studies (Maslow, 1942) found that the greater a woman's dominance needs the more interested she was in sexual contacts, particularly novel and uninhibited ones, although it should be added that dominance in women has not been shown to be specifically related to orgasm capacity. Conventional measures of dominance were obtained in several samples of the present studies by means of the Dominance scale of the Edwards Personal Preference Schedule (1959) and the Dominant scale of the Thurstone Temperament Schedule (1953). In addition, there was available a measure of acquiescence derived from the Bass Famous Sayings Test.[69] Finally, an attempt was made to evaluate feelings of relative superiority to men by asking the women in one sample to judge which of each of 20 pictured paired males and females (faces only) would probably be dominant over the other if they established a relationship. There were also ten paired male and ten paired female faces so as to conceal the intent of the procedure to extract direct comparisons of male and female faces from the women. It was found that orgasm consistency was unrelated to any of the measures concerned with dominance. Within the limits of the instruments used, there is no indication that orgasmic response is in any way a function of how dominant or submissive a woman is.

Body Experiences and Feelings

Because of the writer's special research interests in body attitudes and because of what would appear to be obvious links between sexuality and body experience, a good deal of effort was devoted to finding out whether orgasm consistency is in any way linked to how a woman perceives and experiences her own body. As described in earlier chapters, various techniques have been developed that permit measurement of different aspects of how the individual views his own body. Illustratively, it is now possible to determine an individual's general degree of awareness of his body (as compared to other objects in his environs), the manner in which he distributes his attention to the major sectors of his body, the way in which he defines the boundaries of his body, and so forth. The results pertaining to the relationships of the body image measures to orgasm consistency are now outlined.

In numerous samples, as described in Appendix A, measures were taken of body awareness by means of the Body Prominence technique (Fisher, 1970). This technique is based on asking the individual to list "twenty things you are aware of or conscious of right now" and then scoring the number of times references are made to one's body or body-related functions. The results obtained indicated that women differing in orgasm consistency do not differ in their usual degree of awareness of their body. The woman of low-orgasm consistency is neither more nor less aware of her body than is the woman of high-orgasm consistency.

Attention was also directed to how each woman experiences the boundaries of her body. Fisher and Cleveland (1968) found that persons differ in the degree to which they perceive the boundary regions of their bodies as definite and protective versus vague and fragile.[70] They differ in how clearly they see themselves as separate individuals. Persons with definite boundaries have been observed to be particularly goal oriented, autonomous, and capable of coping efficiently with stress. Analysis of findings pertinent to boundary definiteness in multiple samples indicated that orgasm consistency was unrelated to the state of the body boundary. This was a bit surprising because Fisher (1970) found, in a study involving men, that sexual responsiveness was positively correlated with the definiteness of their body boundaries. It is not presently clear why results for the two sexes should differ so.

This would also be a logical point to indicate that the Witkin rod and frame measure (Witkin, et al., 1962), which is also considered to tap boundary differentiation, was administered in two samples and failed to correlate significantly with orgasm consistency. The Witkin procedure involves adjusting a luminous rod to a vertical position in a dark room lacking spatial clues. Incidentally, aside from boundary differentiation it is said to tap a basic field dependence-independence dimension that relates to one's ability to make judgments in an independent, autonomous fashion.

Although orgasm consistency is not directly correlated with the state of a woman's body boundaries, there is one interesting positive finding that should be cited concerning its relationship to the change in boundary produced by removing one's clothing. It should be noted, however, that an attempt to cross-validate this finding has not yet been made. In Sample 1 boundary definiteness was measured during one session when the women were fully clothed and again on a second occasion (five days later) just after they experienced a gynecological examination and were covered only with a sheet. Barrier scores were derived from inkblot responses produced by the women on the two occasions. It was considered that the conditions during the second session in which the women were practically nude, created a situation in which each woman was forcefully and vividly confronted with her own body in a fashion at least partially analogous to the way she does so when she engages in sexual intercourse (unclothed in a context with sexual connotations). When the shifts [71] in Barrier score from the clothed to the unclothed condition were correlated with orgasm consistency, it was found that the greater a woman's orgasm consistency the less likely she was to suffer disruption of her boundary during her unclothed state ($x^2 = 5.6$, $df = 1$, $p < .02$).[72] Apparently, the woman with low-orgasm consistency found it relatively difficult to maintain her individuation when exposed to the conditions in the second session.[73] Why should the woman with low-orgasm consistency be the one whose boundaries are particularly disturbed in this context? It would not be logical to offer an explanation in terms of greater susceptibility to stress because reactions to other stress conditions (for example, watching a threatening film, being in the hospital for a delivery) did not correlate with orgasmic capacity. Similarly, since orgasm capacity is not correlated in any consistent fashion with disturbed response to sexual stimuli (for example, sexual pictures presented at high speed), it would not be logical to offer an explanation phrased in terms of disturbance aroused by the sexual implications of having had a gynecological examination and having removed one's clothing. However, one might conjecture that the reason why the low-orgasmic woman was particularly thrown out of equilibrium by the removal of her clothing was because of the significance of being vividly confronted with her own body as a perceptual object. The very act of focusing sharply on her own body could require withdrawing some of her investment from outside objects, and it is the possible loss of outside objects which, as shown earlier, particularly troubles her. Apropos of this point, one is reminded that when women (Sample 7) were asked to describe their subjective experiences during the process of trying to attain orgasm, a sizable number emphasized the importance of being able to focus on their own body sensations and to exclude outside stimuli. Here too, then, it might be the heightened focus on one's own body, with the necessarily accompanying withdrawal of attention from outside objects, that would threaten the low-orgasm woman. This is, of course, pure speculation.

Fisher (1970) has described a method for determining how one characteristically distributes one's attention to the various sectors of one's body. This method is based on asking a person to indicate for each of a series of 108 paired body areas (for example, arm as compared to head, heart as compared to stomach) which he is most aware of at that time. It has been shown that persons have rather consistent ways of distributing their attention to their bodies. Some are highly aware of the back of the body and relatively low in their awareness of the front; others have heightened awareness of the head and limited awareness of the legs, and so forth. These patterns of awareness have been shown to be meaningfully related to personality traits and the existence of specific kinds of conflicts.

It was found in several samples that orgasm consistency was not related to the manner in which a woman distributes her attention to the following body areas: head, front versus back, right versus left, eyes, mouth, stomach, heart, and legs. Interestingly, it was also found not to be related to a woman's relative awareness of her breasts or vagina.[74]

In three samples the women were asked to rate the inside of their body. They indicated on rating scales (Osgood, Suci, and Tannenbaum, 1957) how they experienced the inside of the body with reference to such continua as the following: small-large, fast-slow, light-heavy, weak-strong, pleasant-unpleasant, cold-warm. These ratings were obtained because, as indicated earlier, the psychoanalytic literature makes reference to the idea that a woman's feelings about the inside of her body may influence her sexual responsiveness. However, orgasm consistency proved not to be reliably correlated with any of the "inside of body" ratings obtained.

One of the questions that was explored was whether women who differ in orgasm capacity also differ in their clothing attitudes and behavior. Do they choose their clothing with different values and expectations in mind? For example, does the high-orgasmic woman exceed the low-orgasmic woman in choosing her clothing for its decorative, "dress up" impact, or its conformity to style, or its "figure-revealing" qualities? Aiken (1963) has standardized a questionnaire that measures a number of aspects of clothing attitudes.[75] It asks for true or false responses to such statements as the following:

I like close-fitting, figure-revealing dresses.
I approve of the bikini bathing suit and wouldn't mind wearing one myself.
I buy dresses for comfort rather than appearance.

This questionnaire was administered in Sample 3; orgasm consistency turned out to be unrelated to any of the clothing attitude scores derived.

An inquiry pertinent to body attitudes, but also bearing on degree of psychological maladjustment, was undertaken that sought to ascertain whether orgasm consistency is related to the presence of disturbing or distorted body experiences. Is the low-orgasmic woman especially likely to feel that something is wrong with her body? Does she regard her body with the same sense of strangeness and discomfort that one often finds in psychiatric patients? The Fisher (1970) Body Distortion Questionnaire lends itself well to probing such questions by making an inventory of the presence of a variety of possible disturbances in body perception (for example, feelings of body strangeness, depersonalization, peculiar skin sensations) that have been shown to occur significantly more often in neurotic and schizophrenic persons than in normals.[76] When applied in a number of samples of women, none of these categories of disturbance could be shown to be linked with orgasm consistency. These findings not only further indicate the absence of correlation between orgasmic capacity and the way in which a woman experiences her body but also reinforce earlier findings that such capacity is apparently not a function of amount of psychological disturbance.[77]

Finally, it should be reported that when the women in several samples were asked to detail their most often occurring body illness and symptoms, neither the frequency nor the body locale of these symptoms was correlated with orgasm consistency.[78] The woman who has had numerous physical complaints is not less likely to be orgasmic than the one with few such complaints.

Other Trait, Personality, and Attitudinal Attributes

A quick enumeration is now made of the various traits and personal characteristics that were measured in the women studied and that failed to correlate with orgasm consistency.

Orgasm consistency was found not to be correlated with the following:

Degree of interest in achievement.[79,81]
Motivation to be orderly and precise.[79]
Concern about helping and supporting others.[79]
Interest in being sociable and friendly.[79,80]
Impulsivity.[79,80]
Desire to exhibit oneself and be the center of attention.[79]
Interest in understanding others and identifying with them.[79]
Sensitivity to stimuli with sexual connotations.[82]
Interest in new, exciting experience.[83,85,86]
Investment in activities that involve physical activity—with high output of energy and use of large muscle groups.[84] (Incidentally, orgasm consistency is unrelated to amount of interest and participation in sports.)
Motivation to be supported in a state of passivity by others.[83]
Preference for meditative and reflecting thinking and for dealing with theoretical rather than practical problems.[84]
Tendency to move and work rapidly and to feel restless when quiet.[84]
Inclination to be cheerful and to have an even disposition.[84]
Attitudes that emphasize being defensive, guarded, self-repressive, and avoiding self-exposure.[87]
Concern with guilt.[88]
"Anal character" traits that revolve about concern with dirt, frugality, and thrift.[89]

A number of inquiries were also made with reference to the following:

Ease of discussing sex with each parent.
Frequency of seeing parents nude during childhood.
Apparent happiness of parents' marriage.
Frequency with which parents used spanking as a form of punishment.
Expressed preference for male as compared to female role in life.
Attitudes toward husband and men in general.
Degree of favoring liberal attitudes toward sex in movies and novels.
Age began drinking alcohol, usual amount of alcohol consumption, and degree to which enjoy alcohol.
Age began smoking, usual number of cigarettes smoked per day, and degree to which enjoy smoking.

Orgasm consistency was found to be unrelated to any of these variables.

It should be explicitly noted that an examination of the negative findings has not disclosed any finding that obviously challenges the writer's theory that orgasm consistency is linked to concern about object loss.

Physiological Responsiveness

Elaborate attempts were made to discern whether a woman's orgasm consistency is tied to the actual physiological response characteristics of her body. Does the woman who tends to show heightened physiological response have a greater likelihood of reaching orgasm than the woman whose responses are muted? In other words, are there obvious gross differences in physiological responsiveness among women who differ in their orgasmic capacity? Even further, are orgasmic differences paralleled by differences in the relative excitability of different areas of the body? For example, does the woman with low-orgasm capacity show herself to be particularly less arousable in body areas directly involved in sexual contacts (vagina, breasts) than in "nonsexual" body areas (hands)?

Detailed descriptions are provided in Appendices A–C of the multiple physiological measures that were secured from the women as they reacted to a succession of situations. These measures included the Galvanic Skin Response, skin resistance, heart rate, temperature, and stomach motility. Skin resistance was measured at such diverse sites as arms, legs, breasts and labia; whereas temperature was determined at sites such as mouth, rectum, vagina, hands, breasts, and legs. The measures were taken in several samples and under numerous conditions. They were obtained during rest, while undergoing a gynecological examination, while doing arithmetic problems, during the course of listening to an erotic passage that was being read, in the course of observing a movie of a birth, and so forth. Measures were computed that reflected not only the degree of body excitation at specific sites but also the relative excitation of sites in different locations (for example, skin resistance of hand minus skin resistance of leg, vaginal temperature minus rectal temperature).

A thorough analysis of the data gathered did not uncover even one noteworthy trend. Orgasm consistency was unrelated to any of the physiological measures across the many situations in which they were obtained. A woman's orgasm consistency was not correlated with how physiologically aroused she was while at rest, during stress, or while listening to erotic material.[90] Her orgasmic capacity was also not correlated with the relative physiological arousal of such body areas as the vagina, rectum, labia, and breasts. Within the limits of the measurement techniques that were employed, it seems reasonable to say that women who differ in orgasm consistency do not differ correspondingly in their physiological reactivity.

Spontaneous Self-Descriptive and Interview Material

A good deal of the information collected about the women was derived from fairly impersonal, objective procedures. As already shown, this kind of information has provided interesting insights into factors that apparently influence orgasmic consistency. However, it seemed important to obtain, in addition, personalized reports in which a woman could freely describe herself with some of the coloring and drama of spontaneous speech. If one secures extensive self-descriptions from women differing in orgasmic consistency, do subtle stylistic or other sorts of distinctions between them emerge that were not detected by more objective measurement techniques?

Two different approaches were used in obtaining personalized self-descriptions from the women. One involved what was essentially a self-interview. Each woman who participated in this phase was seated alone in a room with a tape recorder and asked to speak freely for about an hour about her background. She was provided with a written outline (see Appendix I) and instructed to speak in a definite sequence about such topics as the following: setting of her early life, her father, her mother, her husband, her own personality, sexual attitudes, pregnancy experiences, love, embarrassing experiences, body changes during adolescence.

A second approach made use of a more conventional interview arrangement. Some of the women were interviewed intensively by a man and another sample by a woman.[91] These interviews sometimes involved three separate sessions, were minimally of two hours' duration, and were tape-recorded. They were conducted in a completely unstructured fashion and were simply directed to eliciting a maximum amount of information. There was some emphasis on finding out about sexual attitudes and how they had evolved.

These two interview procedures were applied only to women at the extremes of orgasm consistency—that is, those either very high or very low. Twenty-six women were involved in the self-interview procedure and 22 in the conventional interview. Requests for women to participate in the interviews were made after all of the formal objective measures had been completed. Only about 5 percent of the total number of women who were asked to return for the interviews refused to do so. It was explained to each woman that although she had originally agreed to take part in the study, the interview was "extra" (for which there was additional financial remuneration), and she was urged to feel free to refuse to respond if she had any reservations about talking openly and frankly about herself. Analysis of the tapes was largely impressionistic. The writer listened to each tape and made detailed notes concerning the content, particularly with reference to how father, mother, and husband were portrayed. It should be added that subsequent to each of the original conventional interviews, the interviewer had written several pages in which a formulation was offered concerning the life style and principal problems of the woman in question. Despite a detailed and patient review of all of this interesting and often fascinating material, it was not possible to detect gross or pervasive life style differences between those at the extremes of high- and low-orgasm consistency. However, there were a few discriminating trends that should be described.

Description of Father

First of all, it was found that in the self-interviews the high- and low-orgastic women depicted their fathers somewhat differently.[92] A majority of the low-orgasm consistency women described their fathers as unavailable for a substantial or consistent relationship. In the low-orgasm group, three women indicated their fathers had died when they were extremely young; one noted that her father had divorced her mother early in childhood; three emphasized the father's unavailability because of his job (for example, traveling salesman), which required him to be away from home for long time periods, and four specifically depicted the father as being seriously alcoholic and therefore very erratic in the way he related. In other words, 11 of the 12 low-orgasm women indicated the absence of a meaningful relationship with their fathers. One finds, by way of contrast, that in the high-orgasm group two women said that their fathers died at an early age, one reported that her father traveled extensively, and one identified her father as an alcoholic. Overall, only four of the 14 women depicted their fathers as being unavailable for a substantial relationship. The difference between the high- and low-orgasm consistency groups in this respect was found to be statistically significant ($x^2 = 10.4$, $df = 1$, $p < .005$). It will be recalled that earlier in this chapter it was similarly found on the basis of an analysis of autobiographies (from a different sample) that low-orgasm women exceeded high-orgasm women in describing their fathers as being unavailable for a relationship because of early death or chronic absence from the family.

Another difference that emerged in perusing the descriptions of the fathers offered by the high- and low-orgastic groups pertained to the frequency with which the fathers were described as ones who valued morality, honesty, and strictness in adhering to rules. Seven of the 12 fathers in the high-orgastic group were depicted as having such values, whereas only one of the 14 fathers in the low-orgastic group was so presented. This difference is statistically significant ($x^2 = 5.6$, $df = 1$, $p < .02$, with Yates' correction). Congruent with this finding, it should be pointed out that data based on the Roe and Siegelman' (1963) Parent-Child Relations Questionnaire that were reviewed earlier in this chapter (involving other samples of women) indicated that the high orgastic recalled their fathers as being less

"Casual" and more "Demanding" than did the low orgastic. The term "Demanding" refers to modes of behavior that have to do with setting definite standards and expecting conformance to certain values.

The two sets of findings just presented reinforce what was said earlier about the difference in the kind of relationship with the father that existed for the high-orgastic versus low-orgastic women. In order to convey more vividly the nature of this difference verbatim extracts from the descriptions of their fathers obtained from five of the low- and five of the high-orgasm women are presented.

Low Orgasm

Subject 1
There's not much I can describe or say about my father, having never known him except for the things that my mother has told me about him. And I'm sure that I was envious of other children who did have fathers and I didn't, and it sort of was a joke that my mother would say to me, "Well, you find someone that you like for a father. You pick him out and we'll see what we can do." However, I know from my mother's attitude how much she had loved my father and there was just never another man that could take his place. And she was never interested in anyone else.

Subject 2
My father, like I say, was in the Army. . . . I don't know whether he enjoyed his Army life or not. I suspect that in the beginning he did but he grumbled a lot about it. But then that doesn't always necessarily mean that a person doesn't like it. I think sometimes grumbling with him was just a habit because he grumbled about everything. As far as beliefs, he talked a lot about being honest and about not stealing or lying or cheating people, although he was never honest—as I got older I realized that he wasn't even honest with himself. Maybe he didn't even know it, I don't know. He was very dictatorial. He was usually kind to me. I only remember one spanking I ever got. The things that he did were all emotional. He was so strict and sometimes unreasonable and sometimes he would tell you that you could do something and then five minutes before you got ready to go he'd change his mind, and you never got an explanation for it, but his only explanation for it was, "I said so, therefore that's the way it is. . . ." He drank quite heavily and life was really pretty miserable when he was around. . . . He just drank all the time and was quite brutal— not to me but to my mother. . . . I enjoyed school and I didn't particularly enjoy being around him. He seemed to have—oh, faith in me. He was proud of me. I could tell this. Whenever I did anything that he especially liked he always bragged about it to his friends and always introduced me to people that he brought around. I really think he could have been a very nice person if he hadn't had this drinking problem, but when he was doing that he wasn't even worth being around.

Subject 3
My father is—I would say he is a rather unusual person. He is quite intelligent; he has many, many talents—probably too many for his own good. His interests and work vary from time to time. He went to drama school. He was also a motorcycle and car racer, mechanic and an engineer. He had a home repair shop for many years and he really excelled with this. . . . I think he was a bit selfish in that his interests came before the interest of his family, and I

think that affected his relationship with my mother and with the children. He's a very flamboyant character. He drinks a great deal; as a matter of fact, he's an alcoholic and probably has been for many years and now, because of that, he finds it difficult to hold a job. He's usually quite cheerful; he likes to tell jokes; at least he's cheerful on the outside—I don't know how he feels on the inside. I respect his intelligence: I respect his talents; and when I was younger he took a great deal of interest in my talents and abilities and he tried to work with me in these. He had me take flute lessons for years, and I think I did quite well at it. I know I wouldn't have if he didn't take the interest in that. He also was interested in my art work, and I think I sort of inherited a little bit of his mechanical skill, although not nearly as much as he has. He's really a very colorful character.

Subject 4

Now to describe my father. Well, he was a very good-natured man. He drank a lot; in fact, I'd say he was an alcoholic. He had many different jobs as far back as I can remember, one after another. We lived with my aunt until I was 16 years old, and then my mother and father, my brother and I moved to an apartment. My father had no particular interests, I don't believe, except drinking, although he was a very kind and good-natured man and I loved him very much. His work: he was a mechanic and he worked for many different garages here in the city. . . . He never went to church, as far as I can remember, but I do remember him talking about God and things. Problems: well, his problems were drinking. As far as his relationship with me, I would say we had a good relationship. I can remember as a little girl I was always happy with him but embarrassed when I saw him coming home drunk or if he took me out some place while he was drinking. But later on after he became ill and stopped drinking, . . . I felt very sorry for him; he could not work any more. All he did was sit at home and watch television and he seemed to enjoy just staying at home. And, as I say, we were friendly and I know my father loved me as I loved him. I would not say we were very close as far as carrying on a conversation with each other to any extent, but just a comfortable relationship.

Subject 5

My father's main characteristic was that he was an alcoholic and naturally didn't make things too pleasant in the home and didn't do anything for our relationship. His work: he was an architect and he was pretty good in his work, but if he hadn't been good he never would have stayed on his job because he was always sleeping it off and not going in and so on. He wasn't religious; I don't believe he had any—I don't know whether he believed in God or not, to tell the truth. He never went to church or anything. I suppose he must have believed in something. Well, his problems were whatever made him drink and then the problems resulting from that, of course, didn't do anything for his marriage relationship or any other kind of relationship. He always made a big thing about how I was supposed to—well, first of all, he was always saying how I was planned—I wasn't an accident and then he wanted me to be a boy and he was always trying to—as if he never knew who I was. He was always acting as if I was a boy and he seemed to think I should be interested in engineering and mechanical things that I had not the slightest aptitude for and he was always—on the rare occasions when he did want to be nice I think he couldn't understand why my mother and I and my brother didn't just turn into the big happy family, which you just don't forget things overnight. So I wouldn't say that we had a particularly good relationship but then there could be worse, I'm sure, because if it hadn't been for the drinking he wouldn't have been too bad a person. As far as discipline and so on is concerned I don't think we had any problem there. I mean whatever I did was never good enough; no matter what grades I got, why, he thought I should have something better, but then he always went and bragged to everybody else about how good I was, so he was kind of two-faced about that.

High Orgasm

Subject 1

My father is a fairly elderly person. . . . And he worked for a large company all of his life since I remember him. . . . He's the sort of person that likes to do work around the house. We had a fairly large home and on weekends he would always be out in the summer, painting or cutting the hedge or mowing the lawn, or doing some kind of work to keep the house up. He was very meticulous about the way the place looked. Everything had to be painted before it got to look bad and the lawn always had to look nice—weeds out and things like that. He liked to play golf. He used to play once a week and when I was little before we had a television set, he used to come home and spend most of the evening reading the newspaper or magazines or something like this. Later, when we got the television when I was about eight, he spent a fair amount of time watching the television at night. I think he's a very—a terribly conservative person in his beliefs. He was born in Scotland and . . . was in the First World War and then he moved to the United States where he met my mother. My father always expected a lot from his children, to the point where I think he was almost blind to some of our faults, and if you ever mentioned things to him like the fact that you might not be as bright as he thought you were or something like this, he always accused us of being too modest. My father wasn't a cold person. He was fairly warm but I can never remember him as the type of person that I would ever go to with a problem and discuss it with him. I think in a way he always looked down on people that were kind of pals to their children. He always used to comment that children had all the pals they needed but they needed a father and he was a father to his children. I can't remember any real problems he had.

Subject 2

My father—he's head of a section in a manufacturing corporation. He's interested in sports. Since he's become a Protestant he's a very good Protestant. Oh, he and I—we get along pretty well. I love him a lot but I get exasperated at him at times. I lived with him while my husband was overseas for six months and finally I left because he told me that if I couldn't raise my children the way he wanted them raised I could leave. I said, "Well, I'll leave then."

Subject 3

My father is a kindly person, strong headed; I always felt that I shouldn't contradict him. It either made him—well, he seemed to be quite angry if he was argued with. He is a bus driver, that's how he earned our keep most of the years we were growing up. . . . And he's a strong believer in being honest and loyal to your country. He's a very patriotic person. Honesty was encouraged in our home, and he was very honest with his children, and I always remember admiring him, and I found it very easy to talk with him on almost any problem as I grew up in my teen-age years, and problems with fellows and dates and necking and kissing—I could talk to him about very freely. I could tell I could go to him with any of the problems, and religion plays a very strong part in his life and my life because of my parents. And he was always interested and busy in civic affairs and is on the school board. . . . I think he finds it difficult to be effective by giving people work. It's easier for him to do it himself than to give it or to trust others with it.

Subject 4
My father was . . . a very loving man and he had a pretty tough childhood, as I can understand, although he's never said it outright. . . . My dad has many interests but most of them are involved in the outdoors. He loves to fish and loves to hunt. He's the type of person who could be perfectly happy in a one-room shack in the middle of a forest . . . because he's a real true woodsman. His work—he works in an automobile factory. He's been doing this for a number of years. . . . His beliefs: he's quite a devoted Christian, I feel. Politically he's definitely a conservative, not an extremist. His problems: my dad's the sort of guy who doesn't look like he's got any problems but I'm sure he does and I never realized this about him until I was quite grown. But he appears to be a very happy person and he enjoys life and he enjoys people. And concerning his relationship with me, I guess I almost feel as if he has a better relationship with me than he does with my two brothers. I was his only daughter, his pride and joy. He sang to me, he rocked me, he played with me. He did all kinds of things.

Subject 5
My father . . . was not born in this country. He has ideas that stem from more of a Victorian upbringing, strictness and moral dictates. He's interested in very serious subjects. He's a doctor. He likes nature; he likes to garden; he likes animals; I guess I acquired my interest in these things from being around him, although we didn't do that much together. That was just communicated to me, I think, more than being involved with these things together. I don't know what his beliefs are. Primarily, I guess, in general, they are, abide by the golden rule; he has a great deal of belief in doing good to others. He doesn't like to cut corners; he doesn't like to lie or to cheat to gain any ends. He doesn't pay any attention to other people around him who are perhaps involving themselves in this kind of means to attain what they want, and this has been a problem in his work because others have advanced beyond him because he has followed this virtuous sort of a pattern. His relationship with me is practically nonexistent. We didn't spend much time together when I was a child and consequently I formed ideas contrary to his as far as traditional and conventional moralities go. Because we didn't spend time together and he didn't have time to grow with me and to understand me, we don't have a relationship now. At the time when he would have spent time with me I had formed other friends and desired other companions so we were just ready at the wrong time for each other.

Description of Mother

A surprising trend was also observed in the self-interview material for the low- and high-orgastic women to differ in their descriptions of mother. The low orgastic typically made specific reference as to whether their relationship with their mothers had been close or distant. Eleven of the 12 in this group used terms such as "We were very distant" or "We were always close." About half emphasized closeness and the other half distance. Only four of the 14 high-orgastic women explicitly referred to the closeness-distance factor in their descriptions of their mothers. This difference between the groups was statistically significant ($x^2 = 10.4$, $df = 1$, $p < .005$). What might such a difference mean? One can only speculate. However, it is interesting that the low-orgastic women, who have been previously described as concerned about the potential loss of love objects, should be the ones who focus on whether their mothers were close or distant. Is this focus an expression of an underlying fear of loss? Even a description of the mother as "very close" could be either a compensatory form of self-reassurance or a reflection of the fact that mother and daughter sought compensatorily to maintain closeness because they so much feared potential separation. However, it should be emphasized that in the absence of other more objective data to support these impressionistic qualitative observations, they can only be regarded as unsubstantiated hints.

In order to communicate more directly the nature of some of the descriptions of the mothers, five excerpts from the low-orgasm and five from the high-orgasm groups are now presented.

Low Orgasm

Subject 1

She always dedicated her life to the church and to making a livelihood for us. She sacrificed many things for me and I seemed to be her whole interest and desire, which would seem natural after my father died, that I was the only one left. So we were always very close to one another and shared things together and did things together.

Subject 2

My mother was—she was a good person. She had a high school education. She worked . . . before she got married. She was good to us children. In fact, she was what you call an indulgent mother, I think, because she was sort of on the opposite scale from my father. He was all discipline and she was very little. She had a very strong belief in God and a great deal of faith, and I think that this probably was a help for her. I don't think my mother and father were very happily married. They were so different in so many ways. He was quite social in his mind and she was definitely a home body, and her big dream in life was to have a great big, huge family, and he thought that—well, they eventually had five children and he was absolutely embarrassed about it because he thought that this was almost animal for people to have such huge families. . . . She was good to me and we were always very close, she and I. We were always able to talk about things and all of the knowledge I ever got about sex or this type of thing always came from mother because she was very honest about it usually. At least she tried to be, I think. She was scared to death of my father. I mean really terrified of him, and all he had to do was snap his fingers and she started looking around to see what for. But life was pretty hectic those last few years at home.

Subject 3

My mother, on the other hand, is very quiet, subdued usually. She doesn't have very many interests. She's an excellent worker. . . . She doesn't have very many other outside interests except perhaps reading newspapers and clipping articles and sending them to me or to friends or other members of the family. I don't feel terribly close to my mother. She was always a rather difficult person to talk to because she didn't seem to take that much interest in us. I wouldn't say that she really neglected us in any way. It's just that it wasn't very easy to talk with her. So, in many respects, I felt closer to my father, and once in a while I would feel closer to my mother in the fact that we commiserated about my father at times—about his actions and about how it was affecting the family. I feel that I was the luckiest of the two children in the family in that I was able to go to college and meet nice people and everything.

Subject 4

As for my mother, my mother—as far as her interests—she at the present time is working part time as a sales clerk. . . . She did drink a little bit after my father died but not to any great extent. Before my father died she took very good care of him. She stayed at home when he was sick, . . . and I remember she had hard times a lot of times. Her problems right now or any problems she ever did have, I would say were with my father's drinking because of his having one job after another and therefore financial difficulties. . . . After my father died, she started work that she is still doing and is quite independent now and comfortable in her own apartment. And she goes out once in a while with a cousin. She visits me. I would say we have a good relationship. Not an intimate one but a loving, friendly relationship. She's very good hearted and kind, as was my father, and I love her very much, as I did my father.

Subject 5

My mother's interests—she is a card player and . . . this is kind of her main interest in life. She works in department stores. She used to have a stationery shop . . . when I was little and then after we moved, she worked at somebody else's. She's always worked except for a brief . . . period when I was in my teens. . . . And she goes to church sometimes. I mean I'm sure she has —she's not what you call organized religious, . . . but she certainly has a moral code and so on. I couldn't tell you exactly what it is. As far as problems are concerned, her main problem was her husband. She stayed with him for many years and she finally left him when I was a freshman in college. And then he died a short time after that—a couple of years after that, and I think she always had trouble kind of reconciling the whole situation—whether she should stay or she shouldn't stay or whatever like that. I think that we had a very good relationship. I always felt comfortable around my mother and always thought we had a very good relationship. She was never possessive or anything like that and though at times I resented her leaving him with me when she went away for a weekend or something, actually it was always better when she was gone, so I kind of felt ambivalent about that. I think—she's not exactly the warmest person in the world as far as physical affection is concerned, but that's just her nature and I wouldn't say it did anything in particular to our relationship.

High Orgasm

Subject 1

My mother was born in Italy and she's much younger than my father. She came to this country . . . and took a job working in a clothing store. . . . She met my father in this store. . . . My mother's main interest was her family. She never seemed to have a lot of outside interests. . . . She never did things without the family. She was a very domestic person. She used to do a lot of sewing; sewed almost all of our clothes when we were young and was a very thrifty person in this way. And she used to do a lot of cooking and canning and gardening and it seemed like she spent all of her time doing things around the house. When I was in high school she took a job managing an office. . . . And she seemed to like this job. Mom was always a very—I could almost say a weak person in that she—you could get her to do almost anything. I can remember when I was little she'd—if ever she didn't want you to do something you could always talk her into it. No matter what it was, she would always come around to your side of the story, and she used to aggravate my father a little bit because he was much stricter. Somehow she never seemed to put her foot down.

Subject 2

My mother—she's quiet while my father is outspoken. He's loud. In fact, my whole family's very loud, excluding my mother. She's very quiet; she sticks to herself a lot. She does have some friends in the neighborhood but she's not the type to gossip. She feels sorry for herself a lot. She likes to sew and she likes to cook but she doesn't like to do housework which is just about my same problem. Problems: well, I guess they have only one and that's the younger sister that I have. And my mother's very religious.

Subject 3

My mother is a real home body and I think she had a deep love and affection for us. She was very, very patient with us. I don't remember getting very many spankings from either my mother or my father. Sometimes I feel they were unjust in that I remember my brothers and sisters found it very, very funny to tease me and I would feel deeply rejected and I would scream and yell and bite my tongue and beat on the nearest person when I was teased, and, consequently, my mother, irritated with the noise, spanked me instead of the others and I thought that was terribly, terribly unjust. I resented it all my life and I still do, and I find teasing is a very difficult thing for me to take or I cannot take a joke played on me very well. But my mother was very careful to make sure we understood what she was trying to explain to us. And she had odd ideas that I think were very unhealthy in some respects, and one of her statements was, "A man doesn't have to have intercourse every night; sometimes he can walk around the block." If she hadn't said this to me it would probably have saved a lot of problems in my marriage. I have a lot of respect for my mother and I enjoy her and respect her more now that I'm grown up; yet I find myself wanting her in times of trouble and worry; I want to run to her and climb up on her lap and suck my thumb. And yet when I'm with my mother now I find it extremely difficult to communicate with her, and we do not have a very satisfactory relationship and it's—even though I miss being away from her I think it's probably a better thing that we have short visits together rather than living fairly close, although I could be wrong. I'd like to try the other method and see if it worked.

Subject 4

My mother is a little bit more of a go-getter than my dad. She very definitely has more of a domineering personality. My mother is very well educated, not through college or anything of this sort but self-educated. She's tremendously efficient and really has worked hard from the day I remember her working. And I guess this is somehow the way I'm like her. The two of us are always doing something and doing more than what we can. My mother is quite outgoing and both my parents are loads of fun. My mother has—oh, a variety of interests. And she and my dad, but particularly she, are involved in club work quite a bit. My mother . . . has a very good job. . . . She's really sharp.

Problems: I don't know—I guess the biggest problem both my parents have had has been a financial one because we've never had much money at all and they've had quite a few problems getting myself and my sisters through college. They're still having problems getting them through. That should pass in a couple of years when everybody graduates. My mother's relationship to me has always been excellent. I never went through the period when I hated my mother. We get along very well.

Subject 5
My mother is not particularly interested in too many other things other than domestic life. She wanted to raise a family. She's very neat and clean and a good cook and an excellent seamstress. She, I think, would be creative if she had outlets for her creativity—if she had been trained; she didn't go to college or very far in high school and she came to this country quite late in life, so that she didn't really have opportunities to take advantage of; but I think she could have achieved more than she has. . . . Her beliefs are, I guess, general, conventional attitudes toward life. She never communicated them to me to that great extent. There is not that much communication in my family, as a matter of fact. Her problems have been that of living with a marriage that is not workable and very unhappy. Similarly, my father has been plagued with this. They stayed together, I think, merely because of myself and my younger sister. They seem to subscribe to the idea that this is a sensible thing to do—remain together for the sake of the children. I, however, disagree, having lived within this kind of environment and realizing its hazards. My mother and I were never particularly close either. Whether this was her fault or something in my personality make-up, I don't know. I'm not very open. And perhaps there were times when I could have given more that I did to establish a relationship with her. However, I'm only becoming lately and recently aware of these things— when it's almost too late, actually.

Description of Husband

There were no other categories that would distinguish the self-interview productions of the high- and low-orgastic women. These highs and lows could not be differentiated in terms of expressed sexual attitudes, how they adapted to their adolescent body changes, their portraits of their husbands, and so forth. By way of illustration, note the similarities in what they say about their husbands.

Low Orgasm

Subject 1
My husband and I met in college when I was a freshman and he was a freshman. . . . Actually, we didn't have any real serious problems that arose. It seemed to be—he told me when he saw me he realized that I was the girl for him. However, I didn't have this same feeling. I enjoyed going with him. We went to church together. We went to the matinee dances. We went to most of the activities together and had a good wholesome relationship. He's a very likeable person—not the tall, dark, and handsome type that my first boyfriend was, but he has a very nice personality and anyone that even meets him now likes him and he gets along well with people. He has a good physical appearance.

. . . I guess the things that we have had the most difficulty in agreeing about could be maybe the discipline of our children and how we should work things out together before we actually have certain problems arise. We've never really had any financial disagreements with regard to the use of our money because we've always felt that this was something that was jointly ours and we have everything in common together with our banking and checking accounts together and our home, our car, everything we have we share together because we feel that this sort of a thing is important in a marriage, although we show him respect and he is the head of our household and he's the one who makes the final decisions.

Subject 2

Like I said, I met my husband when he was in the Army. I went to a dance and he was there and he asked me for a date and I accepted. I was very impressed with him. Up to that time I had just about made up my mind that there weren't many worthwhile men in this world but when I went home I told my cousin whom I was living with at this time that I finally met somebody that I think I could stand to be married to. When he got out of the Army—well, we were engaged—and then he got out of the Army . . . and we were married. . . . We've had—at least from what I've seen—we have just about one of the happiest marriages that I've ever seen. We have our problems, of course. You just can't have two people living in a house together and not have problems, but we seem to be able to get most things straightened out. We've never had a fight; disagreements, yes, arguments, yes, and sometimes we get angry, but never a knock-down battle type of thing. He's a pretty calm person and he won't usually stand and argue with me. He'll just let me cool off and then he'll come back and talk about it later. . . . He's a very gentle person, very good to me. Gives me quite a bit of leeway to do just about what I want as long as I do the few things that he asks which is to keep up a neat home and cook his meals and take care of his clothes—I mean the things that any man would ask of a wife. He's very undemanding. He's very good with the children, very gentle and playful, and, in fact, they get all of the rough house and silly business with him more than from me. I think—it's a funny thing, too, but the things that we have the arguments about and the disagreements about are usually ways to handle the children, I guess.

Subject 3

I met my husband . . . in college. . . . We didn't have very many dates as such; we didn't go to the movies or shows or to clubs or out to eat a lot. We did spend a great deal of time together, though, and although we only knew each other for about four months before we got married, I think we got to know each other quite well during that time. We listened to music a lot and we read sometimes and we went to a couple of plays, and I think we did a few odd-ball things. . . . Our courtship was short. He was proposing to me—I guess he started proposing to me about two months after we met, but I had been engaged the year before to another fellow and that had broken up, and I was still quite shy about getting involved again, so I kept saying no, although I did enjoy his company, but I didn't feel that I was quite ready to get married; I wanted to make certain that this was the right thing and it took a while. But when I finally did say yes, we were married shortly afterward. The problems that arose were, I think, primarily financial. My husband was just a graduate student here and we knew things were going to be pretty rough financially when we got married, but we decided that we would go ahead and that we would make out. And we did. . . . I think my husband is handsome and I think he has a very nice personality. He's cheerful and he likes to make jokes quite often and wisecracks and puns, and I do too. He's very serious about his studies, which is one thing that I admire about him. I like a man that knows what he wants to do and goes ahead and does it.

Subject 4

As for my husband I met him at a party. Our courtship—well, I met him in June, and we were married in November. About the biggest problem that arose, I would say, was the religious problem. He was Baptist at the time and I was Episcopalian. . . . There was a little disagreement here, but we did compromise. . . . My husband, as far as his physical appearance, is tall . . . and a very nice built man, neat in his appearance. As for his personality, he's very friendly and honest and kind.

Subject 5

My husband—I had met him—he ate in the same restaurant where I did . . . and I used to date his cousin but our courtship really didn't start until our senior year. . . . He asked me to a basketball game. . . . He got serious and all of a sudden we were going together, the next thing you know. Problems: well, we didn't have any problem with religion because he never pushed it. He just said, well, you know I'd have to sign a paper but he didn't care whether I converted or not, and I think because of the fact that he took a completely hands-off attitude that's why I was able to be interested in it because he never let religion come into our relationship as a boy and girl, so we never had discussions or fights or anything over that and it never got involved with the two of us personally so that any decision that I made was my own rather than something connected with being in love and so on. Problems that arose mostly were with my family. They didn't care too much for him, to say the least— him or his religion both—they don't like him personally. And I thought we got along all right, though I never thought he was perfect and I realized that he was not the warmest personality in the world, not the—well, kind to think of other people first, let me put it that way. . . . And personality-wise, he's kind of erratic. He's either very voluble and excitable or else he's completely dead to the world.

High Orgasm

Subject 1

I met my husband on a blind date. His roommate was engaged to my cousin. He was—let's see—he was really kind of fun on that first night. It was a rainy night; we went to the movies and walked all the way downtown; there were no busses running; and from that time on I think I only had one other date with another fellow and he never dated another girl after we started going together. We got engaged eight months later but didn't get married until over a year later. . . . He's a very easygoing fellow, although sometimes it irritates him when people take advantage of him, but I think he lets them take advantage of him a lot of the time. He likes to do outside reading, although he doesn't seem to get much time to do it. He likes to work with people. He's always been fairly liberal politically but I think he's changing somewhat, although he denies this. He was raised in a very strict home . . . and until he was in high school he never went to movies and his family forbid drinking or smoking—anything like that. The only problem that we had during the courtship was over religion. He was much more religious than I was. I hadn't been to church in ages and didn't have any plans for going to church regularly. I think we agreed on our philosophy toward religion and it was just the practice that we didn't agree on. I never seemed to practice very much and that was the one problem.

Subject 2

I met my husband in Texas where he was stationed. I met him at a party. . . . We didn't know each other very long. We knew each other about five months, and we got married. We had relations before we got married. The only problem I have ever had is that I get very, very jealous and he is just the opposite. . . . He is very egotistical. He gets along well with children. The only arguments we ever have are about him not spending enough time with his family because it's school, baseball games, etc., etc. But we've ironed those out pretty well. Personality-wise: everyone seems to like him. He's very sarcastic —the two of us are when we get together; we're very, very sarcastic with each other but mainly because there's someone else around. He is not a very romantic fellow. He's not one to put his—to say I love you once in a while—it's a very seldom thing. Really the most important thing that my husband and I have difficulty in agreeing about is how to discipline the children and we still haven't ironed that one out yet.

Subject 3

I met my husband through a friend of mine. . . . We corresponded . . . and talked about a lot of lovely, unrealistic, rosy, romantic things that we saw eye to eye on in many ways. . . . We really didn't know each other too well when we married. He made me uneasy in many ways, but I felt very strongly that this was something that I should do. He was a good person and a very brilliant person. All in all, I think I made a very wise choice. He's not the most beautiful person in the world but he's not an ugly person. He's rather an appealing person. I think his personality probably makes him more appealing, although he is rather shy and in some instances he has an awfully lot of finesse. Most of the time he gets along very well with people at work, with everybody but me, it seems. . . . He's a kind person and believes that kindness is better than gruffness. He likes things quiet and relaxed and not demanding and not pushing. Both of us are quite within ourselves in many ways and definitely— he's definitely not an extrovert but he's not an introvert and he's quite a bright person, in my viewpoint.

Subject 4

I met him at a party. He was quiet, reserved. . . . We started to date and continued for quite a while. I don't remember agreeing about much; I just remember disagreeing about a lot of things. I was very religious at this time and he wasn't. We disagreed about religion. And, oh, he used to go with a girl . . . and he always seemed to be flirting with her and we disagreed about that quite a bit. And I guess we didn't agree very much the first time. We broke up after four months because I felt he was flirting with the other girl too much one night and then I started to go with him again. . . . And he didn't realize it, but I was chasing him. I was quite subtle about it. I knew how to get around him and I still do sometimes. And I snagged him again and we went together for a while and then we broke up because he was such a creep. . . . But somehow we got back together again and I really don't remember what we disagreed about or agreed about. We just disagreed about all kinds of things. I guess I'm describing my husband and my courtship. Problems that arose: we had all kinds of problems but none of them were really that serious. . . . He's relatively quiet with strangers. He's become much more outgoing in the years that I have known him. His mother seems to think that I've been a very good influence because he used to be very unsociable and very reserved, but now he enjoys people, he enjoys being with a group and he's usually quite good in a group, particularly if it's a relatively well-educated group. . . .

Subject 5

I met my husband in college. It was a light relationship at first and all the way, on my part. I think to a great extent I was merely having fun. . . . He is pleasant looking. His personality is that of a good person. He's decent and honorable. He enjoys sports a great deal—working on mechanical things. He enjoys animals and the outdoors, children. He wants to have a good job, a nice home, a good family. His personality and mental make-up do not run deep but he is a very loyal person and a very dependable person. So this, to an extent, compensates for his lack of esthetic training and self-expression on subjects that are closer to my heart and to my interests than physical activity.

Views about Sex

The lack of difference between the high- and low-orgastic women may be illustrated too by quoting their views about "sex" and the expression of sexual feelings.

Low Orgasm

Subject 1

Concerning my attitudes toward love, sex, and the expression of sexual feelings, I feel that my whole outlook stems from the fact that I was brought up in a home without any brothers or without a father and it has been stressed to me over and over again that the important thing about our life is that we should have children and that's our purpose. So perhaps my own feeling and attitude is brought about by this and maybe it is a little off-balance in the fact that my mother was alone and without a husband for so long and she felt that she could do without this sexual experience of a husband and perhaps her attitudes and ideas have rubbed off on to me, that I can take it or leave it. Actually, I could probably go on and on and on without a sexual act. I don't have that great of a desire for sexual intercourse and many times I feel that I am inadequate to my husband because of this and I wish that I did have stronger sexual feelings. However, I do love my husband greatly and I like to embrace him and I want him to kiss me and love me but I don't feel that I respond and take the initiative in these acts in our intimate feeling together as I should. Sometimes I think that I'm just a cold cucumber but I try to show warmth and love and understanding toward my husband, and I feel perhaps when we were first married I did this more so than I do now and other things have sort of taken the place of this, perhaps my attention and feelings toward my children. But I think we have to broaden ourselves so that we can take them into our lives and still not neglect our husbands. However, I feel that sex, as I stated before, is not the ultimate that we're here for and, of course, this also comes out of our religious training and background. We're here to prove ourselves, to see if we'll choose right and do the things that our Father in Heaven wants us to do, and rearing a family and having children is part of this experience, and our ultimate goal is to so live that we might have our children and our family eternally, that even though we die we'll still have our husbands and our children in the next world and forever.

Subject 2

I think sex can be a very lovely thing in its place and it belongs with married people and nowhere else. I believe that it isn't only for having children. Of course, it's very necessary for bringing children into the world for people to have sexual relations but I think it can be a builder in your marriage. I think it draws you together and I think that when people start degrading it and making dirty remarks about it, it makes me angry because I don't think it's the sort of thing to poke fun at. I think they act like little kids—you know, when they giggle about things. I don't think people like that are grown up when they start making these silly remarks and telling silly jokes. I have a very strong feeling of the home with people being married and rearing families. I don't see how society can exist without it and I feel badly when I hear people talking about —oh, you hear weird ideas of people about free-love type of thing where men and women can just live together and no responsibility, no ties. I think they've lost the whole meaning of sex. I think it's overrated on one side and underrated on another. I think it's just a normal, natural thing that people should come to accept and enjoy and quit talking about it. I've never felt embarrassed toward my husband. I've never felt embarrassed about anything we've done together. I never will because he's my husband and it's natural. And this is the thing that I hope to imbue in my children to help them to accept it as just a natural, normal, happy thing that belongs in a certain place.

Subject 3

My attitudes about love, sex, and the expression of sexual feelings I would say are quite normal. It's certainly right to express your sexual feelings to your partner—your husband or wife—and I think that people should not be timid about this. Love certainly is a very important part of life. It is throughout the animal kingdom, and there's no reason why it should be repressed. I don't think that people should think that it's dirty or anything like that. It's perfectly natural and very important and very enjoyable. I think, on the whole, I feel very happy about love and sex and the expression of sexual feelings.

Subject 4

As far as summarizing my attitudes toward love, sex, and the expression of sexual feelings, well, my attitudes toward love, as far as a husband and wife relationship is, as I said before, it's just a compassion, a genuine concern and care for the one you love, caring how he feels when he's hurt, whether he feels good or bad or happy or sad, sharing your life together, raising your children together, bringing them up in as happy a home as possible where there's love and devotion and goodness. As far as my attitudes toward sex, summarizing them, I would say somewhere along the way I got a very mixed up feeling on sex. I know as a young girl when I was dating, I always enjoyed going out and, well—what would you call it—making out after a date, just kissing and maybe light petting—I know I enjoyed this. However, I believe I was not educated on sex the way I should have been, otherwise I may have had a different outlook on it, I don't know. Right now I know I am depriving my husband of a lot in our marriage because I just don't know how to help myself want sex more. I would like to be loving and feel and enjoy sex and experience orgasm which I don't believe—maybe I have once or twice within the last year. I just wish I could be a better sexual partner to my husband. As far as sexual feelings, well, I would say again when I was younger, during my teen-age years, perhaps when I had steady boyfriends and when I was engaged the one time, I did enjoy sexual feelings. . . . I don't know—as far as sexual feelings I'm very, very mixed up. I would say to summarize that it is of great importance to be told what is expected in life, to be told when one is developing and growing into maturity what is happening to one's body, that it is nothing to be afraid of or embarrassed of, that it is just natural, that sex is nothing to be afraid of or embarrassed about or to feel wrongly about, that it is really a beautiful part of love and marriage.

Subject 5

Well, I think I have a pretty healthy attitude toward love and sex and the expression of sexual feelings—a lot healthier than my husband. He has some kind of a problem along that line. But I—as I say, I'm not unconventional as to how to do it. I mean, I like one standard position, all the standard things—I'm not an experimenter, shall we say. I guess that's the end of it.

High Orgasm

Subject 1

I think as far as love, sex, and the expression of sexual feelings go, I'm a very moral person. I believe that sex should be restricted to a married couple, and I think that if it is there's a real warmth of having one partner that you love very much and who understands you and whom you know, and saving this for just this one person as something very special that you don't do with anyone else.

Subject 2

Love, sex, and the expression of sexual feelings. I think it's fine. I am very romantic. I like sex. I like intercourse, I mean. I enjoy it. I think the most wonderful thing that ever happened to me was when I got married. I don't know what I'd say about my attitudes on the expression of sexual feelings. I'm free. I do whatever I feel like doing. Anything that would make my husband happy is fine with me. There are a few things I don't like but—I don't know. I don't know whether to say anything more. I think I've talked about everything that's on the papers and—let's see. I guess that's all.

Subject 3

How would I summarize my attitudes toward love, sex, and the expression of sexual feelings? I like it. Even though my husband and I fight about it. We do have different views. I am not a cold person. Sometimes I feel very dumb, and I don't think we need to have intercourse as often as we do sometimes, and sometimes it's the method in which it is approached that bothers me. But love is a warm feeling and it is a trusting, and it's being able to open up and be yourself without getting your feelings hurt or crushed or criticized. I think love is accepting one another, what they believe, and I think sex is an expression of this love and can be a very satisfying thing and can be a release of emotions and tension, and I think it brings a husband and wife closer together and should be done only in love, not to settle arguments, although it can be a help in this area. And I think if you feel you need to express yourself sexually you should feel free to do so as long as it doesn't embarrass or injure the feelings or physical being of your partner. And that's—I hope that's satisfactory. I have lots more to say but I've run out of time.

Subject 4

My attitudes toward love, sex and the expression of sexual feelings. Fine. I think love is great and sex is great, and the expression of sexual feelings is great. I feel they're healthy and natural and I certainly enjoy them and I think I will continue to for the rest of my life.

Subject 5

My attitudes toward love, sex, and the expression of sexual feelings. I believe in the great power of love toward the achievement of happiness. Simple good feelings between people can do more to advance our civilization in the most important way—not in the sense of technical advancement or scientific discovery. I think that just a general social concern and sensitivity between people is the most important thing we should be working toward at this time before we get to the moon. Sex is an enjoyable and a very transcendent act. It, I think, is one of the closest acts that we have to nature. I don't agree with the role it has been forced to take as something forbidden, something to be snickered at—we have in the books and the movies and the records. I think it should be put on a higher plane than our society puts it, but this, of course, has to begin between two people. It starts in the intimacy between two people and their attitude toward what they're feeling. I think that the individual can influence society—not necessarily the society influencing the individual in all cases. And I personally would like to see sexuality put on a level of appreciation as we place beautiful artistic endeavors, beautiful music, literary expression, because it is an elevating thing. It is something that takes us away from the banality of everyday activity and simple earthly thoughts. It is something that could almost be looked upon with a religious attitude—a sort of a reverence and a deep appreciation that it is available to us—sexual fulfillment and emotional development and expansion, achievement in the sense of loving and communicating this love to a whole family that you have produced—to whole humanity in which you live, I think, can be the greatest thing that we could achieve.

Voice Quality

In the course of reviewing the taped interview and self-descriptive material obtained from the women particularly high or low in orgasmic consistency, the writer became aware of an apparent difference in the voice quality of the two groups. The high orgasmic seemed to be characterized by a greater range of tones and by a greater flexibility in the way they used their voices. They seemed to introduce more variations in their voice styles by use of emphasis, prolonging words, sighs, and perceptible expiration or inspiration of breath as a dramatic counterpart to their words. To put it in another way, the low orgasmics' voices seemed to be overcontrolled, narrow, and somehow mechanical in quality. To determine whether the writer's impressions were valid, a study was undertaken in which judges were asked to blindly evaluate taped excerpts of six high- and six low-orgasm-consistency women selected randomly from the total array of 26 tapes available.[93] A two-minute sample of each was used, and this sample was, in all instances, taken from the same initial point in the self-descriptions when the subjects had been asked to describe the setting of their early childhood.[94] Each judge was introduced to the rating task by first letting him hear several repetitions of a low- and several of a high-orgasm-consistency voice. The differences between the two in voice range and flexibility were pointed out sufficiently so that the judge seemed reasonably certain of the nature of the distinction. The judge was then left alone in a room and requested to make four decisions concerning each of the twelve randomly arranged voices. He rated each voice (on a five-point scale) with reference to its degree of constriction in range; how "natural" versus "artificial" it sounded, and the extent to which it was characterized by "expressive sounds and interesting shifts in rhythm (sighs, inspiration of air, prolonging words, placing emphasis on specific words)," which represented a way of dramatizing and emphasizing what was being communicated. Finally, he was asked to decide for each voice whether it was more like the "rich" or "constricted" voice that had been initially presented to him as a judgmental standard.

A total of six judges evaluated the tapes.[95] It was found that they could significantly distinguish the high- and low-orgasmic voices in terms of how constricted in range they sounded. The high orgasmic were consistently seen as having *less* constricted voices than the low orgasmic.[96] The high orgasmic were also seen as having more "natural" sounding voices than the low orgasmic and as more often using emphatic or dramatizing sounds such as sighs and deep breaths, and these differences were statistically significant. However, the raters were able to do only slightly better than chance in their judgments of which tapes sounded like the original "rich" versus "constricted" models that had been presented to them. When it was established that the voices of the low-orgasmic women were more constricted or narrow in range, less natural sounding, and less characterized by expressive sounds and interesting shifts in rhythm than those of the high orgasmic, the literature concerned with voice quality and personality was examined to see if there were any previous analogous findings. The only directly pertinent study that was found was one by Rousey and Moriarty (1965), who correlated personality and voice attributes in a sample of children who had been intensively observed from a variety of perspectives for many years. One of the hypotheses they were able to support was that (p. 37), "Restriction of range of the voice occurs in individuals whose normal expression of the sex drive is constricted by emotional factors." They suggest that the ability to make full use of one's voice reflects an analogous freedom to be sexually expressive. This may very well turn out to be a reasonable assumption.

However, if so, it is a bit puzzling that in the present studies other personality measures tapping the dimension of spontaneity and freedom to respond did not correlate with orgasm consistency. As one can see in Appendices A–G, there were scales that presumably tap tendencies to be overly self-controlled or self-inhibiting, but they were not significantly linked with the orgasm index. It is possible, of course, that voice constriction is a better measure of general emotional constriction than were the standard tests and procedures that were used. Obviously, further study of this whole issue is required. But if it were true that the low-orgasmic woman is more emotionally constricted than the high-orgasmic woman, how would this fit with the formulation concerning the role of fear of loss of objects in orgasm inhibition? One possibility that comes to mind is that a woman who, as a child, doubted the "permanence" of the important figures in her world might be fearful of "opening up" in her emotional involvements with them. That is, she might restrict her emotional commitments and expressions to a narrow, rather superficial, band because she was frightened of the ultimate disappointment that would result from a deeper involvement. Presumably, her emotional constriction is finally echoed in her constricted, artificial, nonvarying voice style. But this is merely speculation on the writer's part.

Overview

The task of pinpointing the kinds of personal qualities that are correlated with differences in ability to respond consistently to orgasm has proven to be an elusive one. There are so many things with which orgasm consistency is *not* linked. Particularly noteworthy is the fact that it does not seem to be related to maladjustment or psychological disturbance, at least in the sense that such terms are conventionally understood. This is congruent with the conclusion reached, in an earlier chapter, based on a review of the empirical literature concerned with sexual responsiveness in women, that there does not appear to be a relationship between the "mental health" of a woman and her ability to attain orgasm. To know that a woman is unusually tense or even unusually anxious does not predict her orgasm capacity.

Another stereotype that has been challenged by the present findings is that orgasmic ability is somehow a derivative of a woman's degree of "femininity." No correlations of significance have been obtained between orgasm consistency and various standard measures of femininity. One cannot judge a woman's orgasm capacity in terms of how interested she is in "feminine" things or endorses values customarily considered to be womanly. It is pertinent to this point that no differences could be detected between high- and low-orgasmic women with reference to their attitudes toward clothes, use of cosmetics, or other aspects of personal adornment. Further, judges who carefully studied pictures in which the appearance and dress style of a sample of women could be observed did no better than chance in deciding how orgasmic they were. It will be recalled, in this same vein, that orgasm consistency was unrelated to such actual physical parameters as a woman's height, weight, breast size, age she began to menstruate, the amount of pain she experiences during menstruation, and so forth. It was also unrelated to how much she enjoys physical activity as indicated by her frequency of participation in sports. Finally, it was not reliably tied to how her body responds physiologically (for example, heart rate, vaginal temperature) to a range of conditions (for example, rest, stress, erotic) in a laboratory situation. In short, there does not seem to be any way of predicting how orgastic a woman will be on the basis of information about her appearance and other physical attributes, or the manner in which she treats and adorns her body, or the speed with which her body developed secondary sex characteristics.

A salient negative finding is the fact that a woman's orgasm consistency is unrelated to how friendly or unfriendly, hostile or nonhostile, she is. This was found to be true despite the fact that an unusually serious attempt was made to comprehensively evaluate each woman's hostility characteristics. An inclusive repertoire of procedures was utilized that measured overt friendliness (as judged by observers), self-rated friendliness, and amount of hostile feeling and hostile fantasy. The findings obtained suggest that a woman's habitual level of anger and her style of coping with anger do not play a role in her orgasm consistency. As noted earlier, one cannot tell from a woman's degree of aggressiveness or dominance whether she has high- or low-orgasm capacity. Analogously, women scoring high on sociability, cheerfulness, and desire to help others do not differ in orgasmic capacity from those who score low on such variables. It is of parallel pertinence that orgasm consistency was found not to be related to how active and achievement oriented, as compared to passive and dependent, a woman is.

One cannot foretell a woman's orgasm consistency from how "free" or impulsive or emotional she is. Orgasm consistency did not differ for women who make decisions slowly and carefully as contrasted to those who respond quickly, on the spur of the moment. It did not differ for those who prefer a constricted, safe, unexciting style of life as compared to those who constantly seek excitement and new adventure. Relatedly, high- and low-orgasmic women could not be differentiated with reference to the amount of emotion or excitement in the stories they created or in any of the other fantasy material they produced. Orgasmic capacity seems to have little to do with a woman's conventionality or unconventionality. The woman whose interest patterns resemble those of the typical housewife is just as likely to be orgasmic as the woman whose interests are more unique or exotic. Apropos of this matter of conventionality, it will be recalled, too, that religiosity and church attendance were not correlated with orgasm capacity. In fact, the extremeness of a woman's beliefs about sexual freedom seem unrelated to the orgasm index. High- and low-orgasmic women do not differ in their opinions about how much sexual freedom there should be or the manner in which sex education should be given. They also do not differ in the amount of enjoyment they state they derive from reading literary material with sexual content. Tangential to this point, it is also interesting that they do not differ in terms of how permissive they recall their parents to have been about sexual matters (for example, talking freely about sex or permitting body exposure in the home). The woman who perceives her parents as having been puritanical about sex is just as likely to be consistently orgasmic as the woman who characterizes her parents as extremely liberal about sex! [97] Of course, this finding clashes with most accepted views concerning this matter. It is almost a truism in the clinical literature that parents who are narrow and secretive about sex will produce sexual dysfunction in their children. The data from the present study raise doubt about complacently accepting such a dictum. Indeed, one is reminded at this point that religiosity and church attendance, which might be regarded as roughly indicative of degree of acceptance of puritanical standards about sex, have not been reliably linked with orgasm consistency either in the present study or in the Kinsey, et al. (1953) surveys.

It may be concluded that there is no evidence that orgasm capacity occurs more often in the dramatic, adventurous, emotional woman than in the conventional, timid, orderly woman. A woman's ability to attain orgasm is apparently not defined by such stylistic elements.

Miscellaneous other negative findings catch one's eye as one surveys the array of results. It is interesting to learn that orgasm consistency is not significantly related to whether a woman is "extroverted" and outwardly oriented versus "introverted" and reflective. It is also intriguing to note that orgasm consistency is not correlated with any of the several measures of guilt that were used. This last finding does not fit well with the considerable emphasis that some psychoanalytic theorists have placed upon guilt as an explanation for "frigidity" in women. No evidence has emerged that orgasm consistency is related to how narcissistic or self-centered a woman is. This too represents a divergence from some psychoanalytic formulations that would link "frigidity" with an exaggerated narcissism that prevents investment of feeling or love in others. It is also worth mentioning that orgasm consistency is completely unrelated to how much a woman smokes or drinks alcoholic beverages.

Let us turn now to the more positive results that have been presented in this chapter and ponder their implications. In different ways the central communication of the findings has been that the prime difference between women who are high and low in orgasmic consistency concerns their anxiety about losing what they love. The low-orgasmic woman, as contrasted to the high-orgasmic, feels that persons she values and loves are not dependable, that they may unpredictably leave her. She seems to be chronically preoccupied with the possibility of being separated from those with whom she has intimate relationships. Converging lines of information point to this fact. One finds that the low-orgasmic woman exceeds the high-orgasmic woman in the frequency with which she projects themes of separation and loss into her spontaneous story productions and themes of death into her inkblot fantasies. When asked to recall things that happened in early childhood she more often conjures up memories involving loss of important adult figures. Furthermore, she seems to come more often from a family in which the father was literally or psychologically absent (for example, dead, frequently away from home) and in which he adopted a casual, perhaps uninterested ("I'm not really concerned about how you conduct yourself") attitude toward her. As indicated by the findings derived from the earlier cited study of pregnant women, she is also more likely to become concerned about being deserted in times of stress, as suggested by the fact that the low-orgasmic pregnant woman was observed to be more preoccupied than the high-orgasmic with a sense of being alone and deserted when she entered the hospital for her delivery. There were other, more tangential, findings that were interpreted to have analogous meaning. For example, the relatively greater skin responsiveness and sensitivity of the low-orgasmic woman was viewed as possibly indicative of a special "readiness" to make contact with others that reflected her concern about losing love objects. Similarly, her relatively low inclination to persist at tasks in the face of difficulty (as defined by the Endurance scale from the Edwards Personal Preference Schedule) was interpreted as lack of faith in objects and in their likelihood of "paying off."

Before proceeding further it is important to comment on the fact that it was concern about loss of the father, or the feeling that the father did not really care that characterized the low orgasmic rather than an analogous concern about the mother. If it eventually turns out that this is solidly true, it would have implications for past theorizing about the relative importance of relationships with the mother and father for the girl in her ability to evolve sexual identity. There has been increasing evidence in the literature that the father plays a crucial role in this respect. Kohlberg (1966) and Johnson (1963) have been particularly prominent in insisting on this point. As pointed out in an earlier chapter, studies by Sopchak (1952), Osgood, Suci, and Tannenbaum (1957) and others have offered empirical data indicating the considerable prominence of the father in the girl's sex typing. The findings in the present studies would seem to be in accord with the position that the father is a fundamental "catalyst" or shaper in the girl's learning how to relate to a man sexually and to respond to sexual stimulation.

How is concern about loss of objects translated into diminished orgasm consistency? There are a number of explanatory models that one might consider, some more fanciful than others. The simplest possibility would revolve about the concept of generalized anxiety. One could merely assume that chronic concern about loss of objects is disturbing and leads to a general build-up of anxiety that ultimately interferes with the physiological processes involved in attaining orgasm. After all, it is a well-documented fact that anxiety can disrupt many kinds of physiological and motoric sequences. However, the simple anxiety model is not very tenable because it has been shown that high- and low-orgasmic women do not differ in their *overall* levels of anxiety, as measured by a variety of techniques.

One could quite fancifully speculate that since intercourse is an act that is usually seen as having obvious life creative functions, it is particularly disturbing to those who have conflicts related to death and object loss, which represent the opposite pole of creation. That is, an act that denotes creation of new life could, in terms of its antithetical meaning, activate and reinforce anxieties that involve concern about the death or loss of important objects. The low-orgasm capacity of the woman with concern about loss (death) would derive, then, from the fact that each time she engaged in intercourse the meaning of the act (with reference to the creation-death concept) would arouse a special, focal species of anxiety that would interfere with what would otherwise be a "natural" sequence of arousal. This model does not make any assumptions about differences in *general* levels of anxiety between the low and high orgasmic, but only with regard to differences in anxiety aroused by an act with a specific kind of meaning. Presumably, only stimuli that stirred feelings pertaining to creation-death (or loss) would evoke a differential quantity of anxiety in high- as compared to low-orgasmic women.

A third model to consider derives directly from psychoanalytic theory. Freud (1949a,b) proposed that separation anxiety (fear of object loss) represents at one level a fear of nonsatisfaction, a sense of danger about the *build-up of tension* from a need that remains unsatisfied because of the absence of an important person (for example, mother) who previously took responsibility for it. More specifically, he suggested that when a child loses an important figure for any length of time he begins to build up intense, almost intolerable internal tensions as the result of unfulfilled needs that are suddenly no longer cared for, and he learns to equate such intolerable body tensions with the concept of object loss. Object loss becomes identified with the danger of being overwhelmed by an excess of body excitation stemming from unsatisfied wants. If one were to accept Freud's formulation concerning the nature of this anxiety about loss, it would provide a fairly logical sounding framework for interpreting the findings of the present studies concerning the link between fear of loss of object and orgasmic difficulties. Since the low-orgasmic women were found to be concerned about object loss (separation anxiety) one could say that, in Freud's terms, they were really fearful of an uncontrollable accumulation of internal tension (such as presumably arises from needs that are not properly cared for). One is then confronted with the obvious fact that the attainment of orgasm is a process that involves, for most persons, a uniquely enormous buildup of tension or excitation. There are probably few life experiences that set in motion such a dramatic upsurge of excitation in the normal individual. Putting these observations together, one could theorize that the woman who fears object loss has difficulty attaining orgasm because the thing she most specifically fears is the type of accumulation of tension that is basic to becoming sexually aroused. Presumably, the very act of becoming charged with excitation would, at some level, be interpreted as a reinstatement of a feeling state that signifies losing important love objects. This would, indeed, be an attractive theory if there were some supportive empirical evidence for Freud's equation of separation anxiety and fear of being overwhelmed by unsatisfied body tensions.

Another possible approach to the findings of the present study would be within the framework of analyses that have underscored the symbolic death implications to the individual of the blurring (and even loss) of consciousness that occurs during orgasm. There is good evidence that the state of consciousness is affected by a buildup of sexual excitation and that there may even be momentary lapse of reality contact during orgasm (Kinsey, et al., 1953; Masters and Johnson, 1966). Psychoanalytic theorists (particularly Keiser, 1952) and others have suggested that the individual may unconsciously experience an analogy between such blurring of consciousness and dying.[98] There are actually descriptions in the clinical literature of persons who seemed to be frightened by orgasm because of its death implications. If it were true that orgasm has death connotations, one could understand why the woman whose inkblot responses are characterized by an unusual amount of concern about death imagery and who in other ways is preoccupied with the potential loss that death (or other forms of separation) can bring, would find orgasm threatening and actually want to avoid it.

The writer would like to propose an explanatory framework that overlaps with certain aspects of those just reviewed. Some of its elements have already been touched upon in earlier comments. This model begins with the earlier described fact that when a sample of women were asked to describe the process of attaining orgasm they often referred to how important it was to detach their attention from their surroundings and to focus intensely upon themselves. Attaining orgasm seemed to be facilitated by inhibiting awareness of what is "out there" and concentrating upon the subjective experience resulting from the generation of sexual excitation. Relatedly, when such women were asked to list the conditions that they preferred during intercourse they often directly or indirectly referred to a desire to feel secure against intrusion or distraction. For example, they preferred that other persons not be close by and that there not be any distracting noises in the vicinity. Such preferences undoubtedly reflect, to some extent, not wanting one's sexual activity to be detected by others, but there also seemed to be an important element of a desire to be insulated and protected from distraction.[99] The process of becoming sufficiently excited to reach orgasm probably requires a woman to diminish her awareness of other objects and intensify her focus upon her own arousal. In that sense, attaining orgasm means, at least for a short period, giving up some measure of one's attachment to objects "out there." Also, certainly to the degree that a buildup of sexual excitation blunts the clarity of consciousness or awareness, it means a "fade out" of other objects, which become psychologically more vague and distant.[100] If a woman feared loss of objects, any condition that caused them to fade and become more distant in such a fashion could be threatening to her—because of the loss implied. With this perspective, one can understand why the woman who is concerned about themes of separation and loss should be inhibited about reaching orgasm. For her the orgasm experience would mean losing a hold on that which already seems to be undependable. To expose herself to orgasm (or presumably any condition that means withdrawing attention from "out there") is to confront herself with a state of things that she particularly fears. Although the explanatory framework just sketched emphasizes the role of fading consciousness and the need to withdraw attention from outside objects as major elements in interfering with orgasm attainment in the woman with separation anxiety, it does not rule out the impact of other factors mentioned earlier. For example, it could well be true that the creative significance of the act of intercourse, via its associated antithetical meanings, does conjure up the theme of death (that is, the continuum of creation-death) and therefore is disturbing to the woman with separation anxiety who is concerned about death as a representation of loss. Similarly, it could well be true, as Freud theorized, that separation anxiety is primarily a fear of an uncontrollable accumulation of internal tension (presumably associated with the loss of an important figure whose task it was to satisfy the need producing the tension). One of the factors that might inhibit orgasm in the woman with separation anxiety would thus be her desire to avoid the kind of buildup in body tension that means danger to her.

What is central to the formulation that has been offered is the idea that orgasm difficulty in women is fundamentally a function of anxiety about the lack of permanence of love objects. The conditions that might feed into such anxiety could range widely. Any feelings or fantasies created by the nature of the intercourse situation that somehow intensify anxiety about loss and related themes such as death could contribute to inhibiting sexual responsiveness in the woman who is already concerned about such themes.

It is important to assert that the woman who is concerned about object loss does not represent a particular personality type. As shown by the research presented in this chapter, she is not characterized by any one trait or specific cluster of traits. There are probably innumerable ways in which a woman could adapt to anxiety about loss. She could be very careful and guarded about how she set up relationships with others. She might also cope with her concern by compensatorily being very outgoing and seeking to cement every possible contact. She might just as adequately be dependent or independent, friendly or aggressive, and so forth. Similarly, one would have to say that just because a woman has anxiety about loss of objects does not mean that she is weaker or more maladjusted or more neurotic than the average woman. There is no single problem or conflict that has been shown to predominate among those who are most psychologically distressed. It is likely that most women with anxiety about object loss develop adequate defenses for coping with it. They probably learn to cope with such anxiety and to keep its influence from intruding significantly into most situations. One may theorize that only in very specialized contexts where there is a dramatic loss of investment in outside objects or in which fantasies about death are mobilized does the anxiety about object loss seriously intrude into a woman's ability to function adequately.

A final matter to consider derives from an earlier review chapter in which it was pointed out that there is evidence in the literature (Kinsey, et al., 1953) that the higher a woman's educational level or socioeconomic status the more orgasmically consistent she tends to be. If one now looks at this fact in the context of the material presented in this chapter, the idea occurs that a woman who grows up in a home of low educational or socioeconomic status is particularly likely to encounter experiences that would foster separation anxiety. She would probably more often have a father who died early or who was an alcoholic or who deserted the family. Perhaps she would also be more likely to encounter catastrophic threats such as sudden loss of all family income, death of other family members, and unexpected shifts in living arrangements that would reinforce her feeling that objects and relationships are not dependable. To be low in educational or socioeconomic status is to increase the likelihood that a woman will live through events that give her a distrust in the stability of the world.

N O T E S

1. Orgasm is meant in the special context of this chapter to refer to attainment of orgasmic excitement by any means that two heterosexual sex partners prefer.

2. It is important to note at this point that the stability (test-retest reliability) of the self-ratings of orgasm consistency was examined in two studies. In both studies the women were seen twice. It was found in Sample 4 ($N=32$) that the test-retest scores (week intervening) correlated .89 ($p<.001$). In Sample 5 ($N=30$) the test-retest scores (about three days intervening) was .93 ($p<.001$). Apparently, women are very consistent over an interval of three to seven days in reporting their orgasm consistency.

3. One of the negative findings that should be mentioned is the fact that orgasm consistency does not relate to type of contraception used. That is, one cannot account for differences in orgasm consistency in terms of factors linked with the relative effectiveness of various contraceptive techniques (for example, the degree to which they make a woman feel she is safe from unwanted pregnancy).

4. The inkblot task required each woman to look at a series of inkblots and to offer an imaginative interpretation of what each blot looked like to her.

The Thematic Apperception Test involves creating imaginative stories about a series of pictures (for example, male and female figures standing near each other).

5. The median Death score in this sample and the remainder to be described was consistently 0 or 1. The range was typically about 0–6.

6. Chi-square was used here and in several subsequent analyses because the distributions of scores were so skewed.

Note also that in all of the analyses to follow the orgasm consistency scores have been transformed so that a high score indicates high-orgasm consistency.

7. That is, the scorer was not aware of the orgasm ratings of the women as he evaluated their inkblot responses.

8. In Sample 5 an attempt was made to determine if orgasm consistency is related to a woman's degree of fear of death as she would report it in direct response to a questionnaire. The Boyar (1964) Fear of Death Scale, which was the questionnaire employed, asked each individual to rate how much she agreed with such statements as the following: "I have moments when I get really upset about dying"; "Not knowing what it feels like to die makes me anxious." Scores from the Boyar scale

had only a chance correlation with orgasm consistency. One must conclude that although orgasm consistency correlates with preoccupation with death imagery (as elicited by inkblots), it is not related to amount of consciously and explicitly experienced concern about death.

9. The median score was 1 (range 0–5) and was based on an analysis of six stories. The score distribution was seriously skewed.

10. In Sample 2 the women were asked to write stories about the following ten themes: a girl and her father, a girl and her mother, a girl and her boyfriend, a boy and his father, a woman in serious trouble, a woman and her husband, a girl and her sister, a woman and her child, a family, a woman looking for a job. In Sample 4 only the first eight of these themes were requested. The women were given five minutes to write each story.

11. Analyses involving the total sample did not show significant differentiation with reference to Separation scores. Only when the extreme orgasm categories were compared were significant Separation score differences obtained.

12. Yates' correction has been used whenever the expected frequency in a cell falls below 5. Note further that tests of significance throughout this book are two-tailed unless otherwise specified.

13. In Sample 2 the median Separation score for the low-orgasm woman was 5.0 and that for the high-orgasm woman 3.0. The equivalent scores in Sample 4 were respectively 5.0 and 2.0.

14. Italics added by the writer.

15. The median Separation score was 0 and the range was 0–1. Scorable protocols were obtained from 38 women. An independent scorer who evaluated 20 of the protocols attained 93 percent agreement with the present writer.

Chi-square was used to evaluate the findings because the Separation score distribution was so skewed.

16. The median was 0 (range 0–1). Some typical statements of father Separation were as follows: "My father worked long hours and had little time for his family"; "My parents were divorced when I was six and I lived with my mother"; "My father died when I was in the sixth grade"; "My father traveled and was away from home quite a bit."

17. A number did not write such accounts because the decision to obtain descriptions of the delivery was not made until after the study had already begun.

18. Two judges who independently appraised 20 of the delivery descriptions for the occurrence of the two categories of response attained 96 percent agreement concerning the presence of explicit statements indicating a desire to have one's husband present during the delivery and 87 percent agreement concerning statements pertaining to feeling lonely, deserted, and mistreated.

The median response frequency in both categories was 0.

19. An exploratory analysis should be outlined that concerned the frequency with which women explicitly mentioned the exit of the child from their bodies during the delivery. Explicit mention is exemplified by such statements as, "I felt it come out"; "The doctor pulled it out"; "It squeezed out." On the basis of the fact that the low-orgasmic woman seems to have a need to hang on to objects and not to lose them, it was speculated that she would react to delivery as a process of losing an internalized object of value. Therefore, she would presumably be relatively defensive about clearly visualizing the passage of the child out of her body. This would too clearly specify a kind of loss. When the delivery descriptions of the high- and low-orgasmic women were analyzed for the presence of explicit statements about the passage of the child out of the mother's body, it was found that there was a borderline trend for the high-orgasmic group to make more such statements ($x^2 = 3.0$, $df = 1$, $p < .10$). This finding is sufficiently interesting to encourage further exploration of the relationship between orgasm consistency and the symbolic significance assigned to the delivery process in terms of object loss.

20. The high- and low-orgasmic women did not differ in number of previous pregnancies. Therefore, one cannot attribute the results obtained to lesser or greater familiarity with the experiences involved in coming into the hospital and being delivered of the child.

21. All correlations reported in this chapter are Pearson product-moment coefficients.

22. The number of women for whom Parent-Child Relations scores were available was so small because the questionnaire had been mailed to the women almost a year subsequent to the original study, and by that time many had moved and were no longer available to participate.

23. Throughout the book the N upon which a correlation is based is not specifically cited unless it departs considerably from the total N for the sample in question. The N's for each sample are presented in Chapter 7.

24. Orgasm consistency was not significantly correlated with ratings of the father that were obtained in terms of simple six point continua administered in several samples.

There were also no significant correlations between orgasm consistency and the speed or content of free associations to stimulus words with father connotations (Sample 5).

25. Roe and Siegelman (1963) did find that the Casual and Demanding scores were polar opposites.

26. Dr. Frank Johnson suggested to the writer that this pattern of findings might be interpreted, within a psychoanalytic framework, to mean that orgasm consistency is lower in the woman whose father behaved like a permissive peer rather than a father and who, in so doing, encouraged guilt arousing (Oedipal) sexual fantasies.

27. Chi-square was employed because of the presence of skewed scores.

28. The tachistoscopic technique that involves asking an individual to identify words or pictures at speeds as fast as 1 millisecond is fully outlined in Appendix A.

29. As described in Appendix B, the series of pictures was taken from the Blacky test (Blum, 1949), which presumably taps attitudes about major themes that are significant within the psychoanalytic framework.

30. Active: To be restless when quiet. To like to be "on the go."

Vigorous: To participate actively in sports and work involving large muscle groups and great expenditure of energy.

Impulsive: To be happy-go-lucky and of an acting-on-the-spur-of-the-moment disposition.

Dominant: To think of oneself as a leader who takes initiative and responsibility.

Stable: To be usually cheerful and of even disposition. To remain calm in a crisis.

Sociable: To enjoy the company of others and to make friends easily.

Reflective: To like meditation and reflective thinking. To enjoy dealing with theoretical rather than practical problems.

31. Achievement, Deference, Order, Exhibition, Autonomy, Affiliation, Intraception, Succorance, Dominance, Abasement, Nurturance, Change, Endurance, Heterosexuality, Aggression. The names of the various dimensions convey fairly clearly what each is considered to measure.

32. It should be pointed out that this was the abbreviated sample ($N=24$), which was contacted by mail almost a year subsequent to the time they were seen in the laboratory.

33. The mean percentiles and standard deviations of the Endurance scores in Samples 2, 3, and 4 were respectively 51.9 ($\sigma=30.9$), 49.1 ($\sigma=25.3$), 39.6 ($\sigma=27.3$).

34. It is interesting that in one study Terman (1951) found, on the basis of women's self-ratings, that those with orgasm difficulties were characterized by less "persistence" than those without orgasm difficulties.

35. Words in parentheses inserted by the author.

36. The cotton was a strip three inches in length and two inches in width. It was lightly applied to traverse a distance equal to the width of the wrist in one second.

37. A modified method of limits was employed, with four alternating ascending and descending determinations at each site. The mean of all trials represents the mean pressure threshold for that site.

38. All of the values cited for tickle and light touch measures actually represent overall averages for all trials in which measures were secured.

39. In Sample 2 wrist response to tickle was not studied. Only cheek, breast, and thigh sites were appraised.

40. Women in four of the samples (2, 3, 4, 5) were asked to rate themselves with respect to how ticklish they were. In all of these samples there were significant positive correlations between self-ratings of ticklishness and the quickness with which stroking was perceived as tickle. But duration of tickle produced by stroking as well as threshold for light touch were not significantly correlated with self-ratings of tickle. Orgasm consistency was not significantly correlated with self-ratings of tickle.

41. No consistent relationships were found between threshold for experiencing tickle and duration of tickle. Further, only chance correlations occurred between the tickle measures and touch threshold measures.

42. The following are some representative average values for time required for the stroking to be perceived as tickle. (Those women who did not experience tickle within 60 seconds were arbitrarily assigned a value of 65 seconds.)

Wrist	9.2 seconds
Cheek	19.6 seconds
Breast	14.9 seconds
Thigh	13.5 seconds

Representative values for tickle duration are as follows. (It is important to note that these values are based only on those women who were able to begin perceiving tickle within one minute after stroking began.)

Wrist	11.6 seconds
Cheek	11.2 seconds
Breast	13.3 seconds
Thigh	14.1 seconds

Representative average touch threshold values are as follows:

Wrist	3.7 [Log 10. Force (.1 mg.)]
Breast	3.8 [Log 10. Force (.1 mg.)]
Thigh	3.8 [Log 10. Force (.1 mg.)]

43. One of the two correlations involving tickle threshold for breast was significant. It could be argued that if breast threshold had been measured in a third sample a significant correlation might have been obtained with a consequent total of two of three significant coefficients. This may be so. However, it has been arbitrarily decided to regard as nonsignificant those results in which only one of two values bearing on the same issue attains a level of statistical significance.

44. It should be added that measures of tickle response were secured during nonmenstrual and menstrual times of the cycle. No consistent relationships were found between orgasm consistency and shifts in tickle response from the nonmenstrual to menstrual phases.

45. It is true, of course, that duration of tickle on the cheek also correlated with orgasm consistency. But here too one notes that there is likely to be relatively less embarrassment evoked by cheek stroking than breast or thigh stroking.

46. Autokinetic movement refers to the fact that when an individual observes a

pinpoint of light in a dark room it appears to move, even though it is actually stationary.

47. This is the apparatus used by Witkin, et al. (1962) to study field independence. Further details concerning it may be found in Appendix B.

48. In order to control for the possible influence of handedness on measures of right-left directionality, only right-handed women were employed in all of the studies described.

49. As will be seen, although this is a logical assumption, it has not been possible to show a significant relationship between orgasm consistency and a conventional questionnaire measure of femininity (California Psychological Inventory Scale [Gough, 1957]). However, the meaning of femininity as it is defined by such a questionnaire is different from the meaning as defined by right-left directionality, as indicated by the fact that femininity scores based upon the two different approaches do not correlate significantly. A discussion of the possible meaning of femininity as defined in terms of the right-left directionality concept is presented at a later point.

50. The mean right-left rod and frame score in Sample 2 was .03 ($\sigma=6.1$) and in Sample 3 was -2.6 ($\sigma=15.0$).

51. In the one instance (Sample 5) where the right minus left tickle and rod and frame scores were both available, they were found to correlate .26 (p<.10).

52. In order to control for the possible influence of handedness, only right-handed women were studied.

53. Chi-square was employed because of the skewed character of the right-left difference scores in this sample.

54. The mean right-left tickle threshold scores were 3.8 ($\sigma=7.8$), .5 ($\sigma=9.4$), and 1.1 ($\sigma=5.7$) respectively in Samples 3, 4, and 5.

55. No consistent relationships were found between orgasm consistency and right-minus-left differences in duration of tickle.

56. No correlations were found between orgasm consistency and a woman's description of how she and her parents reacted psychologically to her first menstruation.

57. In Sample 1 a gynecological examination was performed for each woman, and no relationship was observed between orgasm consistency and the appearance of the vaginal walls, the occurrence of obvious pelvic pathology, or the *ph* of the vagina.

58. Ratings of a woman's sexual responsiveness were made by judges who had observed them for several hours in the laboratory as well as by judges who had available pictures of each woman. None of these ratings was significantly correlated with orgasm consistency.

59. Formal measures of interest and value patterns were taken not only with the Strong but also the Allport-Vernon-Lindzey (1960) Study of Values scales described in Appendix A. These measures diversely evaluate such dimensions as interests in specific vocational specialties, preferences for activities involving people rather than "things," preferences for aesthetic experiences, motivation to gain power over others, and so forth. No consistent correlations between such interest measures and orgasm consistency could be demonstrated. Apparently, one cannot predict orgasm potential from a knowledge of the values and interests of a woman.

60. It was suggested earlier on the basis of the positive correlation observed between orgasm consistency and left directionality in spatial perception that orgasm consistency may be linked with one *special* aspect of femininity, namely, being "soft" and unguarded in interpersonal contacts.

61. It should be added that no differences in orgasm consistency could be detected among Protestants, Catholics, and Jews.

62. In most samples the women rated themselves as being moderately religious. However, the mean frequency of church attendance was said to be 1.5 times per month. The average Allport-Vernon-Lindzey (1960) Religious score was slightly below the average for college populations.

63. This task requires the individual to write in beneath each of a series of numbers a corresponding code symbol. Scores are computed based on the number of correct code substitutions made within the time limit.

64. The title is "Signal 30."

65. However, this finding cannot be given much weight in view of the fact that Digit Symbol performance did not show a significant decrement after the stress was introduced. One is left in the position of having evidence that the intended stress was not stressful to the average woman exposed to it.

66. The learning task in each case was to look for one minute at a list of 20 words typed on a sheet of paper and then to recall as many of these words as possible during a subsequent five-minute period. Each list consisted of ten words with emotional content and ten that were neutral. In Sample 2 four separate lists were learned, with two containing sex words, one guilt words, and one food words. In Sample 3 the list contained sex words, and in Sample 4 one list contained sex words and another presented pregnancy related words.

67. More details concerning the analysis of the autobiographies are presented in the later chapter dealing with clitoral-vaginal preferences.

68. More detailed descriptions of the specific indices that were computed are presented in the chapter dealing with clitoral-vaginal preferences.

69. This measure is based upon the frequency with which an individual *agrees with* a series of proverbs. A high score implies the opposite of a high dominance score.

70. Fisher and Cleveland (1968) devised a method for measuring boundary articulation that is based on an analysis of the imaginative images produced by an individual when responding to inkblots. They compute an index called the Barrier score, which is equal to the number of inkblot responses given in which protecting and containing properties are ascribed to the periphery of the percept. Some examples of percepts with such qualities are cave with rocky walls, mummy wrapped up, man in armor, bed covered with a blanket.

71. It should be repeated that baseline Barrier scores were not correlated with orgasm consistency.

72. A product-moment correlation coefficient, as contrasted to the chi-square value, did not attain statistical significance. The skewed nature of the Barrier shift scores probably accounts for this difference.

73. Shifts in general body awareness (Body Prominence) from the first to the second session were also analyzed with reference to orgasm consistency, but the relationship proved not to be statistically significant.

74. Awareness of breasts and vagina was measured with a special questionnaire developed especially for the present studies. See Appendix A.

75. It measures the following dimensions: Decoration in Dress, Comfort in Dress, Interest in Dress, Conformity in Dress, and Economy in Dress.

76. It evaluates the following variables: Boundary Loss, Blocked Body Openings, Depersonalization, Sense of Smallness, Sense of Largeness, Feelings of Being Dirty, Unusual Skin Sensations, and Total Distortions.

77. Responses to body distortion were also measured in two samples in which the women were asked to describe the apparent changes in their appearance while viewing their own full-length mirror image through aniseikonic lenses (Appendix C). Orgasm consistency was not correlated with overall readiness to perceive aniseikonic distortions or the susceptibility of specific body areas (for example, pelvis, breasts) to such distortion. It should be added by way of clarification of the aniseikonic lens measure that previous research (Fisher, 1970) has shown that the greater a person's anxiety about an object he views through aniseikonic lenses the *less* likely he is to perceive it as altered or changed in appearance.

78. As mentioned earlier, it was found in Sample 1 that orgasm consistency was unrelated to previous history of gynecological difficulties.

79. As measured by the Edwards Personal Preference Schedule.

80. As measured by the Thurstone Temperament Schedule.

81. Thematic Apperception Test.

82. Orgasm consistency related only irregularly to measures based on response to stimuli with sexual connotations as well as to other measures depicting amount of sexual content in fantasy productions. It was negatively correlated (Sample 1, $r = -.36$, $N = 39$, $p < .05$) with number of sexual themes in Thematic Apperception Test stories, spontaneous stories (Sample 2, $r = -.33$, $N = 41$, $p < .05$), and Holtzman Inkblots (Sample 6, $r = -.33$, $N = 48$, $p < .025$). One must add that there were several samples in which orgasm consistency had only chance relationships with amount of sex content in inkblot responses, several in which it had chance relationships with sex content in word completions, and one in which it had no relationship with the nature of the associations given to words with sexual connotations.

When the women were asked to identify pictures with heterosexual themes (for example, two people kissing) presented at high speed (tachistoscopically), it was found in one study that the greater their orgasm consistency the more quickly they correctly identified the picture (Sample 1, $r = -.27$, $N = 38$, $p < .10$), but in another the trend was in the opposite direction (Sample 2, $r = .48$, $N = 37$, $p < .01$). In a third instance (Sample 2), when the women were asked to identify words (rather than pictures) with sexual connotations presented tachistoscopically, orgasm consistency had a chance correlation with speed of correct perception.

Further, in one sample (Sample 2) a woman's orgasm consistency was found to be positively correlated ($r = .29$, $N = 41$, $p < .10$) with a tendency to recall more nonsexual than sexual words when asked to learn a list, half with and half without sexual meaning. However, in other samples this finding did not hold up.

The results enumerated suggest that although women varying in orgasm consistency do differ in their responses to some perceptual and fantasy tasks involving sexual stimuli, the nature of this difference will vary as a function of the specific structure of the task and is really quite irregular.

83. As measured by the Edwards Personal Preference Schedule.

84. As measured by the Thurstone Temperament Schedule.

85. As measured by the New Experience Questionnaire.

86. Attempts were made in several samples to relate orgasm consistency to the degree to which an individual tends to magnify rather than reduce the intensity of sensory experiences (Petrie, 1967). The two variables were found to be unrelated.

87. As measured by the Minnesota Multiphasic Personality Inventory (Hathaway, 1951) L, K, and R scales.

88. As measured by chain associations to words with guilt connotations and selective memory for guilt words.

89. As measured by the Murray-David Affect scales.

90. Orgasm consistency was also unrelated to the variability of physiological response within the specific conditions and across conditions.

91. The male interviewer was the present writer and the female interviewer was Rhoda Fisher.

92. Little will be said about the material obtained via the conventional interviews. There are trends that could be cited that seem to support some of the self-interview findings. However, it is difficult to make use of the conventional interview data or even to cite illustrations from them because of the obvious biases introduced by the interviewers. Again and again, as one listens to the tape recordings, it is apparent that the interviewers interjected their biases in terms of the questions they asked as well as at what points they chose to interrupt the free flow of a woman's verbalizations.

93. These were the tapes that the women made while sitting alone in a room and talking into a microphone about themselves, as they successively dealt with various topics suggested by a written outline.

94. It should be indicated that the writer and other judges were unable to distinguish the high- and low-orgasm women in terms of the *content* of the taped excerpts.

95. Two were experienced clinical psychologists with the Ph.D. degree, three were graduate students in psychology, and one was a graduate student in Special Education.

96. The mean constriction rating for the high orgasmic was 2.4 and that for the low orgasmic was 3.4. The difference, as indicated by a *t*-test, was statistically significant ($t = 2.7$, $p < .05$). Each of the six raters consistently perceived the voices of the low orgasmic as more constricted than those of the high orgasmic. The mean rating for the high-orgasmic group with regard to how natural their voices sounded was 2.5 and the mean rating for the low-orgasmic group was 3.2. The difference between them was significant ($t = 2.4$, $p < .05$). Furthermore, the mean rating of the high-orgasmic group's voices with regard to how often interesting rhythms and emphases were employed was 1.8 and the mean rating for the low-orgasmic group was 2.5. This difference too was significant ($t = 2.3$, $p < .05$).

97. Strictly speaking, this could be said to be true only within the limits of the degree of puritanical restriction likely to have occurred in the families in which the women in this sample grew up. It is conceivable that more extreme puritanical conditions than those represented in the present sample might have a negative impact on orgasmic ability.

98. Orgasm has been referred to in French as *La petite mort* ("the little death") because of the experienced blurring of consciousness.

99. It is relevant to this point that studies (Kinsey, et al., 1953) of animals have shown that the female is often quite distractible while engaged in intercourse. Her sexual response can apparently be easily inhibited by noises and other stimuli in her vicinity.

100. Kinsey, et al. (1953) comment in some detail about the anoxia produced by sexual excitement and the consequent diminished sensory sensitivity.

9

THE PERSONAL CORRELATES

OF HOW ORGASM

IS EXPERIENCED

A decision that was made in the course of designing the present studies was not to rely entirely on "performance" measures of sexual responsiveness. It is tempting to reduce sexual response to such indices as orgasm consistency and intercourse frequency. However, sexual arousal is obviously a complex psychological experience; and although two women may both attain orgasm with equal frequency, one could consistently *feel* satisfied and the other unsatisfied after orgasm. Or one may focus upon how relaxed she feels during the postorgasmic state whereas the other feels primarily "weak" or "tense" or "guilty."

Does personality play any role in the subjective quality of a woman's sexual arousal as well as in her postorgasm feelings?

To measure the feelings and moods associated with each woman's sexual response, she was asked to arrange a series of terms in the order in which they seemed to describe her inner feelings during and after orgasm. She was asked, first, to put in rank order ten terms that were descriptive of how she feels during orgasm. Then, she designated the rank order of a series of ten other terms with reference to her feelings five minutes *after* orgasm.[1]

An analysis was undertaken to determine if there are any consistent relationships between personality measures and the particular feeling states typifying a woman during and after orgasm. It was found that in only a small number of instances were there noteworthy consistencies. However, they are interesting consistencies that are well worth reporting.

Amount of Satisfaction

On the basis of her ranking judgments each woman indicated how "Unsatisfied" she felt during orgasm and five minutes afterward.[2] The writer regarded the amount of satisfaction versus dissatisfaction experienced during sexual interaction among the most important of the feeling states sampled. As in most instances where an activity is directed at satiating a specific appetite or need, the question of satisfaction is necessarily in the foreground. Whatever other feeling states are elicited by orgasm, one would expect that it would be of paramount interest to the woman involved whether it satisfied her, whether it left her with a sense of having attained what she sought or expected. Apropos of this point, it is pertinent to recall that degree of satisfaction during and after orgasm was the only feeling state found to be significantly correlated with an ability to attain orgasm consistently. As one scans the correlates of the degree to which each woman indicates she feels satisfied during and after orgasm, only three correlates emerge with real consistency. There is a clear trend, such that the greater a woman's feeling of being satisfied the less repressive she is in her attitudes toward her own feelings and emotions, the more spontaneous she is about expressing impulses, and the more she has aspirations to exercise personal power. More specifically, the rank assigned to the term "Unsatisfied" during orgasm was negatively correlated with the Repression scale [3] of the Minnesota Multiphasic Personality Inventory (Hathaway, 1951) and positively correlated with the Political score of the Allport-Vernon-Lindzey (1960) Study of Values.[4] It also showed a weak trend to be positively correlated with the Impulsive scale of the Thurstone (1953) Temperament Schedule.[5] Analogously, the rank assigned to the term "Unsatisfied" five minutes after orgasm was negatively [6] correlated with the Repression scale, and positively with the Impulsive [7] and Political scores.[8] Although the relationships are far from perfect in their continuity, one cannot but be impressed with their overall consistency across both the results for the *during* orgasm and also *after* orgasm ratings.

To understand the meaning of these findings one needs to review the nature of the three measures that showed consistent relationships to amount of satisfaction. The Repression scale of the Minnesota Multiphasic Personality Inventory is considered to measure degree of "dependence upon mechanisms of denial and rationalization and to a lack of effective self-insight" (Dahlstrom and Welsh, 1960, p. 84). It is stated that the greater one's Repression score the more one holds feelings and impulses under tight control and refrains from externalizing or acting out affects and impulses. At another level, the person with a high Repression score has been defined as one who is "acquiescent" in orientation (Edwards and Abbott, 1969).

The Impulsive score of the Thurstone Temperament Schedule is stated to be a measure of the degree to which a person behaves in a "happy-go-lucky, daredevil, carefree, acting-on-the-spur-of-the-moment" fashion.

The Political score of the Study of Values is defined as measuring how motivated one is to exercise power. The person with a high Political score is depicted as one who wishes for "personal power" and "influence."

What do the Repression, Impulsive, and Political parameters have in common? One might say that they all directly or indirectly tap a dimension of self-expressiveness. The Repression score presumably evaluates the extent to which an individual applies restraints to herself, inhibiting not only awareness of her own motives but also the acting out of impulses and wishes. The Impulsive score portrays how easily the individual allows herself to respond spontaneously and to do things on impulse. Relatedly, the Political score might be said to evaluate how much a woman is invested in attaining roles that will permit her to acquire the power to act out her wishes. The common element would seem to be how easily or readily the individual takes self-expressive or self-assertive action. It could be said, then, that the more satisfied a woman feels during and shortly after orgasm the more likely she is to be the sort of person who is nonrepressive toward her own wishes, impulses, and aspirations. Why should satisfaction be linked with such a nonself-inhibiting orientation? One possible interpretation would be that the sheer intensity of feeling aroused during intercourse and its relatively uncontrolled expression at the point of orgasm are threatening to a woman who usually tries to maintain restraint over self-expression. The unrestrained release represented by orgasm might be experienced as sufficiently alien to create discomfort and an underlying sense of dissatisfaction. The dissatisfaction could be regarded as a woman's negative response to a "breakdown" in her usual repressive style of adaptation. One may presume that the woman with a self-inhibiting orientation would, at the height of her sexual excitement, be torn between her wish to obtain intense release and her anxiety about relaxing inhibitions.[9] Such conflict could "spoil" the orgasm experience.

Weak and Tired

While analyzing the correlates of various modes of experiencing orgasm it was observed that a few of these modes were particularly likely to typify the woman who avoids awareness of her body, especially its sexual attributes. More specifically, there seemed to be evidence that the more a woman feels either weak or tired during orgasm the more she is inclined to evade awareness of her body experiences. Several measures obtained from the women were aimed at evaluating body awareness. These measures were as follows: Body Prominence, Breast Awareness, and Vaginal Awareness.

Body Prominence is an index of how generally aware a woman is of her body. It is based on the frequency with which she mentions her own body or related body processes when asked to list spontaneously all of the "things" that are immediately within her awareness at a particular time. (See Appendix A for details concerning this measure.) The writer has shown elsewhere (Fisher, 1970) that degree of body awareness in women is positively linked with a clear sense of identity and individuation. Breast and Vaginal Awareness were ascertained by means of a task that asks each woman to make a series of judgments in which she indicates whether she is more aware of her vagina (or her breasts) than each of a number of other body areas (for example, head, arm). (See Appendix A.) These two measures were developed in order to be able to evaluate the degree to which a woman is aware of regions of her body that have explicit sexual significance. It was presumed that unusually low awareness of such regions might indicate reluctance to assimilate the sexual attributes of one's body into the body scheme. However, it should be added that neither Breast nor Vaginal Awareness has been found to be significantly correlated with any of the major indicators of sexual responsiveness (for example, orgasm consistency) that have already been considered up to this point. On a purely exploratory basis it was found that the measures just listed were related in a similar fashion to two of the various modes of experiencing orgasm that had been sampled. It was observed that degree of body awareness is low in those who feel either weak or tired during orgasm. More specifically, amount of weakness felt during orgasm was negatively related to Body Prominence and degree of awareness of the sexualized body areas. This same pattern of relationships held for how tired one feels during orgasm.[10] Although the relationships involved are far from substantial and have gaps in them here and there, they do hold together as a noteworthy trend. There does seem to be evidence that a woman who is particularly preoccupied with feelings of being tired or weak during orgasm tends to avoid awareness of her body, both generally and also specifically with reference to the sexual areas. One may speculate that the woman who usually avoids awareness of her body finds the intensified and unescapable body experiences produced by orgasmic arousal to be unpleasant. It may be taxing to her to accommodate to a kind of awareness that her defenses usually evade. The sense of being taxed and strained by intense orgasmic body sensations may reflect itself in feelings of tiredness and weakness. As discussed in detail at a later point, many of the disturbing effects of sexual arousal seem to stem from their thrusting emotions, sensations, and fantasies into explicit awareness that are usually carefully controlled and filtered.

Miscellaneous Observations

Aside from the few positive results that have been cited, one may say that the specific feeling states stirred up in a woman during orgasm do not seem to be linked with her general personality or attitudinal characteristics. There are no consistent correlates of whether a woman feels or does not feel "ecstatic" or "embarrassed" or "guilty" or "strange" during the orgasmic sequence. Some of these negative findings are interesting because they do not conform to commonsense expectation. The intensity with which a woman feels guilty after orgasm is not related to her religiosity, frequency of church attendance, or the importance her parents placed upon religion. How embarrassed a woman feels during and after orgasm is apparently not correlated with the amount of sexual experience she has had (for example, as defined by the number of years of marriage), the attitudes of her parents toward sexual matters, the manner in which she received her early sex education, or the attitude toward nudity that prevailed in her home as she was growing up. How tense a woman feels during and after orgasm does not seem to be linked to her *general* level of anxiety or disturbance. The degree to which alien and nonego-syntonic feelings (as represented by rankings of terms such as "strange" and "not myself") are aroused during the orgasmic process is largely unrelated to measures of anxiety and body image disturbance. It is not clear why such relationships as those enumerated that might logically have been expected to be significant did not appear. One might ask whether the disparities could be caused by some basic lack of reliability in the ranking procedure that the women used in order to describe their orgasmic feeling states. However, this is unlikely because the test-retest reliabilities (one week intervening) of the majority of the terms ranked fell within an acceptable range (.70–.80). Another explanatory possibility is that the women's feelings at the height of arousal are considerably affected by the behavior and attitudes of their husbands. That is, one husband might act in such a way as to make his wife feel embarrassed or guilty and another might carefully protect her against such feelings. If the husband's influence in this respect were of large proportions, this would, of course, mask any effects that a woman's own personal attributes had upon her mode of experiencing arousal.[11] There is no way to evaluate, within the context of the present studies, the plausibility of such a possible explanation. A third point to consider is that the feelings produced during orgasm may be so unique, so different from any other psychological state encountered in the average woman's life, that their specific quality is not tied to her personal attributes as they are manifested in her usual style of behavior, which, after all, occurs in relatively nonaroused contexts. The uniqueness of the emotions elicited during orgasm may render them relatively unpredictable from other aspects of a woman's behavior patterns.

NOTES

1. The actual instructions given were as follows:

This question concerns your usual feelings and sensations during orgasm. Below are listed ten words or phrases frequently used to describe such feelings. Put a 1 in front of the word best descriptive of your own feelings, a 2 in front of the word second most descriptive and continue to assign such numbers until you put 10 in front of the least descriptive of how you usually feel.

_____Strange _____Ecstatic _____Slightly embarrassed
_____Happy _____Tense _____Weak _____Tired
_____Unsatisfied _____As if I would burst _____Not like myself

The same instructions were given for a second task that "concerns your usual feelings and sensations five minutes after you have experienced orgasm." The terms that were arranged in rank order were as follows:

_____Not like myself _____Satisfied _____Happy _____Weak
_____Tense _____Unsatisfied _____Tired _____Relaxed
_____ Slightly embarrassed _____Slightly guilty

2. Although the material to be described is based on the rank order assigned to the term "Unsatisfied," it should be noted that the term "Satisfied" was also included in the series pertaining to feelings five minutes after orgasm. However, its inclusion was intended as a check on the consistency with which the ranking judgments were made. Obviously, if a woman put the term "Unsatisfied" low in rank order, she should have put "Satisfied" high. Without exception, this was found to be true in all of the samples. The women were, indeed, consistent in their judgments.

3. Rank of Unsatisfied during orgasm showed the following negative relationships with Repression: $x^2 = 6.1$, $df = 2$, $p < .05$, Sample 1; $r = -.24$, $p < .20$, Sample 2; $x^2 = 9.0$, $df = 2$, $p < .02$, Sample 3; and $r = -.37$, $p < .025$, Sample 4. The correlations in the other samples did not even approach statistical significance.

Note that all correlations cited in this chapter are Pearson product-moment coefficients. Note further that chi-square has been employed in all instances where score distributions are seriously skewed.

4. Rank of Unsatisfied during orgasm was correlated .40 ($p < .01$) with Political in Sample 3 and .57 ($p < .001$) in Sample 5. The correlations in Samples 1 and 2 did not even approach significance.

5. Rank of Unsatisfied during orgasm had the following positive relationships to Impulsive: $x^2 = 6.3$, $df = 2$, Sample 1; $r = .26$, p .10, Sample 2. In Samples 5 and 6 the relationship did not even approach significance.

6. Rank of Unsatisfied five minutes after orgasm had the following negative relationships with Repression: $x^2 = 6.2$, $df = 2$, $p < .05$, Sample 1; $r = -.32$, $p < .05$, Sample 2; $x^2 = 4.0$, $df = 1$, $p < .05$, Sample 3; $r = -.27$, $p < .10$, Sample 5. The relationships in the other three samples did not even approach significance.

7. Rank of Unsatisfied after orgasm had the following positive relationships with Impulsive: $x^2 = 2.5$, $p > .20$, Sample 1; $r = .32$, $p < .05$, Sample 2; $r = .34$, $p < .05$, Sample 6. The relationship for Sample 5 did not even approach significance.

8. Rank of Unsatisfied five minutes after orgasm was correlated with Political as follows: .35, $p < .05$, Sample 2; .63, $p < .001$, Sample 3; .44, p .025, Sample 5. The correlation for Sample 1 did not even approach significance.

9. There are interesting trends for amount of dissatisfaction both during and after orgasm, to be correlated with certain physiological measures. The *rank* of Unsatisfied during orgasm was correlated .34 ($p < .05$) in Sample 1 and .27 (not significant) in Sample 2 with GSR amplitude during stress. The equivalent correlations for *rank* of Unsatisfied (with GSR amplitude) after orgasm were as follows: .28 ($p > .10$), Sample 1 and .37 ($p < .10$), Sample 2. These are barely borderline trends, but worth mentioning in terms of future research possibilities.

Rank of Unsatisfied during orgasm was correlated as follows with temperature of hand minus temperature of leg during stress: .34 ($p < .05$), Sample 1; .37 ($p < .025$), Sample 3. The correlation in Sample 2 did not even approach significance.

Rank of Unsatisfied after orgasm was correlated as follows with temperature of hand minus temperature of leg during stress: .39 ($p < .05$), Sample 1; .31 ($p < .05$), Sample 3. The correlation in Sample 2 did not even approach significance.

The trends involving hand minus ankle temperatures are rather substantial. It would appear that the more satisfied a woman feels both during and after orgasm the relatively greater the temperature of her hand than her leg. More is said about this at a later point.

10. Rank of weakness had the following relationships with Body Prominence: $r = .36$, $p < .05$, Sample 1; $r = .27$, $p < .10$, Sample 2; $r = .26$, $p < .10$, Sample 3; $r = -.45$, $p < .01$, Sample 5. The relationship for Sample 6 did not approach significance.

Rank of weakness had the following relationships with Breast awareness: $r = .34$, $p < .10$, Sample 1; $r = .41$, $p < .01$, Sample 3. The correlation for Sample 2 did not even approach significance.

Rank of weakness had the following relationships with Vaginal awareness: $r = .30$,

p .10, Sample 1; $r = .34$, $p < .05$, Sample 3. The relationship in Sample 2 did not even approach significance.

Rank of tiredness during orgasm had the following relationships with Body Prominence: $r = .42$, $p < .01$, Sample 2; $r = .29$, $p < .10$, Sample 3; $r = .32$, $p < .05$, Sample 6. The correlations for Samples 1 and 5 did not approach significance.

Rank of tiredness during orgasm did not correlate significantly with Breast awareness in any of the samples. But it had the following relationships with Vaginal awareness: $r = .39$, p .01, Sample 2; $r = .25$, p .10, Sample 3. The correlation in Sample 1 did not approach significance.

11. The fact that the women's rankings of the various descriptive terms were not significantly correlated with their ratings of several husband attributes (for example, how easy he is to communicate with about sexual matters) would tend to argue against this view; but, on the other hand, only a relatively small and perhaps insufficient number of judgments were obtained with regard to the husbands.

10

CLITORAL-VAGINAL PREFERENCE AND REGULATION OF TENSION

It was reported in earlier chapters that the women who were studied differ considerably in their preferences for clitoral as compared to vaginal stimulation. Some prefer no clitoral stimulation (even finding it painful) and others cannot attain orgasm without it. Overall, there was a trend for the women in the various samples to feel that clitoral stimulation contributes more than vaginal stimulation to orgasm. Indeed, almost 30 percent of the women regarded clitoral stimulation as contributing "much more" than vaginal, whereas only 7 percent stated that vaginal stimulation contributes "much more" than clitoral. Largely because of statements by psychoanalytic theorists a good deal of controversy has arisen concerning the significance of a woman's preference for clitoral as compared to vaginal stimulation. Such theorists favor the view that when a woman can reach orgasm via vaginal stimulation this is a sign of her personal maturity, but when she can reach orgasm only through direct clitoral stimulation they regard this as evidence of personal immaturity.[1] The complex psychoanalytic rationale for this view was reviewed in an earlier chapter and will not be restated again at this point. In any case, psychoanalytic theory has led to the assignment of good connotations to vaginal responsiveness and bad ones to clitoral arousal. This is true despite the evidence presented by Kinsey, et al. (1953) and Masters and Johnson (1966) that a large proportion of the physiological arousal that contributes to orgasm (even when it is delivered by the penis inserted in the vagina) directly or indirectly involves the clitoris. It is particularly remarkable how widespread has been the acceptance of assumptions about the "more mature" nature of vaginal arousal in the absence of any empirical evidence to support them. The literature is replete with clinical vignettes and strongly phrased opinions presumably demonstrating the maturity of a vaginal orientation, but they only bear witness to an intense belief in certain theoretical propositions. Actually, the writer has been unable to find a single scientific study pertinent to this matter of maturity-immaturity.

The opportunity to obtain empirical information about the psychological and physiological correlates of clitoral-vaginal preferences was provided by the data collected in the seven samples of women who were studied. One of the prime sexual response indices that was derived concerned relative preference for vaginal as compared to clitoral stimulation in attaining orgasm. It was based upon each woman's reply to the following inquiry:

> This question concerns the relative importance of clitoral as compared to vaginal stimulation in your attaining orgasm. Put a circle around the appropriate number.
> 1. Clitoral stimulation contributes much more than vaginal stimulation.
> 2. Clitoral stimulation contributes somewhat more than vaginal stimulation.
> 3. Clitoral stimulation contributes a little more than vaginal stimulation.
> 4. Vaginal stimulation and clitoral stimulation make an equal contribution.
> 5. Vaginal stimulation contributes a little more than clitoral stimulation.
> 6. Vaginal stimulation contributes somewhat more than clitoral stimulation.
> 7. Vaginal stimulation contributes much more than clitoral stimulation.

Each woman's score could range from 1 to 7.[2]

An issue that immediately arises is whether responses to this question were influenced by the desire to make a good impression. Would most women, for example, be inclined to exaggerate the importance to them of vaginal stimulation because of the widely accepted assumption that vaginal responsiveness is better than clitoral responsiveness? There is fairly convincing evidence that the care that was taken to establish a trusting relationship with the women during the course of the studies paid off and that they responded to the clitoral-vaginal questionnaire in a truthful fashion. The evidence derives from several levels. First, the predominant trend across samples was not to emphasize the importance of the so-called good vaginal stimulation in achieving orgasm but rather that of clitoral arousal. There were considerably more who reported that clitoral stimulation was particularly important to them than who reported that vaginal stimulation was of such importance. Secondly, as shown earlier in Table 6–2, the replies of the women to the clitoral-vaginal question were not significantly correlated with measures of the degree to which they were trying to make a good impression (Minnesota Multiphasic Personality Inventory K and L scores). Thirdly, when intensive individual interviews were undertaken with a number of the women, no gross discrepancies were detected between what they said about their clitoral-vaginal preferences and what they had originally indicated about this matter in their questionnaire responses.

Relationship to Other Aspects of Sexual Behavior

As noted earlier, a woman's clitoral-vaginal preference seems to be unrelated to most other aspects of her sexual behavior and attitudes. Illustratively, this preference is not correlated with her orgasm consistency,

preferred or actual intercourse frequencies, self-rating of sexual responsiveness, strength of orgasm, number of intercourse positions used per
month, or length of foreplay. It should be added that clitoral-vaginal preference is also not correlated with age, number of children, number of
years of marriage, age of onset of menses, and other developmental indices. However, beginning with the first study undertaken, an interesting
trend appeared with regard to the correlation of clitoral-vaginal preference
with the quality of the orgasm experience. It will be recalled that each
woman was given ten descriptive phrases (for example, ecstatic, happy,
weak, tense, unsatisfied) and asked to rank them in terms of how well they
depicted her experience during orgasm. One of the terms that the women
ranked in describing their experience during orgasm showed consistencies
in its correlations with the clitoral-vaginal index.[3] As shown in Table
10–1, there was a statistically significant (or borderline significant) trend in

TABLE 10-1
Correlations of Clitoral-Vaginal Index with Degree to Which
Orgasm Experienced As "Ecstatic" and "Happy"

Sample	Ecstatic (Rank)	Happy (Rank)
1 (N = 31)	$.37^a$ ($p < .05$)	$.02^c$ (N.S.)
2 (N = 39)	$-.11$ (N.S.^{b})	$-.24$ (N.S.)
3 (N = 42)	$.26$ ($p < .10$)	$-.31$ ($p < .05$)
4 (N = 40)	$-.16$ (N.S.)	$-.26$ ($p < .10$)
5 (N = 29)	$.39$ ($p < .05$)	$-.09$ (N.S.)
6 (N = 41)	$.25$ ($p > .10$)	$-.40$ ($p < .01$)
7 (N = 40)	$-.04$ (N.S.)	$.04$ (N.S.)

[a]The more positive the correlation the greater the trend for
vaginal preference to be accompanied by a designation of the term
"ecstatic" as *not* descriptive of the orgasm experience.
[b]N.S. = Does not even attain .20 level.
[c]The more negative the correlation the greater the trend for
vaginal preference to be accompanied by a designation of the term
"happy" as descriptive of the orgasm experience.

four of the seven samples such that the greater a woman's clitoral preference the more likely she was to experience orgasm as having an *ecstatic*
quality. Incidentally, there were also significant (or borderline) trends in
three of the seven samples such that the greater a woman's vaginal preference the more likely she was to experience orgasm as having a *happy* quality. That is, the woman with clitoral preference emphasizes the ecstatic nature of the orgasm experience, whereas the woman with vaginal preference
has a tendency to focus upon the fact that it makes her feel happy. It is the
difference with regard to the experience of orgasm as ecstatic that hints at
what will be presented as one of the major psychological differences between those who have vaginal versus clitoral preferences. In dictionary
terms, ecstatic means "being in a state beyond all reason and self-control,
as when obsessed by a powerful emotion." In other words, the woman with

the clitoral orientation exceeds the woman with the vaginal orientation in "feeling" orgasm in a powerful, overwhelmingly exciting fashion. The vaginal orgasm might be said to be more muted or dampened in its impact. This finding that portrayed the vaginally oriented woman as experiencing her arousal in a relatively more muted fashion took on interesting significance when viewed in the context of findings shortly to be presented concerning the greater prevalence of feelings of body depersonalization in the vaginal as compared to the clitoral oriented.

Depersonalization

In the course of measuring several dimensions of body experience that were thought to play a role in sexual responsiveness, the Fisher (1970) Body Distortion Questionnaire was administered to the women in five of the seven samples. As outlined in Appendix A, this questionnaire is designed to measure a number of parameters of unusual or distorted body experience. It evaluates eight different parameters by inquiring concerning distortions in body perception that diversely involve feelings of increase or decrease in body size, sensations that one's body openings are blocked, feelings of being dirty, and so forth.[4] One of the dimensions measured, called Depersonalization, taps the extent to which one perceives one's own body as alien or foreign, lacking sensory vividness. A high score for this dimension is obtained by responding positively to such statements as the following:

My body feels like a nonliving object.
My hands feel like they are not mine.
My body feels "dead."
I feel distant from my own body.
I seem less aware of my body.
My body is less sensitive than it usually is.

It reflects the perception of one's body as lacking vitality or arousal or "alive" quality.

As shown in Table 10–2, a trend was found for Depersonalization to be positively correlated with the degree to which a woman expresses a vaginal preference. In three of the five samples the correlations are either at significant or borderline significant levels. This means that the greater a woman's vaginal preference the more likely she was to indicate that she perceived her body as somehow "dead," "distant," and deficient in the kind of intensity that defines feeling "alive." [5] This finding impressed the writer as having an intriguing congruence with the fact that the woman with high vaginal awareness tended to describe her orgasm as lacking "ecstatic" quality. Just as the high-vaginal woman apparently experiences the body state called orgasm in a nonecstatic fashion, she also refers to her body as

TABLE 10-2
Correlations of Clitoral-Vaginal Preference with Depersonalization

Samples		Correlations	
1 (N = 31)		.17[a]	N.S.[b]
2 (N = 39)		.34	$p < .05$
3 (N = 42)		.27	$p < .10$
4	Not administered		
5 (N = 30)		.16	N.S.
6 (N = 38)		.40[c]	p .01
7	Not administered		

[a]The more positive the correlation the greater is the trend for those who are most vaginally oriented to report feelings of body depersonalization.

[b]N.S. = Does not even attain the .20 level of significance.

[c]Based on responses to the Body Distortion Questionnaire when the individual was no longer pregnant.

lacking experiential intensity in a more general characteristic fashion. This is a congruence that early in the sequence of studies suggested the possibility that the more vaginally oriented a woman is the more she might have a need to dampen or decrease the intensity of her body experiences. The perception of orgasm as lacking "ecstatic" quality might be regarded as one manifestation of a broader adjustment strategy. In fact, as described shortly in more detail, the idea was entertained that it might be a manifestation of an even more pervasive inclination to maintain a regulated ceiling on the intensity of sensory input from the environment.

Awareness of Fetus

Findings obtained from one sample (Sample 6) of women who were pregnant provided an opportunity to test in a unique way the relationship between degree of vaginal preference and the tendency to depersonalize or mute body experience. Each woman in this sample was asked to rate on a five-point scale the frequency with which she thought about the fetus inside of her body. The developing fetus represents a new major source of body experience to the pregnant woman. If the formulation presented concerning the muting of body experience is valid, one would expect that the greater a woman's vaginal orientation the less often she would think about the fetus. That is, she would mute or depersonalize it as an experiential source. This view was tested by correlating the clitoral-vaginal index with the frequency with which each woman indicated she thought about the fetus. The two measures proved to be significantly correlated in the predicted direction ($-.31$,[6] $p < .05$).[7] It was indeed true that the greater a woman's vaginal preference the more likely she was to mute her awareness of the fetus within her body.

Measures of Body Sensation

To explore the finding that dampening of body experience is progressively greater as a woman's orientation is more vaginal at another level, several measures concerned with perception of body stimulation were appraised. If such a dampening process occurs, one might expect that it would manifest itself in a reduced sensitivity to stimulation applied to the body.

This possibility was examined with reference to threshold for the perception of light-touch stimuli. In four samples the women were asked to report (with their eyes closed) whenever they could feel the touch of a series of graded nylon filaments (varying in the pressure they produced) that were applied to a number of body sites. (for example, wrist, thigh). Details of the procedure are presented in Appendix A. The sensitivity with which a woman can perceive touch applied to her skin would seem to bear on the issue of how intensely she experiences body sensations. If she is inclined to mute body sensations one might expect that she would be less sensitive to light-touch stimuli. When the clitoral-vaginal index was correlated in the three samples with the light-touch thresholds, two significant or near significant positive values were found. The index was positively correlated ($r = .33$, $N = 30$, $p < .10$) with the threshold for correctly perceiving touch on the thigh in Sample 1 and was also positively correlated ($r = .37$, $p < .025$) with the threshold for perceiving touch on the wrist in Sample 3. That is, the greater the vaginal preference the *less* sensitivity there was to the touch stimuli. No correlations of significance emerged in Samples 2 or 4. Since the findings approached significance for only two of several different body sites, they can only be considered as suggestive.

The opportunity to consider the relationship of clitoral-vaginal preference to sensitivity to tickle was also available in the data. It will be recalled (as described in detail in Appendix B) that in several samples the skin on various body areas (for example, cheeks, breasts, thigh) was stroked with a piece of cotton and determinations were made of how long it required for the stroking to evoke tickle sensations and how long such sensations persisted. In terms of the model proposed with reference to touch threshold, one might expect that the greater a woman's vaginal preference the less sensitive she would be to the tickle stimulation. However, analysis of the data indicated that the clitoral-vaginal index did not have consistent significant relationships with any of the tickle measures.

A third approach to this issue revolved about a technique that is concerned with whether the individual deals with sensory stimulation in an "augmenting" or "diminishing" fashion. This technique, developed by Petrie (1967), is described in detail in Appendix B. It presents each woman with a task in which she first (with her eyes blindfolded) feels a standard block with her fingers and judges its size. She then receives touch and kinesthetic stimulation to her fingers by rubbing another block, and finally judges again the size of the original standard block. This is done several times with different sized blocks. Scores are computed that indicate the degree to which the stimulation produced by repeatedly rubbing a block results in increasing or decreasing the apparent size of the standard block. An increase is referred to as "augmenting" and a decrease as "diminishing." Petrie has proposed that the degree of augmenting or diminishing shown in this size judgment task is a valid indicator of augmenting-diminishing propensities in general. She also presents tentative evidence that augmenting and diminishing relate respectively to seeking and avoiding stimulation. The augmenting-diminishing task, as presented in four of the present samples, was comprised of three sets of trials. For each set there was first judgment of a standard block, stimulation of the fingers by rubbing another block, and finally rejudging the original block. It was anticipated, of course, that the greater a woman's vaginal preference the more she would be a diminisher rather than an augmentor. In none of the four samples was the *average* augmenting-diminishing score significantly correlated with clitoral-vaginal preference. However, a more detailed look at the findings revealed a trend in the predicted direction that is worth mentioning. In two of the four samples (Samples 2 and 6), when only the initial set of trials involving the first standard block were employed, there were significant or near significant positive correlations $(r = .38, p < .025; r = .29, p < .10)$ between the tendency to be a diminisher and degree of vaginal orientation.

Generally, the material reviewed with respect to sensitivity to stimuli applied to the body is not very promising. Perhaps the finding indicating that sensitivity to touch applied to the skin tends to be lower in women who are more vaginally oriented merits further attention.

Muting of the World

The fact that the more vaginally oriented woman perceives her body as depersonalized or muted in its intensity raises the question whether she might also experience other (nonbody) aspects of the world in an analogously muted fashion. Could her subdued mode of "feeling" her body be part of a more general inclination to minimize the intensity of the experienced world—indeed, to reduce input from it? One of the major ways in which this possibility was explored was to compare the imaginative story productions of high-clitoral-preference women with those of high-vaginal-preference women. Three sets of stories were obtained from different samples. One set (Sample 1) consisted of responses to six Thematic Apperception Test pictures (Appendix A). A second set (Sample 2) was comprised of ten spontaneous stories that the subjects composed when asked to "make up" and write out stories about a series of themes.[8] A third set (Sample 4) consisted of eight spontaneous stories about a sequence of themes.[9] The question was whether the stories of high-clitoral and high-vaginal women in the three samples could be distinguished on the basis of how excitement and tension were handled. If the assumption about their differential muting attributes were correct, one would expect that tension would be minimized and regulated to a greater extent in the stories of the high-vaginal than in those of the high-clitoral women. In order to explore this possibility, some of the Thematic Apperception stories collected in Sample 1 were impressionistically evaluated by judges to ascertain whether they could distinguish those produced by high-vaginal versus high-clitoral women on the basis of how excitement and tension were portrayed. Judges were asked to read stories with an eye to the following:

Evaluate them and decide the degree to which tension is minimized, differences patched up, and excitement reduced. Or, to put it in another way, try to distinguish the extent to which each group of stories contains tension (for example, conflict). Note the degree to which things are not smoothed over and the degree to which characters are definitely and clearly emotional. Note the extent to which disillusionment, pain, suffering, and other affects are not denied or minimized.

Each judge was presented with ten sets of stories, five from randomly selected, extreme high-vaginal women, and five from extreme high-clitoral women. The judge was told that five sets of stories represented women who wanted to minimize excitement and five sets represented women who had no such motivation. After reading each set of stories he was to decide whether it was primarily in one category or the other. Two judges who blindly sorted the ten sets of Thematic Apperception stories both did better than chance in differentiating the clitoral and vaginal protocols; each correctly sorted eight of the ten sets of stories. Encouraged by this finding, a formal scoring system was developed for defining whether any given story glosses over or minimizes tension. Stories with any of the following attributes were considered to be "glossing over" in character:

No one in the story experiences a difficulty or problem.
Emphasis is placed upon how happy and satisfied the story characters are.
When a problem or difficulty is mentioned, it is explicitly dismissed as minor.
There is a "they lived happily ever after" type of ending to the story.

Each story was scored separately, and a total index was computed equal to the number of stories classified as "glossing over." Two judges who independently evaluated 15 sets of stories attained 83 percent agreement. The scoring scheme was applied blindly to the other two sets of stories that had been collected (the spontaneous stories about specified themes such as "A girl and her mother," "A girl and her father"). No consistent relationships between the glossing over scores and clitoral-vaginal preference could be detected in the total samples. However, the decision was made to examine those women with more *extreme* clitoral or vaginal preferences (rating 1 and 2 versus 5, 6, 7 respectively). Because the numbers in the extreme vaginal category were found to be very limited, Samples 2 and 4 were combined for purposes of the present analysis. When the extreme-clitoral and extreme-vaginal women were compared with reference to their glossing over scores,[10] the vaginal women were noted at a statistically significant level to have the higher scores ($x^2 = 4.6$, $df = 1$, $p < .05$).[11] This result was in the predicted direction. The vaginally oriented women did dampen excitement and tension in their stories to a greater extent than did the clitorally oriented.[12] The vaginally oriented women projected into their imaginative productions a vision of the world, perhaps wishfully, as a place in which people do not have to put up with much frustration or pain or unpleasant affect. The difference in character between the vaginal and clitoral fantasy perspective can be made more concrete by quoting some representative stories given by each group. First, examine the following examples (all elicited by the same Thematic Apperception picture) from the vaginal extreme.

Example 1
It is a fall evening and this woman has completed her day's activities, and has the children tucked soundly in bed. The weather is quite warm and she is tired. They live on a farm and have worked hard physically all day. The husband left right after the evening meal to do some church work and as the children are asleep and the last of the dishes put away, this woman sinks into a chair reminiscing over the day's activities and awaiting the return of her husband so they might spend a few moments together before retiring to bed.

Example 2
The young woman is portrayed as pensive. Her thoughts are of another day, another time, another place. Her memories take her to the small town where she spent her early years. The simplicity of that life seems far away now—and far beyond her reach. The sad realization has come to her that the only reality lies in the quiet of the ocean shore and the wind in the trees.

Example 3
A woman sitting, looking very pensive. She is an older woman, not a girl. I would surmise that she is sitting there at the end of the day, thinking over the day's activities. She doesn't look sad or happy—she looks content. She looks as though she feels tired because of a busy day with hard but satisfying work.

The themes are about as subdued as one can imagine. Now, scan some examples (elicited by the same Thematic Apperception picture) from the clitoral extreme.

Example 1
Mrs. X is sitting waiting for her laborer husband to come home from work. They live in a semirundown tenement in a large city. Mrs. X is quite different in looks and temperament than her husband. Possibly she is from the country and not used to the brutalization of emotions and compassion that occurs in the city. She may never accustom herself to it either.

Example 2
This is a young woman who is living around 1850. She is a farmer's wife on one of our desolate Western plains. This morning her husband went to the only

town to sell their crop. It has been a bad year and without a good price they are going to have to admit defeat and go back East. It is late now, after 8:00 P.M. He should have been back before 6:00 P.M. She is waiting and wondering. Their whole future depends on the news he brings home. She is impatient to know but is still a little reluctant to learn if it is bad news. She wonders over and over her life with her husband and wonders what the future will be like.

Example 3

A woman is sitting backward on a chair—deep in thought. She has been doing some cleaning in her home; has on old clothes and has paused a moment in her work to think. She is thinking about her husband who has taken a trip and about her children who are in school. She thinks about what the future holds for her. Should she think about a career outside her family—and what is her major area of interest? She thinks about what her husband is doing and hopes that he will return soon. She thinks about how quickly her children are growing. In a few years they will be finished with school and she will be bored sitting at home all day long.

Here one sees persistent nonresolution of tension; there is no quiescence.

If, as indicated by the results derived from this story analysis, clitoral-vaginal preference is associated with a dimension having to do with the regulation of tension or excitement, might one also find it linked with preferences for quiescent versus stimulating environments? Logically, one might assume that a woman's wish to dampen tension would be expedited by carefully controlling the stimulation impinging upon her from her environs. One would expect that the greater a woman's vaginal orientation the more she would be inclined to seek conditions in which she would not be exposed to tension arousal. It was possible to look into this question in terms of information that had been obtained in two samples concerning preferences for exciting versus unexciting conditions. The information was derived from a questionnaire designed to evaluate how much the individual prefers new and novel experiences as compared to familiar and safe activities. This Sensation-Seeking Scale (Zuckerman, Kolin, Price and Zoob, 1964) asks for preferences with regard to such alternatives as the following:

I am invigorated by a brisk, cold day.
I can't wait to get into the indoors on a cold day.

I would like to learn to fly an airplane.
I would not like to learn to fly an airplane.

I would prefer living in an ideal society where everyone is safe, secure, and happy.
I would have preferred living in the unsettled days of our history.

One might expect that a person who was interested in "dampening" experience would express preference for safe, nonexciting activities. The Sensation-Seeking Scale was administered in Samples 3 and 5. When the clitoral-vaginal index was correlated with the scores derived from the scale in these samples, only chance relationships were found. The difference in orientation between the vaginally and clitorally oriented toward tension, which was evidenced during the analysis of the imaginative stories, did not appear [13] when this orientation was defined by responses to explicit questions about whether one prefers low- or high-exciting conditions.[14]

Anxiety

It was discerned early in the course of the present studies that anxiety is positively correlated with degree of vaginal preference. As defined by a rather wide repertory of measures, anxiety was found to be greater in those women who were more vaginally rather than clitorally oriented. The material pertinent to this matter is now reviewed.

Ratings

Ratings of anxiety based on the repeated observations of at least two independent judges were available from three samples.[15] In Samples 1, 2, and 3 multiple personnel (physicians, nurses, technicians) spent time with each woman in the psychological laboratory as she proceeded through different phases of the experimental procedure. Following their contact with each woman on a given day, all personnel who had interacted with her rated her apparent degree of anxiety (on a five-point scale).

In Sample 1 four judges made ratings (1 = high anxiety) across five different sessions.[16] When the average anxiety scores of the women were correlated with their clitoral-vaginal preferences, a significant relationship was found ($r = -.36$, $p < .05$). The greater a woman's vaginal orientation the more anxious she was rated.

Four raters observed each woman in Sample 2 across four sessions. The average anxiety ratings for all observers across all sessions proved to have only a chance relationship with the clitoral-vaginal index.[17]

In Sample 3 two raters became acquainted with each woman during the course of two sessions. The average anxiety score was found to be significantly correlated ($r = -.29$, p .05) in the expected direction with clitoral-vaginal preference.[18] Once again the greater a woman's vaginal preference the greater was the anxiety attributed to her.

Thus, in two of three samples (in which anxiety ratings were derived from multiple observers) the results depicted the vaginal woman as more anxious than the clitoral one.

Delivery Disturbance

The women in Sample 6 were pregnant. After they delivered, they returned a month later for a second visit to the laboratory and at that time were asked to rate (on a five-point scale, with 5 indicating high disturbance) how "disturbed" they felt during the actual process of delivery.[19] Congruent with the anxiety results just reviewed, it was found that the greater a woman's vaginal orientation the more "disturbed" [20] she was during delivery ($x^2 = 8.3$, $df = 2$, $p < .02$).[21]

Anxiety in Autobiographical Descriptions

The women in Sample 3 were requested to write an autobiography. As described in Appendix C, they were told to discuss a range of topics and to make their accounts conform to a standard number of pages. In reading through their autobiographies, it was apparent that they differed in their frequency of references to feelings and symptoms of disturbance. Episodes of psychological distress were focused upon by some, whereas others described their past as lacking such disturbance. The following brief excerpts from some of the autobiographies illustrate the kinds of distress mentioned by some.

I am terrified of dying.
I could not be away from home because I became too nervous.
I had an emotional collapse.
I had terrible nightmares.
I was very lonely and depressed.

It was rare for any individual to refer to more than one such episode or example of disturbance. Two judges who independently evaluated 20 autobiographies attained 92 percent agreement as to whether a definite incident involving disturbance had been mentioned. When the presence or absence of mention of psychological distress was related to the clitoral-vaginal index, a significant relationship was found ($x^2 = 5.7$, $df = 1$, $p < .02$).[22] The greater a woman's vaginal preference the more likely she was to indicate that she had experienced a psychological disturbance.

Anxiety Scale

In Samples 4 and 5 an attempt was made to relate the clitoral-vaginal index to a formal self-report measure of anxiety (Murray-David Anxiety Scale). Each woman was asked to respond to a questionnaire that asked whether she agreed with such statements as the following:

We are surrounded by all sorts of dangers.
There are times when one is almost paralyzed by fear, sudden and senseless.
There is plenty to worry about in this life.

Contrary to the trend reported for other measures of anxiety, the scores derived from this Anxiety questionnaire were found not to be significantly correlated with the clitoral-vaginal index.

It is also pertinent that the Stability scale of the Thurstone (1953) Preference Schedule that is said to measure "emotional stability" proved to be unrelated to clitoral-vaginal preference in the three samples (1, 2, 6) in which it was administered.

Digit-Symbol Performance

As recounted in detail in Appendix E, the women in Sample 5 were asked to perform a task taken from the Wechsler Adult Intelligence Scale (1955). This task involves writing next to a series of numbers randomly arranged in sequence certain code symbols that are defined as associated with them. Each woman performed this task under relatively quiet baseline conditions. A condition intended to produce stress was then imposed on her, and she went on to repeat the task so that the disruptive impact upon it by the stress could be ascertained. More specifically, each woman worked for 90 seconds on the Digit-Symbol task, was then exposed to a five-minute segment of a movie that portrays automobile accidents in graphic and gory detail, and immediately afterward repeated the Digit-Symbol task, with the film and its sound track continuing. Scores were computed to determine the degree to which performance subsequent to the stress film deteriorated.[23] Unfortunately, as earlier noted, these scores indicated that the stress did not, on the average, produce decrement in performance. One is left in the position of not being able to accept the task, in the present context, as a valid measure of stress effects. Therefore, one cannot assign any significance (relative to stress effects) to the fact that clitoral-vaginal preference scores were found to have only a chance relationship with the performance decrement scores.

Birth Film Stress

Another stress to which one sample (Sample 3) of women was exposed was a brief film directly portraying a birth. This film provided a view of a woman in the delivery position with her genitals exposed, and pictured the birth of the child and the subsequent ejection of the afterbirth. Shortly after seeing the film, each woman was asked to write a description of what had most impressed her about it and the impact it had made upon her. Very few referred to the birth itself as unpleasant or disturbing, but a considerable number specifically indicated that the sight of the afterbirth was unpleasant, disgusting, and in some instances nauseating. The sequence in the film concerned with the afterbirth expulsion was typically quite threatening. With this perspective, each woman's written description of the film was analyzed to evaluate how disturbing the afterbirth had been. The description was rated on a three-point scale (0 = No sign of disturbance; 1 = Mild disturbance; 2 = High degree of disturbance). Two judges who independently evaluated ten of the descriptions attained 77 percent agreement in their ratings. When the disturbance scores were related to the clitoral-vaginal index, they were found to be positively linked at a borderline level of significance ($x^2 = 2.8$, $df = 1$, p .10). The greater a woman's vaginal preference the more disturbed was her apparent response to the afterbirth in the film.[24]

Learning Performance

It is well documented (Lazarus, 1966) that anxiety can interfere with learning. Since a number of learning tasks had been administered in several samples, it was possible to ascertain whether women differing in clitoral-vaginal preference also differ in learning facility—and therefore perhaps by implication in anxiety level. Learning tasks had been administered in three of the samples. In Sample 2 the women were asked to learn three lists of words, each containing ten words with emotional connotations and ten of a neutral character. In one list the emotional words pertained to sexual themes (for example, kiss, nude, love), in another guilt themes (for example, judge, wrong, verdict), and in a third food references (for example, beef, honey, hash). Each list contained 20 words and was presented in typed form to each woman individually who was given one minute to study it. The list was then removed, and the woman was then allowed five minutes to write down on a sheet of paper as many of the words on the list as she could remember. Detailed lists of the words used in this sample and in others to be mentioned may be found in Appendices B, C, and D.

In Sample 3 the women were asked to learn only the 20 word list containing the sex words.

In Sample 4 the women learned the sex word list as well as a second list in which the emotional words pertained to pregnancy themes (for example, birth, baby, diaper).

When the *total* number of words correctly learned by each woman was tabulated, it was found that degree of vaginal preference was correlated $-.27$ ($p < .10$) with it in Sample 2, and $-.38$ ($p < .025$) with it in Sample 3. In Sample 4 there was an analogous significant negative relationship ($x^2 = 5.2$, $df = 1$, $p < .025$).[25] That is, across all three samples the trend is for increasing vaginal orientation to be accompanied by decreased learning facility.[26]

Unpleasant Inkblot Imagery

Still another way in which the anxiety issue was explored was via the character of the responses the women produced when asked to respond imaginatively to a series of inkblots (Holtzman, et al., 1961).[27] The women in various samples responded individually to a series of 25 blots. Following a lead provided by the work of DeVos (1952), it was decided to compute an index of discomfort or disturbance based on the number of inkblot images with negative or unpleasant connotations. An image was considered to have discomfort connotations if it concerned any of the following themes: sadness, hostility, pain, body destruction, illness, storms, explosions and damaging fire, natural disasters (for example, earthquakes), monsters (and similar figures, such as ghosts, skeletons, goblins), ugliness in any form (for example, ugly face), disappointment or failure, dislike (for example, "I don't like this inkblot").

Two judges independently scoring 20 protocols attained 84 percent agreement in their judgments. The amount of unpleasant imagery in the inkblot protocols of the extreme clitoral (ratings 1 and 2) and extreme vaginal (ratings 5, 6, 7) groups across Samples 1, 2, 3, and 5 was scored. When the clitoral-vaginal preferences scores were related to the inkblot discomfort scores, a significant positive relationship was found between degree of vaginal preference and number of unpleasant images ($x^2 = 5.0$, $df = 1$, $N = 111$, p .025).[28] Once again it was the woman who was more vaginally oriented who evidenced the greater signs of discomfort.

Summary of Anxiety Findings

A fairly convincing spectrum of findings supports the notion that the vaginally oriented woman exceeds the clitorally oriented woman in the intensity of her anxiety. This difference has been discerned not only in overt behavior but also at the level of fantasy. More specifically, it has been detected with respect to the following: ratings of multiple observers concerning amount of anxiety displayed; self-ratings of amount of anxiety experienced during delivery; disturbance expressed about the afterbirth seen in a birth film; previous incidents of psychological distress mentioned in autobiographies; learning of words in an emotional context; and amount of unpleasant imagery in inkblot responses. In three instances the findings did not conform to the expected pattern. In two of these instances the anxiety or disturbance measures involved formal self-report questionnaires. In the third instance, namely, that based on the Digit-Symbol task, there was evidence that the intended stress had not actually produced a decrement in the performance of the group.

It is, of course, an intriguing question as to why there should be a link between clitoral-vaginal preference and anxiety. This question is discussed at a later point.

Personality and Value Measures

It will be recalled that a number of self-report personality tests (for example, Edwards Preference Schedule, 1954) as well as value measures (Allport-Vernon-Lindzey Study of Values, 1960) were administered to women in several of the samples. The scores derived from these tests almost entirely failed to correlate consistently with clitoral-vaginal preferences. However, the trend concerning the Aesthetic score of the Allport-Vernon-Lindzey (1960) Study of Values is worthy of mention. The person with a high Aesthetic score is considered to be one who is "interested in grace and symmetry." He finds his "chief interest in the artistic episodes of life." He is dedicated to beauty and the enjoyment of impressions. One might say that an Aesthetic orientation involves a focus upon, and sensitivity to, those aspects of the world that relate to beauty and graceful configuration. In two of three samples in which the clitoral-vaginal index was correlated with the Aesthetic score, a significant negative relationship was found. In Sample 3 the correlation was $-.33$ ($p<.05$) and in Sample 5 it was $-.38$ ($p<.05$). In Sample 2 the correlation was not significant. The implications of this relationship are not clear. At this point one can only suggest that an Aesthetic orientation implies a sensitivity to, and interest in, sensory nuances (configurations, patterns) that may be antithetical to the "muting" orientation that seems to be characteristic of the vaginally oriented woman. If so, the inverse correlation between degree of vaginal preference and Aesthetic score would take on some logic.

Attitudes toward Father

Symbolic Love Reward

As outlined in Appendix B, the Parent-Child Relations Questionnaire (Roe and Siegelman, 1963) was used to measure the attitudes of women in several samples toward their fathers and mothers. Only one of the various measures derived from this scale resulted in consistent findings. In two of three samples in which it was administered the Father Symbolic Love Reward scores were negatively related to the clitoral-vaginal index. In Sample 3 the relationship was significant ($r=-.44$, $p<.01$); in Sample 4 it was also significant in the same direction ($x^2=8.1$, $df=2$, $p<.02$).[29] In Sample 2 the relationship was significantly reversed ($r=.45$, $N=22$, $p<.05$). It is not apparent as to why this reversal occurred.[30] In any case, the results for two of the three samples indicate that the greater a woman's vaginal orientation the less she regarded her father as having shown the kind of behavior toward her that is included in the category of Symbolic Love Reward. This category is defined by Roe and Siegelman (1963) as follows (p. 357): "The parents using this kind of reward praise their children for approved behavior, give them special attention, and are affectionately demonstrative." Those women who ascribed high Symbolic Love Reward behavior to the fathers had to respond affirmatively to such statements as the following:

My father compared me favorably with other children when I did well.
My father told me how proud he was of me when I was good.
My father praised me in front of my friends.

They perceive their fathers as having given them special attention, praise, and approval for "good" behavior. The more vaginally oriented a woman the less she recalls having received such "rewards" from her father.

Image of Father in Imaginative Stories

An attempt was also made to analyze all spontaneous stories (for example, "story about girl and her father") involving figures labeled as fathers. No relationships could be discerned between various attributes (hostility, dominance) assigned to such figures and the clitoral-vaginal index.[31]

Negative Results

It must be stressed that the clitoral-vaginal index lacked consistent relationships with many measures. A woman's relative preference for clitoral as compared to vaginal stimulation was not correlated with such variables as the following: gross physical attributes (for example, height, weight, breast size), age of menarche, number of children, age, degree of pain and discomfort during menstruation, numerous personality parameters, measures of interest patterns, parental attitudes toward sex, religiosity, measures of body perception (for example, boundary definiteness), eating and food attitudes, and guilt.[32]

Physiological Reactivity

The elaborate physiological investigations undertaken in Samples 1, 2, and 3 have already been outlined in Appendices A, B, and C. They included measures of heart rate, Galvanic Skin Response, skin resistance and temperature on numerous body sites, and stomach motility. None proved to be consistently correlated with the clitoral-vaginal index.[33]

Overview

What are the major elements that can be isolated from the material sifted in this chapter? Is there any directionality to the uniformities that have been detected?

There seems to be good reason for concluding that the more a woman prefers vaginal stimulation the greater is her level of anxiety. The strongly vaginally oriented woman is tense and has a low threshold for feeling disturbed. This was demonstrated not only in her overt behavior but also her fantasies. As reported, the relatively high anxiety of the vaginally oriented woman was detected by multiple observers who got to know her while she was in the psychology laboratory. It was also revealed in her self-ratings of how disturbing it was to experience the stress of being delivered of a child in the hospital. Variously, too, it was revealed in her difficulty in dealing with learning tasks, in her inkblot responses suggestive of discomfort and dysphoria, and in her autobiographical accounts of past emotional turbulence. These findings, as already mentioned, represent a reversal of what might have been expected within the framework of most current theories of female sexuality. It has been fashionable to regard a vaginal orientation as being indicative of maturity and good adjustment while assuming that a clitoral preference denotes inadequacy in personality development. Obviously, the facts, as they have emerged in the present studies, blatantly contradict existing theories. If these facts receive support from other investigators, a gross revision of such theories will be required. If anxiety is greater in those who are more vaginally oriented, the question arises as to its origin. Unfortunately, there is no solid information available to answer this question. But one can speculate that some of the "muting" and depersonalizing strategies found to be characteristic of the vaginally oriented serve as defenses against their anxiety. Their inclination to mute their experiences was primarily revealed in the imaginative stories they produced. Typically, they portrayed situations in which either there was very little tension or, if it was of substantial proportions, it was quickly reduced in a "they lived happily ever after" fashion. These stories could, of course, be largely wishful and the vaginally oriented woman might actually have little ability to mute tension-producing stimuli.

There were clearer indications that the vaginally oriented react in a denying (muting) fashion toward their own body experiences. In several samples degree of vaginal preference was positively correlated with Depersonalization (as measured by the Fisher [1970] Body Distortion Questionnaire). The vaginally oriented perceive their own bodies as "foreign," "strange," and "dead." They concur with statements such as "I feel distant from my own body." They disown their own bodies—denying them self quality. It is a reasonable speculation that they defensively react to their own body experiences in this fashion as a means of denying or controlling those aspects that are threatening or anxiety provoking. Perhaps they are seeking to evade awareness that certain anxiety-producing events occurring in their own bodies really involve self. If one scans past findings concerning the Depersonalization measure, one finds that an intensified sense of body depersonalization is most likely to occur when an individual feels that unusual things are happening to her body over which she has no control. For example, Fisher (1970) reported that Depersonalization scores were unusually high in persons while they were being hypnotized and given the suggestion that they could not control certain parts of their bodies. Fast and Fisher (1971) noted that Depersonalization was elevated in persons who had been injected with epinephrine (without being aware of its identity) and felt the effects sweeping over them. Clausen (1971) similarly found Depersonalization sharply intensified in women who were asked to ingest a drug (Pentobarbital) whose nature was unknown to them. All of these instances have in common the creation of a situation in which the individual cannot account for the unexpected and nonvoluntary things happening to his body—and in which there is consequently a reaction of "This can't be my body. It feels foreign and distant from me." In short, the individual disowns his body because it is perceived as the site of alien events. There are suggestions that this disowning process proceeds to the point where the individual loses some elements of the vividness and personalized awareness that permeate most persons' body perceptions.

The vaginally oriented woman may perceive her body in a depersonalized manner because it is so chronically the site of anxiety. Her anxious feelings about the world are probably represented at the body level by unpleasant sensations (muscle tension, stomach discomfort) that persist, are not easily explainable, and are not much influenced by conscious intent. One would theorize that she feels seized or taken over by these body anxiety sensations in the same fashion as those women who develop body depersonalization when they feel their bodies being taken over by the effects of a drug or hypnotic suggestion. It may be that after the vaginally oriented woman has experienced and tried to defend herself against the unpleasant sensations of anxiety for long periods of time she begins to generalize her antipathy so that it includes any kind of extreme excitation. That is, she finds that any sudden or major "stirring up" of her body resembles the body arousal linked with anxiety and calls forth defensive depersonalization. One hint that this may be so was provided by the earlier cited findings that the greater a woman's vaginal orientation the less she tends to describe orgasm as feeling "ecstatic." The vaginally oriented woman might be thought of as wanting to avoid such an extreme of body excitement as denoted by the term "ecstatic." "Controlling" her sexual arousal so that it remains below ecstatic intensity prevents it from attaining a level of body excitement that is associated with anxiety.

Why should a preference for vaginal rather than clitoral stimulation be linked with such attributes as high-anxiety level, desire to mute experience, and depersonalizing of one's own body? At this point, one can only enumerate some possibilities.

1. The simplest explanation would be that vaginal stimulation, while sufficient to produce orgasm, doesn't create a mass of body excitement as great as that aroused by direct clitoral stimulation. If so, the vaginal orientation could be regarded as part of an adjustment strategy directed at controlling anxiety by keeping all excitation below certain levels. The plausibility of this explanation would depend heavily upon whether vaginal excitation is somehow more controlled and less sweeping than clitoral excitation. Although the findings of Masters and Johnson (1966), and Kinsey, et al. (1953) as well as some of the qualitative reports obtained in the present study concerning the subjective experiences associated with vaginal versus clitoral stimulation hint that such may be true, it must be regarded as far from established.

2. A second possibility to consider is that the vaginally oriented

woman, because of her depersonalized body orientation, requires the unique condition of the penis being inserted into her body in order to build up feelings of sexual arousal. That is, her depersonalized way of experiencing her body might make her relatively unresponsive to sexual stimulation unless it was delivered in a way that had unusually intense psychological connotations. The specific act of intercourse, with its special significance, might be necessary to break through the coldness or unresponsiveness possibly associated with a depersonalized set. Perhaps direct clitoral stimulation lacks the definition of a full or real sexual contact and therefore lacks the psychological intensity necessary to "get through" a depersonalized way of interpreting body events. One might say that feeling the penis inserted, with its connotations of unique intimacy, would be necessary for the depersonalizing woman to personalize sexual stimulation.[34]

3. Another perspective on the possible relationship between vaginal orientation and the importance of penile insertion in achieving arousal derives from the relationship that was found between clitoral-vaginal preference and perception of the father. It will be recalled that the greater a woman's vaginal preference the *less* she tended to remember her father as having given her praise and reward for doing well or conforming to his expectations. That is, she recalled having had difficulty in eliciting a positive response from him. If it is assumed that such a relationship with her father actually existed, the possibility arises that it became a prototype for her interactions with men in general. Thus, the greater a woman's vaginal preference the less she might expect men to respond positively when she did things to please them. Is it possible that this relationship could be a causal one, with the attitude toward men influencing the degree of vaginal preference? Apropos of this, it is interesting that Greenacre (1966) proposed that a girl may have fantasies that involve (p. 149) "hanging on to the father with an oral-vaginal babyish grasp." She implied, as has also been theorized by others (Fenichel, 1945), that the vagina can be assigned symbolic meanings and be used to express attitudes toward men. It might be that a woman whose experiences with her father had led her to expect that men would not respond positively would need an extra amount of commitment from a man before she could relate sexually to him in a positive manner. This "extra commitment" might symbolically require insertion of his penis into her vagina. She might need this special sign of intimacy from him to believe that he really intended to be friendly and to bestow affection upon her.

4. It is worth considering the possibility too that a woman who chronically depersonalizes her body (who feels distant from it) might have a relatively hazy concept of it, particularly those areas such as the vagina, which are difficult to perceive visually.[35] If so, the act of intercourse, which would suddenly articulate the vagina and give it clear spatial form, would articulate the sexual potential of her body and make it possible for her to tune in on sexual stimulation in a focused fashion. But merely stimulating the clitoris, without the spatial definition of the vagina caused by penile in-

sertion, might fail to highlight the hazily perceived pelvic region sufficiently to permit focusing on the arousal in that region.

None of the explanatory possibilities just considered is completely convincing. It will require considerably more investigation and thought with reference to this problem before a more sharply defined formulation can be derived.

NOTES

1. Interestingly, they have said little or nothing about the significance of a woman being unable to attain arousal or orgasm from direct clitoral stimulation.

2. The test-retest reliability of the clitoral-vaginal rating was evaluated in Sample 6. It was found that the test-retest coefficient (several months intervening) was .78 (Pearson product-moment) in a subsample of 23 women from whom such data were obtained.

3. One may also mention a potentially interesting borderline finding involving the degree to which women rated themselves as feeling "unsatisfied" *during* orgasm. When only those with extreme vaginal-clitoral ratings (ratings of 1 and 2 versus 5, 6, 7) were compared across all seven samples, it was found that the vaginally oriented judged themselves more dissatisfied than the clitorally oriented ($t=1.7$, $N=167$, $p<.10$). This finding, if further substantiated, would be paradoxical in view of the popular assumption that orgasm produced largely by penile stimulation of the vagina is superior in quality to orgasm produced by direct clitoral stimulation.

4. Depersonalization, Large, Small, Boundary Loss, Dirty, Blocked Openings, Skin, Total Number of Distortions.

5. An attempt was also made to determine if the clitoral-vaginal index was correlated with a woman's *general* level of awareness of her body (irrespective of whether it is experienced as excited or depersonalized). The Body Prominence technique (described in Appendix A), which measures awareness of one's own body as compared to other aspects in one's environs, did not show any consistent correlation with clitoral-vaginal preference.

The clitoral-vaginal index was also unrelated to the amount of grooming attention a woman directs to her own body as defined by the frequency with which she wears jewelry, purchases new dresses, has her hair "done," and so forth (see Appendix K).

6. All correlations reported in this chapter are Pearson product-moment coefficients. N's will not be cited unless they deviate grossly from the sample sizes listed in Chapter 7.

7. Within the context of this particular sample the frequency with which the women thought about the fetus was not correlated significantly with the stage of pregnancy that they were asked to make their rating about this matter.

8. The themes were as follows: A girl and her father, a girl and her mother, a girl and her boyfriend, a boy and his father, a woman in serious trouble, a woman and her husband, a girl and her sister, a woman and her child, a family, a woman looking for a job.

9. The themes involved the first eight employed in Sample 2.

10. The median in the vaginal group was 6 and the median in the clitoral group was 4.

11. Chi-square was used because of the skewed nature of the distribution of glossing over scores.

12. The difference in "dampening" orientation does not apply to sensitivity to sexual stimuli presented tachistoscopically at high speed. As described in Appendix A, the women in three samples were shown pictures depicting sexual themes, along with pictures of other themes, and their ability to accurately identify their content at high-speed exposures was evaluated. It was found in Sample 1 that the greater a woman's vaginal orientation the more quickly she perceived the sexual theme ($r = -.38$, $p < .05$). In Sample 2 the relationship was reversed ($r = .35$, $p < .05$). In Sample 3 the relationship was of a chance order.

13. This was true even when the extremes of the clitoral-vaginal range were analyzed.

14. The Change score of the Edwards (1959) Preference Schedule, which also measures preference for environmental variation and change, was found in several samples not to be significantly correlated with the clitoral-vaginal index.

15. There were several samples in which anxiety ratings by only one observer (who had a relatively brief contact with each woman) were available. These ratings did not correlate in any consistent way with the clitoral-vaginal index. However, they are not considered to be comparable to the anxiety ratings based on multiple raters who observed each woman on multiple occasions.

16. The mean anxiety rating was 2.6 ($\sigma = .6$).

17. The mean anxiety rating was 3.3 ($\sigma = .6$).

18. The mean anxiety rating was 3.5 ($\sigma = .7$).

19. The mean disturbance rating was 2.0 ($\sigma = .8$).

20. The self-ratings of delivery disturbance were found not to be significantly correlated with measures of response defensiveness (namely, K and L scales of the Minnesota Multiphasic Personality Inventory).

21. Chi-square was employed because the distribution of disturbance scores was skewed.

22. There was no relationship between the K and L scales of the Minnesota Multiphasic Inventory and whether a woman admitted to past psychological difficulties. That is, the admission of past difficulty did not seem to be a function of willingness to confess bad things about oneself.

23. The prestress mean was 64.5 ($\sigma = 6.4$) and the poststress mean was 71.1 ($\sigma = 9.6$).

24. The rated degree of disturbance about the afterbirth was found not to be significantly correlated with measures of response defensiveness (K and L scales of the Minnesota Multiphasic Personality Inventory).

25. Chi-square was used because of the skewed nature of the recall scores in this sample.

26. One cannot explain this relationship in terms of gross intellectual differences between the clitoral and vaginally oriented. Amount of education was not significantly correlated with the clitoral-vaginal index. Furthermore, one cannot explain the relationship in terms of the clitorally oriented being more cooperative (or less resistive) than the vaginally oriented. Ratings of the behavior of the clitoral- versus vaginal-oriented women while they were in the laboratory did not indicate differences in amount of hostility displayed. Also, when requests were made to write stories or other kinds of descriptions, there were no differences in the amount of energy the clitoral- and vaginal-oriented women were willing to invest in the tasks (as defined by the number of words they wrote).

27. The women were asked to look at inkblots and to write descriptions of what they looked like or appeared to represent.

28. Chi-square was employed because of the skewed character of the inkblot imagery scores.

29. Chi-square was used because of the skewed nature of the Symbolic Love Reward scores in this sample.

30. The significant reversal in one sample certainly complicates the interpretation of the results. It would be on the conservative side to assert only that the clitoral-vaginal index has *some* kind of a relationship with the Symbolic Love Reward score. However, the writer has chosen to emphasize the two negative, as compared to the one positive, relationships. This choice was partially encouraged by the small size and select nature of the group in Sample 4. These 22 women comprised about half of the original Sample 4. They were the ones who responded to a questionnaire mailed to them some time after their original participation in the study.

31. No significant relationships were found between the clitoral-vaginal index and the speed or nature of free associations (Sample 5) to words referring to father or words referring to mother.

32. One borderline result pertaining to religion might well be worth further exploration. It was found that when all Catholics and all Protestants across the seven samples were compared, the Catholics were relatively more vaginally oriented, at a borderline level of significance ($t = 1.8$, $p < .10$).

33. However, it should be mentioned as a lead for further investigation that a significant trend was found in Sample 1 for the more vaginally, as compared to clitorally, oriented woman to have relatively lower hand than leg temperature in the rest condition. In Sample 2 this finding for the rest condition did not hold up, but it was found at a significant level that the greater a woman's vaginal orientation the more she responded to the reading of an erotic passage from a book by showing a shift toward relatively higher temperature in the leg than the hand. No significant relationships between the clitoral-vaginal index and the difference between the hand and leg temperature were observed in Sample 3.

34. The lack of response of the clitorally oriented woman to vaginal stimulation could possibly be viewed as reflecting two facts: First, the vagina has few sensory receptors (Kinsey, et al., 1953) and therefore does not easily provide a primary site for sexual arousal; secondly, the arousal it does provide is relatively less intense than that rising from direct manual clitoral arousal and therefore is less valued or attended to.

But one must ask why the relatively greater concentration of sensory receptors in the clitoris does not make it easier for the depersonalized woman to react more to clitoral as compared to vaginal stimulation. Once again, it seems necessary to appeal to the idea that a woman with a depersonalized attitude toward her body responds best not to stimulation of the greatest sensory intensity but rather stimulation that is most personalized, most psychologically suggestive that one's own body can be viewed in a nondepersonalized fashion. It may be that in the act of having another commit his body to hers in such a uniquely intimate way during intercourse, the depersonalized woman finds the needed proof that her own body (and its arousal) is "real" and worth relating to.

35. This speculation is, however, not supported by the fact that the clitoral-vaginal index proved not to be significantly related to degree of vaginal awareness (as measured by the Sexual Body Focus Questionnaire).

11

INTERCOURSE FREQUENCY

AND NARCISSISM

Frequency of intercourse differs a good deal among the individual women in each sample. Whereas some reported frequencies as low as zero or one per week, others specified ten or more per week. However, the overall mean values for each of the seven samples studied were rather similar, clustering at three to four times per week. The reports obtained from the women concerning intercourse frequency were, as indicated earlier, not correlated significantly with measures of defensiveness (namely, Minnesota Multiphasic Personality Inventory K and L scales) or intent to make a good impression.[1] They probably accurately reflect true intercourse rates.[2]

Sex Behavior Correlates of Intercourse Frequency

It would be well at this point to review the sex behavior correlates of intercourse frequency. What can one say about a woman's sexual attitudes and reactions on the basis of a knowledge of how often she has intercourse? As noted earlier, intercourse frequency has only a chance relationship with orgasm consistency and clitoral-vaginal preference. But it is correlated with how sexually responsive a woman considers herself to be. The more sexually responsive she rates herself the greater is her intercourse rate.

There are several other significant correlates of intercourse frequency, some of which have not been previously described.

In five of the seven samples it was positively correlated (at significant or borderline levels) with number of different intercourse positions used per month.[3] In four of the seven samples it was positively correlated (at significant or borderline levels) with frequency of intercourse during menstruation.[4]

Another significant trend (in four of seven samples) that was found indicated that the greater a woman's intercourse frequency the more likely she is to sleep in the nude.[5]

Further, in four of seven samples it was noted that the higher a woman's intercourse rate the less likely she is to experience feelings of embarrassment (as defined by a ranking judgment) during intercourse.[6] This is the one and only qualitative *feeling* aspect of the sexual arousal experience that proved to be related to how frequently a woman has intercourse.

There were several interesting findings concerning the relationships of intercourse frequency to indices concerned with intercourse rates *preferred* by self and also husband. One finds that in all samples a woman's intercourse frequency is positively and significantly correlated with her own *preferred* frequency [7] as well as with her estimate of her husband's *preferred* frequency.[8] But interestingly, it is also positively correlated in five of seven samples (at significant or borderline levels) with her estimate of her husband's preferred intercourse minus her own preferred rate.[9] That is, the greater her reported actual frequency the more she indicates that her husband's preferred frequency exceeds her own preferred rate.

This last finding suggests, of course, that the greater a woman's intercourse frequency the more she perceives her husband as preferring a greater amount of intercourse than she does. Does this mean that women with higher intercourse rates feel that to some extent they are pressured by their husbands into having more intercourse than they prefer?

Narcissism [10]

No formal hypotheses were formulated with regard to possible personality or perceptual correlates of intercourse frequency.

However, as the accumulated results from the various samples were scanned, they suggested that the greater a woman's intercourse frequency the more narcissistic or self-focused she is.

One line of evidence with regard to this view derives from findings concerning the amount of energy each woman devotes to self-grooming and enhancing her appearance. A questionnaire was administered in four samples (2, 3, 4, 5) that inquired concerning a range of body enhancing procedures. The following exemplify the questions asked: [11]

How often do you go to a hairdresser per month?
How many times per day, on the average, do you change your make-up?
What articles of jewelry do you frequently wear?
How many different kinds of perfume do you currently have?
How many times per month do you "do your nails" or get a manicure?
How many times per week do you rub your entire body with creams, powders, or colognes?

The responses to these and a series of related questions were coded and converted into a total index (Body Attention score). The greater the Body Attention score of a woman the greater is the effort she presumably devotes to maintaining and improving her appearance. It was found that intercourse frequency was positively and significantly correlated with Body Attention in Samples 3 and 4 (.30, $p < .05$ and .41, $p < .05$, respectively).[12] In Samples 2 and 5 the correlations were not significant. The appearance of positive findings in two of four samples is noteworthy and certainly indicative of a significant trend.[13]

The narcissism and interest in self-display implied by these results were also suggested by some findings from the Edwards (1954) Personal Preference Schedule. One dimension measured by this schedule is called Exhibition. To obtain a high Exhibition score one has to express positive preferences for such activities as the following:

To have others notice and comment upon one's appearance.
To say things just to see what effect it will have on others.
To be the center of attention.
To talk about personal achievements.

In other words, a high score means that the individual describes herself as self-centered and doing things to attract attention.

Intercourse frequency was found to be positively and significantly related to the Exhibition score [14] in Sample 2 ($x^2 = 4.2$, $df = 1$, $p < .05$) [15] and also Sample 4 ($r = .30$, $p.$ 05). The relationship in Sample 3 was of a chance magnitude. Overall, one can say that the greater a woman's intercourse frequency the more she is depicted by the Edwards Preference Schedule as being invested in a narcissistic, self-display style of behavior.

It is pertinent to this same issue that there was a borderline trend observed for intercourse frequency to be positively linked with difficulty in correctly identifying a picture with a narcissistic theme presented tachistoscopically. In three samples the women were asked to view a series of pictures presented at high speed (Appendix A). One of the pictures portrayed a person looking at herself in a mirror and was designed to tap attitudes concerned with narcissism and self-display.[16] In Sample 1 the greater a woman's intercourse rate the more difficulty she had in correctly identifying the Narcissism picture ($r = .30$, $p < .10$). This was also true in Sample 2 ($r = .41$, $p < .01$), but the relationship in Sample 4 was of a chance order.

In Sample 2 the women responded to a series of words presented tachistoscopically, of which two had narcissistic connotations (self, mine). Intercourse frequency was not significantly correlated with the relative degree of difficulty the women had in correctly perceiving the narcissistic words.

The overall results involving perception of narcissism themes presented tachistoscopically are, at best, of a borderline character.[17] But they were in the direction of indicating that those who have the higher intercourse rates have relatively more difficulty in correctly recognizing narcissism representations. This might be interpreted as indicative of greater anxiety about narcissism among those with higher intercourse rates. But this would not be justified, since anxiety about a stimulus may be shown either through a repressive or sensitized mode of perceptual response. The tachistoscopic findings do reinforce others cited above indicating that intercourse rate and behavior relevant to narcissism are *somehow* tied together.

It is pertinent to this matter to return momentarily to the earlier-cited finding that the greater a woman's intercourse rate the less embarrassed she feels during intercourse. Embarrassment has been referred to by several writers (Sattler, 1966; Heider, 1958; Baldwin, 1955) as a feeling especially likely to reflect one's concern about being looked at or observed. It is said to be a response to feeling that one is the focus of attention of others, and it has been speculatively linked with anxiety about exhibitionistic impulses. If so, it would obviously have to do with matters of self-display and narcissism. Thus, the fact that intercourse frequency was related only to the embarrassment dimension and not to any of the others that were used by the women to describe their feelings during intercourse could be attributed to the special concern about self-display presumably implicated in becoming embarrassed. This would provide another bit of evidence concerning the existence of a special link between intercourse frequency and issues pertaining to narcissistic self-display.[18]

A woman who is narcissistic in her orientation might, almost by definition, be expected to be self-indulgent. That is, one would anticipate that she would tend, to a special degree, to do things that were self-gratifying. An opportunity to evaluate this possibility was provided by information derived from the Average Week technique that was applied in two samples. This technique (Appendix B) involved asking each woman to write a description of how she spends an average week. The specific instructions were as follows: "Describe a typical week in your life. Give an account of the routine aspects of it as well as some of the high spots. Go into detail. You will have 15 minutes to write. Be sure to fill two pages." The descriptions obtained in this manner were blindly coded for all statements pertaining to a number of categories.[19] One of the categories, which is labeled "Entertainment," includes all references to activities that are usually regarded as having an entertainment function. For example, it includes references to watching television, attending movies, concerts, and other shows, going to parties, reading novels, and listening to records. In other words, it embraces activities in which a woman is doing things to amuse or indulge herself. It was found that intercourse frequency was positively correlated with Entertainment in Sample 2 ($r = .30$, $p.05$) and also Sample 3 ($r = .34$, $p < .05$). The greater a woman's intercourse rate the greater the percentage of her week she described herself as spending in self-indulgent activities.[20]

After pulling together the disparate clues that have been reviewed, one has to consider seriously the possibility that attitudes about self-display, narcissism, and self-gratification play a part in a woman's intercourse frequency. Admittedly, the data are tentative and circumstantial, and should be regarded with skepticism until there is further, more solid affirmation.

Attitude toward Husband and Men in General

There was a significant trend, cited earlier, for a woman's intercourse rate to be positively correlated with her estimate of her husband's preferred intercourse rate. This is one indirect indication, as has been observed by others (Terman, 1938, 1951), of the obvious fact that the husband plays an important role in setting his wife's intercourse rate. It would be of value to know more about the relationship between a woman's intercourse rate and her perception of her husband's attributes. However, in view of earlier negative findings concerning the minimal role of husband characteristics in the wife's sexual responsiveness, little information in this area was collected. Data were secured concerning each woman's estimate of how well she communicates with her husband about sexual matters, amount of time he requires to attain orgasm, frequency with which she agrees to his requests for intercourse, and how much they disagree with each other about a variety of issues. None of these ratings pertaining to husband correlated significantly, across multiple samples, with intercourse frequency.

Quite a number of ratings and judgments were obtained from the women that concerned their attitudes toward men in general. Indices were derived that touched upon attitudes concerning the relative superiority of men to women, envy of the male role, preferences for aggressive versus nonaggressive men, and preferences for traditional versus nontraditional modes of relating to men. None of these indices was consistently and significantly correlated, across multiple samples, with intercourse frequency.

Physiological Arousal

Whereas measures of physiological arousal have not turned out to be related to such parameters of sexual behavior as orgasm consistency and clitoral-vaginal preference, there is some evidence of augmented physiological response in those women with higher intercourse rates. As described in Appendices A, B, and C, a considerable variety of physiological measures were obtained from the women in Samples 1 and 2 as well as a limited number from those in Sample 3. The measures in Samples 1 and 2 included heart rate, Galvanic Skin Response, skin resistance and temperature (on upper and lower body sites).[21] In Sample 1 stomach motility was also measured. The measures taken in Sample 3 were restricted to skin resistance and temperature on a number of body areas. It should be added that whenever physiological arousal was evaluated, measures were taken over a range of conditions (for example, rest, threatening stress, sexually significant).

The following noteworthy relationships were discerned between intercourse frequency and indices of physiological response.

In both Samples 1 and 2 the amplitude of the Galvanic Skin Response (GSR) during an initial rest phase was positively correlated with intercourse frequency ($r = .29$, $p = .10$; $r = .38$, $p < .025$, respectively). The initial rest phase in which this relationship was found occurred during each woman's first experimental session. After electrodes had been placed on her arms and legs, she was told to relax and was left alone for a period of time.[22] Also, in these two samples GSR amplitude during a phase of the procedure in which sexually stimulating conditions were introduced was positively correlated with intercourse frequency ($r = .28$, p .05; $r = .26$, $p < .10$, respectively). The sexually stimulating condition in Sample 1 [23] was the initiation of a gynecological examination; and in Sample 2 [24] it involved the placement of probes and electrodes in the vaginal and labial areas and a period in which the skin in the thigh area was stroked in order to measure tickle threshold. In both instances the woman was nude, except for a sheet that covered her. However, it should be added that in Sample 2 intercourse frequency was correlated only .10 with GSR amplitude during the phase when a passage by D. H. Lawrence describing an intercourse scene was read aloud.

Another interesting trend involved the relationship of intercourse frequency to the hand temperature minus leg temperature. In Sample 1 the correlation was .39, $p < .025$ during the presumably sexually significant pelvic examination, but there were only chance correlations between the variables during rest and other nonsexual conditions. In Sample 2 intercourse frequency and the hand minus leg temperature were correlated .30 ($p < .05$) during the reading of the D. H. Lawrence sexual passage. The average of all hand minus ankle recordings made during session 2 was also significantly correlated with intercourse frequency ($r = .40$, $p < .01$), but during session 1, which was a rest session (and during which each woman was fully clothed), the two variables had only a chance correlation. In Sample 3 intercourse frequency and hand temperature minus ankle temperature had only chance correlations across the various conditions, including those considered to have special sexual connotations (for example, watching a movie depicting a birth). The highest correlation in Sample 3 was between intercourse frequency and hand minus ankle temperature obtained while the light touch threshold on the breast was being determined ($r = .12$, not significant).[25]

No consistent correlations were observed between intercourse frequency and skin resistance or heart rate or stomach motility or other temperature measures.

As defined by magnitude of GSR responses, there is apparently a positive correlation between intercourse frequency and autonomic arousal, both during a "rest" condition with no explicit sexual connotations and another one with very explicit sexual significance. It is interesting that Zuckerman (1971) in a review of physiological measures of sexual arousal in humans commented on the special sensitivity of GSR magnitude to sexual excitement. This might help to explain the specific correlations involving GSR that were obtained during the explicit sexual excitement conditions, but would not seem to clarify such GSR correlations as they appeared in the "rest" conditions. One could, of course, conjecture that even the condition that was defined as "rest" had unusual sexual connotations because it took place the first time that each woman came to the laboratory to participate in a study that had been defined as having to do with sex. This "rest" condition involved lying down and having electrodes attached to the legs and arms and might, in the context of a "sex study," have aroused sexual fantasies. In other words, one could conjecture that both the "rest" and sexually explicit experimental conditions elicited sexual fantasies and feelings, and that these were particularly well detected by the GSR magnitude measure.

The relationship observed between intercourse frequency and hand temperature minus leg temperature is discussed in greater detail at a later point when the overall physiological findings are integrated.

Miscellaneous Findings

One other positive finding concerning intercourse frequency should be mentioned, but can only be reported as a disparate bit of knowledge.

In one of the samples (2) the women were rated by each of the four technicians with regard to how sexually responsive they appeared to be. The technicians were instructed to make their judgments quite impressionistically and to use any cues that they wished. It was found that a woman's intercourse frequency was positively and significantly correlated ($r = .32$, $p < .03$) with how sexually responsive she was rated.[26] Apparently, the technicians were able to pick up cues (which, by the way, they could not specify) from the behavior and appearance of the women that turned out to be related to how frequently they have intercourse. When several raters who had never personally seen the women in Sample 2 were asked to look at front and back colored pictures of them and to rate their apparent degree of sexual responsiveness, the judgments made turned out not to be correlated with intercourse rate.[27] One could, on this basis, deduce that the cues that successfully categorized women with reference to intercourse rate were not primarily those related to appearance or clothing (as they would be distinguishable in a photograph), but rather those derived from observation of movement and expressive behavior.

Overview

The yield from this chapter has been sparse. It has been difficult to isolate characterological attributes that go along with varying intercourse rates. This may be partially because of the fact that such rates are influenced by husband's expectations. It will be recalled that the greater a woman's intercourse frequency the more she specified that her husband's *preferred* intercourse rate exceeded her own preferred. This would suggest that she feels pressured to conform to his expectations in this respect. If so, her actual intercourse rate would only be partially determined by her own wants and attributes.

However, it is interesting that even within the limitation of this fact, there was a fairly convincing train of evidence that indicated that intercourse rate tended to be higher in the woman who is more narcissistically oriented. She is more likely to devote energy to grooming herself and enhancing her attractiveness. She is more likely to fill her time with activities that are self-indulging.[28] She is more likely to describe herself as a person who enjoys being the center of attention and who seeks ways of exhibiting herself. Interestingly, too, she is more likely to emphasize that she is *not* embarrassed during intercourse. That is, she underscores the fact that she does not feel awkward or anxious about her nudity and other kinds of self-display that occur at the time of intercourse. In short, it is the woman who prefers situations in which she gets the opportunity for narcissistic gratification and self-exhibition who is most likely to engage frequently in intercourse.

Why should such a relationship exist? One of the simplest and most economical explanations would be that the narcissistic woman particularly searches out experiences that will make her the focus of attention and enable her to be the recipient of stimulation signifying admiration. Just as she enthusiastically invests energy in grooming and enhancing her own body, she is drawn to situations in which others will provide her with analogous sensations. Her special enjoyment of the self-enhancing attention associated with intercourse would motivate her in the direction of seeking it frequently.

NOTES

1. The reliability of intercourse frequency reports was evaluated in two samples (4, 5) by asking a segment of the women in each to give repeat reports on a second occasion. In Sample 4 the time intervening between first and second reports was seven days, whereas in Sample 5 it was about three days. The test-retest reliability coefficients in Samples 4 and 5 were respectively .92 ($N=32$) and .93 ($N=29$). These coefficients indicate a high degree of reliability over a short period of time.

2. No consistent relationships were found between intercourse frequency and age, amount of education, number of children, religiosity, religious affiliation, and number of years married. It should be kept in mind, though, that the samples were chosen so as to be quite limited in their range for a number of the variables just enumerated.

3. Sample 2: $r = .57$, $p < .001$; Sample 3: $r = .33$, $p < .05$; Sample 4: $r = .25$, p .05; Sample 5: $r = .40$, $p < .05$; Sample 7: $r = .24$, $p < .10$. All correlations cited in this chapter are Pearson product-moment coefficients. N's will be cited only when they depart grossly from the sample sizes shown in Chapter 7.

4. Sample 2: $r = .52$, $p < .001$; Sample 3: $r = .35$, $p < .025$; Sample 4: $r = .32$, $p < .05$; Sample 5: $r = .38$, $p < .05$.

5. Sample 2: $r = .46$, $p < .01$; Sample 3: $r = .51$, $p < .001$; Sample 4: $r = .43$, $p < .01$; Sample 5: $r = .51$, $p < .01$.

6. Sample 2: $r = .33$, $p < .05$; Sample 4: $r = .45$, $p < .01$; Sample 5: $r = .36$, $p < .05$; Sample 6: $r = .32$, $p < .05$.

7. Sample 1: $r = .59$, $p < .001$; Sample 2: $r = .71$, $p < .001$; Sample 3: $r = .80$, $p < .001$; Sample 4: $r = .85$, $p < .001$; Sample 5: $r = .91$, $p < .001$; Sample 6: $r = .74$, $p < .001$; Sample 7: $r = .76$, $p < .001$.

8. Sample 1: $r = .64$, $p < .001$; Sample 2: $r = .70$, $p < .001$; Sample 3: $r = .84$, $p < .001$; Sample 4: $r = .82$, $p = .001$; Sample 5: $r = .84$, $p < .001$; Sample 6: $r = .77$, $p < .001$; Sample 7: $r = 72$, $p < .001$.

9. Sample 1: $r = .33$ $p < .05$; Sample 3: $r = .31$, $p < .05$; Sample 4: $r = .24$, $p < .10$; Sample 5: $r = .29$, p .05; Sample 6: $r = .28$, p .05.

10. The term "narcissism," as here used, is not intended to have negative connotations. Although it is recognized that the term suffers from negative overtones, it was not possible to find a better one.

11. See Appendix K for more details.

12. The mean Body Attention scores in Samples 3 and 4 were 79.1 ($\sigma = 23.3$) and 80.1 ($\sigma = 25.8$), respectively.

13. Although intercourse frequency was positively correlated with amount of grooming attention a woman devotes to her body, it was not correlated with her habitual degree of *general* awareness of her body (as measured by Body Prominence).

No consistent correlations have been found between general body awareness and the self-grooming index. Furthermore, general body awareness in women has not been observed to be linked with measures of narcissism.

14. The mean percentile Exhibition score in Sample 2 was 53.5 ($\sigma = 29.1$) and in Sample 4, 45.9 ($\sigma = 31.0$).

15. Chi-square was used in this instance because the distribution of Exhibition scores was moderately skewed.

16. Other pictures portrayed themes of heterosexuality, hostility, dependency, and achievement.

17. Intercourse frequency was not significantly correlated with other indices that have tangential narcissistic connotations (namely, clothing preferences, self-ratings of one's own body, dominance).

18. Psychoanalytic theory (Fenichel, 1945) assumes that self-display or exhibitionistic behavior represents, at one level, a seeking for reassurance. To be looked at presumably provides a defense against fears of desertion and loss. An analysis was undertaken of the relationship of intercourse frequency to the frequency with which references to seeing and being observed occurred in the inkblot fantasies of the women. Protocols were blindly scored for references to eyes, seeing, reflections, obscuring of view, looking, and X-ray pictures. It was found in Samples 1 and 3 that the higher the intercourse frequency the greater was the number of such references ($x^2 = 6.4$, $df = 1$, $p < .02$; $x^2 = 7.3$, $df = 1$, $p < .01$, respectively). In Sample 2 the relationship was not significant.

19. For example, eating or oral gratification, sports, cleaning activities.

20. This self-indulgence does not seem to apply to oral gratification, as such. Intercourse frequency is not significantly correlated with measures of the amount or variety of food eaten, nor is it correlated with apparent amount of enjoyment obtained from eating. Similarly, it is not consistently related to smoking or drinking behavior.

21. For example, hand, leg, vagina, labia, breast.

22. In Samples 1 and 2 the measures were based on four one-minute samples taken from a total 15-minute period.

23. Based on three one-minute samples of time.

24. Based on four one-minute samples of time.

25. No significant relationships were observed between intercourse frequency and skin resistance of the hand minus skin resistance of the leg.

26. The sexual-responsiveness rating was not correlated with orgasm consistency.

27. These ratings of the pictures were also not correlated with orgasm consistency.

28. With reference to self-indulgence, it is interesting that Schwartz, Hershenson, and Shipman (1971) found that obese married women had a greater desire for coitus than married nonobese women. However, it should be reiterated that intercourse frequency was not consistently correlated in the present studies with measures of eating behavior and eating attitudes.

12

MASTURBATION AND

BEING MESSY

Only limited masturbatory activity was reported among the samples of married women that were studied. Although, as shown by Kinsey, et al. (1953) masturbation is widely prevalent among women, it occurs with low frequency (less than once per month) among those who are married and have regular intercourse available to them. The average woman in the six samples in which masturbation was investigated by the writer indicated that she masturbates only "rarely"; and thus conforms to the Kinsey, et al. norms.[1] Few aspects of sexual behavior turned out to be consistently related to either a woman's frequency of masturbation or the amount of satisfaction she reported deriving from it. The masturbation parameters were not correlated with orgasm consistency, actual or preferred intercourse frequency, and the quality of the orgasmic experience.[2] This would suggest that such masturbation as does occur is in no obvious way a compensation for lack or deficit in other sectors of sexual experience. The masturbation measures were also not correlated with rate of sexual maturation (as defined by age of menarche), sources of early sex information, and early dating frequency.[3] Furthermore, these measures were not correlated with number of years of marriage, number of children, and religious membership (for example, Catholic versus Protestant). Interestingly, too, they were not linked with a number of direct and indirect measures of anxiety and maladjustment that were employed. That is, there is no indication that they reflect the "mental health" of a woman. Of course, one should keep in mind that the women studied had very low masturbation rates. Only a few of the women seemed to attach really substantial importance to masturbation as a significant source of gratification. It would therefore be hazardous to generalize from the present study to women who do have high masturbation rates.

There were a few indices of sexual behavior and sexual attitude that were found to be related to masturbation behavior.

Masturbation frequency proved to be positively correlated with the following:

The degree of importance ascribed by each woman to sex in her own life.[4]
The extent to which movies and novels about sex provide enjoyment.[5]

The degree to which there is belief that sexual freedom in our culture should be increased.[6]
The amount of time spent thinking about sex.[7]
The frequency of intercourse during menstruation.[8]

As for the index of satisfaction obtained from masturbation, it was found that the greater such satisfaction the stronger was the belief that sexual freedom should be increased in our culture.[9] It was not correlated with any of the other sexual parameters.

No easy generalization presents itself with regard to the correlations just enumerated. One could say that there is a trend for those who indicate a positive investment in masturbation to express attitudes that favor explicit sexual freedom and open awareness (and appreciation) of that which has sexual significance.

In initially pondering the possible personality concomitants of masturbation behavior in women, the existing literature pertinent to this matter was surveyed. A few empirical studies (Terman, 1938, 1951; Landis, et al., 1940) had systematically appraised the personality attributes of women differing with reference to masturbation, but the results were uniformly not promising. A considerable number of theoretical and clinical publications, which speculated concerning the psychological determinants of masturbation (Masters, 1967; Arlow, 1953; Eidelberg, 1945; Freud, 1925), presented a formidable array of assertions and theories. As one examines them, one finds that certain statements recur more than others. For example, it is often said that a very low incidence of masturbation during childhood signifies too great a repression or denial of sexual urges, and a high masturbation rate in an adult is usually interpreted as indicative of an avoidance of "genuine" heterosexuality. Other speculative themes that are prominent in this literature concerning masturbation are as follows:

It represents a way of obtaining release of sexual tension without the necessity of forming a relationship with another person, and therefore permits avoidance of deep personal involvement.

It provides a form of sexual experience in which the individual retains control over the tempo and nature of what occurs and need not be exposed to the unexpected, messy events that can occur during intercourse.

It often arouses intense guilt because it is so disapproved by most parents and is linked early in life with being sinful, and is accompanied by unconscious fantasies that symbolically impart to it a grossly forbidden significance.

It encourages feelings of unreality by not only permitting retreat from the usual intimacy of the two-person sexual transaction but also by requiring the individual to split her identity by simultaneously playing two roles: the one who is delivering stimulation and also the one receiving it.

What most impressed the writer as he became acquainted with this literature was the rather pervasive way in which masturbation was described as eliciting feelings of being sinful and dirty. Although different mechanisms and models were offered to account for this effect, the observation that masturbation is associated with being unclean was recurrent. It was in the context of this impression that the exploratory findings bearing on the relationships between masturbation behavior and personality measures were first examined in Sample 2.[10]

Being Messy

Several of the measures obtained in Sample 2 that seemed especially pertinent to feelings of being unclean were scanned on an exploratory basis to ascertain their relationships to the two masturbation indices (masturbation frequency, masturbation satisfaction). They included the following:

Order scale of the Edwards Preference Schedule, which taps how important it is to the individual to avoid disarray and disorder.

Clean scale (Murray-Harvard Questionnaire), which evaluates the amount of importance attached to keeping oneself clean.

Dirt score, which is based on how frequently remarks about dirt and messiness are made in spontaneous reports of what one is experiencing.

Amount of effort devoted to cleaning (antidirt) activities (for example, bathing, cleaning clothes) as determined from a written account of how one spends an average week.

Speed at which there is accurate identification of a picture (Blacky Anal Sadism) with dirt or anal connotations that is presented tachistoscopically.[11]

Response to jokes with dirt or anal themes.

Degree to which one's own body is perceived as dirty.

All of these measures may be found described in detail in Appendices A through G.

From this array several were noted to be correlated significantly (or at a borderline level) with one or both of the masturbation indices.

Masturbation frequency and masturbation satisfaction were correlated with the Edwards Order score $-.32$ (p .10) and $-.38$ ($p < .10$) respectively. That is, in each instance there was a borderline significant trend, such that the higher a woman's Order score the lower were her masturbation scores. To clarify the meaning of this relationship let us consider first the nature of the Edwards Order score, which is based on a series of decisions as to whether certain needs or preferences particularly characterize oneself. Those obtaining a high score on Order must frequently assert that they have special needs (Edwards, 1959, p. 11):

To have written work neat and organized, to make plans before starting on a difficult task, to have things organized, to keep things neat and orderly, to make advance plans when taking a trip, to organize details of work, to keep letters and files according to some system, to have meals organized at a definite time for eating, to have things arranged so that they run smoothly without change.

In other words, the less a woman is motivated to masturbate the more she depicts herself as preferring a way of life that is orderly, systematic, and not messy.

A second pertinent finding in Sample 2 indicated that masturbation frequency and masturbation satisfaction were correlated with the Murray-Harvard Clean scale $-.37$ ($p<.025$) and $-.25$ ($p>.10$), respectively. That is, there was a trend such that the less a woman's investment in masturbation the greater was her concern about keeping things clean. The Clean score is based upon agreement or disagreement with the following statements:

"Cleanliness is next to Godliness" is a foolish saying.
Soiled hands or dirty fingers bother you very little.
You feel very uneasy in a dirty place.
You like to have your room cleaned every day.
You like to wash your hands before every meal.

None of the other measures relevant to the issue of feelings of being unclean or in disarray was correlated significantly with either of the masturbation indices in Sample 2. However, the two sets of findings involving the Edwards Order score and the Murray-Harvard Clean score were encouraging in suggesting that there was a relationship between masturbation behavior and what, for lack of better terminology, will be referred to as one's orientation to being messy. These initial findings indicated that the more a woman is oriented toward being messy (unclean, disorderly) the more she involves herself with masturbation.

The two measures of orientation toward being messy were also used in subsequent samples, and these results are now reviewed. First, let us consider those concerning the Edwards Order score. Masturbation frequency turned out to be correlated $-.30$ ($p<.05$) with Order in Sample 3 and $-.24$ ($p>.10$) with it in Sample 4.[12] Masturbation satisfaction was found to be correlated $-.32$ ($p<.05$) with Order in Sample 3 and $-.34$ ($p<.05$) with it in Sample 4. Obviously, there was a consistent confirming trend for a woman's masturbation investment to be inverse to her motivation to be orderly (not messy).

When one looks at the additional results involving the other measure of orientation to being messy, that is, the Clean scale, one finds that masturbation frequency was correlated $-.29$ (p .05) and $-.27$ (p .10) with Clean scores in Samples 3 and 6, respectively; but had only chance relationships with them in Samples 4, 5, and 7. Masturbation satisfaction was correlated $-.39$ ($p<.01$), $-.29$ (p just short of .05), and $-.32$ (p .05) in Samples 3, 4, and 6 respectively.[13] The correlations for Samples 5 and 7 were not significant.

In general, the findings look promising. Apparently, the more important it is for a woman to keep her world neat and clean the less likely she is to engage in, or enjoy, masturbation. This could mean that those who avoid masturbation do so because they see it as something that is dirty and makes them feel uncomfortably unclean. Note that this is the only aspect of sexual behavior studied by the writer that has turned out to be related to feelings about dirt and contamination. This is surprising because the term "dirty" is, in a derogatory context, often applied publicly to various aspects of sexual behavior. Religious declarations about sex have for centuries conveyed the evaluation that it is dirty. One might, therefore, have anticipated that such variables as difficulty in attaining orgasm or unusually low intercourse rates would be tied to feelings that sex is besmirching. In fact, no such relationships were discerned. Of course, this implies that masturbation has greater connotations of being a dirty activity than do conventional sexual behaviors such as heterosexual intercourse.

Religion

The fact that a concept of sex as dirty is often prominent in religious systems led to a special inquiry into whether measures of religiosity were correlated with masturbation behavior. One might expect those who are most religious would be most negative toward masturbation. But examination of the findings indicated that the masturbation indices were not consistently correlated with church membership, self-ratings of religiosity, and frequency of church attendance of self or of one's parents. That is, masturbation behavior did not seem to be linked to the degree to which a woman was invested in conventional religious beliefs and practices. However, there was one formal questionnaire measure of religiosity that was employed in several samples that was not so much concerned with conventional religiosity as with a broad orientation emphasizing the existence of God and devotion to religious ideals. This was the Religious subscale of the Study of Values scale (Allport, Vernon, Lindzey, 1960). It proved to be negatively correlated ($-.31$, $p<.05$) with masturbation frequency in Sample 3 and unrelated to it in Samples 2 and 5. Further, it was correlated $-.49$ ($p<.001$) and $-.35$ ($p<.05$) with masturbation satisfaction in Samples 3 and 5 respectively, although lacking correlation in Sample 2. Overall, there does seem to be a significant trend, such that the greater a woman's religiosity the less the satisfaction she derives from masturbation. It is a bit puzzling as to why a relationship between religiosity and masturbation behavior can be discerned by use of the Study of Values measure but not in terms of indicators of more conventional religiosity (for example, frequency of church attendance). No reasonable explanation offers itself, except the speculation that the Study of Values may be a more sensitive and reliable measure of a basic *religious orientation* toward life, whether it gets translated into conventional religious behavior or not.

The uniqueness of these findings involving the Religious orientation needs to be underscored. None of the various other aspects of sexual behavior studied has shown consistent ties to religiosity.

Attitudes toward Parents

Since masturbation behavior did show some degree of relationship to an aspect of religiosity, the question arose whether it might also be related to how moralistic one's parents were perceived to be. That is, if it is assumed that religious standards and values represent moral imperatives that are imposed (largely via one's parents), might it not be expected that masturbation would be inverse to how moralistically one's parents behaved? Among the ratings that each woman had been asked to make of each of her parents, one concerned how moral the parents' orientation had been.[14] When the findings were examined, it was observed that the more a woman portrayed her mother as moralistic the less was her masturbation frequency in Sample 2 ($-.47$, $p < .025$) and Sample 5 ($-.39$, $p < .05$). The relationship in Sample 6 was not significant. As for masturbation satisfaction, it likewise tended to be negatively correlated with the mother's degree of moralism ($-.37$, p. $< .10$, Sample 2; $-.35$, p .05, Sample 5; not significant in Sample 6). The trend certainly suggests that the more a woman thinks of her mother as being morally strict the less is the satisfaction that she derives from masturbation. However, it should be added that masturbation behavior was unrelated to how moralistic her *father* was considered to be. This is particularly noteworthy because it is the first instance in which some aspect of a woman's sexual behavior turned out to be more correlated with her mother's rather than her father's attributes (as she views them). It has been paradoxically true, as noted earlier, that such variables as orgasm consistency have been more linked with the father's perceived characteristics than the mother's.

The relatively greater importance of the mother's as compared to father's perceived qualities with reference to masturbation behavior is brought home when one reviews some of the other findings involving ratings of one's parents. Thus, masturbation frequency was found to be positively correlated with the degree to which the mother was described as behaving in a neglecting,[15] egocentric,[16] distant,[17] hostile,[18] and nonloving fashion.[19] These correlations are in some cases quite low or borderline in value, but the overall directionality of the findings is sharp. The more a woman depicts her mother as an unfriendly and neglecting person the more she masturbates.[20] Analogous findings for masturbation satisfaction were lacking. The only consistency even worth mentioning was a weak trend for masturbation satisfaction to be greater in those who recall the mother as having been neglecting.[21]

No consistent correlations could be detected between the masturbation indices and any of the ratings or evaluations of the father. There was not even a trend for the findings to parallel those involving perception of the mother. Masturbation was *not* more frequent or more satisfying in those who perceived their fathers as negative and unloving.

The rather unique positive association between masturbation frequency and perceiving one's mother as unfriendly and neglecting calls to mind those theories that conceptualize masturbation in adults as an activity that provides sexual arousal without the necessity of giving oneself to another —without the need to give up any of one's independence. That is, if a woman were reared by a mother who kept pushing her away and refusing to relate to her with any warmth, might she not, on the basis of this proto-type experience, feel that she could not expect mutuality in relationships with others and, therefore, that she should seek gratification in as *independent* a fashion as possible. Masturbation might be especially attractive to someone with such an orientation as it permits gratification in a context where one need relate only to self and can be unconcerned about the "other." [22] Although this may be true it should be cautioned that there is no evidence that the woman who enjoys masturbating is so distrustful of personal involvement that she cannot form the kind of intimate relation-ship with a man that occurs during intercourse leading to orgasm. One can only speculate that if a woman has had a history of feeling neglected by her mother she may have a special need to prove to herself periodically that she is capable of satisfying herself without the assistance of an outside agent (namely, mother). If so, the masturbation would not only be a sexual act but also a means of expressing a special kind of autonomy.

Miscellaneous Findings

Several other findings should be enumerated simply because they may provide leads for future research.

One has to do with the relationship between the masturbation indices and interest in new, exciting, and stimulating experiences. In several sam-ples the women were asked to respond to the Zuckerman, Kolin, Price, and Zoob (1964) Sensation-Seeking Scale, which seeks to ascertain the de-gree to which an individual prefers the exciting, unfamiliar, and thrilling as compared to the routine and predictable. Masturbation frequency proved to be positively related to the Sensation-Seeking score in all three of the samples in which it had been obtained.[23] Masturbation satisfaction also showed an analogous, but less consistent trend in its relationship with the Sensation-Seeking score.[24] In other words, the greater a woman's in-vestment in masturbation the more she describes herself as a person who enjoys novelty and stimulation rather than routine. This raises the possibil-ity that another element that contributes to masturbatory behavior in mar-ried women is simply a desire for variety. Women with a strong need for "something different" may, despite the availability of regular intercourse, choose to masturbate in order to vary the nature of their sexual experi-ences.

There are also hints of possible physiological differences that parallel variations in masturbatory behavior. In Samples 2 and 3 a variety of physiological measures, described in Appendices B and C, were taken from each woman.[25] One measure that seems to show particular promise in its link with masturbation is skin resistance. This measure is based upon the degree of resistance of the skin to the passage of a very small current. The greater the resistance the less physiologically active is the skin at that site. It has been shown that conditions that alert or arouse an individual produce a decrease in skin resistance. In both Samples 2 and 3 skin resistance was recorded from both the hand and ankle (among other sites), and an index was constructed (hand resistance minus ankle resistance) that was intended to compare the degree of physiological arousal of "upper" as compared to "lower" body sectors. This was done in a purely exploratory fashion, with the rationale that since the upper and lower areas of the body differ in their sexual connotations, it might be of interest to determine if there are upper versus lower differences in physiological arousal. No consistency has previously been found in the relationship of the skin resistance of the hand minus ankle to parameters such as orgasm consistency or intercourse frequency. But a trend of borderline magnitude was found for masturbation satisfaction (not masturbation frequency) to be positively correlated (in both samples) with the degree to which physiological arousal of the hand (upper sector) is greater than that of the ankle (lower sector.)[26] This relationship is discussed at a later point when an attempt is made to integrate all of the physiological findings.

A final point concerns differences in skin sensitivity to light touch and to stroking (tickle) among those varying in masturbation behavior. There was a clear finding that the greater a woman's masturbation frequency the more sensitive she was to light touch applied to her wrist. That is, the woman with greater frequency of masturbation demonstrated, while blindfolded (see Appendix A), an unusual ability to detect very faint touch stimuli.[27] The degree of satisfaction from masturbation showed an analogous trend in its relationship to ability to detect faint touch stimuli on the wrist.[28] Furthermore, there were signs (at a borderline level) that the greater a woman's masturbation satisfaction the longer the tickle persists when it is produced by stroking her skin with a piece of cotton (see Appendix B).[29] Masturbation frequency also tended (at a borderline level) to be positively correlated with such tickle persistence.[30] These findings suggest that the greater a woman's investment in masturbation the greater is the sensitivity of her skin to light touch as well as the longer the time that the tickle persists once it is applied. Whether her skin sensitivity in this respect plays some role in her masturbatory inclination remains to be seen.

Overview

Within the limitations imposed by the narrow (but probably normal for married women) range of masturbatory investment found in the six samples, one can say that the presence or absence of masturbation does not seem to be a function of other aspects of a woman's sexual behavior. It is not related to whether she does or does not attain orgasm consistently, whether her intercourse rate is high or low, and so forth. This strongly suggests that one cannot regard masturbation in married women as a compensation for a lack in other aspects of their sexual experiences. Such women do not, in general, seem to masturbate because their sex life is deficient in some way. It should be added too that masturbatory behavior seems to have little to do with how anxious or maladjusted a woman is. One cannot say that the presence of masturbation in a married woman indicates that she is somehow emotionally uncomfortable.

The woman who is relatively invested in masturbation does state that sex plays a particularly important role in her life. She indicates that she devotes a lot of thought to sex, that she likes to read material with sexual themes, and that she wishes in general that there were more sexual freedom in the culture. This could mean that sex has unusual prominence for her as a theme for fantasy and preoccupation. But it should be said again that there are no indications that she does in reality involve herself in more, or a greater variety of, other sexual behaviors than does the average woman.

One of the major findings that was uncovered was that masturbation investment is linked with personal attitudes about cleanliness. It was demonstrated that the less a woman is interested in masturbation the more motivated she is to avoid doing things that are messy and unclean. One deduction to be drawn from such a finding is that those who refrain from masturbation do so, at least partially, because it is an act that has unusually strong connotations of the unclean. This is congruent with the fact that in most cultures masturbation is still vividly identified with sinful dirtiness. Indeed, data have been presented in this chapter that indicate that the more religious a woman's attitudes (as defined by belief in God and the importance of religious devotion, but not in terms of formal religious observance), the more negative is her orientation toward masturbation. To some extent, then, avoidance of masturbation by married women probably reflects a fear of doing something besmirching and immoral in the religious sense.[31] At another level, one might say that it reflects a restricted concept of what is acceptable or proper behavior.

Directly apropos of this matter of restriction was the finding that indicated that the more intense a woman's interest in doing new (nonroutine) and exciting things the more she is attracted to masturbation. In other words, if a woman wants to escape restriction and explore the new she is particularly positive toward masturbatory gratification. Perhaps masturbation serves her with some element of the novelty that she seeks.[32]

Truly surprising was the earlier described observation that a woman's investment in masturbation is larger to the degree that she depicts her mother as having been distant, unloving, and neglecting. However, as one contemplates this finding, it does seem to support those theorists who conceptualize masturbation as a means of getting sexual gratification without having to give up one's independence. If one assumes that a woman who has had an antagonistic pattern of experiences with her mother will, because of the prototype nature of this relationship, be concerned with ways of asserting her independence, it is understandable why she might be attracted to a form of sexual gratification that is a declaration of self-sufficiency. It has been cautioned, though, that no evidence exists that the woman who likes masturbation is deficient in her ability to enter into, and enjoy, orthodox sexual intercourse. What has been proposed is that masturbation provides such a woman with a periodic opportunity to reassure herself that she can attain gratification on her own and that she retains the option of not counting on personal intimacy with another to allay her needs. It may be a matter of importance that whereas previously cited sexual behaviors (for example, orgasm consistency) in women that specifically involve intimacy with a man were found to be related to attitudes toward the father, masturbatory activity, which really pertains to a relationship with one's own body, is tied to attitudes toward the mother. Several theorists (Fenichel, 1945) have pointed out that during the child's earliest years he is so close to the mother (as she feeds, cleans, and comforts him) that he may initially have difficulty in differentiating his body from hers. He may experience his body as belonging at least partially to her. Perhaps traces of such attitudes persist into adulthood and the average woman feels (unconsciously?) that her body still "belongs" a bit to her mother. If so, it should not be so surprising that when she has to decide whether to relate to her own body via masturbation, her attitudes toward her mother become involved. That is, if she did, indeed, view her body as being partially her mother's domain, she might very well act out toward it in ways that would be influenced by how she feels about her mother. Her masturbation might symbolically be a way of saying to mother, "You don't own my body."

The major overall conclusion to be drawn from the various studies is that married women who refrain from masturbation probably do so because the act has unusual connotations of being disorderly, unclean, and immoral. However, at the same time, there are indications that other elements are involved. One should keep in mind that amount of investment in masturbation has been found to be related to the degree to which the mother is perceived as neglecting and unloving and also how much interest there is in new and novel experiences. It is likely that each married woman's masturbation behavior is governed significantly by the interaction of at least the three elements just enumerated.

NOTES

1. Masturbation ratings were not consistently correlated with the Minnesota Multiphasic measures of response defensiveness (K and L scales). Therefore, one may assume that they are not seriously distorted by defensive motivation to "make a good impression."

2. The two basic masturbation measures employed were as follows. One was derived from each woman's estimate of the frequency with which she currently masturbates (1 = I never masturbate; 2 = Rarely; 3 = Once in a while; 4 = Quite often; 5 = I masturbate with great frequency). The second was derived from her evaluation of the degree to which she obtains satisfaction from masturbation (1 = No satisfaction; 2 = Some satisfaction; 3 = Fair amount of satisfaction; 4 = Lot of satisfaction; 5 = Intense satisfaction).

3. Since masturbation in women tends to be clitorally focused, one might have expected to find some relationship between the masturbation parameters and clitoral-vaginal preference. However, in fact, no consistent correlates between them could be detected.

4. The correlations in Samples 2, 6, and 7 were respectively .28 ($p < .10$), .38 ($p < .025$), and .36 ($p < .05$). The correlations in the other three samples were not significant.

All correlations cited in this chapter are Pearson product-moment coefficients. N's will not be cited unless they depart grossly from those listed for each sample in Chapter 7.

5. The correlations in Samples 4, 6, and 7 were respectively .44 ($p < .01$), .27 ($p < .10$), and .37 ($p < .025$). Those for the remaining samples were not significant.

6. The correlations in Samples 4, 5, 6, and 7 were respectively .45 ($p < .01$), .45 ($p < .001$), .52 ($p < .001$), and .36 ($p < .025$). Those for the remaining samples were not significant.

7. The correlations in Samples 3, 4, 5, and 6 were respectively .35 ($p < .025$), .29 ($p < .10$), .33 ($p < .10$), and .36 (p .025). Those for the remaining samples were not significant.

8. The correlations in Samples 3, 4, and 6 were respectively .44 ($p < .01$), .27 ($p < .10$), and .40 (p .025). Those in the remaining samples were not significant.

9. The correlations in Samples 3, 4, 5, 6, and 7 were respectively .26 ($p < .10$), .55 ($p < .001$), .33 ($p < .10$), .33 (p .05), and .30 ($p < .10$). The correlation in Sample 2 was not significant.

10. Questions concerning masturbation were not asked in Sample 1.

11. Apparatus that shows pictures or words at very high speeds (for example, one-thousandth of a second).

12. A chi-square analysis indicated that the two variables were significantly related ($x^2 = 6.3$, $df = 2$, $p < .05$).

13. A chi-square analysis indicated that this relationship was significant ($x^2 = 7.0$, $df = 2$, $p < .05$).

14. 1 = Very moralistic; 6 = Very unmoralistic.

15. Masturbation frequency was correlated .56 ($p < .01$) with the Roe and Siegelman (1963) Mother Neglecting score in Sample 2 and .30 ($p < .05$) in Sample 3. The correlation in Sample 4 was significantly in the opposite direction. The Neglecting score reflects the degree to which the parent is regarded as one who pays little attention to his child, "giving him a minimum of physical care and no affection" (p. 357).

16. Masturbation frequency was correlated .34 (p .05) with how egotistic (self-centered) mother was rated in Sample 5 and there was a trend in the same direction (.22, $p > .10$) in Sample 6. The equivalent correlation in Sample 2 did not even approach significance.

17. Masturbation frequency was correlated .53 ($p<.01$) with how distant mother was perceived to be in Sample 2, and the equivalent correlation in Sample 5 was .38 ($p<.05$). The correlation in Sample 6 was not significant.

18. Masturbation frequency was correlated .42 ($p<.05$) with the degree to which mother was rated as hostile in Sample 2 and the equivalent correlation in Sample 5 was .26 ($p>.10$). The correlation in Sample 6 did not even approach significance.

19. Masturbation frequency was correlated $-.51$ ($p<.01$) with the Roe and Siegelman (1963) Symbolic Love Reward score in Sample 2 and $-.24$ ($p>.10$) in Sample 3. The correlation in Sample 4 did not even approach significance.

20. It should be added that in one of the tasks used in Sample 5 in which each woman was asked to give a series of free associations to words referring to the mother and father, there was a borderline trend ($r=.31$, $p<.10$) for number of *negative* references to the mother given by a woman to be positively correlated with the amount of satisfaction she derives from masturbation.

21. Masturbation satisfaction was correlated .36 ($p<.10$) with the Roe and Siegelman (1963) Mother Neglecting score in Sample 2 and .30 ($p<.05$) in Sample 3. The corresponding correlation was significantly in the opposite direction in Sample 4.

22. However, there is no evidence that masturbatory behavior is correlated with *general* indices of hostility or aggressiveness. The independence referred to seems to be quite specialized in the form it takes.

23. $r=.27$, p .10, Sample 2; $x^2=3.9$, $df=1$, $p<.05$, Sample 3; $r=.44$, $p<.01$, Sample 6. [Chi-square was used in Sample 2 because of the skewed nature of one of the distributions of scores.]

24. $r=.23$, $p>.10$, Sample 3; $r=.39$, $p<.025$, Sample 6; the correlation in Sample 2 did not even approach significance.

25. Although physiological measures were obtained in Sample 1, the masturbation ratings were not secured in this sample.

26. Masturbation satisfaction was correlated $-.38$ ($p<.05$) during rest with the hand minus ankle skin resistance index in Sample 2. It also showed a variety of borderline correlations in the same direction (for example, $r=-.24$, $p<.20$ during determination of touch threshold on breast). In Sample 3 masturbation satisfaction showed such correlations as the following with the skin resistance of the hand minus the skin resistance of the ankle: $r=-.28$, $p<.10$, grand means of all sessions; $r=-.28$, $p<.10$, all stress sessions; $r=-.34$, $p<.05$, during breast stroking; $r=-.31$, $p<.05$, during rest. It should be added that comparisons of upper and lower body sectors based on the temperature of the hand minus that of the ankle do not correlate significantly with masturbation satisfaction.

27. Masturbation frequency correlated $-.38$ ($p<.025$) with light touch threshold in Sample 2 and $-.27$ ($p<.10$) in Sample 3. The relationship in Sample 4 was not significant.

28. Masturbation satisfaction was correlated $-.43$ ($p<.01$) with touch threshold in Sample 2 and had a relationship with it in the same direction in Sample 3 ($x^2=4.7$, $df=1$, $p<.05$). The relationship for Sample 4 was not significant.

29. Masturbation frequency was positively correlated with reported persistence of tickle in Sample 2 ($r=.46$, $p<.10$, cheek) and Sample 3 ($r=.69$, $p<.001$, average of all parts tickled). These two variables were not, however, significantly linked in Samples 4 and 5.

30. Masturbation frequency was positively correlated with reported persistence of tickle in Sample 2 ($r=.45$, $p<.025$, cheek) and Sample 3 ($r=.36$, $p<.025$, average of all parts tickled). The two variables were not significantly related in Samples 4 and 5.

31. The masturbation indices were not significantly correlated with a few measures of guilt that were obtained.

32. This may have pertinence to the Kinsey, et al. (1953) observation that

amount of masturbation is positively correlated with education both premaritally and during marriage. If one thinks of the woman with the higher educational level as more interested in learning about, and exploring, multiple aspects of the world, one could regard her greater amount of masturbatory behavior as partially reflecting this orientation.

Apropos of the concept of seeking new experience, one should also note that Maslow (1942) found that women who were "masturbators" had had sexual intercourse with a wider range of men than had "nonmasturbators." Incidentally, Maslow also found that "masturbators" had higher levels of self-esteem (more "dominance-feeling") than "nonmasturbators."

13

MENSTRUATION, PREGNANCY, AND CONTRACEPTION

This chapter embraces several topics that concern the reproductive functions of women. The critical question that is pursued is whether a woman's sexual behavior is related in any way to her psychological adaptation to her reproductive capacities. One version of this question would be to ask whether women differing in orgasm consistency show logically related differences in how they experience menstruation or the manner in which they react to the whole process of containing the growing fetus. Another important matter that is considered concerns whether a woman's mode of adaptation to her reproductive functions can be related in any way to her personality characteristics. For example, is the woman who experiences menstruation as painful or who develops great anxiety during pregnancy less feminine than one who has no such difficulties? As described in earlier review chapters, a considerable superstructure of theory and speculation has grown up about such questions. There is an influential, half-accepted "scientific" folklore that would portray women as consistent in how they deal with their sexual and reproductive capacities. It is widely accepted in some circles (for example, psychoanalytic theorists) that a woman who is disturbed about her sex role will have menstrual difficulties and probably cope poorly with the demands of pregnancy. A woman who reports an unusual amount of menstrual pain automatically becomes suspect as a carrier of serious sexual conflicts. Considerable opportunity was provided the writer in the course of studying the various samples to gather information bearing on issues of this sort. The women were asked to give detailed data concerning their menstrual patterns and several studies were performed in which psychological measures were obtained on the same women during both menstrual and nonmenstrual phases. Also, it will be recalled that one sample of women was studied during pregnancy and again a month after delivery. The menstrual and pregnancy measures that were secured included not only an array of objective tests but also personal accounts of feelings and fantasies.

A concise overview of what came out of these inquiries follows.

Menstruation

Two sources of information were available concerning the menstrual behavior and attitudes of the women who were investigated. One was based on their replies to a number of questions that variously inquired concerning amount of menstrual pain, mood changes associated with menstruation, degree of menstrual irregularity, and duration of menstrual flow.[1]

A second source was provided by measures taken in three samples of various psychological dimensions during menstruation as well as at other times, either before or after menstruation. These measures made it possible to ascertain whether menstruation alters particular aspects of psychological functioning.

It would be well to begin by defining the norm or typical menstrual experiences across the samples. One can see in Table 13–1 that the average woman in the various samples did not find menstruation to be a very disturbing experience. She reported only mild pain that usually dissipates in about 15 to 16 hours, and she indicated experiencing only mild to moderate change in her mood.[2] She also indicated that her onset of menstrual flow is highly regular, typically varying only a few days from the expected date.[3]

TABLE 13-1
Self-Reports Concerning Menstrual Experiences

	Sample 1		Sample 2		Sample 3		Sample 4		Sample 5		Sample 6		Sample 7	
	M	σ	M	σ	M	σ	M	σ	M	σ	M	σ	M	σ
Length of cycle—days	28.7	2.6	29.8	4.1	29.2	3.0	30.5	5.7	27.4	5.0	31.3	11.3		
Degree of regularity (1 = regular)	2.8	.8	1.9	.8	1.9	.7	1.9	.8	1.6	.6	2.0	.8		
Number of days of flow	a		5.0	1.4	5.4	1.6	5.2	1.0	4.9	1.0	5.0	1.3		
Degree of pain (1 = none)			1.9	.9	2.2	.8	2.5	1.1	2.1	.9	2.5	1.1		
Duration of pain (hours)			15.8	17.8			18.9	21.3	17.3	16.3				
Weight fluctuation (pounds)			2.7	1.6			3.0	1.7	3.2	1.8				
Mood change (1 = none)			2.3	.7	2.5	.9	2.6	.8	2.4	.6	2.5	.9		
Age of menarche	12.2	1.3	12.4	1.2	12.3	1.2	12.6	1.3	12.1	1.2	12.6	1.4	12.3	1.(
Woman's reaction to first menses (1 = happy)	3.0	1.1	2.9	1.0	2.4	1.1			2.6	1.0	2.3	1.1	2.3	1.
Mother's reaction to first menses (1 = happy)	2.9	.7	2.6	.7	2.3	.7			2.4	.6	2.4	.8	2.4	.
Father's reaction to first menses (1 = happy)					2.9	.4			2.8	.5	2.8	.5	2.9	.

aWhere values are not presented for a particular sample it is because the pertinent question was not asked in that sample.

The women in Sample 2 were asked to write a personalized account of how they actually experienced the onset of menstruation. They were instructed: Describe briefly what feelings, body sensations, and thoughts you had with the start of your present menstrual period.

They were asked to write their descriptions within a day after the onset of their period. A number of representative excerpts are presented in order to illustrate the wide range of reactions and to point up how relatively well adapted most of the women are to the menstrual events.

Excerpt 1

I felt quite normal. I knew the day it was expected and it simply came. The only thought I had was that I'm almost out of Tampax and I don't like spending the money on something as unexciting as that.

Excerpt 2

A day or two prior to my period, I begin to wonder "when" and feel a little insecure because my period will start at any time of day or night without warning and I will just gush forth. This particular period there was relatively no increase in nervous tension. In fact I felt marvelous.

The day prior to the start of my period . . . and the first day of my period there was a great desire for sexual relations on my part—I would say unusual for me, and would attribute this to my general attitude of feeling well, healthy, and happy.

Excerpt 3

Although I usually get some slight advance warning, such as fatigue the day before, this time it came on suddenly (which has also happened before). The first day I was slightly fatigued and had a mild headache part of the day. After the first day I practically never feel anything at all.

Excerpt 4

No body sensations other than slight cramps. I thought that another month had gone by and I'm not pregnant!

Excerpt 5

My period started yesterday and I knew it had started because of a feeling of slight pressure. Because I had planned a trip for the time when I normally expect my period, I delayed my period by taking a contraceptive pill for three additional days. I did worry a little about this tactic and wondered if it would have any effect on my period. I didn't expect to delay it till after I returned home. My feelings during my period are the same as any other time. My husband says he cannot tell from my emotional state whether I am menstruating or not.

Excerpt 6

Except for a few stomach cramps I believe I felt the same—. I guess I have a secret desire to be pregnant again. Each month I hope I don't get my period for that reason. It's funny when you think that I take the pills every month faithfully. My period is so slight that it hardly alters my life at all and that is fine with me.

Excerpt 7

I felt like my body wanted me to calm down. Like all my energies slowed down. I've never had cramps or pain. I become quite emotional and tears flow easily at the slightest wrong word or confusion. I compose myself but keep it all inside for a while. I feel a tingling sensation in my thighs in the beginning and become quite bloated and I retain my fluids (like my eyelids, hands), once in a while in my ankles. I sometimes feel like being completely alone, away from noise, people, phones, and everyone's problems. Once I got one strange sharp pain like a nerve was being pinched through my ovaries. Like a needle pushed through.

Excerpt 8

I have absolutely no physical feelings with it but I was very glad that it was here because it means I'm not pregnant. I just couldn't handle having a child right now. I guess I feel happier than usual because of this. I'm usually rather depressed but this time it seems as though a great weight had been lifted from my shoulders.

Excerpt 9

I had gone shopping—when I arrived home I discovered I had begun to menstruate. I was not at all uncomfortable—I had felt extremely tired—that day and the day before. Other than that, I didn't notice any physical change. My moods shift easily at this time—yet I wouldn't say I am depressed. At times I feel edgy!

Excerpt 10

1. Once again I was glad that I wasn't pregnant.
2. Wish it would have waited one more day because my husband got back *that* day.
3. More relaxed feeling.
4. First couple of days, I feel the world could fall apart and I wouldn't care.
5. Sometimes I feel my bottom is so heavy that it is going to drop off.
6. Smell sometimes bothers me.
7. Wish I could take a bath morning, noon, and evening.
8. Always feel like I am getting cleaned out.

Excerpt 11

I felt extremely large and heavy. My stomach was very puffy and had a slight amount of stomach cramps and backache. I was relieved when I got my period to know I was safe for one more month, but was also rather disgusted with the whole ordeal. As a matter of fact I dread it. Again I was relieved to have it end and start taking pills again.

Excerpt 12

First reaction that it was exactly on time—as usual—which amazes me how regular the human body can be. It meant relief from the stuffy feeling that I have about two–three days prior to its onset.

Excerpt 13

The first day brought slight cramps and a mild backache. Aspirin and a night's rest completely eliminated these symptoms. It is usual to feel "steamy" in the early stage of a period.

This time I felt an extreme fullness as if the flow would be excessive. It is not. The "fullness" included thighs, as well as abdomen. There was also an excessively warm feeling that usually accompanies the feeling of fullness. This is not synonymous with "bloat."

Thoughts were exhilarating, satisfying; much work accomplished—assignments successful.

Excerpt 14

I had little reaction and a very slight flow. The experience was hardly noticeable except that my breasts were slightly swollen and sore.

Excerpt 15

My back hurt slightly in the small of it. I get a little happier at the beginning because I suppose it is cleaning me out and I feel this more than some people. Sexually I am more aroused and more easily.

The range of reactions to menstruation is striking. One woman barely notices it, for another it signifies the passage of an additional month in which she did not get pregnant. But for still another woman it brings disappointment at not having achieved pregnancy. We find too that some women are primarily concerned about the inconvenience menstruation introduces by interfering with intercourse. There are others who perceive menstruation largely in terms of it being an unexpected event that can cause embarrassment and arouse disgust. It is further interesting that some women are particularly taken with a sense of being cleansed or "cleaned out" by the menstrual process. In general, the data suggest that the average woman studied reacts to menstruation as a well routinized event that causes her some pain and inconvenience, but not a great deal. This is not to deny that there were some extreme cases in which pain and other complaints were quite severe; but even in such instances one is impressed with the acceptance and adaptation that have occurred.[4] The apparent limited impact of menstruation upon the average woman in the samples studied was reaffirmed by the findings that came from comparing scores obtained during menstruation and at other times (before or after menstruation). The following variables were examined during menstrual and nonmenstrual phases: body-boundary definiteness (Barrier); light-touch threshold; general amount of body awareness (Body Prominence); number and types of distortions in body experience (Body Distortion Questionnaire); response to tickle; amount of oral, sexual, and hostile content in inkblot images; amount of oral and hostile content in word constructions; accuracy in making spatial judgments in the dark (Rod and Frame task). After examining the array of results, one must conclude that no menstrual versus nonmenstrual differences were significantly and consistently demonstrated. It was remarkable how similar were the menstrual and nonmenstrual scores.[5]

Without reservation, it can be said that there is little, if any, relationship between a woman's sexual response attributes and her *mode* of experiencing menstruation. The measures of menstrual discomfort (for example, pain, mood change) or irregularity were not reliably related to such sexual indices as orgasm consistency or intercourse frequency. They were also not related to how unsatisfied, tired, tense, guilty, embarrassed, strange, or excited a woman feels during and after orgasm. Furthermore, they were not linked to how much a woman prefers clitoral versus vaginal stimulation, the intensity of her orgasms, her degree of satisfaction from masturbation, the degree to which she favors freedom in sexual behavior, or any of the other sexual indices. It would appear that the manner in which the women respond sexually and feel about sexuality is not predictive of their menstrual discomfort or irregularity. A highly sexually responsive woman seems to have the same probability of finding menstruation painful or irregular as does the woman who is very unresponsive sexually. Interestingly, menstrual discomfort and irregularity were found not to be related to how disturbing a woman recalls her first menstruation to have been to herself or to her parents. They were also unrelated to the way in which she acquired her early knowledge about sex or her recall of how permissive her parents were about sexual matters.

Much information was, of course, available that permitted an evaluation of whether the nature of a woman's menstrual experiences is linked to her personality attributes. However, despite the fact that a formidable battery of personality measures was employed that sampled behavior at several levels, not a single consistent correlation could be established between menstrual discomfort and personality. Women differing in amount of menstrual discomfort did not differ with respect to such dimensions as degree of femininity, aggressiveness, sociability, passivity, guilt, masochism, and anxiety about sexual themes. It was especially noteworthy that menstrual discomfort was unrelated to measures of anxiety and personal disturbance.[6] The woman who usually operates at a high level of anxiety or tension is not the one most likely to feel pain and mood changes during menstruation. There was also no apparent connection between menstrual discomfort and the attributes she ascribed to her parents.

It will be recalled that in an earlier chapter it was concluded that there was more evidence that menstrual irregularity is linked with personal disturbance than is menstrual discomfort. However, the present results failed to support this view. Menstrual irregularity was not consistently correlated with the various measures of anxiety and disturbance (for example, anxiety ratings by laboratory personnel) which had been obtained.[7] The failure to find a link between menstrual irregularity and any of the psychological measures in the writer's studies therefore contradicts the previous trend in the literature. As already noted, this may be because of the rather limited range of amenorrhea in the samples of women studied, or it may be because of some defect in the methodology of the studies that is not readily apparent. Or it may represent the more stringent demand of the studies that the same results be duplicated over successive studies.

Overview of Menstrual Experience

The results that have been outlined can be succinctly coded into the generalization that the amount of menstrual discomfort and irregularity that a woman experiences bears no relationship to her sexual responsiveness, sexual attitudes, personality traits, or level of anxiety.[8] However, one must immediately introduce the modifying statement that this seems to be true within the limitation of the narrow range of menstrual disturbance found among the samples of married women that were studied. Possibly women who represent more extreme examples of menstrual discomfort or irregularity might be found to be characterized by special sexual or personality attributes.[9] This possibility does not detract from the value of knowing that the variations in menstrual experience that occur within a circumscribed "normal" range are not linked with sexual or personality or "mental health" variables. The generally negative findings of the present studies must be given special weight because they are based on rather unique *multiple* samples. Most, if not all, of previous studies in this area have been based on one, or at the most two, samples. The present studies have asked the question whether there are relationships pertinent to menstrual experience that will show themselves in repeated trials. A negative reply has presented itself.

Despite the logical appeal of the idea that because menstruation is a function of a woman's reproductive system and sexual behavior makes use of parts of the sexual anatomy they should be interrelated, the fact remains that such a proposition has been extremely difficult to defend scientifically. Perhaps this is not surprising if one considers that the present studies have shown that even different aspects of sexual behavior that might logically have been thought to be linked (for example, orgasm consistency and intercourse frequency) have turned out to be correlated at only a chance level.

Pregnancy

The writer concluded in an earlier chapter that it has not been shown that women are *generally* more upset during pregnancy than when they are nonpregnant. There also seemed to be no consistent proof that any one phase of pregnancy is more disturbing to the woman than any other. Some reasonable evidence did emerge that in the *immediate postdelivery period* women feel less anxious and more secure than they do during pregnancy. However, even this trend seemed to be contradicted by the fact that there is an unusual frequency of psychosis in the postpartum period. An opportunity to find out more about such phenomena was afforded by a study that the writer conducted in Sample 6 for which the women were recruited by an advertisement placed in the Syracuse University student newspaper.[10] The advertisement offered a sum of money to pregnant women who would participate in a project that would involve their coming to the laboratory both during pregnancy and a month following delivery. The women finally recruited proved to be very similar in their social attributes and sexual behavior to the nonpregnant women in the other samples. As described in Appendix F, each woman responded to a number of procedures and tests both during and after pregnancy.[11] These procedures were largely designed to evaluate whether there are shifts in the content of fantasy, perception of one's own body, and degree of preoccupation with specific need themes from the pregnant to the nonpregnant state. They variously included the Holtzman, et al. (1961) inkblots, the Fisher (1970) Body Distortion Questionnaire, a measure of general body awareness (Body Prominence), and a word construction task (Appendix F), which was scored in terms of the numbers of oral (food), hostile, and sexual themes elicited. It was found that of the multiple change scores examined, only two were statistically significant. The Barrier score, which measures how well differentiated and protective a woman perceives her body boundary to be, *declined* significantly from the pregnant to nonpregnant state.[12] Furthermore, the total number of distortions in body feelings (for example, depersonalization, feeling dirty, strange skin sensations) declined significantly from the pregnant to the nonpregnant state.[13] There were no real changes in number of inkblot references to sex, hostility, orality, or masculine as compared to feminine figures. Also, there were no shifts in the general amount of body awareness (as indicated by Body Prominence) or in the number of word construction references to orality, hostility, and sex. The fact that there was a significant decline in the total number of distorted body experiences suggests that a woman does, indeed, feel more comfortable about her body one month postpartum than she does while she is pregnant. She perceives fewer events in her body that strike her as alien or strange. It was a bit puzzling to find, in apparent contradiction to this result, that the women experienced their body boundaries as less clearly defined post than during pregnancy. This would apparently imply a decline in body security, and the writer would have interpreted it in just such a fashion. However, it should be noted that in a previous study, Edward (1969) also found a decline in Barrier when he evaluated women during and shortly after pregnancy. Edward proposed that this decline might simply represent the fact that once a woman's body has ejected the fetus it is no longer the special protective container that it was. Its emphatic function in providing protective boundaries for the fetus has lapsed, and this sudden lapse may register as a feeling that one's boundaries are no longer as sharply defined as they once were. This is an interesting speculation. It is pertinent to add at this point that when the various scores of the pregnant women were compared to those of similar samples of nonpregnant women, not a single score consistently differentiated the two groups.[14] Measures of personality, aggression, feelings of personal stability, interest in new experience, repressive tendencies, and diverse other factors did not distinguish the pregnant women. What is particularly surprising is that the pregnant women did not differ from the nonpregnant women in the general amount of body awareness and number or specific categories of distorted body experience. Apparently the gross body changes produced during pregnancy do not produce significant disturbance in the body scheme of the average woman. She seems to adapt to these changes sufficiently so that they do not appear to be alien or strange. In fact, her adaptation seems to be so complete that her *general level* of awareness of her body does not exceed that of the nonpregnant woman!

The results of the present study conform to many previous reports indicating that pregnant women are not readily distinguishable from nonpregnant women in terms of their psychological states. Such results place an even greater burden of proof upon those who have speculated that pregnancy is a time of unique psychological turmoil and preoccupation with special conflicts. One finding that invites comment is the decline in the Total Body Distortion score from the pregnancy to the postpartum phase. This shift, which indicates a decrease in disturbed body experience, seems to be superficially logical in terms of the idea that the woman's body in the postpartum phase becomes more like her normal body. But one must remember that the average Total Body Distortion score in the pregnant phase, although high, was not significantly greater than that found in other comparable nonpregnant women. In other words, the postpartum phase reduced the amount of body experience distortion to a point where it was *less than normally observed.*[15] Actually, when the postpartum Total Distortion score was compared with those in two other samples of nonpregnant women, it was found to be significantly lower than both. What this suggests is that the immediate postpartum period may, because of its abrupt and novel contrast with the preceding nine months, induce quite special (even "supernormal") feeling states. However, one would speculate that this contrast effect soon dissipates and that retest several months later would reveal no differences from the "normal" state. It was suggested by the writer in an earlier chapter that this very process of abrupt change, even when it is in a positive direction, may introduce instabilities that have something to do with the upsurge of psychosis in postpartum women.[16]

The Delivery Experience

In any analysis of the changes that occur in a woman as she moves from the pregnant to the postpartum state, one must give thought to the effects of the delivery experience itself. How great is the impact upon a woman of what happens to her during the time that her child is being born? One finds that almost nothing is actually known about what happens psychologically in the course of this process. Although various observers have described in general terms the nature of the woman's experiences during delivery, little is available in the literature concerning how she actually *feels* and *personally witnesses* it all. Special attention is devoted to this matter because it is the writer's view that insufficient recognition has been given to the real proportions of the adaptation it requires from the average woman, and, therefore, insufficient recognition has been given to the role of the delivery experience in subsequent vulnerability to serious psychological regression (such as is exemplified by postpartum psychosis).[17]

It was with the intent of finding out more about the psychological impact of the delivery experience that the writer asked each of the pregnant women who constituted Sample 6 to write a detailed account of her delivery as soon as possible after the event. The actual instructions to her were as follows:

As soon as possible after your delivery write several pages in which you describe your experience. Describe in detail the emotions and body sensations you experienced and also the thoughts and images that passed through your mind.

She was to bring her account of the delivery when she returned to the laboratory for reevaluation one month subsequent to delivery. These accounts proved to be frank and detailed. They provide a rare first-person perspective that really brings home the astonishing vicissitudes of the delivery process. Segments of a representative series are now presented.

Excerpt 1

My feelings were immense relief—finally after all these months I was going to have the baby. I prayed that it would be healthy, perfect and beautiful. I knew the percentage of women having deformed or retarded children wasn't really that large, but nevertheless I was worried that maybe something had gone wrong. Also, since my cramps still weren't very painful, I believe I more than half convinced myself that I'd be one of the few with a very easy and painless labor and delivery. This being my first baby, I was unprepared for everything. . . . The nurses were very nice and helped me to relax. I had thought I'd be terribly embarrassed knowing I would have to be shaved and receive an enema—but realized at the time that this was just a job to the nurses and that there really was no need to be self-conscious. . . . The doctor came in and asked me how the pain was. I'll never forget how I felt when the nurse said that my pains hadn't been too bad yet! I thought I was in agony! From about 9:00 P.M. till about 7:30 A.M. that day, I found out that the nurse's remarks were true. I never, never imagined that it would be possible to feel such pain. All I thought about and wanted was the spinal. I could imagine how an addict must feel when he needed a fix. I had been so determined not to yell—but the last three hours—I couldn't care less. I just wanted the shot, wanted someone to help, something that would take the pain away. I remembered the stories of how women said they hated their husbands or hated the baby. I kept thinking that I wouldn't be like that—and even though the pain was unbearable I still was glad about the baby. I really couldn't understand how anyone could blame it on their husbands—after all, I'm sure—even if he'll admit it that he was worried to death. All I wanted was that shot—I kept praying that they'd give it to me. The nurse kept telling me to bear down and not waste the pain—I wondered how many children she had and if she had ever gone through it. Finally my water broke—and they took me into the delivery room.

Excerpt 2

I was put in a room with two beds separated by a canvas partition. There was a patient in the other bed but she was very quiet. There was also a patient in the labor room across the hall. She was moaning and yelling and I was a little frightened by the sounds she made, but more than that I felt disgusted at her behavior. I told myself that I was not going to behave like that no matter how bad the pains got. During my pregnancy I dreaded the shave prep and enema that I knew I must have in the labor room. However, it was all done so quickly and efficiently that I didn't mind it at all. After a while my pains grew stronger and seemed to be lasting longer. I was given a shot that relaxed me and although each pain seemed unbearable, I knew it would soon go away and I was able to relax and almost sleep in between pains. A doctor came in every once in a while and gave me a rectal examination. This was very painful and I asked him to wait until my contraction passed, but he said he couldn't. When my doctor came in to examine me I felt very relieved to see him. I felt less afraid and was willing to do whatever he said. At this point my doctor and a nurse had me bear down with each contraction. I had to do this about four times and I cried because the pain was so great. They kept making me push and coaxing me and I prayed that it would soon be over. The nurse said she could see my baby and if I would push once more they would take me into the delivery room. The pain seemed constant now, never letting up. I lifted myself onto the operating table and rolled on my side for the anesthesiologist to inject the saddle block into my spine. I waited what seemed a long time but could feel no needle going in me. My doctor told me later the anesthesiologist couldn't get the needle in and that this sometimes happened. I was rolled over and my legs were tied to two bars at the end of the bed. I wanted to push now. The pain made me want to bear down but the nurses told me not to push. I was told to take deep breaths, but this was very difficult; then I was told to pant. I was extremely frightened at this time. A gas mask was put over my nose and mouth and I wanted to pass out. I remember thinking, "I must be dying. If I am I'll just have to die because I can't stand it any longer." The gas gave me the effect of being suspended somewhere—not really alive. I could hear deep long moans and I realized they must be coming from me, but I wasn't aware that I was moaning. I had no more pain. I could feel the baby coming out and I felt it stretching me. I had an impulse to close my legs but I couldn't. The next thing I remember is opening my eyes and hearing a baby cry.

Excerpt 3

I was prepared by my nurse and then my doctor came to examine me. My bag of waters needed to be punctured, so that was my first strange sensation. By that time, lying on my back was very painful, and I found it difficult to concentrate on anything but that each time that it became a necessity. But when my bag of waters was broken my attention was diverted. The puncture itself was somewhat painful, but flow of the warm fluids soothed the pain and felt very good. I am so conditioned to disposing my fluids into the toilet that I felt very strange about lying in a pool of wetness. Later on in the day I had the same feeling when I was unable to control myself and urinated during a contraction. There were so many more important things to think about!

At any rate, the day seemed to be progressing well—I did my breathing exercises and stayed calm during contractions—until the early afternoon. Some time between one and two o'clock the pain started to become unbearable and my cool exterior little by little became undone. Doing the breathing exercises became a chore, and at best I could only do them incorrectly. I wanted very badly to succeed in keeping my head; I didn't want to be a coward. Most of this was because my husband was taking it very hard. I wanted to have him there but not for the purpose of torturing him. Sometime during the afternoon, I am told that I became delirious, failing to recognize people and making little sense when I spoke. I was penetrated twice by hypodermic needles for the pain, had a catheter between my legs, had an intravenous in my hand, was carried off to be X-rayed once, and later in the afternoon had an oxygen mask over my face.

Excerpt 4

In the wheelchair at the hospital I lost some more water, but not as much as it felt like; I had visions of a water trail behind me and was a little embarrassed about that. . . . I changed into the hospital gown, was "prepped" and then checked rectally—which caused more water to gurgle out. The contractions were still mild. . . .

I had taken classes that taught the proper breathing for labor, so I began to

breathe with contractions just for practice. . . . The doctor tried to check me
. . . but my uterus would not cooperate and contract. He wanted to break the
water bag more thoroughly, but could not do it without a contraction. He was
a jovial doctor, and after holding his finger in my vagina for about five minutes
he said his hand was getting tired. He finally gave up, and he told my husband
in the waiting room to go home because I was just "piddling around."

. . . The contractions began to hurt along the whole lower part of the uterus,
as for very strong cramps. I began shallow breathing to relieve the pain. The
contractions didn't seem right to me. They hit hard and suddenly, rather than
the buildup I had experienced before. Also, I knew them by the lower pain
only; my stomach felt flabby and loose to my mind. . . . I was too busy
"breathing" to talk to the nurse, but I wasn't good enough at it to look relaxed
or comfortable. The pressure rectally and even more so along the front ridge
under my stomach became almost unbearable. I felt like crying that I couldn't
stand any more and live, but I kept panting and made no noise. (I was also
feeling proud that I could at least keep silent.) . . . The doctor arrived in the
labor room on time, just barely. I was beginning to lose control of myself.
When I was told to sit up for my spinal, I remember whimpering and draping
myself like a doll over the nurse.

What heavenly relief with the spinal! The doctor (I think) used a tool to
turn the baby before he came out. He had been face up in labor (a more painful
position for me.) Then out he came, and the doctor got him to cry before
plopping him on my stomach. There was a thud of disappointment that it was
another boy, and I didn't feel as related to him as I wanted to.

Excerpt 5

During the night I was examined by doctors several times, until I finally
asked them to examine me rectally instead of vaginally, which had become increasingly painful. Labor progressed, but not well enough, so the doctor broke
the membranes and some water trickled out. This was not at all painful, and I
was continually thankful that he explained everything he was doing and had to
do as he went along. This process appeared to stimulate dilation and soon my
contractions were every minute or so and exceptionally intense. I have never
felt such agonizing pain, and whether it was because I was so tired by this time
or because I have a low pain threshold, I began to scream with the severe contractions. I tried to remember how to breathe properly but breathing didn't
seem to help. The nurse looked very disapproving and even went next door to
explain to the woman laboring there that this was my first baby and I was
frightened. I couldn't believe that she was apologizing for me, and I was just
steamed and then angry, especially since she didn't try to help me by telling
me how to breathe or position myself. The doctor said nothing, just kept his
hand on my uterus and encouraged me by his presence. Unfortunately, I was the
only one in real labor at this point, and my husband could hear me in the waiting room. . . .

Then suddenly I moved into the second stage of labor and felt an overwhelming desire to push. The sharp searing pains of my earlier contractions
gave way to great rolling motions of my uterus that caused me to groan as I
exhaled. I remember finding it difficult to catch my breath and being conscious
of the tremendous effort I was exerting to push, but being relieved that these
contractions *were* endurable. In fact, compared to the end of the first stage of
labor, they were actually relaxing. After a great deal of supervised pushing I
was transferred to a stretcher and taken to the delivery room and given a saddle block.

Excerpt 6

Once at the hospital, I was taken directly up to the labor room; my husband accompanied me as far as he could and then waited. I was put into a labor room and given a gown. My pulse, blood pressure, etc. was taken. After this my husband came in to see. As he came in a contraction was just reaching its peak and I could not speak, except in a hoarse whisper. My husband looked absolutely miserable and helpless. I assured him I was alright and he should leave as there wasn't anything he could do. I thought it silly to make him suffer with me, especially when I knew I was capable of taking care of myself. After he left I thought that despite all I had read, no one was really prepared to have a baby.

The nurse came in to shave my pubic hair. She was a jolly, very patient woman. She kept me from constantly thinking about the pain by talking and even joking a bit. Also, she explained the things she did.

Being shaved was very unpleasant; the warm water was nice and the razor didn't pull. It was rather odd to feel the hair be shaved in such an unusual area, but it seemed rather relaxing. When finished the nurse left. . . .

The time seemed interminable. Nothing would alleviate the pain and I thought that I hadn't expected or desired this much agony, even though I did want a baby. The nurse then proceeded to give me an enema, which was a new, most unpleasant experience. I was prepared for the tube in my rectum, but not for the bloated feeling when the water was forced in. This feeling of fullness increased my pain. I felt absolutely miserable and yet I had to sit on a bedpan to wait on my intestines to empty. Soon the first rush came; it felt like it was just falling out uncontrollably. I found this to be very unpleasant; however, the movements were tolerable, although the pains were not. If anything they seemed worse and were not relievable. I kept my attention focused on the clock as much as possible and when the time was up (the nurse had said it would take about ten minutes) I buzzed for the nurse. Just as she came in I started again, which made me feel embarrassed, but she waited calmly until I was through. Then she cleaned me up; I felt sorry for nurses, as I could never stomach having to do such things. Next, she poured some blue, sterile solution over my genital area warning me it would feel cold; however, my body was shocked and jerked a little.

Soon after this my doctor came in. I immediately felt relieved and secure; I knew he would help me. At this time I became only half aware of those around me and more aware of the pain. I found it more difficult to breathe and I wanted to scream. I started moaning loudly and holding my breath and tightening up. My doctor calmed me, telling me to breathe deeply. I did the best I could, for I wanted to make my delivery as easy as possible.

Next I remember seeing the nurse hand my doctor a long piece of metal similar to the dipstick used in a car. With it he broke my water, which spurted out forcefully causing everyone to jump back. At this time I noticed the young intern standing at the end of the bed. He was watching me very intently. Our eyes met and we stared at each other for several moments. I felt very strange about him. He appeared to be very curious, yet empathetic and slightly frightened. It is difficult to explain; it seemed he was interested in me, yet aloof.

The pain was now unbearable. I asked my doctor if he could make the pain stop. He said I was going through the worst part, going to the second stage, and that surprisingly things would get better. However, I could not be placated and again asked him to make the pain stop. My doctor now told me to hold my breath and push as hard as I could and that I would be given a shot to ease the pain. I did so, but trying to take a breath seemed to tear me apart. The nurse gave me a shot in the buttocks. I asked how long it would be before the pain would ease and she told me it would take effect in about 15 minutes, but I would deliver before then. I resigned myself to the fact that the pain would not stop.

Excerpt 7

The pains started to get very strong. I was in real pain and all of a sudden for the first time I got scared. I knew I was just starting my labor and I couldn't imagine my pains getting any worse. I began to grab on to the sheets as hard as I could, I tried different positions but whatever I did just seemed to make it worse. Finally I pulled myself together after about 30 minutes of twisting and turning. I was once a technician in a program where I learned the importance of lying as still as possible and trying to relax between and during contractions. So I made up my mind I was going to do it and I was very successful. All I thought about, all I concentrated on was totally relaxing. I wouldn't even allow myself to clench my fist a little. Toward the end of my labor the pain got so bad I felt my entire body was going to explode any second. When I felt a pain starting I would slowly count to myself. I would tell myself by the time I got to 10 the pain would be gone. It seemed to help me a little.

At around 6:30 P.M. they told me to start pushing. From then on everything was very easy. Because I relaxed through my labor I had plenty of strength left for pushing. I had the baby's head down in 20 minutes. They brought me into the delivery room where I had a "natural child birth" (this is what I wanted). From the time they brought me into the delivery room until the time I delivered my baby I felt nothing but complete happiness because I knew the baby was going to be born any minute. . . .

Excerpt 8

I was definitely aware of some kind of inexpressible physical change, but in order to prevent becoming unduly excited and to keep from getting my hopes up for naught, I continued to dismiss the pains as insignificant. . . .

By this time I was feeling quite lightheaded and very emotional, not really frightened but overawed in anticipation of the monumental event that really did seem on the very brink of occurring now. For a moment I was afraid I would cry, but in the great concentration that was required of me from then on I completely forgot this fear. I was wheeled into a rather stark room, the labor room, containing only a bed and a strange clock that was numbered from one to 15 and that, I decided, must be for timing contractions. A nurse . . . told me to get undressed and into a gown. My whole being felt numb and unreal except for my abdomen and insides. Nothing of me existed except for the pains. From this point on everything had a dreamlike quality. I undressed very awkwardly and gingerly. The nurse listed all of my clothing and possessions on a piece of paper. We discovered that my purse was missing. I couldn't remember whether I'd left it downstairs or in the car. The nurse said they'd call down and have my husband look for it. The missing purse continued to bother me until my husband later told me that he had found it. I was told to lie on the bed where I was shaved. . . . Blood pressure was taken frequently from this time until after the birth of the baby. A couple of other nurses were in and out. I was given an enema and sent to the adjoining ladies' room. On top of the labor pains the enema was a very unpleasant experience and I hated every minute of it. I could hear a woman groaning and even screaming somewhere nearby. I was determined not to scream or be cowardly in any way. I walked back to the bed and got onto it. A young, pretty nurse came in. She stayed with me until I went to the delivery room. She timed my pains and talked to me. The pains were very close together now. The nurse explained that soon I would begin to feel like pushing and to tell her when so that she could help me.

Excerpt 9

The sensations during labor were varied. At times I felt like there was ice on the outsides of my thighs. My body really felt like it was no longer a part of me—I felt somehow disconnected from my body. The "pains" were feelings of heat or fire in my lower back. I remember consciously counting and breathing deeply during each contraction so as to remain in control of myself. I wanted to remain "rational."

I had very few thoughts about the baby itself. I was more concerned that my husband didn't know what was happening.

The most fantastic part of the whole experience was toward the end when the urge to bear down begins. Your body *does* become something apart from you. The urge and the bearing down process is uncontrollable. I distinctly remember thinking during labor that the whole process was ridiculous and I certainly wouldn't be doing it again. It's amazing how this feeling leaves so quickly.

Excerpt 10

Labor pains were quite severe—I screamed with practically every contraction—I knew screaming wouldn't help the pain any but I still screamed. One nurse scolded me and right then and there I decided I disliked her immensely. I wanted it to be over with. I felt I couldn't take any more. At one time my entire body became numb—my skin prickled—my heart was racing and I felt I was floating in another world. I tried to talk but couldn't. I became frightened. I wanted my husband—I thought I was dying. Apparently I hyperventilated. After what seemed like an eternity I came out of it and I was quite relieved to find out I was still alive. It was the weirdest sensation I have ever felt in my entire 22 years.

Excerpt 11

As the nurse wheeled me down the hall to the labor rooms, all I could think of was that I didn't want to leave my husband. Once in the labor room I started to shake. I was slightly cold but I was really shaking uncontrollably. I admit I was a little nervous but I don't think I was that nervous. Because of this shaking the nurse had a hard time prepping me. All this time I didn't think the labor pains were that hard. After my enema I had to walk to the bathroom; once in there all I could hear was a woman in the next room yelling. This made me very mad because I think all that screaming is unnecessary, plus it seemed to make my pains seem worse. After I got back in bed my labor started to get bad. So I started to kick the guard rails on the bed. Like I said before I don't like screaming so I keep quiet and kick instead. I kicked for quite a while and was just about to ring for the nurse to get me something to help with the pain when she came in; but didn't seem to help. . . . When final stage labor started I was hoping that it wouldn't last too long because I didn't think I could take it without breaking down. Then the nurse came in and checked me, when she said it wouldn't be much longer. I was so relieved that the pain seemed more tolerable. Then all of a sudden I had to bear down and I knew the end was almost near. I knew I wasn't supposed to push so I rang for the nurse. After she checked me she looked at me and said, "Let's go." I was so happy and the labor seemed so short. . . . It seemed that the nurse was running me down the hall. I could feel the baby coming and all the pain didn't bother me. Next I remember the anesthesiologist coming, he was in a big hurry to get to me. The nurse wanted to check me again but she couldn't because the baby was already there. Then I started asking for my doctor, I was afraid he wasn't at the hospital yet. He was but he was still scrubbing up. I couldn't wait to get the spinal injection because then I knew I could relax and the baby would be born in a few minutes. The spinal took effect fast except for my right leg. It felt like the baby was pressing on a nerve in my leg, the top of my leg seemed cramped, I kept trying to rub it and I wasn't supposed to. So finally the nurse held my hand down. My body felt like it was gently rocking on the table as the doctor pulled out the baby. As I watched the doctor bring out the baby, I asked him what the baby was. He said, "Here, you can see for yourself." It was wonderful looking up and seeing your baby that had just been born. I was surprised to find that the baby was a girl. . . .

I was anxious to get to recovery so I could see my husband and the baby again. The thing I remember best in recovery was reaching down and feeling my stomach. It was so hollow I couldn't believe it. After visiting with my husband I kept falling asleep. But when I would wake up I kept thinking this must be a dream. It didn't seem possible that it was all over and that I had a beautiful baby girl.

An impressionistic analysis of all of the delivery protocols ($N = 37$) led the writer to the following classification of the typical problems faced during delivery.

1. A major problem is one that is often encountered by any hospital patient. This relates to being placed in a semipublic context where the usual standards of body modesty are abolished and frequent intrusions into one's body are made. The extent to which this occurs with the delivering woman is more extreme than usual because she is repeatedly called upon to expose her genitals, to allow fingers and instruments to be introduced into her vagina and rectum, and finally to be placed in the revealing (and psychologically vulnerable) delivery position (in stirrups) while she is conscious and often in the presence of others who are largely strangers.

2. Another major problem relates to pain. Not only does the average woman experience pain greater than that she has ever before encountered but it also usually persists for an extended period of time. This pain rapidly takes on intolerable intensity, and the woman begins to doubt that she can sustain it. She feels that it is "inhuman" for anyone to be expected to undergo such an experience. She becomes terribly angry about being expected to suffer so unreasonably. She is deeply impressed by the uncontrollable nature of her suffering. She knows there is no way of "turning off" the birth process once it has started. It should be added that she does know that drugs can relieve her, and is caught in the bind of wanting complete drug induced relief and yet knowing that sedation will be limited in order to facilitate the birth. Correlated with the experience of being confronted with inevitable pain one detects a special attitude toward time. Usual standards of time seem to dissolve. There is an overwhelming desire for time to pass instantaneously, but instead it has zero velocity. It becomes a malevolent force.

3. Another problem emphasized by the women in their descriptions is fear of loss of self-control. This fear is initially heightened by the enema

usually given after admission to the hospital, which produces sensations of being without a functioning anal sphincter. It creates sensations of fluids moving in and out of one's body without any way of regulating them. Other factors that contribute are the breaking of the amniotic sac that results in a gush of leakage, the muscle spasms that surge unpredictably through the body, the persisting unstoppable ("I can't do anything about it") nature of the pain, the occasional loss of bladder control, being surrounded by other women whose cries indicate that they are no longer able to contain their expressions of disturbance, hearing oneself moan and scream despite attempts to inhibit such behavior, reduced level of consciousness and ego stability resulting from drugs, fatigue, and weakness, and the sensation that body processes are occurring (particularly uterine contractions) that are too powerful to be regulated voluntarily.

4. Finally should be mentioned the build-up of anxiety about possibly sustaining serious injury or death. Few women involved in the painful delivery sequence do not entertain some fantasies that they will be grossly injured ("ripped") or suffer a complication that will be fatal. Relatedly, it is common to find fantasies that the child to be brought forth will be badly injured or deformed.

There is no question but that a woman is exposed to qualitatively unique and quantitatively intense stresses during the delivery experience. The delivery descriptions that were just presented testify to this convincingly. Is it possible that we have underestimated the seriousness of the damage that may be done to a woman's personality defenses and control as the result of the delivery demands? At the very least, they probably leave her unusually vulnerable to other stresses that may be encountered in the first week or two postdelivery.[18]

Relationships to Sexual Behavior

In accord with the major objective of this book, attention is now turned to the question whether there is any relationship between a woman's pattern of sexual behavior and the way she copes with her pregnancy experiences.[19] The data collected from Sample 6 offered the opportunity to examine this question. There were a number of prime indices that were computed for the pregnant women that depicted how disturbing they found pregnancy, delivery, and the postpartum period to be. One index, Pregnancy Discomfort, was based on a series of questions concerning how much pain, discomfort, and illness each woman indicated she encountered during her pregnancy.[20] A second index, Delivery Disturbance, summarized her reports of how disturbing the delivery experience had been.[21] A third index, Postdelivery Disturbance, portrayed how disturbed she felt one week following delivery.[22] Information was also obtained from each woman concerning amount of weight change during pregnancy, total length of labor, seriousness of any labor complications that developed, number of days spent in the hospital postdelivery, and number of days postdelivery required to feel "normal" again. There was also available the Total Body Distortion Questionnaire score indicating how disturbed a woman felt about her body experiences during pregnancy.[23]

How is orgasm consistency related to the measures just enumerated? It was found that the greater a woman's orgasm consistency the *greater* was her Total Pregnancy Discomfort ($r = .30$, p .05); but the fewer were the number of body image distortions she experienced during pregnancy ($r = -.32$, p .05), and the less the time she spent in the hospital after delivery ($r = -.28$, $p < .10$). There is inconsistency here, insofar as the greater a woman's orgasm consistency the less difficulty she had, as defined by number of body experience distortions during pregnancy and the amount of time she spent in the hospital postdelivery, but the more difficulty as computed in terms of anxiety, vomiting, fatigue, and pain experienced during the pregnancy. One of the immediate facts that this apparent inconsistency leads one to is that a woman's reports of how she fared during the various stages, proceeding from pregnancy through delivery to the postpartum period, do not show much in the way of consistent relationships with each other: A woman may report that she had no difficulty during pregnancy but did experience much disturbance during delivery as well as during the postpartum period.[24] Or she may report much delivery disturbance and little at any other phase. Or she may have many distortions in body perception during pregnancy but not a corresponding amount of anxiety or pain at the same time. The apparent independence of the reports about different phases of the pregnancy sequence may reflect the fact that each phase makes different kinds of demands upon a woman. For example, the actual period of pregnancy may for most women be a time in which they can be self-indulgent and dependent, whereas the time of delivery may represent a sudden traumatic period of stress in which her tolerance for pain and suffering is tested; the postpartum period may particularly call upon the ability to assimilate radical changes in self or to be nurturant. Since the findings involving orgasm consistency were based on only one sample, they must be regarded with caution. Similarly, one must also keep in mind that orgasm consistency was completely unrelated to quite a number of the measures of adaptation to various phases of the pregnancy process. The finding that the woman with the higher orgasm consistency is likely to experience the greater amount of disturbance during the pregnancy phase is hardly one that would have been predicted; just the opposite would have been unanimously anticipated among most theorists. It is difficult to conjure up a reasonable explanation for this finding. One is tempted, though, to offer a speculation that derives from the fact that orgasm consistency has been shown to be linked to degree of concern about loss of love objects. Is it possible that when the woman of low-orgasm consistency, who particularly has problems about object loss, finds herself pregnant, she derives reassurance from the fact that she suddenly possesses a new "love object" that is uniquely hers and uniquely under her control because it is contained within her body? The pregnancy phase, by providing this kind of special reassurance to her, might make her feel unusually comfortable and stable.

An examination of the correlates of intercourse frequency in Sample 6 indicated that it had only chance correlations with all of the prime indices of disturbance during the various phases of the pregnancy process.

Similarly, the degree to which a woman prefers clitoral versus vaginal stimulation was unrelated to the pregnancy measures.

Several interesting links were observed between the pregnancy indices and how a woman feels shortly after orgasm. It will be recalled that each woman who was studied was asked to put in rank order ten terms descriptive of how she feels at the time of orgasm and another ten terms with reference to her feelings five minutes after orgasm.[25] One of the prime dimensions that was examined with this procedure was how *satisfied* each woman is during and after orgasm. She expressed her degree of satisfaction by the rank she assigned to the term Unsatisfied (in each of the two arrays of ten terms). Although amount of satisfaction during orgasm was not correlated with any of the pregnancy indices, the amount experienced five minutes *after* orgasm was related to two of the major ones. The more satisfied a woman feels *after* orgasm the less was her disturbance during pregnancy ($r = -.45$, $p < .01$) as well as one week following delivery ($r = -.30, p .05$).

Several other relationships involving feelings during and after orgasm should be enumerated:

The less ecstatic a woman feels during orgasm the greater was her disturbance during delivery ($r = .48, p < .01$).

The less tired a woman feels during orgasm the less was her disturbance during pregnancy ($r = -.32, p < .05$).

The less happy a woman feels after orgasm the greater was her disturbance one week after delivery ($r = .36, p .025$).

The less relaxed a woman feels after orgasm the greater was her disturbance during pregnancy ($r = .36, p .025$).

The less guilty a woman feels after orgasm the less disturbed she felt during pregnancy ($r = -.29, p < .10$) and during delivery ($r = -.36, p .025$), and the less time she spent in the hospital following her delivery ($r = -.40, p .01$).

These scattered results do not really add up to much. They merely suggest a trend for pregnancy disturbance to be less in those women who experience orgasm more positively and with a greater sense of satisfaction. The two orgasmic feeling states that were most related to pregnancy disturbance were degree of guilt and degree of dissatisfaction felt five minutes after orgasm.

A sweep through the results involving the numerous other sex behavior variables turned up the following items:

The greater a woman's feeling that sex is one of life's most important experiences the less was her delivery disturbance ($r = -.39, p .01$) as well as her postdelivery disturbance ($r = -.33, p < .05$).

The more a woman continues to be interested in sexual intercourse during pregnancy the less her degree of disturbance one week following delivery $(r = -.36, p. 025)$.

But interestingly there were no significant correlations between the amount of fear a woman usually has about becoming pregnant during intercourse and the various indices of pregnancy disturbance.

The greater a woman's feeling that she is losing her body boundaries (based on the Boundary Loss score of the Body Distortion Questionnaire) during pregnancy the more disturbed she felt one week after delivery $(r = .42, p < .01)$ and the greater the number of days she spent in the hospital postdelivery $(r = .54, p < .001)$.

One of the strangest findings that emerged was that the greater the number of intercourse positions a woman indicates she and her husband use per month the *greater* was her pregnancy disturbance $(r = .45, p < .01)$! No reasonable explanation for this observation even begins to present itself.[26]

A final point of some interest is that pregnancy disturbance was positively correlated with the reported amount of menstrual irregularity $(r = .33, p .05)$ and the amount of menstrual pain $(r = .32, p < .05)$.[27] These two findings should definitely be pursued in more intensive studies. They suggest that those who have difficulties in the functioning of the reproductive system prior to pregnancy are those most likely to have difficulty during pregnancy.

Overview of Pregnancy Experience

Only a few of the large number of relationships that were scanned even hint of a possible bridge between a woman's sexual behavior and her response to the phases of pregnancy. One might say that there was a trend worthy of additional study for the woman who experiences orgasm in the most satisfied terms to have the least amount of pregnancy disturbance. But at the same time, one is confronted with such incongruities as the fact that it is the woman with high-orgasm consistency as well as the woman who makes use of a large number of intercourse positions who shows high pregnancy disturbance. Actually, it is entirely possible that the small number of significant results obtained were only chance occurrences. One is left in the frustrating position of having to declare that the findings derived from the pregnant sample have failed to demonstrate convincingly that a woman's response to pregnancy can be predicted from her sexual behavior, and yet with the reservation that there are a few trends that pique one's interest and hint that better studies might turn up more substantial relationships.

Contraception

Because rather good information was secured from most of the women concerning the contraceptives they used, it was possible to probe the issue whether sexual responsiveness has anything to do with the mode of contraception employed.[28] Does the woman who relies on an oral contraceptive display sexual behavior different from the woman who does not? Indeed, do women who favor any particular kind of contraception differ in sexual behavior or attitudes from those favoring any other kind? As defined by the results obtained from the seven samples studied, one can give unequivocal negative answers to all of these questions. The women in the various contraceptive categories were found not to differ from each other in orgasm consistency, actual and preferred intercourse frequencies, clitoral-vaginal preference, feelings during and after orgasm, masturbation frequency or satisfaction, and attitudes toward sex freedom.[29] Apparently, a woman's sexual response attributes do not result in her selectively choosing one form of contraception over another. It would also seem proper to say that continuing use of one form of contraception does not diminish or enhance sexual responsiveness as compared to the continued use of other forms of contraception. These findings might superficially be viewed as not supporting previous studies (Landis, Poffenberger and Poffenberger, 1950; Terman, 1938; Rainwater, 1965; Ferber, Tretze, and Lewit, 1966), which reported that fear of pregnancy based on distrust of the form of contraception employed inhibited sexual responsiveness.[30] However, one of the questions asked of the women in the various samples studied was how satisfied they were with their present contraceptive techniques. The great majority indicated they were quite satisfied. The women using oral contraceptives were no more satisfied than those using other forms of contraception. This would imply, then, that the women in the several contraceptive categories did not differ in how "good" or dependable they regarded their modes of contraception to be. Therefore, they probably did not differ significantly in how anxious they were about the possibility of getting pregnant during intercourse. If so, the present findings that the various contraceptive groups did not differ in sexual behavior would not bear on previous reports that distrust of a form of contraception can interfere with sexual responsiveness. They would simply indicate that different forms of contraception in which there is equal trust do not affect sexual behavior differentially.

One other matter that should be reported is that there were no consistent relationships between preferred form of contraception and a range of personality and attitudinal measures. In other words, one cannot say that the women who were studied chose one form of contraception versus another because of specific traits, conflicts, or attitudes toward the world. It is likely, instead, that a woman's choice of a contraceptive is strongly influenced by other factors such as her husband's preferences, advice given by her gynecologist, and informal information from friends.[31]

NOTES

1. Some of the major questions involving menstruation that were asked were as follows:

Age you first began to menstruate: _____.
Circle the number that best describes your reaction to your first menstruation.

Very happy	Quite happy	Indifferent	Quite upset	Very upset
1	2	3	4	5

Circle the number that best describes your mother's reaction.

Very happy	Quite Happy	Indifferent	Quite upset	Very upset
1	2	3	4	5

Circle the number that best describes your father's reaction.

Very happy	Quite happy	Indifferent	Quite upset	Very upset
1	2	3	4	5

Usual length of menstrual cycle (in days) from the first day of one period to the first day of next period: _____.
Degree of menstrual regularity:
1. Completely regular
2. Quite regular but maybe a few days early or late
3. Quite irregular but have some pattern
4. Totally irregular
Usual number of days of menstrual flow: _____.
Degree of menstrual pain:
1. No pain
2. Mild pain
3. Moderate pain
4. Severe pain
Duration of maximum menstrual pain: _____.
Amount of weight fluctuation during menstrual cycle (in lbs.): _____.
Mood change with menstrual period:
1. None
2. Mild
3. Moderate
4. Severe

See Appendix H for more details.

2. These menstrual reports were given in an open, nondefensive fashion. None of the menstrual measures was consistently correlated with indexes of response defensiveness (namely, K and L scales of the Minnesota Multiphasic Personality Inventory).

3. This regularity typified those women whose cycle was not regulated by an oral contraceptive and was also recalled as having been characteristic of self previous to taking an oral contraceptive by those who were using that technique.

4. Intensive interviews with some of the women who experience considerable pain during menstruation revealed that they respond to such pain as a routinized fact of life and are rarely alarmed by it.

5. Two studies have been conducted by the writer in which various psychological

measures obtained from *unmarried* women have been related to the number of days since they last finished menstruating. One of the tasks used in these studies was based upon Kuethe's (1962) work and involved placing miniature cut-out human figures on an unstructured felt background. It was found consistently and significantly in both studies that the closer a woman was to her next time of menstruation the further apart she placed two of the figures, one representing a mother and the other a child. This relationship was not found for the placement of other pairs of figures (for example, man and woman, father and child, woman and woman). Therefore, the interesting possibility arises that as the time of menstruation approaches and the *unmarried* woman is about to be confronted with a clear signal as to whether she is pregnant, her anxiety about the whole matter of becoming a mother (and having a relationship with a child) increases and evidences itself in her putting increased distance between the mother and child cut-out figures.

6. However, a significant trend appeared for degree of menstrual pain to be positively correlated with amount of pain expressed during a gynecological examination ($r = .31$, p .05, Sample 1) and self-rated amount of physical discomfort during pregnancy (.32 p <.05, Sample 6).

Note that all correlations cited in this chapter are Pearson product-moment coefficients. $N's$ will not be specifically cited unless they deviate grossly from the sample sizes listed in Chapter 7.

7. In a previous study by Fisher and Osofsky (1967), which was cited in the chapter reviewing the menstrual literature, it was found that the woman most likely to develop amenorrhea under stress is the one who has poorly defined body boundaries as well as a relatively limited awareness of her body. It is therefore interesting that in two samples Body Prominence was negatively and significantly correlated with degree of irregularity. The Barrier score showed this negative relationship in only one sample. It is difficult to compare the present findings with those from the Fisher and Osofsky study because the latter involved unmarried girls who had left home to attend nursing school and who under the impact of this stress experience were averaging a considerable amount of irregularity.

8. Two other negative findings should be mentioned that bear on previous reports in the literature.

First, no support was obtained for Shipman's (1964) observation that certain personality characteristics are related to the age of onset of menses. In fact, no consistent perceptual or physiological correlates of how early or late menstruation began could be established.

Secondly, no support was detected for Peskin's (1968) report that the number of days of menstrual flow is linked to a specific personality orientation. Number of days of flow did not correlate consistently, across samples, with any of the multiple personality and perceptual measures.

9. The writer's review of the literature in an earlier chapter suggested that menstrual irregularity was linked with psychological variables, but that this was probably not true for menstrual discomfort and pain. The failure to find a link between menstrual irregularity and any of the psychological measures in the writer's studies therefore contradicts the previous trend in the literature. As already noted, this may be because of the rather limited range of amenorrhea in the samples of women studied by the writer. Or it may be because of some defect in the methodology of the writer's studies that is not readily apparent. Or it may represent the more stringent demands of the writer's studies that the same results be duplicated over successive samples.

10. *Wanted for Study of Pregnancy Attitudes*

Women, 18 to 40 years of age, with minimum of high school education who are now pregnant.

Participants will be paid $20.00 for two sessions involving answering questionnaires. Total time about four hours.

11. Women at any stage of pregnancy from the second to ninth month were allowed to participate. The average number of months the women had been pregnant was 6.0 ($\sigma=2.6$). Any test score that proved to be significantly correlated with stage of pregnancy was not used.

12. The mean Barrier score during pregnancy was 7.63 ($\sigma=3.45$) and postpregnancy it was 6.00 ($\sigma=6.65$). The t value for this difference is 2.6 ($p<.02$). The Penetration score that McConnell and Daston (1961) and Edwards (1969) both found to decline from the pregnancy to postpartum phase also declined in the present study but not significantly.

13. The mean total Body Distortion score during pregnancy was 13.63 ($\sigma=8.12$) and postpregnancy it was 7.79 ($\sigma=7.58$). The t value for this difference is 3.6 ($p<.001$).

14. As described in Appendix F, a considerable array of test scores was obtained from the pregnant women. Aside from the inkblot, word construction, and body-image measures already enumerated, they included personality parameters (for example, Stability, Dominance, Sociability), indexes of hostility, food preferences, desire for new experience, repression, and cleanliness.

15. Simple test-retest with the Body Distortion Questionnaire does not produce a decrease in the Total Distortion score.

16. The feeling of being radically changed would be expected to be at its height within the first few days after delivery.

17. Davids, Devault, and Talmadge (1961a) found that women who had had a difficult delivery showed significant cognitive deficit (as evidenced by a decline in intelligence test scores) even a month after their delivery experience.

18. At the same time, there must be a great sense of relief in the postpartum period about having overcome the unpleasant demands of the delivery and this may play a role in the "supernormal" feelings that seem to evolve at this time.

19. Note that in none of the seven samples studied were there consistent correlations between the sexual measures and such variables as the following: age first became pregnant; how long after marriage first pregnancy occurred; amount of fear of becoming pregnant during intercourse; recalled length of labor. There was also a lack of significant relationship between the Blau, et al. (1964) Maternal Attitude to Pregnancy Instrument scores in Sample 1 (Appendix A) and the sex behavior measures.

20. The questions variously concerned vomiting, fatigue, muscle pain, headache, internal pain, and fear. Neither this index nor any of the others concerned with pregnancy were significantly correlated with measures of response defensiveness such as the L and K scales of the Minnesota Multiphasic Personality Inventory.

21. This index was based on replies to questions about amount of fear, irritability, self-control, and anxiety experienced during delivery.

22. This index was based on replies to questions about how tense, irritable, depressed, and weak the woman felt one week after delivery.

23. As shown in Appendix F, other measures of response to pregnancy and delivery were obtained, but they are not pertinent to the issue of how much difficulty a woman had in adapting to the phases of the pregnancy process.

24. Disturbance during pregnancy has only chance correlations with disturbance during or postdelivery. A positive correlation ($r=.31$, $p<.05$) was found between delivery and postdelivery disturbance, but the magnitude of the correlation is so small that one cannot regard the two variables as having much of a relationship.

25. Some examples of the various terms ranked are as follows: unsatisfied, tired, weak, ecstatic, strange, as if I would burst.

26. A particularly high correlation ($r=.54$, $p<.001$) was found between number of positions used and amount of vomiting (which is one of the subsidiary measures included in the total pregnancy disturbance score).

27. Although information was obtained in several samples as to whether the

women had breast-fed versus bottle-fed their children, it was not possible to analyze the data meaningfully because only a small minority had not used breast-feeding for at least a time.

28. About 50–60 percent of the women in the various samples were relying on an oral contraceptive. The remainder were about equally distributed in the diaphragm, foam, IUD, and condom categories, or some combination of them.

29. In two samples the data analyses were complicated by the fact that there were significant trends for the oral contraceptive users to be younger than those using other forms of contraception. In these instances further data analyses were carried out within age subgroups.

30. Bialos and the writer, in an unpublished study involving over 40 subjects, found that when women shifted from other forms of contraception to an oral contraceptive they showed no general significant changes in mood or sexual responsiveness during two subsequent follow-up periods. This is not to deny, as shown by several publications (Herzberg and Coppen, 1970; Grounds, Davies, and Mowbray, 1970) that some individual women may evidence gross changes in mood and psychological behavior after starting or stopping an oral contraceptive. Particularly exaggerated effects have been reported in psychiatric patients (Kane, Treadway, Ewing, 1969).

31. Incidentally, no consistent support was found for the earlier cited report of Rodgers and Ziegler (1968) that women who continue to use an oral contraceptive are more ascendant (dominant) in their orientation than those who discontinue its use.

14

DIVERSE AND NEGATIVE

FINDINGS

A hodgepodge of topics is sorted through in this chapter. The material presented includes what appear to be interesting but tentative positive findings as well as many findings pointing to the absence of relationships among important parameters.

Traditional versus Nontraditional Feminine Attitudes

The concept of the feminine role is in transition and the question arises whether there are differences in sexual responsiveness between those adhering to the traditional values of femininity and those identified with newer definitions. Is the woman whose orientation matches that of the "typical housewife" characterized by a particular pattern of sexual behavior? Does the woman who believes that the husband should have greater power than the wife in the family differ sexually from the woman who rejects such a concept? Does the woman who believes that the male has a more satisfying role in life than the female differ in her sexual attitudes from the woman with the obverse view? Tentative answers to such questions were provided by several lines of inquiry that were undertaken.

In Sample 2 a direct effort was made to ascertain how certain aspects of authoritarian versus nonauthoritarian ideological orientation were related to sexual behavior. Two scales, Traditional Family Ideology and Politico-Economic Conservatism were administered (Levinson and Huffman, 1955). The Traditional Family Ideology Scale measures how much importance is attached to strong male as well as parental authority in the family, exaggerated masculinity and femininity, and old-fashioned child rearing discipline. A high score is obtained by indicating agreement with such statements as the following:

Some equality in marriage is a good thing, but by and large the husband ought to have the main say-so in family affairs.

Women who want to remove the word "obey" from the marriage service don't understand what it means to be a wife.

The Politico-Economic Scale taps attitudes in terms of how much agreement is expressed with such statements as the following:

When private enterprise does not do the job, it is up to the government to step in and meet the public's needs for housing, water power, and the like.
Men such as Henry Ford or J. P. Morgan, who overcame all competition on the road to success, are models for all young people to admire and imitate.

This scale essentially evaluates how much one is loyal to a capitalistic versus socialistic model of how economic matters should be conducted.

The degree to which a woman favors the traditional family ideology proved to be correlated with a number of the sexual measures, but not with most of the principal indices. It was not significantly correlated with orgasm consistency, intercourse frequency, and masturbation behavior. However, it was related to several of the variables having to do with the quality of orgasmic and postorgasmic feelings. The higher a woman's Traditional Family Ideology score the more she indicated that during orgasm she felt "not like myself" ($-.36$, p .025) and "slightly embarrassed" ($r = -.45$, $p < .01$), and during the postorgasm period (five minutes after orgasm) she felt "not like myself" ($-.34$, $p < .05$), not "satisfied" ($r = .35$, $p < .05$), and not "happy" ($r = .32$, $p < .05$).[1] In other words, the more traditionally oriented woman was inclined to emphasize that the orgasm experience made her feel as if something alien were happening to her ("not like myself," "embarrassed") and left her feeling somewhat unsatisfied. Other scattered correlations should be mentioned. The higher a woman's Traditional Family Ideology score:

The less often she thinks about sex ($r = -.34$, $p < .05$).
The less frequently she engages in intercourse during her menstrual period ($r = -.40$, $p < .01$).
The less the time she prefers for foreplay ($r = -.42$, $p < .01$).
The less importance she assigns to sex in her life ($r = -.43$, $p < .01$).
The less freely she communicates with her husband about sex ($r = .39$, p .01).
The less often she sleeps in the nude ($r = -.32$, $p < .05$).
The greater her preference for vaginal stimulation ($r = .34$, $p < .05$).[2]

It should be added that a woman's degree of menstrual pain and irregularity were not significantly related to her Traditional Family Ideology score.

The Politico-Economic Conservatism score was also not significantly correlated with any of the prime sexual indices (namely, orgasm consistency, intercourse frequency, clitoral-vaginal preference, and masturbation behavior); and did not show any consistent relationships with the manner in which the orgasmic and postorgasmic phases were experienced (as defined by the rankings of descriptive phrases). The only significant correlations observed indicated that the greater a woman's conservatism the less often she thinks about sex ($-.37$, $p < .025$) and the less often she engages in intercourse during her menstrual period ($-.33$, $p < .05$).

Another approach to the question under discussion that was undertaken in Sample 2 involved the Housewife scale of the Strong Vocational Interest Blank (1966), which measures how closely a woman's expressed pattern of interests matches that of the average housewife. The higher a woman's Housewife score the more one may regard her as conforming to a conventional feminine orientation. This score proved not to be correlated with any of the major indices of sexual responsiveness. However, the greater a woman's Housewife orientation the less likely she was to experience orgasm as "ecstatic" ($.37$, $p < .025$) and the more likely she was to feel Unsatisfied in the postorgasm period ($-.30$, p $.05$).[3] Further, the higher her score:

The fewer the number of intercourse positions she uses per month ($-.31$, $p < .05$).
The less easily she communicates with her husband about sex ($.31$, $p < .05$).

One of the special techniques employed in Sample 2 to get at attitudes about female versus male power relationships was taken from an earlier study by Fisher (1965). This technique (described in Appendix B) was based on asking each woman to look at a series of 40 paired pictures of faces (20 of which involved a female versus a male, 10 a male versus a male, and 10 a female versus a female), and to guess in each instance which of the two pictured persons would be more likely to be dominant over the other. A score was computed equal to the number of times the male was designated as dominant over the female. It was then possible to ascertain whether the degree to which a woman views the male as dominant over the female is correlated with her sexual behavior. Completely negative results were obtained. There were only a few minor significant correlations that are not even worth mentioning.

Still another approach to the matter of whether attitude toward the feminine role is related to sexual behavior was undertaken in four samples (3, 4, 5, 6) by asking each woman to rate (five-point scale) the degree to which she considers a man's role in life to be more satisfying than a woman's. These ratings did not show any consistent significant correlations with the various sexual measures.

A number of other related negative findings should be mentioned. Thus, no consistent correlations could be discerned between any of the sexual measures and the following variables:

Degree to which a woman believes that a successful marriage requires the husband to be the major authority figure in the family.
Extent to which a woman usually expresses disagreement with her husband.
How much a woman prefers an aggressive versus nonaggressive man.
How much a woman believes that sexual freedom should be increased in our society.[4]

The *total* yield is not impressive. The degree to which a woman identifies with conventional feminine attitudes and standards (at least within the
range represented in the present samples) does not seem to play a really
important part in her sexual responsiveness. Orgasm consistency, intercourse frequency, and clitoral-vaginal preference proved to be almost completely unrelated to how conventionally a woman conceptualizes the feminine role. There were a few trends, particularly involving degree of belief
in the ideology of the traditional family, which suggest that the more traditional woman may (in contrast with the less traditional one) be a bit more
embarrassed by sex, less consciously preoccupied with it, less comfortable
with nudity, less satisfied with orgasm, more vaginally oriented, and less
accepting of intercourse during menstruation. Even these differences must
be viewed as rather tentative because they are based upon only one sample. The range of attitudes represented in the present studies with regard
to the feminine role was rather limited. Possibly, one might discover that
in comparing cultures that differed dramatically in the degree of freedom
and mobility given to women, larger differences in sexual responsiveness
would become apparent.[5] In any case, it can be said that within the range
of sex role attitudes that one finds in well-educated, middle-class women
and looking at the total array of findings, sexual behavior is probably not
significantly linked to the degree of adherence to the conventional feminine
role. It remains to be seen whether attitudes specifically concerned with
conformance to traditional family ideology have a more significant influence on sexual behavior and feelings.

Parents' Attitudes toward Sex and the Body

A number of inquiries were made across the various samples with regard
to parental attitudes toward sex, menstruation, and nudity, as well as the
parental role in sex education. These inquiries, based on each woman's
memory of her parents, involved the following matters:

Parents' attitudes about their daughter's first menstruation.
Which of the parents provided sexual information.
How much the parents approved or disapproved of sex.
How openly affectionate the parents were toward each other.
Whether the parents' marriage was a happy one.
Whether the parents could talk easily about sex and the body.
Whether mother considered it natural to see her daughter nude.
How comfortable the parents were about touching their daughter's body.

No consistent relationships could be found between any of these variables and the entire array of sexual measures. There is no indication that
the extent to which parents were free or liberal in their attitudes toward
their daughter (as she recalls it) about sex or body contact played a part in

her ability to be sexually responsive, in her preferences for particular modes of stimulation, in her menstrual experiences, and even in her liberality of sexual standards.

Influence of Critical Psychosexual Experiences

The women in all of the samples were asked to report how they felt at several, what are usually considered to be critical, times in psychosexual development. They were to rate their reactions (namely, their amount of disturbance) to their first menstruation, their first serious date, and their first intercourse.[6] It was found that such reports of degree of disturbance did not correlate consistently with any of the sexual measures. The amount of trauma produced by such experiences as first menstruation or first intercourse did not have a detectable impact upon subsequent sexual behavior. It will be recalled that in a previous chapter no evidence could be mustered to support the notion that such experiences have a lasting traumatic impact upon sexual behavior. Of course, one can take the position that reports by women of how they felt many years earlier are likely to be inaccurate. However, even within the context of such inaccuracy one might at least expect that the differentiation between those reporting no trauma and those reporting a high amount of trauma would be meaningful. Yet, an analysis of these extreme categories also did not turn up any differences in sexual behavior.

Cigarette Smoking

The women in four of the samples (2, 3, 4, 5) were asked to indicate the average number of cigarettes per day they smoke, the age they first began smoking, and how much they enjoy smoking. These indices of smoking behavior were, by and large, found to be unrelated to the manifold sex behavior measures. Only one consistent trend was detected. The number of cigarettes smoked correlated positively (at significant or borderline levels) with strength of orgasm in three samples.[7] The greater the number of cigarettes smoked by a woman the stronger she reported her orgasms to be. This is an interesting finding that deserves further investigation. One could speculatively suggest that the relationship between the two variables reflects their shared commonality with reference to allowing oneself to be "seized" by a kind of body arousal. That is, one could say that the greater the number of cigarettes smoked by a woman the more she has "surrendered" control of herself to a tension; analogously one could regard a woman who attains the more extreme states of orgasmic excitement as having "surrendered" to the loss of her usual controls. This analogy, as stated, is not terribly convincing, but there may be a kernel of truth in it.

Consumption of Alcohol

Data were also collected in four samples (2, 3, 4, 5) with regard to age began drinking, number of drinks consumed per week, and amount of liking for alcohol. There was almost a complete absence of significant correlations between these variables and the various sex behavior measures. Three trends are, however, worth mentioning. First, it was found in two samples that the greater the amount of alcohol consumed by a woman the more unsatisfied she feels five minutes *after* orgasm.[8]

Secondly, the isolated curious trend should be mentioned that in three samples there was a positive correlation between the amount of alcohol consumed by a woman and the number of minutes of stimulation she customarily receives before attaining orgasm.[9]

Finally, in three samples it was observed that the earlier the age at which a woman began to drink alcohol the higher was her usual preferred intercourse rate.[10]

These findings must be viewed as tentative, and there is little point in weaving possible explanations until they are confirmed by further work.

Attitudes toward Parents

It is surprising how minimally sexual behavior turned out to be related to attitudes toward one's parents. Despite attempts to measure attitudes toward the mother and father in multiple ways (both at a conscious and unconscious level), the results have been largely negative. It is true that a few sexual variables (for example, orgasm consistency) were linked with feelings about one or the other of the parents, but they were exceptions. Such diverse aspects of sexual behavior as intercourse frequency, importance ascribed to sex, feelings during and after orgasm, and intensity of orgasm have proven to be unrelated to such measures as feelings about parents, apparent liberality of parents about sex and nudity, frequency with which parents used spanking as a form of punishment, and response of parents to their daughter's first menstruation. It should be added that the various measures pertaining to menstruation (for example, amount of pain, irregularity) also failed to be consistently linked with the measures of attitudes toward one's parents. How are such findings to be interpreted? One could dismiss them and assert that their sparseness simply reflects the inadequacy of the measures of attitudes toward parents that were employed. However, in view of the fact that there were instances in which these measures were apparently sufficiently "sound" to show a pattern of consistent relationship with a sexual variable, one wonders whether the results can justifiedly be dismissed on the basis of inadequacy. Other possible explanations offer themselves. Perhaps the lack of relationship truly indicates that many aspects of a woman's sexual behavior, as such, are learned outside of the family from interactions with male and female peers whose values may be quite different from those of her parents. If so, one would have to question theories that trace most aspects of a woman's sexual behavior back to events that occurred in her early interactions with her parents. But still another way of interpreting the lack of relationship would be to accept the possibility that parents' attitudes do play an important role in their daughter's sexual behavior, but that they do so in such a complex fashion that they cannot be detected by the techniques that were used. For example, it is possible that an extremely conservative and restrictive attitude about sex by a girl's parents might cause her to become similarly conservative, but it also might stimulate her to resist their orientation and to move to a polar opposite, free kind of sexual behavior. Or it is possible that in one family the father's attitudes would be most influential, whereas in another the mother's might be. It is with such potential complexity in mind that one must interpret the largely negative results obtained in a modest and questioning fashion.

Intensity of Arousal

The women in six samples (2, 3, 4, 5, 6, 7) were asked to report about the intensity of their excitement as they engaged in intercourse in a number of ways. They rated the degree to which such excitement made their thinking and their body movements become uncontrolled; in addition they rated the intensity of their orgasms on two different kinds of scales. An analysis of such ratings failed to turn up a single consistent personality, attitudinal, or value orientation correlate. Significant findings would appear in one sample but disappear in the next. There is nothing positive that can be said that would be truly valid. One can only conclude on the basis of the results obtained that the sheer intensity of the excitement aroused during intercourse is not a function of personality traits (for example, impulsivity or sociability), anxiety level, hostility, mode of organization of the body image, amount of guilt, sensory sensitivity of the skin to touch or tickle, interest in new experience, and tendency to augment versus diminish sensory input. Of course, it is possible that the failure to pin down correlates of degree of excitement during intercourse is caused by the ambiguity involved in defining the continuum of low to high excitement. What appears to be extreme arousal to one individual may appear only moderate to another. This difficulty in definition may be significant in view of the fact that the arousal state elicited by intercourse in women is quite different from that typifying the vast proportion of their everyday experiences. As such, it is a sector of experience in which they probably have relatively little experiential expertness. This factor might also play a role in the results obtained with reference to other sex behavior variables in which a woman's judgment about the character of her sexual experience was required. For example, it might affect judgments about the experience of orgasm, whether it has "ecstatic" or "embarrassing" or "as if burst" qualities. This is a matter that awaits more careful scrutiny.

Repeated Orgasms in a Limited Period of Time

One finds differences among the women in the frequency with which they have more than one orgasm in a relatively brief period of time. In view of the Masters and Johnson (1966) report that women do not have the sort of refractory period of response to sexual stimulation that men do, one might expect that all women could potentially have many orgasms during a limited time span. The question arises, then, as to why there are differences in the frequency of such orgasm experiences. In the present samples there were no indications that such differences are caused by age, number of years of marriage, or number of pregnancies. The negative results with respect to age and number of years of marriage are noted in order to indicate that "multiple" orgasms are not simply a function of amount of sexual experience or practice. The negative result pertaining to number of pregnancies is mentioned in relation to Sherfey's (1966) hypothesis that the increase in pelvic vascularity resulting from pregnancy plays a significant part in orgasmic potential.

On the positive side, a few variables showed consistent trends to be related to frequency of "multiple" orgasms. In two of the four samples in which the Barrier score was obtained, it proved to be positively correlated ($r = .30$, $p < .05$, Sample 3; $r = .50$, $p < .01$, Sample 5) with such frequency. It will be recalled that the Barrier score (Appendix A), which is derived from inkblot responses, defines the degree to which one perceives the boundaries of one's body as well articulated, differentiating self from others, and providing protection from intrusion. Perhaps, then, it can be said that the woman who achieves multiple orgasms feels more secure about her body than does the woman who does not do so. This must be stated tentatively because not only was the Barrier relationship found in only two of four samples but also there were no consistent correlations between frequency of "multiple" orgasm and any of the Body Distortion Questionnaire scores (Appendix A) that tap boundary disturbance or other kinds of body anxiety. However, even further, it is pertinent (to the possible role of body attitudes) that a woman's frequency of "multiple" orgasms was found to be positively and significantly correlated with her degree of awareness of her breasts [11] and her vagina in two of three samples.[12] That is, the woman who attains frequent orgasms in a relatively limited period of time is likely to be one with a clear awareness of the sexual sectors of her body.

Finally, in the interest of future research possibilities, it should be indicated that in all three samples in which measures of the set to augment versus diminish sensory input were obtained, frequency of "multiple" orgasm tended to be positively correlated with an augmenting orientation, but only as defined by the first set of trials in the augmenting-diminishing procedure (see Appendix B for clarification).[13] It will be recalled that an augmenter is one who increases the intensity of what she perceives or experiences. There is an appealing logic to the idea that the woman who enhances sensory input is also the one characterized by multiple orgastic response. But it must be emphasized that these findings are barely borderline. They are cited because they deserve further thought.

Number of Intercourse Positions

Number of positions used during intercourse is another aspect of sex behavior that was found to be linked to the definiteness of the body boundary, as measured by the Barrier score (Appendix A). The greater the number of positions that a woman and her husband use during intercourse the more definite her body boundary tends to be (in two of four samples).[14] Does this mean that the woman who feels insecure about her body finds putting it into a variety of positions while she is sexually aroused particularly threatening? Since it has also been shown in previous work that amount of awareness of one's muscles is relatively high in those with definite boundaries, it is interesting that in the one sample in which the Life Style Scale (Mackler and Shontz, 1964) scale (Appendix B) was administered, which measures how much each woman enjoys kinesthetic experiences (that is, those involving muscle sensations), a significant positive correlation was found between number of positions and Kinesthesia ($r = .39$, p .01, Sample 2).[15] Obviously, since variations in intercourse positions involve gross changes in muscular experience, one might expect that a woman who enjoys kinesthetic sensations would be particularly motivated to experiment with such positions. However, it must be added that number of positions used was not consistently correlated with amount of participation, or interest in, athletics.

It is also worthy of note that number of positions was not significantly related to age, amount of sexual experience (as defined by years of marriage), or total pregnancies. Further, it was not related to interest in new experiences (as defined by the Zuckerman, et al. [1964] Sensation-Seeking Scale) or tendencies to augment versus diminish sensory input.

Dating History

One of the surprising results that has presented itself is that no aspect of sexual behavior is consistently correlated with a woman's previous history of dating. It is not possible to predict her sexual responsiveness in the marital situation on the basis of the age at which she first began to date, the frequency of her dating at various phases of her life, the frequency with which she dated regularly ("steady") with one boy, or the fact that she previously attained sufficient intimacy with a man to become "engaged" to him. Previous dating behavior apparently does not foretell such aspects of sexual behavior as orgasmic consistency, intercourse frequency, clitoral-vaginal preference, number of intercourse positions used, liberality of sexual standards after marriage, masturbation satisfaction, foreplay preferences, and feelings about nudity. It also does not foretell usual intensity of menstrual pain or menstrual regularity. Some of the implications of these findings have already been discussed in Chapter 8 in relation to the fact that dating behavior was discovered not to be correlated with orgasm consistency.

One of the important conclusions that may be drawn from the findings is that sexual responsiveness is basically not a derivative of how much practice a woman has had in relating to her male peers. A woman who has had little practice in heterosexual type contacts turns out to be just as orgasmic as the woman who has had a history of intensive interactions with male peers. One is reminded of the Kinsey, et al. (1953) findings that indicate that even the opportunity for intensive practice of intercourse (as in the first year of marriage) really produces only a small to moderate increase in sexual responsiveness in women.

Hostility

Early in the series of studies there were results that suggested that hostile women might be less sexually responsive than nonhostile women. However, as information from successive samples has been collected, this idea has not been confirmed. Multiple measures of anger and aggression have failed to show consistent correlations with any of the sexual behavior indices. This is true despite the use of an exhaustive assemblage of techniques for measuring hostility that have diversely looked at a woman's own evaluation of her hostility behavior, the ratings by observers of how aggressively she conducts herself, and the amount of hostility in her fantasies as elicited by pictures and inkblots. There is no sign that the irritable woman suffers from diminished orgastic capacity, nor is there any evidence that the aggressive woman has either more or less intercourse per week than the nonaggressive one.[16] Furthermore, a woman's degree of hostility does

not seem to play a role in her clitoral versus vaginal stimulation preferences, in her likelihood of having "multiple" orgasms, in the liberality of
her sexual standards, in her likelihood of agreeing to intercourse during
her menstrual period, in her preferred modes of foreplay, in her degree of
dissatisfaction after orgasm, in the type of contraception she uses, and in
her response to her menstrual period. This is not a pattern of results that
one would have intuitively predicted. For example, one might have expected the angry woman to have orgasm difficulties or to be characterized
by reduced intercourse rates. However, if one looks carefully at the few
studies in the literature that have explored the relationship of hostility in
women to sexual parameters, the findings have been mixed. Winokur (in
Winokur, 1963) reported that when 20 married couples were asked to estimate how often they had been angry in a two-week period and to estimate
their frequency of intercourse during this same period, the two classes of
events had only a chance relationship. This was true despite the fact that
when explicitly questioned about this issue, the individuals expressed the
belief that when they are angry they are less "sexually active." But, to
further complicate things, about half of the 17 women who described
themselves as becoming more irritable and quarrelsome premenstrually
also said that they were more receptive to sexual relations at this time.
That is, the irritability was accompanied by *higher* rather than lower sexual receptivity. Relatedly, one should also keep in mind that there are
studies (Barclay and Haber, 1965) in which women seemed to find hostility
sexually arousing. In short, previous observations do not support a simple
theory about hostility as either inhibiting or facilitating sexual responsiveness. It might "feel" as if it were inhibitory, but at the same time arouse
sexual fantasies. Or it might heighten sexual responsiveness while at the
same time interfering with the initial sociability needed to initiate intercourse.

Self-Rating of Sexual Responsiveness

A woman's rating of her own overall sexual responsiveness (five-point
scale, Appendix J) turned out, as earlier indicated, to be correlated with a
wider range of the various major indices of sexual behavior than did any
other single index.[17] But despite this fact, it does not show many consistent
relationships with the manifold personality and perceptual tests that were
administered. Scattered findings are individually interesting, but they do
not fit or coalesce sensibly. Consider the following:

In three samples the women were asked to rate how they experience the
inside of their body (Appendix C). They expressed their feelings in terms
of such continua as pleasant-unpleasant, sharp-dull, strong-weak. It was
found (at significant or borderline levels) in two of the three samples that
the more sexually responsive a woman considers herself to be the more she

rates the inside of her body as feeling "pleasant" [18] and "active" (rather than passive).[19]

In three of seven samples there were significant or near significant negative correlations between how sexually responsive a woman considers herself to be and her Repression score of the Minnesota Multiphasic Personality Inventory.[20] The Repression score is defined as an index of the degree to which an individual depends upon denial, repression, and rationalization for coping with problems, and the degree to which she lacks insight about her own motives and feelings. The trend was for those who viewed themselves as low in sexual responsiveness to have limited awareness of their own motivations and to take a denying, repressive attitude toward their own impulses. It must be underscored, though, that the findings represent only a borderline trend.

It is apropos to add at this point that sexual responsiveness was positively correlated with the Zuckerman, et al. (1964) Sensation-Seeking Scale (Appendix B) in two of three samples in which it was administered.[21] The more a woman rates herself as sexually responsive the more she indicates that she enjoys novel experiences. This finding is obviously congruent with the fact that those women who rate themselves as most sexually responsive are least repressive of their own impulses.

It is additionally pertinent to this whole issue of the relationship of self-rated sexual responsiveness to being sex expressive and "open" to excitement that borderline positive correlations were found (in two of three samples) between degree of self-rated sexual responsiveness and the Exhibition score (Appendix C) of the Edwards Preference Schedule.[22] The Exhibition score is basically a measure of the degree to which one likes to do and say things that will make one the center of attention.

Another finding that should be mentioned concerns the woman's perception of her father. One of the dimensions that each woman rated concerned how emotional as compared to calm she considers her father to be (Appendix A). In two out of four samples it was found that the more sexually responsive a woman regards herself to be the more she views her father as being on the calm side.[23] This, by the way, was not true with respect to her ratings of the mother. Such a finding represents another paradoxical instance in which there are more significant relationships between a woman's sexual behavior and her attitude toward her father than between her sexual behavior and her attitude toward her mother.

A final matter of interest is the observation that self-rated sexual responsiveness proved to be positively and significantly correlated ($r = .49$, p .001) with the pooled ratings of sexual responsiveness (Appendix B) of all the technicians who had administered tasks to each woman in one of the two samples (2).[24] The more sexually responsive [25] a woman judged herself to be the greater the responsiveness attributed to her by the laboratory observers.[26]

The disparate findings that have been enumerated are not easy to interpret. It is hoped, however, that they will provide leads for further studies.

If one had to extract some generality, one might conclude that the tendency for self-rated sexual responsiveness to be positively linked with the Exhibition and New Experience scores and negatively with the Repression score indicated that overall responsiveness was likely to be greater in those women who have the "freedom" to be expressive and to expose themselves to new or stimulating events. But this can be regarded as little more than a speculation.

Ordinal Position

No consistent relationships were found between ordinal position in the family and any of the sex behavior measures. For example, a woman's sexual behavior turned out not to be correlated with whether she was the oldest or the youngest or the only child in her family.

Clothing Choices

Middle-class women obviously differ in their clothing strategies. Some choose their clothes primarily as a means of attracting attention, others are chiefly interested in being "comfortable," and still others are motivated by the wish to conform to the current fashion. Do such clothing strategies reflect a woman's sexual attitudes or sexual responsiveness? As described in Appendix C, Aiken (1963) constructed a questionnaire that analyzes clothing preferences and choices with reference to five dimensions: conformity, interest, comfort, decoration, and economy. The women in one sample (3) responded to this questionnaire; their scores for the various clothing dimensions could therefore be related to their sex behavior indices.

No correlations of significance could be detected between clothing attitudes and the major measures of sexual responsiveness. Whether a woman is primarily interested in clothing as a mode of self-display or a means of affirming her conformity to current fashions tells us nothing about her orgasm consistency, her intercourse frequency, her feelings during and after orgasm, and her preference for clitoral versus vaginal stimulation. The relatively few noteworthy correlations between clothing attitudes and sexual parameters that did emerge were of a minor character. They may be summarized as follows:

The greater a woman's inclination to choose her clothes so as to conform to current standards the less likely she is:

To assign high importance to sex as a life experience ($r = -.40$, $N = 30$, $p < .05$).
To want sex freedom increased in our culture ($r = -.40$, $N = 30$, $p < .05$).

To experience more than one orgasm in a one-hour period ($r = -.54$, $N = 30$, $p < .01$).

To obtain satisfaction from masturbation ($r = -.33$, $N = 30$, $p < .10$).

To lose control of her thinking during intercourse ($r = -.35$, $N = 30$, p .05).

Proceeding further, one finds that the greater a woman's interest in her clothes as a means of self-decoration or attracting attention the more likely she is to emphasize the importance of sex in her life and to endorse liberal sex standards.[27] Just the opposite pattern typifies the relationship between the extent to which a woman believes that economy should be her chief basis for selecting clothes and the importance she ascribes to sex in her life.

No correlations of consequence were found between the degree to which clothes are chosen because they are "comfortable" and any of the sexual variables.

If the questionnaire used to measure clothing preference strategies is a valid one, it would appear that little can be discerned about a woman's sexual responsiveness from her clothing attitudes.

Preferred Intercourse Frequency

The women in all samples were asked to state the number of times per week they prefer having intercourse. Their preferred frequencies were found not to be consistently related to any of the major sexual responsiveness, personality, perceptual, and physiological measures. There were one or two minor trends that are simply worth mentioning. It has already been noted in this chapter that the greater a woman's preferred intercourse frequency the earlier is the age at which she began to drink alcohol. Also, a barely borderline trend was observed such that the greater a woman's preferred frequency the higher was her score on the Negativism scale of the Buss-Durkee Hostility Scale.[28] That is, the higher her preferred frequency the more likely she was to describe herself as using negativistic strategies, such as working slowly or doing the opposite of what is expected, when angry at someone. If this barely borderline observation were to be supported by future work, it would raise the question whether a woman's intercourse frequency preferences might in some indirect ways be influenced by hostile intent.

Physiological Response

Scattered references have been made throughout this book to the physiological measures that were obtained (primarily in Samples 1, 2, and 3). An attempt is now made to pull together the diverse findings involving these physiological measures. It will be recalled that the following parameters were sampled: Galvanic Skin Response, heart rate, temperature (hand, leg, breast, vagina, rectum, mouth), and skin resistance (hand, leg, labia, breast). Stomach motility was also determined in one sample. Physiological recordings were obtained under varying conditions: rest, stress, and sexually arousing conditions.

The overall mean values and standard deviations for each physiological measure for various samples are presented in Tables 14–1, 14–2, and 14–3. More detailed analyses of mean values and change scores for each of the specific conditions introduced in each sample have also been made. One of the prime questions that was investigated was whether conditions presumed to be sexually arousing differ in their physiological impact from those that seem to produce arousal primarily as the result of stress which is nonsexual in character.[29] Generally, one has to give a negative answer. None of the physiological indices successfully differentiated the sexual excitement from the nonsexual excitement conditions.[30] One should add that the temperature of the vagina (as well as that of the rectum) were the least sensitive to change in conditions. The skin resistance of the labia was among the most sensitive of the indicators of change. However, at the same time, it should be emphasized that when the women were asked to perform an arithmetical task, this produced greater labial excitation (as defined by skin resistance) than did listening to a sexual passage from D. H. Lawrence. The inability of the physiological measures to distinguish the sexual and nonsexual responses may, as already indicated, be caused by the fact that the so-called sexual conditions were not sufficiently "sexual" and actually involved other affects such as anxiety. This is a possibility that has to be considered. But at the same time, one should note that

TABLE 14-1

Overall Means and Standard Deviations of Physiological Parameters (Sample 1)

Variable	Session 1			Session 2			Session 3		
	M	σ	N	M	σ	N	M	σ	N
GSR frequency	1.61	1.75	41	2.06	1.24	42	3.88	2.08	37
GSR amplitude[a]	.68	.51	41	.55	.24	42	3.89	2.87	37
Heart rate	71.52	11.27	42	74.26	11.21	42	77.80	11.18	34
Temperature[b]									
Hand	28.19	4.34	42	28.39	4.11	42	29.67	3.67	40
Leg	29.11	1.71	42	29.88	1.98	42	29.24	1.66	40
Rectum	—	—	—	37.21	.18	42	37.18	.36	42
Vagina	—	—	—	37.18	.18	42	37.18	.26	42
Hand minus leg	−.92		42	−.49		42	.43		40
Skin resistance[c]									
Hand	18.45	8.63	41	14.31	5.00	42	12.25	5.84	39
Labia	—	—	—	10.71	5.51	40	9.78	5.84	38
Breast	—	—	—	21.03	7.39	41	19.43	6.90	38
Leg	26.06	10.12	39	18.77	5.76	42	18.23	9.26	39
Hand minus leg	−7.61		39	−4.46		42	−5.98		39

[a]Millivolt units (an excursion of 1 microvolt or larger was scored as a response).
[b]Degrees Centigrade.
[c]10,000 Ohm units.

TABLE 14-2

Overall Means and Standard Deviations of Physiological Parameters (Sample 2)

Variable	Session 1			Session 2		
	M	σ	N	M	σ	N
GSR frequency	5.28	2.88	32	5.24	2.99	36
GSR amplitude[a]	.13	.09	32	.07	.05	36
Heart rate	75.03	7.15	29	69.17	7.54	34
Temperature[b]						
Hand	29.37	2.96	40	29.73	2.91	43
Leg	27.91	2.55	40	29.42	1.98	43
Oral[c]	36.39	.39	37	—	—	—
Rectal	—	—	—	36.97	.53	40
Vaginal	—	—	—	37.05	.26	41
Hand minus leg	1.46		40	.31		43
Skin resistance[d]						
Hand	23.93	12.67	41	16.83	10.07	42
Leg	39.67	32.29	40	34.82	32.21	41
Labia	—	—	—	9.61	7.97	37
Hand minus leg	−15.74		40	−17.99		41

[a]Millivolt units (an excursion of 1 microvolt or larger was scored as a response).
[b]Degrees Centigrade.
[c]Oral temperature was also recorded in Sample 4: Mean = 36.04, σ = .60.
[d]10,000 Ohm units.

TABLE 14-3

Overall Means and Standard Deviations of Physiological Parameters (Sample 3)

Variable	Session 1		
	M	σ	N
Temperature[a]			
Hand	29.79	4.09	43
Leg	29.28	1.64	43
Breast	33.63	.78	43
Hand minus leg	.51		43
Skin resistance[b]			
Hand	23.10	10.37	41
Leg	36.25	12.84	41
Breast	28.20	10.61	41
Hand minus leg	−13.15		41

[a]Degrees Centigrade.
[b]10,000 Ohm units.

Zuckerman (1971) after reviewing the literature concerned with physiological responses to sexual stimuli, concluded that it has not been demonstrated that such responses differ in magnitude from those to nonsexual stressful or anxiety-producing stimuli. The writer's findings are congruent with this general conclusion.[31]

An interesting question is whether the erogenous zones characteristically, over a range of situations, show greater or less activation than the nonerogenous zones of the body.[32] As defined by skin resistance values, there were consistent and significant trends for the activation levels of the labia to be higher than the levels for the hand and leg. However, the activation level of the breast, as defined by skin resistance, was found to be consistently lower than the hand (but not consistently higher or lower than the leg). No difference could be discerned between the activation levels of the vagina and rectum, as defined by temperature. In general, then, only the labia seemed to be uniquely and consistently high in amount of activation.

Attempts by the writer to discover sexual behavior correlates of the diverse physiological measures have met with only slight success. Looking back over previous chapters dealing with the major sexual response indices, one finds that several trends (largely of a borderline character) were detected:

1. The less satisfaction a woman says she derives from orgasm the relatively lower is her hand as compared to her leg temperature.
2. The less the satisfaction a woman states she derives from masturbation the less is the arousal of her hand as compared to her leg (as defined by higher hand than leg skin resistance).
3. The greater a woman's intercourse frequency the greater is the temperature of her hand as compared to her leg.
4. The more sexually responsive a woman rates herself the higher is her rectal temperature.

What is interesting about these trends is that three of the four listed involve physiological measures in which the activation level of an upper body sector is compared with that of a lower body sector.[33,34] This suggests that future work concerned with the physiological correlates of individual differences in sexual responsiveness in women should look more closely at differences in upper-versus-lower body activation. It is pertinent to this matter that the writer reported in previous studies (Fisher, 1970) that women differ significantly from men in the degree to which their hands are more physiologically activated than their legs (as defined by skin resistance measures). One cannot avoid remarking that this pattern of relatively greater hand than leg activation that typified women (and girls at some age levels) was the one that was associated in the present studies with being satisfied during and after orgasm, deriving satisfaction from masturbation, and having a relatively high intercourse rate.

In pondering the possible mechanisms of such upper-versus-lower activation differences, it is obvious that the lower region of the body is much more associated with sexuality than is the upper region. Also, of course, the reproductive system is in the lower body sector. Possibly, then, long-term differences in sexual attitudes or ability to obtain satisfaction from sexual stimulation result in differential preparatory physiological sets in the sexual as compared to nonsexual body areas. For example, the unsatis-fied woman might be chronically prepared for finding more satisfying sex-ual stimulation and so the lower part of her body would remain relatively highly activated.[35] This is, of course, pure speculation.

Detailed analyses of the correlations of various measures of activation of sexual areas (vagina, labia, rectum, breasts) with the entire available range of personality, sex behavior, and perceptual variables revealed al-most nothing of significance. But one may simply mention the following scattered findings for their future research potential:

1. There was a consistent, statistically significant trend (in Samples 1 and 2) such that the higher a woman's vaginal temperature the less likely she was to describe herself (through a ranking of various terms) as feeling happy during orgasm.

2. Also, there was a consistent significant trend (in Samples 1 and 2) such that the higher a woman's rectal temperature the more likely she was to describe (through rankings of various terms) her orgasm as an "as if I would burst" experience.

3. There was a consistent (significant) positive correlation (Samples 1 and 2) between labial skin resistance and an index of the degree of con-cern about the fragility of one's body boundaries (Penetration score).

Other Sex Behavior Measures

There were diverse subsidiary self-report measures of sexual behavior whose correlational patterns were scanned. Nonsignificant findings pre-dominated. One or two leads of interest that did emerge deserve brief de-scription.

Think about Sex

The women in six of the samples were asked to rate on a five-point scale (1 = Never; 5 = A large part of the time) how often they think about sex. It was found that in four of the samples there was a negative correlation between this index and the Clean score (which, as described in Appendix B, measures how much effort is put into keeping things clean and neat).[36] Most of these correlations were of borderline significance, but their consis-tency is noteworthy. Apparently the greater a woman's interest in keeping her world clean and "tidied up" the less she thinks about sexual things.

Length of Climax

The women in several samples were asked to estimate the duration (in seconds) of their average orgasm. In two of the samples in which this information was obtained the Witkin, et al. (1962) rod and frame procedure (Appendix B) was administered. This procedure evaluates the degree to which spatial judgments can be accurately made in the presence of distracting visual cues. It has been described as a measure of how well an individual can differentiate cues from a context or be "field independent." Women have been found to perform less well on the task than do men. In the present study, it was observed in two samples that the greater the amount of error in rod and frame judgments the longer was the reported length of orgasm ($r = .35$, $p < .05$, Sample 2; $r = .27$, $p < .10$, Sample 3).

Negative Findings

One important negative finding that should be particularly mentioned involves a number of questions from the Bernreuter questionnaire that Terman (1938, 1951) reported to differentiate orgasmic from nonorgasmic women across two studies. Six such questions were administered by the writer to the women in Sample 5.[37] The derived scores were found to have only chance relationships with major sex behavior measures such as orgasm consistency, intercourse frequency, and clitoral-vaginal preference. Thus, the writer was not able to cross-validate the efficacy of these six items, which were the only ones out of a much larger number that Terman found capable of making successful discriminations in the two samples he studied. This is one more demonstration of the difficulty of obtaining consistent results in this area of research.

The following sex behavior variables all proved to be essentially unrelated to the numerous personality, perceptual, and other measures available:

Minutes of stimulation necessary before attains orgasm.
Rankings of body areas in terms of where foreplay excitement experienced.
Rated importance of sex.
Time after marriage before first climax.
Amount of vaginal pulsation.
How feel when nude before other women.
Minutes of foreplay preferred.
Frequency of pain during intercourse.
Age married.
Number of years married.
Amount of vaginal lubrication.
Amount of imagery during orgasm.
How would feel about total loss of sex gratification.
Preferred frequency of intercourse minus actual frequency of intercourse.

Husband's preferred frequency of intercourse (as estimated by wife) minus
     wife's preferred frequency of intercourse.[38]
Vaginal awareness.
Breast awareness.
Amount of enjoyment of breast stimulation.

NOTES

1. All correlations in this chapter are Pearson product-moment coefficients. N's
will not be cited unless they deviate grossly from those listed for each sample in
Chapter 7.

2. This isolated finding regarding clitoral-vaginal preference is intriguing. Unfortunately, it was not pursued further to determine whether it would stand up to
cross-validation. If one wanted to speculate about its possible implications, one could
not avoid noting the analogy between the vaginally oriented woman being relatively
more identified with traditional family ideology and her previously observed tendency to mute and "gloss over" her experiences. It could be said that the traditional
family ideology orientation implicitly contains within itself an adherence to certain
conventionalized ("This is the way it is") modes of interpretation and the shutting
out of the new, the strange, or the esoteric.

3. As already indicated, standard measures of femininity (for example, Femininity
scale of Gough [1964] California Psychological Inventory) do not correlate consistently with any of the sexual variables.

4. Analysis of extreme scores for the various parameters did not yield any better
results than the use of the entire range of scores. In all of the other subsections to
be presented in this chapter it can be assumed that analyses of extreme scores were
undertaken.

5. One is immediately reminded of Rainwater's (1965) observations that women
in lower-class cultures seem to be particularly limited in their sexual responsiveness.

6. These ratings were not significantly correlated with measures of response defensiveness (namely, L and K scales of the Minnesota Multiphasic Personality Inventory).

7. $r = .37, p < .025$, Sample 3; $r = .30, p < .10$, Sample 4; $r = .36, p$ $.05$, Sample 7.

8. $r = -.53, p < .01$, Sample 3; $r = -.35, p < .05$, Sample 4.

9. $r = .32, p < .10$, Sample 2; $r = .47, p < .01$, Sample 4; $r = .37, p < .05$, Sample 5.

10. $r = -.35$, $p < .05$, Sample 2; $r = -.38$, $p < .025$, Sample 3; $r = -.33$, $p < .05$,
Sample 4.

11. $r = .33, p < .05$, Sample 2; $r = .37, p < .025$, Sample 3.

12. $r = .35, p$ $.05$, Sample 2; $r = .44, p < .01$, Sample 3.

13. $r = .10$, not significant, Sample 2; $r = .25$, $p < .10$, Sample 3; $r = .28$, $p < .10$,
Sample 4.

14. $r = .39, p$ $.01$, Sample 2; $r = .37, p < .025$, Sample 3.

15. However, only borderline and inconsistent positive correlations were obtained
with the Vigorous score of the Thurstone (1953) Temperament Schedule.

16. Apropos of the dimension of aggression, it can be added that none of the sexual behavior parameters was consistently correlated with achievement motivation or
masculinity-femininity.

17. The test-retest reliability of this index (one week intervening) was .84 in one
sample and .94 in another (three days intervening). It was not consistently correlated
with measures of response defensiveness (namely, L and K scales of the Minnesota
Multiphasic Personality Inventory).

18. $r = .43$, $p < .01$, Sample 4; $r = .32$ $p < .10$, Sample 5. Note that for convenience of interpretation the self-ratings of sexual responsiveness have been transformed so that a high score indicates high responsiveness.

19. $r = .29$, $p < .10$, Sample 4; $r = .38$, $p < .05$, Sample 5.

20. $r = -.29$, $p < .10$, Sample 2; $r = -.56$, $p < .001$, Sample 4; $r = -.27$, $p < .10$, Sample 7.

21. $r = .38$, p .025, Sample 2; $r = .28$, $p < .10$, Sample 6.

22. $r = .37$, $p < .10$, Sample 2; $r = .27$, $p < .10$, Sample 4.

23. $r = .39$, $p < .05$, Sample 2; $r = .40$, $p = .05$, Sample 5. It should be noted that a nonsignificant correlation of .22 was found in Sample 1.

24. There are also significant findings that involve relationships between self-rated sexual responsiveness and rectal temperature. Sexual responsiveness was found to be positively related to rectal temperature during stress in Sample 1 ($x^2 = 3.8$, $df = 1$, p .05) and in Sample 2 ($r = .30$, $p < .10$).

25. Self-rated sexual responsiveness was found to be positively and significantly correlated with rated happiness of marriage ($r = .33$, $p < .05$) in Sample 2. Other measures of sexual responsiveness were not significantly correlated with marital happiness. This was the only sample in which ratings of marital happiness were obtained because, as indicated in earlier chapters, this variable has already been intensively explored and studied.

26. When the laboratory personnel were asked to define how they made their judgments, they could not give meaningful statements. They indicated that the judgments were "intuitive" and not based on obvious attributes such as beauty, friendliness, or mode of dress.

27. This statement is a condensation of a number of discrete findings; and specific correlation coefficients will not be cited.

28. $r = .21$, not significant, Sample 1; $r = .25$, p .10, Sample 2; $r = .29$, p .05, Sample 3; $r = .04$, not significant, Sample 6.

29. In Sample 1, the gynecological examination and the first exposure of the genitals to the physician are considered to have had significant sexual overtones. A task that involved doing arithmetic problems was considered to be nonsexual and stressful. There were also nonsexual and nonstressful rest periods. In Sample 2 listening to a passage from D. H. Lawrence concerning sexual intercourse was regarded as sexually stimulating. Rest and stress conditions were represented respectively by periods of being alone (when told to "relax") and periods when judgments were requested by the female technician concerning the intensity of touch stimuli. In Sample 3 the viewing of a film depicting birth was regarded as having significant sexual overtones; this was confirmed for the majority of women by written descriptions obtained from them concerning their responses to, and fantasies about, the film. Nonsexual stresses were again represented by tasks in which the female technician asked for judgments concerning the intensity of various stimuli.

It must be acknowledged that it is difficult to be even moderately certain concerning the character of the impact of the various experimental conditions. It is obviously very difficult to create a sexually stimulating situation in a laboratory setting that does not also evoke apprehension and embarrassment. However, there were certain conditions (for example, listening to a passage from D. H. Lawrence) that, in all probability, aroused sexual affects; and others (for example, doing arithmetical computations) that were stressful and nonsexual in their connotations. Still others (for example, sitting quietly with clothes on in a room) were probably relatively nonstressful and nonsexual in their significance.

30. Analyses were made of change scores corrected for baseline effects. Also, the possibility of "channeling" effects was appraised.

31. The findings concerning the labia and other sexual areas remind one of the emphasis that Kinsey, et al. (1953) and Masters and Johnson (1966) place upon the

idea that sexual arousal involves the total body and is not restricted primarily to one organ or one body sector.

32. Another question of interest concerns the degree to which the levels of activation of sexual body areas are correlated with the activation levels of nonsexual body areas. A sweep of the data indicates that vaginal temperature, skin resistance of the labia, and both temperature and skin resistance of the breast are not consistently (across several samples) correlated with such other measures as GSR, heart rate, temperature of hand, leg, and mouth, and skin resistance of hand and leg. Apparently, the activation levels of the sexual areas are unrelated to the activation levels of the nonsexual areas. It should be added that the measures of activation of the sexual areas are also not consistently correlated with each other. One exception is vaginal temperature, which was found to be significantly correlated with rectal temperature in Samples 1 and 2 (.67 and .66 respectively).

33. Measures of hand or leg activation by themselves do not correlate significantly with the sexual response indices just enumerated. Only the hand minus leg measures are significantly linked with them. It should be added that none of the other physiological measures was consistently correlated with any of the sex behavior measures.

34. It is presumed that if one body region has a lower temperature than another it is less physiologically activated.

35. The normal pattern, as shown in Tables 14–1, 14–2, and 14–3, is for the leg to be somewhat less activated than the hand. During stress of any kind the difference diminishes considerably, but still remains.

36. $r = -.28$, $p < .10$, Sample 2; $r = -.32$, $p < .05$, Sample 3; $r = -.24$, p .10, Sample 6; $r = -.25$, $p < .10$, Sample 7.

37.

1. Do you often feel just miserable?	Yes No	?
2. Do you often experience periods of loneliness?	Yes No	?
3. Do you frequently feel grouchy?	Yes No	?
4. Do you lack self-confidence?	Yes No	?
5. In your work do you usually drive yourself steadily?	Yes No	?
6. Can you be optimistic when others about you are greatly depressed?	Yes No	?

38. For future research possibilities, it should be mentioned that this index was negatively and significantly correlated in three samples with general body awareness, as measured by Body Prominence (Appendix A). No ready explanation for this relationship offers itself.

15

A SUMMING UP OF

FEMININE SEXUALITY

The main purpose of this whole enterprise has been to arrive at reasonable conclusions about what influences sexual responsiveness in women. A considerable literature has been minutely pored over, and a fairly large number of women have been questioned, probed, and tested. These efforts were made on the assumption that many of our theories and widely accepted ideas about the determinants of female sexual behavior are probably erroneous and need revision. Hopefully, the revision can be accomplished by scientific observation and reason. The pressure for such revision comes not only from scientific tradition but also the practical importance of being able to make available accurate information about sexuality. A tremendous volume of pseudofact is being transmitted to people of all age levels about the nature of sexual response; one would guess that this encourages irrational behavior in the sexual domain. This point applies doubly to the behavior of many professionals (psychoanalysts, counselors) who have subjected patients and others seeking help to unreasonable expectations about how they should behave sexually. One can, for example, only lament the number of women in psychoanalytic treatment who have been given to understand that they cannot join the ranks of the "normal" until they learn to attain orgasm primarily through vaginal stimulation. The need for making available accurate information about sexuality is dramatized when one finds, upon scanning the existing literature, that no scientific reports are to be found about exactly how the majority of persons go about having sexual intercourse. Actually we still know little about the specific kinds and amounts of foreplay employed, their sequence, the emphasis placed on direct clitoral versus vaginal stimulation, and the relative timing of each partner's orgasm. In other words, what occurs during intercourse in the average instance has remained somewhat obscure. This is particularly true if one asks questions concerning the typical feelings and fantasies that are aroused during intercourse. Intercourse as a psychological phenomenon has not been studied scientifically.

This chapter is devoted to pulling together the conglomeration of information about sexual responsiveness in women that has accumulated. Earnest efforts are made to bridge between the work of previous investigators and the findings of the present studies. Broad generalizations about the nature of feminine sexuality are offered, and answers are formulated to a variety of questions concerning factors that play a role in a woman's sexual behavior and attitudes.

The Feminine Sexual Potential

It would be well at this point to discredit long extant beliefs concerning woman's inferiority in experiencing sexual stimulation and to challenge the supposition that woman has an inferior concept of her own sexual attributes. Masters and Johnson (1966) have already presented evidence that a woman's orgasm is physiologically analogous in many ways to that of the man. They have also found that women are potentially capable of having a greater number of orgasms per unit time than men can. However, despite this fact two ideas persist that portray women as sexually inferior in a psychological sense. One of these ideas, which was partially energized by Kinsey, et al. (1953), is that women are less sexually aroused than men by psychosexual stimuli, particularly if they are visual in nature. It is asserted, for example, that pictures depicting nudity or sexual themes evoke relatively little sexual response from women; the implication has been therefore drawn that women are less sexually arousable (less sensitive to sexually stimulating things) than men. The second of these ideas, which was given a pseudoscientific rationale by Freud, is that a woman typically has a negative attitude toward her own body because she sees it as inferior to the phallic body of the man. Presumably, she feels deprived or "castrated" because she lacks that superior organ, the penis. The underlying assumption has been that having a vagina rather than a penis is a badge of inferiority and a cause for disturbance. It is not an exaggeration to say that Freud pictured the young female child as merely a castrated version of the male child. The view has been widely propagated that a woman experiences her body in a more disturbed and unsatisfied fashion than a man does. These two ideas reverberate in multiple other notions about the psychological sexual inferiority of the woman. Illustratively, one can find assertions that sexual arousal is less important to women than to men, or that the orgasm experience is a more "natural" thing for men than for women, or that women frequently cannot enjoy sex (and being a woman) because of "penis envy."

The writer was able to show in the literature review presented in earlier chapters that the actual facts do not support these notions about women's sexual deficiencies. Consider for a moment the idea that women are less aroused than men by psychosexual stimuli. With an increasing influx of relevant information, it is becoming obvious that women do respond with excitement to all kinds of psychosexual stimuli, including visual ones. Although there are *overall* average trends for men to report slightly more sexual excitement than women to pictures depicting nudity, it is also true that many individual women report more excitement than do many men. Actually, some women have reported a level of excitement that is attained by few men. One must keep in mind, too, that it is deceptive to compare the average reports of men and women concerning the excitement evoked in them because cultural standards disapprove of women talking as openly as men about experiencing sexual excitement. Probably, as it becomes more respectable for a woman to say that even nontraditionally romantic sexual material excites her, the small average differences between the reports of women and men with respect to amount of sexual arousal evoked by visual stimuli will disappear from research studies.

Let us appraise, too, the widely accepted stereotype that the average woman perceives her body as sexually inferior to that of the man, and consequently finds it a source of discomfort and anxiety. The scientific findings overwhelmingly contradict this concept of feminine inferiority. One can, on the contrary, make out a good case for the assertion that men are more insecure and anxious about their bodies than are women. As described in an earlier chapter, several lines of evidence point in this direction. It will be recalled that men have more anxiety than women about possibly sustaining body damage; they have more fantasies about body injury and seem to be more threatened by situations (for example, hospitalization) with special body implications. They even dream more about body injury than do women. There is also evidence men have less clearly defined body boundaries than women; this suggests that men feel relatively more concerned about outside forces possibly intruding upon their bodies. Furthermore, one should mention that men seem less comfortable than women about focusing attention upon their own bodies. It is acceptable that a woman should lavish interest upon her body and experiment with its adornment, but a man who behaves equivalently is viewed with suspicion. Such differences in body attitudes between women and men have been described by a number of researchers. Interestingly, they have been detected even in early childhood. One is reminded that some observers (Katcher and Levin, 1955; Katcher, 1955) report that girls arrive at a realistic notion of the difference between masculinity and femininity and between female and male genitals earlier than do boys. It was the writer's conclusion, after reviewing all available studies, that the average woman is more "at ease" with her own body than is the average man. She not only feels less body threat but can more clearly see a relationship between her body and her primary life roles. As Douvan and Adelson (1966) and others have shown, most young women still *primarily* have a goal of marrying and becoming mothers. A woman can easily discern a link between the sexual and reproductive aspects of this role and the related aspects of her own body. Her body "makes sense" to her as one of the prime means to become what she wants to become. This is probably much less true for the man. Many of man's most important life goals revolve about attaining vocational success and often these goals call for activities that require little body strength or prowess. The businessman or the lawyer or the clerk cannot conjure up much of a logical connection between his body attributes and his vocational identity, which for most men is basic to their self-definition. The woman can more easily integrate her body meaningfully into the pattern of her life than can the man. It is the man, rather than the woman, who is more likely to feel insecure about his body and alienated from it.[1]

The material presented indicates with clarity that there is no factual basis for regarding women as psychologically less sexually secure or able than men. To continue to promulgate ideas about such alleged inferiority would seem to be an expression of antifeminine prejudice.

What Determines How Sexually Responsive a Woman Will Be?

There is no question but that the women studied by the writer were "sexually responsive." Although a sizable percent of the women studied did not attain orgasm *consistently* during intercourse, it was also true that, on the average, they experienced their sexual encounters positively. The average woman enjoyed intercourse and considered the sexual dimension of her life to be a major source of gratification. She did not find intercourse painful and was not particularly concerned about getting hurt or becoming unexpectedly pregnant when she was vaginally penetrated. She spent quite a bit of time thinking about sex and preferred to have intercourse with considerable frequency. She did not feel that her husband was making inordinate sexual demands upon her. After orgasm she described herself as feeling satisfied, happy, and relaxed. A picture emerges in which sexual stimulation and all that is associated with it have a clear positive valence in the lives of the married women who were studied. Sex was largely perceived by them as a source of fun and enjoyment. This positive picture contrasts with the rather grim and negative portrayals found in many clinically oriented sources in which some writers have depicted the sexual life of the average woman as a maze of difficulties, conflicts, and threatening consequences. Of course, one could object that the writer's samples are hardly representative of women in general; it could be argued that studies of women from lower socioeconomic groups would uncover more negative attitudes. This cannot be denied, and one will have to suspend judgment until data equivalent to the writer's are obtained from other strata of the culture. But it should be added that other studies of middle-class women (for example, Ard, 1962; Terman, 1938) have also found that, on the average, such women regard sexual transactions as enjoyable. Schaefer (1964) reported that even in a sample of troubled women who had sought psychotherapeutic treatment, sexual gratification was a significant component of life. Although the marital sexual relationship is a complicated one and often calls for new adaptations, it apparently is very rewarding to many.

Some of the confusion in the literature about how much satisfaction women obtain from sexual stimulation derives from the subjective nature of "satisfaction." It is difficult to pin this term down, and so the temptation is great to use fairly simple indices such as orgasm consistency or intercourse frequency as measures of a person's sexual experiences. Those who have criticized the Kinsey, et al. (1953) and Masters and Johnson (1966) work because it emphasizes the measurement of orgasm would be less vociferous if they were personally confronted with the responsibility of deciding how to evaluate an individual's response to sexual stimulation. The writer attempted to add new complexity to this evaluation process by asking the women studied to rank various descriptive terms with reference to how well they portrayed feelings during and after orgasm. Other ratings involving attitudes toward sexual gratification and related issues were also secured. However, these procedures were really quite crude in the face of the complex phenomena they were supposed to evaluate. Experiences during sexual arousal can potentially be scaled on a range of dimensions. Not only are there the obvious ones involving amount of excitement, tension, release, and gross "satisfaction," but also the following:

Feelings of tenderness and love toward the sex partner.
Feelings of unique intimacy.
Satisfaction from body nudity and display.
Enjoyment in being an object of admiration.
Satisfaction from being sexually competent.
Sensations of a unique kind of self "release."
Emphatic definition of one's sex identity.
Fantasy and imaginative role playing (for example, pretending to have a novel sex partner).
Satisfaction related to the act of creation and reproduction.
Enjoyment of muscular and kinesthetic variations.

This list could obviously be extended further. One cannot deny that those aspects of sexual experience that have been measured so far are only a small sample of the total possible. However, it should be pointed out that the same criticism can be made with reference to research dealing with all the other major forms of gratification. Only a few aspects of such experiences as eating, listening to music, vigorously participating in a sport, or working have ever been explored. The difficulties that plague the study of sexual experience are similar to those that have held up the study of all forms of gratification. They may be somewhat more extreme in the sexual realm because of the special reluctance of many persons to discuss their sexual feelings, but even this difference is rapidly disappearing as sex becomes an increasingly acceptable public topic.

Obviously, one cannot really treat sexual responsiveness as a unitary entity. There are many ways of defining what happens during a sexual interaction. Sexual stimulation has complex effects and each individual may selectively focus on one effect as compared to another. Sexual arousal can stir up a variety of fantasies; it may or may not eventuate in orgasm; the orgasm itself may be strong or weak; the orgasm may be enjoyable or even unenjoyable; the orgasm may be followed by relaxation or even by increased tension; there may be no orgasm but the unresolved build-up of sexual excitement may somehow be an intriguing experience; the closeness of one's body to the sexual partner may be more prominent in awareness than the orgasm attained.[2] Not only do different women have different ways of enjoying (and not enjoying) sexual stimulation, but it is also probable that they individually fluctuate to some extent in their own pattern of enjoyment over a series of sexual contacts. The psychological complexity of sexual arousal in a woman cannot be overemphasized. It is too easy to slip into simplistic notions that women are neatly ordered into "sexy" and "nonsexy" categories. The real complexity of the matter can perhaps best be conveyed by stating that one can easily accept the possibility that there are instances in which the extremely "sexy" woman who always achieves intense orgasms may not derive as much satisfaction out of intercourse as the apparently less "sexy" woman whose orgasms are inconsistent and of lesser strength. Measures of different aspects of the response to sexual stimulation either do not correlate with each other, or, if they do, the correlations are of low magnitude. A woman may be high in terms of one index of responsiveness and low in terms of another. She may obtain much satisfaction from orgasm but *prefer* to engage in intercourse infrequently. She may rarely attain orgasm and still *actually* have a high intercourse rate. Whether she attains orgasm may be unrelated to most of the qualitative sensations that she has during orgasm (for example, feeling tense or depersonalized).

When referring to a woman's sexual responsiveness, care must be taken to specify a particular aspect or dimension. One can refer to her orgasm consistency or her intercourse frequency or her likelihood of feeling "ecstatic" during orgasm or the frequency of intercourse she prefers or the number of different intercourse positions she uses, but one would rarely be able to make the statement that she is *generally* high or low with respect to most of these dimensions. In an earlier chapter it was noted that although a conclusion of this sort may appear to be unreasonable when applied to sexual behavior, it would not seem so if applied to another kind of appetite, such as eating. The average person's "responsiveness" to food could probably not be adequately described by terms such as "high" or "low." One may enjoy food a great deal and yet eat only small quantities, or one may intensely enjoy a narrow spectrum of foods and dislike most others, or one may relish eating but begin to feel discomfort from it when the digestive processes get under way, or one may get more satisfaction from the social context of eating than from the food itself. This general perspective does not mean that certain aspects of sexual responsiveness cannot be viewed as being relatively more important than others. There is probably little question that the average woman places high value during intercourse on becoming highly excited, attaining orgasm, and finally arriving at a feeling of satisfaction. She probably also attaches a fair amount of importance to the frequency with which she engages in intercourse. Certain aspects of sexual arousal may, on the contrary, be ascribed low importance. In all likelihood, the average woman engaging in regular intercourse does not attend to whether her orgasm is of extremely high as compared to moderate intensity, does not care about the amount of her vaginal lubrication, as long as it exceeds a certain minimum, is not terribly concerned about the matter of multiple orgasms, and does not have a large investment in using many as compared to few intercourse positions.

Attainment of orgasm is one of the prime ways of defining sexual responsiveness. This is true despite the often discussed fact that there are other important feelings and sensations linked with intercourse that, in individual cases, may be even more important than the orgasm itself. In general, orgasm is a major criterion of sexual responsiveness, whether one evaluates it from the private perspective of the individual's own feelings or that based on more public norms and expectations. Because it is assigned so much importance, as compared to other kinds of feelings and sensations, there has been surprise, amounting almost to consternation, at the repeated research findings that about 30 percent of all married women either do not ever attain orgasm or do so only occasionally. These findings have been interpreted by some to mean that a large segment of women in our culture do not get very aroused by, or really enjoy, sexual stimulation. Observations from the writer's studies would argue that this is an overstatement. It will be recalled that the women in the seven samples did generally value sexual stimulation and did assign considerable importance to it in their lives, despite their not infrequent difficulties in achieving orgasm. But there still remains the puzzling question as to why so many women lack the ability to mass their excitement to the orgasm threshold. One of the most popular explanations is that many women are brought up puritanically and have so much anxiety and inhibition about sexual matters that they respond negatively when exposed to sexual stimulation. A second explanation places the burden of failure upon the male partner who is portrayed as inadequate in his sexual approach; he is said to be too aggressive and shocking in his sexual behavior or not willing to deliver sexual stimulation for a sufficiently sustained period or not bestowing it in the correct proportions to certain anatomical areas as compared to others (for example, clitoral versus vaginal).

The explanation based on puritanical upbringing is difficult to sustain in the face of several contradictory facts. First of all, no one has been able to detect a convincing link between orgasm consistency and religiosity, except perhaps in a few extreme instances. Terman (1938, 1951) could find no significant correlations between orgasm indices and measures of religiosity (such as church attendance, religious affiliation); this was essentially true also in the Kinsey, et al. (1953) study (except for a small, extremely devout Catholic sample). It will also be recalled that the writer failed to find a significant correlation, across numerous samples, between orgasm consistency and indices of religiosity based on church attendance, self-ratings, and a formal measure of religious values. There were similar negative results in relating orgasm consistency to the woman's recall of how religious her parents had been. Since it is logical to assume that the amount of puritanical inhibition about sex that a woman would encounter in her family as she grew up would be positively related to the religiosity of the family atmosphere, the lack of correlation between orgasm consistency and religiosity is not congruent with the "puritanical" hypothesis. This hypothesis is further contradicted by the writer's findings that a woman's recall of how permissive versus repressive her parents had been about sex does not correlate with her orgasm consistency. It is additionally pertinent that several studies (including the writer's) have shown that the extent to which a woman recalls her parents as having personally participated in giving her sexual information is quite unrelated to her sexual responsiveness. The "puritanical" hypothesis would, on the contrary, lead one to expect that since parents who refrain from giving information about sex probably are inhibited about sexuality, their children would have difficulties in sexual interactions.

Other measures of sexual enjoyment (for example, satisfaction after orgasm, self-rated sexual responsiveness) have also turned out to be unrelated to recall of how one's parents behaved with respect to sexual matters. A woman's ability to be sexually responsive is apparently not linked with the adequacy of the sex information provided by her parents, how openly they talked to her about sexual matters, their attitudes about nudity and the display of one's body, their degree of open display of affection toward each other, and their reaction to the onset of her menstruation. In other words, there is no empirical support for the idea that the parents' *formal* or *explicit* behavior with regard to sexual matters has a profound effect upon their daughter's psychological sexual development. The parent who is open about sexual matters and who provides explicit sexual information is no more likely to produce a daughter without sexual response difficulties than the parent who is reserved in his communications about sex. Such data raise questions about the emphasis that some have placed upon the importance of the parent's providing formal instruction about sexual matters to their children. Formal information about sex may facilitate certain aspects of adaptation to sex role, but on the basis of the presently available findings one would have to be skeptical that such information will make a fundamental difference in a woman's ability to enjoy sexual stimulation.

The notion that a woman's orgasm difficulties reflect her husband's poor love-making techniques also does not stand up well against the available research evidence. The extensive studies by Terman (1938, 1951), in which wives and their husbands were evaluated in detail, turned up few, if any, consistent correlations between diverse husband attributes (including sexual behavior) and wife's orgasmic ability.[3] It is also true that Kinsey, et al. (1953) and others have generally been unable to show that a woman's orgasm consistency is related to several different aspects of the husband's sexual behavior (for example, how long he persists in applying sexual stimulation to his wife). In the present writer's studies there were no consistent correlations between variables that certainly reflect the husband's sexual behavior (number of intercourse positions, amount of foreplay, and duration of sexual stimulation) and the wife's orgasm consistency. However, such findings are not meant to imply that a husband's particular pattern of sexual behavior does not importantly affect the content and "feel" of his wife's sexual experiences, but only that it does not play a decisive role in whether she will reach orgasm. The probable picture that emerges is that beyond the point of delivering a certain necessary minimum of stimulation the husband's *sexual* behavior is of secondary importance as to whether his wife will build up to orgastic excitement. At a later point, the potential role of the husband's personality in this orgastic process is further considered. Of course, there can be no certainty on this matter until other studies are carried out in which more detailed information is obtained about male sexual behavior and its effect on female orgasm. In this respect, it might have been informative if the women in the writer's studies had been asked to provide more data relative to this area, for example, whether their orgasm consistency has changed with different sex partners and if so, why this was so.

Let us review the factors that have been empirically shown to be correlated with a woman's orgasm consistency. The results of the writer's studies are first considered, but it must again be cautioned that whereas they represent statistically significant findings, they are of limited magnitude and should be regarded as tentative in nature. One of the primary findings was that the greater a woman's feeling that love objects are not dependable (that they are easily lost or will disappear) the less likely she is to attain orgasm. Women with orgasm difficulties were found to produce an elevated number of projective test themes referring to death and separation. Also, there was actual evidence that such women are likely to have suffered the literal loss (through death) or functional loss (because of long periods of absence from home) of their fathers during childhood. These and related findings were explained in terms of a model that focuses upon the blurring of consciousness and the diminished "hold" upon what is "out there" by a woman as her sexual excitement mounts to the point of orgasm. It was theorized that the woman who feels that objects are undependable and who fears their loss finds the blurring of her relationships with objects that is produced by sexual excitement so threatening that she has to "turn it off." Presumably, she is made so uncomfortable by the loss implications of her excitement that the process of building up to orgasm is inhibited or blocked. It is essential to add that the concern about loss of objects is not a sign of personality disturbance. That is, there was no indication that women who do not attain orgasm consistently are *generally* more anxious or in poorer "mental health" than women who do reach orgasm consistently. Concern about loss of objects may be viewed as one problem among many other kinds of psychological difficulties that afflict humans, and need be neither more nor less burdensome than other varieties of problems. Furthermore, one may suggest that although a woman is especially concerned about object loss she can still learn to cope with it through compensatory defenses, which would make it possible for her to function just as well as persons without such concern in most contexts (with the exception of situations involving buildup of sexual excitement). The fact that the writer did not find greater *general* psychological disturbance in low- as compared to high-orgasmic women certainly fits with the majority of previous studies that have failed to demonstrate that a woman's sexual responsiveness has anything to do with how psychologically disturbed she is. There is, for example, no consistent evidence in the literature that schizophrenic women are less sexually responsive than those who are nonschizophrenic. It is doubtful that the myth that orgasm consistency reflects mental health will die easily. The psychiatric literature is saturated with belief in this concept. It has been perpetuated by endless anecdotes and case studies, and has become an article of faith. One would guess that if observers had been as alert to detect exceptions to the equation between orgasm ability and psychological disturbance as they were to amass support for it, the clinical literature would now contain as many negative as positive reports. There is really no persuasive reason for viewing low-orgasm consistency in a woman as just another example of her general inability to cope adequately with the world. Such a view only perpetuates the stereotype that a woman's orgasm capacity is an index of her general superiority-inferiority as a functioning person. If analogous reasoning were applied to a woman's enjoyment of eating or sleeping or physical exercise, it would evoke only amusement.

It is even possible to propose speculatively that certain kinds of disturbance in psychological functioning might facilitate orgasm. If it is assumed that the increasing excitement that leads to orgasm becomes ultimately inhibiting to many women because it causes a threatening blurring of their perceptual "hold" on objects, the question arises whether those who have had previous "practice" with such blurring experiences might be less threatened by them. One way in which "practice" of this kind might have been obtained would be through previous psychopathological experiences. A woman who has had over the years to cope with the impact of intense anxiety or with psychotic-like distortions of the world might gradually adapt to the experience of having a tenuous "hold" on objects. The blurring of perception produced by sexual excitement would, then, be a familiar phenomenon to her, and so there might be a lower probability that it would have an acute disturbing or inhibiting effect. Such a formulation could possibly help to explain puzzling reports in the clinical literature about certain schizophrenic women who appear to be unusually orgasmic. Perhaps some schizophrenic women are able to derive from their history of fluid and fluctuating reality contact the "skill" to immerse themselves in, and let themselves be carried away by, other varieties of experiences that blur contact with objects. They would therefore not be particularly alarmed by alterations in perception that are caused by intense sexual arousal. Of course, this immediately raises the question whether women who have had histories of epileptic seizures or who have intensively cultivated the use of consciousness altering drugs experience the perceptual blurring of sexual excitement as an old, familiar phenomenon. If so, how does it affect their orgasm potential? In effect, what the writer proposes is that although confidence in the stability of love objects may be the principal facilitator of orgasm, there may be a paradoxical opposing familiarity with the instability of consciousness that can also facilitate orgasm. Although it may turn out that only a relatively small percent of women become highly orgasmic by means of the instability route, it is a matter of considerable theoretical importance that should be studied.

Another point about the writer's findings that needs underscoring is that orgasm consistency was found *not* to be related to a host of variables that have often been cited in the literature as contributing to "frigidity." For example, orgasm consistency turned out not to be related to degree of femininity (as conventionally defined), attitudes toward the mother, aggressiveness, passivity, guilt, religiosity, recalled attitudes of parents toward sex, impulsivity, and narcissism. One cannot glibly speak of orgasm as more likely to occur in women with certain personality traits as compared to others. The likelihood of orgasm is no greater in the forceful than the passive, in the feminine than the not so feminine, in the sociable than the shy, in the extraverted than the reflective, in the self-centered than the altruistic, in the conservative than the liberal, and in the calm than the anxious. What has emerged from the writer's findings is that orgasm consistency tends to be diminished in women with a specific kind of uncertainty about people (that they cannot be depended upon to remain available for relationships). However, this type of uncertainty can apparently exist in women of diverse personalities. One would presume that there are potentially an infinite number of ways in which it can be dealt with, contained, and expressed.

If it has not already become obvious, it should be pointed out that the concept of fear of loss of love object bears a remarkable resemblance to the concept of fear of loss of love or separation from love object that was described in an earlier review chapter as a species of anxiety particularly characteristic of women. Although concern about body damage has been found to typify men, women have been observed in several studies (for example, Bradford, 1968) to be especially sensitive to potential separation from those with whom they have close relationships. This sensitivity has been detected in their responses to questionnaires about the kinds of things they fear. It has also evidenced itself in the themes of stories they create and in brief samples of their stream of thought. Bradford (1968), as earlier noted, stated (p. 88): "It might be argued that from infancy on, females are encouraged to be people and home oriented; that parents tend to use withdrawal of love rather than physical punishment in disciplining girls and thus their extreme sensitivity to this threat. . . ."

One cannot but be impressed with the fact that a species of anxiety that has been identified in the literature as typifying women should turn out to be a significant element in interfering with their attainment of orgasm. If Bradford is correct in his statement that threatened withdrawal of love is one of the common ways of disciplining girls, it would follow that an "anti-orgasm" vector is built right into the current modal style of rearing girls. Perhaps this accounts for the high frequency with which orgasm difficulties are encountered in women. It is a paradox that the very socialization experiences that give rise to certain aspects of what we call a feminine orientation may simultaneously be generating an incapacity to cope with the conditions associated with orgasmic levels of excitement. If there are any cultures in the world in which the socialization of the girl does not involve focusing her anxieties upon potential separation from love objects, they would provide a unique opportunity to evaluate the role of fear of loss of love objects upon orgasm consistency. Obviously, one would expect orgasm consistency rates to be unusually high in such cultures. The writer would urge that cross-cultural studies pertinent to this matter be given high priority.

Relevant to this same issue, the thought presents itself that even *within* our culture it might be possible on the basis of an analysis of child-rearing practices to demonstrate changes over the last several generations in the degree to which girls are instilled with anxiety about separation from love objects. If so, one would conjecture that it would be found that there has been a gradual decline in the practice, and so there should be a perceptible parallel increase in orgasmic consistency. One is reminded, in this respect, that Kinsey, et al. (1953) reported that orgasm consistency rates for married women were higher in women born after 1900 than before that date, and in fact show a trend to increase in succeeding generations after 1900.

If concern about loss of love objects does actually contribute to a woman's orgasmic difficulties, does this not raise the possibility that the behavior of her sex partner, who is, after all, one of the most important in the class of current "love objects," may also be significantly involved? [4] This question is asked in the face of the fact that previous intensive studies (for example, Terman, 1938, 1951) have not been able to demonstrate that a wife's orgasmic capacity is correlated in any noteworthy way with the attributes of her husband. These studies have not only examined reports of the sex behavior of the husband but have also examined measures of his personality, social status, and the like. Even so, one must question whether they concerned themselves sufficiently with patterns of husband behavior that might particularly affect a woman's feelings about loss of sex object. For example, since men probably also vary in their anxiety about potential loss of love object, is it possible that a husband with high concern of this kind might reinforce an analogous concern in his wife—and in so doing decrease her orgasm consistency? But if his anxiety about object loss were unusually low he might also communicate this feeling to his wife and in the process give her reassurance that would counter her own uncertainties about loss. Perhaps a husband can intensify or decrease his wife's concern about object loss in terms of how much his work keeps him away from home or how often he communicates in an empathic fashion with her or the degree to which he expresses anger by sulking and going off by himself rather than openly ventilating it. Such behavior patterns and others of a related order are difficult to measure and one can definitely say that they have not been adequately evaluated in previous studies of how husband attitudes and wife orgasm consistency are correlated.[5] It would seem to be sensible at this point to suspend judgment about the husband's potential impact, by means of his general conduct and emotional stance, upon certain of his wife's emotional attitudes that probably influence her orgasmic potential. Apropos of this matter, one is reminded that Masters and Johnson (1970) state that successful treatment of a woman with orgasmic problems requires that she be seen conjointly with her husband (as a "unit"). They see the husband as playing a significant part in helping his wife to overcome orgasm inhibitions. It should be cautioned that this view is based on clinical observation and still awaits empirical support.

How does the concept that orgasm consistency is influenced by feelings about the dependability of love objects fit with previous empirical findings in this area? As one looks back over the earlier meager positive results that have been obtained (for example, Terman, 1938, 1951; Thomason, 1951), there is little that is directly congruent with this concept. There are two instances (Terman, 1938, 1951; Thomason, 1951) in which low-orgastic women have been described as lacking in individualism and self-confidence. One might somehow think of such qualities as indicating a poor sense of identity and this identity variable might, in turn, be remotely linked with being concerned about whether there are dependable love objects around, but the train of reasoning is quite unconvincing. One would have to say flatly that there is little or nothing in the previous empirical literature that is directly supportive of the "loss of objects" hypothesis. However, it should be underscored that this lack of support is simply due to the fact that previous investigators have not designed their studies to look at the role of concern about loss of objects in orgasm consistency. There is an important sense in which previous studies do support the writer's findings. They discovered that many personality and background variables are *not* correlated with orgasm consistency, and they were unable to isolate a specific, circumscribed *personality trait* as typifying the woman who is orgastically low. That is, they have not been able to associate orgasmic ability with a particular type of personality.

More successful than the psychologically-oriented studies have been several concerned with the relationship of orgasm consistency to broad sociological variables such as education and social class. An earlier review of the literature indicated that with increasing education or increasing social class women show greater orgasm consistency. Kinsey, et al. (1953) have detected such positive correlations between orgasm consistency and both social class and education.[6] It has already been suggested that these correlations may indirectly support the writer's formulation that concern about object loss interferes with orgasm. One can reason that the more limited a woman's education or the lower her social class the more likely she is to have come from an economically deprived background in which uncertainty about loss would be magnified. This uncertainty might stem from the greater probability of occurrence of such events as sudden loss of family income, desertion by father, and serious illness among family members. The lower socioeconomic family context is one in which there is less assurance that one's parents will be able to provide necessary resources and that they will remain consistently available for relationships. Chronic exposure during childhood to unpredictability might instill the sort of concern about loss of objects that has been found to be correlated with low-orgasm consistency.

It must be reiterated that not a particle of data has been uncovered that would indicate that the likelihood of being orgastic is a function of rate of physiological maturation or gross physical attributes. Orgasm consistency is, for example, not correlated with age of menarche and age of development of axillary or pubic hair. It is also not related to indices of body size (for example, height, weight, breast size), menstrual characteristics (namely, irregularity, duration of flow), and a variety of measures of autonomic response at multiple sites on the body. Quite surprising is the fact that it is not correlated with indicators of amount of arousal or activation of the genital and breast regions (for example, as ascertained by vaginal and breast temperatures) under various conditions. One should add that those researchers who have evaluated the evidence with respect to the influence of hormonal factors on the sexual responsiveness of women have not been able to discern convincing relationships. Generally, it can, with justification, be said that no convincing relationships have yet been established between orgasm consistency in women and specific physiological or constitutional factors. This does not, of course, rule out the possibility that there really are such factors or that genetic influences may be of some importance. However, the burden of proof rests upon those who would appeal to them as explanatory concepts.

Little, if anything, is known about whether orgasm is more likely to occur at certain times in the menstrual cycle as compared to others. Unfortunately, no questions were included in the writer's studies that directly touch on this matter. Inquiries were made about whether general sexual responsiveness varied in some lawful fashion during the cycle. A definite trend was found for the women studied to be relatively more responsive during the week before the onset of menstruation as well as the week following the cessation of menstruation. The augmented responsiveness in the week preceding menstruation was explained as being the result of an anticipation of sexual deprivation during menstruation (during which intercourse either ceases or is considerably reduced for many). The peak of responsiveness following menstruation was attributed to the actual deprivation that does occur during menstruation. Support for this last explanation was found in the data.

If orgasm capacity were to vary in a similar fashion (that is, paralleled reports of sexual responsiveness) it would mean, of course, that an additional element governing the attainment of orgasm in women pertains to how sexually deprived they feel. But we do not know whether orgasm capacity varies in an analogous fashion. It is important to note, too, that no direct information is available about the effects of actual sexual deprivation upon orgasm capacity. If a woman has not had a sexual experience for a long period of time, is she more likely to attain orgasm than if she has recently had such an experience? Two facts come to mind that would lead the writer to conjecture that amount of deprivation does not generally affect orgasm capacity. First, there is no indication that unmarried women who have much less regular intercourse than married women, and who are therefore more "deprived," attain orgasm in a greater percentage of their intercourse contacts. In fact, as already described, the opposite seems to be true. Secondly, the writer found no consistent relationships between orgasm consistency and intercourse rates. Presumably, a woman who had intercourse with low frequency would come to each sexual encounter in a greater state of want than the woman who engaged frequently in intercourse. If relative deprivation did increase orgasm consistency, and all other things were equal, one might expect at least a low positive correlation between these two indices. The facts did not support this expectation. But we are dealing only with tangential deductions and speculations. Obviously, there is a need for more direct studies of how various amounts of sexual deprivation affect orgasm capacity in both sexually experienced and inexperienced women.

A key question that arises in discussing a woman's orgasm consistency concerns how early in her development it is determined. Do her childhood relationships with her parents already define whether she will be "high" or "low"? Are the early years of her heterosexual liaisons of crucial importance? Is the whole process actually unpredictable because single dramatic or traumatic events (such as first intercourse experience) have significant impact? If childhood relationships are important, to what degree can their influence be altered by adult love relationships and adult sexual experiences? These are the questions that one would like to be able to answer. They cannot all be fully and adequately dealt with on the basis of our current knowledge, but there is a fair amount of information that permits partial replies. First of all, it seems fair to say that there are research findings that indicate that early interactions with parents do play a role in a woman's later ability to be orgastic. These findings specifically involve her relationships with her father. The writer's studies indicated a trend for a woman's orgasm consistency to be positively correlated with her recall of how demanding and definite (as contrasted to casual and permissive) her father's expectations of her had been. If one accepts the fact that her perception of her father's behavior toward her mirrors, to some extent, how he treated her as she was growing up, one would have to conclude that during childhood she was already having social experiences that would influence her later orgastic potential. If one had to speculate what she was learning from these interactions with her father, it would be that he was sufficiently seriously interested in her as a person to expend a good deal of energy in guiding and helping her to structure her life. If he was obviously seriously interested in guiding her, she could, even if she resented his authoritarianism and his intrusiveness, feel that he was *dependably* invested in her. Incidentally, the fact that a woman's perception of equivalent qualities in her mother was found not to be correlated with her orgasm consistency suggests that it is particularly the father's dependability that is important in shaping her orgasm potential. The most obvious way to explain this differential would be to point to the fact that her orgasm potential does, after all, express itself in her interactions with a male sex partner, and so it would be logical that her feelings about the dependability of the prime male figure in her early life should be the specific ones to carry over to her later sexual relationship with men. In any case, all that we can say is that to some significant but unknown degree the nature of a woman's transactions with her father as she is growing up will probably affect her orgasm capacity.[7] Because of the imperfect techniques available for measuring the variables involved, one cannot begin to define realistically how influential these early transactions are. They could be enormously important and even *the prime determinant* of orgasmic potential. This remains to be seen.

Indeed, one is tempted to ascribe great importance to this kind of early socialization influence because there have been so few, if any, other influences that have shown even a hint of a link to orgasm consistency. In earlier chapters it was noted that there is little evidence that the average woman's orgasm potential is shaped by one or a few special traumatic sexual episodes. For example, unmarried women who find it necessary to obtain an abortion, which would certainly be a severe traumatic event, do not later, in their first year of married intercourse, show lowered orgasm consistency. Women who report childhood episodes in which they were raped or forcefully seduced are not less orgasmic than women who indicate they did not suffer in this fashion. The writer could find no consistent correlations in his data between orgasm consistency and how a woman experienced such major sex development landmarks as her first menstruation, first serious date, and first intercourse. Those who recalled their first intercourse as extremely unpleasant were no less orgasmic than those who remembered it as being very pleasant. The temptation to minimize the influence of actual sexual learning experiences, as such, upon orgasm capacity is encouraged by the findings, across several studies, that a girl's dating history gives no hint as to her orgasm consistency. How early a girl begins to date, or the average frequency with which she dates at different phases of her adolescence and early womanhood, or the seriousness of her dating (as defined by "getting engaged") do not foretell her orgasm behavior. This was apparent in Terman's (1938, 1951) data as well as those of the writer and others. Whatever a girls learns about heterosexual behavior and about relating to a male intimately from her dating experiences does not seem to affect her orgasm potential. This is a truly remarkable finding and difficult to believe. One is reluctant to accept the message that a girl's history of sexual experience and her apparent capability of attracting and pleasing males count for nought in her later ability to achieve orgasm during regular intercourse.

The crucial question must then be asked whether sexual practice does materially affect orgasm consistency. This is the pivot on which wavers the decision about how modifiable orgasm capacity is once a girl's basic socialization experiences have occurred. It will be recalled that Kinsey, et al. (1953), who have published the most reliable data bearing on this matter, reported that practice derived from regular married intercourse did have an appreciable effect on the likelihood of attaining at least *"occasional"* orgasm. Illustratively, whereas 75 percent of married women attained at least occasional orgasm during the first year of marriage, this increased to 83 percent by the fifth year, and 89 percent by the twentieth year. In other words, there was a 14 percent increase in this "at least occasional" orgasm category over a 20-year span. Another way to look at this result is that it represents a 14 percent decrease in those who "never" attain orgasm. Note too that over the span of the first three months of marriage there was an analogous 10 percent decrease in the "never" attain orgasm category. But approaching the Kinsey, et al. data from another perspective, one finds that the percent of women who attained orgasm in "nearly all" (90–100 percent) of their coitus increased only 8 percent from the first to the twentieth year of marriage. In other words, 20 years of practice produced an 8 percent increment in those able to attain orgasm with high regularity. It is of further interest that whereas 39 percent of married women attained orgasm 90 to 100 percent of the time during their first year of marriage, this value increased to only 40 percent by the fifth year of marriage. After five years of practice only a 1 percent increase could be detected! Even after ten years of practice the increase was only 3 percent. If one looks at the less extreme category of those women able to attain orgasm 60–89 percent of the time, one finds only a 3 percent improvement after five years of practice and a 5 percent improvement after ten years.

These rates of improvement strike the writer as being quite small. However, it should be acknowledged that Kinsey, et al. (1953) chose a different interpretative framework. They stated (p. 384): "These data provide impressive evidence that experience and psychological reconditioning may, in the course of time, improve the ability of the female to respond to the point of orgasm in her marital coitus." The Kinsey, et al. view seems exaggerated in its optimism. If after five years of practice only 1 percent of the women studied show an increase in being really consistently orgasmic, or if after five years of practice only 8 percent of those who are *totally* nonorgasmic begin to have an occasional orgasm, how can one attribute much influence to practice effects? The role of practice is detectable but otherwise of small proportions. Overall, it is the writer's impression that practice may, to a limited degree, decrease a woman's likelihood of *never* reaching orgasm during intercourse, but that it has minimal effect on her probability of attaining orgasm with high consistency. Intensive practice can help a woman who has serious difficulty in attaining orgasm at all to build up an orgasmic level of excitement occasionally, but it seems rarely to transform her into one who achieves orgasm with great consistency.

Incidentally, there is another factor to consider that cautions one to conservatively interpret even the small practice effects observed by Kinsey, et al. One must consider the possibility that with increasing duration of marriage there is greater assurance on a woman's part that her husband is a dependable love object (that he can be counted upon to remain with her), and it may be her diminished concern about his dependability, rather than practice effects, which facilitates her achievement of orgasm. Indeed, as one further scans the Kinsey, et al. data concerned with practice effects, other questions arise.[8] For example, is it really logical to attribute any of the gains in orgasm consistency that may occur beyond the fifth year of marriage to practice? Would one not expect the potential maximum facilitation because of practice to have already been approached in the first five years of marriage when youthful vigor and intercourse rates are at their height? Another question that presents itself is why the apparent effect of practice should register primarily in terms of facilitation of the nonorgasmic woman to the point where she can be occasionally orgasmic? If practice is a prime factor in reaching orgasm, why does it so rarely enable a woman with low-orgasm consistency to become highly consistent?[9] In the writer's opinion; this last question is of paramount import and stands as an impressive objection to any theory that underscores the role of practice, as such, in shaping orgasm potential.

If one respects the information presented and the train of logic pursued, it becomes difficult to evade the conclusion that a woman's orgasm potential is probably determined by conditions relatively early in her life, well before she becomes sexually active. We know practically nothing about the specific socialization conditions that facilitate or inhibit orgasm potential. The only hint we have is that certain attitudes on the father's part may be especially critical. Apparently, a woman's orgasm potential is at least partially a function of whether she was able to perceive her father as dependably interested in her. It remains a mystery why the mother's attitudes have not been implicated in the shaping of orgasmic potential. Despite an earlier attempt to cope with this puzzle by suggesting that it is, after all, logical that a mode of response to a current male love object should be particularly linked to experiences with the original prime male love object (father), it still seems strange that feelings about the original feminine model (mother) should not also be implicated. Of course, the present studies have dealt only with a woman's *recall* of her mother's qualities and it is possible that, if more direct study of the mothers themselves had been possible some significant correlations between a woman's orgasm consistency and her mother's attributes would have been obtained. One can also speculate that the difficulty in detecting the influence of the mother may stem from the fact that those of her attributes that are important involve not so much specific traits or qualities as her attitude toward her husband. Illustratively, if the mother relates to the father in a way that suggests that the mother thinks the father to be a dependable person and that his love can be counted upon, this might convey to her daughter the message that not only her father but also men in general can be taken as dependable love objects. Clarification of this issue would appear to be an important area for research exploration.

In originally offering a model to explain the possible influence of a woman's feelings about love object dependability upon her orgasm consistency, emphasis was placed upon the fact that the process of attaining orgasm involves a retreat from what is "out there" induced not only by diminished sensory acuity but also by focusing upon immediate body experiences that diminish awareness of outside objects. It means, for the average woman, giving up her perceptual hold on the usual world of objects and allowing herself to be "carried away" by sensations that are aroused in her by a man's behavior. The writer earlier conjectured that if a woman has preexisting doubts about the dependability of love objects the process of becoming sexually excited is disturbing to her not only because it results in a less articulated perceptual "hold" on objects in general, but also because, while in this less articulated condition, she has to "trust" the behavior of a man who, by means of his stimulating behavior, exerts control over her state of consciousness and the clarity of her object relations. Presumably, if she finds such conditions too threatening she will develop anxiety that inhibits the buildup of sexual excitement and blocks orgasm. One cannot help wondering whether the woman with low-orgasm consistency might not also have difficulties in other situations in which the action of some outside male agent produces changes in her level of consciousness or exerts control over the way she experiences the world. For example, would she find a hypnotic induction procedure particularly threatening? Would she respond with special negativism to medical procedures that produced loss of consciousness or called for "submission" to a physician who would be in a position to do radical things to her that she could not control? Would she be the one who would be most resistive to taking a drug or other medications prescribed for her that might have unpredictable effects? Might her anxiety about losing her perceptual hold on objects make her avoid such conditions as loss of sleep, extreme fatigue, and intake of substances that really alter her awareness? Some doubt is cast on this last possibility by the fact that no relationships were found by the writer between orgasm consistency and amount of use of (or liking for) alcohol. These thoughts might, in some ways, imply that the woman with low-orgasm consistency is concerned about potential loss of self-control, but it would be more accurate to characterize her concern as a fear of finding herself completely alone (without the support of a man who really cares). If so, one could expect that orgasm would be facilitated by any conditions that increase a woman's feeling that the man with whom she is having sexual intercourse can be counted on to be loyal and to maintain steadfast interest in her. What are the practical implications of this generalization? Consider some illustrative formulations.

1. A woman will probably be more orgastic with a man when her relationship with him has been formally stabilized (as through marriage).
2. A woman should be less orgastic in transient, temporary sexual liaisons.
3. Increasing duration of marriage (within certain age limits) should increase orgasm consistency.
4. Conditions that magnify the probability of a husband having to be absent unpredictably (for example, war duty, job responsibilities) should decrease the wife's orgasm consistency.
5. A wife's discovery of her husband's infidelity with other women should decrease her orgasm consistency.
6. Wives who find themselves in competition with other wives (as in a polygamous culture) should manifest decreased orgasm consistency.
7. A woman whose husband cannot give up close investment in his mother, and who is therefore uncertain of his investment in her as his wife, should have special orgasm difficulties.[10]
8. Although one would be tempted to argue that the birth of a child would help to reassure a woman about the stability of her marriage and therefore to enhance her orgasm consistency, there are also other repercussions of a birth (for example, its possible estranging effect on the husband who sees the new child as a competitor) that prevent such a simple generalization. Perhaps one could say that if a child is born to a marriage and the husband is genuinely pleased by the event (does not feel seriously competitive with the child), this may, through its further formalization of the long-term nature of the marriage, increase the wife's orgasm potential.

These various conditions would be expected to have a significant impact upon orgasm consistency mainly in women with a moderate to high amount of concern about object loss. Those with a low degree of such concern would probably be less sensitive to fluctuations in external conditions that bear on object dependability. It should be possible to test the propositions that have been presented by measuring changes in orgasm consistency in women (high and low in their concern about object loss) under such conditions as pre- versus postmarriage, early versus late in marriage, and husband frequently absent versus husband seldom absent.

The Clitoral-Vaginal Controversy

Rarely have there been so many opinionated assertions based on absolutely no evidence as one finds in the literature dealing with clitoral versus vaginal arousal. It was largely within psychoanalytic circles, at Freud's behest, that the myth evolved that enjoyment of vaginal stimulation by a woman is more mature or healthy than is enjoyment of direct (manual or oral) clitoral arousal. The clitoris was considered to be a phalliclike organ, and preference for direct clitoral stimulation was labeled as unfeminine. Even the Masters and Johnson (1966) report that a major part of the arousal produced by movements of the penis in the vagina is achieved indirectly through clitoral stimulation has not done much to discourage the view that "clitoral" orgasm is somehow inferior. Masters and Johnson (along with Kinsey, et al.) went so far as to propose that vaginal stimulation, *as such,* adds little to the total arousal elicited by intercourse. They pointed out that sensory receptors are almost absent from the vaginal wall and therefore discounted the role of sensations from the vagina in building up to orgasmic excitement. This extreme position does not appear to be justified. Women can distinguish the patterns of sensations they experience from direct vaginal versus direct clitoral stimulation, and they often have strong preferences for one or the other. Although the vaginal wall may have few sensory receptors, there is no question that the kinesthetic sensations produced by penile intromission can be perceived and have highly erotic significance. One must also assume that there is major arousing significance for many women in the mere fact of being vaginally penetrated. The writer's studies clearly demonstrated that women differ considerably in the degree to which they prefer direct clitoral versus vaginal stimulation during intercourse. Some prefer only direct vaginal stimulation and even find direct clitoral arousal to be unpleasant. Others get "nothing" out of penile intromission and extract all of their sexual excitement from direct manual manipulation of the clitoris. However, the information collected did indicate that the average woman tends to rate manual clitoral manipulation as a particularly important component of the arousal sequence and 19 percent consider it absolutely essential for reaching orgasm. When asked to choose between having either clitoral or vaginal stimulation, 64 percent gave their vote to clitoral. Thirty percent of women in one sample indicated that even while penile intromission is occurring they require the final assistance of direct clitoral manipulation in order to reach their orgasm threshold. There is no question but that the average woman finds direct manual clitoral manipulation a sizable component of the stimulation needed to reach orgasm.

The woman who prefers manual clitoral stimulation does not differ in her orgasm consistency from the one preferring vaginal modes of arousal. Either form of stimulation is just as effective as the other when judged in terms of orgasm attainment. It is also extremely important, in view of past speculations that vaginally focused stimulation produces a "better" orgasm, to add that no correlations were found by the writer that would favor such a conclusion. Actually, if there is a "better" species of orgasm linked with one or the other mode of stimulation, the findings favor the direct clitoral species. It will be recalled that the writer detected a trend across multiple samples such that the greater a woman's clitoral preference the more she described her orgasms as having "ecstatic" qualities; whereas the greater her vaginal preference the more she tended to choose the word "happy" as descriptive of her feelings during orgasm.[11] Apparently, the clitorally oriented woman experiences a higher charge of whatever is encompassed by the term "ecstatic" than does the vaginally oriented woman.[12] This difference eventually turned out to be congruent with other data analyses that suggested that there might be a basic difference in the clitorally versus vaginally oriented women with respect to the way they modulate arousal or excitement. Early in the writer's studies an important differentiation between the clitorally and vaginally oriented women was detected with respect to how they experience their bodies. Fairly convincing evidence was obtained that the greater a woman's vaginal orientation the more likely she is to report (when responding to the Body Distortion Questionnaire [Fisher, 1970]) that her body feels "distant," "not mine," and diminished in sensitivity. The more vaginally oriented woman seemed to perceive her body as lacking vitality, sensitivity, and the quality of vividness or aliveness that one's own body customarily has. Analogous to this finding, other results obtained by the writer indicated that the more vaginally oriented woman is inclined to "dampen" excitement and to minimize the potentially arousing aspects of what she perceives. When constructing imaginative stories she minimizes and mutes tension or crisis. Problems within her stories are resolved in a "they lived happily ever after" fashion. While casting about for an explanation as to why the vaginally oriented woman is inclined to mute experience, a logical possibility presented itself in terms of the finding that she is more anxious than the clitorally oriented. As defined by several different measures, amount of anxiety was observed to be positively linked with strength of vaginal preference. This suggested that the muting of both body and nonbody stimuli by the vaginally oriented women might be a defense against anxiety. They might learn to dampen the intensity of what they experience in an attempt to evade the chronic unpleasant sensations associated with anxiety.

The writer would caution that although the vaginally oriented have been described as more anxious than the clitorally oriented, this in no way is meant to imply that they are less "healthy" or that they are seriously maladjusted. There is no intent to replace the equation between vaginal response and maturity that has so long been common in the psychoanalytic literature with a reverse equation. The women who were studied were without gross psychiatric symptomatology and generally functioned at what would be considered a "normal" level. There is no justification for labeling the vaginally oriented women as really disturbed or maladjusted. It should be added that the fact that the vaginally oriented woman is more anxious or has experienced more psychological distress than the clitorally oriented does not mean that she is less mature or that she is somehow psychologically inferior. The women with these differing orientations may simply differ in how their tension shows itself when they run into difficulties. For example, those with a clitoral preference may channel their disturbance into preoccupation with minor body complaints or defensive compulsiveness rather than anxious distress.

Several possible hypotheses were proposed earlier by the writer to explain why a vaginal orientation should be linked with the "muting" style of coping with stimuli. Briefly they were as follows:

1. Vaginal stimulation may generally produce less intense excitement than manual clitoral stimulation and therefore be less threatening to a woman who wants to keep her experiences muted or subdued.

2. The vaginally oriented woman's depersonalized way of experiencing her body might make her relatively unresponsive to sexual stimulation unless it was delivered in a way that had unusually intense *psychological* connotations. The specific act of intercourse, with its special significance of intimacy, might be necessary to get through the coldness or unresponsiveness possibly associated with a depersonalized set. Perhaps direct clitoral stimulation lacks the *personalized* psychological intensity produced by penile penetration and cannot overcome a depersonalized body set.

3. Another possibility is that the vaginally oriented woman who, as shown by the writer's findings, has a tendency to recall her father as not having been willing to respond *positively* to her, needs an extra commitment from a man, in the form of penile penetration, before she is willing to respond to him.

4. Finally, the possibility was considered that the vaginally oriented woman, because of her depersonalized way of experiencing her body, may have an unusually hazy concept of her genital area and so require the active articulation of the vaginal space by the penis in order to be able to "tune in" on sensation in the genital region in a focused fashion.

When the writer scanned the empirical differences that he had found between the vaginally and clitorally oriented women, he was particularly impressed with the potential explanatory value of the fact that there was a greater sense of body depersonalization in the former group. The vaginally oriented woman indicated with fair consistency that she felt estranged and distant from her body, as if it did not belong to her personally. The possible utility of such depersonalization in defending against anxiety has already been discussed. Some other possible implications also came to mind. A depersonalized feeling about one's body might be a way of denying responsibility for what happens to, or is experienced via, the body. It could be a means of denying responsibility for the general realm of body events. In other words, depersonalization might represent a rejection of the somatic dimensions of self. What might motivate a woman to do this? One possibility would be that she grew up in a highly puritanical family in which the body was portrayed as a bad object, a source of evil. Depersonalization would be a way of denying ownership of the bad object. However, this does not seem to be a likely explanation in view of the fact that clitoral-vaginal preference was found to be uncorrelated with any of the measures of religiosity and formal church behavior that were employed and that one would expect to be linked with puritanical socialization. Another alternative that was pondered is that the depersonalized attitude might be a way of steeling self against anticipated attack upon, or exploitation of, one's body. A woman who expects that her body will be the target of great hostility or that it will be misused in some way might want to disown it, not as a bad object but rather as one that will incur unpleasantness. It is as if she felt, "I am certain my body is going to get hurt or be exploited, so I want to be as little associated with it as possible." Such an attitude might possibly be instilled by having to endure long periods of illness in oneself or in some important family member. It could derive too from a sadomasochistic concept of femininity, especially its sexual aspects. There might be a vivid belief that sexual intercourse is painful and involves potential body damage and danger. The male sex partner would be visualized as destructive and exploiting. There is little in the way of empirical data either to affirm or reject this possibility. If it were to turn out to be reasonable, it might have implications for the vaginal versus clitoral preference. Perhaps a woman who visualizes sexual stimulation as being inextricably linked with a situation in which a man aggresses against her by literally penetrating her body cannot build up sexual excitement unless the act of penetration occurs. It may be necessary for her to know that she is penetrated and thus to give the sex partner's approach to her some potential meaning of "forcible entry" or body exploitation before she can assimilate stimulation as being really sexual.

These were some of the possibilities and speculations that were entertained by the writer as he considered the significance of the findings relating to depersonalization. However, none could be affirmed or disaffirmed on the basis of the actual empirical findings available. Furthermore, none of the findings offered clarification as to why the clitorally oriented woman does not enjoy vaginal stimulation.

To seek additional clarification, another line of analysis was undertaken that involved considering in more detail the exact nature of what clitoral and vaginal stimulation mean. If one accepts the observations of Kinsey, et al. (1953) and Masters and Johnson (1966), it would have to be agreed that penile intromission delivers a large amount of stimulation to the clitoris. The vaginally oriented woman does receive a substantial quantity of clitoral stimulation. However, this occurs indirectly. The stimulation is delivered by the penis (by traction exerted on the wings of the clitoral hood) rather than by direct manual manipulation. Relatedly, direct manual arousal of the clitoris produces vaginal excitation and pulsation and, as excitement builds up, a variety of kinesthetic sensations in the pelvic musculature that may be analogous to some of the sensations induced by penile penetration. Clearly, there are common elements in the two forms of sexual stimulation. One would have to say that the vaginally oriented woman experiences many of the arousal elements that are basic to the clitoral orientation and likewise one would have to agree that the clitorally oriented woman builds her excitement on sensations and cues that are not dissimilar from those utilized by the vaginally oriented woman. Whether a woman is clitoral or vaginal in preference, she does receive stimulation of the clitoris, does experience vaginal changes and pulsations, and does become aware of a muscle tension build-up, with accompanying intense kinesthetic sensations. One should add that the overlap between the clitoral and vaginal orientations is further fostered by the fact that a majority of persons engaging in sexual relationships use both direct clitoral and vaginal stimulation successively and simultaneously, resulting in a complex blend of the two. Even psychologically the clitorally and vaginally oriented women experience much in common. In both instances, there is typically an interaction with a man who is sexually aroused and who is interested in eliciting as much excitement or response as possible. What, then, is the nature of the experiential distinction that the clitoral as compared to the vaginal oriented woman is reacting to during sexual interaction? Obviously, this distinction relates primarily to the fact that in one case the stimulation that is most preferred is delivered by the penis while it is inserted in the vagina, and in the other case the preferred stimulation is manually (orally) delivered to the clitoral region. Penile intromission is particularly valued in the one instance, whereas manual stroking of the clitoris seems primary in the other instance. The problem of explaining vaginal versus clitoral orientation becomes one of clarifying the differential significance of the male sex partner inserting his penis into the vagina as compared to his using his hand to stimulate the clitoris.

Can one not conceptualize this difference in terms of role differences? [13] The woman who is receiving stimulation from a man who has his penis inserted in her vagina is engaged in an act of *mutual* stimulation. At the same time that the man is trying to bring her to orgasm she is doing likewise for him. It is a transaction in which they are both closely and equally involved. This contrasts with the situation in which manual clitoral stimulation is applied by a man. In this instance the woman is receiving stimulation intended to arouse her to orgasm; and although the man may also be receiving arousing stimulation from her, it is usually not immediately intended to produce orgasm in him as such. The woman occupies the role of the principal receiver; the man's is the relatively more detached role. He will have either already attained orgasm or will do so after she has reached orgasm. What this means is that the vaginally oriented woman is stimulated to orgasm during a transaction in which the sex partner is equally involved as a giver and taker. The clitorally oriented woman is aroused to orgasm in a context where she is the primary receiver and her sex partner is in many respects a spectator or onlooker. If this analysis is correct, it means that the greater a woman's clitoral orientation the more she prefers achieving orgasmic excitement in a context in which she is the central object, in which her partner is clearly separate and largely giving his attention to her. The vaginally oriented woman could be said to prefer that her orgasmic excitement be generated in an interchange in which she is not the observed object, but rather "fused" with a partner who is as equally involved as she is.

Related to this formulation is another obvious difference between the conditions of vaginal versus direct clitoral stimulation. In the first instance the primary aspect of the sexual transaction involves vaginal penetration and a resultant unique closeness of two bodies. In the second instance, the bodies of the two sex partners are more clearly separate. On this basis, too, one can say that delivery of manual clitoral stimulation leaves the male sex partner relatively more psychologically detached than does delivery of vaginal stimulation. There is great intimacy in both contexts, but there are differences in the degree to which the woman can think of herself as a "separate" entity. How do such formulations relate to other differences between the clitorally and vaginally oriented woman that have appeared in the writer's data? They immediately seem to lead right back to the greater tendency of the vaginally oriented woman to experience her body as depersonalized. The essence of the depersonalized feeling is that one's body is alien, distant, and not truly a part of self. In other words, there is a sense of not having full ownership of one's own body. This may represent a belief on the part of the vaginally oriented woman that she has no right to feel that her body belongs to herself or to enjoy body experiences that only gratify her personally. She might, then, further believe that an intense body experience such as sexual arousal should occur only when someone else, a male sex partner, becomes so closely involved with her body that he is sharing in the responsibility for it. In other words, when her body is fused sexually with his, she can think of her sexual arousal as a joint event. She can perceive the experience as not primarily for her own satisfaction but also for another. At the other extreme, the clitorally oriented woman would, from this viewpoint, have the opposing need to experience her body autonomously and to be reassured that an event such as intense sexual excitement belonged clearly and personally to her. She would be a person who would have a negative response to conditions that seriously challenged her sense of body autonomy.

How might such attitudinal differences between the vaginally and clitorally oriented woman with respect to the autonomy of her body arise? There is no solid information available upon which to construct an answer. One can only speculate that parental attitudes play a prime role. The vaginally oriented woman could be pictured as having grown up in a family in which she was made to feel that she was obligated to her parents and had only limited rights to enjoy anything unless they approved or could derive indirect profit from it themselves. That is, she would be made to feel that her parents had important proprietary rights over her—and her body. The sense of not having body autonomy might be particularly fostered if the parents promulgated strict rules about various kinds of body activities. For example, if they emphasized that she could use her body for sexual purposes only under special conditions that they would spell out, they would be giving her the message that, in this realm, her body really was only partially under her own control. They would, in essence, be telling her that an important aspect of her body functioning was alienated from her own decision making. It is possible that similar feelings of not being in possession of one's body could be encouraged by parents who demanded strict adherence to certain standards about eating or who enforced elaborate arbitrary rituals with regard to toilet training. The basic attitude would be shaped that one dare not have a really important or dramatic body experience unless it was approved by, or shared with, some other significant figure. What can one say about the possible socialization background of the clitorally oriented woman? It is quite conceivable that she too grew up with parents who made the same demands for proprietary rights over her body as have been speculatively attributed to the parents of the vaginally oriented woman. However, instead of acquiescing to these demands, she may have rejected them and adopted compensatory defenses built around the idea that she would not permit intrusion upon the autonomy of her body. This would mean that she would be wary of situations in which her perception of her body as a clearly separate entity might be violated. One can also conceive of such an orientation being encouraged in a family setting in which there was an exaggerated, and probably defensive emphasis placed on being autonomous and not allowing one's individuality to be encroached upon by others. It will be a difficult task to test this formulation empirically. There might be multiple patterns of parental behavior that would encourage either a loss of sense of body ownership or an opposite exaggerated feeling of body autonomy. Such attitudes could be a function of the parents' moralistic expectations about sex or their special ideas about eating and adoption of their perfectionistic demands for control of anal functions and maintenance of body cleanliness. One can also think of manifold other possibilities, for example, the parental assumption that the child's body has to be carefully watched and controlled in order to protect it from accidents or other physical trauma. The various ways in which parental control over the body might be exercised would make it difficult to specify a particular parental attribute that would be predictive of a daughter adopting a clitoral versus vaginal orientation. The difference in body attitude between those with clitoral versus vaginal preferences specifically involves the dimension of depersonalization. There were no discernible differences with respect to other body attitude dimensions (for example, general body awareness, body-boundary differentiation, or feelings about the body interior). However, if one portrays the clitorally oriented woman as being particularly uncomfortable about conditions that threaten to compromise her sense of body autonomy, would this not lead one to expect that she would have special feelings of potential body vulnerability, and by implication, poorly defined body boundaries? Whereas this may sound like a logical deduction, previous empirical findings argue against it. These findings (Hammerschlag, et al., 1964; Fisher, 1967) emerged from studies that were indirectly concerned with what kinds of women are most resistive to assuming the role of a medical patient. The studies indicated that the greater the definiteness of a woman's body boundaries the longer she delays in seeking treatment for early symptoms of cancer of the breast and cervix. It was concluded that the woman with well-defined boundaries is especially loath to assume the role of patient, which implies partially sharing the ownership of her body with the physician who would be treating her. In other words, reluctance to give up body autonomy does not mean that one necessarily has poorly differentiated boundaries. In the context of the cancer studies just mentioned, it actually had the opposite significance. It is pertinent too that no correlations have been found in previous studies (Fisher, 1970) between feelings of body depersonalization and boundary differentiation.

The entire question of clitoral versus vaginal preference is obviously extremely complex. Only a small beginning has been made in understanding its psychological components. What are some of the key issues and problems that remain to be further investigated? Consider the following:

1. We need to know more about the specific fantasies and concerns that characterize the clitorally and vaginally oriented when they are sexually aroused. Do they, for example, differ in how passive or submissive they feel? Do their existing differences in feelings of body depersonalization become even more accentuated? Would one find that the vaginally oriented women show a relatively greater decrease in their sense of boundary differentiation during sexual excitement?

2. Much more needs to be learned about whether parents of the clitorally versus vaginally oriented woman differ in the communications they give about body autonomy. Studies should be undertaken in which parental behavior pertinent to body control can be examined minutely. If one were to construct a composite index of all of the major ways in which a parent may deny a child proprietary rights over his own body, would the parents of vaginally oriented women obtain higher scores than the parents of clitorally oriented women? Would the difference apply more to fathers than mothers?

3. Do the clitorally and vaginally oriented women "choose" different kinds of men when they marry? Perhaps the vaginally oriented woman is more likely to prefer a man who gives her the message that he expects to have "proprietary" rights over her body or that he expects her to be willing to fuse her identity with his to a considerable degree. The clitorally oriented woman may look for a rather aloof man who is more willing to be a "spectator" of her feelings and passions.

Sexual Appetite

One of the questions that was explored throughout the writer's studies concerns the relationship of sexual appetite to other forms of appetite. Does the woman who has high orgasm consistency or who has a high intercourse rate show special gusto with reference to other gratifications? Many other forms of "appetite" have been appraised. Measures were taken of satisfaction derived from eating and the range of foods enjoyed. Information was also obtained about consumption of alcohol and cigarette smoking, and determinations were made of the amount of enjoyment of athletics and of the use of the large muscles of the body. Systematic inquiry was undertaken about how much new experience and novelty (and the accompanying excitement) were sought after, and measures were made of amount of time spent per week in seeking entertainment (for example, watching television), amount of effort devoted to narcissistically oriented self-grooming activities, and preferences for visual versus kinesthetic experiences. An analysis of the data emanating from these diverse measures has failed to establish more than a few isolated links between sexual appetite and other forms of appetite. It was found that the greater a woman's intercourse frequency the more she devotes herself to grooming and beautifying her body as well as the more time she spends during an average week in entertaining activities (for example, watching television and going to parties). There was also a borderline trend for *preferred* intercourse rate to be greater in those women who began to drink alcoholic beverages at a relatively early age, but this trend was not correlated with amount of alcohol consumed. Finally, one should mention a borderline trend for strength of orgasm to be positively correlated with number of cigarettes smoked. Overall, though, there does not seem to be any indication that the woman who particularly enjoys or responds to sexual stimulation has correspondingly enhanced appetites in other realms. The "sexy" woman is not likely to enjoy food more than the less "sexy" one, and is also not more likely to enjoy alcohol or smoking or athletic activities. Sexual appetite cannot be easily conceptualized as a manifestation of a more generalized zest for gratification. It is important to add that the data have not even hinted of a *compensatory* relationship between the area of sexual gratification and other modes of gratification. That is, there is no sign that the woman who has difficulty in reaching orgasm or who feels unsatisfied after orgasm is inclined, by way of compensation, to be unusually interested in food. Nor is she unusually invested in alcohol or smoking. If an inability to attain sexual satisfaction does result in compensatory forms of behavior, they lie outside of the wide repertory that was studied. It is pertinent to this same point that one cannot even say (in terms of the data collected) that lack of satisfaction from sexual interaction raises amount of tension, as far as it is detectable in the form of anxiety or hostile irritability or achievement fantasies or even general body awareness. Such findings, if affirmed by further studies, would seem to have considerable relevance for theories that view sexual tension in the context of a hydraulic system—such that if the tension does not find outlet in one sector it will increase the pressure in another. The writer's findings would suggest, on the contrary, that within the range of sexual gratification characterizing the married women who were studied, there was adaptation to the level of available satisfaction. There were no indications that women with very low orgasm rates were more tense or irritable or more invested in other appetites such as eating than women with high orgasm rates. This is a fairly radical conclusion, but one that is congruent with the facts. It must be cautioned that one cannot validly apply such a perspective to women who almost totally lack opportunity for heterosexual intimacy. Perhaps there are certain minimum quantities of sexual contact that are necessary to prevent the buildup of disturbing tension. Although there would probably be individual differences in this area, one wonders whether the average woman might not quite successfully adapt to rates of sexual interaction that are considerably below current averages for married women.

With respect to the matter of the effects associated with different quantities of sexual contact, we do not know such simple things as whether there are changes in tension levels of women as they shift from the state of limited sexual contact usually typifying the unmarried role to the state of considerable sexual contact accompanying marriage. We do not know whether the shift results in an increase or a decrease in other areas of appetite. We do not know in what ways a woman feels differently after intercourse producing orgasm versus intercourse that does not eventuate in orgasm. If there are such different feelings, are they transitory or do they last for long periods? In a related vein, we do not know whether a woman who usually fails to attain orgasm learns to focus in a compensatory fashion upon other aspects of the sexual experience. Perhaps she begins to "tune in" more to the sheer intimacy of each sexual contact or the skin sensations it creates or to the "feel" of being penetrated. Conceivably, she might even begin to develop a special "taste" for the quality of heightened tension that is never directly or grossly relieved. She might learn to enjoy her own more gradual strategies (both during and after intercourse) for dissipating her sexual arousal.

The question of how much sexual contact a woman "needs" leads logically to the matter of intercourse frequency. As reported earlier, the writer and other investigators have found enormous differences in women's intercourse rates. Although there is little doubt that the husband's preferences are important determiners of such differences in rates, the writer's studies suggest that another significant factor is a woman's interest in narcissistic gratification. Evidence was found that the greater a woman's intercourse rate the more energy she invests in body-enhancing procedures (for example, buying new clothes, grooming, and applying cosmetics) and the more she seeks out activities that will "entertain" her. In addition, the women with higher intercourse rates were discovered to be inclined toward exhibitionism, to prefer situations in which they are the center of attention. These findings intimated that one of the elements motivating higher intercourse rates is a need for large amounts of attention. The intercourse situation is one in which a woman may find not only sexual stimulation but also the close attention of another who communicates admiration and lavishes interest on her body. The fact that narcissistic and exhibitionistic wishes seem to play a part in intercourse frequency raises the more general issue of what are the major components of gratification that the average woman seeks in a sexual contact. What is the weight that she assigns to sexual arousal, as such, as compared to variables such as an opportunity for intimacy or interaction with a man who invests his attention in her? We do not have scientific information that would even begin to clarify this matter. It is a safe guess, though, that one would probably find that individual women differ considerably as to which components of intercourse they most value. Furthermore, one would conjecture that at different stages of her life a woman might change with respect to the component that was most important to her. Sexual arousal might be the most prominent element in the early stage of marriage; intimacy might become particularly important following the death of some important figure (for example, a parent); and narcissistic gratification derived from being the focus of the partner's attention might gain ascendancy after events signifying failure or loss of self-esteem. It is well to keep in mind the potential diversity of the psychological elements associated with intercourse that may appeal to a woman. In addition to those mentioned, one might, by way of illustration, enumerate the following ways in which a woman could utilize intercourse:

To reassure herself of her femininity.
To dispel her boredom.
To gain power over her sex partner.
To affirm her attractiveness.
To obtain unusual or even painful sensory experiences.
To find release from her own usually overrigid self-control.
To be held and comforted.

Returning to the eating analogy, which the writer has often cited, it would come as no surprise if one stated that people eat not only to gratify hunger but also diversely because they enjoy the taste, find the social interactions during meals to be gratifying, like the range of sensory experiences they obtain, and find that the routine of eating is an interesting ritual that often relieves boredom.

One form of sexual gratification found by the writer to be very infrequently utilized by the married women in the various samples was masturbation. The average woman said she masturbates "rarely." Relatedly, Kinsey, et al. (1953) found masturbation (to orgasm) to occur, on the average, about once or twice a month in married women.[14] Nevertheless, it is of interest that married women masturbate at all, in view of the fact that they have regular intercourse available. Although some of such masturbatory behavior might be attributed to factors such as the wish for sexual stimulation when the husband is absent from home (for example, away on a business trip), there are suggestions that other factors also play a role. It will be recalled that the writer's findings indicated that women who were least likely to masturbate and who say they least enjoy it are characterized by certain attributes. There was evidence that the more a woman refrains from masturbation the more she is opposed to greater freedom in sexual matters; the less explicitly she acknowledges the importance of sex in her life; the more she prefers a routine that is orderly, systematic, and not messy (unclean); the more she expresses belief in the existence of God and in religious ideals (but is not more religious as defined by formal religious behavior such as church attendance); the more she recalls her mother as having been moralistically strict; the less she enjoys new and novel experiences; and the less she recalls her mother as having been distant, unloving, and neglecting. When the last finding pertaining to the mother was originally interpreted, emphasis was placed on the fact that this was the first instance in which a measure of sexual behavior was significantly linked with attitudes toward the mother rather than the father. In view of the fact that those women who were most inclined to masturbate perceived their mothers as rejecting and unloving, it was proposed that masturbation might be a way of asserting the independence of one's body from mother, a declaration of freedom from her and an assertion of ability to be separate from her. The underlying note of defiance in masturbation is also implied in the fact that amount of masturbation was found to be positively correlated with declaring that there should be more sexual freedom in our culture and in the rejection of orderly, clean, and regulated ways of doing things. There does seem to be a note of self-assertion in the attitude of the woman who is inclined toward masturbation. At the same time, it must be cautioned that there is no evidence that she is *generally* hostile or aggressive or antagonistic to an unusual degree. Her defiance seems to be confined to limited sectors of attitude and behavior. One might almost say that she finds it sufficiently expressive of her defiance to engage periodically in masturbation. The association of masturbation with that which is bad, messy, and immoral needs to be reiterated. Apparently, one of the factors that inhibits masturbation is that it is perceived both figuratively and literally as a "dirty" thing. As noted earlier, this is the only aspect of sexual behavior that was found by the writer to be related to attitudes about being dirty. It is also the only aspect found to be linked with certain aspects of religiosity. Interestingly, Kinsey, et al. (1953) also found the amount of masturbatory behavior to be clearly lower in the religiously devout than nondevout.[15] But they found few, if any, relationships between religiosity and other aspects of sex behavior (except homosexuality and premarital sex contacts). A similar lack of relationship between religiosity and most aspects of sexual behavior has characterized the writer's data. One must also call attention to the link between desire for new and novel experience and masturbatory behavior; the greater a woman's interest in such novel experience the more likely she is to masturbate. From this view, a married woman who masturbates may partially be doing so simply because she wants a change in her usual mode of experiencing sexual arousal. One is reminded at this point that Kinsey, et al. (1953) found that masturbation was positively related to a woman's educational level, even after her marriage and the availability of regular intercourse. If one thinks of the woman who seeks higher amounts of education as being particularly motivated to broaden her perceptions of the world and to learn about its diversity, one could interpret the positive correlation between educational level and amount of masturbation as a reflection of the general relationship between interest in new experience and masturbatory frequency.

Obviously, multiple factors contribute to a woman's motivation to masturbate. Kinsey, et al. (1953) have shown that she will turn to masturbation when other forms of sexual gratification are not available. The writer's data indicate, in addition, that she may turn to masturbation as a way of expressing independence and defiance, and as a way of introducing novelty into her sex life. At the same time, impulses to masturbate growing out of such motivations must overcome inhibitory feelings that define masturbation as dirty and immoral. Amount of masturbation probably represents, then, in each individual case a unique balance among the factors cited that both positively motivate as well as inhibit masturbatory interest. Another point that needs to be reiterated is that masturbation in married women does not appear to be a compensation for deficiencies in other aspects of sexual behavior. Masturbation frequency turned out not to be related to orgasm consistency and was also unrelated to preferred and actual intercourse frequencies, strength of orgasm, amount of satisfaction derived from orgasm, and many other indices concerned with sexual responsiveness. One cannot justifiedly think of the woman who masturbates with relatively high frequency (at least if she is not too extremely beyond the range found in samples of normal married women) as trying to obtain substitute gratification for failure in her sexual intercourse encounters. Masturbatory behavior, as it was reported in the various samples studied, is also unrelated to anxiety level or other measures having to do with one's "mental health." There is no support for considering masturbation, in any general sense, a sign of disturbing psychological tensions. This does not rule out the possibility that some individual women might utilize masturbation as a channel for releasing disturbing affect or acting out conflictual wishes, but, of course, any segment of behavior can be adapted to such ends.

Little is known about how married women define their masturbatory activity within the context of their marriage relationship. We do not have data about whether they keep their masturbation secret from their husbands. Do they ever masturbate in the husband's presence? Do they discuss masturbation with their husbands as freely as they discuss other aspects of sexuality? Such information would provide a more accurate basis for evaluating the role of masturbation in the average woman's life. If one had to guess, it is probably likely that most wives conceal their masturbation and rarely talk openly about it. They are probably reluctant to discuss it with their husbands not only because of its "dirty" connotations but also because it could easily be interpreted as depreciatory of the husband's sexual prowess. One negative result with respect to the masturbation findings deserves special comment. The writer discovered that neither masturbation frequency nor amount of satisfaction from masturbation was significantly related to clitoral-vaginal preference. There was not even a hint of a relationship. One might have expected that the clitorally oriented woman who particularly enjoys manual manipulation (which is usually focused in the clitoral area) would also have a special liking for masturbation, which is also manual in character, and in most instances directed to the vicinity of the clitoris (Kinsey, et al., 1953). The fact that this expectation was not fulfilled suggests that the two modes of excitation, although involving analogous anatomical areas, are quite different psychologically. But is this true? It was proposed earlier that what is typical of the clitorally oriented woman is that she prefers a sexual context in which she can feel that she has full possession of her own body, that it is not fused with the body of another. If so, would not the masturbatory situation, which does not involve a sex partner at all, be an even clearer instance of what the clitorally oriented woman prefers? Does this not imply a considerable similarity between the two forms of sexual stimulation? Perhaps so, but the similarity may be only superficial. First of all, there is evidence that although the clitorally oriented woman wants to maintain a sense of being in full possession of her own body, one of the motivations for masturbation is to express a defiant independence (of her mother). That is, masturbation goes a step beyond the simple assertion of self-ownership to a more defiant rejection of any outside hold on one's body. Masturbation may represent psychologically a more radical position with respect to how one wants one's body to be related to others (at a sexual level) than the clitorally oriented woman seeks.

Laing (1959) and others have pointed out another aspect of masturbation that may differentiate it psychologically from the needs of the clitorally oriented woman. In analyzing the act of masturbation they have been impressed with how often it takes on an unreal quality and involves relating to a fantasied or imaginary partner. That is, in the process of masturbating there is an isolation from others and a deviation from accepted norms that imparts to it an unusual aura of unreality. Laing states (p. 40): "The awareness the masturbator has of his body is complicated by the fact that his body has been seduced from real action into participation in an imaginary situation." He adds, "The body as used in the act of masturbation is employed with the express intention of gaining satisfaction by eliminating the problems of coping with other real bodies. . . . The 'real' other person who is the object of desire becomes merely the shadow of the imagined other. This is one of the problems the masturbator runs into: his imagination casts its shadow over him. . . ." One of the implications of this view is that during masturbation a woman would find that her body takes on somewhat strange, unreal qualities, and in that sense might seem to belong less to herself than it usually does. Relatedly, Laing and others (Masters, 1967) have also remarked that during masturbation the individual is forced to take several divided perspectives toward his own body. He is simultaneously the recipient of stimulation, the giver of stimulation, and perhaps in fantasy still another figure who has been brought into the act. This could mean that masturbation encourages a division of identity as well as multiple modes of regarding or experiencing one's own body. The clitorally oriented woman, who has been speculatively portrayed as motivated to maintain a clear sense of "My body belongs to me," might find the unreality of the masturbatory situation and its encouragement of multiple modes of experiencing one's body to be unacceptable. What about the vaginally oriented woman? One would presume that although the sharing of her body with others, which she could achieve through fantasy during masturbation, might please her, she would find the literal isolation of her body (and the obvious fact that its experiences would be her sole responsibility) to be unpleasant.

A final matter of interest with regard to masturbation derives from the Kinsey, et al. (1953) observation that of the 62 percent of their total sample of women who reported ever having masturbated, only 4 to 6 percent did not attain orgasm. That is, about 96 percent of these women could reach orgasm through their self-stimulation. The 4 to 6 percent who could not reach orgasm may be contrasted with the considerably higher percentages who fail to achieve orgasm while stimulated by a male sex partner. Even after five years of marriage 17 percent of married women have not had an orgasm during their sexual contacts with their husbands. One possible explanation of this difference might be that the 68 percent of women who do report masturbating represent a special selective sample with unusual orgastic potential and that their superiority in this respect would also be evidenced in their sexual response to a male partner. That is, only 4 to 6 percent of them would be completely nonorgastic with a sex partner. However, this is unlikely for two reasons.[16] First, the writer found in his samples that frequency of masturbation had only a chance relationship to orgasm consistency. Furthermore, in the Kinsey, et al. data one finds that even of those women with considerable masturbatory experience prior to marriage, 16 percent still achieved no orgasms at all during the first year of marriage. This 16 percent clearly exceeds the 4 to 6 percent who cannot achieve orgasm through masturbation. There is no obvious simple way to dismiss the apparently greater ability of women to attain orgasm during masturbation than in interaction with a male sex partner.[17] One must conclude that the presence of the male sex partner introduces an antiorgasm influence. Is this antiorgasm influence merely caused by the poorer stimulation techniques of the male as compared to those that a woman can bring to bear on her own body? That is, are women simply more skillful in how they apply stimulation to their own genital areas? Although this may be true in some cases, it is doubtful that it is generally true. One notes, for example, that even among extremely well-educated women, who would presumably have husbands who are well educated (and highly intelligent), 15 percent fail (Kinsey, et al., 1953) to attain orgasm at all after five years of marriage. One would be skeptical that the majority of husbands of such educational (and intellectual) attainment would have neglected during a five-year time span to learn a good deal about stimulating their wives. It is unlikely (although admittedly debatable) that failure to reach orgasm in such a sample would, in any major way, be caused by lack of technique on the husband's part.

There is probably more logic in attributing the male sex partner's antiorgasm effect to his psychological impact. In view of the writer's findings that inhibition of orgasm in women is correlated with fear of loss of objects, one can even specifically suggest that the male partner's negative effect is caused by the concern he arouses about such loss. In many cases the presence of the male sex partner appears to increase the woman's concern about object loss beyond the level that is present when a woman stimulates herself sexually. Although certain difficulties related to role and feelings of unreality were mentioned as possibly arising during a woman's sexual self-stimulation, they seem to have less orgasm inhibiting power than does the presence of the male sex partner. One could say that she finds herself a more dependable object to which to relate than she does a man. It is pertinent to this matter that Kinsey, et al. (1953) found that women with extensive homosexual experience produce higher orgasm rates in their female sex partners than do men in their female sex partners after five years of marriage. Since in this homosexual instance and in that of self-stimulation the person delivering the stimulation is female, the question arises whether the orgasm-inhibiting effect of the male is somehow caused by his being of a different sex. Kinsey, et al. specifically propose that a female may be more capable than a male of stimulating a female adequately because she has a better understanding of the feelings, sensations, and anatomy involved—and therefore has better stimulation techniques. They state (pp. 467–468):

The higher frequency of orgasm in the homosexual contacts may have depended in part upon the considerable psychologic stimulation provided by such relationships, but there is reason for believing that it may also have depended upon the fact that two individuals of the same sex are likely to understand the anatomy and physiologic responses and psychology of their own sex better than they understand that of the opposite sex.

The writer has already enunciated reasons why explanations of orgasm differences in terms of "technique" seem inadequate. One is left with the obvious alternative of having to ask whether the process of interacting with a male figure sexually does not itself have a negative impact upon a wide range of women. This calls to mind again that the writer's data indicated that orgasm consistency is related to certain attitudes toward the father, but not toward the mother. It may be that socialization experiences in our culture engender in a majority of women certain negative feelings toward the father that later cause them to respond in specifically negative ways (among, of course, other positive ways) to the *intimate* presence of any masculine figure. One must underscore that this entire discussion has been concerned with the negative impact of the masculine presence upon orgasm. It goes without saying, of course, that unique positive feelings and satisfactions are probably derived from sexual intimacy with a male partner, and it is unlikely that either masturbation or homosexual stimulation (in the present cultural climate) provide these satisfactions.

Psychoanalytic Theory

Most of the major theories concerning the psychological factors in sexual behavior are directly or indirectly of psychoanalytic origin. The core aspects of these theories were reviewed in earlier chapters, and so the pertinent details are not repeated at this point. It is simply noted that psychoanalysts such as Freud, Ferenczi, Fenichel, and Hitschmann have attributed women's problems in sexual responsiveness primarily to variables such as Oedipal conflict, guilt, fear of body damage (resulting, for example, from penetration or pregnancy), and fixation at immature psychosexual levels. How have such concepts fared in the light of the empirical information that has become available? Quite generally, one can say that a reasonable amount of support may be found for the general psychoanalytic view that difficulties in sexual response are caused, at least in part, by psychological factors. Certainly, the writer's findings pertaining to concern about object loss in orgasm consistency are congruent with such a view. Some of the observations of Kinsey, et al. (1953), which implicate social class and educational level in orgasm attainment, are indirectly supportive of the view insofar as they make clear that a woman's sexual responsiveness is tied to her social history. The writer's data indicating a correlation between orgasm potential and attitudes toward the father also analogously reinforce the general psychoanalytic position. Actually, the writer's earlier reasoned out conclusion that orgasm potential is probably shaped by socialization experiences relatively early in a girl's life fits well with the psychoanalytic perspective. Although the empirical findings support psychoanalytic theory in its *general* emphasis on the importance of early socialization influences, they rarely fit with more specific psychoanalytic formulations. One of the first major disparities that should be mentioned involved the analytic notion that sexual responsiveness is a fundamental indicator of psychological maturity and "mental health." The analytic view is that psychosexual maturity is reflected in the ability to attain orgasm and even more specifically in the ability to have a so-called vaginal orgasm. The vaginal orgasm has been treated in the analytic literature as one of the prime signs of whether a woman is truly mature and possessed of a sound ego structure. It has already been pointed out in several contexts that the real facts are otherwise. A woman's orgasm consistency is not linked with how psychologically immature or disturbed she is. As for the vaginal orgasm, not only is there now considerable skepticism that such a species really exists in pure form but there is also evidence that preference for vaginal as compared to clitoral stimulation is linked with variables (for example, depersonalized body attitudes and elevated anxiety) that would hardly be classified as indicative of superior ego strength.

Another major analytic proposition asserts that a woman's difficulties in reaching orgasm stem from her inability to resolve her Oedipal conflicts. Presumably, the nonorgasmic woman experiences her current sexual relationship in distorted, anxiety-provoking, guilt-evocative terms that derive from the fact that she equates it with her original Oedipal involvement with her father (and the jealous, competitive mother). It is difficult to judge in a straightforward way whether the empirical findings support such a formulation. One of the problems in rendering a judgment is the simple fact that there are many combinations of Oedipal elements and even more complex permutations as to how they may be potentially expressed. For example, Oedipal difficulties with the father may theoretically be expressed in both overattachment and unusual hostility toward him. Things are similarly complicated with respect to how Oedipal difficulties with the mother are supposedly manifested. Since the writer found evidence that orgasm consistency with the current sex partner is related to attitudes toward the father, one could argue that the Oedipal formulation has gained some support, insofar as a tie between feelings toward the father and behavior with respect to a contemporary sex object was affirmed. However, since feelings about the mother are also a basic component of the Oedipal dilemma, and since the writer detected no correlations between orgasm consistency and attitudes toward the mother, one could argue that the findings, at this level, do not support the overall model about how Oedipal factors inhibit sexual responsiveness. The truth is that one will have difficulty in arriving at any clear-cut decisions with respect to this matter until more precise hypotheses can be extracted concerning the relationship of sexual behavior to the manner in which the father and mother are perceived. Another factor often mentioned in the psychoanalytic literature as important in inhibiting a woman's orgasm potential is fear of being penetrated. It is said that anxiety about the consequences of the penis entering her body not infrequently prevent a woman from becoming sexually aroused during intercourse. Presumably the penetrating penis stirs up fantasies about internal injury, potential body damage consequent to becoming pregnant, and so forth. Relatedly, it has often been said in the analytic literature that most women envy the penis, and that this envy may evoke competitive fantasies that, when intensified by sexual interactions, interfere with loving and being loved, and thus prevent orgasmic levels of excitement. No support has been found in the empirical data for either of these two formulations. Several measures of body anxiety and concern about body vulnerability proved to have only chance correlations with orgasm consistency. Also, a number of indices were utilized (for example, ratio of male to female figures in inkblot images, degree of femininity of interests, and feelings about male versus female superiority) that indicated no relationships of consequence between orgasm consistency and attitudes with regard to male-female competition.[18]

In general, one would have to declare that psychoanalytic concepts about sexual responsiveness in women have been largely unsupported by the available empirical evidence. It is apropos to add that in previously reviewing the existing literature concerned with male-female differences, no support was found for the psychoanalytic proposition that a woman experiences her body as castrated and inferior to that of the man. In fact, the woman was found to have less body anxiety than the man and probably a greater sense that her body is meaningfully tied to her identity and life goals. The scientific findings challenge the psychoanalytic concepts so sharply in several areas that one must begin to regard them with skepticism.

The Feminine Image

Certain psychological qualities accompany being a woman in Western culture. These qualities, which were previously described, cohere around several themes: interest in close interpersonal involvement with others, nurturant orientation, relative lack of investment in hostile and aggressive modes, delay in final role structuring until marriage, close identification of one's body with prime life goals, and relative feelings of inhibition about motility in space. What has emerged surprisingly from the writer's data is that orgasm consistency and other measures of sexual responsiveness are only slightly related to whether a woman fits the feminine image as defined by such themes.[19] Aggressive women seem to be just as sexually responsive as the nonaggressive women. Similarly there are no apparent differences in ability to attain sexual arousal in those low versus high in nurturance, sociability, body security, and sheer femininity of interests. One must conclude that sexual responsiveness is not *generally* a function of how well a woman conforms to the usual definition of the feminine life style. A number of techniques were employed by the writer to find out the degree to which the women in the samples studied reject conventional femininity and are actually interested in emulating masculine values. It will be recalled that questionnaires were administered that evaluated amount of satisfaction with the feminine role, acceptance of established definitions of the woman's place in the family, political-economic conservatism, and so forth. The measures derived from these questionnaires had no consistent or generalized relationships with the repertory of sex responsiveness indices. A woman can be in revolt against the societal definition of femininity and still be highly responsive sexually. The woman who fits the feminine model perfectly may be seriously lacking in her ability to become sexually aroused. Those qualities that figure most perceptibly in a woman's ability to enjoy sexual stimulation seem not so much to be linked to definitions of femininity as anchored in broader attitudes that cut across sex classification. Factors such as concern about loss of objects, feelings of body depersonalization, religiosity, and amount of faith in the father are important in the psychological make-up of any human being, regardless of sex. It is difficult to think of a single measure specifically tapping an aspect of femininity that was consistently correlated with measures of sexual responsiveness.

This point is pertinent to other formulations that have indirectly tied sexual responsiveness to femininity through the functioning of the reproductive system. As outlined earlier, it has been popular to theorize that the woman who is adequate sexually will experience a minimum of difficulties in those physiological systems that concern reproduction and define her structurally as a woman. Presumably, the sexually adequate woman would have relatively few menstrual symptoms, would easily conceive, would have a minimum of pregnancy complications, and so forth. Such theorizing proceeds explicitly or implicitly on the premise that sexual responsiveness and the functioning of the reproductive system should be related either because they both involve pelvic organ systems or because they are both important aspects of a larger phenomenon called femininity. It is a plausible line of thought but when one looks at the available scientific information dealing with this issue, one finds little that is convincing. There is no solid support for the view that amount of menstrual pain and discomfort and degree of menstrual irregularity are related to sexual responsiveness. Interestingly, it is also true that no convincing evidence can be mustered that menstrual discomfort is greater in women who are seriously maladjusted than in those without psychiatric symptomatology. There may be some evidence of a positive relation between menstrual irregularity and psychological tension, but at best it is of a borderline character.[20] In studying a sample of pregnant women the writer did detect a few borderline trends that would suggest that a woman's adaptation to pregnancy depends upon the same factors that influence sexual responsiveness. Although there were some significant correlations between sexual response indices and measures of adjustment to the demands of pregnancy, they were scattered and await more convincing support.

One is left with the overall impression that it would be well to challenge skeptically anyone who forcefully claims that a woman who has difficulties in being sexually responsive will be particularly susceptible to menstrual, pregnancy, and other pelvic malfunctions. An intriguing thing that was discovered in the course of analyzing various findings pertaining to pregnancy was that the pregnant woman is probably no more psychologically disturbed than the nonpregnant woman. Although some have urged that pregnancy is a time of profound and unusual turmoil for the average woman, one finds upon close examination that even when empirical studies underlie this view they have neglected to use adequate control groups. It is possible to find considerable anxiety and psychopathology in pregnant women, but just as much can probably be found in nonpregnant women. The pregnant woman may have different kinds of concerns than the nonpregnant woman, but it is doubtful that she has a greater total amount of disturbance. One should add that if pregnancy were as disturbing a process as some would have us believe, it is unlikely that pregnancy rates would be as high as they are. The fact is that the majority of women probably look forward eagerly to the child-bearing experience. It is of further pertinence that the writer could detect few consistent differences between the psychological state of menstruating women and those not menstruating.[21] Such findings suggest that women learn to adapt rather quickly to the demands associated with their reproductive functions. Both popularly and clinically it has been fashionable to portray the menstruating or pregnant woman as existing in a state of delicate balance, but this is not a reasonable stereotype. In fact, the writer has suggested that a function such as menstruation takes on important femininity-defining significance and, in addition, may, because of its regular cyclic nature, introduce a stabilizing rhythm into the life of the average woman. It is true that clinicians not infrequently encounter women who complain about discomfort associated with various aspects of their reproductive systems, but they also encounter many who have discomfort in their nonreproductive systems. The ratio of reproductive to nonreproductive complaints probably conforms to the ratio of the total anatomical size of the reproductive systems to that of the nonreproductive. Although certain of the physiological changes that occur in a woman's body are stressful, there is no reason to assume that they are, in any general sense, seriously threatening. A person is capable of adapting well to profound alterations in his body, especially if the adaptation occurs over a relatively long period of time. It is too easily overlooked that even those who have gross body deformities and serious physiological difficulties usually learn to cope with them without persistent serious disturbance. The stress arising from menstruation and pregnancy is almost certainly considerably less than that derived from such gross kinds of body difficulties. The major adaptation problem associated with pregnancy may actually be the abrupt change in state that occurs when the child is delivered. Suddenly, the average woman experiences a gross alteration in her appearance, she is no longer the container for her child, she no longer has the special status and privileges of the pregnant, and she is confronted with new arduous duties involved in the care of the newborn. All of this happens in just a matter of minutes and hours. Few life changes of equal magnitude are condensed into such a tiny time interval. Even if some of the alterations are perceived favorably, they are radically abrupt. It was earlier conjectured by the writer that this may be the cause of the relatively high psychosis rate in postpartum women.

Although the writer has clearly suggested that the average pregnant woman is probably not more disturbed psychologically than the average nonpregnant woman, it must be admitted that this represents an oversimplification of the actual empirical findings, which are confusing. It is true that no solid evidence exists that pregnant women are more disturbed than nonpregnant women. It is also true that no consistency has been demonstrated in a pattern of either increasing or decreasing disturbance *within* the period of pregnancy itself. However, there are fairly good indications that when women are evaluated during pregnancy and again shortly after delivery they show a decrease in disturbance. They seem to be less anxious and more positive toward self during the postpartum period. It must also be pointed out, however, that there is a paradoxical increase in psychosis rate during the postpartum period. This is a seemingly contradictory package of observations. The writer has proposed that one possible way of resolving the contradiction is by assuming that during the postpartum period a woman may interpret the sudden and dramatic transformations that have occurred in herself in such a positive fashion that she may, for a while, actually feel better than she usually does. She feels "supergood," so to speak. One would expect that after several months her psychological state would level off to return to its "normal" level. Some empirical support for this view is provided by the writer's earlier described finding that a month after delivery women not only show less overall disturbance in body experience than they did during pregnancy but also less than normal nonpregnant women usually do. But to proceed further and try to account for the increase in psychosis during the postpartum phase, one may offer the speculation that certain women are unusually vulnerable to the impact of quick dramatic changes in their state, even when some of the changes have positive connotations, and are thus thrown into serious disequilibrium by the transformations initiated by the delivery. In other words, it is theorized that even changes that have "good" connotations may be severely disturbing to some women simply because of the magnitude of the alterations in self that they produce. This is, of course, only speculation, and it remains to be seen how it will stand up to empirical check.

A final point to add that is pertinent to the matter of pregnancy is that fear of accidental pregnancy does not seem to play an appreciable part in inhibiting sexual responsiveness. There were no consistent correlations in the writer's data between any of the indices of sexual responsiveness and self-reported fear of becoming pregnant. Of course, it must be kept in mind that this negative result was obtained with samples of middle-class women who were largely satisfied with their contraceptive procedures. In women who either had no contraception available or whose contraception was seriously inadequate, one might expect fear of pregnancy to intrude significantly and interfere with sexual arousal. However, even in this more extreme group one wonders how strong the impact of fear of accidental pregnancy would be once the arousal process had started. Although it might affect intercourse rate, would it prevent orgasm once intercourse had begun? One reason for being skeptical about this point derives from a report by Gebhard, et al. (1958) that women who have had an abortion (to terminate an unwanted pregnancy) do not have lower orgasm rates during their first year of marriage than other comparable women. It might have been expected that such women would be unusually anxious about becoming accidentally pregnant and that this anxiety would somehow interfere with their enjoyment of sexual stimulation. In any case, as contraceptive technology continues to become more efficient, whatever role fear of accidental pregnancy has had in modifying sexual arousal should practically disappear.

Sex and Other Appetites

In essence, this book has examined the nature of one appetite as it occurs in women. How far can the findings be generalized to other appetites such as eating, drinking, seeking of new experience, and so forth? This is difficult to say. But it might prove to be an interesting and profitable exercise to assume that they are of wider significance and to follow their implications through. What are some of these implications?

1. First, if one considers that no consistent correlations were obtained between most of the major sex behavior indices and those measuring other appetites (for example, interest in eating, amount of drinking), it seems logical to conjecture that the various appetites represent fairly distinct, independent systems.

2. If one further considers that most of the major indices of sexual behavior were not consistently correlated with each other, it is also possible to conclude that each appetite system is organized in complex ways, with many inconsistent and even contradictory elements being simultaneously present. The same overall conclusion has been arrived at by others who have examined need systems (for example, Allport, 1949; Murray, 1938). Simple models based on the idea that an individual is consistently high or low in his use of, or enjoyment from, the multiple possible channels available for satisfying a specific appetite have turned out not to fit the facts.

3. Since several of the sexual measures were linked with attitudes toward parents, it is logical to generalize that other appetites will, at least in part, be influenced by early socialization experiences. Certain patterns of interaction with one's parents will tend to energize or inhibit specific appetites. There is already a fair amount of evidence in the literature that the intensity and modes of expression of various appetites are detectably influenced by childhood experiences (Jones, 1968; Murray, 1938; Whiting and Child, 1953).

4. A number of the sexual measures turned out to be correlated with personality attributes. By analogy, then, one would expect other appetites

and their modes of expression to be linked with personality parameters. Moderate support for this formulation may be found in the existing literature (for example, Jones, 1968; Murray, 1938; Miller and Swanson, 1960).

5. In view of the fact that the measures of sexual behavior did not relate significantly to the state of a woman's "mental health," it might be logical to expect that other appetite systems would not reflect maladjustment. It is doubtful, for example, that most aspects of eating behavior are linked to indices of anxiety or personal disturbance. However, a moment of reflection suggests that such a generalization may not hold up empirically for such appetites as consumption of alcohol or drugs.

6. Although some instances were observed in which amount of sexual imagery and fantasy (as defined, for example, by number of references to sex themes in inkblot responses) or sensitivity to stimuli with sexual connotations (such as presented tachistoscopically) were correlated with measures of sexual satisfaction and orgasm consistency, these were few and irregular. There do not seem to be direct or compensatory relationships between habitual modes of sexual satisfaction and preoccupation with sexual fantasies or themes. Although this is surprising, it may simply be another example of the fact that the individual learns to adapt to and accept long prevailing conditions. It should be added, though, that all of the women studied were married and were receiving at least some amount of regular sexual experience. It is possible that if women were studied who were extremely deprived of sexual interaction, evidence would be found for the presence of compensatory sexual imagery.

One should note, apropos of the whole issue of the relationship between appetite satisfaction and imagery pertaining to the appetite, that studies that have looked at the results of relatively brief periods of deprivation (for example, of food or sleep) upon fantasy have found them to be very complex and inconsistent (Saugstad, 1966). Both with reference to short- and long-term appetite satisfaction it seems premature to posit any simple pattern of fantasy or perceptual sensitivity effects.

7. Finally, attention should be called to the importance that was deductively assigned to change in state of consciousness (or perceptual sensitivity) as a factor in orgasm attainment. It seemed as if concern about the perceptual fading of objects was significant in inhibiting orgasmic excitement. The question arises whether the perceptual changes arising from the processes linked with other appetites may not have important feedback effects. For example, do some persons find their enjoyment of food inhibited because of the sleepy, less aroused state produced by filling up of the stomach? They may have a need to remain alert, and the soporific effects of the food may be experienced as incongruent and unpleasant. Or do some individuals avoid their appetite for new experiences because in the process they become so aroused and alert that they cannot maintain their "shutting out" attitude toward certain classes of stimuli?

These generalizations represent only rough analogies. It is not clear that they articulate much in the way of new thought, but they are offered in the spirit of seeking maximum systematization of the results that were obtained.

Practical Implications

If one takes the liberty of projecting from the results and generalizations presented in this book, a number of practical implications can be derived. These implications, which are offered in a tentative way, go beyond the actual facts and should be approached with caution.

Pathways to Sexual Adequacy

One of the prime deductions to be made from the findings is that many pathways are open to a woman in the process of becoming a sexually adequate person. She need not grow up with any special set of traits in order to be sexually responsive. Likewise, she need not conform to any fixed stereotype of what is feminine. Perhaps even more importantly, her sexual responsiveness does not depend upon her achieving a certain fixed amount of practice in dating or heterosexual contacts as she grows up. Many different kinds of women with many different kinds of dating patterns have been found to be equally orgastic. An immediate implication of these findings is that parents, psychiatrists, and others who are involved in the guidance or treatment of girls should be modest in their assertions about how any specific girl needs to behave in order to grow up to be a sexually adequate person. Perhaps only the most extreme kinds of deviance in sexual behavior should be viewed as indicating a "defect" in sexual development. There would seem to be little rationale in assuming that the developing girl is headed for disaster in her future sex role simply because she is shy with boys or does not easily wear certain of the standard trappings of femininity. Of course, it is still possible that the girl who is troubled with shyness and difficulties in relating to male peers may be headed for other kinds of adjustment difficulties. A condition that can be regarded as a signal for potential future sexual difficulties is the existence of a distant, noninvolved relationship with the father. It will be recalled that it was found that if a woman perceives her father as not having invested serious interest in her she tends to experience orgastic difficulties. Therefore, if a girl has a father who is absent from home for long periods of time or whose work absorbs too great a part of his energies or who is psychologically difficult to relate to because of his own symptomatology (for example, alcoholism), serious thought ought to be given to the impact it will have upon her future sexual adaptation. Perhaps with an awareness of such potential complications, special remedial measures might be undertaken.

Sex Education

Debate has raged interminably about the role of formal sex education in the child's long-term sexual development. Also, there have been conflicting opinions about how important it is for the parents as compared to other agents to supply the child with information about sexual matters. If one uses as a criterion the adult sexual adequacy of a woman, the overall scientific findings indicate that the nature of *formal* sex education is relatively unimportant. Neither in the writer's studies nor in those of others (Terman, 1938, 1951) has a woman's ability to enjoy sexual intercourse turned out to be related to the manner in which she received her early sex education. It made no difference whether she obtained her information from her mother or books or friends or a formal course in school. This is not to argue against giving accurate sexual information to children. Such information could in many instances help to correct inaccurate concepts of sexuality and relieve the individual of the need to go through a lot of unnecessary anxiety provoking trial and error learning on his own. That is, sex education would help to clarify *cognitively* the essential nature of the sexual act and its relationship to reproduction. The benefit would be informational at an intellectual level. It is doubtful that formal sex education does much in terms of the individual's "emotional" sexual development. It will be recalled that in the writer's data there were no consistent relationships between a woman's sexual responsiveness and her recall of how openly her parents talked about sex or were comfortable with nudity. This suggests that much of what parents do that is *directly* concerned with sexual matters may have little to do with how comfortable their children will eventually be with sexual excitement. One would speculate that this is so because there are so many different reasons why parents may be open and explicit as opposed to closed and noncommunicative about sex. In some instances the difference may actually reflect degree of comfort with sexuality. But in other instances, facade or compensatory behavior is probably involved. A parent may be very "open" about sexual matters simply because he has read a book that insists that it is important to do so. Or he may be "open" about sex as a way of forcefully denying real anxiety and insecurity in this area. On the other hand, the parent may be "closed" about sex not because he is specifically ashamed of it but rather because he is restrained in communicating about any matters with personal or intimate connotations. One gets the impression from the available data that the really important things that a girl learns about sex from her parents are only minimally contained in those communications and behaviors that are clearly "about sex." Probably much more is learned from those aspects of their behavior indicating how much they are capable of intimacy, trust, and dependability.

Sexual Adequacy

Women have been the targets of many unreasonable ideas about how they should behave sexually. For centuries they have been educated to believe that they are sexually inferior to men. They have been told that they are only castrated versions of men and that they are not really as sensitive to sexual stimuli as men. Pseudoscientific pronouncements have been utilized to reinforce such beliefs. As already shown, the empirical findings have not supported assumptions about women being sexually defective. It is true that women are less consistently able to attain orgasm in heterosexual intercourse than are men. However, it is highly probable that this is a reflection of certain special kinds of fears about separation from love objects that are generated by the way in which girls are socialized in most cultures. One would expect the orgasm consistency differential between the sexes to diminish (as it may already show signs of doing in the Kinsey, et al. [1953] data) when the feminine role is less radically defined in terms of dependence and winning the love of a protector.

One of the most radical sources of feelings of sexual inadequacy in women has been the proscription that sexual arousal through direct clitoral stimulation does not have the same validity as arousal elicited by vaginal stimulation. Women have been led to believe that they are neurotic, unhealthy, and immature if they prefer clitoral to vaginal stimulation. Once again the empirical facts indicate how badly they have been misled. Women who favor direct clitoral stimulation are in no way unusually immature or maladjusted. It is obvious from both the quantitative and qualitative material collected by the writer that each woman has fairly special patterns of preference about attaining arousal, and that there is no basis for asserting that any one pattern is "healthier" than another. Furthermore, the writer's data indicate that direct clitoral manipulation plays a far larger role in attaining orgasm than previously suspected. Only 20 percent of a sample questioned indicated that they never require the assistance of a final "push" from *direct* clitoral stimulation in order to attain orgasm while engaged in intercourse. Only 7 percent of the women in several samples endorsed the statement that vaginal stimulation contributes "much more" to orgastic arousal than does clitoral stimulation. Sixty-four percent of one sample indicated that if they had to choose between clitoral and vaginal stimulation, they would settle for the clitoral. One can only guess that the elaborate fictions invented by men about the superiority of the so-called vaginal orgasm reflect the fact that they themselves enjoy a sexual relationship with a woman more when the penis is vaginally inserted than when it is not. In any case, there is no longer any rational reason for burdening women with restrictions on what is the "proper" way for them to reach orgasm in a relationship with a man.

Sex and "Mental Health"

Until evidence to the contrary appears, it must be urged that those who make decisions about whether women are psychologically maladjusted and in need of treatment not use sexual responsiveness as one of their judgmental criteria. The available findings simply do not indicate a convincing relationship between degree of psychological disturbance and almost any aspect of sexual behavior. Obviously, this conclusion clashes with some of the major viewpoints prevailing among professionals who dispense psychotherapeutic treatment. However, it is now clearly necessary to articulate a challenge to those who use limited sexual responsiveness in a woman as a sign of her poor "mental health." The accumulated empirical observations place the burden of proof upon them. This is not to argue that psychotherapeutic techniques may not help women with orgastic difficulties, but only that such difficulties should be regarded as occurring within a limited region of the personality and need not be representative of the state of other personality regions.

There has also been an unfortunate tendency to associate most of the reproductive functions of the human female with pathological psychological states. It has been customary to portray the menstruating or pregnant woman as being in a delicately balanced and troubled psychological condition. However, the studies to be found in the literature that bear on such phenomena do not support this idea. It may be true that women are more troubled than usual during the premenstrual phase and the postpartum phase, but this does not seem to be true during the major portions of menstruation or pregnancy. The clarification of this point is really important because many women maintain their psychological stability during menstruation and pregnancy despite being indoctrinated with false expectations that things must go psychologically wrong at these times. One cannot help but wonder whether the idea that a woman's reproductive functions are disturbing to her psychologically have not been promulgated by men who perceive the events that occur in women's bodies as terribly different from those occurring in their own bodies—and, therefore, suggesting a strange, alien, and disturbing quality.

Treatment of Orgasm Difficulties

What deductions can be made from the findings that might be helpful in assisting an adult woman who has difficulty in attaining orgasm? This is a complex question because there are so many different levels at which "assistance" might be provided. It could be offered in relatively simplistic ways involving direct intervention in immediate family and living arrangements, at one extreme, and esoteric psychotherapeutic procedures, at the other extreme. One can only review some of the possibilities that take on pertinence in the light of the fact that orgasm difficulties were observed to be linked to concern about the instability or potential loss of love objects. It will remain for future work to define the utility of these possibilities.

1. At the simplest level, one might begin by determining whether the husband (or sex partner) of the woman with orgastic problems engages in modes of behavior that dramatize his lack of dependability. Is he away for long periods of time? Does he fluctuate markedly in his acceptance of his wife? Does he engage in maneuvers that chronically intimate that he plans to separate if things are not done his way? It is conceivable that if such behavior patterns were called to the husband's attention (for example, in the context of joint marital therapy) that sufficient change could be induced to relieve some of the wife's feelings that he is undependable. This, in turn, might sufficiently reduce her overall concern about potential object loss to help increase her ability to tolerate orgastic excitement.

2. A second possible approach would be in terms of individual psychotherapeutic exploration that focused on issues of object loss. This would particularly involve an analysis of the woman's feelings and fantasies about her father, who, it will be recalled, seemed to play a selectively important role in those attitudes that inhibit orgasm. The essence of such psychotherapeutic work would be to make the woman aware of her original uncertainty about her father's lack of dependability and give her insight into her tendency to overgeneralize what seemed to be true of him to her current heterosexual transactions.

3. A third treatment alternative the writer would propose for consideration (and empirical evaluation) aims to cope directly with the perceptual "fading" process that has been presumed to elicit orgasm inhibition in women who are particularly concerned about object loss. It was theorized earlier that when a woman is sensitive to object loss, she finds a build-up of sexual excitement to be threatening because it is accompanied by diminished perceptual sensitivity and a retreat from what is "out there," which results in a feeling of having a less secure perceptual hold on objects and therefore less actual attachment to them. The question arises whether the woman with orgastic difficulties could be helped if she were made explicitly aware of the perceptual changes accompanying sexual excitement as well as interpretation of these changes. If she could more directly face up to the perceptual "fading" process and become aware of her irrational assumptions concerning its significance, she might learn to master its threatening implications. Indeed, if she could be assigned the task of repeatedly building up sexual excitement (for example, through masturbation) and studying the perceptual changes produced, she might gradually become less sensitized to their impact—and so ultimately less likely to become inhibited as orgasm approaches.

Nonsexual Functions of Sex

There are hints here and there in the writer's findings that sexual behavior serves other needs than those that would be considered sexual in the strict sense of the term. For example, intercourse rates were found to be correlated with certain indices of narcissism. Furthermore, masturbation frequency was found to be correlated not only with interest in novel experience but also with wishes having to do with demonstrating one's independence from one's mother. Of course, many other theorists and clinicians have pointed out the nonsexual satisfactions or purposes that sexual behavior may serve in the life of an individual. The writer would like to suggest that insufficient recognition has been given to nonsexual derivatives of various sexual behaviors. Actually, most persons probably tend to feel guilt or a sense of inappropriateness when they become aware of such nonsexual derivatives in their own lives. But one wonders whether discomfort of this sort might be partially dispelled if there were wider explicit recognition of the nonsexual functions of sex. The woman who gets the urge to masturbate because she is seeking a novel experience or because she has the desire to affirm again her independence of her mother need not intrinsically have a greater sense of inappropriateness than she does when she eats to allay a *general* feeling of uneasiness or takes a shower to help her articulate her body boundaries. This statement is made, of course, entirely from a nonmoralistic perspective and would not apply within the context of religious beliefs, which, because they define nonsexual uses of sex as immoral, produce guilt and discomfort.

Education

The more educated a woman is, the less she typifies the usual stereotypes about femininity. It is a characteristic finding in studies that evaluate degree of femininity, as defined by interest patterns, that women with much education are "less feminine" than those with limited education. A widely accepted belief is that a well-educated woman has somehow lost an important component of her womanhood. Education is thought to masculinize a woman and to diminish her likelihood of being passionate. It is an interesting commentary on the divergence between speculative assumptions and real fact that empirical studies have shown just the opposite to be true. As already described in detail, Kinsey, et al. (1953) discovered that orgasm consistency is positively related to amount of education. They also reported that the difference between women with low and high amounts of education does not disappear even after many years of sexual practice in marital intercourse. Possible reasons for the greater orgasm consistency of the well-educated woman have already been discussed by the writer.[22] What is important from a practical point of view is that women have been misled concerning the impact that education might have upon them as sexual persons. They have been led to fear that the educational process would make them all "brain" and diminish their body sexuality proportionately. One can only say that it is time to emancipate them from this belief by a straightforward reassurance that it is untrue. There are analogous beliefs to the effect that if women aspire to roles or types of work that are conventionally masculine they will somehow lose their sexuality. Although no scientific information is available about whether women in more "masculine" occupations are less sexually responsive than women in conventional sex status roles, one would doubt it in view of the writer's findings that measures of masculinity of interest were unrelated to sexual responsiveness indices. It is very unlikely that the housewife or the feminine-looking model are more orgastic than the woman engineer or taxi driver.

Sexual Practice Effects

Comment should be made about the practical implications of the relatively minimal role that sheer amount of sexual practice (as in marital intercourse) has been found to play in orgasm consistency. Years of marital intercourse seem to have rather unimpressive effects on orgasm attainment. It will also be recalled that measures of the elaborateness of the sexual stimulation delivered to women were found by the writer and others (Kinsey, et al., 1953) to be uncorrelated with sexual responsiveness. For example, the writer noted that number of intercourse positions and length of foreplay had only chance correlations with orgasm consistency. A primary deduction to be made from such material is that the ability to be sexually responsive cannot be learned by an adult woman in the way that she learns other motor skills. It is doubtful that she can really improve her sexual responsiveness significantly by reading books on sexual technique or experimenting with a variety of stimulation procedures.[23] Beyond a moderate level of knowledge concerning primary erogenous zones, the factors facilitating sexual arousal seem to be largely interpersonal, involving feelings of intimacy, closeness, and dependability. Women with orgasm difficulties probably try to convince themselves that if they could only master some new sexual technique all would be well. Or they may irrationally criticize their sex partners for not being sufficiently expert to stimulate them properly. In other words, the attainment of orgasm is too often perceived as a motor act that can be mastered in the same way as any muscular maneuver. For what it is worth, one should add that the writer found no significant correlations between sexual responsiveness and amount of investment in athletic activities. It is doubtful that sexual responsiveness is any more a function of motor skill than is the ability to enjoy eating.

Pregnancy

Part of the folklore about female sexuality is that a woman does not reach genuine sexual maturity until she has had the experience of bearing a child. This concept has probably motivated many women with orgasm difficulties to become pregnant. Sherfey (1966) has even given the concept an apparent scientific basis by proposing that pregnancy, by increasing the vascularity of the pelvis, augments "orgasmic competency." She declares at one point (p. 90): "Many women experience their first coital orgasm after their first pregnancy." There were no indications in the writer's findings that women who had had one or more pregnancies were any more orgasmic than those who had never been pregnant. There were no differences between these categories either with respect to orgasm consistency or other measures of sexual responsiveness.[24] One can imagine that bearing a child might in certain individual instances increase a woman's orgasmic consistency, but if so, the writer would attribute it to a sense of increased security about being part of a stable family group. That is, the birth of a child might signal to a woman that her marriage did, indeed, have permanence and that her husband could be counted on to maintain their liaison. However, it is also possible to imagine that the birth of a child would alienate a husband and cause the wife to feel more insecure about her marriage and her husband. This could conceivably eventuate in diminished orgasmic consistency. But, in general, the writer would maintain that it is unlikely that any one psychological or physiological event will drastically alter a woman's sexual responsiveness. It is unrealistic to advise a woman with an orgasm problem that if she would only become pregnant or find a new sex partner or shift from an "outside" job to being a housewife that her ability to respond to orgasm would be significantly augmented. Such advice has no foundation in fact.

Priority Problems in the Study of Female Sexuality

One of the benefits of a thorough analysis of any sector of knowledge is that it clarifies not only what is understood but also what is not understood. If one looks back at the review of the sex behavior literature and the findings collected by the writer, it becomes clear that there are certain prime questions concerning female sexuality that deserve priority in future studies. A number of these questions are specified.

High priority should be assigned to learning more about the conditions that facilitate or inhibit a woman's orgasm potential.

1. Cross-cultural studies are badly needed in which orgasm consistencies of women reared under different conditions can be compared. Special attention should be given to looking at cultures that differ in how much they try to instill anxiety in girls about loss of love and love objects as a means of maintaining control over them. This would provide an opportunity for directly evaluating the writer's formulation that concern about object loss plays a significant role in orgasm potential.

2. It would be helpful if fathers of women with contrasting orgasm consistencies were studied. To what degree do such fathers differ in the amount of interest they have invested in their daughters? How much do they vary from each other in traits such as dependability, self-confidence, and conscientiousness? On the basis of such information one could test the writer's tentative conclusion that a woman's orgasm potential is significantly linked to whether she experienced her father as a dependable love object.

3. A related question that needs to be probed is the possible role of the husband (or sex partner) in a woman's orgasm capacity.[25] It is important to find out whether her feelings about her husband's dependability as a love object influence her orgasm potential. This would probably necessitate a study of married couples. The attributes of the husband reflecting his de-

pendability would be correlated with his wife's orgasm behavior. One would want to evaluate the husband with respect to traits such as conscientiousness and ability to identify with his wife, and one would also want to ascertain how much confidence she had in him.

Parallel to such inquiries, it would be informative to have a sample of wives keep "diaries" in which they would record their orgasm behavior over a period of time and simultaneously, for the same period, report the major events and feeling states in their lives. Various questions could be investigated. Does orgasm consistency decline when the husband is planning to be away from home for a while? Do crises in the family, such as illness of children or financial difficulties, affect orgasm capacity? If a woman loses one of her close friends does this adversely affect her orgasm response by increasing her uncertainty about the dependability of objects? [26] Does successful achievement influence a woman's orgasm potential? Do periods of sexual deprivation increase subsequent orgasm potential? It is the writer's view that naturalistic studies of this sort should be given particular priority.

4. Detailed and finely etched reports must be secured from a variety of women concerning the perceptual changes that occur as excitement builds up to orgasmic levels. This information is necessary, first of all, to gain a better understanding of how sexual excitement diminishes the woman's perceptual hold on objects. Furthermore, it might prove of value in helping to develop practical procedures that would enable women with orgasm difficulties to recognize and adapt to experiential "object fading."

5. Finally, controlled evaluations are needed of possible treatment procedures for increasing orgasm consistency in women who have response difficulties. Treatments ranging from the simple to the complex should be appraised. For example, one could compare joint counseling designed to reduce the frequency with which a woman's husband displays behavior demonstrating his lack of dependability (such as being away from home frequently) with a more complex procedure that focuses on the history of a woman's relationships with her father and the fantasies she entertains about his lack of dependability.

The matter of clitoral versus vaginal preference should probably also be given priority in future studies as it has valuable theoretical and practical implications.

1. Detailed descriptions and ratings need to be obtained of the manner in which women experience their sex partners in the clitoral-versus vaginal-stimulation situation. In line with the formulations previously spelled out by the writer, does one actually find that the vaginally oriented woman feels more "fused" with her sex partner and less responsible for her arousal, whereas the clitorally oriented feels more autonomous and self-responsible for her sexual excitement?

2. Is it possible to find cultures that clearly differ in the degree to which

women prefer vaginal versus clitoral stimulation? If so, what are the differences between them in the way they rear girls? Do they, as would be expected from the writer's formulations, place contrasting amounts of emphasis on how much a girl is really an individual who should be in charge of her own body?

3. Much more has to be learned about whether clitoral-vaginal preferences are modified by sexual experience. Is there a shift toward greater vaginal preference in the average marriage as a woman has an increasing amount of experience with vaginal stimulation? The fact that the writer did not find a significant correlation between length of marriage and clitoral-vaginal preference would argue against this possibility. However, no information was obtained from the *individual* woman as to whether she had observed a change in her clitoral-vaginal orientation over the course of her marriage.

4. Another question to be probed is whether the average woman has observed her clitoral-vaginal preference to change vis-à-vis different sex partners. That is, does a woman find that she is quite responsive to vaginal stimulation with one man and unresponsive with another? If so, what attributes characterize one partner as compared to the other?

Relatedly, there should be a study of the husbands of women who differ in clitoral-vaginal orientation. Do such husbands differ in their attitudes about feminine autonomy and the need for a wife to "fuse" with her husband?

Many other problems could be mentioned that are important to clarify and are in need of investigation. The following are a few illustrations of the diversity that come to mind: We need to know more about the conditions that increase or decrease intercourse rates. Is intercourse used as a means of narcissistic enhancement at times when life events are threatening self-esteem? It would be of theoretical import to find out whether a woman's sexual responsiveness is related to any aspect of the sexual behavior of her parents (for example, their intercourse rate) and more specifically the orgasm consistency of her mother. One wonders whether low or high sexual responsiveness shows up consistently in families over several generations. What does the nonorgasmic woman derive from her sexual contacts? What kinds of sensations and experiences does she selectively highlight in order to make intercourse satisfying?

Hopefully, the coming years will see a large increase in the amount of scientific energy devoted to clarifying such questions.

N O T E S

1. One wonders whether the difference in body security between men and women may not become even greater if machines make further inroads on the male's need to have body strength and prowess in order to be a "successful" person. However, the machine shows little likelihood of modifying the need for a woman to be attractive in order to marry and to possess a functional reproductive system in order to become a mother.

2. Hollender (1970) has documented the paramount importance of body closeness, as such, to some women as they engage in intercourse.

3. The one exception to this statement is Terman's findings (1938, 1951) in two studies that husbands of nonorgastic women tend to have had more strict religious training than husbands of orgastic women. If one assumes that strictness in religious training carries with it learning a puritanical attitude toward sex, the possibility arises that there may be a special puritanical quality in the sexual behavior of the husband of the low orgastic woman that inhibits her. However, none of the available indices of husband's sexual behavior (for example, duration of stimulation he provides), which might be expected to reflect puritanical attitudes, has turned out to be correlated with orgasm consistency.

4. Kinsey, et al. (1953) found evidence that some women are more orgasmic in extramarital affairs with other men than they are with their own husbands. However, overall, there does not seem to be a significantly higher rate of orgasmic attainment in extramarital than in marital intercourse.

5. Note that when the women in one of the samples studied by the writer were asked to describe the conditions that facilitate orgasm, they particularly emphasized the importance of something occurring that made them feel that they had a "good relationship" with their husbands.

6. Note that Kinsey, et al. (1953) reported that the differences in orgasm consistency between women of contrasting educational levels are not erased by the practice effects of five or even ten years of marital intercourse.

7. It is pertinent to this issue that a woman's education and social class, which are also significantly correlated with orgasm capacity, are likely to be particularly influenced by the status and behavior of her father.

8. There is another interesting matter that comes to one's attention when studying the Kinsey, et al. data with respect to the relationship between duration of marriage and orgasm consistency in women of different educational levels. One finds that in the first year of marriage 12 percent more women of high educational level (17 years or more) achieve orgasm with great consistency than do women of low educational level (0–8 years of education). By the fifth year of marriage the difference increases to 13 percent. Practice, rather than decreasing the difference between the groups, actually increases it slightly. In other words, whatever is the nature of the difference in orgasmic capacity between women of low and high educational level, it is not decreased by practice effects.

9. Kinsey, et al. (1953) and others have shown that women who attain orgasm premaritally (whether by masturbation or heterosexual intercourse) are more likely to attain orgasm in marital intercourse. However, it is not clear that this is a practice effect. As pointed out earlier, there may be a selective process such that women who have the greatest orgasmic potential are those most likely to seek out premarital experiences that will provide them with the excitement needed for arousal.

Furthermore, one has to keep in mind that women who had had premarital intercourse without attaining orgasm were not more orgasmic in their first year of marriage than women who had had no premarital intercourse. The premarital practice did not give the one category an advantage over the other.

10. One is reminded of the earlier reported finding that sexual activity is inhibited in marriages where the husband continues to have close relationships with his original family.

11. Masters and Johnson (1966) report that when women were sexually stimulated in a laboratory setting, the orgasms they attained through their partners' manipulating their genitals were usually more intense than those attained through coition.

12. It will also be recalled that a trend of borderline significance was observed for the extreme vaginally oriented to describe themselves as feeling less satisfied during orgasm than the extreme clitorally oriented.

13. I am indebted to Dr. Roger Greenberg for raising a number of questions that led to this line of thought.

14. The rate in unmarried women tends to be between 50 and 100 percent higher.

15. Kinsey, et al. (1953) found no convincing evidence that masturbation frequency was related to whether a woman was Protestant, Catholic, or Jewish. This was also true in the writer's data.

Note that the range of religiosity represented in the Kinsey, et al. samples was probably considerably greater than in the writer's samples.

16. It is true that Kinsey, et al. (1953) found amount of *premarital* masturbation to be positively correlated with orgasm consistency during marriage.

17. Kinsey, et al. (1953) point out that women reach orgasm more quickly during masturbation than during intercourse. Further, Masters and Johnson (1966) state (p. 133): "Understandably, the maximum physiologic intensity of orgasmic response subjectively reported or objectively recorded has been achieved by self-regulated mechanical or automanipulative techniques. The next highest level of erotic intensity has resulted from partner manipulation, again with established or self-regulated methods, and the lowest intensity of target-organ response was achieved during coition."

18. A variety of unsuccessful exploratory attempts were also made to relate sexual responsiveness to responses to phallic inkblot areas.

19. One possible exception to this statement was the writer's finding that orgasm consistency is positively correlated with a left directional bias in spatial perception, which in turn may be linked with a "feminine" kind of softness and nondefensiveness in relating to others.

20. These statements are not meant to imply that psychological vectors may not influence the physiology of the reproductive system. A number of studies were cited earlier in which psychotherapeutic techniques had a demonstrable effect on phenomena such as spontaneous abortion and pregnancy complications.

21. This statement is not meant to challenge the rather formidable evidence that much tension builds up *premenstrually* that is both disturbing and perhaps the cause of various kinds of impulsive acting out.

22. It is also of interest that well-educated women are less modest about being nude during sexual intercourse than are women with limited education.

23. Masters and Johnson (1966) indicate that some of the women who participated in their laboratory sexual studies and who were given the opportunity to "practice" sexually in new ways improved their orgasm consistency. However, they cite only a few individual cases and one cannot ascertain the overall effect of such practice on their experimental population. Furthermore, one does not know whether improvement was a function of practice or an increased sense of object dependability derived from joining the research project and receiving support and reassurance from Masters and Johnson and their associates.

24. However, there is no intent to imply that changes in sexual responsiveness do not occur during pregnancy itself. Masters and Johnson (1966) found, for example, that eroticism tended to decline during the first three months of pregnancy and to increase during the second three months.

25. Systematic inquiry is also needed as to whether women find their orgasm potential to vary markedly with different sex partners. All that we know about this matter at present is based on unreliable anecdotal reports.

26. An interesting experiment would be to obtain repeated samples of inkblot responses from women over a period of time and to determine whether variations in amount of concern about object loss (for example, as defined by death imagery) were predictive of orgasm consistency changes at each time phase.

APPENDICES

The details concerning procedure and measurement techniques used in each of the samples studied are presented in the Appendices that follow. Copies or descriptions of important questionnaires are also included.

APPENDIX A (Sample 1)

The women in Sample 1 were evaluated over the course of five sessions.

SESSION 1 (This session was begun within five days after the cessation of each woman's last menstrual period.)

The following procedures were administered.

1. *Body Prominence Task.* This task measures how aware one is of one's body (Fisher, 1970) as compared to other objects in the world. It was administered by asking each woman to be seated alone in a quiet room and to write on a sheet of paper "Twenty things that you are aware of or conscious of right now." She was told to use "at least several words" in each of her descriptions. Scoring of body awareness is based on the number of direct or indirect references made to one's own body. Details concerning the scoring, reliability, and validity of the Body Prominence technique may be found elsewhere (Fisher, 1970). The protocols obtained by means of this procedure were also scored for the following: Orality (references to oral activities such as eating and smoking); Dirt (references to dirt or antidirt activities); Sex (references to sexual activities). These scores have adequate scoring objectivity (Fisher, 1970).

2. *Body Focus Questionnaire.* This procedure developed by Fisher (1970) measures relative awareness of various sectors of one's own body. It involves presenting the subject with a series of verbal references to paired body regions and asking her to indicate which of the two constituting each pair stands out most clearly in her awareness. Eight scale scores are derived: Front-Back, Right-Left, Heart, Stomach, Eyes, Mouth, Head, Arms. The validity and reliability of these scales have been analyzed elsewhere (Fisher, 1970).

3. *Dating Questionnaire.* This involves an inquiry concerning frequency of dating in high school and college, age at which dating began, and number of times has "gone steady" or been engaged.

4. *Religion Questionnaire.* This form consisted of questions concerning religious affiliation, frequency of church attendance of self and parents, and ratings of degree of one's religiosity.

5. *Body Distortion Questionnaire.* This questionnaire (Fisher, 1970) evaluates the frequency and specific nature of disturbances in body experience. It requires the subject to answer Yes, No, or Undecided to 82 statements referring to a number of different kinds of distorted body experience. The categories of distortion measured are as follows: (a) Large (perception of one's body as unusually large); (b) Small

(perception of one's body as unusually small); (c) Boundary Loss (feeling that one's body boundaries are weak); (d) Dirty (sensations that one's body is dirty or contaminated); (e) Blocked Openings (perception of body "openings," such as throat, eyes, ears, as blocked or "stopped up"; (f) Skin (unusual skin sensations); (g) Depersonalization (feeling that one's body is alien or foreign).

6. *Physiological Measures.* While each woman sat quietly alone in a room for 15 minutes the following physiological measures were obtained: heart rate, Galvanic Skin Response, skin resistance from the finger and ankle, and temperature from the finger and ankle.

Heart rate was determined from a Blocom transducer that was taped to the palmar side of the fourth finger, right hand. Output was recorded on a Grass Polygraph.

G.S.R. was secured from a Grass silver EEG electrode from the palmar side of the right middle finger to an indifferent electrode placed on the upper left arm and recorded on a Grass Polygraph, using sensitivity of 1mv/cm at a chart speed of 6mm/sec. Masking tape with a hole ¼ inch in diameter restricted the area of recording. Contact between the skin and electrode was made with a paste composed of Glycerol and salt.

A Brush Polygraph (Model RP 562100) was used to record skin resistance. Calibration of the amplifiers was to a sensitivity of 1,000 ohms per chart line. Electrodes were of ⅛ inch lead sheeting (½ inch squares). Recording area was restricted by means of Scotch masking tape, with a hole ¼ inch in diameter.

Skin temperature was ascertained by means of the Yellow Springs Telethermometer 46 T U C equipped with a six-channel input. Maximal readable sensitivity is .1° C. The Yellow Springs Thermister (No. 408, Banjo type) was taped to the skin for the skin-temperature measurement. At a later point rectal and vaginal readings were secured with the Yellow Springs Thermister Probe (No. 401).

7. *Holtzman Inkblots (Form B).* Each woman wrote her interpretations of the first 25 inkblots in the larger series of 45 blots (Form B) developed by Holtzman, et al. (1961). The protocols were scored for the following parameters.

A. Barrier: This is a measure of the degree to which the individual perceives the boundaries of her body as definite and clearly differentiating her from nonself objects. Details concerning the scoring validity and reliability of this index may be found elsewhere (Fisher, 1970).

B. Penetration: This score measures the degree to which there is concern that one's body boundaries will be violated or disrupted. Details concerning the scoring, reliability, and validity of this index are presented elsewhere (Fisher, 1970).

C. Hostility: Each response was scored in terms of whether it did or did not depict a clear, overt, aggressive act (for example, "man shooting another," "two people arguing"). Symbolic hostile representations were not scored. Scores could range from 0 through 25. Interscorer agreement between two judges for 25 protocols was 95 percent.

D. Orality: Responses were scored as oral in terms of criteria previously developed in a study by Fisher (1965). The reliability of this scoring system has been shown to be adequate (Fisher, 1965).

E. Masculine versus Feminine Images: An evaluation of the relative representation of male versus female content in the inkblot imagery. This index was equal to the number of inkblot percepts in which a human male figure was specified minus the number in which a female figure was portrayed.

8. *Thurstone Temperament Schedule.* This is a personality questionnaire devised by Thurstone (1953) that involves answering Yes, No or ? to a series of 140 statements. Seven scores are derived: Active: How fast the individual works and moves; how restless she is. Vigorous: How much the large muscle groups are used; degree of participation in sports and work requiring use of tools. Impulsive: Being

"happy-go-lucky," daredevil, carefree, acting-on-the-spur of the moment; making decisions quickly. Dominant: Thinking of self as a leader; wanting to "take charge" and persuade others. Stable: Being cheerful; of even disposition; remaining calm in a crisis. Sociable: Enjoying the company of others; making friends easily. Reflective: Liking meditative and reflecting thinking; enjoying dealing with theoretical rather than practical problems.

9. *Buss-Durkee Inventory.* This questionnaire (Buss and Durkee, 1957) involves answering True or False to 39 statements concerning how one customarily expresses aggression. There are four scales, and an illustrative item from each will be presented. Assaultive (Once in a while I cannot control my urge to harm others); Irritability (I am irritated a great deal more than people are aware of); Negativism (When someone is bossy, I do the opposite of what he asks); Verbal hostility (When I get mad, I say nasty things).

10. Each woman was asked to take home and fill out a questionnaire concerned with her menstrual history and the development of her secondary sex characteristics. A description of this questionnaire may be found in Appendix H.

(All personnel who had contact with each woman rated her [five-point scale] with reference to the following variables: Anxiety, Anger. These ratings were repeated at the end of every session.)

SESSION 2 (Approximately five days later.)

1. *Physiological Recordings.* Each woman removed her clothing, put on a hospital gown, and lay down on an examining table in a shielded room. A nurse placed electrodes and probes for recording the following: Heart rate, Galvanic Skin Response (GSR), skin resistance (finger, breast, labia majora, ankle), temperature (finger, vagina, rectum, ankle). Heart rate and GSR electrodes were the first to be fastened on and recording of these measures was begun while the remainder of the electrode placement procedure was in progress. Recording of the other variables was begun as soon as the appropriate probes had been fastened in place.

The nurse then told each woman to "relax" for a while, and after she left the room, five minutes of recording were taken. Next, a male gynecologist (with the nurse) entered the room and inspected the electrodes. It was noted on the physiological recordings when he lifted the sheet to look at the woman's genital area and check the electrodes. This act was timed to occupy two minutes and was intended to confront each woman with the fact that her nude body was being looked at by a man. The gynecologist and nurse left the room and five more minutes of "rest" were recorded. The gynecologist and nurse returned and went through a procedure that involved determination of touch threshold (by means of a graded series of nylon filaments) for thigh and wrist.[1] Two minutes of physiological recording were taken initially while touch judgments were obtained on the thigh, two more during initial touch judgments on the wrist, and another two minutes for further judgments on the thigh. The gynecologist and nurse left the room and ten more minutes of "rest" were recorded. The electrodes were removed. Each woman rated her own reactions [2] to the procedures, and the gynecologist and nurse independently rated [3] her reactions.

The physiological recordings were analyzed in terms of specific segments, overall means, and change scores.

2. *Body Prominence.* While each woman was still clad only in a hospital gown and covered only with a sheet, she was asked to sit in a chair, and another measure of Body Prominence was obtained (that is, she wrote her responses to the instruction: "List 20 things that you are aware of or conscious of right now").[4]

3. *Body Distortion Questionnaire.*[4]

4. *Holtzman Inkblots (Form A).*[4]

5. *Thematic Apperception Test.* After each woman had put her clothes back on, she was presented with six Thematic Apperception Test (Murray, 1938) pictures (8GF, 2, 4, 10, 13MF, 16) and asked to write an imaginative story about each. A

time limit of five minutes was set for writing each story. The stories that were obtained were scored for the following variables:

Achievement: The degree to which the stories contain themes referring to success, attainment, and goal achievement. Each picture was scored as either containing or not containing an achievement theme; total scores could vary from 0 to 6. Two judges who independently evaluated 15 protocols attained 83 percent agreement in their judgments.

Hostility: The number of stories in which there was explicit reference to aggression (for example, attacking, criticizing). Total scores could range from 0 to 6. Two judges who independently scored 20 protocols attained 95 percent agreement.

Sexual: The number of stories in which there was explicit reference to heterosexual interaction (for example, dating, kissing, proposing). Total scores could range from 0 to 6. Two judges who independently scored 15 protocols reached 92 percent agreement.

SESSION 3 (Approximately five days later.)

1. *Body Prominence* (Already described).

2. *Byrne Food Attitude Scale.* The Byrne Food Attitude scale (Byrne, Golightly, and Capaldi, 1963) was administered. It evaluates liking for food, pleasantness associated with past eating experiences, mother's cooking ability, and importance of food as a reward and comfort. Responses to each item are registered by answering True or False. The higher the score the more the woman was considered to have a positive attitude toward eating and oral experiences in general. Included in the Byrne scale is a list of 103 foods. Each woman indicated which of the foods she likes. The total number of foods liked was determined. This was simply an index of the number of foods positively regarded.

3. *Physiological Recordings.* Another series of physiological measures was obtained. They were the same as those described for Session 2. Recordings were obtained as soon as electrodes and probes were placed (by the same nurse that participated in Session 2) and for five minutes after completion of the "hook-up." The same gynecologist that was involved in Session 2 entered and completed a standard gynecological examination (which included placement of a speculum in the vagina). Recordings were made throughout the examination and for five minutes after it was over, with the gynecologist and nurse out of the room. Each woman then rated her own response to the examination.[5] The nurse returned and placed external electrodes for measuring stomach motility (as described by Davis, Garafola, and Gault [1957]). The nurse left the room and five minutes of "rest" were recorded. The nurse returned and asked each woman to respond to a series of difficult arithmetic problems (intended to produce stress) for two minutes. Recordings were taken during this time and for five minutes afterward (with nurse out of room).

The physiological recordings were analyzed in terms of specific segments, overall means, and change scores.

4. *Murray-Harvard Scales.* Three of the brief Murray-Harvard questionnaires were administered: (a) Anal Preoccupation Scale (sample item: "Nothing is worse than an offensive odor"); (b) Anal Orderliness Scale (sample item: "I am generally methodical and systematic in the way I go about things"); (c) Oral Aggression Scale (sample item: "I can be pretty sarcastic at times").

5. *Tachistoscopic Perception.* Each woman responded to a series of pictures presented tachistoscopically.[6] The pictures, taken from a study by Forrest and Lee (1962), portrayed the following themes (presented in the order listed): Achievement (Figures climbing); Heterosexual 1 (Figures sitting next to each other on bed); Heterosexual 2 (Figures embracing, moon in sky); Hostility (Two figures shooting at each other); Nurturance (Adult figure holding a baby); Narcissism (Figure looking in a mirror). Each picture was presented five times at the following sequence of speeds (.008, .010, .025, .050, .075 seconds). The earliest speed at which it was correctly

identified was determined and code values ranging from 1 to 6 assigned on this basis (1 = correct identification at fastest speed). The values for the two heterosexual pictures were averaged. The coded values for all of the themes were rank ordered (1 = fastest identification). This provided an index of the degree to which each woman responded either selectively slow or fast to each of the major themes.

6. *Sex Superiority Pictures.* This procedure was devised by Fisher (1965) in a previous study to measure the extent to which one sex is perceived as superior to the other in power. It is based on judgments of male and female pictures of faces (front view). Twenty of the pictures involved male-female pairs. Ten involved male-male and ten involved female-female pairs. These like sex pairs were introduced to camouflage the fact that the task was really concerned with male versus female differences. The women were given the instruction to decide for each pair which would probably be the dominant one if they set up a social relationship with each other. The assumption underlying this task was that the greater the number of one sex designated as "dominant," the more that sex was regarded as being superior to the other.

SESSION 4 (Five days later.)

1. *Parental Ratings.* Each woman rated her father and subsequently her mother with reference to 34 attributes (for example, strictness, independence, anger, anxiety, responsibility, fairness). From such ratings the following dimensions were extracted: Moralism (Based on average of ratings for conventionality, strictness, and moralism); Hostility (Based on average of ratings for strictness, coldness, competitiveness, anger, being bossy, frequently administered punishment, aggressiveness, irritability, criticalness, frequently "beat me"); Egotism; Assertiveness; Closeness (To person making the rating); "Interest in me."

2. *Famous Saying Test.* The Bass (1958) Famous Saying Test was administered. It consists of a series of proverbs with which each woman indicated agreement or disagreement. Four scores can be derived: (a) Social Acquiescence (The degree to which there is a tendency to agree or acquiesce); (b) Conventional Mores; (c) Hostility; (d) Fear of Failure.

3. *Sexual Questionnaire.* Information concerning each woman's sexual behavior and attitudes was secured by means of a questionnaire. Details of this questionnaire may be found in Appendix J.

4. *Study of Values.* An analysis of basic value orientation was undertaken by means of the Allport-Vernon-Lindzey (1960) Study of Values. This questionnaire is based on the concept that values may be classified into the following dimensions: Economic, Aesthetic, Social, Political, Religious, and Theoretical.

5. *Maternal Attitude to Pregnancy Instrument.* Blau, et al. (1964) constructed a scale that taps attitudes about different aspects of the pregnancy process. It is based on amount of agreement expressed with statements about pregnancy and related topics. Presumably, it evaluates four dimensions: (a) Positive response to pregnancy, labor, and delivery; (b) Desire to participate actively in labor and breast-feeding and a feeling of looking well during pregnancy; (c) Anxiety about self, relationship to husband, and baby during pregnancy; (d) Acceptance of pregnancy and looking forward to handling the baby.

6. *Word Construction.* Each woman was presented with a sheet with a series of 48 blank lines, each preceded by a letter, and instructed as follows: "Below are a series of blanks and each is preceded by a letter. As quickly as you can, think of a word beginning with each letter and write in the rest of the word." The word completions were scored for the following variables:

Hostility: A word was scored as hostile if it clearly depicted an act of aggression (shoot, slap), hostile feeling (furious, irritated), or means of attack (cannon, grenade). Two independent scorers demonstrated 90 percent agreement in their judgments of 30 protocols.

Orality: A word was scored as having oral implications if it referred to food, eating, biting, smoking, chewing, mouth, or stomach. Two judges who independently evaluated 20 protocols attained 91 percent agreement in their scoring.

Sex: A word was categorized as having sexual connotations if it explicitly referred to love, intercourse, the genitals, dating activities, or reproduction. Two judges who independently evaluated 20 protocols reached 94 percent agreement.

SESSION 5 (Within 1 to 3 days of onset of menstrual flow.)

1. *Lie, K, and Repression Scales of the Minnesota Multiphasic Personality Inventory.* The Lie and K scales are concerned with measuring the degree to which an individual responds to questionnaire inquiries in a defensive, self-protective fashion. The L scale detects gross defensiveness that verges on lying.

The K scale detects more subtle tendencies to put on a "good," socially desirable facade.

The Repression scale is defined as a measure of the degree to which one represses one's own impulses and feelings and avoids acting them out.

2. *Sexual Body Focus Questionnaire.* This measure was constructed by the writer specifically for the present series of sexual studies. Its purpose was to determine the degree to which a woman is aware of two areas of her body that have obvious sexual significance (namely, vagina, breasts). The actual scale is modeled closely after the earlier described Body Focus Questionnaire (Fisher, 1970) in that it asks for a series of judgments regarding whether one is more aware of one body sector as compared to another. Thus, there was one cluster (ten items) that inquired whether the woman was more aware of her breasts than a range of other body areas (for example, arms, head, stomach). Another cluster (ten items) involved the woman comparing her awareness of her vagina with that for a series of other body areas.

3. *Early Sex Memory.* Each woman was asked to list ten memories from her early life that involved events that had sexual significance to her. These memories were evaluated in terms of a pleasantness-unpleasantness scheme. Each memory was classified as being either positive, negative, or neutral in its feeling tone. A memory was considered to be positive if it referred to events that were happy, joyful, successful, or pleasantly arousing. A memory was labeled negative if it involved fear, anger, guilt, injury, punishment, failure, or loneliness. If a memory could not be clearly classified as positive or negative, it was labeled neutral.

Two judges who independently scored 15 protocols attained an overall agreement rate of 74 percent.

4. *Description of Menstrual Experience.* The experimental plan was structured in such a fashion that the first session would occur shortly after the cessation of menstrual flow of the last menstrual period and Session 5 within a few days after the beginning of flow of the next menstrual period. Advantage was taken of the fact that each woman had just begun to menstruate when she came to this session by asking her to write a description of the experiences and sensations associated with menstruation. These descriptions were not quantitatively analyzed.

5. *Self-Interview.* Finally, each woman was asked to provide detailed information, in her own words, concerning many aspects of her life. She was, in fact, requested to speak into a tape recorder, while sitting alone in a room, and to outline a miniature autobiography. Her discussion was guided by a written outline (see Appendix I) that variously called for descriptions with reference to such topics as father, mother, brothers and sisters, husband, children, dating, sexual attitudes, changes in one's body during adolescence, pregnancy, and so forth.

This tape-recorded information was used primarily in a qualitative fashion.

APPENDIX B (Sample 2)

SESSION 1 (This occurred within a few days of the cessation of the last menstrual flow.)

1. *Body Prominence.*[7]
2. *Body Focus Questionnaire.*[7]
3. *Selective Learning.* A learning task was introduced that has been used in previous studies (Fisher, 1970) to measure selective response to sex versus nonsex words. Each woman was given one minute to learn a list of 20 words, ten with and ten without sexual connotations (Fisher, 1970). The list was removed and the woman was given five minutes to recall (by writing on a sheet of paper) as many of the words on the list as possible. A score was computed equal to the number of sex words minus nonsex words recalled.
4. *Spontaneous Stories.* Each woman wrote two spontaneous stories. The first story was to deal with the theme "A girl and her mother" and the second with the theme "A woman and her husband."

This was the first of five occasions, once in each of the five sessions comprising the experimental schedule for Sample 2, in which such stories were composed—with a total of ten finally being obtained. The themes to which the women were asked to address themselves in their stories were formulated by the writer. The purpose of the procedure was to confront each woman with having to create fantasies about a specific series of themes. By specifying each theme, the task sought to prevent evasion in dealing with them. It was intended that such story material would supplement that obtained by means of the Thematic Apperception Test, which is less structured, and might have allowed some women to avoid particular conflictual themes.

Several quantitative scores were derived from the series of stories.

A. Achievement: The same scoring system was used as described for the Thematic Apperception Test in Sample 1.

B. Hostility: The same scoring system was used as described for the Thematic Apperception Test in Sample 1.

Other special purpose scores were derived but they are described within the context of evaluating particular hypotheses taken up in the book.

5. *Holtzman Inkblots (Form B).*[8]
6. *Physiological Recordings.* The following physiological measures were recorded: temperature (hand, ankle, mouth), Galvanic Skin Response, heart rate, and skin resistance (hand, ankle).

Five minutes of recording were taken while each woman sat alone. A one-minute sample was taken when a blindfold was placed on her eyes, in preparation for a series of trials to determine her light-touch threshold. Recordings were continued throughout the light-touch trials. Recordings were also taken for the first minute of a procedure designed to determine threshold for the perception of tickle. (This tickle threshold procedure is described in detail in the section dealing with Session 2.)

The physiological recordings were analyzed with reference to each specific phase, overall means, and change scores.

7. *Tachistoscopic Selectivity.* This procedure has already been outlined in Appendix A. The same pictures and the same themes which were appraised in Sample 1 were explored once again.

8. *Photograph.* Two colored pictures were taken of each woman. One was a full-length front view and the other a full-length back view. The pictures were taken in order to permit an analysis of appearance and posture that would not be influenced by factors of personal acquaintance.

9. *Menstrual and Gynecological History.* The questionnaire dealing with men-

strual history and development of secondary sex characteristics was given to each woman to take home and fill out before the next session. Details are presented in Appendix H.

(All personnel in contact with each woman rated her with reference to the following variables: Anxiety, Hostility. These ratings were repeated at the end of every session.)

SESSION 2 (About seven days later.)

1. *Body Prominence.*[9]
2. *Dating History.*[9]
3. *Spontaneous Stories:* (a) Story about a girl and her father; (b) Story about a girl and her boyfriend.
4. *Selective Learning.*[9] The selective learning task in this instance involved food versus nonfood words (Fisher, 1970).
5. *Byrne Food Scale.*[10]
6. *Touch Threshold* [10] (Determined on the wrist).
7. *Tickle Threshold.* The purpose of this procedure was to evaluate response to tickle. The intent was to measure how quickly a woman experiences tickle when her skin is stroked and how long it will persist with continued stroking.

Tickle was studied by stroking body sites with a strip of cotton (three inches in length and two inches in width). Stroking was lightly applied in a consistent fashion. Each woman reported as soon as the stroking produced a feeling of tickle. She also reported exactly when the feeling of tickle disappeared and was replaced by some other sensation. Stroking was stopped at that moment. If the sensation of tickle persisted beyond one minute, stroking was terminated at that point. Tickle samples were taken at varying numbers of body sites at different points in the experimental procedure. The person administering the procedure used a stopwatch to time the first appearance of tickle and the time of cessation.

In the present instance two tickle measure trials were taken on the right cheek.

8. *Bass Famous Sayings Test.*[11]
9. *Chain Associations.* Selective response to specific themes was sampled in terms of "chain associations" given to a series of words. This procedure has been described by Story (1963). Each woman was requested to give the first 15 words she could think of to each of the following 13 words (listed in the order actually presented): House[n], Taste[o], Love[s], Hit[h], Suicide[m], Candy[o], Sky[n], Stab[h], Sex[s], Swallow[o], Shoot[h], Kiss[s], Hurt-Self[m].

> n = neutral
> o = oral
> s = sex
> h = hostility
> m = masochistic

The time required to give the first association $(T/1R)$ to each word was determined as well as the total time (T/TR) to complete each "chain" of 15 associations. The words were selected to represent four themes (sex, orality, hostility, masochism) and a neutral category. The average $T/1R$ and the average T/TR for each category of words were computed.

10. *Lie, K, and Repression Scales of the Minnesota Multiphasic Personality Inventory.*
11. *Body Distortion Questionnaire.*[12]
12. *Physiological Recordings.* Prior to this period of recording each woman removed her clothing, put on a hospital gown, and lay (with a sheet over her) on an examining table in a shielded room.

The following measures were secured (by a female technician): Temperature (mouth, hand, ankle, rectum, vagina); Galvanic Skin Response; Heart rate; Skin resistance (hand, ankle, labia).

The sequence of periods of physiological recording was as follows:

Five minutes while the woman was alone.

Putting on of blindfold to prepare for light-touch threshold determinations.

Touch threshold on breast, thigh, wrist, breast, thigh, wrist.

Threshold for tickle on right cheek, right breast, right thigh.

Five minutes of recording while the woman was alone.

Five minutes of recording while a passage with explicit sexual imagery from D. H. Lawrence's *Lady Chatterley's Lover* (pp. 141–142, 1968) was read. The passage consisted of a vivid description of an intercourse scene, with considerable detail about the feelings and body sensations aroused (for example, "He too had bared the front of his body and she felt his naked flesh against her as he came into her—there awoke in her strange thrills rippling inside her").

Five minutes of recording while the woman was alone.

Analysis of the physiological recordings was undertaken in terms of values for specific phases, overall means, and change scores.

SESSION 3 (About five days later.)

1. *Average Week.* To obtain quantifiable information concerning how each woman typically spends her time, a procedure devised by Fisher (1970) was utilized. It involves a content analysis of her spontaneous written account of what she does from day to day. The instructions given to each woman were as follows: "Now I am going to ask you to describe an average week in your life. Describe some of the routine aspects as well as some of the highlights. Be complete. You will have 15 minutes to write. Be sure to fill at least a couple of pages."

The written protocols were blindly analyzed for the following content categories: (a) Cleaning activities: for example, cleaning house, washing clothes; (b) Oral gratifications: for example, eating, preparing food, buying food; (c) Entertainment: for example, going to the movies, going to parties, watching television; (d) Sexual: for example, kissing husband, love making, thinking or talking about sex.

Total number of discrete statements concerning each category was determined and expressed as a percentage of total number in all categories. The interscorer reliabilities of all of the categories, except the sexual one, have been shown elsewhere (Fisher, 1970) to be adequate. Two judges who independently scored 20 protocols for sexual statements attained 86 percent agreement.

2. *Selective Learning.*[13] Selective learning with reference to a list containing ten words with guilt connotations and ten without such connotations was evaluated. The list of words has been previously used by Fisher (1970). The score computed was the total number of guilt words minus the total number of nonguilt words recalled.

3. *Sex Proverbs.* Story (1963) described a method for detecting conflict about a theme by asking subjects to interpret proverbs pertaining to the theme. In the present instance it was employed to measure reactions to sexual themes. Each woman was asked to give an interpretation of 14 proverbs. Seven had sexual significance (for example, Under the Empress' skirt there is only the naked skin) and seven had no sexual connotations (for example, There are many ways of skinning a cat). The key measurement was the time $(T/1R)$ required to begin the interpretation of each proverb and the total time (T/TR) to complete each interpretation. The mean $T/1R$ and T/TR values were computed separately for the sexual and nonsexual proverbs. Two indices were then computed: (1) $T/1R$ nonsexual proverbs minus $T/1R$ sexual proverbs; (2) T/TR nonsexual proverbs minus T/TR sexual proverbs.

4. *Cartoons.* In an attempt to find out how each woman would cope with themes (pertinent to sex attitudes and sex role definition) presented in a humorous

context, cartoons concerned with the following categories were collected from magazines: Sexual (four cartoons); Sexual hostility of men toward women (four cartoons); Hostility of women to men (four cartoons); Hostility of men to men (four cartoons).

Each woman was asked to look through the series of cartoons and then to arrange them in rank order (rank 1 = cartoon most liked). The average of the ranks assigned to each category of cartoon was computed.

    5.   *Spontaneous Stories.* The two themes about which stories were created were as follows: (a) Woman and her sister; (b) Woman and her child.

    6.   *Buss-Durkee Hostility Scale.*[14]

    7.   *Word Construction.*[14]

    8.   *Tachistoscopic Perception.*[14] Once again the tachistoscope was used to investigate selective attitudes toward specific themes. In this instance the procedure was very similar to that described in Appendix A with reference to tachistoscopic perception of pictures. However, instead of presenting pictures, words were shown. The following words were presented (in the order listed): Shoot[h], Love[s], Self[n], Food[o], Kiss[s], Hate[h], Candy[o], Sex[s], Mine[n], Kill[h], Soup[o], Mate[s], Chew[o].

$$h = \text{hostility}$$
$$s = \text{sex}$$
$$o = \text{orality}$$
$$n = \text{narcissism}$$

As indicated, several words were averaged to represent each of the following categories: Hostility, Sex, Orality, Narcissism. Each word was shown at five successively slower speeds (.0033, .0034, .0036, .0040, .0045 seconds) and the point at which it was correctly identified was ascertained. The response to each word was coded 1–6, with 1 indicating identification at the fastest speed. The coded values for all the words in a given category were averaged, and these means were then rank-ordered (1 = fastest correct identification).

    9.   *Sex Questionnaires.* Several questionnaires directly or indirectly concerned with sexual behavior and attitudes were administered. An example of the first to be filled out may be found in Appendix J. The others are described in Appendix K.

    10.   *Sexual Body Focus Questionnaire.*[15]

    11.   *Cleanliness, Frugality, Thrift.* Three scales developed by Barnes (1952) for measuring attitudes relating to cleanliness, frugality, and thrift were administered. They involve answering Yes or No to a series of statements. The following are examples of the items comprising each scale.

Cleanliness (five items): You feel very uneasy in a dirty place.

Frugality (eight items): You admire the frugal virtues of the old pioneers.

Thrift (eight items): Many things are more important to you than money.

    12.   *Religious Behavior.*[16]

    13.   *Cigarettes and Alcohol.* A brief questionnaire was used to evaluate age began smoking, age began drinking, current number of cigarettes smoked per day, current number of drinks per week, and ratings of degree to which enjoy smoking and drinking.

(All personnel in contact with each woman rated her with reference to the following: Anxiety, Hostility.)

SESSION 4 (Within one to three days of onset of menstrual flow.)

    1.   *Body Prominence* (Repeated at this point to evaluate impact of the menstrual period).[16]

    2.   *Menstrual Attitudes.*[17] Descriptions of feelings during present menstrual period.

    3.   *Spontaneous Stories.*[17] The two themes about which stories were written were as follows: (a) Boy and his father; (b) A woman in serious trouble.

4. *Selective Memory*.[17] The same list containing sexual and nonsexual words as used earlier in this sample was repeated (to determine if the menstrual period would have an impact on recall of sexual material).

5. *Holtzman Inkblots (Form A)* [18] (Repeated to evaluate effect of the menstrual experience).

6. *Body Distortion Questionnaire* [18] (Repeated to evaluate effect of the menstrual period).

7. *Jokes*. A technique described by Weiss (1954) was administered. This technique is based on eliciting reactions to a series of jokes. The jokes clustered about the following themes: Oral Eroticism, Oral Sadism, Anal Expulsiveness, Oedipal Intensity, Castration Anxiety.

Each woman indicated how much she enjoyed each joke. The mean ratings of all the jokes in each of the specific categories were computed and these means were assigned ranks (rank 1 = least enjoyable).

8. *Touch Threshold* (On wrist).[18] To evaluate test-retest changes related to menstruation.

9. *Tickle Threshold*.[19] To evaluate test-retest changes related to menstruation (measures obtained for right cheek).

10. *Tachistoscopic Perception*.[18] The same basic tachistoscopic technique was employed as earlier described, except that the stimuli consisted of pictures from the Blum (1949) Blacky Pictures series. These pictures were originally drawn to depict crucial conflict areas, as defined by psychoanalytic theory. They show a dog, named Blacky, engaged in various activities that represent the conflict areas. For example, one picture that shows Blacky defecating is intended to tap attitudes about anality. The Blacky pictures that were presented tachistoscopically were as follows: Anal Sadism, Castration Anxiety, Masturbation Guilt, Oral Sadism, Oral Eroticism, Sibling Rivalry.

Each picture was shown six times, at progressively slower speeds (.0023, .0025, .0030, .0035, .0040, .0045 seconds). The first speed at which the picture was correctly identified and the number of times it was correctly identified were determined. The speeds of first correct identification were rank ordered (1 = fastest identification), as were total frequencies of correct identification (1 = largest number of correct identifications). Such tachistoscopic use of the Blacky pictures has been described elsewhere by Fisher (1970).

11. *Early Memories*. Each woman was asked to write down ten early memories. She was to think back on her childhood and describe in detail ten different events that she could recall. A variation of this procedure has been outlined by Holleman (1965). The memories were scored for the following categories:

Sex: Number of memories involving sexual interactions, nudity, "dirty" jokes, and so forth.

Orality: Number of memories involving eating, smoking, biting, or illness related to the gastrointestinal tract.

Achievement: Number of memories that concern winning, getting ahead, striving, working hard, and getting recognition in school.

Phallic: As defined by Holleman, this category includes number of memories in which there is an emphasis on riding vehicles or animals; using tools; hunting, fishing, or shooting; engaging in competitive sports; fighting; wearing uniform or emblems; climbing; participating in initiations and strength-testing rituals.

Body damage: Number of memories about illness, accidents, injury, and hospitalization.

All coding of protocols was done blindly. The total number of references in each scoring category was converted into a percent by dividing by the total number in all the categories.

12. *Study of Values*.[20]

SESSION 5 (Seven days later.)

1. *Life Style Scale* (Mackler and Shontz, 1964). This scale assesses preferences for visual and kinesthetic modes of experience. It ascertains how much special interest there is in seeking visual as well as kinesthetic stimulation. Each woman was asked to read a series of statements and to rate each in terms of "How much is this like you?" The visual statements are exemplified by "Like to watch movies" and "Like to look at store windows"; and the kinesthetic by "Like to practice dance steps or to try out new dance steps" and "Like to run, walk vigorously, or turn swiftly." Not only were separate Visual and Kinesthetic scores computed but also the difference between them (Visual-Kinesthetic).

2. *Draw-a-Person Test*. This is a widely used test that derives conclusions concerning personality from the manner in which an individual draws the human figure (Machover, 1949). Each woman was asked to draw a full-length picture of a person, and when she had completed that task she was then asked to draw a full-length picture of a person of the opposite sex.

Analysis of the drawings concerned the following variables: (a) Height of each figure; (b) Relative height of female as compared to male figure (as an index of the degree to which the power attributes of the male and female role are differentiated); (c) Ratings of femininity of female figure; (d) Ratings of masculinity of male figure; (e) Impressionistic analyses to determine if figure drawings of those with high- and low-orgasm consistency could be discriminated.

3. *Spontaneous Stories.*[21] The themes about which the stories were constructed were as follows: (a) A family; (b) A woman who has just obtained a job.

4. The Witkin, et al. (1962, 1954) Rod and Frame procedure was administered. It measures a broad dimension relating to field independence versus dependence (clear self-differentiation versus difficulty in differentiating self [or other objects] from the surrounding field). The task posed for each woman was to adjust a luminous rod (in a completely dark room) to a vertical position in the presence of a luminous frame that introduced distracting cues. The rod and the frame were set at various degrees from the true vertical, and the task of the woman was to instruct the experimenter how to move the rod until it was perfectly vertical ("straight up and down"). She gave 12 judgments.

Two scores were derived. One was the total amount of error (deviation from vertical) in the series of judgments. The second was a measure of the degree to which judgments were biased in a right-versus-left direction (number of errors to right of vertical minus number of errors to left of vertical). The right minus left index was introduced because of previous findings by the writer (Fisher, 1970) that right-left differentiation is linked with sex role factors. More is said about this matter in the text of the book.

5. *Augmenting-Diminishing.* Petrie (1967) suggests that persons may be classified in relation to whether they augment (magnify) or diminish (mute) perceptual input. She reports that "augmenters" and "diminishers" differ in their experience of pain, sensory isolation, menstruation, and even sexual stimuli. She further indicates that augmenting-diminishing tendencies can be reliably measured by changes in the perceived size of objects experienced kinesthetically via the hands in a context where special stimulation is applied to the hands. The actual procedure was to present each woman with a task in which first (with her eyes blindfolded) she feels a standard block with her fingers and judges its size, then receives touch and kinesthetic stimulation to her fingers by rubbing another block, and finally judges the size of the original standard block again. Three sets of trials were used. For each set there was first judgment of a standard block, then stimulation of the fingers produced by rubbing another block (for periods varying from 90 seconds to 300 seconds), and finally rejudging the original block. Exact details of the complicated procedure may be found in Petrie's book (1967).

Separate scores were computed for each set of trials as was an overall mean for all trials combined. The scores were in each instance essentially equal to the size ascribed to the standard block after stimulation minus the size attributed to it before stimulation.

6. *Politicoeconomic Conservatism and Traditional Family Ideology.* Two scales taken from Levinson and Huffman (1955) that tap what were considered to be important social attitudes were included in the battery. One was the Politicoeconomic Conservatism Scale and the other the Traditional Family Ideology Scale. Each woman indicated her amount of agreement with a series of statements. An example of a statement from the Politicoeconomic Conservatism Scale is: "When private enterprise does not do the job, it is up to the government to step in and meet the public's needs for housing, water power, and the like."

An example of a statement from the Traditional Family Ideology Scale is: "Some equality in marriage is a good thing, but by and large the husband ought to have the main say-so in family affairs."

7. *Thurstone Temperament Scale.*[22]

8. *Sensation-Seeking Scale.* Zuckerman, Kolin, Price, and Zoob (1964) conceptualize people as differing in the amount of stimulation they seek. They constructed a scale to evaluate relative preference for new and novel experience. The form designed to measure this variable in women contains 30 items. Each woman was asked to indicate for each of 30 pairs of statements which of each pair best expressed her own attitude. An example of a pair is:

I would like a job that would require a lot of traveling.
I would prefer a job in one location.

A score is derived based on the amount of preference for novel and exciting experiences.

9. *California Psychological Inventory Femininity Scale* (Gough, 1964). Only the items comprising the Femininity scale of this questionnaire were administered. The score indicates the degree to which the individual responds to a series of statements concerning her behavior and interests in a manner congruent with the way most women (as contrasted to men) respond to them.

10. *Strong Vocational Interest Blank* (1966). This inventory compares the individual's pattern of interests with those characteristic of a range of occupational groups. For the purposes of the present study only the following scores were computed: Housewife, Social Worker, Artist, Engineer, Femininity-Masculinity. The occupational scores were chosen arbitrarily to represent a diverse range.

11. About nine months after the completion of the study involving Sample 2, the women who had participated were asked, through the mail, to fill out the Edwards Personal Preference Schedule (see Appendix C for description) and to complete a series of ratings of their mother and father (described in Appendix A).

(Because many of the women were wives of students, who left Syracuse University when the semester was over, about one-third of the sample had moved by the time this attempt was made to obtain new data. It was possible to obtain forwarding addresses for only a few of this group).

APPENDIX C (Sample 3)

SESSION 1 (One week before menstruation.)
1. *Body Prominence.*[23]
2. *Body Focus Questionnaire.*[23]
3. *Word Construction.*[23]
4. *Body Distortion Questionnaire.*[23]

5.   *Selective Memory.*[24]
     Sex versus nonsex words.

6.   *Tickle Threshold.* The sites measured and their sequence were as follows: right cheek, left cheek, right wrist, left wrist. Average values for each site and also for right minus left sites were computed.

7.   *Touch Threshold.*[25]

8.   *Holtzman Inkblots (Form B).*[25]

9.   *Lie, K, and Repression Scales of Minnesota Multiphasic Personality Inventory.*[25]

10. *Rod and Frame.*[26]

11. *Augmenting and Diminishing.*[26]

12. *Rating Inside of One's Body.* In order to sample her attitudes toward the inside of her body, each woman was requested to rate the inside of her body on a series of eight continua derived from Osgood, Suci, and Tannenbaum (1957) (for example, small-large, fast-slow, light-heavy).

13. *Breast-feeding.* The following request was made of each woman: "Please indicate whether you have bottle-fed or breast-fed your children."

14. *Male versus Female Role.* Each woman indicated on a six-point scale whether she thought men or women "have a more satisfying role in life."

15. The women were given an envelope that they were told contained a number of questionnaires and instructions to be completed at home before they returned for the next session. The following were included in the envelope:

A. Edwards Personal Preference Schedule: This test was developed by Edwards (1954) to measure a considerable number of personality variables. It presents the individual with an extended series of paired statements (matched for social desirability), and she indicates in each instance which of the two statements is more true of herself. The following fifteen scores are computed: Achievement; Deference; Order; Exhibition; Autonomy; Affiliation; Intraception (To analyze one's motives and feelings, to put oneself in another's place); Succorance (To have others help when one is in trouble, to seek encouragement from others); Dominance; Abasement; Nurturance (To help friends when they are in trouble, to assist others less fortunate); Change (To do new and different things, to meet new people); Endurance (To keep at a job until it is finished, to work hard at a task, to stick at a problem); Heterosexuality; Aggression.

Most of these terms are self-explanatory. Brief notes of clarification have been added where the term does seem to be at all vague.

B. Menstrual History and Development of Secondary Sex Characteristics.[27]

C. Autobiography: In order to secure a personal account of each woman's life that would convey in more qualitative terms her way of life, she was given the following instructions. "Write a history of your life. Fill about three pages with enough material so that the most important events and feelings that have typified your life are described."

Some aspects of these autobiographies were scored quantitatively but details concerning such scoring are provided in the text of the book.

D. Clothing Attitudes: Aiken (1963) constructed a questionnaire that analyzes the principal motives a woman has in her choice of clothing. She responds true or false to a series of statements about clothing. Four dimensions are measured: Decoration in Dress, Interest in Dress, Conformity in Dress, Economy in Dress.

(All personnel who had contact with each woman rated her with reference to the following: Anxiety and Hostility. This was done at the end of every session.)

SESSION 2 (Second day of flow of new menstrual period.)
1.   *Body Prominence* (Retest to evaluate effect of menstruation).[28]
2.   *Word Construction* (Retest to evaluate effect of menstruation).[28]

3. *Ratings of Inside of One's Body* (Retest to evaluate effect of menstruation).[29]
4. *Body Distortion Questionnaire* (Retest to evaluate effect of menstruation).[28]
5. *Holtzman Inkblots (Form A)* (Retest to evaluate effect of menstruation).[28]
6. *Tickle Threshold* (Retest to evaluate effect of menstruation).[30]
7. *Touch Threshold* (Retest to evaluate effect of menstruation).[28]
8. *Sex Questionnaires.*[31]
9. *Aniseikonic Lenses.* It has been demonstrated that aniseikonic lenses not only cause distortions in the perceptual field but that such distortions are influenced by psychological factors. Wittreich and Radcliffe (1955) were able to show specifically that anxiety about a perceptual target inhibits perceiving it as distorted when viewed aniseikonically. Fisher and Richter (1969) reported that anxiety about a sector of one's own body may inhibit perceiving that sector as altered when it is viewed aniseikonically in a mirror. The writer secured reports from each woman regarding the distortions in the appearance of regions of her body when she perceived them aniseikonically in a mirror. The procedure was as follows. Each woman was brought into a room, asked to put on a pair of aniseikonic lenses, and encouraged to become familiar with the perceptual alterations they produced. Then, she was asked to stand five feet from a full-length mirror, to describe the changes the lenses produced in her appearance, and finally to rank six different body areas in terms of the degree to which they appeared to be distorted. The ranking procedure was assisted by a schematic drawing of a human figure that was divided into head, arm, chest, abdomen, pelvic, and leg areas. Each area was numbered, and the task was to give the number of the region most changed, the number of the area second most changed, and so forth. When this procedure was completed, each woman was given a second set of aniseikonic lenses, and a second ranking of body distortion effects was obtained. The average alteration rank for each body area was computed. The smaller the average, the greater is the alteration that occurred and therefore presumably the less the anxiety linked with a given body region.
10. *Rod and Frame* (Retest to evaluate effect of menstruation).[32]
11. *Augmenting and Diminishing* (Retest to evaluate effect of menstruation).[32]
12. *Parent-Child Relations Questionnaire.*
Father Form

Roe and Siegelman (1963) evolved a questionnaire for evaluating attitudes toward one's parents. A wide range of statements are offered concerning parental behavior ("especially about the time before you were 12"). The task is to indicate (on a four-point scale) how truly these statements apply to one's parent. There are separate questionnaires for Father and Mother. Responses are scored in terms of the following complex dimensions:

Protective: Refers to parents who are seen as giving the child's interests first priority; being very indulgent; providing special privileges.

Demanding: Depicts parents who promulgate high standards of accomplishment, set up strict regulations, and demand obedience.

Rejecting: Portrays parents who are rejecting, who are cold and hostile to their child, who derogate him, who leave him alone.

Neglecting: Refers to parents who pay little attention to the child, who give him a minimum of physical care and no affection.

Casual: Depicts parents who give attention to the child if they are not busy with something else. They do not give much thought to him specifically, but deal with him in the context of general situations.

Loving: Portrays parents who are warm and loving to the child; who try to help him through problems; who encourage independence.

Symbolic-Love Reward: "Parents using this kind of reward praise their children for approved behavior, give them special attention, and are affectionately demonstrative" (p. 357).

Direct-Object Reward: "These include tangible rewards such as gifts of money or toys, special trips, or relief from chores" (p. 357).

Symbolic-Love Punishment: "Such punishments include shaming the child before others, isolating him, and withdrawing love" (p. 357).

Direct-Object Punishment: 'These include physical punishment, taking away playthings, reducing allowance, denying promised trips, and so on" (p. 357)

13. *Study of Values.*[33]
14. *Cigarettes and Alcohol.*[34]
15. *Menstrual Feelings.*[33] Spontaneous description.

SESSION 3 (Five days after cessation of menstrual flow.)
1. *Body Prominence.*[33]
2. *Tickle Threshold* (Cheeks, wrist).[34]
3. *Sexual Body Focus Questionnaire.*[33]
4. *Average Week.*[34]
5. *Parent-Child Relation Questionnaire, Mother Form.*
6. *Physiological Recordings.*

The following physiological parameters were recorded while each woman was lying on an examining table: Temperature (Hand, Leg, Breast), Skin Resistance (Hand, Leg, Breast).

There was an initial rest period recording of ten minutes during which the woman was left alone by the female technician who had attached the electrodes and probes. The technician returned and a recording was made while she determined light touch threshold on the breasts. A one-minute rest recording followed. Further recordings were then made while tickle thresholds were secured on the cheeks, breasts, thighs, and feet (soles). This was followed by another five-minute rest period.

A special condition was introduced at this point. A birth film, without a sound track, was shown that depicted a close-up view of the emergence of a baby from the vagina and then the expulsion of the afterbirth. The film lasted five minutes. Recordings were taken throughout this time. The purpose of the film was to provide a setting in which reactions to material referring to birth and reproduction could be evaluated.

Shortly afterward, each woman was asked to rate (on a five-point scale) the degree to which she enjoyed the birth film. She was also asked to describe in her own words the kinds of feelings and body sensations evoked by the film.
7. *Byrne Food Attitude Scale.*[35]
8. *Buss-Durkee Hostility Scale.*[35]
9. *Sensation Seeking Scale.*[36]
10. *Frugality, Thrift, Cleanliness.*[36]
11. *Cartoons.*[36]
12. *Aniseikonic Lenses* (Set of the lenses was readministered).[36]

APPENDIX D (Sample 4)

1. *Tickle Threshold.*[36]
2. *Oral Temperature.* A three-minute recording of oral temperature while the woman was sitting quietly.
3. *Touch Threshold.*[35]
4. *Lie, K, and Repression Scales of Minnesota Multiphasic Personality Inventory.*[35]
5. *Cigarettes and Alcohol.*[36]

6. *Frugality, Thrift, Cleanliness.*[36]

7. *Tachistoscopic Perception.*[37] The stick-figure drawings developed by Forrest and Lee (1962) were used. The following pictures were represented: Nurturance: Adult holding baby. Heterosexual: Figures on bed. Hostility: Figures shooting at each other. Nurturance: Adult figure and a baby. Narcissism: Figure looking in a mirror.

8. *Selective learning.*[38] Sexual versus nonsexual words.

9. *Selective learning.*[38] Pregnancy versus nonpregnancy words. The list consisted of ten words that directly or indirectly referred to birth, babies, and pregnancy; and ten neutral words.

10. *Sex Questionnaires.*[39]

11. *Figure Placement Procedure.* Kuethe (1962) theorized that an individual's attitudes about others may be appraised in terms of the social schemas that characterize his thinking. Presumably, one can tell a good deal about his attitudes by analyzing his concepts of what kinds of figures should be closely and distantly related in space. Kuethe concretized this rationale by means of a procedure that involves placing cut-out felt figures upon a simple unstructured felt background. Such placements may then be analyzed by measuring the distances between specific figures.

Four sets of figures were presented to each woman for placement on a felt background. The sets were considered to represent specific themes (which are indicated in each instance): adult male, adult female (heterosexual); adult woman, child (mother-child); adult male, child (father-child); young male, young female (heterosexual). The distance between each two figures was measured. It was considered that the closer the placement of any two figures the more positive was the feeling about closeness or intimacy between such figures.

12. *Spontaneous Stories.*[40] Four stories were obtained, each based on one of the following four themes: (a) woman and her husband; (b) girl and her boyfriend; (c) woman and her child; (d) a family.

13. *Augmenting-Diminishing.*[40]

14. *Aniseikonic Lenses.*[41]

15. *Murray-Harvard Anxiety Questionnaire.* Each woman indicated her degree of agreement with a series of statements concerning anxiety. Samples:

We are surrounded by all sorts of dangers.

In our American culture the fear of failure is inevitable, ever present, and incurable.

A total anxiety score was computed.

16. *Ratings of Inside of One's Body.*[41]

17. Each woman was asked to take home, fill out, and return by mail the following questionnaires:

A. Edwards Preference Schedule.[41]

B. Parent-Child Relations Questionnaire (Father and Mother Forms).[41]

C. Menstrual Questionnaire.[42] This was an abbreviated version of the Menstrual History form used in Sample 1.

D. Spontaneous Stories: [43] Four story themes (1) girl and her mother; (2) woman and her husband; (3) girl and her father; (4) girl and her boyfriend.

E. Retest of Sexual Questionnaire: Several self-reports concerning sexual behavior repeated to obtain test-retest reliability information.

F. Sports Questionnaire: Brief series of questions concerning frequency with which participates in, and enjoys, sports.

APPENDIX E (Sample 5)

1. *Body Prominence.*[44]
2. *Tickle Threshold.*[45]
3. *Thrift, Frugality, Cleanliness.*[45]
4. *Lie, K, and Repression Scales of Minnesota Multiphasic Personality Inventory.*[44]
5. *Ratings of Inside of Own Body.*[46]
6. *Byrne Food Attitude Scale.*[44]
7. *Holtzman Inkblots (Form B).*[44]
8. *Chain Associations.*[45] The Chain Association technique was applied to obtain information about attitudes toward the mother and father. Each woman was asked to give ten associations to each of the following words: House, Father, Sky, Mother, Cloud, Dad, Tree, Water, Mom, Father's first name, Mother's first name.

The average time to produce the first association (T/1R) for the father words was computed, and the same computation was made with reference to the mother and also neutral words. The average time (T/TR) to produce the total number of associations for the father words was computed, and the same calculation was carried out for the mother and neutral words.

9. *Augmenting-Diminishing.*[47]
10. *Sexual Questionnaires.*[48]
11. *Birth Film.*[49]
12. *Digit-Symbol Performance.* This procedure measured response to stress. It is based on a task taken from the Wechsler Adult Intelligence Scale (1955) which involves writing next to a series of numbers randomly arranged in sequence code symbols that are defined as associated with them. Each woman first performed the task under quiet baseline conditions. Then a stress (movie depicting bloody accident) was imposed on her, and she went on to repeat the task so that the amount of disruption of the stress upon her performance could be measured. Scores were computed that indicated the degree to which performance subsequent to the stress film deteriorated (average of two post-stress trials minus average of two baseline trials).

13. *Sensation-Seeking Scale.*[47]

(Ratings of hostility and anxiety were made by all personnel who had had contact with each woman.) Each woman was requested to take home a series of questionnaires; to fill them out; and to return them within ten days. The questionnaires were as follows:

A. Menstrual History (Abbreviated version of form described in Appendix H).
B. Study of Values.[50]
C. Ratings of Parental Attributes.[51]
D. Fear of Death Scale: This scale was constructed by Boyar (1964). It called for each woman to indicate her degree of agreement with such statements as the following: "I have moments when I get really upset about dying"; "Not knowing what it feels like to die makes me anxious." The higher the score the greater the expressed fear of death.
E. Murray-Harvard Anxiety Scale.[52]
F. Cigarettes and Alcohol.[53]
G. Terman Questionnaire: Contains the questions that Terman (1951) found to distinguish most consistently between orgastic and nonorgastic women.
H. Retest of Sex Questionnaire: Several of the sex behavior themes were presented to evaluate test-retest reliability. Informal inquiry suggested that the average woman responded to this form about three to five days after she received it.

APPENDIX F (Sample 6)

SESSION 1

This was the sample of pregnant women. They were pregnant when seen for this first session.

1. *Body Prominence.*[51]
2. *Holtzman Inkblots (Form B).*[51]
3. *Body Focus Questionnaire.*[51]
4. *Word Construction.*[51]
5. *Body Distortion Questionnaire.*[51]
6. *Menstrual History.* Abbreviated version of questionnaire (see Appendix H).
7. *Pregnancy Associations.* Each woman was given the following instructions: "List 20 thoughts or feelings or body sensations you have had at any time during your pregnancy." These spontaneous productions were analyzed in terms of the following categories: (a) References to fetus: Total number, number favorable. (Two raters who independently evaluated 20 protocols attained 72 percent agreement in the Favorable category.) (b) References to husband: Total number, total favorable. (Two raters who independently evaluated 20 protocols attained 77 percent agreement for the Favorable category.) (c) References to own body: Total number, total favorable. (d) References to possible injury or disfigurement to self or fetus. (e) References to one's mood: Total favorable. (Two raters who independently evaluated 20 protocols attained 83 percent agreement for this category.)
8. *Pregnancy Questionnaire.* Several kinds of information were requested of each woman: (a) Ratings of her own body; (b) Ratings of the fetus; (c) Frequency of occurrence of various symptoms (for example, vomiting); (d) Feelings and mood during pregnancy.
A more detailed description of the kind of information obtained may be found at the end of the section dealing with Sample 6.
9. *Sexual Questionnaires.*[54]
10. *Lie, K, Repression Scales of Minnesota Multiphasic Personality Inventory.*[55]
11. *Frugality, Thrift, Cleanliness.*[56]
12. *Byrne Food Attitude Scale.*[55]
13. *Buss-Durkee Hostility Scale.*[55]
14. Each woman was asked to return to the laboratory one month subsequent to her delivery. She was also instructed to bring with her a detailed description of the delivery process. The exact directions to her were as follows:
"As soon as possible after your delivery write several pages in which you describe your experiences. Describe in detail the emotions and body sensations you experienced and also the thoughts and images that passed through your mind.
"Give as much detail as possible."
This material was analyzed in a primarily qualitative fashion. One quantitative analysis that was undertaken has been described in detail in the text.

SESSION 2

1. *Body Prominence.*[55]
2. *Holtzman Inkblots (Form A).*[55]
3. *Word Constructions.*[55]
4. *Body Distortion Questionnaire.*[55]
5. *Delivery Thoughts.* Each woman was asked to "List 20 thoughts or feelings or body sensations you had at any time during the course of your delivery." The same mode of analysis was followed as was applied to the Pregnancy Thoughts.
6. *Delivery Ratings.* Each woman rated her baby and herself for the same vari-

ables as she had rated the fetus and herself prior to delivery. In addition, she rated herself with regard to her feelings, behavior, and difficulties during and after delivery. A description of this questionnaire is presented at the end of this section dealing with Sample 6.

7. *Sexual Questions.* The clitoral-vaginal rating was obtained for retest purposes on a part of the original sample.

8. *Sensation-Seeking Scale.*[57]
9. *Ratings of Parents* [58] (Father Scale, Mother Scale).
10. *Thurstone Temperament Scale.*[58]
11. *Augmenting-Diminishing.*[57]
12. *Aniseikonic Distortion.*[59]

Pregnancy Ratings

SESSION 1

The following are the pregnancy variables with respect to which the women rated themselves: vomiting, fatigue, bleeding, muscle pain, headache, depression, internal pain, and fear. They also rated the degree to which their sexual responsiveness changed during pregnancy.

Furthermore, ratings were obtained of how the unborn child was perceived. These ratings involved the following continua: small-large, fast-slow, light-heavy, sharp-dull, active-passive, weak-strong, pleasant-unpleasant, and cold-warm.

The unborn child was, in addition, rated with respect to how "quiet" it is, how often the mother "thinks about it," and how often the mother "wonders about its sex."

Delivery Ratings

SESSION 2

The delivery variables with respect to which the women rated themselves were anxiety, self-control, and friendliness. They also rated how they felt one week after delivery in relation to the following dimensions: sad-happy, tense-relaxed, weak-strong, irritable-placid, satisfied versus not satisfied with the baby, attractiveness-nonattractiveness of the body, and friendliness-hostility of husband.

The newly born child was rated with respect to the following continua: small-large, fast-slow, light-heavy, sharp-dull, active-passive, weak-strong, pleasant-unpleasant, and cold-warm.

The following questions were asked about the delivery: "How long did your delivery take?" "Were there any complications?"

With regard to the postpartum period, questions were asked about how long it took to "feel like your normal self again," weight changes, whether baby was breast- or bottle-fed, how long it took for intercourse to resume again.

APPENDIX G (Sample 7)

1. *Sex Questionnaires.*[60]
2. *Number of Foods Liked* (From the Byrne Food Attitude Scale).[61]
3. *Ranking of Activities.* This task involved the following set of instructions:

Rank these in the order in which you most enjoy them. Put 1 next to the activity you most enjoy; put 2 next to the activity that is your second preference; and continue until you put 7 next to the activity you least enjoy.

Eating.
Sleeping.
Sexual intercourse.
Participating actively in a sport.
Talking to close friends.
Drinking an alcoholic beverage.
Watching a good program on television.

Each woman's rankings could be used to ascertain the relative degree of satisfaction she obtained from sexual intercourse.

4.   *Frugality, Thrift, Cleanliness.*[62]

5.   *Attainment of Orgasm.* Each woman was instructed as follows:

"Please give a detailed description of how you usually attain orgasm. Describe particularly the body sensations you experience, the thoughts that pass through your mind, your feelings, your attitudes, any difficulties you have, and so forth.

"Also, describe in detail how you feel about five minutes *after* you attain orgasm.

"Please write on the attached blank sheets. Try to fill at least two pages." This material was analyzed qualitatively.

6.   *Lie, K, and Repression Scales of Minnesota Multiphasic Personality Inventory.*[63]

7.   *Thoughts during Intercourse.* The following was requested of each woman:

"Please give at least two examples of thoughts or images or fantasies you have had more than once while having intercourse or during orgasm." This material was used to ascertain the frequency and nature of fantasies occurring during intercourse.

8.   *Orgasm: Self versus Husband.* This brief questionnaire was designed to determine the time relationships existing between a woman's orgasm and that of her husband. It contained the following questions:

A. What percent of the time that you attain orgasm does it occur *at the same time* that your husband attains his orgasm?

B. What percent of the time does your orgasm occur *before* your husband's orgasm?

C. What percent of the time does your orgasm occur *after* your husband's orgasm?

D. What percent of the time that you reach orgasm is the final stage of excitement that actually pushes you to the point of orgasm produced by your husband stimulating your clitoral area with his hand?

E. If you had the choice of receiving only clitoral or only vaginal stimulation, which would you select?

F. What percent of the time is your husband's penis still inserted in your vagina at the moment that you actually have your orgasm?

9.   *Vaginal versus Clitoral Sensations.* Each woman was given the following instructions:

"Describe as best you can the difference between vaginal and clitoral stimulation. Enumerate any differences in body sensation, intensity, mood, and so forth that you can recall." These protocols were analyzed qualitatively.

APPENDIX H

Gynecological History

The gynecological history called for information and quantitative judgments involving the following variables: rate of breast development, onset of menstruation, breast size, dress size, weight, height, development of pubic and axillary hair, facial hair, length of menstrual cycle (if taking oral contraceptives, all judgments involving menstruation were to be based on the facts as they were before such contraception was started), menstrual regularity, duration of menstrual flow, amount of menstrual flow, amount of menstrual pain, type and amount of treatment for menstrual pain, duration of menstrual pain, degree of weight and mood fluctuation during menstruation, frequency and types of contraception utilized, degree of satisfaction with modes of contraception, amount of vaginal discharge, degree of vaginal itching, nature of vaginal discharge, number of pregnancies, number of miscarriages, age first became pregnant, average frequency of visits to gynecologist, types of complaints that prompted visits to gynecologist, and frequency and categories of nongynecological symptoms.

APPENDIX I

Self-Interview Outline

1. Take about 10 or 15 minutes and describe the overall course of your life: when and where you grew up; your neighborhood; interests; hobbies; schools; jobs; friends; marriage; children.
2. Now describe your father; his interests, work, beliefs, problems, and especially his relationship with you.
3. Do the same with regard to your mother.
4. Outline and describe all of the *major* illnesses you have ever had.
5. Describe your first serious boyfriend: how you met him, what he was like, your agreements and disagreements with him, etc.
6. Describe how you met your husband, your courtship, problems that arose, etc. Give detailed description of your husband in terms of his physical appearance and also his personality.
7. Give an example of the sorts of things you and your husband have had the most difficulty in agreeing about.
8. Describe your own personality in as much detail as you can: how you approach people, your ways of dealing with anger, your strengths, weaknesses, etc.
9. Describe the biggest problem you ever had to face.
10. Describe the time you felt most angry in your life.
11. Describe the time you were most embarrassed in your life.
12. What is the saddest thing you have ever experienced?
13. What is the most intense physical pain you have ever experienced? How did it happen?
14. Describe your views on sex education.
15. What is real love, and how can a married couple best keep it alive?
16. What would you like most to change about yourself?
17. Describe in detail how you felt as you grew into adolescence and you began to mature. How did you experience the changes in your body? What problems did they produce? What satisfactions did they produce? What advice would you give about the best ways to help a teen-age daughter?
18. Describe your first pregnancy: how you felt; complications; the delivery; your relationship with your obstetrician; and your husband's behavior during this time.
19. How do you feel about nudity and the exposure of one's body?

20. What are your feelings and reactions when you are at a party where people talk about sex?

21. How would you summarize your attitudes toward love, sex, and the expression of sexual feelings?

APPENDIX J

1. Age you first began to menstruate_____.

2. Circle the number that best describes your reaction to your first menstruation.

Very happy	Quite happy	Indifferent	Quite upset	Very upset
1	2	3	4	5

3. Circle the number that best describes your mother's reaction.

Very happy	Quite happy	Indifferent	Quite upset	Very upset
1	2	3	4	5

4. Circle the number that best describes your father's reaction.

Very happy	Quite happy	Indifferent	Quite upset	Very upset
1	2	3	4	5

5. At what age did you first learn the facts of reproduction?____ Circle the number that best describes how you felt when you learned these facts.

Very pleased	Moderately pleased	Indifferent	Quite worried	Very worried
1	2	3	4	5

Who did you learn these facts from? (Put x in appropriate places)

Mother_____	Girlfriend_____
Father_____	Boyfriend_____
Sister_____	Books_____
Brother_____	Others_____

6. What was your reaction to your first serious date with a boy?

Very happy	Quite happy	Indifferent	Quite tense	Very tense
1	2	3	4	5

7. Circle the number that best completes the following statement as it applies to you: During intercourse I experience orgasm

Always	Nearly always	Frequently	Occasionally	Rarely	Never
1	2	3	4	5	6

8. What was your experience the first time you had intercourse?

Very happy	Quite happy	Indifferent	Quite tense	Very tense
1	2	3	4	5

9. How would you describe your own sexual responsiveness?

I am very much more responsive than the average	I am above average	I am average	I am slightly below average	I am considerably below average
1	2	3	4	5

10. What is your preferred frequency of intercourse per week? (Circle one)
    More [63] 10 9 8 7 6 5 4 3 2 1 0

11. How often do you experience pain during intercourse?

Never	Occasionally	Often	Always
1	2	3	4

12. Please circle the answer or answers that most nearly apply to you: During the menstrual cycle I notice greatest sexual responsiveness at the following times:

    A. During menstruation.
    B. The week after menstruation ceases.
    C. During the middle of the cycle.

    D. The week before menstruation begins.

    E. No differences noted during the menstrual cycle.

13. What is your husband's preferred frequency of intercourse per week? More [63] 10 9 8 7 6 5 4 3 2 1 0

14. This question concerns your usual feelings and sensations during orgasm. Below are listed ten words or phrases frequently used to describe such feelings. Put a 1 in front of the word best descriptive of your own feelings, a 2 in front of the word second most descriptive, and continue to assign such numbers until you put 10 in front of the least descriptive of how you usually feel.

    _____Strange   _____Ecstatic   _____Slightly embarrassed   _____Happy

    _____Tense   _____Weak   _____Tired   _____Unsatisfied

    _____As if I would burst   _____Not like myself

15. This question concerns your usual feelings and sensations five minutes after you have experienced orgasm. Below are listed ten words or phrases frequently used to describe such feelings. Put a 1 in front of the word best descriptive of your own feelings, a 2 in front of the word second most descriptive, and continue to assign such numbers until you put 10 in front of the word least descriptive of how you usually feel.

    _____Not like myself   _____Satisfied   _____Happy   _____Weak

    _____Tense   _____Unsatisfied   _____Tired   _____Relaxed

    _____Slightly embarrassed   _____Slightly guilty

16. What is your average frequency of intercourse per week? More 10 9 8 7 6 5 4 3 2 1 0

17. This question concerns the relative importance of clitoral as compared to vaginal stimulation in your attaining orgasm. Put a circle around the appropriate letter.

    A. Clitoral stimulation contributes much more than vaginal stimulation.

    B. Clitoral stimulation contributes somewhat more than vaginal stimulation.

    C. Clitoral stimulation contributes a little more than vaginal stimulation.

    D. Vaginal stimulation and clitoral stimulation make an equal contribution.

    E. Vaginal stimulation contributes a little more than clitoral stimulation.

    F. Vaginal stimulation contributes somewhat more than clitoral stimulation.

    G. Vaginal stimulation contributes much more than clitoral stimulation.

APPENDIX K

Each woman also rated herself (on either a four- or five-point scale) with respect to the following variables:

How much her parents disapproved of sex.

Degree of embarrassment when nude before other women.

Amount of gratification obtained from sex.

Whether worry about getting pregnant during intercourse.

Amount of interest in sex during pregnancy.

Fear of being hurt during intercourse.

Change in enjoyment of intercourse from first year of marriage to present.

How much would miss loss of sexual gratification.

Preference for aggressive men.

Liking for movies and novels about sex.

Amount of time spends thinking about sex.

Degree to which thinks sexual freedom in our society should be increased.

Frequency with which engages in intercourse during menstruation.
How often refuses husband's request for intercourse.
Degree to which has pictures or images in mind during orgasm.
Frequency with which has more than one orgasm during one-hour span.
Masturbation frequency.
Masturbation satisfaction.
Enjoyment of breast stimulation.
Minutes of stimulation after intercourse begins before attains orgasm.
Minutes of stimulation after intercourse begins before husband attains orgasm.
Number of intercourse positions used during average month.
Amount of foreplay (in minutes) before beginning intercourse.
Nature of parental attitudes toward nudity, talking about sex, touching the bodies
  of other family members, and openly displaying affection.
Happiness of parental marriage.

One series of questions was preceded by the following:

Listed below are explanations of the several technical terms that are used in questions to follow.

1. The *vulva* has two outer lips or folds that surround, and usually touch and cover, the outside or external opening of the female sex organs.
2. The *labia* are the lips or folds of the vulva. Inside the two outside lips, there are two smaller inner lips.
3. Found just inside the vulva and back of the lips is the opening to the *vagina* or birth canal.
4. The *clitoris* is the small, sometimes tiny, bean like body or ridge found inside the vulva, and is located just above the opening to the vagina.
5. The *vagina* is the internal passage inside of which intercourse takes place. The vagina leads to the uterus or womb.
6. The increased moistness or dampness of the vulva and vagina during sexual arousal and intercourse is due to *lubricating fluid* secreted by the female.

During love making but before intercourse actually begins, where do you feel excitement? Rank the following body areas in these terms. Put 1 next to the area in which you feel the greatest excitement, 2 next to the area in which you feel the next greatest amount, and so forth until you put 6 next to the area in which you feel the least excitement.

Breasts.
Outside lips of vulva.
Inside lips of vulva.
Vagina near clitoris.
Clitoris.
Inside vagina.

Included in this form were questions that required ratings (four- or five-point scale) of the following:

Amount of lubricating fluid produced during love making, but before intercourse
  actually begins.
Strength of orgasm.
Amount of control of movements near end of intercourse.
Amount of control of thinking near end of intercourse.
Amount of contraction of vaginal walls during climax.
How freely can discuss sex with husband.
How freely husband can discuss sex with her.

The following specific estimates were also requested:

If your feeling reaches a climax near or at end of intercourse, does your excitement: rise, then die out gradually____; mount to a high tension followed by sudden release ____; rise steadily to a condition of rigidity, followed by a very strong or cataclysmic release ____; increase to a point where release is accompanied by spasms or convulsions____; reach such a high level that release is accompanied by collapse (possibly a faint)____?

About how long does a climax last in seconds: 1 to 5____; 6 to 10____; 11 to 15____; 15 to 20____; more than 20 seconds____? Comment: _____

How soon after marriage did you have your first climax in intercourse? Within 1 month ____; 2 months____; 3 months____; 4 to 6 months____; 7 to 11 months ____; one year____; later____; have never had one____.

There was also included a 15-item questionnaire concerning the degree to which a woman believes that a successful marriage requires that it conform to standard moralistic concepts of husband-wife interaction. The women were asked to rate (five-point scale) the degree to which such conditions as the following are necessary to a successful marriage:

That the husband should be some years older than his wife.

That children should be given religious instruction.

That husband and wife should not have had sexual intercourse with each other before marriage.

Relatedly, judgments were obtained concerning how frequently there is disagreement with husband about 11 different areas: family finances, recreation, religion, demonstration of affection, friends, caring for children, table manners, matters of conventionality, philosophy of life, ways of dealing with in-laws, and intimate relations.

Cosmetics, Clothes, and Body Functions

Each woman was asked to rate herself (five-point scale) with reference to: how ticklish she is, how tight she prefers her clothes to be, and how much perfume she likes to wear.

Then, she was requested to answer the following questions:

How often do you take a bath or shower per week?____

How often do you go to a hairdresser per month?____

How often do you wash your hair per month?____

How many sticks of gum do you chew a week?____

How many days per year do you sleep in the nude?____

How many times per day, on the average, do you change your make-up? ____

How many times per week do you apply a deodorant?____

What articles of jewelry do you frequently wear? Please list them.____

How frequently per week do you wear mascara or eye shadow?____

How many times per week do you rub conditioning or "dry skin" creams into your skin?____

How many times per month do you "do your nails" or get a manicure?____

How many times per year do you go for massages or steam baths?____

How frequently, on the average, do you urinate per day?____

How frequently, on the average, do you defecate per day?____

How many different colors or shades of lipstick do you currently have?____

How many different kinds of perfume do you currently have?____

How many different kinds of face powder do you currently have?____

How many times per week do you rub your entire body with creams, powders, or colognes?____

How often, per year, do you change your hair style?____

How many times per month do you shave your armpits?_____
How often, per year, do you dye your hair a different color?_____
On the average, how many new dresses do you buy a year?_____
On the average, how many new pairs of shoes do you buy a year?_____
How many times per day do you brush your teeth?_____
How many times per week do you use a mouth wash?_____
How many times per month do you shave your legs?_____

NOTES

1. The filaments were calibrated so that the force they exerted was known. Each woman was asked, with her eyes blindfolded, to indicate each time she felt touch on a given body site. A modified method of limits was employed, with four ascending and descending determinations at each site. The mean of all trials represents the mean pressure threshold for that site.

2. Degree of anxiety.

3. Anxiety, Pain, Hostility.

4. These retest measures were administered to evaluate the effects of each woman having removed most of her clothing.

5. Anxiety, Pain (overall, when speculum inserted, when gynecologist's finger inserted, when uterus palpated, when ovaries palpated, rectovaginal examination).

6. The tachistoscope is an instrument that can be used to expose stimuli (for example, pictures, words) at speeds so fast that they are difficult to perceive accurately (for example, one-thousandth of a second). By showing a stimulus at a succession of speeds, it is possible to determine the point at which it is first correctly identified. This information can be used to evaluate whether there is selectively fast or slow response to various themes.

7. Described in detail in Appendix A.

8. Already described in detail in Appendix A.

9. Described in detail in Appendix A.

10. Described in Appendix A.

11. Described in Appendix A.

12. Described in detail in Appendix A.

13. The details of this procedure have already been described in Appendix A.

14. Described in detail in Appendix A.

15. Already described in Appendix A.

16. Already described in Appendix A.

17. Already described in Appendix B.

18. Already described in Appendix A.

19. Described earlier in Appendix B.

20. Already described in Appendix A.

21. Already described earlier in Appendix B.

22. Already described in Appendix A.

23. Already described in Appendix A.

24. Already described in Appendix B.

25. Already described in Appendix A.

26. Already described in Appendix B.

27. Described in Appendix H.

28. Already described in Appendix A.

29. Already described in Appendix C.

30. Shown in Appendix B.

31. Described in Appendices J and K.
32. Already described in Appendix B.
33. Already described in Appendix A.
34. Already described in Appendix B.
35. Already described in Appendix A.
36. Already described in Appendix B.
37. Described in Appendix A.
38. Already described in Appendix B.
39. Descriptions of these questionnaires may be found in Appendices J and K.
40. Already described in Appendix B.
41. Already described in Appendix C.
42. Already described in Appendix H.
43. Appendix B.
44. Already described in Appendix A.
45. Already described in Appendix B.
46. Already described in Appendix C.
47. Already described in Appendix B.
48. Descriptions of these questionnaires may be found in Appendices J and K.
49. Already described in Appendix C.
50. Already described in Appendix A.
51. Already described in Appendix A.
52. Details of this procedure have been described in Appendix D.
53. Already described in Appendix B.
54. Details of these sexual questionnaires may be found in Appendices J and K.
55. Already described in Appendix A.
56. Already described in Appendix B.
57. As described in Appendix B.
58. As described in Appendix A.
59. As described in Appendix C.
60. Details of these questionnaires are presented in Appendices J and K.
61. Already described in Appendix A.
62. Already described in Appendix B.
63. Already described in Appendix A.
64. Values above 10 were scored as 11. It was extremely rare to find values greater than 10.

REFERENCES

Abel, Theodora M., and Joffe, Natalie F. Cultural backgrounds of female puberty. *American Journal of Psychotherapy*, 1950, *4*, 90–113.

Aberle, Sophie D., and Corner, G. W. *Twenty-five years of sex research*. Philadelphia: Saunders, 1953.

Abraham, Hilda C. A contribution to the problems of female sexuality. *International Journal of Psychoanalysis*, 1956, *37*, 351–353.

Abraham, K. Manifestations of the female castration complex (1920). In *Selected papers of Karl Abraham*. New York: Basic Books, 1954.

Abraham, K. *On character and libido development*. New York: Basic Books, 1966.

Abramson, M., and Torqhele, J. R. Weight, temperature changes and psychosomatic symptomatology in relation to the menstrual cycle. *American Journal of Obstetrics and Gynecology*, 1961, *81*, 223–232.

Adams, Abby B. Choice of infant feeding technique as a function of maternal personality. *Journal of Consulting Psychology*, 1959, *23*, 143–146.

Adams, C. R. *Preparing for marriage*. New York: E. P. Dutton & Co., 1951.

Adams, C. R. An informal preliminary report on some factors relating to sexual responsiveness of certain college wives. In M. F. DeMartino (Ed.), *Sexual behavior and personality characteristics*. New York: Citadel Press, 1963, Pp. 208–226.

Adams, C. R., and Lepley, W. M. *The personal audit*. Chicago: Science Research Associates, 1945.

Adorno, T. W., Frenkel-Brunswick, Else, Levinson, D. J., and Sanford, R. N. *The authoritarian personality*. New York: Harper & Row, 1950.

Agoston, T. Some psychological aspects of prostitution: The pseudo-personality. *International Journal of Psychoanalysis*, 1945, *26*, 62–67.

Agoston, T. The fear of post-orgastic emptiness. *Psychoanalytic Review*, 1946, *33*, 197–214.

Aiken, L. R., Jr. The relationships of dress to selected measures of personality in undergraduate women. *Journal of Social Psychology*, 1963, *59*, 119–128.

Allport, G. W. *Personality: A psychological interpretation*. London: Constable, 1949.

Allport, G. W., Vernon, P. E., and Lindzey, G. *Manual for Study of Values*. Boston: Houghton Mifflin Company, 1960.

Anastasiow, N. J. Success in school and boys' sex-role patterns. *Child Development*, 1965, *36*, 1,053–1,066.

Angrilli, A. F. The psychosexual identification of preschool boys. *Journal of Genetic Psychology*, 1960, *97*, 329–340.

Angrist, Shirley S. Role conception as a predictor of adult female roles. *Sociology and Social Research*, 1966, *50*, 448–459.

Apperson, Louise B., and McAdoo, W. G., Jr. Parental factors in the childhood of homosexuals. *Journal of Abnormal Psychology*, 1968, *73*, 201–206.

Ard, B. N., Jr. Sexual behavior and attitudes of marital partners. Unpublished doctoral dissertation, University of Michigan, 1962.

Arlow, J. A. Masturbation and symptom formation. *Journal of the American Psychoanalytic Association*, 1953, *1*, 45–58.

Aronson, H. G., and Glienke, C. F. A study of the incidence of pregnancy following adoption. *Fertility and Sterility*, 1963, *14*, 547–553.

Asch, S. S. Claustrophobia and depression. *Journal of the American Psychoanalytic Association,* 1966, *14,* 711–729.

Bachrach, D. L. Sex differences in reactions to delayed auditory feedback. *Perceptual and Motor Skills,* 1964, *19,* 81–82.

Bailey, Maureen A. Toxemia of pregnancy: Cognitive and emotional effects in children from consistent and non-consistent environments. Unpublished doctoral dissertation, Wayne State University, 1963.

Bakan, D. *The duality of human existence.* Chicago: Rand McNally, 1966.

Bakan, P. Hypnotizability, laterality of eye-movements and functional brain asymmetry. *Perceptual and Motor Skills,* 1969, *28,* 927–932.

Baker, H. J., and Stoller, R. J. Sexual psychopathology in the hypogonadal male. *Archives of General Psychiatry,* 1968, *18,* 631–634.

Baker, R. R. Sex differences in the structure of childhood personality. Unpublished doctoral dissertation, University of Arizona, 1968.

Bakker, C. B., and Dightman, C. R. Psychological factors in fertility control. *Fertility and Sterility,* 1964, *15,* 559–567.

Baldwin, A. *Behavior and development in childhood.* New York: Dryden, 1955.

Balint, A. Love for the mother and mother love. *International Journal of Psychoanalysis,* 1949, *30,* 251–259.

Balint, M. A contribution to the psychology of menstruation. *Psychoanalytic Quarterly,* 1937, *6,* 346–352.

Balint, M. On genital love. *International Journal of Psychoanalysis,* 1948, *29,* 34–40.

Ban, Peggy L., and Lewis, M. Mothers and fathers, girls and boys: Attachment behavior in the one-year-old. Presented at annual meeting of Eastern Psychological Association, New York, 1971.

Bandura, A. Social learning through imitation. In M. R. Jones (Ed.), *Nebraska symposium on motivation.* Lincoln, Neb.: University of Nebraska Press, 1962, Pp. 211–269.

Bandura, A., and Walters, R. H. *Social learning and personality development.* New York: Holt, Rinehart and Winston, 1963.

Banks, A., Rutherford, R. N., and Coburn, W. A. Fertility following adoption. Report of 31 cases. *Fertility and Sterility,* 1961, *12,* 438–442.

Banner, R. H. Anxiety, personality and birth delivery. Unpublished doctoral dissertation, Colorado State University, 1968.

Barclay, A. M., and Haber, R. N. The relation of aggressive to sexual motivation. *Journal of Personality,* 1965, *33,* 462–475.

Bardwick, Judith M. *Psychology of women. A study of biocultural conflicts.* New York: Harper & Row, 1971.

Bardwick, Judith M., and Behrman, S. J. Investigation into the effects of anxiety, sexual arousal, and menstrual cycle phase on uterine contractions. *Psychosomatic Medicine,* 1967, *29,* 468–482.

Barglow, P. Pseudocyesis and psychiatric sequelae of sterilization. *Archives of General Psychiatry,* 1964, *11,* 571–580.

Barker, W. J. Female sexuality. *Journal of the American Psychoanalytic Association,* 1968, *16,* 123–145.

Barnes, C. A. A statistical study of the Freudian theory of levels of psychosexual development. *Genetic Psychology Monographs,* 1952, *45,* 105–175.

Barnett, Marjorie C. Vaginal awareness in the infancy and childhood of girls. *Journal of the American Psychoanalytic Association,* 1966, *14,* 129–141.

Barnett, Marjorie C. "I can't" versus "he won't." *Journal of the American Psychoanalytic Association,* 1968, *16,* 588–600.

Barron, F. *Inventory of personal philosophy.* Berkeley: University of California Press, 1952.

Barrucand, D. La psychogenese des vomissements repetes de la femme enceinte. *Annales Medico-Psychologiques,* 1968, *2,* 617–626.

Barry, H. A., Bacon, M. K., and Child, I. L. A cross-cultural survey of some sex differences in socialization. *Journal of Abnormal and Social Psychology*, 1957, *55*, 327–332.

Bartlet, J. E. The role of society in neurosis and psychosomatic diseases. *Psychotherapy and Psychosomatics*, 1967, *15*, 7.

Barton, D., and Ware, P. D. Incongruities in the development of the sexual system. *Archives of General Psychiatry*, 1966, *14*, 614–624.

Baruch, Rhoda. The achievement motive in women: Implications for career development. *Journal of Personality and Social Psychology*, 1967, *5*, 260–267.

Bass, B. M. Development and evaluation of a scale for measuring social acquiescence. *Journal of Abnormal and Social Psychology*, 1956, *53*, 296–299.

Bass, B. M. *Famous Saying Test*. Missoula, Montana: Psychological Test Specialists, 1958.

Bayer, Leona M., and Reichard, Suzanne. Androgyny, weight, and personality. *Psychosomatic Medicine*, 1951, *13*, 358–374.

Bayley, Nancy. Some psychological correlates of somatic androgyny. *Child Development*, 1951, *22*, 47–60.

Beach, F. A. Characteristics of masculine "sex drive." In M. R. Jones (Ed.), *Nebraska symposium on motivation*. Lincoln, Neb.: University of Nebraska Press, 1956, Pp. 1–32.

Beach, F. A. (Ed.). *Sex and behavior*. New York: John Wiley & Sons, 1965.

Beach, F. A., and Merari, A. Coital behavior in dogs: V. Effects of estrogen and progesterone on mating and other forms of social behavior in the bitch. *Journal of Comparative and Physiological Psychology*, 1970, *70*, 1–22.

Beardslee, D. C., and Fogelson, R. Sex differences in sexual imagery aroused by musical stimulation. In J. W. Atkinson (Ed.), *Motives in fantasy, action, and society*. Princeton, N. J.: D. Van Nostrand, 1958, Pp. 132–142.

Becker, G. Sex-role identification and the needs for self and social approval. *Journal of Psychology*, 1968, *69*, 11–15.

Beier, E. G., and Ratzeburg, F. The parental identifications of male and female college students. *Journal of Abnormal and Social Psychology*, 1953, *48*, 569–572.

Beigel, H. G. Sex and human beauty. *Journal of Aesthetics*, 1953, *12*, 83–92.

Bell, A. P. Role modelship and interaction in adolescence and young adulthood. *Developmental Psychology*, 1970, *2*, 123–128.

Benedek, Therese. Climacterium: A developmental phase. *Psychoanalytic Quarterly*, 1950, *19*, 1–27.

Benedek, Therese. *Studies in psychosomatic medicine. Psychosexual functions in women*. New York: The Ronald Press, 1952.

Benedek, Therese. Psychobiological aspects of mothering. *American Journal of Orthopsychiatry*, 1956, *26*, 272–278.

Benedek, Therese. Parenthood as a developmental phase. *Journal of the American Psychoanalytic Association*, 1959a, *7*, 389–417.

Benedek, Therese. Sexual functions in women. In S. Arieti (Ed.), *American handbook of psychiatry*, Vol. I. New York: Basic Books, 1959, Pp. 727–748.

Benedek, Therese. An investigation of the sexual cycle in women. *Archives of General Psychiatry*, 1963, *8*, 311–322.

Benedek, Therese. Discussion of Sherfey's paper on female sexuality. *Journal of the American Psychoanalytic Association*, 1968, *16*, 424–448.

Benedek, Therese, Ham, G. C., Robbins, F. P., and Rubenstein, B. B. Some emotional factors in infertility. *Psychosomatic Medicine*, 1953, *15*, 485–498.

Benedek, T., and Rubenstein, B. The sexual cycle in women: The relation between ovarian function and psychodynamic processes. Washington, D.C.: National Research Council, 1942.

Bennett, D. H. Perception of the upright in relation to body image. *Journal of Mental Science*, 1956, *102*, 487–506.

Bennett, E. M., and Cohen, L. R. Men and women: Personality patterns and contrasts. *Genetic Psychology Monographs*, 1959, *59*, 101–155.

Bennett, M. C. Exploratory study of masculine-feminine choices of preschool children. Unpublished doctoral dissertation, Claremont Graduate School, 1968.

Bentler, P. M. Heterosexual behavior assessment: I. Males. *Behaviour Research and Therapy*, 1968a, *6*, 21–25.

Bentler, P. M. Heterosexual behavior assessment: II. Females. *Behaviour Research and Therapy*, 1968b, *6*, 27–30.

Berger, C. R. Sex differences related to self-esteem factor structure. *Journal of Consulting and Clinical Psychology*, 1968, *32*, 442–446.

Bergler, E., and Kroger, W. S. *Kinsey's myth of female sexuality*. New York: Grune & Stratton, 1954.

Berkman, P. L. Spouseless motherhood, psychological stress, and physical morbidity. *Journal of Health and Social Behavior*, 1969, *10*, 323–334.

Bermant, G., and Westbrook, W. H. Peripheral factors in the regulation of sexual contact by female rats. *Journal of Comparative and Physiological Psychology*, 1966, *61*, 244–250.

Bernard, Jessie. *The sex game*. Englewood Cliffs, N.J.: Prentice-Hall, 1968.

Bernard, J., and Sontag, L. W. Fetal reactivity to fetal stimulation: A preliminary report. *Journal of Genetic Psychology*, 1947, *70*, 205–210.

Bernreuter, R. G. *The personality inventory*. Stanford, Cal.: Stanford University Press, 1931.

Bertling, Marion H. Some psychic aspects of dysmenorrhea and nausea and vomiting of pregnancy. *American Journal of Obstetrics and Gynecology*, 1948, *56*, 733–737.

Bibring, Grete L. Some considerations in the psychological processes of pregnancy. *Psychoanalytic Study of the Child*, Vol. 14, New York: International Universities Press, 1959, 113–121.

Bibring, Grete L. A study of the psychological processes in pregnancy and of the earliest mother-child relationship. *Psychoanalytic Study of the Child*, Vol. 16, New York: International Universities Press, 1961, 9–45.

Bickers, W. Uterine contraction patterns: Effects of psychic stimuli on the myometrium. *Fertility and Sterility*, 1956, *7*, 268–275.

Bieber, I., and Drellich, M. G. The female castration complex. *Journal of Nervous and Mental Disease*, 1959, *129*, 235–242.

Bieliauskas, V. J. Recent advances in the psychology of masculinity and femininity. *Journal of Psychology*, 1965, *60*, 255–263.

Biller, H. B. Maternal salience and feminine development in young girls. Proceedings, 77th Annual Convention, American Psychological Association, 1969.

Biller, H. B., and Bahm, R. M. Father absence, perceived maternal behavior, and masculinity of self-concept among junior high school boys. *Developmental Psychology*, 1971, *4*, 178–181.

Biller, H. B., and Borstelmann, L. J. Masculine development: An integrative review. *Merrill-Palmer Quarterly of Behavior and Development*, 1967, *13*, 253–294.

Biller, H. B., Singer, D. L., and Fullerton, Maryellen. Sex role development and creative potential in kindergarten age boys. *Developmental Psychology*, 1969, *1*, 291–296.

Biller, H. B., and Weiss, S. D. The father-daughter relationship and the personality development of the female. *Journal of Genetic Psychology*, 1970, *116*, 79–93.

Bion, W. R. The psycho-analytic study of thinking. II. A theory of thinking. *International Journal of Psychoanalysis*, 1962, *43*, 306–310.

Blanton, S. Phallic women. *Psychoanalytic Quarterly*, 1947, *16*, 214–224.

Blau, A., Slaff, B., Easton, K., Welkowitz, Joan, Springarn, J., and Cohen, J. The psychogenic etiology of premature births. A preliminary report. *Psychosomatic Medicine*, 1963, *25*, 201–211.

Blau, A., Welkowitz, Joan, and Cohen, J. Maternal attitude to pregnancy instrument. *Archives of General Psychiatry*, 1964, *10*, 324–331.

Blazer, J. A. Leg position and psychological characteristics in women. *Psychology*, 1966, *3*, 5–12.

Blinder, M. G. Differential diagnosis and treatment of depressive disorders. *Journal of American Medical Association*, 1966, *195*, 8–12.

Blitzer, J. R., and Murray, J. M. On the transformation of early narcissism during pregnancy. *International Journal of Psychoanalysis*, 1964, *45*, 89–97.

Blood, R. O. Jr., and Wolfe, D. M. *Husbands and wives: The dynamics of married living*. London: Collier-Macmillan, 1960.

Bloomingdale, E. C. Psychological aspects of essential dysmenorrhea. Unpublished doctoral dissertation, Radcliffe Graduate School, 1953.

Blum, G. S. A study of the psychoanalytic theory of psychosexual development. *Genetic Psychology Monographs*, 1949, *39*, 3–99.

Blum, G. S. *Psychoanalytic theories of personality*. New York: McGraw-Hill, 1953.

Blum, Lucille H. Sterility and the magic power of the maternal figure. *Journal of Nervous and Mental Disease*, 1959, *128*, 401–408.

Bolles, R. C., Rapp, H. M., and White, G. C. Failure of sexual activity to reinforce female rats. *Journal of Comparative and Physiological Psychology*, 1968, *65*, 311–313.

Bonaparte, Marie. *Female sexuality*. New York: International Universities Press, 1953.

Bonney, M. E. Choosing between the sexes on a sociometric instrument. *Journal of Social Psychology*, 1954, *39*, 99–114.

Borstelmann, L. J., Fowler, J., and McBryde, A. Maternal values, personality and infant feeding behaviors. Presented at annual meeting of American Orthopsychiatric Association, New York City, 1965.

Boss, M. *Meaning and content of sexual perversions*. New York: Grune & Stratton, 1949.

Boyar, J. I. The construction and partial validation of a scale for the measurement of the fear of death. Unpublished doctoral dissertation, University of Rochester, 1964.

Boyd, P. S., and Valentine, M. Word-association test in dysmenorrhoea: A polygraph investigation. *British Journal of Medical Psychology*, 1953, *26*, 58–63.

Brackbill, G. A., and Brackbill, Y. Some reactions to first remembered sexual climax. In M. F. DeMartino (Ed.), *Sexual behavior and personality characteristics*. New York: Citadel Press, 1963; Pp. 227–233.

Bradford, Jean L. Sex differences in anxiety. Unpublished doctoral dissertation, University of Minnesota, 1968.

Bradley, N. The doll: Some clinical, biological and linguistic notes on the toy-baby and its mother. *International Journal of Psychoanalysis*, 1961, *42*, 550–555.

Brennan, J. F. Autoeroticism or social feeling as basis of human development. *Journal of Individual Psychology*, 1969, *25*, 3–18.

Brenneis, C. B. Differences in male and female ego styles in manifest dream content. Unpublished doctoral dissertation, University of Michigan, 1967.

Bressler, B., Nyhus, P., and Magnussen, F. Pregnancy fantasies in psychosomatic illness and symptom formation. *Psychosomatic Medicine*, 1958, *20*, 187–202.

Brew, Mary F., and Seidenberg, R. Psychotic reactions associated with pregnancy and childbirth. *Journal of Nervous and Mental Disease*, 1950, *111*, 408–423.

Brierley, M. Specific determinants in feminine development. *International Journal of Psychoanalysis*, 1936, *17*, 163–180.

Brim, O. G., Jr. Family structure and sex role learning by children: A further analysis of Helen Koch's data. *Sociometry*, 1958, *21*, 1–16.

Brodbeck, A. J. Learning and identification: IV. Oedipal motivation as a determinant of conscience development. *Journal of Genetic Psychology*, 1954, *84*, 219–227.

Broderick, C. B. Sexual behavior among pre-adolescents. *Journal of Social Issues*, 1966, *22*, 6–21.

Broderick, C. B., and Rowe, G. P. A scale of preadolescent heterosexual development. *Journal of Marriage and The Family*, 1968, *30*, 97–101.

Brodsky, S. L. Self-acceptance in pregnant women. *Marriage and Family Living*, 1963, *25*, 483–484.

Brody, H. Psychologic factors associated with infertility in women: A comparative study of psychologic factors in women afflicted with infertility including groups with and without a medical basis for their condition. Unpublished doctoral dissertation, New York University, 1955.

Brody, Sylvia. *Patterns of mothering*. New York: International Universities Press, 1956.

Bromley, Dorothy D., and Britten, Florence H. *Youth and sex*. New York: Harper & Bros., 1938.

Bronfenbrenner, U. Freudian theories of identification and their derivatives. *Child Development*, 1960, *31*, 15–40.

Broverman, Inge K., Broverman, D. M., Clarkson, F. E., Rosenkrantz, P. S., and Vogel, Susan R. Sex-role stereotypes and clinical judgments of mental health. *Journal of Consulting and Clinical Psychology*, 1970, *34*, 1–7.

Brown, D. G. Sex-role preference in young children. *Psychological Monographs*, 1956, *70*, No. 421.

Brown, D. G. Masculinity-femininity development in children. *Journal of Consulting Psychology*, 1957, *21*, 197–202.

Brown, D. G. Sex-role development in a changing culture. *Psychological Bulletin*, 1958, *55*, 232–242.

Brown, D. G., and Lynn, D. B. Human sexual development: An outline of components and concepts. *Journal of Marriage and The Family*, 1966, *28*, 155–162.

Brown, D. G., and Tolor, A. Human figure drawings as indicators of sexual identification and inversion. *Perceptual and Motor Skills*, 1957, *7*, 199–211.

Brown, F., Chase, Janet, and Winston, Judith. Studies in infant feeding choices of primiparae: II. Comparison of Rorschach determinants of accepters and rejecters of breast feeding. *Journal of Projective Techniques*, 1961, *25*, 412–421.

Brown, F., Lieberman, Janet, Winston, Judith, and Pleshette, N. Studies in choice of infant feeding by primiparae: I. Attitudinal factors and extraneous influence. *Psychosomatic Medicine*, 1960, *22*, 421–429.

Brown, Julia S. A comparative study of deviations from sexual mores. *American Sociological Review*, 1952, *17*, 135–146.

Brown, L. B. Social and attitudinal concomitants of illness in pregnancy. *British Journal of Medical Psychology*, 1962, *35*, 311–322.

Brown, L. B. Anxiety in pregnancy. *British Journal of Medical Psychology*, 1964, *37*, 47–58.

Bugental, Daphne E., Love, Leonore R., and Gianetto, R. M. Perfidious feminine faces. *Journal of Personality and Social Psychology*, 1971, *17*, 314–318.

Burgess, E. W. The sociologic theory of psychosexual behavior. In P. H. Hoch and J. Zubin (Eds.), *Psychosexual development in health and disease*. New York: Grune & Stratton, 1949, Pp. 227–243.

Burgess, E. W., and Cottrell, L. S., Jr. The prediction of adjustment in marriage. *American Sociological Review*, 1936, *1*, 737–751.

Burgess, E. W., and Cottrell, L. S., Jr. *Predicting success or failure in marriage*. Englewood Cliffs, N. J.: Prentice-Hall, 1939.

Burgess, E. W., and Wallin, P. Homogamy in personality characteristics. *Journal of Abnormal and Social Psychology*, 1944, *39*, 475–481.

Burgess, E. W., and Wallin, P. *Engagement and marriage*. Philadelphia: J. B. Lippincott, 1953.

Burton, Genevieve, and Kaplan, H. M. Sexual behavior and adjustment of married alcoholics. *Quarterly Journal of Studies on Alcohol*, 1968, *29*, 603–609.

Buss, A. *The psychology of aggression*. New York: John Wiley & Sons, 1961.

Buss, A., and Durkee, Ann. An inventory for assessing different kinds of hostility. *Journal of Consulting Psychology*, 1957, *21*, 343–349.

Bychowski, G., and Deutsch, Helene. In Panel on Frigidity of Women, reported by B. E. Moore. *Journal of the American Psychoanalytic Association*, 1961, *9*, 571–584.

Byrne, D., Golightly, C., and Capaldi, E. J. Construction and validation of the Food Attitude scale. *Journal of Consulting Psychology*, 1963, *27*, 215–222.

Byrne, D., and Sheffield, J. Response to sexually arousing stimuli as a function of repressing and sensitizing defenses. *Journal of Abnormal Psychology*, 1965, *70*, 114–118.

Cabe, P. A. Note on response sets on the rod-and-frame test. *Perceptual and Motor Skills*, 1968, *26*, 94.

Cain, A. C., Erickson, Mary E., Fast, Irene, and Vaughan, Rebecca. Children's disturbed reactions to their mother's miscarriage. *Psychosomatic Medicine*, 1964, *26*, 58–66.

Calderone, Mary S. *Release from sexual tensions*. New York: Random House, 1960.

Caldwell, Bettye M., Hersher, L., Lipton, E., Richmond, J. B., Stern, G. A., Eddy, Evelyn, Drachman, R., and Rothman, A. Mother-infant interaction in monomatric and polymatric families. *American Journal of Orthopsychiatry*, 1963, *33*, 653–664.

Call, J. D. Emotional factors favoring successful breast feeding of infants. *Journal of Pediatrics*, 1959, *55*, 485–496.

Cameron, P. Note on time spent thinking about sex. *Psychological Reports*, 1967, *20*, 741–742.

Carlson, R. Sex differences in ego functioning: Exploratory studies of agency and communion. *Journal of Consulting Psychology*, in press.

Carmichael, L. *Manual of child psychology* (3rd Edition). New York: John Wiley & Sons, 1970.

Carpenter, J., Aldrich, C., and Boverman, H. The effectiveness of patient interviews. *Archives of General Psychiatry*, 1968, *19*, 110–112.

Carter, J. E. Hypnotic induction of labor: A review and report of cases. *American Journal of Clinical Hypnosis*, 1962/63, *5*, 322–325.

Castaldo, V. and Holzman, P. S. The effects of hearing one's own voice on sleep mentation. *Journal of Nervous and Mental Disease*, 1967, *144*, 2–13.

Centers, R., and Blumberg, G. H. Social and psychological factors in human procreation: A survey approach. *Journal of Social Psychology*, 1954, *40*, 245–257.

Chall, L. P. A survey of advances in modern sex research. In A. Ellis and A. Abarbanel (Eds.), *Encyclopedia of sexual behavior*. Vol. 1. New York: Hawthorn Books, 1961.

Chambers, W. R. Brain tumor simulating pregnancy. *American Journal of Obstetrics and Gynecology*, 1955, *70*, 212.

Chapman, L. J., Chapman, Jean P., and Brelje, T. Influence of the experimenter on pupillary dilation to sexually provocative pictures. *Journal of Abnormal Psychology*, 1969, *74*, 396–400.

Chasseguet-Smirgel, Janine (Ed.). *Female sexuality. New psychoanalytic views*. Ann Arbor: The University of Michigan Press, 1970.

Chateau, J. Les attitudes spatiales en fonction des ages et des sexes dans des epreuves labyrinthes. *Enfance*, 1959, *1*, 1–27.

Cheger, Jean G. Cyesis: Social and educational dilemma. Unpublished doctoral dissertation, Wayne State University, 1967.

Chertok, L., Mondzain, M. L., and Bonnaud, M. Vomiting and the wish to have a child. *Psychosomatic Medicine,* 1963, *25,* 13–18.

Chesser, Eustace. *The sexual, marital and family relationships of the English woman.* New York: Roy Publishers, 1957.

Chodoff, P. A critique of Freud's theory of infantile sexuality. *American Journal of Psychiatry,* 1966, *123,* 507–518.

Christensen, H. T. *Marriage analysis.* New York: The Ronald Press, 1958.

Christenson, Cornelia V., and Gagnon, J. H. Sexual behavior in a group of older women. *Journal of Gerontology,* 1965, *20,* 351–356.

Christenson, Cornelia V., and Johnson, A. B. Sexual patterns in a group of older single women. Presented at annual meeting of Midwest Psychological Association, Chicago, 1966.

Clark, A. L., and Wallin, P. The accuracy of husbands' and wives' reports of the frequency of marital coitus. *Population Studies,* 1964, *18,* 165–173.

Clark, R. A. The projective measurement of experimentally induced levels of sexual motivation. *Journal of Experimental Psychology,* 1952, *44,* 391–399.

Clark, R. A. The effects of sexual motivation on phantasy. In D. C. McClelland (Ed.), *Studies in motivation.* New York: Appleton-Century-Crofts, 1955, Pp. 44–57.

Clark, R. A., and Sensibar, M. R. The relationship between symbolic and manifest projections of sexuality with some incidental correlates. *Journal of Abnormal and Social Psychology,* 1955, *50,* 327–334.

Clausen, J. The effects of amphetamine and barbiturates on body experience. Presented at annual meeting of American Psychosomatic Society, Denver, Colorado, 1971.

Clifford, E. Expressed attitudes in pregnancy of unwed women and married primigravida and multigravida. *Child Development,* 1962, *33,* 945–951.

Cohen, H. Physiological test findings in adolescents having ovarian dysgenesis. *Psychosomatic Medicine,* 1962, *24,* 249–256.

Cohen, Mabel B. Personal identity and sexual identity. *Psychiatry,* 1966, *29,* 1–14.

Colby, K. M. Sex differences in dreams of primitive tribes. *American Anthropologist,* 1963, *65,* 1116–1121.

Colley, T. The nature and origins of psychological sexual identity. *Psychological Review,* 1959, *66,* 165–177.

Colson, D. B. The interaction of sex-role conflict with the experimental manipulation of masculinity-femininity test scores of college students. Unpublished doctoral dissertation, University of Cincinnati, 1966.

Comfort, A. *Sex in society.* London: Gerald Duckworth and Co., 1963.

Compton, N. Body perception in relation to anxiety among women. *Perceptual and Motor Skills,* 1969, *28,* 215–218.

Conn, J. Children's awareness of the origins of babies. *Journal of Child Psychiatry,* 1948, *1,* 140–176.

Conn, J. Sexual curiosity of children. *Anerican Journal of Diseases of Children,* 1940a, *60,* 1,110–1,119.

Conn, J. Children's reactions to the discovery of genital differences. *American Journal of Orthopsychiatry,* 1940b, *10,* 747–754.

Conn, J., and Kanner, L. Children's awareness of sex differences. *Journal of Child Psychiatry,* 1947, *1,* 3–57.

Cooper, A. J. Some personality factors in frigidity. *Journal of Psychosomatic Research,* 1969, *13,* 149–155.

Coppen, A. Psychosomatic aspects of pre-eclamptic toxaemia. *Journal of Psychosomatic Research,* 1958, *2,* 241–265.

Coppen, A. Vomiting of early pregnancy. Psychological factors and body build. *Lancet,* 1959, *1,* 172–173.

Coppen, A. The prevalence of menstrual disorders in psychiatric patients. *British Journal of Psychiatry*, 1965, *111*, 155–167.

Coppen, A., and Kessel, N. Menstrual disorders and personality. *Acta Psychotherapeutica, Psychosomatica et Orthopaedagogica*, 1963a, *11*, 174–180.

Coppen, A., and Kessel, N. Menstruation and personality. *British Journal of Psychiatry*, 1963b, *109*, 711–721.

Coriat, I. Sex and hunger. *Psychoanalytic Review*, 1921, *8*, 375–384.

Cottle, T. J. Family perceptions, sex role identity and the prediction of school performance. *Educational and Psychological Measurement*, 1968, *28*, 861–886.

Cottrell, L., Jr. The adjustment of the individual to his age and sex roles. *American Sociological Review*, 1942, *7*, 617–620.

Countryman, F. W., and Countryman, Betty A. Psychological determinants in successful breastfeeding. *Psychotherapy and Psychosomatics*, 1967, *15*, 13.

Cowden, R. C., and Brown, J. E. The use of a physical symptom as a defense against psychosis. *Journal of Abnormal and Social Psychology*, 1956, *53*, 133–135.

Crawford, Mary I. Physiological and behavioral cues to disturbances in childbirth. Unpublished doctoral dissertation, Columbia University, 1968.

Cuber, J. F., and Harroff, Peggy B. *The significant Americans. A study of sexual behavior among the affluent.* New York: Appleton-Century-Crofts, 1965.

Dahlstrom, W. G., and Welch, G. S. *An MMPI handbook.* Minneapolis: University of Minnesota Press, 1960.

Dame, Nenabelle G., Finck, G. H., Reiner, Beatrice S., and Smith, B. The effect on the marital relationship of the wife's search for identity. *Family Life Coordinator*, 1965, *14*, 133–136.

D'Andrade, R. G. Sex differences and cultural institutions. In Eleanor Maccoby (Ed.), *The development of sex differences.* Stanford, Cal.: Stanford University Press, 1966, Pp. 174–204.

Davids, A. A research design for studying maternal emotionality before childbirth and after social interaction with the child. *Merrill-Palmer Quarterly of Behavior and Development*, 1968, *14*, 345–354.

Davids, A., and DeVault, S. Use of the TAT and human figure drawings in research on personality, pregnancy, and perception. *Journal of Projective Techniques*, 1960, *24*, 362–365.

Davids, A., DeVault, S., and Talmadge, M. Psychological study of emotional factors in pregnancy: A preliminary report. *Psychosomatic Medicine*, 1961a, *23*, 93–103.

Davids, A., DeVault, S., and Talmadge, M. Anxiety, pregnancy, and childbirth abnormalities. *Journal of Consulting Psychology*, 1961b, *25*, 74–77.

Davids, A., and Holden, R. H. Consistency of maternal attitudes and personality from pregnancy to eight months following childbirth. *Developmental Psychology*, in press.

Davids, A., Holden, R. H., and Gray, Gloria B. Maternal anxiety during pregnancy and adequacy of mother and child adjustment eight months following childbirth. *Child Development*, 1963, *34*, 993–1002.

Davids, A., and Mahoney, J. T. Personality dynamics and accident proneness in an industrial setting. *Journal of Applied Psychology*, 1957, *41*, 303.

Davids, A., and Rosengren, W. R. Social stability and psychological adjustment during pregnancy. *Psychosomatic Medicine*, 1962, *24*, 579–583.

Davids, A., and Silverman, M. A psychological case study of death during pregnancy. *Journal of Abnormal and Social Psychology*, 1960, *61*, 287–291.

Davidson, Maria. Predictions in fertility. *Eugenics Quarterly*, 1961, *8*, 92–96.

Davis, H. V., Sears, R. R., Miller, H. C., and Brodbeck, A. J. Effects of cup, bottle and breast feeding on oral activities of newborn infants. *Pediatrics*, 1940, *3*, 549–558.

Davis, Katharine B. *Factors in the sex life of twenty-two hundred women.* New York: Harper & Bros., 1929.

Davis, Maxine. *The sexual responsibility of women.* New York: The Dial Press, 1956.

Davis, R. C., Garafolo, L., and Gault, F. An exploration of abdominal potentials. *Journal of Comparative and Physiological Psychology,* 1957, *50,* 519–523.

Davis, R. C., Garafolo, L., and Kveim, K. Conditions associated with gastrointestinal activity. *Journal of Comparative and Physiological Psychology,* 1959, *52,* 446–475.

Davis, R. E., and Ruiz, Rene A. Infant feeding method and adolescent personality. *American Journal of Psychiatry,* 1965, *122,* 673–678.

Day, M. E. Attention, anxiety and psychotherapy. *Psychotherapy: Theory, Research and Practice,* 1968, *5,* 146–149.

Day, M. E. An eye-movement indicator of individual differences in the physiological organization of attentional processes and anxiety. *Journal of Psychology,* 1967, *66,* 51–62.

Day, M. E. An eye-movement phenomenon relating to attention, thought, and anxiety. *Perceptual and Motor Skills,* 1964, *19,* 443–446.

Dean, S. J., Martin, R. B., and Streiner, D. L. The use of sexually arousing slides as unconditioned stimuli for the GSR in a discrimination paradigm. *Psychonomic Science,* 1968, *13,* 99–100.

Dearborn, L. Masturbation. In M. F. DeMartino (Ed.), *Sexual behavior and personality characteristics.* New York: Citadel Press, 1963, Pp. 239–254.

De Beauvoir, Simone. *The second sex.* New York: Alfred A. Knopf, 1952.

Dedman, Jean. The relationship between religious attitude and attitude toward premarital sex relations. *Marriage and Family Living,* 1959, *21,* 171–176.

DeLevita, D. J. *The concept of identity.* New York: Basic Books, 1966.

DeLucia, L. A. Some determinants of sex-role identification in young children. Unpublished Master's thesis, Brown University, 1960.

DeMartino, M. F. (Ed.). *Sexual behavior and personality characteristics.* New York: Citadel Press, 1963.

DeMartino, M. F. Dominance-feeling, security-insecurity, and sexuality in women. In M. F. DeMartino (Ed.), *Sexual behavior and personality characteristics.* New York: Citadel Press, 1963, Pp. 113–143.

De Monchaux, Cecily. The psychoanalytic study of thinking. *International Journal of Psychoanalysis,* 1962, *43,* 311–314.

Destounis, N. Complications of pregnancy—a psychosomatic approach. *Canadian Psychiatric Association Journal,* 1962, *7,* 279–290.

Deutsch, Helene. *Psychology of women.* Vols. I and II. New York: Grune & Stratton, 1944–1945.

Devereux, G. The psychology of feminine genital bleeding. An analysis of Mohave Indian puberty and menstrual rites. *International Journal of Psychoanalysis,* 1950, *31,* 237–257.

De Vos, G. A quantitative approach to affective symbolism in Rorschach responses. *Journal of Projective Techniques,* 1952, *16,* 134–150.

De Wit, G. A. *Symbolism of masculinity and femininity.* New York: Springer Publishing Co., 1963.

Diamant, L. Premarital sexual behavior, attitudes, and emotional adjustment. *Journal of Social Psychology,* in press.

Diamond, M. (Ed.). *Perspectives in reproduction and sexual behavior.* Bloomington, Ind.: Indiana University Press, 1968.

Dickinson, R. L., and Beam, Lura. *A thousand marriages. A medical study of sex adjustment.* Baltimore, Md.: The Williams and Wilkins Co., 1931.

Didato, S. V., and Kennedy, T. M. Masculinity-femininity and personal values. *Psychological Reports,* 1956, *2,* 231–234.

Diggory, J. C. *Self-evaluation: Concepts and studies.* New York: John Wiley & Sons, 1966.

Dingwall, E. J. *The American woman.* New York: Rinehart and Co., 1956.

Doherty, Anne. Influence of parental control on the development of feminine sex role and conscience. *Developmental Psychology,* 1969, *2,* 157–158.

Doorbar, Ruth R., and Coke, Esther U. Frigidity: Summary of some issues raised during the discussion period. *Quarterly Review of Surgery, Obstetrics and Gynecology,* 1959, *16,* 262–263.

Doty, Carol N., and Hoeflin, Ruth M. A descriptive study of thirty-five unmarried graduate women. *Journal of Marriage and The Family,* 1964, *26,* 91–94.

Douglas, G. Puerperal depression and excessive compliance with the mother. *British Journal of Medical Psychology,* 1963, *36,* 271–278.

Douglas, G. Some emotional disorders of the puerperium. *Journal of Psychosomatic Research,* 1968, *12,* 101–106.

Douvan, Elizabeth. Sex differences in adolescent character processes. *Merrill-Palmer Quarterly of Behavior and Development,* 1959–60, *6,* 203–211.

Douvan, Elizabeth, and Adelson, J. *The adolescent experience.* New York: John Wiley & Sons, 1966.

Drellich, M. G., and Bieber, I. The psychologic importance of the uterus and its functions. *Journal of Nervous and Mental Disease,* 1958, *126,* 322–336.

Duffy, J. Masturbation and clitoridectomy. *Journal of the American Medical Association,* 1963, *19,* 246–248.

Duke, J. D. Lateral eye movement behavior. *Journal of General Psychology,* 1968, *78,* 189–195.

Dunbar, F. *Emotions and body changes.* New York: Columbia University Press, 1954.

Duncan, C. H., and Taylor, H. C., Jr. A psychosomatic study of pelvic congestion. *American Journal of Obstetrics and Gynecology,* 1952, *64,* 1–12.

Duryea, W. R. Sex-role preference in children: Individual and group administration of the IT Scale for Children. *Psychological Reports,* 1967, *21,* 269–274.

Duvall, Evelyn M. *Love and the facts of life.* New York: Associated Press, 1963.

Edlundh, K., and Jansson, B. Pelvic congestion syndrome—a preliminary psychiatric report. *Journal of Psychosomatic Research,* 1966, *10,* 221–229.

Edwards, A. L. *Edwards Personal Preference Schedule* (manual). New York: Psychological Corporation, 1954. (Revised 1959.)

Edwards, A. L., and Abbott, R. D. Further evidence regarding the *R* scale of the MMPI as a measure of acquiescence. *Psychological Reports,* 1969, *24,* 903–906.

Ehrhardt, A. A., and Money, J. Progestin-induced hermaphroditism: IQ and psychosexual identity in a study of ten girls. *Journal of Sex Research,* 1967, *3,* 83–100.

Ehrmann, W. *Premarital dating behavior.* New York: Henry Holt and Co., 1959.

Ehrmann, W. Social determinants of human sexual behavior. In G. Winokur (Ed.), *Determinants of human sexual behavior.* Springfield, Illinois: Charles C. Thomas, 1963, Pp. 142–163.

Eichorn, Dorothy H. Biology of gestation and infancy: Fatherland and frontier. *Merrill-Palmer Quarterly of Behavior and Development,* 1968, *14,* 47–81.

Eidelberg, L. A contribution to the study of the masturbation phantasy. *International Journal of Psychoanalysis,* 1945, *26,* 127–137.

Eisenbud, R. J. Factors influencing the repudiation of femininity: A comparison of professional and homemaking women. Unpublished doctoral dissertation, Radcliffe, Graduate School, 1951.

Eisenstein, V. W. Dreams following intercourse. *Psychoanalytic Quarterly,* 1949, *18,* 154–172.

Eisenstein, V. W. (Ed.). *Neurotic interaction in marriage.* New York: Basic Books, 1956.

Eisler, R. M. The relationships among thematic sexual responses, sexual conflict, sex of examiner, and arousal under varying conditions of stimulus relevance. Unpublished doctoral dissertation, State University of New York at Buffalo, 1967.

Eisler, R. M. Thematic expression of sexual conflict under varying stimulus conditions. *Journal of Consulting and Clinical Psychology*, 1968, *32*, 216–220.

Eisner, Betty G. Some psychological differences between fertile and infertile women. *Journal of Clinical Psychology*, 1963, *19*, 391–395.

Elder, G. H., Jr., and Bowerman, C. E. Family structure and child-rearing patterns: The effect of family size and sex composition. *American Sociological Review*, 1963, *28*, 891–905.

Elias, G. A measure of homelessness. *Journal of Abnormal and Social Psychology*, 1952, *47*, 62–66.

Elkan, E. Evolution of female orgastic ability: A biological survey. *International Journal of Sexology*, 1948, *2*, 1–13.

Elkan, E. Orgasm inability in women. *International Journal of Sexology*, 1951, *4*, 243.

Ellis, A. Questionnaire versus interview methods in the study of human love relationships. II. Uncategorized responses. *American Sociological Review*, 1948, *13*, 61–65.

Ellis, A. A study of the love relationships of college girls. *International Journal of Sexology*, 1949a, *2*, 1–6.

Ellis, A. A study of the love emotions of American college girls. *International Journal of Sexology*, 1949b, *3*, 15–21.

Ellis, A. Love and family relations of American college girls. *American Journal of Sociology*, 1950, *55*, 550–558.

Ellis, A. Is the vaginal orgasm a myth? In A. P. Pillay and E. Ellis (Eds.), *Sex, society and the individual*. Bombay: *International Journal of Sexology*, 1953, pp. 155–162.

Ellis, A. (Ed.). *Sex life of the American woman in the Kinsey report*. New York: Greenberg, 1954.

Ellis, A. Guilt, shame, and frigidity. *Quarterly Review of Surgery, Obstetrics and Gynecology*, 1959, *16*, 259–261.

Ellis, A., and Abarbanel, A. *The encyclopedia of sexual behavior*. Vols. I and II. New York: Hawthorn Books, 1961.

Ellis, A., Doorbar, Ruth R., Guze, H., and Clark, L. A study of sexual preferences: Preliminary report. *International Journal of Sexology*, 1952, *6*, 87–88.

Ellis, Evelyn. Social psychological correlates of upward social mobility among unmarried career women. *American Sociological Review*, 1952, *17*, 558–563.

Ellis, H. *Studies in the psychology of sex*. Vol. 4. Philadelphia: F. A. Davis Co., 1921.

Ellison, Carice. Psychosomatic factors in the unconsummated marriage. *Journal of Psychosomatic Research*, 1968, *12*, 61–65.

Emmerich, W. Young children's discriminations of parent and child roles. *Child Development*, 1959a, *30*, 402–419.

Emmerich, W. Parental identification in young children. *Genetic Psychology Monographs*, 1959b, *60*, 257–308.

Engels, W. D., Pattee, C. J., and Wittkower, E. D. Emotional settings of functional amenorrhea. *Psychosomatic Medicine*, 1964, *26*, 682–700.

Engstrom, L., Geijerstam, G., Holmberg, N. G., and Uhrus, K. A prospective study of the relationship between psycho-social factors and course of pregnancy and delivery. *Journal of Psychosomatic Research*, 1964, *8*, 151–155.

Epstein, LaRene S. Dreams of pregnant women. Unpublished doctoral dissertation, University of Kansas, 1969.

Epstein, S., and Smith, R. Thematic apperception, Rorschach content, and ratings of sexual attractiveness of women as measures of the sex drive. *Journal of Consulting Psychology*, 1957, *21*, 473–478.

Erickson, Marilyn T. Relationship between psychological attitudes during pregnancy and complications of pregnancy, labor, and delivery. *Preceedings of American Psychological Association,* 1965, *1,* 213–214.

Erickson, Marilyn T. Method for frequent assessment of symptomology during pregnancy. *Psychological Reports,* 1967, *20,* 447–450.

Erikson, E. H. Sex differences in the play configurations of pre-adolescents. *American Journal of Orthopsychiatry,* 1951, *21,* 667–692.

Fagot, Beverly I., and Patterson, G. R. An in vivo analysis of reinforcing contingencies for sex-role behaviors in the pre-school child. *Developmental Psychology,* 1969, *1,* 563–568.

Farnsworth, P. R. *The social psychology of music.* New York: Dryden, 1958.

Fast, G. J., and Fisher, S. The role of body attitudes and acquiescence in epinephrine and placebo effects. *Psychosomatic Medicine,* 1971, *33,* 63–84.

Fauls, Lydia B., and Smith, W. D. Sex-role learning of five-year-olds. *Journal of Genetic Psychology,* 1956, *89,* 105–117.

Faust, Margaret S. Developmental maturity as a determinant in prestige of adolescent girls. *Child Development,* 1960, *31,* 173–184.

Feldenkrais, M. *Body and mature behaviour.* London: Routledge and Kegan Paul, 1949.

Feldman, S. S. Anxiety and orgasm. *Psychoanalytic Quarterly,* 1951, *20,* 528–549.

Felkder, D. W., and Hunter, D. M. Sex and age differences in response to cartoons depicting subjects of different ages and sex. *Journal of Psychology,* 1970, *76,* 19–21.

Fellows, R., and Cerbus, G. HTP and DCT indicators of sexual identification in children. *Journal of Projective Techniques and Personality Assessment,* 1969, *33,* 376–379.

Fenichel, O. *The psychoanalytic theory of neurosis.* New York: W. W. Norton & Co., 1945.

Ferenczi, S. Thalassa: A theory of genitality. Albany: *Psychoanalytic Quarterly,* 1938.

Ferenczi, S. *Sex in psychoanalysis.* New York: Basic Books, 1950.

Ferguson, L. W. Correlates of marital happiness. *Journal of Psychology,* 1938a, *6,* 285–294.

Ferguson, L. W. Correlates of woman's orgasm. *Journal of Psychology,* 1938b, *6,* 295–302.

Fernberger, S. W. Persistence of stereotypes concerning sex differences. *Journal of Abnormal and Social Psychology,* 1948, *43,* 97–101.

Ferreira, A. J. The pregnant mother's emotional attitude and its reflection upon the newborn. *American Journal of Orthopsychiatry,* 1960, *30,* 553–561.

Ferreira, A. J. Emotional factors in prenatal environment. *Journal of Nervous and Mental Disease,* 1965, *141,* 108–118.

Feshbach, Norma D. Sex differences in children's modes of aggressive responses toward outsiders. *Merrill-Palmer Quarterly of Behavior and Development,* 1969, *15,* 249–258.

Fink, P. J. Correlations between "actual" neurosis and the work of Masters and Johnson. *The Psychoanalytic Quarterly,* 1970, *34,* 38–51.

Fish, Kathleen D. Paternal availability, family role structure, maternal employment, and personality development in late adolescent females. Unpublished doctoral dissertation, University of Massachusetts, 1969.

Fisher, Rhoda L. The effect of a disturbing situation upon the stability of various projective tests. *Psychological Monographs,* 1958, *72,* No. 467.

Fisher, S. Achievement themes and directionality of autokinetic movement. *Journal of Abnormal and Social Psychology,* 1961, *63,* 64–68.

Fisher, S. Developmental sex differences in right-left perceptual directionality. *Child Development,* 1962, *33,* 463–468.

Fisher, S. A further appraisal of the body boundary concept. *Journal of Consulting Psychology*, 1963, *27*, 62–74.

Fisher, S. Sex differences in body perception. *Psychological Monographs*, 1964, *78*, No. 591.

Fisher, S. Body sensation and perception of projective stimuli. *Journal of Consulting Psychology*, 1965a, *29*, 135–138.

Fisher, S. Sex designations of right and left body sides and assumptions about male-female superiority. *Journal of Personality and Social Psychology*, 1965b, *2*, 576–580.

Fisher, S. Body attention patterns and personality defenses. *Psychological Monographs*, 1966, *80*, No. 617.

Fisher, S. Motivation for patient delay. *Archives of General Psychiatry*, 1967, *16*, 676–678.

Fisher, S. *Body experience in fantasy and behavior*. New York: Appleton-Century-Crofts, 1970.

Fisher, S., and Cleveland, S. E. *Body image and personality*. New York: Dover Press, 1968.

Fisher, S., and Osofsky, H. Sexual responsiveness in women. Psychological correlates. *Archives of General Psychiatry*, 1967, *17*, 214–226.

Fisher, S., and Osofsky, H. Sexual responsiveness in women: Physiological correlates. *Psychological Reports*, 1968, *22*, 215–226.

Fitzgerald, J. E., and Webster, Augusta. Hyperemesis gravidarum. *American Journal of Obstetrics and Gynecology*, 1938, *36*, 460.

Fitzherbert, Joan. Scent and the sexual object. *British Journal of Medical Psychology*, 1959, *32*, 206–209.

Flapan, M. A paradigm for the analysis of childbearing motivations of married women prior to birth of the first child. *American Journal of Orthopsychiatry*, 1969, *39*, 402–417.

Fliess, R. *Erogeneity and libido*. New York: International Universities Press, 1956.

Ford, C. S. A brief description of human sexual behavior in cross-cultural perspective. In P. Hoch and J. Zubin (Eds.), *Psychosexual development in health and disease*. New York: Grune & Stratton, 1949, Pp. 79–84.

Ford, S., and Beach, F. A. *Patterns of sexual behavior*. New York: Harper & Bros., 1951.

Forrest, D. W., and Lee, S. G. Mechanisms of defense and readiness in perception and recall. *Psychological Monographs*, 1962, *76*, No. 523.

Foss, B. M. (Ed.). *Determinants of infant behaviour*. New York: John Wiley & Sons, 1961.

Fox, H. M. Narcissistic defenses during pregnancy. *Psychoanalytic Quarterly*, 1958, *27*, 340–358.

Fox, W. I. Psychological factors in childbirth. Unpublished doctoral dissertation, New York University, 1964.

Franck, K., and Rosen, E. A projective test of masculinity-femininity. *Journal of Consulting Psychology*, 1949, *13*, 247–256.

Freed, S., and Kroger, W. S. Psychologic manifestations of the menstrual cycle. *Psychosomatic Medicine*, 1950, *12*, 229–235.

Freedman, L. Z. Childbirth while conscious: Perspectives and communication. *Journal of Nervous and Mental Disease*, 1963, *137*, 372–379.

Freedman, L. Z., and Ferguson, Vera M. The question of "painless childbirth" in primitive cultures. *American Journal of Orthopsychiatry*, 1950, *20*, 363–372.

Freedman, L. Z., Redlich, F. C., Eron, L. D., and Jackson, Edith B. Training for childbirth. Remembrance of labor. *Psychosomatic Medicine*, 1952, *14*, 439–452.

Freedman, M. B. The sexual behavior of American college women: An empirical study and an historical survey. *Merrill-Palmer Quarterly of Behavior and Development*, 1965, *11*, 33–48.

Freedman, R., and Coombs, Lolagene. Childspacing and family economic position. *American Sociological Review*, 1966, *31*, 631–648.

French Institute of Public Opinion, The. *Patterns of sex and love: A study of the French woman and her morals*. New York: Crown Publishers, 1961.

Freud, S. Hysterical phantasies and their relation to bisexuality. *Collected papers*. Vol. 2. London: Hogarth Press, 1925a.

Freud, S. Fragment of an analysis of a case of hysteria. *Collected papers*. Vol. 3. London: Hogarth Press, 1925b.

Freud, S. Three contributions to the theory of sex. In A. A. Brill (Ed.), *Basic writings of S. Freud*. New York: Modern Library, Inc., 1938.

Freud, S. *Inhibitions, symptoms, and anxiety*. London: Hogarth Press, 1949a.

Freud, S. *Three essays on the theory of sexuality*. London: Imago Publishing Co., 1949b.

Freud, S. *Collected papers*. Vol. 5. J. Strachey (Ed.). New York: Basic Books, 1959.

Freud, S. Female sexuality. In H. M. Ruitenbeek (Ed.), *Psychoanalysis and female sexuality*. New Haven, Conn.: College and University Press Services, 1966, Pp. 88–105.

Freund, K. Diagnosing homo- or heterosexuality and erotic age-preference by means of a psychophysiological test. *Behavior Research and Therapy*, 1967, *5*, 209–228.

Fried, Edrita. *The ego in love and sexuality*. New York: Grune & Stratton, 1960.

Fried, P. H., and Rakoff, A. E. Pseudocyesis: A clinical endocrine study. *A.M.A. Archives of Neurology and Psychiatry*, 1951, *65*, 120–123.

Friedgood, H. B. Neuro-endocrine and psychodynamic factors in sterility. *Western Journal of Surgery, Obstetrics and Gynecology*, 1948, *56*, 391–398.

Friedman, L. J. *Virgin wives*. London: Tavistock Publications, 1962.

Friedman, S. M. An empirical study of the castration and oedipal complexes. *Genetic Psychology Monographs*, 1952, *46*, 61–130.

Fries, M. E. Psychosomatic relationships between mother and infant. *Psychosomatic Medicine*, 1944, *6*, 159–162.

Fromm, E. Sex and character. *Psychiatry*, 1943, *6*, 21–31.

Fryrear, J. L., and Thelen, M. H. Effect of sex of model and sex of observers on the imitation of affectionate behavior. *Developmental Psychology*, 1969, *1*, 298.

Gagnon, J. H. Sexuality and sexual learning in the child. *Psychiatry*, 1965, *28*, 212–228.

Galbraith, G. G. Variation in sexual behavior to word association stimuli under conditions of sexual arousal, guilt, and situational expectancies for censure. Unpublished doctoral dissertation, Ohio State University, 1964.

Galbraith, G. G., Hahn, K., and Leiberman, H. Personality correlates of free-associative sex responses to double-entendre words. *Journal of Consulting and Clinical Psychology*, 1968, *32*, 193–197.

Ganley, Barbara. Sex roles and differences in moral behavior. Unpublished doctoral dissertation, Stanford University, 1968.

Gantt, W. H. Extension of a conflict based upon food to other physiological systems and its reciprocal relations with sexual functions. *American Journal of Physiology*, 1938, *123*, 73–74.

Garai, J. E. Sex differences in mental health. *Genetic Psychology Monographs*, 1970, *81*, 123–142.

Garai, J. E., and Scheinfeld, A. Sex differences in mental and behavioral traits. *Genetic Psychology Monographs*, 1968, *77*, 169–299.

Gebhard, P. H. Factors in marital orgasm. *Journal of Social Issues*, 1966, *22*, 88–95.

Gebhard, P. H., Pomeroy, W. B., Martin, C. E., and Christenson, Cornelia V. *Pregnancy, birth and abortion*. New York: Harper & Bros., 1958.

Gelfman, M. A post-Freudian comment on sexuality. *American Journal of Psychiatry*, 1969, *126*, 651–657.

Gerdine, P. V., Jr. Patterns of ego function in psychophysiological skin disorders. Unpublished doctoral dissertation, Boston University Graduate School, 1964.

Gershman, H. The evolution of gender identity. *American Journal of Psychoanalysis*, 1968, *28*, 80–90.

Gewirtz, J. L. Mechanisms of social learning: Some roles of stimulation and behavior in early human development. In D. A. Goslin (Ed.), *Handbook of socialization theory and research*. Skokie, Ill.: Rand McNally and Co., 1969, Pp. 57–212.

Gewirtz, J. L., and Stingle, Karen G. Learning of generalized imitation as the basis for identification. *Psychological Review*, 1968, *75*, 374–397.

Gidro-Frank, L., Gordon, Thelma, and Taylor, H. C., Jr. Pelvic pain and female identity. *American Journal of Obstetrics and Gynecology*, 1960, *79*, 1,184–1,202.

Gildea, Margaret, Glidewell, J. C., and Kantor, Mildred B. Two approaches to the study of maternal attitudes. *Psychiatric Research Reports*, 1960–63, *13–16*, 182–206.

Gillespie, W. H. Concepts of vaginal orgasm. *International Journal of Psycho-Analysis*, 1969, *50*, 495–497.

Ginsparg, Sylvia L. Post-partum psychosis. Unpublished doctoral dissertation, Washington University, 1956.

Glenn, J., and Kaplan, E. H. Types of orgasm in women: A critical review and redefinition. *Journal of the American Psychoanalytic Association*, 1968, *16*, 549–564.

Gleser, Goldine C., Gottschalk, L. A., and Watkins, J. The relationship of sex and intelligence to choice of words: A normative study of verbal behavior. *Journal of Clinical Psychology*, 1959, *15*, 182–191.

Glick, I. D., Salerno, L. J., and Royce, J. R. Psychophysiologic factors in the etiology of pre-eclampsia. *Archives of General Psychiatry*, 1965, *12*, 260–266.

Goldberg, S., and Lewis, M. Play behavior in the year-old infant: Early sex differences. *Child Development*, 1969, *40*, 21–31.

Goldman, G. D., and Milman, D. S. (Eds.). *Modern woman*. Springfield, Ill.: Charles C. Thomas, 1969.

Goode, W. J. The theoretical importance of love. *American Sociological Review*, 1959, *24*, 38–47.

Goodenough, Evelyn W. Interest in persons as an aspect of sex difference in the early years. *Genetic Psychology Monographs*, 1957, *55*, 287–323.

Goodman, Carolyn. A study of psychological factors in different fertility and family planning types. Unpublished doctoral dissertation, Columbia University, 1967.

Goodrich, W., Ryder, R. G., and Raush, H. L. Patterns of newlywed marriage. *Journal of Marriage and The Family*, 1968, *30*, 383–391.

Gordon, R. E., and Gordon, Katherine K. Social factors in the prediction and treatment of emotional disorders of pregnancy. *American Journal of Obstetrics and Gynecology*, 1959, *77*, 1,074–1,083.

Goshen-Gottstein, Esther R. Courtship, marriage and pregnancy in "Geula." A study of an ultra-orthodox Jerusalem group. *The Israel Annals of Psychiatry and Related Disciplines*, 1966, *4*, 43–66.

Gottschalk, L. A., and Auerbach, A. H. *Methods of research in psychotherapy*. New York: Appleton-Century-Crofts, 1966.

Gottschalk, L. A., Gleser, Goldine C., and Springer, K. J. Three hostility scales applicable to verbal samples. *Archives of General Psychiatry*, 1963, *9*, 254–279.

Gottschalk, L. A., Kaplan, S. M., Gleser, Goldine C., and Winget, Carolyn M. Variations in magnitude of emotion: A method applied to anxiety and hostility during phases of the menstrual cycle. *Psychosomatic Medicine*, 1962, *24*, 300–311.

Gottschalk, L. A., Titchener, J. L., Piker, Helen N., and Stewart, Sarah S. Psychosocial factors associated with pregnancy in adolescent girls: A preliminary report. *Journal of Nervous and Mental Disease*, 1964, *138*, 524–534.

Gough, H. G. *Manual for the California Psychological Inventory.* Palo Alto, Cal.: Consulting Psychologists Press, 1957. (Revised 1964.)

Graham, D. T., Kabler, J. D., and Graham, Frances K. Physiological response to the suggestion of attitudes specific for hives and hypertension. *Psychosomatic Medicine*, 1962, *24*, 159–169.

Graham, S. R. The effects of psychoanalytically oriented psychotherapy on levels of frequency and satisfaction in sexual activity. *Journal of Clinical Psychology*, 1960, *16*, 94–95.

Grant, V. W. *The psychology of sexual emotion.* New York: Longmans, Green and Co., 1957.

Gray, Susan W. Masculinity-femininity in relation to anxiety and social acceptance. *Child Development*, 1957, *28*, 203–214.

Gray, Susan W. Perceived similarity to parents and adjustment. *Child Development*, 1959, *30*, 91–107.

Gray, Susan W., and Klaus, R. The assessment of parental identification. *Genetic Psychology Monographs*, 1956, *54*, 87–114.

Grayson, H. T., Jr. Psychosexual conflict in adolescent girls who experienced early parental loss by death. Unpublished doctoral dissertation, Boston University Graduate School, 1967.

Greaves, D. C., Green, P. E., and West, L. J. Psychodynamic and psychophysiological aspects of pseudocyesis. *Psychosomatic Medicine*, 1960, *22*, 24–31.

Green, A. W. The "cult of personality" and sexual relations. *Psychiatry*, 1941, *4*, 344–348.

Green, W. A. Early object relations, somatic, affective and personal: An inquiry into the physiology of the mother-child unit. *Journal of Nervous and Mental Disease*, 1958, *126*, 225–253.

Greenacre, Phyllis. The biological economy of birth. *Psychoanalytic Study of the Child*, Vol. 1, New York: International Universities Press, 1945, Pp. 31–51.

Greenacre, Phyllis. Special problems of early female sexual development. In *Trauma, growth, and personality.* New York: W. W. Norton & Co., 1952.

Greenacre, Phyllis. Early physical determinants in the development of the sense of identity. *Journal of the American Psychoanalytic Association*, 1958, *6*, 612–627.

Greenacre, Phyllis. Special problems of early female sexual development. In H. M. Ruitenbeek (Ed.), *Psychoanalysis and female sexuality.* New Haven, Connecticut: College and University Press, 1966, Pp. 140–160.

Greenberg, N. H., Loesch, J. G., and Lakin, M. Life situations associated with the onset of pregnancy. I. The role of separation in a group of unmarried pregnant women. *Psychosomatic Medicine*, 1959, *21*, 296–310.

Greenblatt, R. B. Syndrome of major menstrual molimina with hypermenorrhea alleviated by testo-sterone propionate. *Journal of the American Medical Association*, 1940, *115*, 120–125.

Greenson, R. R. Forepleasure: Its use for defensive purposes. *Journal of the American Psychoanalytic Association*, 1955, *3*, 244–254.

Gregory, B. A. J. C. The menstrual cycle and its disorders in psychiatric patients. I. Review of the literature. *Journal of Psychosomatic Research*, 1957a, *2*, 61–79.

Gregory, B. A. J. C. The menstrual cycle and its disorders in psychiatric patients. II. Clinical studies. *Journal of Psychosomatic Research*, 1957b, *2*, 199–224.

Grimm, Elaine R. Psychological tension in pregnancy. *Psychosomatic Medicine*, 1961, *23*, 520–527.

Grimm, Elaine R. Psychological investigation of habitual abortion. *Psychosomatic Medicine*, 1962, *24*, 369–378.

Grimm, Elaine R. Psychological and social factors in pregnancy, delivery, and outcome. In S. A. Richardson and A. F. Guttmacher (Eds.), *Childbearing—its social and psychological aspects.* Baltimore, Md.: The Williams & Wilkins Co., 1967, Pp. 1–52.

Grimm, Elaine R., and Venet, Wanda R. The relationship of emotional adjustment and attitudes to the course and outcome of pregnancy. *Psychosomatic Medicine,* 1966, *28,* 34–49.

Grinder, R. E. (Ed.). *Studies in adolescence.* New York: The Macmillan Co., 1963.

Grinder, R. E., and Schmitt, Sue S. Coeds and contraceptive information. *Journal of Marriage and The Family,* 1966, *28,* 471–479.

Groat, H. T., and Neal, A. G. Social psychological correlates of urban fertility. *American Sociological Review,* 1967, *32,* 945–959.

Gross, L. A hypothesis of feminine types in relation to family adjustment. *American Journal of Orthopsychiatry,* 1950, *20,* 373–381.

Grounds, D., Davies, B., and Mowbray, R. The contraceptive pill, side effects and personality: Report of a controlled double blind trial. *British Journal of Psychiatry,* 1970, *116,* 169–172.

Guardo, Carol J. Developmental aspects of self-identity. Presented at annual meeting of Rocky Mountain Psychological Association, Salt Lake City, 1970.

Gundlach, R. H., and Riess, B. F. Birth order and sex of siblings in a sample of lesbians and non-lesbians. *Psychological Reports,* 1967, *20,* 61–62.

Gunter, Laurie M. Psychopathology and stress in the life experience of mothers of premature infants. *American Journal of Obstetrics and Gynecology,* 1963, *86,* 333–340.

Gustafson, J. E., Winokur, G., and Reichlin, S. The effect of psychic-sexual stimulation on urinary and serum acid phosphatase and plasma nonesterified fatty acids. *Psychosomatic Medicine,* 1963, *25,* 101–105.

Gutmann, D. L. Women and the conception of ego strength. *Merrill-Palmer Quarterly of Behavior and Development,* 1965, *11,* 229–240.

Gynther, M. D., and McDonald, R. L. Personality characteristics of prisoners, psychiatric patients, and student nurses as depicted by Leary system. *Journal of Genetic Psychology,* 1961, *64,* 387–395.

Hain, J. D., Linton, P. H., Eber, H. W., and Chapman, Melinda M. Menstrual irregularity, symptoms and personality. *Journal of Psychosomatic Research,* 1970, *14,* 81–87.

Hall, C. S. Strangers in dreams: An empirical confirmation of the Oedipus complex. *Journal of Personality,* 1963, *31,* 336–345.

Hall, C. S., and Van de Castle, R. L. *The content analysis of dreams.* New York: Appleton-Century-Crofts, 1966.

Hall, D. E., and Mohr, G. Prenatal attitudes of primiparae: A contribution to the mental hygiene of pregnancy. *Mental Hygiene,* 1933, *17,* 226.

Hall, Marjorie, and Keith, R. A. Sex-role preference among children of upper and lower social class. *Journal of Social Psychology,* 1964, *62,* 101–110.

Hamblin, R. L., and Blood, R. O., Jr. Premarital experience and the wife's sexual adjustment. *Social Problems,* 1956, *4,* 122–130.

Hamburger, W. W. The occurrence and meaning of dreams of food and eating. *Psychosomatic Medicine,* 1958, *20,* 1–16.

Hamilton, G. V. *A research in marriage.* New York: Albert and Charles Boni, 1929.

Hammerman, S. Masturbation and character. *Journal of the American Psychoanalytic Association,* 1961, *9,* 287–311.

Hammerschlag, C. A., Fisher, S., DeCrosse, J., and Kaplan, E. Breast symptoms and patient delay: Psychological variables involved. *Cancer,* 1964, *17,* 1,480–1,485.

Hampson, J. L., and Hampson, J. G. The ontogenesis of sexual behavior in man. In W. C. Young (Ed.), *Sex and internal secretions.* Baltimore, Md.: The Williams and Wilkins Co., 1961, Pp. 1,401–1,432.

Hampson, J. G., and Money, J. Idiopathic sexual precocity in the female. *Psychosomatic Medicine,* 1955, *17,* 16–35.

Hardenbergh, E. W. The psychology of feminine sex experience. In A. P. Pillay and

A. Ellis (Eds.), *Sex, society and the individual*. Bombay: *International Journal of Sexology*, 1953, Pp. 110–117.

Hardy, K. R. An appetitional theory of sexual motivation. *Psychological Review*, 1964, *71*, 1–18.

Hardy, K. R. Sexual appetite and sexual drive: A reply. *Psychological Reports*, 1965, *17*, 11–14.

Harlow, H. F. The heterosexual affectional systems in monkeys. *American Psychologist*, 1962, *17*, 1–9.

Harmon, Lenore W. Anatomy of career commitment in women. *Journal of Counseling Psychology*, 1970, *17*, 77–80.

Harrington, C. C. *Errors in sex-role behavior in teen-age boys*. New York: Teachers College Press, 1970.

Harris, D. B. Sex differences in the life problems and interests of adolescents. *Child Development*, 1959, *30*, 453–459.

Hart, H. H. Maternal narcissism and the Oedipus complex. *International Journal of Psychoanalysis*, 1958, *39*, 188–190.

Hart, R. D. Monthly rhythm of libido in married women. *British Medical Journal*, 1960, *1*, 1,023–1,024.

Hartley, Ruth E. Children's concepts of male and female roles. *Merrill-Palmer Quarterly of Behavior and Development*, 1959–60, *6*, 83–91.

Hartley, Ruth E. A developmental view of female sex-role definition and identification. *Merrill-Palmer Quarterly of Behavior and Development*, 1964, *10*, 3–16.

Hartley, Ruth E. Children's perceptions of sex preference in four culture groups. *Journal of Marriage and The Family*, 1969, *31*, 380–387.

Hartley, Ruth E., Hardesty, F. P., and Gorfein, D. S. Children's perceptions and expressions of sex preference. *Child Development*, 1962, *33*, 221–227.

Hartley, Ruth E., and Klein, A. Sex-role concepts among elementary-school-age girls. *Marriage and Family Living*, 1959, *21*, 59–64.

Hartmann, E. Dreaming sleep (the D-state) and the menstrual cycle. *Journal of Nervous and Mental Disease*, 1966, *143*, 406–416.

Hartrup, W. W., and Zook, E. A. Sex-role preferences in three- and four-year-old children. *Journal of Consulting Psychology*, 1960, *24*, 420–426.

Harvey, W. A., and Sherfey, Mary J. Vomiting in pregnancy. *Psychosomatic Medicine*, 1954, *16*, 1–9.

Hastings, D. W. *Impotence and frigidity*. Boston: Little, Brown and Company, 1963.

Hathaway, S. R., and McKinley, J. C. *The Minnesota Multiphasic Personality Inventory manual*. (Revised.) New York: The Psychological Corporation, 1951.

Hauser, S., and Hobart, C. Premarital pregnancy and anxiety. *Journal of Social Psychology*, 1964, *63*, 255–263.

Hayman, Anne. Some aspects of regression in non-psychotic puerperal breakdown. *British Journal of Medical Psychology*, 1962, *35*, 135–145.

Hayward, E. P. Types of female castration reaction. *Psychoanalytic Quarterly*, 1943, *12*, 45–66.

Heider, F. *The psychology of interpersonal relations*. New York: John Wiley & Sons, 1958.

Heilbrun, A. B., Jr. Parental identification and college adjustment. *Psychological Reports*, 1962, *10*, 853–854.

Heilbrun, A. B., Jr. An empirical test of the modeling theory of sex-role learning. *Child Development*, 1965, *36*, 789–799.

Heilbrun, A. B., Jr. Sex-role identity in adolescent females. A theoretical paradox. *Adolescence*, 1968a, *3*, 79–88.

Heilbrun, A. B., Jr. Sex role, instrumental-expressive behavior, and psychopathology in females. *Journal of Abnormal Psychology*, 1968b, *73*, 131–136.

Heilbrun, A. B., Jr., and Fromme, D. K. Parental identification of late adolescents and level of adjustment: The importance of parent-model attributes, ordinal position, and sex of the child. *Journal of Genetic Psychology*, 1965, *107*, 49–59.

Heiman, M. Reproduction: Emotions and the hypothalamic-pituitary function. *Fertility and Sterility*, 1959, *10*, 162–175.

Heiman, M. Sexual response in women. *Journal of the American Psychoanalytic Association*, 1963, *11*, 360–385.

Heiman, M., and Kleegman, Sophia J. Insemination: A psychoanalytic and infertility study. *Fertility and Sterility*, 1966, *17*, 117–125.

Heinstein, M. I. *Childrearing in California. A study of mothers with young children.* Berkeley, California: Department of Public Health, 1965.

Heinstein, M. I. Expressed attitudes and feelings of pregnant women and their relations to physical complications of pregnancy. *Merrill-Palmer Quarterly of Behavior and Development*, 1967, *13*, 217–236.

Heise, D. R. Cultural patterning of sexual socialization. *American Sociological Review*, 1967, *32*, 726–739.

Hellkamp, D. T. Perceptual response sets on the rod-and-frame task in a college sample. *Perceptual and Motor Skills*, 1968, *27*, 591–594.

Helper, M. M. Learning theory and the self concept. *Journal of Abnormal and Social Psychology*, 1955, *51*, 184–194.

Helper, M. M., Cohen, R. L., Beitenman, E. T., and Eaton, Louise F. Life-events and acceptance of pregnancy. *Journal of Psychosomatic Research*, 1968, *12*, 183–188.

Helson, Ravenna. Generality of sex differences in creative style. *Journal of Personality*, 1968, *36*, 33–48.

Heltsley, Mary E. Religiosity and premarital sexual permissiveness. Unpublished doctoral dissertation, Pennsylvania State University, 1968.

Herschberger, Ruth. Sexual differences and character trends. *Psychiatry*, 1943, *6*, 301–305.

Herzberg, Brenda, and Coppen, A. Changes in psychological symptoms in women taking oral contraceptives. *British Journal of Psychiatry*, 1970, *116*, 161–164.

Hetherington, E. Mavis. A developmental study of the effects of sex of the dominant parent on sex-role preference, identification, and imitation in children. *Journal of Personality and Social Psychology*, 1965, *2*, 188–194.

Hetzel, B. S., Bruer, Brigid, and Poidevin, L. O. S. A survey of the relation between certain common antenatal complications in primiparae and stressful life situations during pregnancy. *Journal of Psychosomatic Research*, 1961, *5*, 175–182.

Heyder, D. W., and Wambach, Helen S. Sexuality and affect in frogmen. *Archives of General Psychiatry*, 1964, *11*, 286–289.

Hilgard, E. R. *Theories of learning.* New York: Appleton-Century-Crofts, 1948.

Himelhoch, J., and Fava, Sylvia (Eds.). *Sexual behavior in American society.* New York: W. W. Norton & Co., 1955.

Hirst, J. C., and Strousse, Flora. The origin of emotional factors in normal pregnant women. *American Journal of Mental Science*, 1938, *196*, 95–99.

Hirt, M., Kurtz, R., and Ross, W. D. The relationship between dysmenorrhea and selected personality variables. *Psychosomatics*, 1967, *8*, 350–353.

Hitschmann, E. Freud's conception of love. *International Journal of Psychoanalysis*, 1952, *33*, 421–428.

Hitschmann, E., and Bergler, E. Frigidity in women—restatement and renewed experiences. *Psychoanalytic Review*, 1949, *36*, 45–53.

Hobbs, D. F., Jr. Transition to parenthood: A replication and an extension. *Journal of Marriage and The Family*, 1968, *30*, 413–417.

Hoch, P. H., and Zubin, J. (Eds.). *Psychosexual development in health and disease.* New York: Grune & Stratton, 1949.

Hodge, R. S., Walter, V. J., and Walter, W. G. Juvenile delinquency: An electrophysiological, psychological, and social study. *British Journal of Juvenile Delinquency*, 1952, *3*, 155–172.

Hoffman, D. T. Sex differences in preferred finger tapping rates. *Perceptual and Motor Skills*, 1969, *29*, 676.

Hoffman, Lois W., and Hoffman, M. L. (Eds.). *Review of child development research*. Vol. 2. New York: Russell Sage Foundation, 1966.

Holleman, J. L. Explorations in human development with an early memories inventory. Unpublished doctoral dissertation, University of Oklahoma, 1965.

Hollender, M. H. Women's fantasies during sexual intercourse. *Archives of General Psychiatry*, 1963, *8*, 86–90.

Hollender, M. H. The need or wish to be held. *Archives of General Psychiatry*, 1970, *22*, 445–453.

Hollender, M. H., Luborsky, L., and Harvey, Roberta B. Correlates of the desire to be held in women. *Psychosomatic Research*, 1970, *14*, 387–390.

Hollender, M. H., Luborsky, L., and Scaramella, T. J. Body contact and sexual enticement. *Archives of General Psychiatry*, 1969, *20*, 188–191.

Holter, Harriet. *Sex roles and social structure*. Oslo: Universitetsforlaget, 1970.

Holtzman, W. H., Thorpe, J. S., Swartz, J. D., and Herron, E. W. *Inkblot perception and personality*. Austin, Texas: University of Texas Press, 1961.

Holzberg, J., and Plummer, J. Sex differences in schizophrenics: Satisfactions with body parts. Unpublished paper, Wesleyan University, 1964.

Honigmann, J. J. Cultural dynamics of sex. *Psychiatry*, 1947, *10*, 37–47.

Honzik, Marjorie P. Sex differences in the occurrence of materials in the play constructions of preadolescents. *Child Development*, 1951, *22*, 15–35.

Hooke, J. F., and Marks, P. A. MMPI characteristics of pregnancy. *Journal of Clinical Psychology*, 1962, *18*, 316–317.

Hooper, D., and Sheldon, A. Evaluating newly-married couples. *British Journal of Social and Clinical Psychology*, 1969, *8*, 169–182.

Hornberger, R. H. The projective effects of fear and sexual arousal on the rating of pictures. *Journal of Clinical Psychology*, 1960, *16*, 328–331.

Horney, Karen. Die Angst vor der Frau. *Zeitschrift fur Psychoanalyses*, 1932, *13*, 1–18.

Horney, Karen. The denial of the vagina. *International Journal of Psychoanalysis*, 1933, *14*, 57–70.

Horney, Karen. *New ways in psychoanalysis*. New York: W. W. Norton & Co., 1939.

Horney, Karen. *The collected works of Karen Horney*. Vol. I. New York: W. W. Norton & Co., 1937–1945.

Horney, Karen. *Feminine psychology*. New York: W. W. Norton & Co., 1967.

Housman, H. S. A psychological study of menstruation. Unpublished doctoral dissertation, University of Michigan, 1955.

Israel, L., Jacquot, J. P., Sichel, J. P., and Locquet, R. Psychological aftereffects of gynecological interventions. *Annales Medico-Psychologiques*, 1966, *2*, 688–689.

Ittelson, W. H., and Kutash, S. B (Eds.). *Perceptual changes in psychopathology*. New Brunswick, N.J.: Rutgers University Press, 1961.

Ivey, M. E., and Bardwick, Judith M. Patterns of affective fluctuation in the menstrual cycle. *Psychosomatic Medicine*, 1968, *30*, 336–345.

Jackson, E. B., Wilkin, L. C., and Auerbach, H. Statistical report on incidence and duration of breast feeding in relation to personal-social and hospital maternity factors. *Pediatrics*, 1956, *17*, 700–715.

Jacobson, L., Kau, L., and Nilsson, A. Post-partum mental disorders in an unselected sample: Frequency of symptoms and predisposing factors. *British Medical Journal*, 1965, *1*, 1640.

Jakobovits, L. A. Evaluational reactions to erotic literature. *Psychological Reports,* 1965, *16,* 985–994.

James, Alice, and Pike, Ruth. Sexual behavior of couples receiving marriage counseling at a family agency. *Journal of Sex Research,* 1967, *3,* 232–238.

Jarrahi-Zadeh, A., Kane, F. J., Jr., Van De Castle, R. L., Lachenbruch, P. A., and Ewing, J. A. Emotional and cognitive changes in pregnancy and early puerperium. *British Journal of Psychiatry,* 1969, *115,* 797–805.

Jaynes, R. V. Acceptance of oral contraception by private patients. *Obstetrics and Gynecology,* 1962, *24,* 512.

Johnson, Miriam M. Instrumental and expressive components in the personalities of women. Unpublished doctoral dissertation, Radcliffe College, 1955.

Johnson, Miriam M. Sex role learning in the nuclear family. *Child Development,* 1963, *34,* 319–333.

Johnson, O., and Knapp, R. Sex differences in aesthetic preferences. *Journal of Social Psychology,* 1963, *61,* 279–301.

Johnson, R. C., Johnson, Carol, and Martin, Lea. Authoritarianism, occupation, and sex role differentiation of children. *Child Development,* 1961, *32,* 271–276.

Johnson, W. R. Hypnotic analysis of the recognition of a sex symbol. *Journal of Sex Research,* 1967, *3,* 229–231.

Jones, A. Sexual symbolic response in prepubescent and pubescent children. *Journal of Consulting Psychology,* 1961, *25,* 383–387.

Jones, E. The early development of female sexuality. In H. M. Ruitenbeek (Ed.), *Psychoanalysis and female sexuality.* New Haven, Connecticut: College and University Press, 1966, Pp. 21–35.

Jones, H. E. *Motor performance and growth.* Berkeley, Cal.: University of California Press, 1949.

Jones, Mary C. Psychological correlates of somatic development. *Child Development,* 1965, *36,* 899–911.

Jones, Mary C. Personality correlates and antecedents of drinking patterns in adult males. *Journal of Consulting and Clinical Psychology,* 1968, *32,* 2–12.

Jones, Mary C. and Bayley, N. Physical maturing among boys as related to behavior. *Journal of Educational Psychology,* 1950, *41,* 129–148.

Jones, Mary C., and Mussen, P. H. Self-conceptions, motivations, and interpersonal attitudes of early and late maturing girls. In R. R. Grinder (Ed.), *Studies in adolescence.* New York: The Macmillan Co., 1963, Pp. 454–465.

Jonowsky, D. S., Gorney, R., and Mandell, A. J. The menstrual cycle. Psychiatric and ovarian-adrenocortical hormone correlates: Case study and literature review. *Archives of General Psychiatry,* 1967, *17,* 459–469.

Jordan, B. T., and Butler, J. R. GSR as a measure of the sexual component in hysteria. *Journal of Psychology,* 1967, *67,* 211–219.

Josselyn, Irene M. Cultural forces, motherliness and fatherliness. *American Journal of Orthopsychiatry,* 1956, *26,* 264–271.

Kagan, J. The concept of identification. *Psychological Reports,* 1958, *65,* 296–305.

Kagan, J. Acquisition and significance of sex typing and sex role identity. In M. L. Hoffman and Lois W. Hoffman (Eds.), *Review of child development research.* New York: Russell Sage Foundation, 1964, Pp. 137–168.

Kagan, J., and Lemkin, Judith. The child's differential perception of parental attributes. *Journal of Abnormal and Social Psychology,* 1960, *61,* 440–447.

Kagan, J., and Moss, H. A. The stability of passive and dependent behavior from childhood through adulthood. *Child Development,* 1960, *31,* 577–591.

Kagan, J., and Moss, H. A. *Birth to maturity. A study in psychological development.* New York: John Wiley & Sons, 1962.

Kalin, R. Effects of inhibition on thematic apperception. Presented at annual meeting of Eastern Psychological Association, New York City, 1966.

Kalka, Beatrice S. A comparative study of feminine role concepts of a selected group of college women. Unpublished doctoral dissertation, Oklahoma State University, 1967.

Kammeyer, K. Birth order and the feminine sex role among college women. *American Sociological Review*, 1966, *31*, 508–515.

Kammeyer, K. Sibling position and the feminine role. *Journal of Marriage and The Family*, 1967, *29*, 494–499.

Kane, F. J., Jr., Harman, W. J., Jr., Keeler, M. H., and Ewing, J. A. Emotional and cognitive disturbance in the early puerperium. *British Journal of Psychiatry*, 1968, *114*, 99–102.

Kane, F. J., Jr., Lipton, M. A., and Ewing, J. A. Hormonal influences in female sexual response. *Archives of General Psychiatry*, 1969, *20*, 202–209.

Kane, F. J., Jr., Treadway, C. R., and Ewing, J. A. Emotional change associated with oral contraceptives in female psychiatric patients. *Comprehensive Psychiatry*, 1969, *10*, 16–30.

Kanin, E. J. An examination of sexual aggression as a response to sexual frustration. *Journal of Marriage and The Family*, 1967, *29*, 428–433.

Kanin, E. J., and Howard, D. H. Postmarital consequences of premarital sex adjustments. *American Sociological Review*, 1958, *23*, 556–562.

Kaplan, A. J., and Schobpach, R. Pseudocyesis: A psychiatric study. *A.M.A. Archives of Neurology and Psychiatry*, 1951, *65*, 120–123.

Kaplan, E. H. Congenital absence of the vagina. *Psychoanalytic Quarterly*, 1970, *34*, 52–70.

Kapp, F. T., Hornstein, S., and Graham, Virginia T. Some psychologic factors in prolonged labor due to inefficient uterine action. *Comprehensive Psychiatry*, 1963, *4*, 9–18.

Karacan, I., Heine, W., Agnew, H. W., Jr., Williams, R. L., Webb, W. B., and Ross, J. J. Characteristics of sleep patterns during late pregnancy and the postpartum periods. *American Journal of Obstetrics and Gynecology*, 1968, *101*, 579–586.

Kartchner, F. D. A study of the emotional reactions during labor. *American Journal of Obstetrics and Gynecology*, 1950, *60*, 19–29.

Katcher, A. The discrimination of sex differences by young children. *Journal of Genetic Psychology*, 1955, *87*, 131–143.

Katcher, A., and Levin, M. Childrens' conceptions of body size. *Child Development*, 1955, *26*, 103–110.

Kau, L., Jacobson, L., and Nilsson, A. Post-partum mental disorders in an unselected sample: The influence of parity. *Journal of Psychosomatic Research*, 1967, *10*, 317–325.

Kaye, H. E., Berl, S., Clare, J., Eleston, Mary R., Gershwin, B. S., Gershwin, Patricia, Kogan, L. S., Torda, Clara, and Wilburn, Cornelia B. Homosexuality in women. *Archives of General Psychiatry*, 1967, *17*, 626–634.

Keiser, S. Psychopathology of orgasm. *Psychoanalytic Quarterly*, 1947, *16*, 378–390.

Keiser, S. Body ego during orgasm. *Psychoanalytic Quarterly*, 1952, *21*, 153–166.

Keiser, S. Female sexuality. *Journal of the American Psychoanalytic Association*, 1956, *4*, 563–574.

Kelley, K. Sterility in the female with special reference to psychic factors. Part I: A review of the literature. *Psychosomatic Medicine*, 1942, *4*, 211–222.

Kelley, K., Daniels, G. E., Poe, J., Easser, Ruth, and Monroe, R. Psychological correlations with secondary amenorrhea. *Psychosomatic Medicine*, 1954, *16*, 129–147.

Kelly, E. L. Personality as related to source and adequacy of sex instruction. In Q. McNemar and Maud A. Merrill (Eds.), *Studies in personality*. New York: McGraw-Hill, 1942, Pp. 147–158.

Kelly, J. V. Effect of fear upon uterine motility. *American Journal of Obstetrics and Gynecology*, 1962a, *83*, 576–581.

Kelly, J. V. Effect of hypnotically induced anxiety on uterine muscle. *American Journal of Obstetrics and Gynecology*, 1962b, *83*, 582–587.

Kenyon, F. E. Studies in female homosexuality—psychological test results. *Journal of Consulting and Clinical Psychology,* 1968, *32,* 510–513.

Kenyon, F. E. Homosexuality in the female. *British Journal of Hospital Medicine,* 1970, *3,* 183–206.

Kepecs, J. G., and Robin, M. Studies in itching: I. Contributions to an understanding of the physiology of masochism. *Psychosomatic Medicine,* 1955, *17,* 87–95.

Kepecs, J. G., and Robin, M. Studies in itching: II. Some psychological implications of the interrelationships between the cutaneous pain and touch systems. *Archives of Neurology and Psychiatry,* 1956, *76,* 325–340.

Kepecs, J. G., Robin, M., and Munro, Clare. Response to sensory stimulation in certain psychosomatic disorders. *Psychosomatic Medicine,* 1958, *20,* 351–365.

Kepecs, J. G., Robin, M., and Munro, Clare. Tickle in atopic dermatitis. *Archives of General Psychiatry,* 1960, *3,* 243–251.

Kestenberg, Judith S. Vicissitudes of female sexuality. *Journal of the American Psychoanalytic Association,* 1956a, *4,* 453–476.

Kestenberg, Judith S. On the development of maternal feelings in early childhood. *Psychoanalytic Study of the Child,* 1956b, *11,* 257–291.

Kestenberg, Judith S. Menarche. In S. Lorand and H. Schneer (Eds.), *Adolescents. Psychoanalytic approach to problems and therapy.* New York: Paul B. Hoeber, 1961, Pp. 19–50.

Kidd, Aline H., and Rivoire, Jeanne L. *Perceptual development in children.* New York: International Universities Press, 1966.

Kilpatrick, D. G., and Cauthen, N. R. The relationship of ordinal position, dogmatism, and personal sexual attitudes. *Journal of Psychology,* 1969, *73,* 115–120.

Kilpatrick, D. G., Cauthen, N. R., Sandman, C. A., and Quattlebaum, L. F. Dogmatism and personal sexual attitudes. *Psychological Reports,* 1968, *23,* 1,105–1,106.

Kinsey, A. C., Pomeroy, W., and Martin, C. *Sexual behavior in the human male.* Philadelphia: W. B. Saunders Company, 1948.

Kinsey, A. C., Pomeroy, W., Martin, C., and Gebhard, P. *Sexual behavior in the human female.* Philadelphia: W. B. Saunders Company, 1953.

Kirkendall, L. A., and Libby, R. W. Interpersonal relationships—crux of the sexual renaissance. *Journal of Social Issues,* 1966, *22,* 45–59.

Kirkpatrick, C., Stryker, S., and Buell, P. An experimental study of attitudes towards male sex behavior with reference to Kinsey findings. *American Sociological Review,* 1952, *17,* 580–587.

Kitay, P. M. A comparison of the sexes in their attitudes and beliefs about women. *Sociometry,* 1940, *34,* 399–407.

Klatskin, Ethelyn H., and Eron, L. D. Projective test content during pregnancy and postpartum adjustment. *Psychosomatic Medicine,* 1970, *32,* 487–493.

Klausner, S. Z. Inferential visibility and sex norms in the Middle East. *Journal of Social Psychology,* 1964, *63,* 1–29.

Kleegman, Sophia J. Frigidity in women. *Quarterly Review of Surgery, Obstetrics and Gynecology,* 1959, *16,* 243–248.

Klein, Henriette R., Potter, H. W., and Dyk, Ruth B. *Anxiety in pregnancy and childbirth.* New York: Paul B. Hoeber, 1950.

Klein, S. D. A developmental study of tactual perception. Unpublished doctoral dissertation, Clark University, 1963.

Klein, Viola. *Feminine character.* London: Kegan, Paul, Trench, Trubner and Co., 1946.

Klein, Viola. *The feminine character. History of an ideology.* New York: International Universities Press, 1949.

Kline, C. L. Emotional illness associated with childbirth. *American Journal of Obstetrics and Gynecology,* 1955, *69,* 748–757.

Knapp, P. H. Some riddles of riddance. *Archives of General Psychiatry,* 1967, *16,* 586–602.

Knapp, R. H., and Ehlinger, Linda A. Sex differences among schizophrenics in the interpretation of the human dyad. *Journal of Psychology*, 1963, *56*, 473–478.

Knobel, M. Preventive psychotherapy in pregnancy. *Psychotherapy and Psychosomatics*, 1967, *15*, 34.

Koch, Helen A. A study of some factors conditioning social distance between the sexes. *Journal of Social Psychology*, 1944, *20*, 79–107.

Kockelmans, J. J. Merleau-Ponty on sexuality. *Journal of Existentialism*, 1965/66, *6*, 9–29.

Kogan, Kate L., and Jackson, Joan K. Conventional sex role stereotypes and actual perceptions. *Psychological Reports*, 1963, *13*, 27–30.

Kogan, W. S., Boe, E. E., and Gocka, E. F. Personality changes in unwed mothers following parturition. *Journal of Clinical Psychology*, 1968, *24*, 3–11.

Kogan, W. S., Boe, E. E., and Valentine, Betty L. Changes in the self-concept of unwed mothers. *Journal of Psychology*, 1965, *59*, 3–10.

Kohlberg, L. Moral development and identification. In H. W. Stevenson (Ed.), *Child psychology: The sixty-second yearbook of the National Society for the Study of Education*. Chicago: University of Chicago Press, 1963, Pp. 277–332.

Kohlberg, L. Development of moral character and moral ideology. In M. L. Hoffman and Lois Hoffman (Eds.), *Review of child development research*. New York: Russell Sage Foundation, 1964, Pp. 383–432.

Kohlberg, L. A cognitive-developmental analysis of children's sex-role concepts and attitudes. In Eleanor Maccoby (Ed.), *The development of sex differences*. Stanford, California: Stanford University Press, 1966, Pp. 82–173.

Komarovsky, Mirra. Functional analysis of sex roles. *American Sociological Review*, 1950, *15*, 508–516.

Komarovsky, Mirra. *Women in the modern world*. Boston: Little, Brown and Company, 1953.

Komarovsky, Mirra. Learning the feminine role. In E. M. Schur (Ed.), *The family and the sexual revolution*. Bloomington: Indiana University Press, 1964, Pp. 213–223.

Korchin, S. J., and Heath, Helen A. Somatic experience in the anxiety state: Some sex and personality correlates of "automatic feedback." *Journal of Consulting Psychology*, 1961, *25*, 398–404.

Krich, A. M., and Mead, Margaret (Eds.). *Women: The variety and meaning of their sexual experiences*. New York: Dell Publishing Co., 1953.

Kroger, W. S., and LeLee, S. T. The psychosomatic treatment of hyperemesis gravidarum by hypnosis. *American Journal of Obstetrics and Gynecology*, 1946, *51*, 544–552.

Kroger, W. S., and Peacock, J. F. Psychophysiological effects with an ovulation inhibitor. *Psychosomatics*, 1968, *9*, 67–70.

Kroth, J. A. Relationship between anxiety and menarcheal onset. *Psychological Reports*, 1968, *23*, 801–802.

Kubie, L. S. Psychiatric implications of the Kinsey report. *Psychosomatic Medicine*, 1948, *10*, 95–106.

Kuder, G. *Kuder Preference Record*. Vocational. Form CH. Chicago, Ill.: Science Research Associates, 1948.

Kuethe, J. L. Social schemas. *Journal of Abnormal and Social Psychology*, 1962, *64*, 31–38.

Kupperman, H. S. Hormonal aspects of frigidity. *Quarterly Review of Surgery, Obstetrics and Gynecology*, 1959, *16*, 254–257.

LaGrone, C. W. Sex and personality differences in relation to feeling for direction. *Journal of General Psychology*, 1969, *81*, 23–33.

Laing, R. D. *The self and others*. London: Tavistock Publications, 1959.

Laitman, M. Psychodynamic factors associated with functional infertility in married couples: A comparative study of psychological factors in a group of fertile married couples and a group of infertile married couples without a medical basis for their conditions. Unpublished doctoral dissertation, New York University, 1957.

Lakin, M. Assessment of significant role attitudes in primiparous mothers by means of a modification of the TAT. *Psychosomatic Medicine*, 1957, *19*, 50–60.

Lamb, C. W. Personality correlates of humor enjoyment following motivational arousal. *Journal of Personality and Social Psychology*, 1968, *9*, 237–241.

Lamkin, F. D. Masculinity-femininity of preadolescent youth in relation to behavior acceptability, tested and graded achievement, inventoried interests and general intelligence. Unpublished doctoral dissertation, University of Virginia, 1967.

Lampl-De-Groot, Jeanne. The evolution of the Oedipus complex in women. In H. M. Ruitenbeek (Ed.), *Psychoanalysis and female sexuality*. New Haven, Connecticut: College and University Press, 1966, Pp. 36–50.

Landis, C., Landis, Agnes T., and Bolles, M. M. *Sex in development*. New York: Paul B. Hoeber, 1940.

Landis, C., and Bolles, M. Marjorie. *Personality and sexuality of the physically handicapped woman*. New York: Paul B. Hoeber, 1942.

Landis, C., Bolles, M. Marjorie, and D'Esopo, D. A. Psychological and physical concomitants of adjustment in marriage. *Human Biology*, 1940, *12*, 559–565.

Landis, J. T. Length of time required to achieve adjustment in marriage. *American Sociological Review*, 1946, *11*, 666–677.

Landis, J. T., Poffenberger, S., and Poffenberger, T. The effects of first pregnancy upon the sexual adjustment of 212 couples. *American Sociological Review*, 1950, *15*, 767–772.

Landis, J. T. Intent toward conception and the pregnancy experience. *American Sociological Review*, 1952, *17*, 616–620.

Landy, F., Rosenberg, B. G., and Sutton-Smith, B. The effect of limited father absence on cognitive development. *Child Development*, 1969, *40*, 941–944.

Lane, R. W. The effect of preoperative stress on dreams. Unpublished doctoral dissertation, University of Oregon, 1966.

Langer, Marie. *Motherhood and sex*. Buenos Aires: Editorial Nova, 1951.

Langer, Marie. Sterility and envy. *International Journal of Psychoanalysis*, 1958, *39*, 139–143.

Langner, L. *The importance of wearing clothes*. New York: Hastings House, 1959.

Lansky, L. M. Mechanisms of defense: Sex identity and defenses against aggression. In D. R. Miller and G. E. Swanson (Eds.), *Inner conflict and defense*. New York: Holt, Rinehart and Winston, 1960, Pp. 272–288.

Lansky, L. M. The family structure also affects the model: Sex-role identification in parents of preschool children. *Merrill-Palmer Quarterly of Behavior and Development*, 1964, *10*, 39–50.

Lansky, L. M. Some comments on Ward's (1968) "Variance of sex-role preferences among boys and girls." *Psychological Reports*, 1968, *23*, 649–650.

Lanval, M. *An inquiry into the intimate lives of women*. New York: Cadillac Publishing Co., 1950.

Lawrence, D. H. *Lady Chatterley's lover*. New York: Bantam Books, 1968.

Lawrence, G. L. Behaviors and attitudes of college females differing in parent identification. Unpublished doctoral dissertation, George Peabody College for Teachers, 1968.

Laws, D. R., and Rubin, H. B. Instructional control of an autonomic sexual response. *Journal of Applied Behavior Analysis*, 1969, *2*, 93–99.

Lazarus, A. A. The treatment of chronic frigidity by systematic desensitization. *Journal of Nervous and Mental Disease*, 1963, *136*, 272–278.

Lazarus, R. S. *Psychological stress and the coping process*. New York: McGraw-Hill Book Co., 1966.

Lazarus, R. S., Eriksen, C. W., and Fonda, C. P. Personality dynamics and auditory perceptual recognition. *Journal of Personality*, 1951, *19*, 471–482.

Lazowick, L. M. On the nature of identification. *Journal of Abnormal and Social Psychology*, 1955, *51*, 175–183.

Lederer, W. *The fear of women*. New York: Grune & Stratton, 1968.

Lehfeldt, H., and Ellis, A. (Eds.). Symposium on aspects of female sexuality. *Quarterly Review of Surgery, Obstetrics and Gynecology*, 1959, *16*, 217–263.

Lehfeldt, H., and Guze, H. Psychological factors in contraceptive failure. *Fertility and Sterility*, 1966, *17*, 110.

Leiman, A. H., and Epstein, S. Thematic sexual responses as related to sexual drive and guilt. *Journal of Abnormal and Social Psychology*, 1961, *63*, 169–175.

Leonard, Marjorie R. Fathers and daughters. *International Journal of Psycho-Analysis*, 1966, *47*, 325–334.

Lerner, B., Raskin, R., and Davis, Elizabeth B. On the need to be pregnant. *International Journal of Psycho-Analysis*, 1967, *48*, 288–297.

Leslie, G. R., and Johnsen, Kathryn P. Changed perceptions of the maternal role. *American Sociological Review*, 1963, *28*, 919–928.

Lessler, K. J. The anatomical and cultural dimensions of sexual symbols. Unpublished doctoral dissertation, Michigan State University, 1962.

Lessler, K. J., and Erickson, Marilyn T. Response to sexual symbols by elementary school children. *Journal of Consulting and Clinical Psychology*, 1968, *32*, 473–477.

Leventhal, D. B., Shemberg, K. M., and Van Schoelandt, S. Kaye. Effects of sex-role adjustment upon the expression of aggression. *Journal of Personality and Social Psychology*, 1968, *8*, 393–396.

Leventhal, H., and Mace, W. The effect of laughter on evaluation of a slapstick movie. *Journal of Personality*, 1970, *38*, 16–30.

Levi, L. Sympatho-adrenomedullary activity, diuresis, and emotional reactions during visual sexual stimulation in human females and males. *Psychosomatic Medicine*, 1969, *31*, 251–268.

Levin, Rachel B. An empirical test of the female castration complex. *Journal of Abnormal Psychology*, 1966, *71*, 181–188.

Levinger, G. Systematic distortion in spouses' reports of preferred and actual sexual behavior. *Sociometry*, 1966, *29*, 291–299.

Levinson, D. J., and Huffman, Phyllis E. Traditional family ideology and its relation to personality. *Journal of Personality*, 1955, *23*, 251–273.

Levitt, E. E., and Lubin, B. Some personality factors associated with menstrual complaints and menstrual attitude. *Journal of Psychosomatic Research*, 1967, *11*, 267–270.

Levitt, E. E., Lubin, B., and Zuckerman, M. A simplified method of scoring Rorschach content for dependency. *Journal of Projective Techniques*, 1962, *26*, 234–236.

Levy, D. M. Control-situation: studies of children's responses to the differences in genitalia. *American Journal of Orthopsychiatry*, 1940, *10*, 755–762.

Levy, D. M., and Hess, Audrey. Problems in determining maternal attitudes toward newborn infants. *Psychiatry*, 1952, *15*, 273–286.

Levy, Judith M. Phenomenological aspects of childbearing. Unpublished doctoral dissertation, University of Florida, 1969.

Lewis, Anne, and Hoghughi, M. An evaluation of depression as a side effect of oral contraceptives. *British Journal of Psychiatry*, 1969, *115*, 697–701.

Lewis, E. C. *Developing woman's potential*. Ames, Iowa: Iowa State University Press, 1968.

Lewis, Selma A. Experimental induction of castration anxiety and anxiety over loss of love. Unpublished doctoral dissertation, Yeshiva University, 1969.

Lidz, T. Emotional factors in the etiology of hyperthyroidism occurring in relation to pregnancy. *Psychosomatic Medicine*, 1955, *17*, 420–427.

Lightenstein, H. Identity and sexuality. A study of their interrelationship in man. *Journal of the American Psychoanalytic Association*, 1961, *9*, 179–260.

Lin, Yi-guang. Age and sex differences in the dimensionalities of the self concept. Unpublished doctoral dissertation, University of Michigan, 1962.

Livson, N., and Bronson, Wanda C. An exploration of patterns of impulse control in early adolescence. *Child Development,* 1961, *32,* 75–88.

Locke, H. J., and Karlsson, G. Marital adjustment and prediction in Sweden and the United States. *American Sociological Review,* 1952, *17,* 10–17.

Locke, H. J., and Williamson, R. C. Marital adjustment: A factor analysis study. *American Sociological Review,* 1958, *23,* 562–569.

Loesch, J. G., and Greenberg, N. H. Some specific areas of conflicts observed during pregnancy: A comparative study of married and unmarried pregnant women. *American Journal of Orthopsychiatry,* 1962, *32,* 624–636.

Loftus, T. A. Psychogenic factors in anovulatory women. III. Behavioral and psychoanalytic aspects of anovulatory amenorrhea. *Fertility and Sterility,* 1962, *13,* 20–28.

Loiselle, R. H., and Mollenauer, Sandra. Galvanic skin response to sexual stimuli in a female population. *Journal of General Psychology,* 1965, *73,* 273–278.

Lomas, P. The husband-wife relationship in cases of puerperal breakdown. *British Journal of Medical Psychology,* 1959, *32,* 117–123.

Lomas, P. Defensive organization and puerperal breakdown. *British Journal of Medical Psychology,* 1960a, *33,* 61–66.

Lomas, P. Dread of envy as an aetiological factor in puerperal breakdown. *British Journal of Medical Psychology,* 1960b, *33,* 105–112.

Lomas, P. The concept of maternal love. *Psychiatry,* 1962, *25,* 256–262.

Lorand, S. Contributions to the problem of vaginal orgasm. *International Journal of Psychoanalysis,* 1939, *20,* 432–438.

Lorand, S. *Technique of psychoanalytic therapy.* New York: International Universities Press, 1946.

Lott, D. F., and Brody, P. N. Support of ovulation in the ring dove by auditory and visual stimuli. *Journal of Comparative and Physiological Psychology,* 1966, *62,* 311–313.

Lowry, R. J. Male-female differences in attitudes towards death. Unpublished doctoral dissertation, Brandeis University, 1965.

Lu, Y. C. Parent-child relationship and marital roles. *American Sociological Review,* 1952, *17,* 351–361.

Luckey, Eleanore B. Marital satisfaction and parent concepts. *Journal of Consulting Psychology,* 1960, *24,* 195–204.

Luckey, Eleanore B. Marital satisfaction and personality correlates of spouse. *Journal of Marriage and The Family,* 1964, *26,* 217–220.

Ludwig, A. O., Murawski, B. J., and Sturgis, S. H. *Psychosomatic aspects of gynecological disorders.* Cambridge, Mass.: Harvard University Press, 1969.

Lukianowicz, N. Sexual drive and its gratification in schizophrenia. *International Journal of Social Psychiatry,* 1963, *9,* 250–258.

Lukianowicz, N. "Body image" disturbances in psychiatric disorders. *British Journal of Psychiatry,* 1967, *113,* 31–47.

Lundberg, F., and Farnham, Marynia F. *Modern woman: The lost sex.* New York: Harper & Bros., 1947.

Lynn, D. B. A note on sex differences in the development of masculine and feminine identification. *Psychological Review,* 1959, *66,* 126–135.

Lynn, D. B. Sex differences in identification development. *Sociometry,* 1961, *24,* 372–383.

Lynn, D. B. Sex-role and parental identification. *Child Development,* 1962, *33,* 555–564.

Lynn, D. B. Divergent feedback and sex-role identification in boys and men. *Merrill-Palmer Quarterly of Behavior and Development,* 1964, *10,* 17–23.

Lynn, D. B. *Parental and sex role identification.* Berkeley, California: McCutchan Publishing Corp., 1969.

Lynn, D. B., and Sawrey, W. L. The effects of father-absence on Norwegian boys and girls. *Journal of Abnormal and Social Psychology,* 1959, *59,* 258–261.

Lynn, Rosalie. Sex-role preference and mother-daughter fantasies in young girls. Unpublished doctoral dissertation, University of Denver, 1961.

McBrayer, Caroline T. Differences in perception of the opposite sex by males and females. *Journal of Social Psychology,* 1960, *52,* 309–314.

Maccoby, Eleanor E. (Ed.). *The development of sex differences.* Stanford, Cal.: Stanford University Press, 1966.

Maccoby, Eleanor E., Wilson, W. C., and Burton, R. V. Differential movie-viewing behavior of male and female viewers. *Journal of Personality,* 1958, *26,* 259–267.

Mackler, B., and Shontz, F. C. An assessment of sensory style. *Perceptual and Motor Skills,* 1964, *18,* 841–848.

MacLean, P. D. The limbic system with respect to two basic life principles. In M. A. B. Brazier (Ed.), *Central nervous system and behavior.* New York: Josiah Macy, Jr. Foundation, 1959, Pp. 31–118.

MacLean, P. D. New findings relevant to the evolution of psychosexual functions of the brain. *Journal of Nervous and Mental Disease,* 1962, *135,* 289–301.

MacLeod, A. W. Some psychogenic aspects of infertility. *Fertility and Sterility,* 1964, *15,* 124–134.

Malerstein, A. J. Post-hysterectomy pseudocyesis or phantom visceral organ. *American Journal of Psychiatry,* 1963, *119,* 1102–1103.

Malm, M., and Jamison, O. G. *Adolescence.* New York: McGraw-Hill, 1952.

Malmquist, C. P., Kiresuk, T. J., and Spano, R. M. Personality characteristics of women with repeated illegitimacies: Descriptive aspects. *American Journal of Orthopsychiatry,* 1966, *36,* 476–484.

Mann, E. C. Psychiatric investigation of habitual abortion, preliminary report. *Obstetrics and Gynecology,* 1956, *7,* 589.

Mann, E. C. The role of emotional determinants in habitual abortion. *Surgical Clinics of North America,* 1957, *37,* 447–458.

Marchand, W. E. Analgesic effect of masturbation. *Archives of General Psychiatry,* 1961, *4,* 137–138.

Margoshes, A., and Litt, S. Sexual appetite and sexual drive. *Psychological Reports,* 1965, *16,* 713–719.

Marmor, J. Some considerations concerning orgasm in the female. *Psychosomatic Medicine,* 1954, *16,* 240–245.

Marshall, Rose N. Psychological aspects of infertility in marital pairs: A comparative study. Unpublished doctoral dissertation, Columbia University, 1967.

Martin, B. Expression and inhibition of sex motive arousal in college males. *Journal of Abnormal and Social Psychology,* 1964, *68,* 307–312.

Maslow, A. H. Dominance, personality and social behavior in women. *Journal of Social Psychology,* 1939, *10,* 3–39.

Maslow, A. H. Self-esteem (dominance-feeling) and sexuality in women. *Journal of Social Psychology,* 1942, *16,* 259–294.

Maslow, A. H., Rand, H., and Newman, S. Some parallels between sexual and dominance behavior of infra-human primates and the fantasies of patients in psychotherapy. *Journal of Nervous and Mental Disease,* 1960, *131,* 202–212.

Masserman, J. H. (Ed.). *Sexuality of women.* New York: Grune & Stratton, 1966.

Masters, R. E. L. *Sexual self-stimulation.* Los Angeles, Cal.: Sherbourne Press, 1967.

Masters, W. H., and Johnson, Virginia E. *Human sexual response.* Boston: Little, Brown, and Company, 1966.

Masters, W. H., and Johnson, Virginia E. *Human sexual inadequacy.* Boston: Little, Brown, and Company, 1970.

May, R. Sex differences in fantasy patterns. *Journal of Projective Techniques and Personality Assessment*, 1966, *30*, 576–586.

May, R. Deprivation-enhancement fantasy patterns in men and women. *Journal of Projective Techniques and Personality Assessment*, 1969, *33*, 464–469.

Mazen, F. R. A. Communicator similarity and acceptance of recommendations: A study of attitudes and behavior of pregnant women. Unpublished doctoral dissertation, Yale University, 1967.

McCance, R. A., Luff, M. C., and Widdowson, E. E. Physical and emotional periodicity in women. *Journal of Hygiene*, 1937, *77*, 571–611.

McCandless, B. R. Rate of development, body build and personality. *Psychiatric Research Reports*, 1960–63, *13–16*, 42–62.

McClelland, D. C. The harlequin complex. In R. White (Ed.), *The study of lives*. New York: Atherton Press, 1963, Pp. 94–119.

McClelland, D. C. Wanted: A new self-image for women. In R. J. Lifton (Ed.), *The woman in America*. Boston: Houghton Mifflin Company, 1964, Pp. 173–192.

McClelland, D. C., and Watt, N. F. Sex-role alienation in schizophrenia. *Journal of Abnormal Psychology*, 1968, *73*, 226–239.

McConnell, O. L., and Daston, P. G. Body image changes in pregnancy. *Journal of Projective Techniques*, 1961, *25*, 451–456.

McCulloch, D. J., and Stewart, Joan C. Sexual norms in a psychiatric population. *Journal of Nervous and Mental Disease*, 1960, *131*, 70–73.

McDonald, R. L. Fantasy and the outcome of pregnancy. *Archives of General Psychiatry*, 1965a, *12*, 602–606.

McDonald, R. L. Personality characteristics, cigarette smoking, and obstetric complications. *Journal of Psychology*, 1965b, *60*, 129–134.

McDonald, R. L. Personality characteristics in patients with three obstetric complications. *Psychosomatic Medicine*, 1965c, *27*, 383–390.

McDonald, R. L. The role of emotional factors in obstetric complications: A review. *Psychosomatic Medicine*, 1968, *30*, 222–237.

McDonald, R. L., and Christakos, A. C. Relationship of emotional adjustment during pregnancy to obstetric complications. *American Journal of Obstetrics and Gynecology*, 1963, *86*, 341–348.

McDonald, R. L., and Gynther, M. D. Relations between self and parental perceptions of unwed mothers and obstetric complications. *Psychosomatic Medicine*, 1965, *27*, 31–38.

McDonald, R. L., Gynther, M. D., and Christakos, A. C. Relations between maternal anxiety and obstetric complications. *Psychosomatic Medicine*, 1963, *25*, 357–363.

McDonald, R. L., and Parham, K. J. Relation of emotional changes during pregnancy to obstetric complications in unmarried primigravidas. *American Journal of Obstetrics and Gynecology*, 1964, *90*, 195–201.

McElroy, W. A. A sex difference in preferences for shapes. *British Journal of Psychology*, 1954, *45*, 209–216.

McKee, J. P., and Sherriffs, A. C. The differential evaluation of males and females. *Journal of Personality*, 1957, *25*, 356–371.

McKee, J. P., and Sherriffs, A. C. Men's and women's beliefs, ideas, and self-concepts. *American Journal of Sociology*, 1959, *64*, 356–363.

McNeill, D., and Livson, N. Maturation rate and body build in women. *Child Development*, 1963, *34*, 25–32.

Mead, Margaret. *Sex and temperament in three primitive societies*. New York: Morrow, 1935.

Mead, Margaret. *Male and female*. New York: William Morrow & Co., 1949.

Megargee, E. I. Influence of sex roles on the manifestation of leadership. *Journal of Applied Psychology*, 1969, *53*, 377–382.

Meisels, M., and Guardo, Carol J. Development of personal space schemata. *Child Development*, 1969, *40*, 1,167–1,178.

Melges, F. T. Postpartum psychiatric syndromes. *Psychosomatic Medicine*, 1968, *30*, 95–108.

Messer, S. and Lewis, M. Social class and sex differences in the attachment and play behavior of the year-old infant. *Child Development*, in press.

Metzner, R. J., and Golden, J. S. Psychological factors influencing female patients in the selection of contraceptive devices. *Fertility and Sterility*, 1967, *18*, 845–856.

Meyer, W. J. Relationships between social need strivings and the development of heterosexual affiliations. *Journal of Abnormal and Social Psychology*, 1959, *59*, 51–57.

Miller, D. R., and Swanson, G. E. *Inner conflict and defense.* New York: Schocken Books, 1960.

Miller, H., and Wilson, W. Relation of sexual behaviors, values, and conflict to avowed happiness and personal adjustment. *Psychological Reports*, 1968, *23*, 1,075–1,086.

Milton, G. A. The effects of sex-role identification upon problem-solving skill. *Journal of Abnormal and Social Psychology*, 1957, *55*, 208–212.

Mintz, T. Tickle—the itch that moves. *Psychosomatic Medicine*, 1967, *24*, 606–611.

Minuchin, Patricia. Sex-role concepts and sex typing in childhood as a function of school and home environments. *Child Development*, 1965, *36*, 1033–1048.

Mischel, W. A. A social-learning view of sex differences in behavior. In E. E. Maccoby (Ed.), *The development of sex differences.* Stanford: Stanford University Press, 1966, Pp. 56–81.

Money, J. Components of eroticism in man: I. The hormones in relation to sexual morphology and sexual desire. *Journal of Nervous and Mental Disease*, 1961a, *132*, 239–248.

Money, J. Components of eroticism in man: II. The orgasm and genital somasthesia. *Journal of Nervous and Mental Disease*, 1961b, *132*, 289–297.

Money, J. Sex hormones and other variables in human eroticism. In W. C. Young (Ed.), *Sex and internal secretions.* Baltimore, Md.: Williams and Wilkins, 1961c, Pp. 1,383–1,400.

Money, J. (Ed.). *Sex research. New developments.* New York: Holt, Rinehart and Winston, 1965a.

Money, J. The sex instinct and human eroticism. *Journal of Sex Research*, 1965b, *1*, 3–16.

Montague, A. *The natural superiority of women.* New York: The Macmillan Co., 1953.

Moore, B. E. Frigidity in women. *Journal of the American Psychoanalytic Association*, 1961, *9*, 571–584.

Moore, B. E. Frigidity: A review of psychoanalytic literature. *Psychoanalytic Quarterly*, 1964, *33*, 323–349.

Moore, B. E. Psychoanalytic reflections on the implications of recent physiological studies of female orgasm. *Journal of the American Psychoanalytic Association*, 1968, *16*, 569–587.

Moos, R. H. Psychological aspects of oral contraceptives. *Archives of General Psychiatry*, 1968a, *19*, 87–94.

Moos, R. H. The development of a Menstrual Distress Questionnaire. *Psychosomatic Medicine*, 1968b, *30*, 853–867.

Moos, R. H. Assessment of psychological concomitants of oral contraceptives. In H. Salhanick (Ed.), *Metabolic effects of gonadal hormones and contraceptives.* New York: Plenum Publishing Corporation, 1969a, Pp. 676–705.

Moos, R. H. Typology of menstrual cycle symptoms. *American Journal of Obstetrics and Gynecology*, 1969b, *103*, 390–402.

Moos, R. H., Kopell, B. S., Melges, F. T., Yalom, I. D., Lunde, D. T., Clayton, R. B., and Hamburg, D. A. Fluctuations in symptoms and moods during the menstrual cycle. *Journal of Psychosomatic Research*, 1969, *13*, 37–44.

Mordkoff, A. M. Some sex differences in personality correlates of "automatic feedback." *Psychological Reports*, 1966, *18*, 511–518.

Mosher, D. L., and Cross, H. J. Sex guilt and premarital sexual experiences of college students. *Journal of Consulting Psychology*, 1971, *36*, 27–32.

Mosher, D. L., and Greenberg, Irene. Females' affective responses to reading erotic literature. *Journal of Consulting and Clinical Psychology*, 1969, *33*, 472–477.

Moss, H. A., Robson, K. S., and Pedersen, F. Determinants of maternal stimulation of infants and consequences of treatment for later reaction to strangers. *Developmental Psychology*, 1969, *1*, 239–246.

Mowrer, O. H. Identification: A link between learning theory and psychotherapy. In *Learning theory and personality dynamics*. New York: The Ronald Press Company, 1950, Pp. 573–616.

Mudd, Emily H., Stein, M., and Mitchell, H. E. Paired reports of sexual behavior of husbands and wives in conflicted marriages. *Comprehensive Psychiatry*, 1961, *2*, 149–156.

Mullen, F. G. The treatment of a case of dysmenorrhea by behavior therapy techniques. *Journal of Nervous and Mental Disease*, 1968, *147*, 371–376.

Murray, H. A. *Explorations in personality*. New York: Oxford University Press, 1938.

Murphy, G. E., Kuhn, N. O., Christensen, R. F., and Robins, E. "Life stress" in a normal population: A study of 101 women hospitalized for normal delivery. *Journal of Nervous and Mental Disease*, 1962, *134*, 150–161.

Mussen, P. Some antecedents and consequents of masculine sex-typing in adolescent boys. *Psychological Monographs*, 1961, *75*, No. 506.

Mussen, P., and Distler, L. Masculinity, identification, and father-son relationships. *Journal of Abnormal and Social Psychology*, 1959, *59*, 350–356.

Mussen, P., and Rutherford, E. Parent-child relations and parental personality in relation to young children's sex-role preferences. *Child Development*, 1963, *34*, 589–607.

Narjani, A. Considerations on the anatomical causes of frigidity in women. Bruxelles-Medical Bi-weekly Review M and S Science, No. 42, 1924, Bruxelles, Medical and Scientific Print Shop.

Needles, W. The defilement complex: A contribution to psychic consequences of the anatomical distinction between the sexes. *Journal of the American Psychoanalytic Association*, 1966, *14*, 700–710.

Nesbitt, R. E. L., Jr., Hollender, M., Fisher, S., and Osofsky, H. J. Psychological correlates of the polycystic ovary syndrome and organic infertility. *Fertility and Sterility*, 1968, *19*, 778–786.

Neugarten, Bernice L., and Kraines, Ruth J. Menopausal symptoms: in women of various ages. *Psychosomatic Medicine*, 1965, *27*, 266–273.

Newson, L. J., and Newson, E. Breast feeding in decline. *British Medical Journal*, 1962, *2*, 1,744–1,745.

Newton, G., Paul, J., and Bovard, E. W., Jr. Effect of emotional stress on finger temperature. *Psychological Reports*, 1957, *3*, 341–343.

Newton, N. *Maternal emotions*. New York: Paul B. Hoeber, 1955.

Newton, N., Foshee, D., and Newton, M. Parturient mice: Effect of environment on labor. *Science*, 1966, *151*, 1,560–1,561.

Newton, N. R., and Newton, M. Relationship of ability to breast feed and maternal attitudes toward breast feeding. *Pediatrics*, 1950, *5*, 869–875.

Newton, N., and Newton, M. Mothers' reactions to their newborn babies. *Journal of the American Medical Association*, 1962, *181*, 122–126.

Newton, N., and Newton, M. Psychologic aspects of lactation. *New England Journal of Medicine*, 1967, *277*, 1,179–1,188.

Newton, N., Peeler, D., and Newton, M. Effect of disturbance on labor. *American Journal of Obstetrics and Gynecology*, 1968, *101*, 1,096–1,102.

Newton, N., Peeler, D., and Rawlins, Carolyn. Effect of lactation on maternal behavior in mice with comparative data on humans. *Lying-in: Journal of Reproductive Medicine*, 1968, *1*, 257–262.

Nilsson, A., and Almgren, P. E. Psychiatric symptoms during the post-partum period as related to use of oral contraceptives. *British Medical Journal*, 1968, *2*, 453–455.

Nilsson, A., Kau, L., and Jacobson, L. Post-partum mental disorder in an unselected sample. The psychiatric history. *Journal of Psychosomatic Research*, 1967a, *10*, 327–339.

Nilsson, A., Kau, L., and Jacobson, L. Post-partum mental disorder in an unselected sample. The importance of the unplanned pregnancy. *Journal of Psychosomatic Research*, 1967b, *10*, 341–347.

Nissen, H. W., Chow, K. L., and Semmes, J. Effects of restricted opportunity for tactual, kinesthetic and manipulative experience on the behavior of a chimpanzee. *American Journal of Psychology*, 1951, *64*, 485–507.

Nixon, R. E. An approach to the dynamics of growth in adolescence. *Psychiatry*, 1961, *24*, 18–31.

Noyes, R. W., and Chapnick, Eleanor M. Literature on psychology and infertility. A critical analysis. *Fertility and Sterility*, 1964, *15*, 543–558.

Offer, D. Studies of normal adolescents. *Adolescence*, 1966/67, *1*, 305–320.

Offer, D., and Offer, Judith L. Profiles of normal adolescent girls. *Archives of General Psychiatry*, 1968, *19*, 513–522.

Ofstad, N. S. The transmission of self-reinforcement patterns through imitation of sex-role appropriate behavior. Unpublished doctoral dissertation, University of Utah, 1967.

O'Neal, P., Schaefer, J., Bergmann, J., and Robins, E. A psychiatric evaluation of adults who had sexual problems as children: A 30 year follow-up study. *Human Organization*, 1960, *19*, 32–34.

O'Neil, W. M., and Levinson, D. J. A factorial exploration of authoritarianism and some of its ideological concomitants. *Journal of Personality*, 1954, *22*, 449–463.

O'Neill, Marion, and Kempler, B. Approach and avoidance responses of the hysterical personality to sexual stimuli. *Journal of Abnormal Psychology*, 1969, *74*, 300–305.

Orr, D. W. Anthropological and historical notes on the female sexual role. *Journal of the American Psychoanalytic Association*, 1968, *16*, 601–612.

Osgood, C. E., Suci, G. J., and Tannenbaum, P. H. *The measurement of meaning*. Urbana, Ill.: University of Illinois Press, 1957.

Osofsky, H. J. After office hours. Women's reactions to pelvic examination. *Obstetrics and Gynecology*, 1967, *30*, 146–151.

Osofsky, H. J., and Fisher, S. Psychological correlates of the development of amenorrhea in a stress situation. *Psychosomatic Medicine*, 1967a, *29*, 15–23.

Osofsky, H. J., and Fisher, S. Sexual and reproductive correlates of chronic cervicitis. *Obstetrics and Gynecology*, 1967b, *30*, 481–485.

Ostow, M. The erotic instincts—a contribution to the study of instincts. *International Journal of Psychoanalysis*, 1957, *38*, 305–324.

Ostwald, P. F., and Regan, P. F. III. Psychiatric disorders associated with childbirth. *Journal of Nervous and Mental Disease*, 1957, *125*, 153–165.

Ovesey, L. Masculine aspirations in women. *Psychiatry*, 1956, *19*, 341–351.

Paige, Karen E. The effects of oral contraceptives on affective fluctuations associated with the menstrual cycle. Unpublished doctoral dissertation, University of Michigan, 1969.

Paris, Joyce, and Goodstein, L. D. Responses to death and sex stimulus materials as a function of repression-sensitization. *Psychological Reports*, 1966, *19*, 1,283–1,291.

Parsons, L., Whittaker, Joanne O., and Lemon, H. M. Evaluation of electrovaginal potential recordings as a therapeutic guide in gynecological problems. *American Journal of Obstetrics and Gynecology*, 1960, *79*, 736–746.

Parsons, T., and Bales, R. F. *Family, socialization and interaction process.* Glencoe, Illinois: The Free Press, 1955.

Pasamanick, B., Rogers, M. E., and Lilienfeld, A. M. Pregnancy experience and development of behavior disorder in children. *American Journal of Psychiatry*, 1956, *112*, 613–618.

Patt, S. L., Rappaport, R. G., and Barglow, P. Follow-up of therapeutic abortion. *Archives of General Psychiatry*, 1969, *20*, 408–414.

Patterson, Virginia, Block, Jeanne, Block, J., and Jackson, D. D. The relation between intention to conceive and symptoms during pregnancy. *Psychosomatic Medicine*, 1960, *22*, 373–376.

Paulson, M. J. Psychological concomitants of premenstrual tension. *American Journal of Obstetrics and Gynecology*, 1961, *81*, 733–738.

Payne, S. A conception of femininity. *British Journal of Medical Psychology*, 1935, *15*, 18–33.

Peck, A., and Marcus, H. Psychiatric sequelae of therapeutic interruption of pregnancy. *Journal of Nervous and Mental Disease*, 1966, *143*, 417–425.

Perloff, W. H. Role of the hormones in human sexuality. *Psychosomatic Medicine*, 1949, *11*, 133–139.

Peskin, H. Pubertal onset and ego functioning. *Journal of Abnormal Psychology*, 1967, *72*, 1–15.

Peskin, H. The duration of normal menses as a psychosomatic phenomenon. *Psychosomatic Medicine*, 1968, *30*, 378–389.

Petrie, A. *Individuality in pain and suffering.* Chicago, Ill.: University of Chicago Press, 1967.

Pfeiffer, E., Verwoerdt, A., and Wang, H. Sexual behavior in aged men and women. I. Observations on 254 community volunteers. *Archives of General Psychiatry*, 1968, *19*, 753–758.

Philippopoulos, G. S. The analysis of a case of frigidity (psychopathology-psychodynamics). *Psychotherapy and Psychosomatics*, 1967, *15*, 220–230.

Phillips, J. K. A study of the sexual attitudes, behavior patterns, and attitude-behavior pattern inconsistencies of graduate students. Unpublished doctoral dissertation, University of Virginia, 1969.

Pillay, A. P., and Ellis, A. (Eds.). *Sex, society and the individual.* Bombay: International Journal of Sexology, 1953.

Pines, M. "Human sexual response"—a discussion of the work of Masters and Johnson. *Journal of Psychosomatic Research*, 1968, *12*, 39–49.

Pinneau, S. R., and Hopper, H. E. The relationship between incidence of specific gastro-intestinal reactions of the infant and psychological characteristics of the mother. *Journal of Genetic Psychology*, 1958, *93*, 3–13.

Pintler, Margaret H., Phillips, Ruth, and Sears, R. R. Sex differences in the projective doll play of preschool children. *Journal of Psychology*, 1946, *21*, 73–80.

Piotrowski, Z. A. Psychogenic factors in anovulatory women. *Fertility and Sterility*, 1962, *13*, 11–19.

Pishkin, V. Psychosexual development in terms of object and role preferences. *Journal of Clinical Psychology*, 1960, *16*, 238–240.

Pitcher, Evelyn G., and Prelinger, E. *Children tell stories—an analysis of fantasy.* New York: International Universities Press, 1963.

Poffenberger, Shirley, and Poffenberger, T. Intent toward conception and the pregnancy experience. *American Sociological Review*, 1952, *17*, 616–620.

Pohlman, E. *The psychology of birth planning*. Cambridge, Mass.; Schenkman Publishing, 1969.

Pollak, O., and Friedman, A. S. (Eds.). *Family dynamics and female sexual delinquency*. Palo Alto, Cal.: Science and Behavior Books, 1969.

Pomeroy, W. B. An analysis of questions on sex. *Psychological Record*, 1960, *10*, 191–201.

Pomeroy, W. B. Some aspects of prostitution. *Journal of Sex Research*, 1965, *1*, 177–187.

Potter, H. W., and Klein, Henriette R. On nursing behavior. *Psychiatry*, 1957, *20*, 39–46.

Prados, M. Emotional factors in the climacterium of women. *Psychotherapy and Psychosomatics*, 1967, *15*, 231–244.

Preston, Grace A. Parental role perceptions and identification in adolescent girls. Unpublished doctoral dissertation, University of Michigan, 1965.

Purtell, J. J., Robins, E., and Cohen, M. E. Observations on clinical aspects of hysteria. *Journal of American Medical Association*, 1951, *146*, 902–909.

Rabban, M. Sex-role identification in young children in two diverse social groups. *Genetic Psychology Monographs*, 1950, *42*, 81–158.

Rabin, A. I., and Greene, R. J. Assessing motivation for parenthood. *Journal of Psychology*, 1968, *69*, 39–46.

Raboch, J., and Bartak, V. A contribution to the study of the anesthetic-frigid syndrome in women. *Ceskoslovenska Psychiatrie*, 1968a, *64*, 230–235.

Raboch, J., and Bartak, V. The sexual life of frigid women. Sonderdruck aus, *Psychiatrie, Neurologie und medizinische Psychologie*, 1968b, *10*, 368–373.

Rado, S. Evolutionary basis of sexual adaptation. *Journal of Nervous and Mental Disease*, 1955, *121*, 389–396.

Rado, S. Sexual anesthesia in the female. *Quarterly Review of Surgery, Obstetrics and Gynecology*, 1959, *16*, 249–253.

Rainwater, L. Marital sexuality in four cultures of poverty. *Journal of Marriage and The Family*, 1964, *26*, 457–466.

Rainwater, L. *Family design. Marital sexuality, family size, and contraception*. Chicago, Ill.: Aldine Publishing, 1965.

Rainwater, L. Some aspects of lower class sexual behavior. *Medical Aspects of Human Sexuality*, 1968, *2*, 15.

Rangell, L. Clinical communications. The interchangeability of phallus and female genital. *Journal of the American Psychoanalytic Association*, 1953, *1*, 504–509.

Ranker, J. E., Jr. Attitudes toward sex in marriage and patterns of erotic behavior in dating and courtship before marriage. Unpublished doctoral dissertation, University of Southern California, 1967.

Raphael, Dana L. The lactation-suckling process within a matrix of supportive behavior. Unpublished doctoral dissertation, Columbia University, 1966.

Raush, H. L., Goodrich, W., and Campbell, J. D. Adaptation to the first years of marriage. *Psychiatry*, 1963, *26*, 368–380.

Reed, Ruth. Changing conception of the maternal instinct. *Journal of Abnormal and Social Psychology*, 1923, *18*, 78–87.

Rees, L. Psychosomatic aspects of the premenstrual tension syndrome. *Journal of Mental Science*, 1953, *99*, 62–73.

Reevy, W. R. Marital prediction scores of college women relative to behavior and attitudes. Unpublished doctoral dissertation, Pennsylvania State University, 1954.

Reich, Annie. Narcissistic object choice in women. *Journal of the American Psychoanalytic Association*, 1953, *1*, 22–44.

Reich, W. *The function of the orgasm*. New York: Orgone Institute Press, 1942.

Reik, T. *Psychology of sex relations*. New York: Rinehart and Co., 1945.

Reiss, I. L. Premarital sexual permissiveness among Negroes and whites. *American Sociological Review*, 1964a, *29*, 688–698.

Reiss, I. L. The scaling of premarital sexual permissiveness. *Journal of Marriage and The Family*, 1964b, *26*, 188–198.

Reiss, I. L. Social class and premarital sexual permissiveness: A re-examination. *American Sociological Review*, 1965, *30*, 747–756.

Reymert, M. L., and Jost, H. Further data concerning the normal variability of the menstrual cycle during adolescence and factors associated with age of menarche. *Child Development*, 1947, *18*, 169–179.

Reynolds, Evelyn. Variations of mood and recall in the menstrual cycle. *Journal of Psychosomatic Research*, 1969, *13*, 163–166.

Reynolds, S. R. M., Harris, J. S., and Kaiser, I. H. *Clinical measurement of uterine forces in pregnancy and labour*. Springfield, Ill.: Charles C. Thomas, 1954.

Rheingold, Harriet L. *Maternal behavior in mammals*. New York: John Wiley & Sons, 1963.

Rheingold, J. C. *The fear of being a woman*. New York: Grune & Stratton, 1964.

Rholl, K. N. A study of relationships between occupational and marital roles and marital adjustment. Unpublished doctoral dissertation, University of Southern California, 1968.

Richardson, R. A. An investigation into the universality of sexual symbolism. Unpublished doctoral dissertation, Louisiana State University, 1967.

Richardson, S. A., and Guttmacher, A. F. (Eds.). *Childbearing—its social and psychological aspects*. Baltimore, Md.: The Williams and Wilkins Co., 1967.

Richardson, T. A. Hypnotherapy in frigidity. *American Journal of Clinical Hypnosis.*, 1962/63, *5*, 194–199.

Riffaterre, Brigitte B. Determination of pregnancy depression and its relation to marital status and group affiliation in a single ethnic group. Unpublished doctoral dissertation, Yeshiva University, 1961.

Ringrose, C. A. D. Psychosomatic influences in the genesis of toxemia of pregnancy. *Canadian Medical Association Journal*, 1961a, *84*, 647–651.

Ringrose, C. A. D. Further observations on the psychosomatic character of toxemia of pregnancy. *Canadian Medical Association Journal*, 1961b, *84*, 1,064–1,065.

Ripley, H. S., and Papanicolaou, E. N. The menstrual cycle with vaginal smear studies in schizophrenia, depression, and elation. *American Journal of Psychiatry*, 1942, *98*, 567–571.

Robbins, B. The nature of femininity. *Psychotherapy*, 1956, *1*, 99–108.

Robin, A. A. The psychological changes of normal parturition. *Psychiatric Quarterly*, 1962, *36*, 129–150.

Rodgers, D. A., and Ziegler, F. J. Social role theory, the marital relationship, and use of ovulation suppressors. *Journal of Marriage and The Family*, 1968a, *30*, 584–591.

Rodgers, D. A., and Ziegler, F. J. Changes in sexual behavior consequent to use of noncoital procedures of contraception. *Psychosomatic Medicine*, 1968b, *30*, 495–505.

Rodgers, D. A., Ziegler, F. J., Prentiss, R. J., and Martin, P. L. Comparisons of nine contraceptive procedures by couples changing to vasectomy or ovulation suppression medication. *Journal of Sex Research*, 1965, *1*, 87–96.

Rodrigue, E. M. Notes on menstruation. *International Journal of Psychoanalysis*, 1955, *36*, 328–334.

Roe, Anne, and Siegelman, L. A parent-child relations questionnaire. *Child Development*, 1963, *34*, 355–369.

Roemer, H. Schmerzanalyse und Schmerzbeeinflussung in der Geburtshilfe. *Psychotherapy and Psychosomatics*, 1966, *14*, 412–424.

Rose, Annelies A. Menstrual pain and personal adjustment. *Journal of Personality*, 1949, *17*, 287–302.

Rosen, S. Emotional factors in nausea and vomiting of pregnancy. *Psychiatric Quarterly*, 1955, *29*, 621–633.

Rosenberg, B. G., and Sutton-Smith, B. The measurement of masculinity and femininity in children. *Child Development,* 1959, *30,* 373–380.

Rosenberg, B. G., and Sutton-Smith, B. A revised conception of masculine-feminine differences in play activities. *Journal of Genetic Psychology,* 1960, *96,* 165–170.

Rosenberg, B. G., and Sutton-Smith, B. Ordinal position and sex-role identification. *Genetic Psychology Monographs,* 1964a, *70,* 297–328.

Rosenberg, B. G., and Sutton-Smith, B. The measurement of masculinity and femininity in children: An extension and revalidation. *Journal of Genetic Psychology,* 1964b, *104,* 259–264.

Rosenberg, B. G., and Sutton-Smith, B. Family interaction effects on masculinity-femininity. *Journal of Personality and Social Psychology,* 1968, *8,* 117–120.

Rosenberg, B. G., Sutton-Smith, B., and Morgan, E. The use of opposite sex scales as a measure of psychosexual deviancy. *Journal of Consulting Psychology,* 1961, *25,* 221–225.

Rosenblatt, P. C. A cross-cultural study of child rearing and romantic love. *Journal of Personality and Social Psychology,* 1966, *4,* 336–338.

Rosengren, W. R. Some social psychological aspects of delivery room difficulties. *Journal of Nervous and Mental Disease,* 1961a, *132,* 515–521.

Rosengren, W. R. Social sources of pregnancy as illness or normality. *Social Forces,* 1961b, *39,* 260.

Rosenkrantz, P., Vogel, Susan, Bee, Helen, Broverman, Inge, and Broverman, D. M. Sex-role stereotypes and self-concepts in college students. *Journal of Consulting and Clinical Psychology,* 1968, *32,* 287–295.

Rothbart, M. K., and Maccoby, E. E. Parent's differential reactions to sons and daughters. *Journal of Personality and Social Psychology,* 1966, *4,* 237–243.

Rothchild, I. The central nervous system and disorders of ovulation in women. *American Journal of Obstetrics and Gynecology,* 1967, *98,* 719–747.

Rothman, D., Kaplan, A. H., and Nettles, Elizabeth. Psychosomatic infertility. *American Journal of Obstetrics and Gynecology,* 1962, *83,* 373–381.

Rousey, C. L., and Moriarty, Alice E. *Diagnostic implications of speech sounds.* Springfield, Ill.: Charles C Thomas, 1965.

Rubenfeld, F. A. Projection of sexual motivation and racial prejudice. Unpublished doctoral dissertation, Yale University, 1964.

Rubenstein, B. B. An emotional factor in infertility. *Fertility and Sterility,* 1953, *2,* 80–86.

Rubin, B. Psychological aspects of human artificial insemination. *Archives of General Psychiatry,* 1965, *13,* 121–132.

Rudy, A. J. Sex-role perceptions in early adolescence. *Adolescence,* 1968/69, *3,* 453–470.

Ruitenbeek, H. M. (Ed.). *Psychoanalysis and female sexuality.* New Haven, Conn.: College and University Press, 1966.

Rutherford, R. N., Banks, A. L., Coburn, W. A., Williams, J., and Zaffiro, F. H. Psychometric testings in frigidity and infertility. *Psychosomatics,* 1960, *1,* 72–76.

Salber, Eva J., Stitt, Pauline G., and Babbott, Joan G. Patterns of breast feeding. I. Factors affecting the frequency of breast feeding in the newborn period. *New England Journal of Medicine,* 1958, *259,* 707–713.

Salber, Eva J., Stitt, Pauline G., and Babbott, Joan G. Patterns of breast feeding in family health clinic. II. Duration of feeding and reasons for weaning. *New England Journal of Medicine,* 1959, *260,* 310–315.

Salerno, L. J. Psychophysiologic aspects of the toxemias of pregnancy. *American Journal of Obstetrics and Gynecology,* 1958, *76,* 1268–1274.

Salzman, L. Psychology of the female. *Archives of General Psychiatry,* 1967, *17,* 195–203.

Salzman, L. Sexuality. In J. Marmor (Ed.), *Modern psychoanalysis.* New York: Basic Books, 1968, Pp. 123–145.

Sandler, B. Conception after adoption: A comparison of conception rates. *Fertility and Sterility*, 1965, *16*, 313–322.

Sandler, B. Emotional stress and infertility. *Journal of Psychosomatic Research*, 1968, *12*, 51–59.

Sandstrom, C. I. A note on the Aubert phenomenon. *Journal of Experimental Psychology*, 1954, *48*, 209–210.

Sanford, N. The dynamics of identification. *Psychological Review*, 1955, *62*, 106–118.

Sanford, N., Webster, H., and Freedman, M. Impulse expression as a variable of personality. *Psychological Monographs*, 1957, *71*, No. 440.

Sappenfield, B. R. Perception of masculinity and femininity in Rorschach blots and responses. *Journal of Clinical Psychology*, 1961, *17*, 373–376.

Sarlin, C. N. Feminine identity. *Journal of the American Psychoanalytic Association*, 1963, *11*, 790–816.

Sattler, J. M. The relative meaning of embarrassment. *Psychological Reports*, 1963, *12*, 263–269.

Sattler, J. M. A theoretical, developmental, and clinical investigation of embarrassment. *Genetic Psychology Monographs*, 1965, *71*, 19–59.

Sattler, J. M. Embarrassment and blushing: A theoretical review. *Journal of Social Psychology*, 1966, *69*, 117–133.

Saugstad, P. Effect of food deprivation on perception-cognition. *Psychological Bulletin*, 1966, *65*, 80–90.

Schachter, S. *The psychology of affiliation.* Stanford: Stanford University Press, 1959.

Schaefer, Leah C. Sexual experiences and reactions of a group of 30 women as told to a female psychotherapist. Unpublished doctoral dissertation, Columbia University, 1964.

Schafer, R. *Aspects of internalization.* New York: International Universities Press, 1968.

Scheinfeld, A. *Women and men.* New York: Harcourt, Brace and Co., 1943.

Schiebel, D. R. Tactile behavior in psychopathology. Unpublished doctoral dissertation, University of Michigan, 1965.

Schilder, P. *The image and appearance of the human body.* London: Kegan, Paul, Trench, Trubner and Co., 1935.

Schimel, J. L. The psychopathology of egalitarianism in sexual relations. *Psychiatry*, 1962, *25*, 182–186.

Schmidt, G., and Sigusch, V. Sex differences in responses to psychosexual stimulation by films and slides. *Journal of Sex Research*, 1970, *6*, 268–283.

Schneider, S. C. Analysis of presurgical anxiety in boys and girls. Unpublished doctoral dissertation, University of Michigan, 1960.

Schofield, M. *The sexual behaviour of young people.* Boston: Little, Brown and Company, 1965.

Schon, Martha, and Sutherland, A. M. The role of hormones in human behavior. III. Changes in female sexuality after hypophysectomy. *Journal of Clinical Endocrinology*, 1960, *20*, 833–841.

Schon, Martha, and Sutherland, A. M. The relationship of pituitary hormones to sexual behavior in women. In H. G. Beigel (Ed.), *Advances in sex research.* New York: Paul B. Hoeber, Pp. 33–47.

Schopbach, R. R., Fried, P. H., and Rakoff, A. E. Pseudocyesis. A psychosomatic disorder. *Psychosomatic Medicine*, 1952, *14*, 129–134.

Schwartz, B. J. An empirical test of two Freudian hypotheses concerning castration anxiety. *Journal of Personality*, 1956, *24*, 318–327.

Schwartz, R. A., Hershenson, D. B., and Shipman, W. G. The sexual behavior of obese married women. *Proceedings of the Annual Convention of the American Psychological Association*, 1971, *6*, 445–446.

Science News Letter. Eating, fighting and sex. *Science News Letter*, 1961, *79*, 19.

Scott, Eileen M., Illsley, R., and Thomson, A. M. A psychological investigation of primigravidae. *Journal of Obstetrics and Gynecology of the British Empire*, 1956, *63*, 331–343.

Scott, Eileen M., and Thomson, A. M. A psychological investigation of primigravidae. IV. Psychological factors and the clinical phenomena of labour. *Journal of Obstetrics and Gynecology of the British Empire*, 1956, *63*, 502–508.

Sears, Pauline S. Doll play aggression in normal young children: Influence of sex, age, sibling status, father's absence. *Psychological Monographs*, 1951, *65*, No. 323.

Sears, R. R. Relation of early socialization experiences to self-concepts and gender role in middle childhood. *Child Development*, 1970, *41*, 267–289.

Sears, R. R., Maccoby, E. E., and Levin, H. *Patterns of child rearing*. Evanston, Ill.: Row, Peterson, 1957.

Sears, R. R., Rau, L., and Alpert, R. *Identification and child rearing*. Stanford: Stanford University Press, 1965.

Secord, P. F., and Jourard, S. L. The appraisal of body cathexis: Body cathexis and the self. *Journal of Consulting Psychology*, 1953, *17*, 343–347.

Seward, Georgene H. Psychological effects of the menstrual cycle on women workers. *Psychological Bulletin*, 1944, *41*, 90–102.

Seward, Georgene H. *Sex and the social order*. New York: McGraw-Hill, 1946.

Seward, Georgene H. Sex identity and the social order. *Journal of Nervous and Mental Disease*, 1964, *139*, 126–136.

Seward, Georgene H., Bloch, S. K., and Heinrich, J. F. The question of psychophysiologic infertility: Some negative answers. A post-script. *Psychosomatic Medicine*, 1967, *29*, 151–152.

Seward, Georgene H., and Larson, W. R. Adolescent concepts of social sex roles in the United States and the two Germanies. *Human Development*, 1968, *11*, 217–248.

Seward, Georgene H., Wagner, P. S., Heinrich, J. F., Bloch, S. K., and Myerhoff, H. L. The question of psychophysiologic infertility: Some negative answers. *Psychosomatic Medicine*, 1965, *27*, 533–545.

Shader, R. I., DiMascio, A., and Harmatz, J. Characterological anxiety levels and premenstrual libido changes. *Psychosomatics*, 1968, *9*, 197–198.

Shainess, Natalie. A re-evaluation of some aspects of femininity through a study of menstruation: A preliminary report. *Comprehensive Psychiatry*, 1961, *2*, 20–26.

Shainess, Natalie. Psychiatric evaluation of premenstrual tension. *New York State Journal of Medicine*, 1962, *62*, 3,573–3,579.

Shainess, Natalie. The structure of the mothering encounter. *Journal of Nervous and Mental Disease*, 1963, *136*, 146–161.

Shainess, Natalie. Psychological problems associated with motherhood. In S. Arieti (Ed.), *American handbook of psychiatry*. New York: Basic Books, 1966, Pp. 47–65.

Shainess, Natalie. Images of woman: Past and present, overt and obscured. *American Journal of psychotherapy*, 1969, *23*, 77–97.

Shanan, J., Brzezinski, A., Sulman, F., and Sharon, M. Active coping behavior, anxiety, and cortical steroid excretion in the prediction of transient amenorrhea. *Behavioral Science*, 1965, *10*, 461–465.

Shapiro, A., Cohen, H. D., DiBianco, P., and Rosen, G. Vaginal blood flow changes during sleep and sexual arousal. *Psychophysiology*, 1968, *4*, 394.

Shapiro, A., and Swensen, C. Patterns of self-disclosure among married couples. *Journal of Counseling Psychology*, 1969, *16*, 179–180.

Shatin, L., and Southworth, J. A. Sex knowledge, intelligence, and sexual adjustment. *Journal of Social Psychology*, 1961, *54*, 219–233.

Shemberg, K. M., and Leventhal, D. B. Masculinity-femininity and need for social approval. *Journal of Projective Techniques and Personality Assessment*, 1968, *32*, 575–577.

Sherfey, Mary J. The evolution and nature of female sexuality in relation to psychoanalytic theory. *Journal of the American Psychoanalytic Association,* 1966, *14,* 28–128.

Sherriffs, A. C., and Jarrett, R. F. Sex differences in attitudes about sex differences. *Journal of Psychology,* 1953, *35,* 161–168.

Shiloh, A. (Ed.). *Studies in human sexual behavior. The American scene.* Springfield, Illinois: Charles C. Thomas, 1970.

Shipman, W. G. Age of menarche and adult personality. *Archives of General Psychiatry,* 1964, *10,* 155–159.

Shontz, F. C. *Perceptual and cognitive aspects of body experience.* New York: Academic Press, 1969.

Shope, D. F. A comparison of virginal and non-virginal college girls. Unpublished Master's thesis, Pennsylvania State University, 1964.

Shope, D. F. A comparison of selected college females on sexual responsiveness and nonresponsiveness. Unpublished doctoral dissertation, Pennsylvania State University, 1966.

Shope, D. F., and Broderick, C. B. Level of sexual experience and predicted adjustment in marriage. *Journal of Marriage and The Family,* 1967, *29,* 424–427.

Shopper, M. Three as a symbol of the female genital and the role of differentiation. *Psychoanalytic Quarterly,* 1967, *36,* 410–417.

Shuttleworth, F. A biosocial and developmental theory of male and female sexuality. *Marriage and Family Living,* 1959, *21,* 163–170.

Siegman, A. Responses to a personality questionnaire by volunteers and nonvolunteers to a Kinsey interview. *Journal of Abnormal and Social Psychology,* 1956, *52,* 280–281.

Sigusch, V., Schmidt, G., Reinfeld, A., and Wiedemann-Sutor, I. Psychosexual stimulation: Sex differences. *Journal of Sex Research,* 1970, *6,* 10–24.

Silbermann, I. A contribution to the psychology of menstruation. *International Journal of Psychoanalysis,* 1950, *31,* 258–267.

Sim, Myre. Psychiatric disorders of pregnancy. *Journal of Psychosomatic Research,* 1968, *12,* 95–100.

Simon, Lora S. The measurement of approach-avoidance conflict in pregnancy. Unpublished doctoral dissertation, University of Massachusetts, 1964.

Simon, N. M., and Senturia, Audrey G. Psychiatric sequelae of abortion. *Archives of General Psychiatry,* 1966, *15,* 378–389.

Simon, N. M., Senturia, Audrey G., and Rothman, D. Psychiatric illness following therapeutic abortion. *American Journal of Psychiatry,* 1967, *124,* 59–65.

Singer, J. L. *Daydreaming. An introduction to the experimental study of inner experience.* New York: Random House, 1966.

Slater, E., and Woodside, Moya. *Patterns of marriage.* London: Cassell, 1951.

Slater, P. E., and Slater, Dori A. Maternal ambivalence and narcissism: A cross-cultural study. *Merrill-Palmer Quarterly of Behavior and Development,* 1965, *11,* 241–259.

Sloane, R. B., Inglis, J., and Payne, R. W. Personal traits and maternal attitudes in relation to blood lipid levels. *Psychosomatic Medicine,* 1962, *24,* 278–285.

Slote, Geraldine M. Feminine character and patterns of interpersonal perception. Unpublished doctoral dissertation, New York University, 1962.

Smith, Mildred E. P. Maturational crisis of pregnancy: Associated themes and problems. Unpublished doctoral dissertation, Boston University School of Nursing, 1965.

Smith, Nora, Schwartz, Jean R., Mandell, W., Silberstein, R. M., Dalack, J. D., and Sacks, S. Mothers' psychological reactions to premature and full-size newborns. *Archives of General Psychiatry,* 1969, *21,* 177–181.

Smith, S. Age and sex differences in children's opinions concerning sex differences. *Journal of Genetic Psychology,* 1939, *54,* 17–25.

Smith, S. L., and Sauder, Cynthia. Food cravings, depression, and premenstrual problems. *Psychosomatic Medicine,* 1969, *31,* 281–287.

Snyder, J. A. An investigation of certain personality needs and relational patterns in a group of 70 premaritally pregnant girls. Unpublished doctoral dissertation, University of Pennsylvania, 1967.

Soichet, S. Emotional factors in toxemia of pregnancy. *American Journal of Obstetrics and Gynecology,* 1959, *77,* 1065–1073.

Solien de Gonzales, Nancie L. Breast-feeding, weaning, and acculturation. *Journal of Pediatrics,* 1963, *62,* 577–581.

Sontag, L. W. Physiological factors and personality in children. *Child Development,* 1947, *18,* 185–189.

Sopchak, A. L. Parental "identification" and "tendency toward disorders" as measured by the Minnesota Multiphasic Personality Inventory. *Journal of Abnormal and Social Psychology,* 1952, *47,* 159–165.

Sopchak, A. L. Individual differences in responses to different types of music, in relation to sex, mood, and other variables. *Psychological Monographs,* 1955, *69,* No. 396.

Soysa, Nita. Self-concept and role conflict: A study of some aspects of women's self-perception and self-evaluation in relation to their attitudes towards their sex-role. Unpublished doctoral dissertation, Cornell University, 1961.

Spiegel, D. E., Brodkin, S. G., and Keith-Spiegel, Patricia. Unacceptable impulses, anxiety and the appreciation of cartoons. *Journal of Projective Techniques and Personality Assessment,* 1969, *33,* 154–159.

Spiegel, D. E., Olivo, Martha L., and Keith-Spiegel, Patricia. Tactual appeal and aversion: Validation of three predictors. *Journal of Projective Techniques and Personality Assessment,* 1968, *32,* 82–87.

Spinley, B. M. *The deprived and the privileged: Personality development in English society.* London: Routledge and Kegan Paul, 1953.

Spitz, R. A. The primal cavity. *Psychoanalytic Study of the Child,* Vol. 10, New York: International Universities Press, 1955, Pp. 215–240.

Spitz, R. A. Autoerotism re-examined. *Psychoanalytic Study of the Child,* Vol. 17, New York: International Universities Press, 1962, Pp. 283–315.

Spitz, R. A., and Wolf, K. M. Autoerotism. *Psychoanalytic Study of the Child,* Vol. 3, New York: International Universities Press, 1949, Pp. 85–120.

Stein, K. B., and Lenrow, P. Expressive styles and their measurement. *Journal of Personality and Social Psychology,* 1970, *16,* 656–664.

Stein, M. H. The marriage bond. *Psychoanalytic Quarterly,* 1956, *25,* 238–259.

Steinbach, E. *Sex and life: Forty years of biological and medical experiments.* New York: The Viking Press, 1940.

Steinmann, Anne. A study of the concept of the feminine role of 51 middle-class American families. *Genetic Psychology Monographs,* 1963, *67,* 275–352.

Stekel, W. *Frigidity in woman.* New York: Boni and Liveright, 1926.

Sternbach, R. A. *Pain. A psychophysiological analysis.* New York: Academic Press, 1968.

Stewart, H., and Chou, F. Frequency of sex thoughts in males and females: A college sample. Unpublished study.

Stoke, S. M. An inquiry into the concept of identification. *Journal of Genetic Psychology,* 1950, *76,* 163–189.

Stoller, R. J. *Sex and gender.* New York: Science House, 1968a.

Stoller, R. J. The sense of femaleness. *Psychoanalytic Quarterly,* 1968b, *37,* 42–55.

Stone, A., and Ward, Mildred E. Factors responsible for pregnancy in 500 infertility cases. *Fertility and Sterility,* 1956, *7,* 1–14.

Stone, A. A., and Onque, Gloria C. *Longitudinal studies of child personality.* Cambridge, Mass.: Harvard University Press, 1959.

Stone, H. M., and Stone, A. S. *A marriage manual.* (Rev.) New York: Simon and Schuster, 1952.

Story, R. I. The relationship between the effects of conflict arousal and oral fixation on thinking. Unpublished doctoral dissertation, University of Michigan, 1963.

Stott, D. H. Some psychosomatic aspects of casuality in reproduction. *Journal of Psychosomatic Research,* 1958, *3,* 42–55.

Strassburger, F. The "steeple effect": Sex differences in marginal perception and fantasy. *Journal of Nervous and Mental Disease,* 1966, *142,* 228–234.

Stratton, J. R., and Spitzer, S. P. Sexual permissiveness and self-evaluation: A question of substance and a question of method. *Journal of Marriage and The Family,* 1967, *29,* 434–441.

Strodtbeck, F. L., and Creelan, P. G. The interaction linkage between family size, intelligence, and sex-role identity. *Journal of Marriage and The Family,* 1968, *30,* 301–307.

Strong, E. K. *Strong Vocational Interest Blanks Manual.* (Revised by D. P. Campbell.) Stanford: Stanford University Press, 1966.

Stycos, J. M. *Family and fertility in Puerto Rico: A study of the lower income group.* New York: Columbia University Press, 1955.

Sussman, M. B. *Sourcebook in marriage and the family.* Boston: Houghton Mifflin Company, 1963.

Sutton-Smith, B., Roberts, J. M., and Rosenberg, B. F. Sibling associations and role involvement. *Merrill-Palmer Quarterly of Behavior and Development,* 1964, *10,* 25–38.

Sutton-Smith, B., Rosenberg, B. G., and Landy, F. Father-absence effects in families of different sibling compositions. *Child Development,* 1968, *39,* 1,213–1,221.

Sutton-Smith, B., Rosenberg, B. G., and Morgan, E. F., Jr. Development of sex differences in play choices during preadolescence. *Child Development,* 1963, *34,* 119–126.

Suwa, N., Yamashita, I., Ito, K., Yoshimura, Y., and Moroji, T. Psychic state and gonadal function: A psychophysiologic study of emotion. *Journal of Nervous and Mental Disease,* 1966, *143,* 36–46.

Swanson, Ethel M., and Foulkes, D. Dream content and the menstrual cycle. *Journal of Nervous and Mental Disease,* 1968, *145,* 358–363.

Swensen, C. H., Jr. Sexual behavior and psychopathology: A test of Mowrer's hypothesis. *Journal of Clinical Psychology,* 1962, *18,* 406–409.

Swensen, C. H., Jr. Sexual behavior and psychopathology: A study of college men. *Journal of Clinical Psychology,* 1963, *19,* 403–404.

Symonds, P. M. Sex differences in the life problems and interests of adolescents. *School and Society,* 1936, *43,* 751–752.

Taylor, H. C., Jr. Life situations, emotions and gynecologic pain associated with congestion. *Association for Research in Nervous and Mental Disease,* 1950, *29,* 1,051–1,056.

Terman, L. M. *Psychological factors in marital happiness.* New York: McGraw-Hill, 1938.

Terman, L. M. *Studies in personality.* New York: McGraw-Hill Book Company, 1942.

Terman, L. M. Correlates of orgasm adequacy in a group of 556 wives. *Journal of Psychology,* 1951, *32,* 115–172.

Terman, L. M. Marital adjustment and its prediction. In M. Fishbein and E. W. Burgess (Eds.), *Successful marriage.* New York: Doubleday and Co., 1955.

Terman, L. M., and Miles, Catherine C. *Sex and personality.* New York: McGraw-Hill Book Company, 1936.

Terman, L. M., and Oden, Melita H. *The gifted child grows up.* Stanford, Cal.: Stanford University Press, 1947.

Theobald, G. W. A centre, or centres, in the hypothalamus controlling menstruation, ovulation, pregnancy, and parturition. *British Medical Journal,* 1936, *1,* 1,038–1,041.

Thomason, B. Marital sexual behavior and total marital adjustment: A research report. In J. Himelhoch and Sylvia F. Fava (Eds.), *Sexual behavior in American society*. New York: W. W. Norton & Co., 1955, Pp. 153–163.

Thomason, O. B. Differential non-sexual and sexual behavior in the marital adjustment of Penn State alumni. Unpublished doctoral dissertation, Pennsylvania State College, 1951.

Thompson, Clara. The role of women in this culture. *Psychiatry*, 1941, *4*, 1–8.

Thompson, Clara. Penis envy in women. *Psychiatry*, 1943, *6*, 123–125.

Thompson, Clara. *Psychoanalysis: Evolution and development*. New York: Hermitage House, 1950.

Thompson, Clara. Some effects of the derogatory attitude towards female sexuality. In H. M. Ruitenbeek (Ed.), *Psychoanalysis and female sexuality*. New Haven, Conn.: College and University Press, 1966, Pp. 51–60.

Thompson, L. J. Attitudes of primiparae as observed in a prenatal clinic. *Mental Hygiene*, 1942, *26*, 243.

Thurstone, L. L. *Examiner manual for the Thurstone Temperament Schedule*. Chicago: Science Research Associates, 1953.

Tiffany, Frances L. A tension inventory to reveal subjective changes accompanying the menstrual cycle. Unpublished doctoral dissertation, Rutgers, The State University, 1964.

Tiktin, M. Menstrual tensions and marital satisfaction. Unpublished doctoral dissertation, University of Oregon, 1966.

Tonks, C. M., Rack, P. H., and Rose, M. J. Attempted suicide and the menstrual cycle. *Journal of Psychosomatic Research*, 1968, *11*, 319–323.

Treadway, C. R., Kane, F. J., Jarrahi-Zadeh, A., and Lipton, M. A. A psychoendocrine study of pregnancy and puerperium. *American Journal of Psychiatry*, 1969, *125*, 86–92.

Trites, R. L. Response sets on the rod-and-frame test in neurologically impaired Ss. *Perceptual and Motor Skills*, 1969, *29*, 327–333.

Tryon, M. C. Evaluation of adolescent personality by adolescents. *Monograph of Social Research in Child Development*, 1939, *4*.

Tupper, C., and Weil, R. J. The problem of spontaneous abortion. IX. The treatment of habitual aborters by psychotherapy. *American Journal of Obstetrics and Gynecology*, 1962, *83*, 421–424.

Tylden, Elizabeth. Hyperemesis and physiological vomiting. *Journal of Psychosomatic Research*, 1968, *12*, 85–93.

Tyler, E. T., Bonapart, J., and Grant, Jeanne. Occurrence of pregnancy following adoption. *Fertility and Sterility*, 1960, *11*, 581–589.

Udry, J. R., and Morris, Naomi M. A method for validation of reported sexual data. *Journal of Marriage and The Family*, 1967, *29*, 442–446.

Uhr, L. M. Personality changes during marriage. Unpublished doctoral dissertation, University of Michigan, 1957.

Van de Castle, R. L. Some problems in applying the methodology of content analysis to dreams. Presented at University of Cincinnati symposium, Dream Psychology and the New Biology of Dreaming, October, 1967.

Vanden Bergh, R. L., Taylor, E. S., and Drose, Vera. Emotional illness in habitual aborters following suturing of the incompetent cervical os. *Psychosomatic Medicine*, 1966, *28*, 257–263.

Van Lennep, D. J. Projection and personality. In H. P. David and E. Von Bracken (Eds.), *Perspectives in personality theory*. New York: Basic Books, 1957, Pp. 259–277.

Van Ophuijsen, J. H. W. Contributions to the masculinity complex in women. In H. M. Ruitenbeek (Ed.), *Psychoanalysis and female sexuality*. New Haven, Conn.: College and University Press, 1966, Pp. 36–50.

Vener, A. M., and Snyder, C. A. The preschool child's awareness and anticipation of adult sex-roles. *Sociometry*, 1966, *29*, 159–168.

Vogel, Susan R., Broverman, Inge K., Broverman, D. M., Clarkson, F. E., and Rosenkrantz, P. S. Maternal employment and perception of sex-roles among college students. *Developmental Psychology*, in press.

Vroegh, Karen. Masculinity and femininity in the elementary and junior high school years. *Developmental Psychology*, 1971, *3*, 254–261.

Wagman, M. Sex differences in types of daydreams. *Journal of Personality and Social Psychology*, 1967, *7*, 329–332.

Wagman, M. The relationship of types of daydream behavior to selected MMPI scales. *Psychiatry*, 1968, *31*, 84–89.

Wagner, E. E., and Slemboski, Jean. Psychological reactions of pregnant unwed women as measured by the Rorschach. *Journal of Clinical Psychology*, 1968, *24*, 467–469.

Walker, W. L., and Heyns, R. W. *An anatomy for comformity*. Englewood Cliffs, N.J.: Prentice-Hall, 1962.

Wallach, M. A. Two correlates of symbolic sexual arousal: Level of anxiety and liking for esthetic material. *Journal of Abnormal and Social Psychology*, 1960, *61*, 396–401.

Wallach, M. A., and Greenberg, Carol. Personality functions of symbolic sexual arousal to music. *Psychological Monographs*, 1960, *74*, No. 494.

Waller, H. The early yield of human milk, and its relation to the security of lactation. *Lancet*, 1950, *1*, 53–56.

Wallin, P. A study of orgasm as a condition of women's enjoyment of intercourse. *Journal of Social Psychology*, 1960, *51*, 191–198.

Wallin, P., and Clark, A. L. Cultural norms and husbands' and wives' reports of their marital partners' preferred frequency of coitus relative to their own. *Sociometry*, 1958a, *21*, 247–254.

Wallin, P., and Clark, A. L. Marital satisfaction and husbands' and wives' perception of similarity in their preferred frequency of coitus. *Journal of Abnormal and Social Psychology*, 1958b, *57*, 370–373.

Wallin, P., and Riley, Rosemary P. Reactions of mothers to pregnancy and adjustment of offspring in infancy. *American Journal of Orthopsychiatry*, 1950, *20*, 616–622.

Wapner, S., and Werner, H. *Perceptual development*. Worcester, Mass.: Clark University Press, 1957.

Ward, C. H., Beck, A. T., and Rascoe, E. Typical dreams. *Archives of General Psychiatry*, 1961, *5*, 606–615.

Ward, W. D. Process of sex-role development. *Developmental Psychology*, 1969, *1*, 163–168.

Watson, A. S. A psychiatric study of idiopathic prolonged labor. *Obstetrics and Gynecology*, 1959, *13*, 598–602.

Wax, M. Themes in cosmetics and grooming. *American Journal of Sociology*, 1956–57, *62*, 588–593.

Waxenberg, S. E., Drellich, M. G., and Sutherland, A. M. The role of hormones in human behavior. I. Changes in female sexuality after adrenalectomy. *Journal of Clinical Endocrinology*, 1959, *19*, 193–202.

Waxenberg, S. E., Finkbeiner, J. A., Drellich, M. G., and Sutherland, A. M. The role of hormones in human behavior. *Psychosomatic Medicine*, 1960, *22*, 435–442.

Weakland, J. H. Orality in Chinese conceptions of male genital sexuality. *Psychiatry*, 1956, *19*, 237–247.

Weatherley, D. Self-perceived rate of physical maturation and personality in late adolescence. *Child Development*, 1964, *35*, 1,197–1,210.

Weaver, Frances J. Selected aspects of father-daughter interaction and daughter's instrumentalness in late adolescence. Unpublished doctoral dissertation, Pennsylvania State University, 1968.

Webb, A. P. Sex-role preferences and adjustment in early adolescents. *Child Development*, 1963, *34*, 609–618.

Wechsler, D. *The Wechsler Adult Intelligence Scale*. New York: Psychological Corporation, 1955.

Weider, A., and Noller, P. A. Objective studies of children's drawings of human figures. I. Sex awareness and socioeconomic level. *Journal of Clinical Psychology*, 1950, *6*, 319–325.

Weil, R. J., and Stewart, Lucille C. The problem of spontaneous abortion. III. Psychosomatic and interpersonal aspects of habitual abortion. *American Journal of Obstetrics and Gynecology*, 1957, *73*, 322–327.

Weil, R. J., and Tupper, C. Personality, life situation, and communication: A study of habitual abortion. *Psychosomatic Medicine*, 1960, *22*, 448–455.

Weinberg, J. Sexual expression in late life. *American Journal of Psychiatry*, 1969, *126*, 159–162.

Weir, W. C., and Weir, D. R. Adoption and subsequent conceptions. *Fertility and Sterility*, 1966, *17*, 283–288.

Weiss, J. L. An experimental study of the psychodynamics of humor. Unpublished doctoral dissertation, University of Michigan, 1955.

Weiss, P. Some aspects of femininity. Unpublished doctoral dissertation, University of Colorado, 1962.

Weissman, P. Psychosexual development in a case of neurotic virginity and old maidenhood. *International Journal of Psychoanalysis*, 1964, *45*, 110–120.

Weller, R. H. The employment of wives, dominance, and fertility. *Journal of Marriage and The Family*, 1968.

Welsh, G. S., and Dahlstrom, W. G. (Eds.). *Basic readings on the MMPI in psychology and medicine*. Minneapolis: University of Minnesota Press, 1956.

Wenger, Marion A., Averill, J. R., and Smith, D. D. Autonomic activity during sexual arousal. *Psychophysiology*, 1968, *4*, 468–478.

Westoff, C. F., and Potvin, R. H. *College women and fertility values*. Princeton, N.J.: Princeton University Press, 1967.

Westoff, C. F., Sagi, P. C., and Kelly, E. L. Fertility through twenty years of marriage: A study in predictive possibilities. *American Sociological Review*, 1958, *23*, 549–556.

Whalen, R. E. (Ed.). *Hormones and behavior*. Princeton, N. J.: D. Van Nostrand, 1967.

White, Alice M., Fichtenbaum, L., and Dollard, J. Measured relationships between sexual motivation and anxiety. *Journal of Counseling Psychology*, 1967, *14*, 544–549.

White, M. J. Laterality differences in perception: A review. *Psychological Bulletin*, 1969, *72*, 387–405.

Whiting, J. W., and Child, I. L. *Child training and personality: A cross-cultural study*. New Haven: Yale University Press, 1953.

Wilson, W. R. Relation of sexual behaviors, values, and conflicts to avowed happiness. *Psychological Reports*, 1965, *17*, 371–378.

Wineman, Eugenia W. Some psychophysiological correlates of the human menstrual cycle. Unpublished doctoral dissertation, University of California, Los Angeles, 1967.

Winker, J. B. Age trends and sex differences in the wishes, identifications, activities and fears of children. *Child Development*, 1949, *20*, 191–200.

Winokur, G. (Ed.). *Determinants of human sexual behavior*. Springfield, Ill.: Charles C. Thomas, 1963a.

Winokur, G. Sexual behavior: Its relationship to certain affects and psychiatric diseases. In G. Winokur (Ed.), *Determinants of human sexual behavior*. Springfield, Ill.: Charles C. Thomas, 1963b, Pp. 76–100.

Winokur, G., and Gaston, W. R. Sex, anger and anxiety: Intrapersonal interaction in married couples. *Diseases of the Nervous System*, 1961, *22*, 1–5.

Winokur, G., Guze, S. B., and Pfeiffer, E. Developmental and sexual factors in women: A comparison between control, neurotic and psychotic groups. *American Journal of Psychiatry*, 1958–59, *115*, 1,097–1,100.

Winokur, G., Guze, S. B., and Pfeiffer, E. Nocturnal orgasm in women. *Archives of General Psychiatry*, 1959, *1*, 180–184.

Winokur, G., and Werboff, J. The relationship of conscious maternal attitudes to certain aspects of pregnancy. *Psychiatric Quarterly Supplement*, 1956, *30*, 61–73.

Winter, Sara K. Characteristics of fantasy while nursing. *Journal of Personality*, 1969, *37*, 58–72.

Witkin, H. A., Dyk, R. B., Faterson, H. F., Goodenough, D. R., and Karp, S. A. *Psychological differentiation*. New York: John Wiley & Sons, 1962.

Witkin, H. A., Lewis, H. B., Hertzman, M., Meissner, P., Machover, K., and Wapner, S. *Personality through perception*. New York: Harper & Brothers, 1954.

Witryol, S. L., and Kaess, W. A. Sex differences in social memory tasks. *Journal of Abnormal and Social Psychology*, 1957, *54*, 343–346.

Wittkower, E., and Wilson, A. T. M. Dysmenorrhea and sterility personality studies. *British Medical Journal*, 1940, *50*, 586–588.

Wittreich, W. J., and Grace, M. Body image and development. Technical report, March 29, 1955, Princeton University, Contract N6 ONR-270(14), Office of Naval Research.

Wittreich, W. J., and Radcliffe, K. B., Jr. The influence of simulated mutilation upon the perception of the human figure. *Journal of Abnormal and Social Psychology*, 1955, *51*, 493–495.

Wohlford, P., Santrock, J. W., Berger, S. E., and Liberman, D. Older brothers' influence on sex-typed, aggressive, and dependent behavior in father absent children. *Developmental Psychology*, in press.

Woodside, Moya. Orgasm capacity among two hundred English working-class wives. *Marriage Hygiene*, 1948, *1*, 133–137.

Wright, Helena. A contribution to the orgasm problem in women. *International Journal of Sexology*, 1949, *3*, 97–102.

Wylie, Ruth C. *The self concept*. Lincoln, Neb.: University of Nebraska Press, 1961.

Yalom, I., Lunde, D., Moos, R., and Hamburg, D. The "postpartum blues" syndrome: Description and related variables. *Archives of General Psychiatry*, 1968, *18*, 16–27.

Yarros, R. S. *Modern woman and sex. A feminist physician speaks*. New York: Vanguard Press, 1933.

Yazmajian, R. V. Biological aspects of infantile sexuality and the latency period. *Psychoanalytic Quarterly*, 1967, *36*, 203–229.

Zell, J. R., and Crisp, N. E. Psychiatric evaluation of the use of oral contraceptives —a study of 250 private patients. *Obstetrics and Gynecology*, 1964, *23*, 657.

Zemlick, M. J., and Watson, R. I. Maternal attitudes of acceptance and rejection during and after pregnancy. *American Journal of Orthopsychiatry*, 1953, *23*, 570–584.

Zern, D. The relevance of family cohesiveness as a determinant of premarital sexual behavior in a cross-cultural sample. *Journal of Social Psychology*, 1969, *78*, 3–9.

Ziegler, F. J., Rodgers, D. A., and Kriegsman, Sali A. Effect of vasectomy on psychological functioning. *Psychosomatic Medicine*, 1966, *28*, 50–63.

Ziegler, F. J., Rodgers, D. A., and Prentiss, R. J. Psychosocial response to vasectomy. *Archives of General Psychiatry*, 1969, *21*, 46–54.

Zilboorg, G. Malignant psychoses related to childbirth. *American Journal of Obstetrics and Gynecology*, 1928a, *15*, 145–158.

Zilboorg, G. The dynamics of schizophrenic reactions related to pregnancy and childbirth. *American Journal of Psychiatry*, 1928b, *8*, 733–767.

Zilboorg, G. Depressive reactions related to parenthood. *American Journal of Psychiatry*, 1930–31, *10*, 927–962.

Zuckerman, M. Physiological measures of sexual arousal in the human. *Psychological Bulletin, 1971, 75*, 297–329.

Zuckerman, M., Kolin, Elizabeth A., Price, Leah, and Zoob, Ina. Development of a sensation-seeking scale. *Journal of Consulting Psychology, 1964, 28*, 477–482.

Zuk, G. H. Sex-appropriate behavior in adolescence. *Journal of Genetic Psychology, 1958, 93*, 15–32.

NAME INDEX

SUBJECT INDEX